The Nativist Prophets of Early Islamic Iran

Patricia Crone's latest book is about the Iranian response to the Muslim penetration of the Iranian countryside, the revolts triggered there, and the religious communities that these revolts revealed. The book also describes a complex of religious ideas that, however varied in space and unstable over time, has demonstrated a remarkable persistence in Iran across a period of two millennia. The central thesis is that this complex of ideas has been endemic to the mountain population of Iran and has occasionally become epidemic with major consequences for the country, most strikingly in the revolts examined here and in the rise of the Ṣafavids who imposed Shīʿism on Iran. This learned and engaging book by one of the most influential scholars of early Islamic history casts entirely new light on the nature of religion in pre-Islamic Iran, and on the persistence of Iranian religious beliefs both outside and inside Islam after the Arab conquest.

Patricia Crone is Mellon Professor of Islamic History in the School of Historical Studies, Institute for Advanced Study, Princeton. Her numerous publications include *Slaves on Horses: The Evolution of the Islamic Polity* (1980, 2003); *God's Caliph: Religious Authority in the First Centuries of Islam*, co-authored with Martin Hinds (1986, 2003); *Pre-Industrial Societies: Anatomy of the Pre-Modern World* (1989, 2003); and *Medieval Islamic Political Thought* (2005).

The Nativist Prophets of Early Islamic Iran

Rural Revolt and Local Zoroastrianism

PATRICIA CRONE
Institute for Advanced Study, Princeton

CAMBRIDGE
UNIVERSITY PRESS

CAMBRIDGE UNIVERSITY PRESS
Cambridge, New York, Melbourne, Madrid, Cape Town,
Singapore, São Paulo, Delhi, Mexico City

Cambridge University Press
32 Avenue of the Americas, New York, NY 10013-2473, USA

www.cambridge.org
Information on this title: www.cambridge.org/9781107018792

First published 2012
Reprinted 2013

A catalog record for this publication is available from the British Library.

Library of Congress Cataloging in Publication Data

Crone, Patricia, 1945–
The nativist prophets of early Islamic Iran / Patricia Crone.
p. cm.
Includes bibliographical references and index.
ISBN 978-1-107-01879-2 (hardback)
1. Islam – Iran – History. 2. Religion – Iran – History. I. Title.
BP63.I68C76 2012
295′.095509021–dc23 2011033306

ISBN 978-1-107-01879-2 Hardback

Contents

Preface

This is a book about the Iranian response to the Muslim penetration of the Iranian countryside, the revolts that the Muslims triggered there, and the religious communities that these revolts revealed. It is also a book about a complex of religious ideas that, however varied in space and unstable over time, has shown remarkable persistence in Iran over a period of two millennia. The central thesis of the book is that this complex of ideas has been endemic to the mountain population of Iran and has occasionally become epidemic with major consequences for the country, most strikingly in the revolts examined here and in the rise of the Safavids who imposed Shīʿism on Iran.

The revolts to which Part I is devoted have been studied several times before, above all by Sadighi (Ṣadīghī) and Daniel. Though I have added some new material, mostly from Chinese sources and Central Asian archaeology, the main novelty of this part lies in its approach. Part II, on the other hand, tries to do something entirely new. It subjects the religious beliefs of the rebel communities to systematic analysis, traces back the beliefs in question to pre-Islamic times, and seeks to determine their relationship with Zoroastrianism. This part is based on Arabic and Persian sources in combination with a wide array of Pahlavi, Greek, Syriac, Buddhist, Manichaean, and other sources, including Middle Iranian texts recovered from Central Asia, Central Asian archaeology again, and, needless to say, a mass of secondary literature. Part III also tries to do something entirely new, namely to offer a systematic examination of the marital patterns and reproductive strategies discernible behind the accusations of 'wife-sharing' levelled at the rebel communities and related groups, with reference to much the same array of sources as those used in Part II. This is followed by a discussion of the role of the marital patterns in question in the formation of a communist utopian ideal in Sasanian Iran. The final chapter traces the extraordinary continuity of the complex of beliefs and practices from early Islamic down to modern times, with heavy use of secondary literature again.

WHERE TO FIND WHAT IN THE BOOK

The book is addressed primarily to Iranianists and Islamicists, but some parts of it should be of interest to scholars in quite different fields as well, notably specialists in early Christianity, Gnosticism, late antiquity, gender history, the comparative history of empires, and pre-modern communism. They will not want to read the entire book; many other readers probably will not either (though I obviously hope that there are some who will). Accordingly, I here briefly indicate where they can find the material most likely to interest them.

Most readers will probably find it helpful to start with Chapter 1, which introduces the main actors and sets the scene, but they can part company thereafter. For historians of the ʿAbbāsid caliphate the most relevant part of the book is Part I. Historians and sociologists of empires can make do with Chapters 1 and 8, which consider the Arab handling of the natives they had conquered and the latter's reaction in comparison with native responses to incorporation in the European empires. Islamicists interested in extremist Shīʿism and experts in Zoroastrianism (and Iranian religion in general), on the other hand, can proceed to Part II and top it up with the conclusion. Specialists in Judaism, Christianity, and Gnosticism can skip the introduction and go straight to Chapter 14, which discusses the Elchasaite, Manichaean, and early eastern Christian conception of divine incarnation, with an attempt to trace it to its (Mesopotamian) roots in Chapter 15, in the section called 'The Image and the mahdi'. But there should also be something of relevance for specialists in Christianity and Gnosticism in Chapter 10, on cosmology, and in the first pages of Chapter 19, on monotheism, dualism, and the religious trend in later antiquity; those curious to see living versions of Elchasai should read more of Chapter 19, especially the section on the Ahl-i Ḥaqq. Finally, readers in search of marriage patterns and reproductive strategies should go to Chapter 17, while historians and sociologists interested in pre-modern communism should go to the much shorter Chapter 18. All readers should know that every chapter of the book can be read on its own.

ACKNOWLEDGEMENTS

I can say for sure that I would not have written this book if, more than thirty years ago, my colleague in Oxford, John Gurney, had not asked me to teach a course on the transition from pre-Islamic to early Islamic Iran. I taught this course for the thirteen years I spent in Oxford and eventually added the nativist prophets as a special subject. By the time I left Oxford for Cambridge, I knew that I wanted to write a book about the rebellious prophets one day. I must accordingly start by expressing my gratitude to John Gurney for getting me interested in things Iranian and to all the students who took these courses for making the subject so rewarding to teach.

If I had written the book back then it would have consisted of little more than Part I of the present work, for what fascinated me in those days was the nature of the revolts and the fact that one can be deeply influenced by people to whom one is utterly hostile. I was not particularly interested in the religious beliefs that the revolts revealed, except as clues to the social background and motivation of the rebels. Having written about Mazdak, moreover (thanks to the same transition course), I did not think I would have anything to add on the subject of women and property. All this drastically changed when I eventually decided to write. The little book for a wide audience that I had anticipated turned into some kind of monster that dragged me further and further away from my home territory, so that I often despaired of ever getting back. I doubt that I would have persevered with what eventually became Parts II and III if I had not had the good fortune to be at the Institute for Advanced Study, where I had time to fight the monster until I felt I had it under reasonable control.

Reasonable control is one thing, intimate familiarity of the type arising from years of immersion is quite another. Full mastery of the Zoroastrian, Manichaean, Buddhist, Christian, and sundry other literary traditions of relevance to this book is beyond the capacity of a single person and I still feel a certain trepidation about having ventured in where angels fear to tread. I hope I have not made the specialists wince. If I have, I must apologise in advance to the many who have helped me over the years. They include Oktor Skjaervø, a fellow Scandinavian to whom I am much indebted for unfailing assistance in connection with questions of a philological nature; Lance Jenott, who helped with Gnostic matters (disputing the validity of that very label); Kevin van Bladel, from whom I have learned more than the references that the reader will see acknowledged in the footnotes; the graduates with whom I read texts on Khurramism in a seminar at Princeton University in 2009; and countless members of the Institute for Advanced Study, both permanent and transient, whom I have pestered with questions over the years. Of those, my greatest debt is to Masoud Jafari Jazi, whose presence at the Institute greatly improved my knowledge of Persian language and literature, who answered more questions than anyone else, and with whom I had the pleasure of co-authoring an article on a topic connected with this book; he has also kept me abreast of recent publications in Iran. Last but not least, I must thank Michael Cook, Philip Kreyenbroek, and Maria Subtelny for reading the entire typescript and making numerous corrections and suggestions for improvement.

CONVENTIONS

In so far as possible I refer to texts and translations alike even when the texts are in languages (and more particularly scripts) that I do not read. I do this to enable specialists to go straight to the text without having to look up the translations in order to find the reference, which often makes a simple task extremely time consuming. One needs the original to judge an interpretation regardless of whether the non-specialist has simply adopted the position of another specialist or proposed his or her own view. When I refer to texts in languages unknown to me I depend on other people's references, however. They may not always be right, and sometimes I only quote a small section of a longer passage covering several pages and do not know exactly where my section comes. In that case I simply give the reference as I find it: an approximate reference is better than none.

On the question of transcription, I fear I am guilty of much inconsistency. I try to use the transliteration system customary for the particular language involved, including the standard transliteration of modern Persian as if it were Arabic. But I could not bring myself to use the *x* with which specialists in pre-Islamic Iran transliterate the sound that Islamicists reproduce as *kh* because it is so counter-intuitive. I use *kh* in the transliteration of Arabic and Iranian words alike, with one exception: in the transliteration of consonantal skeletons from middle Iranian languages I defer to specialist usage. Further, I use *v* and *w* interchangeably in transliteration from Iranian languages, and a name transliterated with *š* in one place may be transliterated with *sh* in another because the source in the second case is Arabic or new Persian. The names of Sasanian kings are given without diacritics in their popular forms. Following advice once given to me by Sebastian Brock, I omit diacritics in the transliteration of Syriac, though again I may not have been entirely consistent.

I take the liberty of using *hijrī* dates alone in discussions of chronology but no longer take the parallel liberty of using AD dates alone when the dates are routine. Though double dates are cumbersome and impossible to take in at a glance, they have been used throughout in deference to those who view the absence of *hijrī* dates as fraught with symbolic significance. I use the form 365/975f. in preference to 365/975–6 because it minimises the number of figures one has to take in. When I refer to sources in the form 365 = ii, 136, the former figure refers to the text and the latter to the translations; and when references take the form of 160.5 or 160.-5, the former means page 160, line 5 and the latter p. 160, line 5 from the bottom.

Patricia Crone
Princeton, May 2011

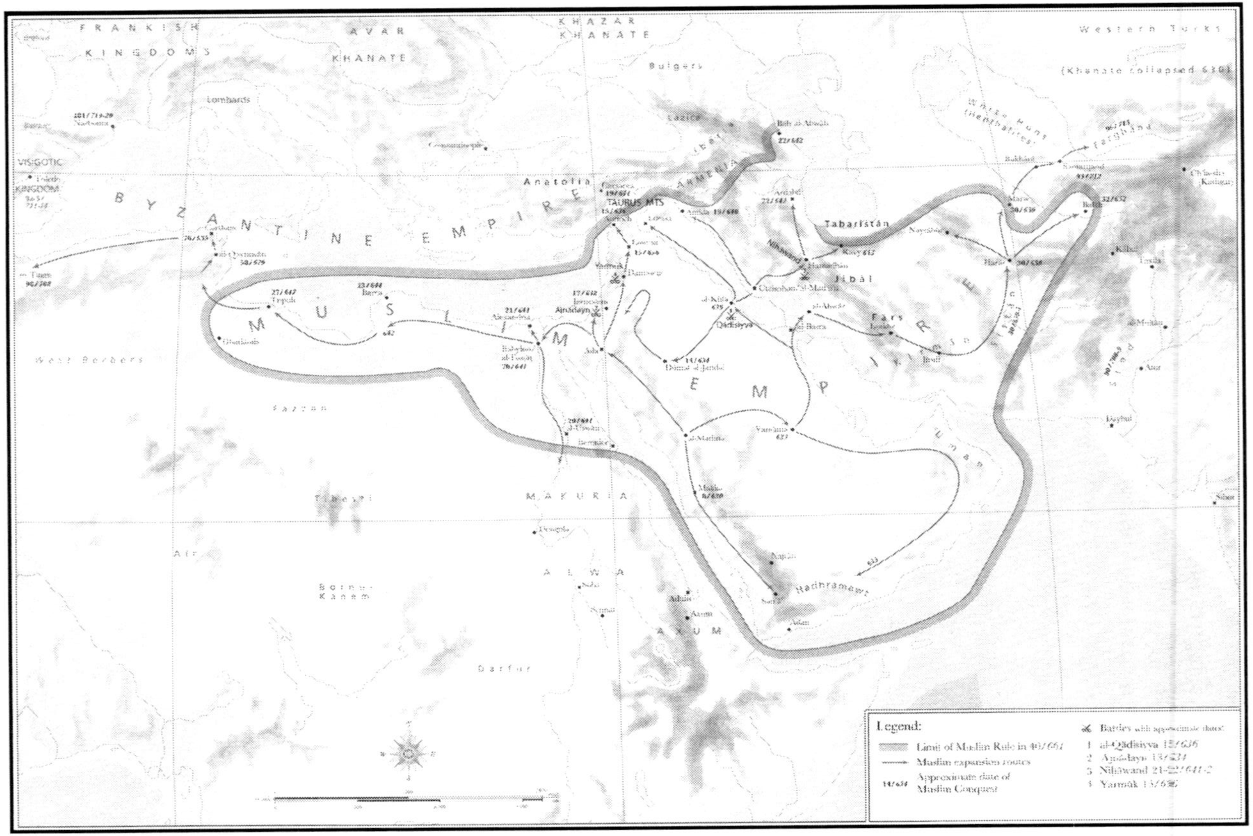

MAP I The early Arab conquests. Adapted from Kennedy, *Historical Atlas of Islam*, 7.

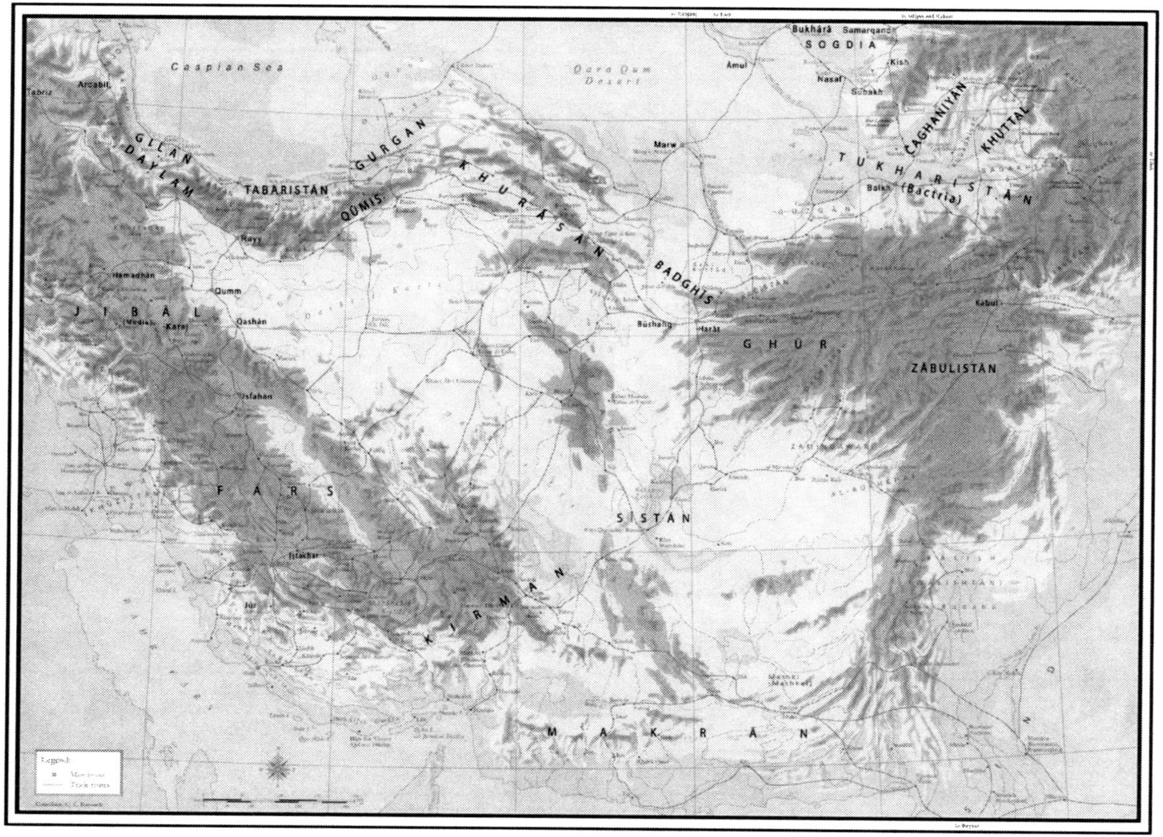

MAP 2 Early Islamic Iran. Adapted from Kennedy, *Historical Atlas of Islam*, 134.

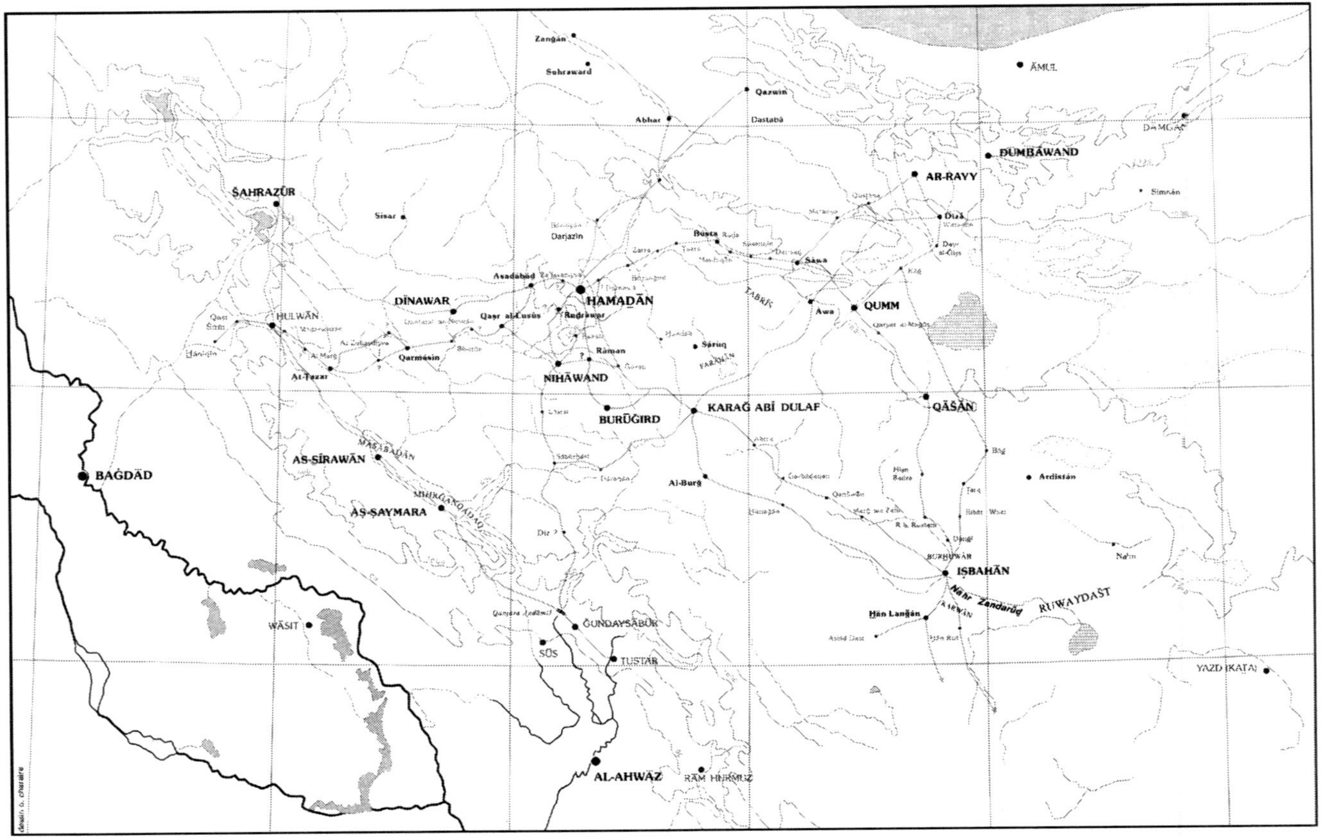

MAP 3 The Jibāl. Adapted from Cornu, *Atlas du monde arabo-islamique*, V.

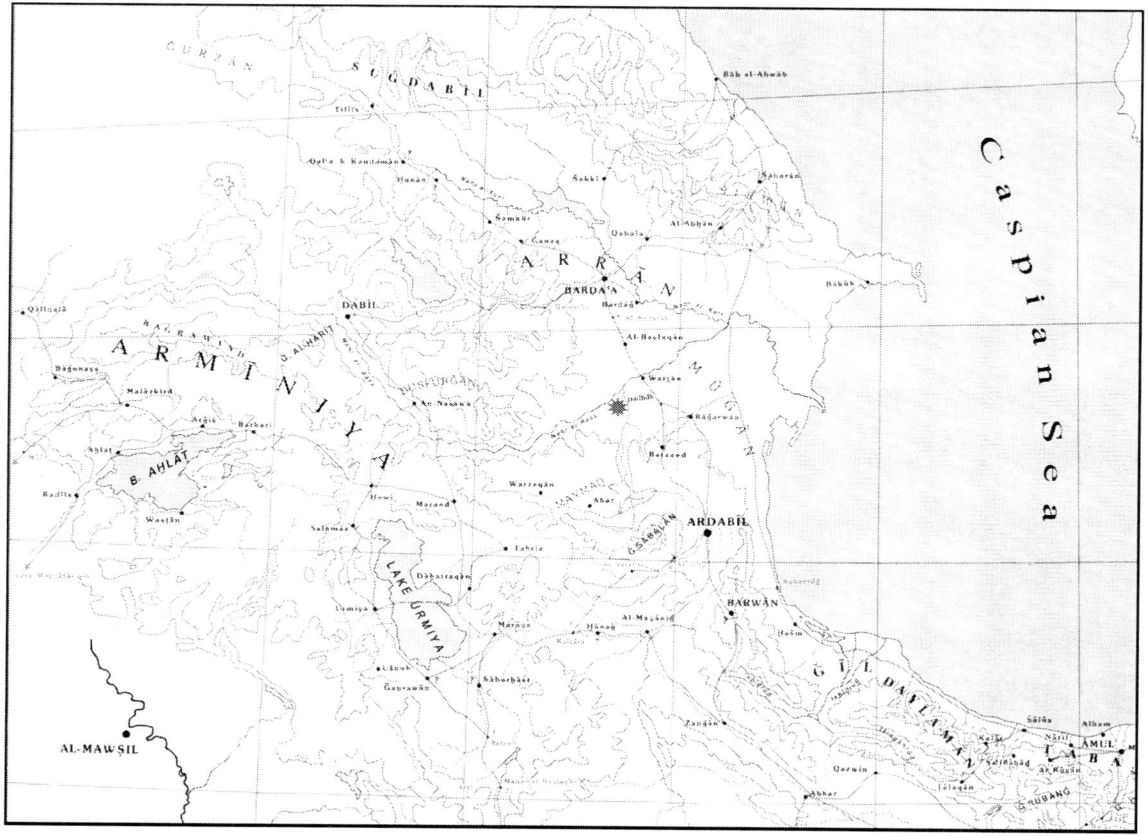

MAP 4 Azerbaijan. Adapted from Cornu, *Atlas du monde arabo-islamique*, XVI.

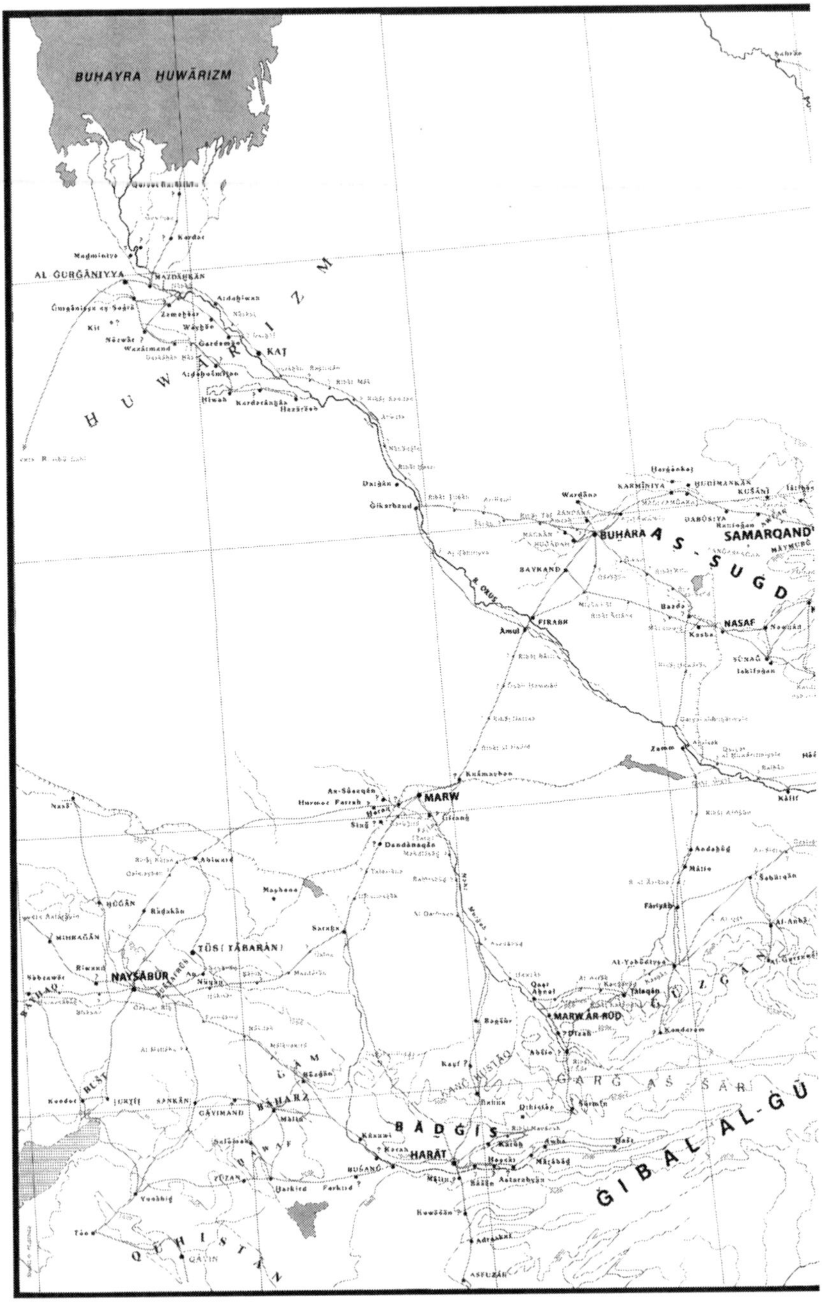

MAP 5 Khurāsān and Transoxania. Adapted from Cornu, *Atlas du monde arabo-islamique*, XVII.

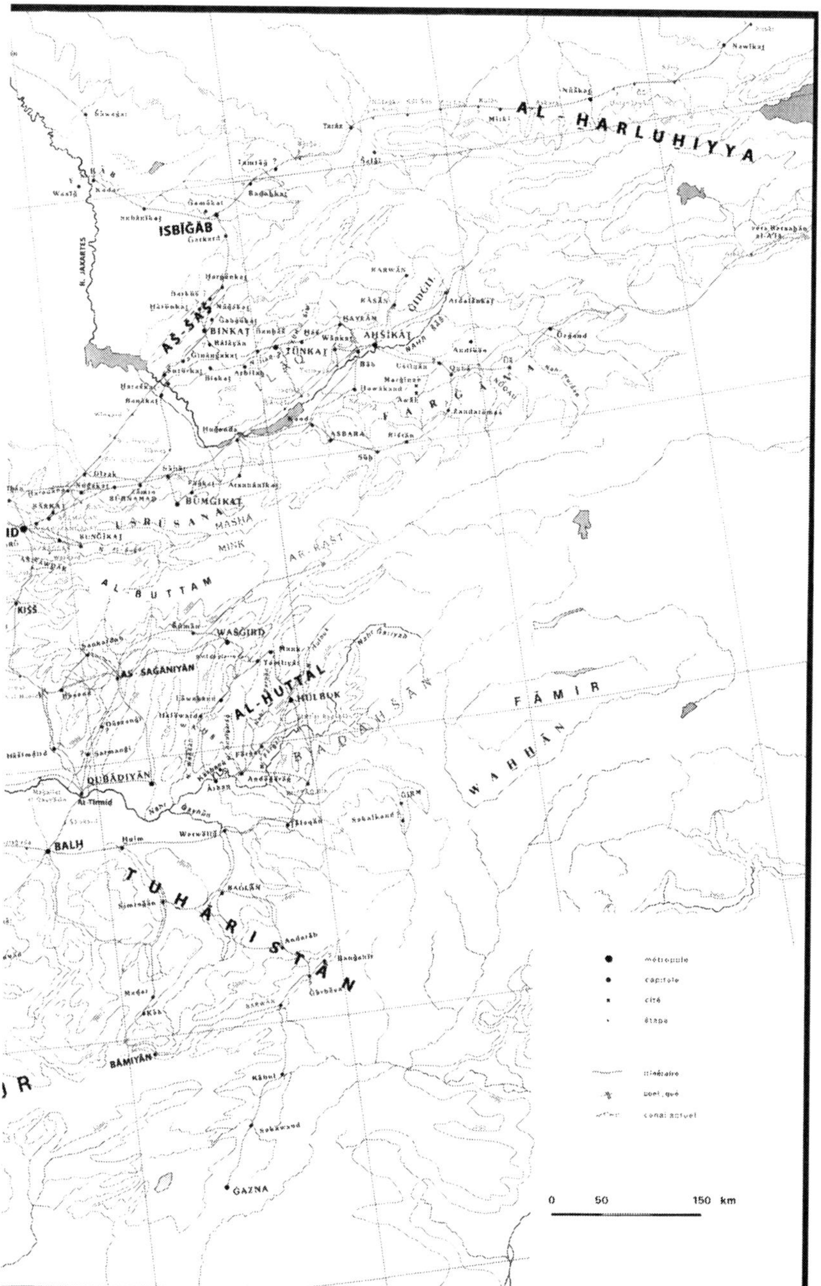
AL-HARLUHIYYA
Taraz
ISBĪĞĀB
N. JAXARTES
AŠ-ŠĀŠ
BINKAṮ
TŪNKAṮ
AHSĪKAṮ
FARĠĀNA
QIDĠIL
KASĀN
Ḫuğanda
ASBARA
USRŪSANA
BUMĠIKAṮ
MASḤA
MINK
AR-RAŠT
AL-BUTTAM
KIŠŠ
WAŠĠIRD
AŠ-ṢAĠĀNIYĀN
AL-ḪUTTAL
HULBUK
BADAḪŠĀN
FĀMIR
WAḪḪĀN
QUBĀDIYĀN
At-Tirmid
BALḪ
Ḫulm
ṬUḪĀRISTĀN
BAĠLĀN
Andarāb
BĀMIYĀN
Kābul
ĠAZNA
métropole
capitale
cité
étape
itinéraire
pont, gué
canal actuel
0 50 150 km

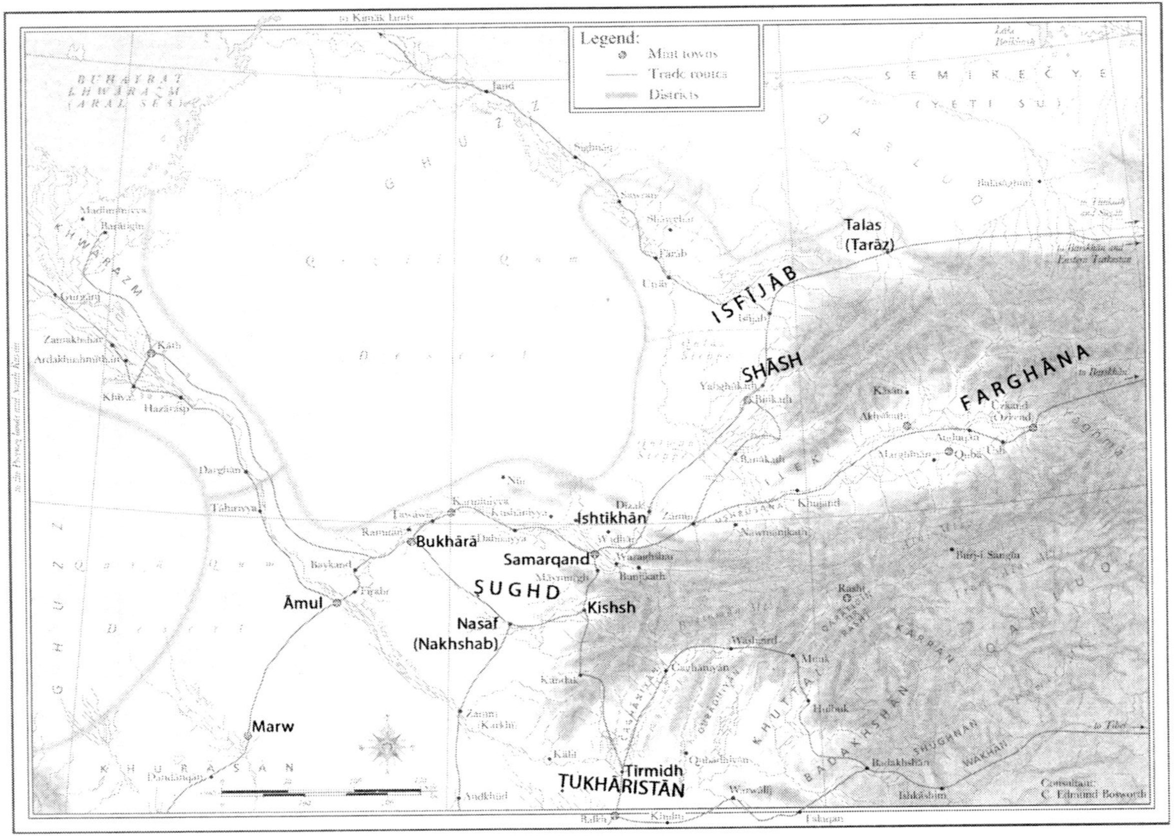

MAP 6 Transoxania. Adapted from Kennedy, *Historical Atlas of Islam*, 41a.

1

Introduction

THE ARAB CONQUEST

In the early seventh century Iran was overrun by Arab invaders who inflicted two crushing defeats on its ruler, Yazdegerd, at Qādisiyya in 16/37 and at Nihāwand in 21/642. The first victory secured them Iraq, then part of the Sasanian empire and the site of its capital, Ctesiphon (Arabic al-Madā'in); the second victory secured them the plateau. The collapse of the Sasanian empire was so swift that a fair number of modern historians have thought that the empire must have been corrupt, practically waiting to fall. It collapsed, we are told, because of the sharp difference between the classes and lack of cooperation between them, the prevalent tendency to fatalism, the numerous heterodoxies, the cupidity and corruption of the priests and their interference in politics, the weaknesses of the government and the exhaustion due to Khusraw II's aimless wars, and, in the final analysis, the material and spiritual bankruptcy of the ruling class.[1]

In actual fact, the key factor in the inability of the Sasanians to survive the Arab onslaught seems to have been the location of their capital. There cannot of course be much doubt that both they and the Byzantines were in a poor state after their twenty-year war, and the Sasanians, who had lost that war, were probably in the worse state of the two; but the Byzantines were equally incapable of defeating the Arabs in battle. They also suffered two decisive defeats, one at Ajnādayn in 13/634 and the other at Yarmūk in 15/636. Yet the Byzantine empire survived. The key difference is that the Byzantine capital was not located in Syria. As Ibn Khaldūn explained, you can nibble at the outlying provinces of an empire without thereby causing it to collapse, but if it loses its capital it is unlikely to survive, however

[1] Thus for example Zarrīnkūb, 'Arab Conquest of Iran', 17; Frye, 'Parthian and Sasanian History', 21; Bahrāmī, *Tārīkh-i Īrān*, 198f.

many of its provinces remain to be conquered. 'When the Muslims took al-Madā'in [Ctesiphon], the whole Persian empire dissolved, and the outlying provinces which remained in Yazdegerd's hand were of no avail to him. By contrast, the centre of the Byzantine state was in Constantinople ... the loss of Syria did not harm them.'[2] The Arabs proceeded to overrun Anatolia without encountering much resistance: every year they invaded, and every year they went back again without keeping their gains. What defeated them there was not the greater social cohesion, religious unity, material welfare, or spiritual health of the Byzantines, but simply the mountainous climate, which would have been a major problem for them in Iran as well if they had not conquered the capital first. Neither the Iranian nor the Anatolian plateau was a region they could conquer piecemeal. However many gains they made in Anatolia, the Byzantine state was still intact, leaving them with the problem of how to keep what they had won when the campaigning season was over. They could try to hang on to their gains by wintering there, but garrisons in Anatolia were cut off from Syria when snow blocked the passes in the Taurus mountains, so that they were left to fend for themselves in a bitterly cold and hostile land. Unlike the Turks, who came from Central Asia, they could not simply move in and occupy the land by settling on it with their families and animals. Both the Arabs and their animals were adapted to hot desert conditions, and their animals died during the Anatolian winters. The only way they could gain permanent control of Anatolia was by destroying the Byzantine empire altogether – that is, by conquering the capital; and this they could not do because the location of Constantinople made it exceptionally difficult to take. If the Sasanian capital had been in Rayy or Nīshāpūr, the Arabs might have found themselves similarly incapable of making permanent gains in the Persian plateau, however easily they could overrun it every year, for the Persian plateau was an equally inhospitable environment to them. But as it was, the very first defeat they inflicted on the Sasanians secured them the capital, and so, as Ibn Khaldūn said, the Persian empire was doomed. Having lost their administrative machinery, their treasury, and most of their personnel, the Sasanians had trouble coordinating the resistance to the invaders. They were now homeless, and as their problems mounted their alliance with the great aristocratic families who controlled the plateau unravelled.[3]

[2] Ibn Khaldūn, *Muqaddima*, III, 7 (ed. Beirut, 179; tr. Rosenthal, I, 329; tr. Cheddadi, 428).
[3] Cf. Pourshariati, *Decline*.

Yazdegerd fled to Iṣfahān, where it was put to him that he should go to Ṭabaristān, an inaccessible mountainous area on the Caspian coast not unlike the Leon and Asturias in which the Christian kings of the Iberian peninsula were to hold out. He decided against it. He would not necessarily have fared any better by going there, for Ṭabaristān did not retain its autonomy for more than a century, and there was no equivalent of Frankish Gaul, let alone the whole of Christian Europe, to the north of it, so that it is hard to imagine an eventual Reconquista from there. Yazdegerd proceeded eastwards via Kerman and Sīstān to Khurāsān, no doubt in the hope of repeating the feat of his ancestor Kavadh, who had regained his throne with Hephtalite help in 498 after having been deposed by his own nobility.[4] Yazdegerd sent appeals for help to the Turkish *khāqān*, the king of Sogdia, and the emperor of China, but he alienated the very men from whom he needed help with his haughty behaviour, and in 651 he was killed by a miller at Marw. The royal family and a number of Iranian nobles fled eastwards, and eventually reached China.[5]

China was not quite so distant a place in those days as one might think. It had come within the purview of the Sasanians close to two centuries before the Arab conquests thanks to its pursuit of an expansionist policy in Central Asia, and there had been a fair number of diplomatic exchanges between the two empires. Yazdegerd II and the emperor of the Wei dynasty had exchanged delegates in 455.[6] Kavadh had sent another embassy which reached China between 518 and 520, apparently bringing Zoroastrianism along with it: the empress dowager Ling is said to have been impressed by this religion.[7] Khusraw I sent two embassies which arrived in 553 and 555 respectively, and the Chinese responded by sending several, one of them to Khusraw II; they also compiled a report on Po-szu (Persia) to acquaint themselves with Persian affairs.[8] By then there was a strong Iranian presence in China, mainly thanks to the Sogdians who dominated the overland trade between Iran and China, and who played a prominent role in its internal trade as well.[9] Labelled Hu (Westerners) by the Chinese, they too

[4] BF, 315; cf. Christensen, *Iran*, 349f.

[5] Tab. i, 2683, 2690ff. His envoys to China reached Changan in 647 (Shinji, 'Zoroastrian Kingdoms', 44); BF, 315f.

[6] Harmatta, 'Inscription', 370f.

[7] Harmatta, 'Inscription', 371; Leslie, 'Persian Temples in T'ang China', 288f. (here dated to between 516 and 519).

[8] Harmatta, 'Inscription', 372f.

[9] De la Vaissière, *Marchands sogdiens*, 109ff.; See also de la Vaissière and Trombert, 'Des Chinois et des Hu'.

had brought their 'Heaven-God' with them. This deity had been exempted from a proscription of heretical cults by about 500, and was approved again in the 570s, though not for the Chinese, who were forbidden to use the Hu places of worship. A bureau for the cultic affairs of the Hu was set up, which lasted, with some reduction in 713f., down to 845.[10] The official history of the Tang reports that one thousand dogs picked the bones of the dead clean in the outskirts of Taiyuan, meaning where the Zoroastrians exposed their dead.[11] The Chinese also wrote several accounts, to which we shall come back, of the religious beliefs and behaviour of the Hu, and made some artistic representations of them.[12]

Yazdegerd III had sent an envoy to ask for Chinese help against the invaders in 638, after his first defeat against the Arabs; but nothing seems to have come of it.[13] His son Peroz settled among the Turks, took a local wife, and received troops from the king of Ṭukhāristān (ancient Bactria); and in 661 he established himself with Chinese help as king of Po-szu (Persia) in a place which the Chinese called Jiling (Chi-ling) and which is assumed to be Zaranj in Sīstān.[14] His campaigns during these years are reflected in Muslim sources which mention revolts in Zaranj, Balkh, Bādghīs, Herat, and Būshanj, and also in Khurāsān, during the First Civil War, in the reigns of ʿAlī (35–40/656–61) and Muʿāwiya (41–60/661–80).[15] They do not remember Peroz himself, but they tell us that when ʿAlī's newly appointed governor of Khurāsān, Khulayd b. Kaʾs, reached Nīshāpūr, he heard that governors of the Sasanian king (*ʿummāl Kisrā*) had come to Khurāsān from Kābul and that the Khurāsānīs had rebelled.[16] Peroz's comeback cannot have been entirely insignificant then, but the entire region was reconquered in the reign of Muʿāwiya. Peroz went to Changan, the capital of the Tang empire, where they gave him a

10 Eichhorn, 'Materialen', 533, 535f.

11 Hansen, 'New Work on the Sogdians', 157; cf. Grenet, *Pratiques funéraires*, 227.

12 See Chapter 5; Mahler, *Westerners among the Figurines of the T'ang Dynasty.*

13 Chavannes, *Documents*, 172; Harmatta, 'Inscription', 373; Shinji, 'Zoroastrian Kingdoms', 44 (the embassy arrived in 639).

14 BF, 316.-2; Chavannes, *Documents*, 172, 257; Harmatta, 'Inscription', 373f.; Shinji, 'Zoroastrian Kingdoms', 45 (here dated 661); cf. the confused Zoroastrian recollection of his activities in *GrBd*, 33, 21: Yazdegerd's son brought a large army to India, but died before he reached Khurāsān.

15 BF, 395, 408.ult., 409.11; Tab. i, 3350, 3389f.

16 Naṣr b. Muzāḥim, *Waqʿat Ṣiffīn*, 12; cf. Dīnawarī, 163, where it is a daughter of Kisrā who had come from Kābul. According to *EI*², s.v. 'Nīshāpūr', Peroz was reputed to have lived for a while at Nīshāpūr, but no source is given.

consolation prize in the form of a grandiose title and permitted him to build a fire-temple in 677.[17]

Peroz had a son called Ni-li-shih, probably Narsai. This son went to Central Asia in 679, accompanied by a Chinese 'Ambassador for Pacifying the Arab States', and stayed for twenty years in Ṭukhāristān without accomplishing anything at all. Eventually he returned to Changan to receive the same consolation prize.[18] The Arabs seem to have confused him with Peroz himself.[19] Later they record the appearance of Peroz's grandson, Khusraw, among the Turks at Kamarja in 110/728f.: he told them that he had come to restore his kingdom. But in 730 and 737 the same Khusraw, if Harmatta is right, paid his respects at the Chinese imperial court, suggesting that he too ended up with a consolation prize in Changan. This was the last attempt at a comeback by the royal family.[20]

Back in Iran, someone who called himself king of Persia sent embassies to China in 722 and 732, and in 744 and 746 the Chinese received envoys from two rulers of Ṭabaristān on behalf of eight kingdoms on the Caspian coast.[21] They had left it a bit late, for in 751 the Chinese themselves were defeated by the Muslims at Talas, and in 755 the Tang empire was shaken to its foundations by the revolt of An-Lushan, or Rokhshan the Bukharan as we might call him, a Sogdian general in the Chinese army.[22] It has been conjectured that some of the refugees from the Sasanian empire were recruited into an auxiliary corps formed to combat him,[23] so that Iranians briefly played a major role in both the military and commercial affairs of China. But though yet another embassy from Ṭabaristān arrived in 755, the 'Black Garment Arabs' – i.e., the ʿAbbāsids – soon annexed Ṭabaristān,[24] and China was now definitely out of action. In 845 there was a backlash against foreigners in China: all foreign religions were

[17] Shinji, 'Zoroastrian Kingdoms', 45; Eichhorn, 'Materialen', 537; cf. Leslie, 'Persian Temples in T'ang China', 286, 289, where this temple is taken to have been Nestorian; Compareti, 'Last Sasanians in China', 206ff.

[18] Chavannes, *Documents*, 173, 258; Harmatta, 'Inscription', 375; Shinji, 'Zoroastrian Kingdoms', 45; Compareti, 'Last Sasanians in China', 209f.

[19] Cf. Ibn al-Faqīh, 209/417, from Ibn al-Kalbī: Qutayba defeated Fīrūz b. Yazdajird and took his daughter, who became the mother of Yazīd III.

[20] Tab. ii, 1518; cf. Gibb, *Arab Conquests in Central Asia*, 71; Harmatta, 'Inscription', 375; Compareti, 'Last Sasanians in China', 210f.

[21] Chavannes, *Documents*, 258; Chavannes, *Notes additionelles*, 70, 76f.; Shinji, 'Zoroastrian Kingdoms', 29ff.

[22] See EI^2, s.v. 'Ṭarāz'; Karev, 'Politique d'Abū Muslim', 11ff.; Pulleyblank, *Rebellion of An Lu-Shan*, 10ff.

[23] Harmatta, 'Inscription', 369.

[24] Chavannes, *Notes additionelles*, 91f.; Shinji, 'Zoroastrian Kingdoms', 29.

proscribed, though the Iranians seem to have kept at least some of their fire-temples.[25] Thirty years thereafter, in 872 or 874, an Iranian aristocrat of the Sūrēn clan buried his daughter and/or wife near Changan and placed a bilingual inscription in Chinese and Middle Persian over her grave. The inscription says that he was a commander in the 'Left Divine Strategy Army' and that his wife and/or daughter had died at the age of twenty-six.[26] This is the last we hear of the refugees in China.

Back in Iran there had been plenty of resistance to the Arabs. The same places had to be conquered again and again, having 'turned traitors' (*ghadarū*) or been 'unfaithful' (*kafarū*) or 'broken their treaty' (*naqaḍū*), as the Muslim sources laconically inform us. Some places seem to have capitulated merely to buy time: Hamadhān, for example, rebelled within a year of having surrendered.[27] In Fārs, the home province of the Sasanians, a certain Māhāk concluded a treaty with the Arabs at Iṣṭakhr in 27/647f., or 28/648f., but broke it again in 29/649f., when the Iṣṭakhrīs killed their fiscal governor. The twenty-five-year-old governor of Basra, ʿAbdallāh b. ʿĀmir, who was laying siege to the still unsubdued Jūr at the time, completed the conquest of Jūr and moved back to reconquer Iṣṭakhr, apparently in 30/650f. or 31/651f.[28] Deeming the lives of all the inhabitants forfeit, he killed 'forty thousand' or 'a hundred thousand', or in other words a huge number, and 'annihilated most of the aristocracy and noble cavalry' (*ahl al-buyūtāt wa-wujūh al-asāwira*).[29] None the less, the inhabitants of Iṣṭakhr rebelled again during the caliphate of ʿAlī.[30] According to the Armenian historian customarily called Sebeos the people of Media – i.e., Jibāl – also rebelled about that time, more precisely in 654. They killed the tax collectors of the Arabs and fled to their mountain fortresses, where the Arabs were unable to dislodge them; the Arabs had been crushing the people of Jibāl with fiscal impositions, he says; they would take a man (as a slave) for every dirham that the locals could not pay, and thus 'they ruined the cavalry and the nobility of the country'. It was for this reason, he says, that the Medians resolved that death was better than servitude and began

[25] Eichhorn, 'Materialen', 538ff.

[26] Harmatta, 'Inscription', 363ff.; Humbach, 'Pahlavi–Chinesischen Bilingue'.

[27] See Fragner, *Hamadān*, 21ff.

[28] In Ibn al-Balkhī, *Fārsnāma*, 116, Jūr is taken in 30, but Iṣṭakhr is only reconquered in 32. Since the first Arab-Sasanian coin from Iṣṭakhr was struck in 31, the reconquest must have taken place earlier (cf. Daryaee, 'Collapse', 17).

[29] BF, 315, 389f. (with the phrase); Tab. i, 2830 (cf. 2828 for Ibn ʿĀmir's age); Ibn al-Balkhī, *Fārsnāma*, 116.

[30] BF, 390.4; Ibn al-Balkhī, *Fārsnāma*, 117.

to recruit and organise troops.[31] Sebeos may be confusing a revolt of mountaineers who fled to inaccessible mountain fortresses with that of the Iṣṭakhrīs, whose cavalry and nobility were annihilated; or perhaps complaints about the ruin of the nobility and cavalry had become a refrain. At all events, there can be no doubt that there was massive resistance. But it was all in vain. The Persian empire could not be saved. 'O men, see how Persia has been ruined and its inhabitants humiliated', as the Arab poet al-Nābigha al-Ja'dī (d. c. 70/690) said in illustration of the ephemeral nature of everything: 'they have become slaves who pasture your sheep, as if their kingdom was a dream.'[32]

IRAN UNDER THE UMAYYADS

Thereafter a ghostly silence descends on the Persian plateau. In so far as we encounter Iranians in the next hundred years it is mostly in Iraq, where the Arabs had founded two garrison cities and where the bulk of the surviving sources for early Islamic history were compiled; but even there the sightings are few and far between. Like other non-Arabs the Iranians had to enter the Muslim community to acquire visibility.

It was overwhelmingly as slaves and freedmen that they did so. It was standard practice in antiquity to enslave captives taken in war. The Arabs followed that practice, and both Muslim and non-Muslim sources give us to understand that the numbers they took were very large indeed. We are not usually offered any figures, but two Greek inscriptions relating to the Arab invasions of Cyprus in the 650s claim that 120,000 captives were carried off in the first invasion and about 50,000 in the second.[33] We are hardly to take these figures at face value. The Romans are said to have enslaved 55,000 captives after their destruction of Carthage in 146 BC, and to have taken 100,000 captives in Severus' war against the Parthians in 198 AD;[34] it seems unlikely that the Arabs should have taken about the same number in two not particularly important campaigns in Cyprus. But the figures do convey a sense of the magnitudes involved. The Islamic tradition gives the total number of fighting men in an Arab garrison city about that time as 30,000 to 60,000, the most common figure being the stereotypical 40,000, encountered in connection with Kufa,

[31] Sebeos, tr. Macler, 143, tr. Thomson, ch. 51 (where 'annihilated' is replaced by 'abolished'), 277 (for the date).

[32] al-Nābigha al-Ja'dī, *Dīwān*, 8:12f.

[33] Feissel, 'Bulletin épigraphique', 380f.; de Gagniers and Tam Tihn, *Soloi*, I, 116ff.

[34] Bradley, *Slavery and Society at Rome*, 33.

Basra, and Fusṭāṭ alike.[35] (Marw, conquered in 31/651, still only had a small garrison, stereotypically set at 4,000.)[36] Again, we are not to take the figures at face value, but if for the sake of argument we do, and assume four dependants for each combatant, the total population of an Arab garrison city in those early days will have been between 120,000 and 240,000. The Greek inscriptions estimate the yield of the two Cyprus campaigns at 170,000, exceeding or approaching the total population of an entire Arab garrison city at the time. There were only three garrison cities and four military districts in Syria in the 650s; and vastly many more captives were taken in the Fertile Crescent and Iran than on Cyprus. Though there was further emigration from Arabia in the early Umayyad period, when Marw became a substantial garrison city, Qayrawān was founded, and a fifth military district was established in Syria, there can be no doubt that the Arabs were a very small minority in the non-Arab Near East. Unreliable though the figures are, they graphically illustrate the fact that the Arabs must soon have been outnumbered by non-Arabs even in their own settlements.

Slaves were generally used in the house, where they did all the work nowadays done or facilitated by machines, and where they serviced the sexual needs of their masters too. Outside the home they supplied skilled labour as scribes, copyists and teachers, and as craftsmen and traders earning money for themselves and their masters, as well as unskilled labour of diverse kinds (again including sexual services); there was little agricultural slavery, no galley slavery, and no slavery for the exploitation of mines that we know of. Since most forms of slavery involved personal human contact with Muslims, most slaves ended up by adopting the religion of their captors, with momentous consequences for the latter. It was not just as Arabs that the conquerors were rapidly outnumbered in their own settlements, it was as Muslims too.

Slaves were often manumitted. It is impossible to say with what frequency (slavery is one of the most under-studied topics of early Islamic history), but freedmen abound in the sources, and the Arabs accepted those of them who had converted as full members of their own polity. The freedman did suffer some disabilities vis-à-vis his manumitter, whose client (*mawlā*) he became, but the effects of this were largely

[35] BA, IVa, 190.17 (Basra on the arrival of Ziyād); Tab. i, 2805.7; Ibn ʿAbd al-Ḥakam, 316 (Fusṭāṭ under Muʿāwiya); *al-Imāma wa'l-siyāsa*, I, 144 (Basra under ʿAlī), 145 (Kufa under ʿAlī).

[36] *EI*², s.v. 'Marw al-Shāhidjān'.

limited to private law; in public law freedmen had the same status as their captors. Of course, whatever the law might say, there was massive prejudice against them.[37] Non-Arab freedmen were casually written off as slaves, awarded less pay in the army than their Arab peers, regarded as less valuable for purposes of blood-money and retaliation, and deemed utterly unacceptable in positions of authority such as prayer leaders, judges, governors, and generals, where their occasional appearance would be greeted with wild abuse. Free or freed, non-Arabs were deemed unsuitable as marriage partners for Arab women; aristocratic Arabs disliked the idea of giving daughters even to 'half-breeds' (sing. *hajīn*), however elevated the fathers.[38] Stories regarding Arab prejudice against their non-Arab clients are legion. Treated as outsiders, the clients (*mawālī*) responded by congregating in their own streets, with their own separate mosques;[39] but they stopped short of forming their own separate Muslim community and, for all the prejudice against them, they rapidly acquired social and political importance. A mere forty years after the conquests, when the Arabs were fighting their Second Civil War, slaves and freedmen participated as soldiers on several sides and played a conspicuous part in the movement that took control of Kufa under the leadership of the Arab al-Mukhtār (66–7/685–7). The slaves and freedmen in this revolt were mostly Iranians captured in the course of Kufan campaigns in north-western Iran, and they spoke an Iranian language ('Persian' to al-Dīnawarī) among themselves.[40] Clients, again many of them Iranians, dominated the civilian sector of Muslim society which emerged after the Second Civil War, and they rose to influential political positions too, though they continued to remain subordinate to the Arabs in military and political affairs throughout the Umayyad period (41–132/661–750).[41]

As might be expected, their rapid rise to prominence was a source of anxiety to the Arabs, who watched their own society being transformed by outsiders and feared losing control of it, both politically and culturally. Patriarchal figures were credited with predictions that things would go wrong when the children of captives became numerous, or when they

[37] The classic study is Goldziher, *Muhammedanische Studien* (ed. and tr. Stern as *Muslim Studies*), I, ch. 3.

[38] Bashear, *Arabs and Others*, 37–40; Crone, 'The Pay of Client Soldiers'; Crone, 'Mawālī and the Prophet's Family', 170f.

[39] Tab. ii, 681.4, iii, 295.12; Dietrich, 'Die Moscheen von Gurgān', 8, 10.

[40] Tab. ii, 724.11; Dīnawarī, 302.7; cf. *EI*², s.v. 'al-Mukhtār b. Abī 'Ubayd'.

[41] Cf. *EI*², s.v. 'mawlā'.

attained maturity.[42] The slaves who had once been Arab property would inherit the world, it was said; non-Arabs would 'kill your fighting men and consume your income [*fay*', lit. booty]'.[43] It might be better to kill nine out of ten captives than to have slaves, it was argued: 'they will not remain loyal and they will embitter your lives'.[44] Clients responded with horror stories about Arab prejudice, crediting past Arab rulers with abortive plans to decimate their ranks, an idea occasionally mentioned in an applauding vein on the Arab side as well.[45] Free converts also became a source of anxiety. It would be the end of the religion when the Arameans became eloquent (in Arabic) and reached a status allowing them to acquire palaces in the provinces, it was said; the caliph ʿUmar reputedly wept on hearing that they had converted to Islam.[46] When al-Ḥajjāj (governor of Iraq, 75–95/694–713) built the new garrison city of Wāsiṭ in Iraq he is said to have cleared the area of Arameans and forbidden them entry into his new city, envisaged as a pure Arab enclave and bastion of colonial rule in Aramean-Iranian Iraq, though the people it was meant to keep out soon settled there as well.[47] Whatever the truth of this story (one out of many involving al-Ḥajjāj and *mawālī*), there is no doubt that the Umayyad regime sometimes tried to stem the tide of free converts, when it came.[48] But despite the advice to cut down on slavery, they never seem to have tried to limit the taking of captives or to exclude freedmen from membership of their community, so the flood of immigrants continued.

By the 120s/740s the Arabs were no longer the people that their grandfathers had been. Many apparent Arabs were actually children of mixed parentage – or not descendants of the Arab conquerors at all, but simply Muslim speakers of Arabic who tried to pass for Arabs, or who did not even try to hide their non-Arab descent.[49] Among the Syrian troops at al-Ahwāz in the 740s, for example, there was a Damascene soldier by the name of Hāniʾ; he was a *mawlā* attached through his patron to a South Arabian tribe, and he married an Iranian woman by whom he fathered a son and a daughter. The daughter married a slave by the name of Faraj

[42] Sayf b. ʿUmar, *al-Ridda wa'l-futūḥ*, 18, no. 21; Abū Zurʿa, no. 1339; Bashear, *Arabs and Others*, 95.

[43] Bashear, *Arabs and Others*, 74, 103.

[44] Kister, 'Land, Property and *Jihād*', 289.

[45] Crone, 'Mawālī and the Prophet's Family'.

[46] Bashear, *Arabs and Others*, 80.

[47] Jāḥiẓ, *Bayān*, I, 275; Wāsiṭī, *Taʾrīkh Wāsiṭ*, 46, no. 13; Ibn al-Faqīh (ed. Hādī), 266; Yāqūt, IV, 886.2, s.v. 'Wāsiṭ'.

[48] See below, pp. 13ff.

[49] Goldziher, *Muhammedanische Studien*, I, 133ff.

al-Qaṣṣār, a fuller to judge by his name, whose owner was a certain Aḥmad b. ʿIṣmat Allāh al-Bākharzī, clearly a non-Arab too. The son rose to fame under the name of Abū Nuwās, one of the greatest Arabic poets.[50] This is how we should envisage much of Muslim society at the time on the ground. Arabic was rapidly becoming a cosmopolitan language rather than a sign of ethnic identity,[51] just as Islam was becoming everyone's property, rather than a religion special to its initial carriers. The political house in which this hybrid society was accommodated, however, was still basically that which had been built for the Arab conquerors three generations previously. It was ruled from Syria, and the Syrian army which policed the empire was dominated by Arab tribesmen from the Syrian desert who came across as increasingly alien to everyone else. Of course, there were also men such as Abū Nuwās's father and other non-Arabs in the Syrian army. There were non-Arab Muslims everywhere. But in terms of organisation and outlook alike, Syria was more closely attuned to the old-fashioned Arab world from which the conquerors had come than to the new society in which their grandsons were living.

THE HĀSHIMITE REVOLUTION

All this changed in the Hāshimite revolution which enthroned the ʿAbbāsid dynasty, a key event in Islamic history and the background to all the revolts studied in this book. The revolutionaries came from Khurāsān, that is, eastern Iran. In the narrow sense Khurāsān was the region between Nīshāpūr and the river Oxus (Jayḥūn, Amu Darya) which had its capital in Marw, plus the north-western part of what is now Afghanistan. Only about a third of that region forms part of Iran today; part of it is in Afghanistan, and the rest, including Marw, is now in Turkmenistan. In the wider sense Khurāsān included Transoxania (Mā warāʾ al-nahr), an open-ended category which stretched all the way to Kāshgar and 'China', that is Chinese-dominated Central Asia,[52] but which normally referred to the region now divided between Uzbekistan and Tajikistan. With the exception of Afghanistan and Tajikistan the dominant languages in all these countries are now Turkic, but in our period the entire region was still predominantly Iranian in both language and culture, though it had a Turkish population as well.

[50] Wagner, *Abū Nuwās*, 15f., 20f.; cf. also Kennedy, *Abu Nuwas*, 1ff.
[51] Cf. the traditions in Bashear, *Arabs and Others*, 56.
[52] Cf. the account of Qutayba's campaign there (Tab. ii, 1275ff.).

When the Arabs conquered Khurāsān in the narrow sense of the word, they left a garrison at Marw, and in 51/671 they moved a large number of Arabs there from, or perhaps just via, Basra and Kufa.[53] These colonists were a long way from home. The Arabs who had settled in Syria, Iraq, and Egypt were linked to their Arabian homeland by deserts which they navigated with ease and which were inhabited by Arabs too; but the colonists in Khurāsān were separated not just from Arabia, but also from their peers in Iraq by the Iranian plateau, a highland region like Anatolia in which, as mentioned before, they did not feel at home. They did briefly found a garrison city in Fārs, at Tawwaj, 'suitable for Arab settlement because of its extreme heat', as Ibn al-Balkhī says; but it was rapidly abandoned in favour of Basra.[54] Arab tribes moved into hot desert areas elsewhere in Iran where they found them,[55] and other settlements were established on the plateau in the course of the Umayyad period.[56] Even so, the Persian plateau remained a solid stretch of non-Arab land quite unlike the deserts between Egypt, Syria, and Iraq. It would be an exaggeration to say that the colonists at Marw were cut off from their fellow Arabs, for there was much coming and going between Khurāsān and other Muslim settlements. But they did form a small drop in a sea of Iranians, and as they expanded into Ṭukhāristān and Transoxania they became increasingly diluted. Necessity forced them quickly to use non-Arab troops, in the form of both non-Muslim allies and client members of the regular army. When we first hear of the client section of the army in Khurāsān, in 96/715, it was commanded by a first-generation Muslim from the Caspian coast, presumably a former prisoner of war, who had come to Khurāsān via Basra, where his patron resided, and who spoke Arabic with an accent.

[53] BF, 410.9; Tab. iii, 81, 155f.; Agha, *Revolution*, 178ff. The number is given as 50,000, apparently including their families, a large number rendered more plausible if we assume them to be fresh arrivals from Arabia.

[54] Ibn al-Balkhī, *Fārsnāma*, 135 (adding that 'Aḍud al-Dawla later settled Arab tribes from Syria there); cf. Hinds, 'First Arab Conquests in Fārs'. For Arab complaints of the bitter cold and snow in Khurāsān, see the poetry in Agha, *Revolution*, 179.

[55] At some point Arab tribes settled in the coastal areas of Fārs (Iṣṭakhrī, 140ff.; Ibn al-Balkhī, *Fārsnāma*, 140). For their presence in eastern Iran, mostly as pastoralists, see Bosworth, *Ghaznavids*, 112.

[56] Rayy allegedly had a *dīwān* by the time of 'Uthmān (BA, V, 41f.), but it was still a *thaghr* as opposed to a *miṣr* in 52 (Tab. ii, 182.16). It did have both a *dīwān* and a governor of its own by 77 (Tab. ii, 996, cf. 1001). For Arabs settling in the Iṣfahān (Jayy) and Hamadhān area see BF, 314.4, 324.8; *Aghānī*, V, 13; Tab. ii, 99f., 994 (year 77, by which time there were governors there); for Qumm see *Tārikh-i Qumm*, 44 (where Ash'arīs arrive at an unspecified date, initially living in tents); for Shīrāz, founded by a relative of al-Ḥajjāj, see Yāqūt, III, 348f., s.v.

That such a man should have been put in charge of Muslim troops a mere fifty years after the conquests is illustrative of the speed with which clients rose in Arab society.[57] Again, the effects were far reaching. By the 120s/740s old Muslim society in Khurāsān consisted of the sons and grandsons of the Arab immigrants and non-Arab freedmen who had been the first settlers there, all of them solidly Muslim, Persian speaking, and with an outlook that set them apart from their co-religionists elsewhere. It was by such men that the upper echelons of the revolutionary armies were dominated.[58]

It was not only as slaves and freedmen that Iranians entered Muslim society, however. As mentioned already, there were also free converts. Some of them were members of the elite, such as cavalry troops who defected to the Arabs during the conquests and occasional aristocrats who opted for a place in the new order.[59] But the free converts one hears about in the first century after the conquests were not usually aristocrats. Rather, they were peasants and other villagers, which is in fact also what most of the captives must have been by origin. From around 80/700 onwards we hear of peasants running away from the land, both in the former Sasanian empire and elsewhere, in order to claim status as Muslims in the Arab garrison cities; here they usually tried to gain membership of the army, a privileged institution at the time. This posed a problem. On the one hand, the Arabs liked their subjects to see the truth of Islam, and in Syria and Khurāsān they also needed soldiers; but on the other hand, the fiscal organisation of the Arab empire rested on the assumption that non-Arabs were non-Muslims who cultivated the land and paid taxes, whereas Arabs were Muslims who fought in the army and consumed the taxes in the form of pay and rations. By the mid-Umayyad period it was becoming clear that the tax system had to be changed to take account of changing conditions, but this was more easily said than done, since it would inevitably mean depriving the Arabs of their freedom from taxation, their most important privilege as tribesmen and conquerors alike. The classical solution was that all taxes were blind to both ethnicity and faith except for *jizya*, identified as the poll-tax, which was to be collected from unbelievers alone. This was apparently worked out, or at least applied, only a few

[57] Crone, 'A Note on Muqātil', 1997, 238f.

[58] Cf. Agha, *Revolution*, ch. 13. For the distinction between old Muslim society in Khurāsān and fresh immigrants/converts see Crone, "Abbāsid Abnā'", 12f.; cf. also the introduction to Crone, *From Arabian Tribes*, viif., on the regrettable tendency to treat non-Arab Muslims as a single, undifferentiated group.

[59] *EIr.*, s.vv. 'Asāwera', 'Ḥamrā'; Pourshariati, *Decline*, 238ff.

years before the revolution.[60] Until then the authorities were in the habit of treating fugitive peasants as illegal immigrants, denying them admission to the army and every now and again rounding them up in order to deport them, so that they could be made to cultivate the land and pay their taxes again (a policy in which the leaders of the native communities had an interest too). This problem is attested in Iraq, Egypt, and Khurāsān (including Transoxania), where it alternated with attempts to consolidate Arab control by promising converts to Islam freedom from taxation.[61]

Conversion and flight from the land went together because peasants were running away from all their taxes, not simply trying to escape the poll-tax from which converts were freed according to the classical rules. Besides, they risked being penalised, both fiscally and otherwise, by their own former co-religionists if they stayed in their villages, especially if there was no Arab settlement in them. After the Hāshimite revolution the garrison cities ceased to be islands of privilege, but until then the whole point of conversion was that it took a man away from the land and into the garrison cities of the conquerors, where he could hope to share their favoured status.

This point is often presented in misleading terms in the modern literature because it is taken to imply that the converts cannot have been sincere, which in its turn is felt to be belittling to Islam. But quite apart from the fact that we are not supposed to rewrite history to fit modern sensibilities, this is mistaken. The fact that conversion enabled people to change their lives for the better in material terms in no way implies that they converted insincerely: it is after all a good deal easier to believe in the truth of ideas that work wonders than it is to deny their truth while still accepting that they have wondrous effects. Immigrants seeking by hook or by crook to gain entry to the wealthy West today are usually firm believers in the capitalist market economy and democratic politics in terms of which Western wealth is commonly explained. Converts trying to secure entry to the privileged ranks of the Muslim conquerors must be presumed similarly to have been convinced of the truth of the religion that was taken to be the key to Muslim power. There may have been people who converted for the material benefit alone: Umayyad governors not unnaturally suspected this.[62] But most converts are likely to have embraced their new life with

[60] Cf. Tab. ii, 1688f.

[61] Cf. Wellhausen, *Kingdom*, 456ff., 477ff.; Gibb, *Arab Conquests in Central Asia*, 69; Crone, 'Qays and Yemen', 14f., 21f., 24, 31; Crone, 'The Pay of Client Soldiers', 297ff.

[62] E.g. Tab. ii, 1354.10.

enthusiasm, exhilarated by the idea that the deity who had allowed the Arabs to conquer the world should be willing to include the defeated peoples among his devotees.

The Arabs (and their clients too) not unnaturally reacted by trying to stem the tide of immigrants, or to get them out again, by imposing tests on them, refusing to register them for payment, or simply deporting them outright.[63] But they were up against the fact that the privileges they were trying to defend were explained in terms of Islam, a religion open to all mankind, so that what would otherwise have been regarded as a perfectly normal imperial reaction was perceived as morally outrageous, and has been so regarded ever since. Inviting the natives in with one hand and trying to keep them out with the other, the Arabs had no hope of keeping their privileged position for long.

The fact that access to the rank of the conquerors lay in conversion, in principle if not always in practice, is a point of major importance. Like so many other imperial powers the Arabs freely recruited soldiers from the conquered population. In addition to individual clients who had passed through slavery and manumission among them they enrolled whole regiments of captives taken during campaigns, and sometimes free peasants too, using tax-freedom for converts as bait. In 77/696f. a Khurāsānī Arab claimed that one could recruit 50,000 superbly obedient soldiers in Khurāsān by simply announcing that all converts to Islam would be freed from their taxes (*kharāj*).[64] In 127/144 Yazīd III's governor of Egypt caused 30,000 Copts to abandon their villages when he promised freedom from taxation to converts in order to raise troops, civil war having broken out.[65] Captives or peasants, all became Muslims in order to fight for the empire. How much they knew or understood about Islam, or even how sincerely they believed in it, does not matter at this point: what does matter is that they all became members of the same political and moral community as their former conquerors.

[63] For all these policies see the material in Crone, 'Qays and Yemen', 14f., 21f., 24, 31.

[64] Tab. ii, 1024.

[65] Kindī, *Governors*, 84ff.; Severus b. al-Muqaffaʿ, *Patriarchs*, in *PO*, V, 116; cf. also Basset, *Synaxaire*, in *PO*, XVI, 233. For the term *Maqāmiṣa* applied to these troops, see the Greek and Arabic versions of the Life of St Stephen cited in Stroumsa, 'Judeo-Arabic Commentary on Genesis', 377f.: here an Egyptian convert from Islam to Christianity is described in Greek as a Hagarene (*magarites*) from among the indigenous (*autokhtonōn*) Hagarenes, presumably meaning a Muslim from among the native, i.e., non-Arab, Muslims (differently Stroumsa); in the Arabic translation, made about 800, this is rendered as *mqmṣ ibn mqmṣ*.

This is distinctly unusual. The Romans also recruited troops from among the conquered peoples for their external expansion and eternal wars, and they did at some point grant citizenship to the Italians among their troops (and to Italians in general); thereafter they granted citizenship to non-Romans who had served for twenty-five years, or performed some exceptional service. But it was not as members of the Roman political and moral community that such troops had fought, nor could they simply choose to become citizens. It was only with the grant of universal citizenship in 211 and the victory of Christianity a century thereafter that all conquered peoples came to form part of the same political and moral community as the conquerors. Or again, the Europeans also enrolled troops from among the peoples they had conquered in Asia, Africa, and elsewhere, both for the policing of their empires and for fighting in what amounted to European civil wars, in the First World War, and, on a much greater scale, the Second. But it was not as members of the same political or moral community as the European powers that these recruits fought either. They were not citizens or Christians (except fortuitously), nor was the aftermath a revolution in Europe itself, but rather independence for the colonies. By contrast, the Muslims hardly ever recruited troops from the conquered lands without converting them (though they did use federate troops in Khurāsān), and Islam was both a political and a moral fellowship.

Conversion to Islam in the sense of a declaration of willingness to join the Muslim community was extremely easy, yet the community to which it secured access was a highly privileged one, the society created by the conquerors for themselves. This is what was so unusual about Umayyad society: rarely have imperial powers set the bar to membership of their own favoured ranks so low. Conversion to Christianity was also easy in the French and the British empires, and where the missionaries were the main disseminators of European knowledge the rural masses often converted, persuaded that Christianity was the key to European strength. But the European empires were not based on Christianity. Conversion did not result in membership of the privileged polity of the conquerors, only of the church, and many reacted by seceding from the church – or from Christianity altogether – on discovering this.[66] By contrast, converts to Islam became members of both the 'church' and the privileged polity, the two being rolled together as the community of believers, so that, prejudice notwithstanding, they could envisage themselves as sharing in the political

[66] See Chapter 8.

structure created by the foreign rulers, not just as having to choose between resisting it and living in perpetual subjection.

This does something to explain the extraordinary fact that the revolution was Islamic. A comparativist would have expected the Arabs simply to have been forced to withdraw, after the fashion of the Mongols in China or the European powers in Asia and Africa, for example. Fighting no less than three civil wars in the century after the conquests, the Arabs seemed positively to invite expulsion: how long can a tiny minority be expected to hang on to power in a foreign land if it fights itself every thirty years? But, thanks to the ease with which outsiders could enter, the Muslim community had already expanded enormously by the time of the Second Civil War, and even more by the time the Umayyads fell. What is more, by drawing in huge masses of low-status people the Arabs had unwittingly turned the social map of the Near East upside down: the peasants and villagers who had come together, voluntarily or by force, in the cities constituted a pool from which a new elite was emerging, at the expense of the Umayyads and non-Arab elites, such as the Iranian aristocracy, alike. The native converts had become the main bearers of the belief system brought by the Arabs: they had taken over as its spokesmen and interpreters. So the outcome of the Third Civil War was not independence for Iran or any other region, but on the contrary a revolution in Arab society itself. 'Noble Arabs and aristocratic Iranians' were killed while 'lowly and ignoble people' rose to high status, as a member of a Sasanian aristocratic family is said to have predicted.[67]

THE RECRUITS

The Hāshimite mission had its centre in Marw and recruited a great many long-standing members of Muslim society there, both Arab and Iranian, suggesting that their intention was focused on the subversion of the ethnically mixed local army in Khurāsān.[68] In fact, however, large segments of the Khurāsānī army remained loyal to the Umayyads, and the figures given for the revolutionary armies, unreliable though they are, leave no doubt

[67] See Chapter 2, p. 32.

[68] Cf. Sulaymān b. Kathīr al-Khuzāʿī, one of their earliest recruits: we know that both his father and his brother had been members of the Khurāsānī army (Tab. ii, 1480, 1595, 1601), and that he himself was also *min ahl al-dīwān* (*AA*, 199). Differently Shaban, *ʿAbbāsid Revolution*, where they recruit Arabs who have dropped out of the army, and Sharon, *Revolt*, where they get their professional fighting force at a late stage by recruiting the Yemeni faction of the army led by al-Kirmānī.

that the missionaries must have drawn extensively on alternative sources of manpower. In an agrarian society the only significant source of manpower is the peasantry, probably some 90 per cent of the population in greater Khurāsān if we include village craftsmen and other providers of rural services in the count. There were some Arab bedouin in the region, but no Arab peasantry in Khurāsān that we know of. It follows that the missionaries must have recruited Iranians. This view, formulated a century ago, was hotly contested for some thirty years, but it has been gaining ground again, and Agha has provided it with rich documentation.[69] The revolutionary armies included recruits from regions in which the Arabs must have been thin on the ground or wholly absent, including regions that had barely been conquered yet, or at least not properly subdued, such as Khwārizm, Khuttal, Farghāna, and Kābul,[70] and perhaps even Isfijāb.[71] Some of the recruits continued to be known by their Iranian names or titles, as did Zuwāra al-Bukhārī, Māhān al-Ṣamghānī, al-Ishtākhan, Turārkhudā, Abrāzkhudā, Sunbādh, and Nīzak.[72] But these recruits mostly belonged to the elite: several of them were local potentates who will have brought their own troops with them.[73] We are less well informed about the social provenance of the rest. We hear of one who was a driver of sheep to Marw,[74] another who was a village headman in Sogdia, and a third who may have been a fuller,[75] but it is rare for their professions to be mentioned. The recruits are often identifiable as Iranians, however, if not always with certainty, by their lack of tribal *nisbas*, the absence of father's names, or by the father's name being Iranian, or by explicit identification of them as Iranians (*ʿajam*) or clients (*mawālī*), or by their appearance in contexts suggesting the same. Most of them must have been men whose enrolment into the Hāshimite movement constituted their entry into Muslim society. They came across to their opponents as little but infidel rabble from the backwoods of Iran: they were derided as *ʿulūj* and *ʿajam*, roughly translatable as non-Arab scum and barbarians, alleged to worship

[69] Agha, *Revolution*, 334ff.

[70] Cf. Dīnawarī, 360 (Khuttalān); YB, 248.16f., 249.17; Ibn Ḥajar, *Tahdhīb*, IV, 163 (Sulaymān b. Dāwūd b. Rushayd al-Khuttalī, *min al-abnā'*, cf. Tab. iii, 319, 427); Samʿānī, *Ansāb*, I, 10.9 (ʿAwf b. ʿĪsā b. Yart b. al-Shanfardān al-Farghānī, *min al-abnā'*).

[71] The people settled in the Ḥarbiyya quarter included those of Asbīshāb, presumably to be read Asbijāb/Isfijāb (on which see *EI²*, suppl, s.v. 'Isfidjāb').

[72] Cf. Crone, "Abbāsid Abnā'", 12. For Nīzak, an associate of Abū Muslim's, see Tab. iii, 100, 108; *ʿUyūn*, 221.

[73] See Chapter 2.

[74] Tab. ii, 1957 (ʿAbdawayh Jardāmidh b. ʿAbd al-Karīm).

[75] See below, pp. 107, 111.

cats and heads, and not to pray; they were 'not *mawālī* that we know', as Naṣr b. Sayyār, the last Umayyad governor of Khurāsān, famously declared; their religion was identified as killing Arabs; they wanted to 'eliminate us'; their Islam was feigned. All this was propaganda, of course, but propaganda only works if it plays on something real; and while the counter-propaganda went to great lengths to deny the charges of unbelief, no attempt was made to rebut the ethnic characterisation.[76] Conservative Muslims had every reason to be scared by these alien avengers whose Islam seems to have consisted primarily in fierce loyalty to their new Muslim leaders, who arrived in their lands dressed all in black, speaking a foreign language, and wielding clubs that they called infidel-bashers against descendants of the very men to whom they owed Islam, expressing their religious hatred of the existing order by digging up the graves of dead Umayyads in Syria in order to inflict post-mortem punishments on them, and appointing non-Arabs to positions in which old-fashioned Muslims still found them utterly unacceptable.[77]

The revolutionaries were well aware of their Iranian past, but it was the rightful position of the Prophet's family, not their ancestral polity, that they wished to restore. On the march to Iraq Qaḥṭaba (himself an ethnic Arab) gave a speech intended to dispel their fear of the Syrians they were about to face in battle. Their forefathers had owned the land, he said, but the Arabs had defeated them, taken their land, bedded their women, and reduced their children to slaves. The Arabs had been fully justified in doing so, Qaḥṭaba said, for back in those days they had been good Muslims whereas the Iranians had been oppressors. Since then, however, the Arabs had themselves become oppressors who acted unjustly, in particular by maltreating the Prophet's family, so now God had authorised the troops to avenge them for him. In other words, the righteous Arabs had turned into Umayyad wrongdoers and so had to be removed by all those whom they had reduced to political impotence: whether the latter were Iranians or ethnic Arabs, all were united in pursuit of vengeance for the Prophet's family, the fountainhead of truth, who had been ousted from their rightful role by the oppressive Arabs now ruling in their stead.[78]

[76] For all this see Agha, *Revolution*, 197–212.

[77] For all this see Wellhausen, *Kingdom*, 493f., 533ff., 552f.; Crone, 'Wooden Weapons', 176ff.; Azdī, 146 (in explanation of the massacre in Mosul discussed in Robinson, *Empire and Elites*, ch. 6).

[78] Tab. ii, 2004f.; *'Uyūn*, 192f.; discussed in Crone, 'Wooden Weapons', 185; Zakeri, *Sāsānid Soldiers*, 280; Agha, *Revolution*, 198f.

The men to whom Qaḥṭaba was speaking clearly saw the Holy Family as typifying their own situation: like the true bearers of the Prophet's message they had been oppressed by the 'Arabs', meaning all those who saw Islam as going hand in hand with a privileged position for its original carriers. The Umayyads were 'Arabs', men such as Qaḥṭaba or the Prophet's family were not. It was the 'Arabs' who had restricted the entry of non-Arabs into Muslim society, taxing converts, and keeping those who were admitted in a lowly position; and it was the Prophet's family that was now letting them in with full membership: Islam as originally preached by the Prophet himself was being restored; everything would come right at the hands of the redeemer from his family, the mahdi whose kingdom they were preparing. Everything did in fact come right for some of them, including Qaḥṭaba's men. Qaḥṭaba himself was drowned in the course of the conquest of Iraq, but his army remained intact and was eventually housed in Baghdad, where the so-called Ḥarbiyya quarter teemed with Iranians full of weird beliefs of the kind that will figure prominently in what follows, notably deification of the redeemer who, when he came, took the form of the ʿAbbāsid caliph.[79]

Things did not come right for the many recruits who stayed in Khurāsān, however. Many of them had been recruited by Abū Muslim, a man of uncertain ancestry who was the actual architect of the revolution and who remained in Khurāsān as governor and general, engaged in imposition of control over the province. In 137/755 Abū Muslim was summoned to a meeting with the caliph al-Manṣūr. Forbidden to take his army with him, he left it at Ḥulwān,[80] on the border between Iran and Iraq, and proceeded with a small number of troops to the caliph's palace at al-Rūmiyya, a city near Ctesiphon (al-Madāʾin) originally built by the Sasanians for the accommodation of captives from the Byzantine empire. Here the caliph had him assassinated, ruining the careers of thousands of men at a stroke. Once Abū Muslim had been disposed of his army ceased to exist, except as a threat to the caliph, who unsuccessfully tried to regulate the movements of the now disbanded troops as they began to drift home.[81] To the troops themselves the murder of their master meant the end of everything they had hoped for, and briefly enjoyed, proving that there was no room for them in Muslim society after all: the new caliph was an 'Arab'

[79] *EI*², s.v. 'Kaḥṭaba'; YB, 248.15–17, on the Ḥarbiyya; also below, pp. 86–91 (on the Rāwandiyya).
[80] BA, III, 246.
[81] See Chapter 2.

too. In effect, they were being sent back to their villages again. This time, however, they had military organisation and training, so they rebelled, demanding vengeance for Abū Muslim and casting him as yet another representative of the truth martyred by the 'Arabs'. As their inflammatory message spread in the countryside Abū Muslim came to be seen as a symbol of Iranian victimhood, his death as the ultimate proof of Arab perfidy;[82] and just as the recruits who had made a good life for themselves in Iraq were prone to deifying their redeemer in the form of al-Manṣūr, so those who were excluded were now prone to deifying him in the form of Abū Muslim.

Their strong sense of victimhood only made sense in the countryside. In the cities the vast majority of non-Arab Muslims were descendants of slaves, and though their ancestors had suffered when they were torn from their homes, Islam had typically been an avenue to liberation and respect for them, as it continued to be for their descendants. They had never been faced with deportation to the villages from which their ancestors had been dragged, and they had no trouble at all distinguishing between Arabs and Islam. When they thought about Abū Muslim it was not as a symbol of Iranian victimhood, but on the contrary as the revolutionary leader who had facilitated the liberation of Islam from the grips of its prejudiced Arab carriers. When they disliked Arabs they would react by asserting their own superior merits as the new bearers of Islam, crediting themselves with greater piety than the Arabs to whom they owed their faith, or casting themselves as the wellsprings of Islamic culture, heirs as they were to long-lived civilisations, and stressing the barbarism in which the pre-Islamic Arabs had supposedly lived. In short, they would become Shuʿūbīs, 'adherents of the cause of the (non-Arab) peoples'; they did not turn against Islam itself. But things looked different to the many whose ancestors had escaped enslavement. Having encountered difficulties when they tried to enter Muslim society voluntarily back in the days of the Umayyads, they were now being excluded again. This was true not just in the sense that Abū Muslim's army had been disbanded, but also in the sense that the Arabs and their many converts were beginning deeply to affect conditions in the countryside. Rural Iranians were being ousted from their very own homes in the sense of their traditional social organisation and way of life. This is why the fate of Abū Muslim spoke so powerfully to so many at the time even when they had not been members of his army: it

[82] Thus even Yaʿqūb al-Ṣaffār, with other examples of how the ʿAbbāsids would kill Iranians who had served them well (*TS*, 267f. = 213).

articulated a widespread sense that Islam was a mere cover for the interests of the rulers and their local representatives. To the victims of ʿAbbāsid policies either Islam was a false religion or else it was being perverted by the ʿArabs', its true form being that expounded by their own Iranian leaders. Accordingly, many of them reacted by rejecting Islam altogether, or at least Islam in its normal form, often (but not always) in the name of vengeance for Abū Muslim.

KHURRAMISM

Many of the rural communities to which Abū Muslim's fate was deeply meaningful were distinguished by a set of beliefs which the Muslims regarded as distasteful. They had many names for adherents of such beliefs, but they often subsumed them under the label of 'Khurramīs' (*Khurramiyya, Khurramdīniyya*). This term is first attested in Khurāsān in 118/736: in that year the leaders of the Hāshimite movement repudiated one of their missionaries, Khidāsh, for having adopted *dīn al-khurramiyya*, the religion of the Khurramīs.[83] Exactly what this religion was is the subject of Part II of this book, but the reader needs some information about it to follow this part as well.

There is general agreement in the medieval and modern literature that Khurramism is related to Mazdakism, a Zoroastrian heresy which had appeared back in the days of the Sasanian empire. The founder of Mazdakism was one Zardūsht, son of Khrōsak or Khurrak, a Zoroastrian heresiarch who was a contemporary of Mani (d. 277).[84] He proposed to remove strife from this world by eliminating desire, not by training people to suppress it, but rather by enabling all to fulfil it in equal measure: the remedy was equal access to the main sources of conflict, namely women and property, coupled with abstention from harm to any living being. Women and property were to be shared; war was evil; and animals were not to be killed for food. His ideals relating to women were taken up by the emperor Kavadh in the first part of his reign (488–96). Kavadh was expelled, returned, and displayed no signs of heresy thereafter. When he died in 531 a Zoroastrian priest by the name of Mazdak also tried to implement Zardūsht's ideas, this time those relating to the sharing of women and

[83] Tab. ii, 1588.

[84] The date is given in the Syriac History of Karkha de Bet Selokh (in Bedjan, *Acta Martyrum*, II, 517; tr. Hoffmann, *Auszüge*, 49). This is the only date given in the sources. It was not known to Yarshater, 'Mazdakism', 996, and does not simply add another 'school of thought' to his conjectures, as Pourshariati assumes (*Decline*, 344f.).

property alike, as the leader of a major revolt in Iraq and western Iran (*c.* 531–40). It is thanks to his revolt that the heresy came to be known as Mazdakism. The two episodes have been conflated in the later tradition, which casts Kavadh as a supporter of Mazdak, and if we had not had contemporary sources placing Kavadh's heretical phase in the first part of his reign we would not have been able to dissociate them.[85] After the suppression of Mazdak's revolt we hear nothing about views of this kind until the mid-eighth century, when they resurface in the Iranian countryside, first in Khurāsān and Transoxania, and soon thereafter in western Iran.

The beliefs we encounter from the mid-eighth century onwards are reminiscent of Mazdakism without quite corresponding to it. On the one hand, Khurramism was distinguished by two beliefs that are not normally associated with Mazdakism, namely periodic incarnation of the divine in human beings and reincarnation of the human spirit. One source does credit both to Mazdak, probably correctly in the case of reincarnation, but the chroniclers of his revolt know nothing about it.[86] On the other hand, the Khurramīs did not subscribe to revolutionary ideas regarding women and property. Countless sources do indeed tell us that they believed in *ibāḥat al-nisāʾ*, literally 'holding women to be lawful (for anyone to sleep with)', and they are sometimes credited with similar views regarding property. The sources normally understand this as the ultimate sign of their Mazdakism. But, as will be seen, what they are referring to is local ideas and practices relating to a village setting, not a utopian or revolutionary blueprint for the reorganisation of Iranian or human society at large. What the Khurramīs, or some of them, did share with Mazdak was the belief that it was wrong to inflict harm on any living being, animals included, except at times of revolt; some of them seem to have been vegetarians. Those in the Jibāl are reported also to have deemed it wrong to speak ill about members of other religious communities as long as the latter were not trying to harm them. They told a Muslim informant that all messengers had received the same spirit even though they had brought different laws and doctrines, and that the followers of all religions were right as long as they believed in reward and punishment (after death). The informant, the tenth-century al-Maqdisī, found them to be extremely clean, tidy, and kind people.[87] Since the Khurramīs combined their seemingly outrageous views on women with neglect of Muslim ritual law in respect of prayer,

[85] On all this see Crone, 'Kavād's Heresy'. It is the chronological disparity that proves the two episodes to be separate, not the absence of Mazdak from contemporary sources on Kavādh, as Pourshariati has me say (*Decline*, 345n.).
[86] See further Chapters 11, p. 228, and 13, p. 255.
[87] Maqdisī, IV, 30f.

fasting, ritual ablution, dietary taboos, and the like even after they had acquired status as Muslims, most sources report on them in a scandalised tone very different from al-Maqdisī's, crediting them with unbridled promiscuity and generally unspeakable behaviour without pausing to consider how communities based on such seeming lack of social restraint managed to survive. There were still Khurramīs in the sixth/twelfth century.[88]

The overlap between the doctrines reported for Mazdak and the Khurramīs is such that they must indeed be related. Since the Khurramīs are not mentioned before the second/eighth century, modern scholars not unnaturally assume them to be some kind of residue of Mazdakism: one term for them that has gained currency in the modern literature is 'neo-Mazdakites'. But there is reason to question this assumption, for Khurramism is far too widely and densely attested to be seen as the residue of a defeated sect. Mazdak rebelled in Iraq and Fārs, and we do hear of Khurramīs in Iraq[89] and Fārs,[90] but it is not where we normally find them. They are well attested, however, from Iṣfahān to the Caucasus in the north, and from the Caucasus in the west to Turkestan in the east. Their presence is most densely reported for the Zagros mountains (the Jibāl), where we hear of them at Iṣfahān,[91] including the districts of Barnadīn/Timidīn, Kāpula, Fābak, Barandīn (or the like), and Būrida/Rawanda,[92] Fahmān, and Qāmidān,[93] as well as al-Burj;[94] at Hamadhān,[95] including Dargazīn, Ansābadh,[96] Karaj Abī Dulaf,[97] the Zazz of Ma'qil, the Zazz of Abū Dulaf,[98] Nihāwand and Dīnawar (Māh al-Kūfa and Māh al-Baṣra);[99] at Shahrazūr;[100] and at Māsabadhān and Mihrijānqadhaq,

[88] See Chapter 9.

[89] Shahrastānī, I, 113 = I, 449; cf. the editorial puzzlement in n. 77, where it is suggested that the reference could be to Iraq 'Ajamī, or that the Khurramīs here stand for Ismailis.

[90] *SN*, ch. 47:4 (314 = 240); Shahrastānī, I, 194 = I, 666.

[91] Tab. iii, 1165; Ibn al-Nadīm, 406.1 = III, 817; MM, IV, §2399 (VI, 187); Mas'ūdī, *Tanbīh*, 353; *SN*, ch. 47:2–5, 13 (312–15, 319 = 239–41, 244); Khwāfī, *Mujmal*, I, 230.ult.

[92] *SN*, ch. 47:2, 3 (313 =239).

[93] YB, 275.

[94] MM, IV, §2399 (VI, 187); Mas'ūdī, *Tanbīh*, 353.

[95] Tab. iii, 1165; Ibn al-Nadīm, 406.1 = II, 817; Mas'ūdī, *Tanbīh*, 353; *SN*, ch. 47:2 (313 = 239).

[96] Yāqūt, II, 569, s.v. 'Darkazīn'; Bundārī, *Mukhtaṣar*, 124.

[97] MM, IV, §2399 (VI, 187); Mas'ūdī, *Tanbīh*, 353; *SN*, ch. 47:2 (313 = 239); Miskawayh, *Tajārib*, I, 278 = IV, 316; IA, VIII, 269 (year 321).

[98] Mas'ūdī, *Tanbīh*, 353. The two Zazzes do not seem to be known to Yāqūt, but he knows of a district called Zazz, assigned by one authority to Iṣfahān, by another to Hamadhān (*Buldān*, 929f., s.v. 'Zazz').

[99] Ibn al-Nadīm, 406.1 = II, 817; Mas'ūdī, *Tanbīh*, 353. For the identification of these places see *Tārīkh-i Qumm*, 61.

[100] Shahrastānī, I, 194 = I, 666.

including Ṣaymara, al-Sīrawān, Qism, Kūdhasht, Arīwajān, al-Radhdh, and Warsanjān.[101] They are also reported at al-Ahwāz in Khuzestan,[102] and even (implausibly) in Baḥrayn.[103] We do not get the same detailed breakdown for their presence on the west–east axis, but we are told that they were found in Armenia and Azerbaijan,[104] in the villages of Rayy,[105] at Dastabā;[106] Qumm and Kashān,[107] Daylam,[108] Jurjān,[109] Khurāsān,[110] and 'the rest of the land of the Iranians and other places', as al-Mas'ūdī puts it. They were known as Bāṭinīs in Khurāsān and elsewhere, he says (apparently without conflating them with Ismailis).[111] A more common name for them in the east is 'White-clothed ones', but they are sometimes identified as Khurramīs or Khurramdīnīs there as well. We encounter them at Balkh (in what is now Afghanistan),[112] in 'the rural areas of the Hephtalites',[113] presumably meaning in Bādghīs or Ṭukhāristān;[114] in Sogdia, including Bukhārā, Samarqand, Kish, and Nasaf,[115] and, beyond the Jaxartes (Syr Darya), in Shāsh,[116] Khujand,[117] Īlāq,[118] Kāsān, and

101 MM, IV, §2399 (VI, 197), here oddly placing al-Radhdh and Warsanjān at Burj, on the other side of Little Lur; Mas'ūdī, *Tanbīh*, 353 (where Warsanjān is placed in Ṣaymara in Mihrijānqadhaq); Maqdisī, IV, 31; Tab. iii, 1165.

102 Ibn al-Nadīm, 406.1 = II, 817; Shahrastani, I, 194 = I, 666.

103 Dhahabī, *Ta'rīkh*, ṭbq xxix, year 286, 28, claims that when Abū Sa'īd al-Jannābī went to Baḥrayn he was joined by remnants of the Zanj and Khurramiyya.

104 Ibn al-Nadīm, 406.1 = II, 817; Mas'ūdī, *Tanbīh*, 353, and many other sources; cf. Chapter 3, on Bābak.

105 MM, II, §868 (III, 27); IV, §2399 (VI, 187); Mas'ūdī, *Tanbīh*, 353; Abū Ḥātim, *Zīna*, 306; Ibn Rizām in Ibn al-Malāḥimī, *Mu'tamad*, 803 ('as for the villages of al-Rayy, they are dominated by the *Khurramiyyat al-majūs*'); Ibn al-Jawzī, *Muntaẓam*, VIII, 39f.; cf. *SN*, ch. 45:1 (279 = 212), where Mazdak's alleged wife Khurrama converts Zoroastrians at Rayy; Chapter 2, on Sunbādh.

106 *SN*, ch. 47:2 (313 = 239); cf. Yāqūt, II, 573, s.v. 'Dastabā'.

107 Mas'ūdī, *Tanbīh*, 353; cf. also Yāqūt, IV, 607, s.v. 'Muqaṭṭa'a'.

108 Ibn al-Nadīm, 406.1 = II, 817.

109 See Chapter 4.

110 Ps.-Nāshi', §52; Mas'ūdī, *Tanbīh*, 353; Chapter 4.

111 Mas'ūdī, *Tanbīh*, 353; MM, IV, §2399 (VI, 188).

112 Ibn al-Nadīm, 408.13 = II, 824; Nashwān al-Ḥimyarī, *Ḥūr al-'īn*, 160; both citing al-Balkhī (Muslimiyya, called Khurramdīniyya by some).

113 al-Muqaddasī, 323 (White-clothed ones).

114 Cf. the Khusrawiyya and Khurramiyya mentioned by al-Tha'ālibī in Chapter 7, p. 150.

115 See Chapter 6, on al-Muqanna'.

116 Shahrastānī, I, 194 = I, 666.

117 *SN*, ch. 46:22 (200 = 228).

118 *Ḥudūd al-'ālam*, 117, §63, cf. 356 (White-clothed ones); Baghdādī, 243 (White-clothed ones, followers of al-Muqanna'); Baghdādāī, *Uṣūl*, 322; Isfarā'inī, *Tabṣīr*, 77; Shahrastānī, I, 194 = I, 666.

Farghāna.[119] In short, their presence stretched from the mountains of Anatolia to those of Tien Shan, far into those parts of Central Asia that, though inhabited by Iranians (and Turks), had never formed part of the Sasanian empire. There are simply too many Khurramīs, in far too many places, for the assumption that they owed their existence to Mazdak to be persuasive. The only regions of Iran in which they do not seem to be attested are Kerman, Sīstān, and Makrān.

Madelung has suggested that we should see Khurramism as a kind of Zoroastrian 'low church', presumably in the sense of Zoroastrianism as understood at the bottom of the social scale.[120] As will be seen, this probably is not quite right either, but it is certainly closer to the truth, for the Khurramīs are consistently identified as peasants, landless labourers, and villagers of other kinds.[121] The point that matters here is that we should envisage Khurramism as an ancient, widely disseminated set of rural beliefs and practices which formed the substratum to Mazdakism rather than the other way round. Zardūsht and Mazdak will have drawn on the ideas that came to be labelled Khurramī; the Khurramīs will not have owed their beliefs to them. But their systematised ideas may well have travelled back to the villages, allowing the villagers to put names to assumptions that they had hitherto taken for granted, and Mazdak may also have gone down in rural memory as a great hero. The relationship between Mazdakism and Khurramism will also be taken up for further discussion in the second part of the book.

It should be clear that Khurramism was not an intrinsically subversive or rebellious creed. On the contrary, its message was as friendly and as pacifist as could be. Its adherents are of course likely to have honoured their own beliefs as much in the breach as in the observance, but the key factor behind their sudden proclivity to revolt was undoubtedly the activities of the Hāshimiyya. We know that Hāshimite missionaries were active among them in Khurāsān from the story of Khidāsh, the missionary who was denounced for having adopted Khurramism: he must have been

119 *SN*, 46:22, 26 (300, 307= 228, 230).

120 Madelung, *Religious Trends*, 2 (where they are nonetheless neo-Mazdakites too). The term 'low church' comes from Anglicanism and Madelung does not say what it would mean in a Zoroastrian context.

121 Muqaddasī, 37.9 (the Khurramdīniyya and Abyaḍiyya are *fī 'l-rasātīq*); MM, IV, §2399 (VI, 187) (most of them are *fī 'l-qurā wa'l-ḍiyā'*); cf. MM, III, 27 (II, §868) (a village in which they make a living removing dead animals: cf. further pp. 259f.); 'Awfī, *Jawāmi'*, ed. She'ar, 272 (*dahqanat va kashāvarzī kunand*); cf. Chapters 3, 6, on the revolts of Bābak and al-Muqanna'.

affected by the people he was meant to convert.[122] Of Abū Muslim we are told that he brought up one Abū Ḥātim, son of one Pīlawayh, both of whom eventually betrayed him, and that the two of them adhered to something 'similar to the religion of the Khurramiyya'.[123] That Khurramīs were being recruited for the Hāshimite armies is also clear from the section of them known as the Rāwandiyya, as well as from the rebel al-Muqannaʿ.[124] Recruitment in the name of Hāshimite Shīʿism was also going on in western Iran, where ʿAbdallāh b. Muʿāwiya was active, and there were Khurramīs in his army too.[125] But it was the Khurāsānīs who had the galvanising effect.

Thanks to the Hāshimite missionaries who toured the villages of greater Khurāsān, throngs of fresh converts to Islam left their villages to enrol in the revolutionary armies, and thousands and thousands of bright-eyed young men full of high hopes were despatched westwards, disseminating their expectation of a new era all the way from Khurāsān to Syria and disrupting the normal channels of authority as they progressed. Disturbances broke out in Khurāsān even before the revolution. The Khurramīs recruited by Khidāsh seceded from the Hāshimiyya when he was executed – convinced, it would seem, that the promises of a new era had been false; and a Zoroastrian by the name of Bihāfarīdh tried to resist the lure of Islam by declaring himself a prophet and preaching a revised form of Zoroastrianism later taken up by Ustādhsīs. But a new sequence of revolts started when Sunbādh rebelled at Rayy in response to Abū Muslim's death, repudiating Islam. In the west we soon hear of Khurramī risings in the Jibāl, upper Mesopotamia, and Armenia, culminating in the revolt of Bābak in Azerbaijan. In the east we hear of Khurramī risings in Jurjān and obscure activities by a certain Isḥāq in Transoxania, culminating in the revolt of al-Muqannaʿ in Sogdia. It is with all these revolts and the nature of Khurramism that this book is concerned.

[122] See further Chapter 4.
[123] Jāḥiẓ, *Ḥayawān*, VII, 83.
[124] See Chapters 4, 6.
[125] See Chapter 4.

I

THE REVOLTS

A. Western Iran

2

The Jibāl

Sunbādh, the Muslimiyya

The Jibāl is part of what was once the Achaemenid satrapy of Media, mostly taken up by the Zagros mountains. The Greeks later distinguished between a major and a minor Media, the minor part being Azerbaijan. In Muslim times Azerbaijan and the Jibāl were always separate provinces, but they were known to speak related languages, which were grouped together, or indeed identified, as Fahlawī (Pahlavi). This name is somewhat confusing, for Pahlavi, meaning 'heroic', originally stood for Parthian, i.e. the language of Khurāsān. Manichaeans writing in Parthian continued to call it *Pahlawānīg*. Already by Mani's time, however, Pahlavi had come to mean Median to others. To complete the confusion, by the fourth/tenth century the term had come to stand for yet another language, Middle Persian, i.e. the language of Pārs/Fārs in the 'middle' period of Iranian language history (roughly from Alexander to the coming of Islam).[1] Median and Persian do not even belong in the same Iranian language group, but the development is irreversible. In the period of interest to us the Pahla region was the Jibāl and Azerbaijan (including Rayy and Iṣfahān according to some, not so according to others),[2] but I shall nonetheless speak of 'Pahlavi books', meaning those composed in the language of Fārs.

After the revolt in Media in the 650s mentioned by Sebeos the Jibāl was reasonably quiet down to the 120s/740s, when it came to form part of a

[1] Ibn al-Muqaffaʿ in Ibn al-Nadīm, 15 = I, 24; Henning, 'Mitteliranisch', 94f.; Lazard, 'Pahlavi, Pârsi, Dari'; *EIr.*, s.v. 'Fahlavīyāt' (Tafazzoli).

[2] Ibn al-Nadīm, 15 = I, 24; Ibn Khurdādhbih, 57; Khwārizmī, 117.2; Ibn al-Faqīh, 209/417 (excludes both Rayy and Iṣfahān); Yāqūt, III, 925, s.v. 'Fahlaw', citing Ḥamza al-Iṣbahānī and Shīrawayh b. Shahrdār (also excludes both); Bīrūnī, *Āthār*, 229.12 = 213 ('Iṣfahān, Rayy and other Fahla countries'). Sayf b. ʿUmar explains *al-Fahlawaj* as the people of Jibāl (Tab. i, 2608, cf. also i, 1993; IA, II, 440, discussed in Pourshariati, *Decline*, 214f., 242, with objections to Sayf's usage).

short-lived principality set up by the ʿAlid rebel ʿAbdallāh b. Muʿāwiya. A great many of the recruits of this rebel were of the Khurramī type;[3] indeed, al-Shahrastānī regards them as the font and origin of all Khurramīs.[4] But though they were recruited in the Zagros mountains they fled with Ibn Muʿāwiya to Khurāsān, where Abū Muslim had Ibn Muʿāwiya killed and apparently took over his troops for use in the revolution. As a result, the subsequent history of these Khurramīs was quite different from that of those who stayed in the Jibāl, and for this reason they are dealt with in another chapter.[5]

SUNBĀDH

When Abū Muslim was killed in 137/755, a friend of his by the name of Sunbādh rebelled at Rayy. Like the other men in Abū Muslim's army Sunbādh came from Khurāsān, more precisely from a village called Ahan or Ahrawāna in the district of Nīshāpūr;[6] but he was no simple villager. According to Niẓām al-Mulk he was the chief (*raʾīs*) of Nīshāpūr;[7] and according to Mīrkhwānd he had hosted Abū Muslim before the revolution. On that occasion he had supposedly foreseen that Abū Muslim would 'kill noble Arabs and aristocratic Iranians'. When Abū Muslim returned to Nīshāpūr as ruler of Khurāsān, i.e., in 131/748f., and helped Sunbādh against some local bedouin, both Sunbādh and his brother joined the revolutionary movement; this was how they came to be in Abū Muslim's army when the latter was killed.[8] The *Tārīkh-i Harāt* tells the story differently. Here it is a certain Fādhūsbān b. Kanāranj, identified as the *dihqān* of Nīshāpūr, who befriends Abū Muslim. It is Fādhūsbān's wife rather than the magnate himself who dreams that the 'great men will suffer decline while lowly and ignoble people will rise to high status', and it is the magnate who helps Abū Muslim against some local bedouin rather than the other way round. Abū Muslim then vows to destroy the quarter of these bedouin, known as Būyābād, which is the point of the story, and there is no reference to Fādhūsbān joining Abū

3 Abū Ḥātim, *Zīna*, 298 (calling them Ḥārithiyya).

4 Shahrastānī, 113 = I, 449, probably on the basis of Abū Ḥātim.

5 See Chapter 4.

6 Tab. iii, 119; IA, V, 481.

7 *SN*, ch. 45:1 (279 = 212).

8 Mīrkhwānd, III, 2558; cf. also *TN*, II, 1093; *EIr.*, s.v. 'Abū Moslem', for the date. In the *Tārīkh-i alfī*, according to Daniel, *Khurasan*, 127, it is Sunbādh himself who 'kills noble Arabs and aristocratic Iranians'.

Muslim when the latter returned. Here as in the first story, however, the magnate and Abū Muslim become friends.[9] Yet another version is given by Ibn al-Athīr, who does not mention any bedouin; here al-Fādhūsbān is identified as the Zoroastrian *dihqān* of Nīshāpūr and here too he helps Abū Muslim, who nobly refuses to seize his wealth when he comes back as the conqueror of Nīshāpūr.[10] There are also versions of the story of Abū Muslim's destruction of the quarter of Būyābād that make no reference to the local magnate.[11]

Fādhūsbān b. Kanāranj is clearly envisaged as a descendant of the *kanārang* who had governed the north-eastern frontier of Iran in Sasanian times. *Kanārang* is a title which was often understood as a name. It was used by the commander (*iṣbahbadh*) of the north-eastern region, centred in Abarshahr, the province in which Nīshāpūr was located.[12] Kanārā was the 'king of Nīshāpūr', as Ibn Khurdādhbih says.[13] Bearers of this name/title participated in Kavadh's wars against Byzantium, intermarried with the Sasanian family, and fought against the Arabs, first at Qādisiyya and thereafter in Khurāsān,[14] when Kanārā lost half of Abarshahr and surrendered two sons to the Arabs as hostages.[15] One of these hostages eventually had a son of his own called ʿUmar b. Abī 'l-Ṣalt b. Kanārā, a client *min al-dahāqīn* who formed part of the Kufan troops sent against the Khārijite rebel Qaṭarī in 77/696f.,[16] and who later participated in the revolt of Ibn al-Ashʿath.[17] Al-Ḥajjāj contemptuously referred to him as a slave.[18] Thereafter the family disappears from view until Abū Muslim's arrival in Nīshāpūr. The three accounts of the Kanārang's friendship with Abū Muslim were perhaps designed to explain why this magnate had been spared when other great men were eliminated by Abū Muslim. Eventually, though, the Kanārang was eliminated, too: he was deprived of the control he retained over part of Nīshāpūr and Ṭūs by Ḥumayd b. Qaḥṭaba, presumably during the latter's governorship of

9 *Tārīkh-i Harāt*, fols. 16pff.
10 IA, V, 480, year 137 (written *al-fādhūsyān*).
11 IA, V, 258; *Tarīkh-i Naysābūr* in Pourshariati, *Decline*, 448.
12 Cf. *EI*², s.v. 'Nīshāpūr'.
13 Ibn Khurdādhbih, 39.11 and n. f; cf. also Justi, *Namenbuch*, s.v. 'Kanārang'.
14 Justi, *Namenbuch*, s.v. 'Kanārang'; Minorsky, 'Older Preface', 163f.; Pourshariati, *Decline*, 266ff.
15 Tab. i, 2886f.
16 Tab. ii, 1019f.; IA, IV, 442 (year 77).
17 Khalīfa, I, 368, 374 (year 82); Tab. ii, 119; IA, IV 494f. (year 83). His father and (in Khalīfa) brother also participated in the revolt.
18 Tab. ii, 1120; Khalīfa, I, 368.

Khurāsān in the reign of al-Manṣūr.[19] Since all versions depict Abū Muslim as a friend of the magnate it is difficult to share Pourshariati's conviction that the story reflects hostility between the two.[20] What it does suggest is that Sunbādh and Fādhūsbān b. Kanāranj were one and the same person.

Fādhūsbān is also a title which doubled as a personal name.[21] The four regions in which the Sasanian empire was divided had a *fādhūsbān* each, we are told,[22] and the name of the *iṣbahbadh* of Khurāsān was Fādhūsbān.[23] The reference is presumably to the Kanārang; Sunbādh certainly claimed the title of *iṣbahbadh*. The astronomical *Book of Nativities* says of itself that it was translated into Arabic by Saʿīd b. Khurāsān-Khurra in the time of Abū Muslim at the request of Sunbādh the *iṣbahbadh*, who realised that Arabic was overtaking Persian;[24] and Sunbādh also called himself the 'victorious ispahbad' (*fīrūz iṣbahbadh*) when he rebelled.[25]

In short, Sunbādh appears to have been the scion of a family endowed with immense power and prestige in Sasanian times, now reduced to a purely local position and uncomfortably perched between descent into obscurity and client status. In Abū Muslim he acquired a useful friend. He may actually have liked Abū Muslim; he probably also hoped that the new era that Abū Muslim promised to inaugurate would enable him and his family to recover prominence. At the very least his friendship with the conqueror of Khurāsān would protect him from elimination along with all the other 'noble Arabs and aristocratic Iranians' who had collaborated with the Umayyad regime. Accordingly, Sunbādh joined the revolutionary movement in 131/748f. Abū Muslim elevated him to the rank of commander (*sipahsālār*), as Niẓam al-Mulk puts it,[26] though in truth Sunbādh was a commander in his own right. He was a Zoroastrian at the time,[27] and

[19] Minorsky, 'Older Preface', 179; cf. Crone, *Slaves*, 188. It is not clear on what grounds Pourshariati places Ḥumayd's activities before Abū Muslim's second visit to Nīshāpūr (*Decline*, 435, 450).

[20] Pourshariati, *Decline*, 448ff. She casts Sunbādh as a Kārinid who re-enacts the career of the god Mithra and Bahrām Chūbīn.

[21] Cf. Justi, *Namenbuch*, s.v. 'patkōspān'.

[22] Tab. i, 892; YT I, 202f.; cf. Tab. i, 2639ff., where *al-fādhūsfān*, understood as a name, is the ruler of Iṣfahān; Gignoux, 'Organisation administrative', 8f., 11, 13, 20, 26 (*pāygō-spān*). Gignoux doubts the reality of the four-fold division.

[23] Ibn Khurdādhbih, 18.

[24] Gutas, *Greek Thought*, 37f. (where 'the possessor of rule' must render *ṣāhib al-dawla*).

[25] Tab. iii, 119; IA, V, 481; Daniel, *Khurasan*, 148, n. 12, with further references.

[26] *SN*, ch. 45:1 (279 = 212).

[27] See the references in n. 31 of this chapter.

whether he ever converted formally to Islam we do not know, but behaviourally at least he became a Muslim. In 137/755 he accompanied Abū Muslim on his fateful march to Iraq out of friendship, without being registered on the military roll.[28] He must have brought his own troops.

Abū Muslim had been forbidden to take his army with him to Iraq, so he left it at Ḥulwān, and this was where Sunbādh received the news of his death.[29] He reacted by beginning to march home, in what state of mind we do not know. When he reached Rayy he was detained by the governor,[30] who had been instructed not to let any of Abū Muslim's troops pass through. Sunbādh protested that he was not on Abū Muslim's military roll and merely wanted to go home, but the governor apparently still refused to let him pass through, so Sunbādh fled at night – clearly not alone, for when the governor caught up with him they fought a fierce battle. The governor's attempt to implement al-Manṣūr's order had produced the very result that al-Manṣūr was trying to forestall: the soldiers in Abū Muslim's army rebelled. Sunbādh defeated the governor and captured him (later having him killed) and went back to Rayy. He now reverted to Zoroastrianism (*ʿāda ilā 'l-majūsiyya*) and declared the dominion of the Arabs to have come to an end (*qad inqaḍā mulk al-ʿarab*).[31] He took to bashing 'Arabs' with wood, a symbolic act demonstrating that the ʿAbbāsids and their supporters were no better than the Umayyads, and persecuted Muslims in every way he could, killing large numbers of them and even forcing a father to eat of the flesh of a slaughtered child, or so it was said.[32] He successfully solicited help from the ruler of Daylam and beat off two local armies, causing a crisis so severe that the annual summer campaign against Byzantium was suspended.[33] The caliph al-Manṣūr sent Khurāsānī troops from Iraq against him under the command of Jahwar b. Marār al-ʿIjlī.[34] 'You will be fighting people bent on eliminating your

[28] BA, III, 246.
[29] This and what follows is based on the earliest source, Madā'inī and others in BA, III, 246f.
[30] BA, III, 246 gives his name as Abū ʿAbda; he is ʿAbd(a) or Abū ʿUbayda al-Ḥanafī in Niẓām al-Mulk and Mīrkhwānd (*SN*, ch. 45:1; *Rawḍa*, III, 2559).
[31] BA, III, 246; cf. *SN*, ch. 45:2 (280 = 213), where he tells Zoroastrians in private that Arab rule is finished, claiming to have found this in a Sasanian book. Other sources omit his repudiation of Islam and simply identify him as a Zoroastrian, e.g. Tab. iii, 119; Maqdisī, VI, 82; *SN*, ch. 45:1 (279 = 212; *TN*, IV, 1093).
[32] BA, III, 246; cf. Crone, 'Wooden Weapons', esp. 182f.
[33] Tab. iii, 121.1 (year 137).
[34] Jahwar b. Marār was a Khurāsānī Arab and participant in the revolution (Tab. iii, 2000f.), not an Arab of western Iran chosen for his lack of sympathy with the Khurāsānī rebels, as proposed by Kennedy, *Early Abbasid Caliphate*, 64, followed by Pourshariati, *Decline*, 438, n. 2506 (where his name has turned into Jawhar).

religion and expelling you from your world (of wealth and power)' (*maḥq dīnikum wa-ikhrājakum min dunyākum*), Jahwar told his men.[35] When the Khurāsānīs arrived local troops were mobilised again, and volunteers also joined, including the famous ʿUmar b. al-ʿAlāʾ, a butcher from Rayy who gathered soldiers of his own and did so well in action that he rose to a distinguished military career.[36] This time Sunbādh was defeated. He and his brother fled to Ṭabaristān (not Daylam, as one would have expected), and here a relative of the local ruler had both of them killed and sent their heads to Jahwar.[37] Unplanned, the revolt had lasted a mere seventy days.[38]

According to Ibn Isfandiyār so many of Abū Muslim's and Sunbādh's troops were killed in the defeat that one could still see their bones on the ground in 300/912f.[39] Al-Madāʾinī gives the number of casualties as 30,000.[40] Later authors make it 50,000 or 60,000, with an unspecified number of women and children taken captive;[41] al-Maqdisī says that Sunbādh's army numbered 90,000 men; and by the time we reach Niẓām al-Mulk the figure has risen to 100,000.[42] The recollection of huge numbers of casualties on the rebel side suggests that villagers from the countryside of Rayy and neighbouring areas had joined Sunbādh on the spur of the moment. In fact, even Abū ʿĪsā al-Iṣfahānī, the Jewish prophet who claimed to be a precursor of the Messiah, seems to have joined him, for al-Shahrastānī says that this Abū ʿĪsā fell in battle against the troops of al-Manṣūr at Rayy, and al-Manṣūr's troops are not known to have fought any other battle at Rayy.[43]

35 BA, III, 246f.

36 *SN*, ch. 45:2; BF, 339; Tab. iii, 136f., 493, 500, 520, 521; Ibn Isfandiyār, I, 176, 180–2, 187; cf. Ibn al-Faqīh, 308f./571, where the new edition adds that he distinguished himself against *al-Daylam*. (There is no basis for Sadighi's assumption, *Mouvements* 144/180, that ʿUmar and his troops were Arabs, unless he just meant Arabised Muslims.)

37 Ibn Isfandiyār, I, 174. In the *Tārīkhnāma*, IV, 1093, followed by Pourshariati, *Decline*, 438, he flees to Jurjān (cf. p. 37).

38 Tab. iii, 120; MM, VI, 189/IV, §2400; IA, V, 481. They have turned into seven years in Niẓām al-Mulk (*SN*, ch. 45:2).

39 Ibn Isfandiyār, I, 174.6.

40 BA, III, 247. By contrast, Jahwar is credited with no more than 10,000 men (Tab. iii, 119) or 20,000 (*ʿUyūn*, 224).

41 Tab. iii, 120; MM, VI, 189/IV, §2400; Fasawī, *Maʿrifa*, I, 6 (year 137); IA, V, 481.

42 Maqdisī, VI, 83; *SN*, ch. 45:2 (280 =213).

43 Shahrastānī, I, 168 = I, 604; cf. Wasserstrom, "Īsāwiyya Revisited', 78, arguing that al-Shahrastānī may have used an ʿIsawī source.

SUNBĀDH'S TRANSFORMATION

The narrative followed so far is that of al-Madā'inī, our earliest source. It may not be entirely right, for if Sunbādh received military assistance from Daylam it is odd that he should have sought refuge in Ṭabaristān. One suspects that the stories of his older relatives have skewed the narrative here, for 'Umar b. Abī 'l-Ṣalt b. Kanārā, who campaigned against Qaṭarī in Ṭabaristān, later sought refuge there together with his father, and they too were killed by the local ruler, who sent their heads to al-Ḥajjāj.[44] In both cases, moreover, the scion of the Kanārā is depicted as inordinately arrogant even in their moment of need for protection. (The theme of the fallen grandee who completes his ruin by continuing to behave as a haughty king also figures in the account of Yazdegerd III's end.)[45] It could admittedly have been the story of Sunbādh that inspired that about 'Umar b. Abī 'l-Ṣalt's last days in Ṭabaristān rather than the other way round, but 'Umar at least had a reason to choose Ṭabaristān. Later sources compound the confusion by having Sunbādh flee to Jurjān, probably thanks to the fact that a revolt broke out there too after Abū Muslim's death.[46] But the story of Sunbādh was to be reshaped in more drastic ways as well.

The later sources do not just inflate the casualty figures, but also change the nature of the revolt in two ways. First, they reverse the direction of Sunbādh's movements, thereby making the revolt more extensive than it actually was. Khalīfa and Ibn Isfandiyār apart,[47] they all have him rebel at Nīshāpūr and go to Rayy, conquering everything on his way,[48] not because they had good information, but rather because they lacked it: they simply inferred that Sunbādh must have rebelled in Nīshāpūr from the fact that this was where he came from. If Sunbādh had actually been at home in Nīshāpūr when Abū Muslim was killed it is hard to see why he should have reacted by marching off to Rayy to fight his decisive battles there. Some sources claim that he seized Abū Muslim's treasure at Rayy,[49] and this is not

44 IA, IV, 494f. (year 83); retold in Minorsky, 'Older Preface', 163f.

45 For Sunbādh's arrogance causing his death see Ibn Isfandiyār, I, 174; for Yazdegerd's see Chapter 1, p. 3.

46 *TN*, IV, 1093; cf. Pourshariati, *Decline*, 438.

47 Thus Khalīfa, II, 637 (year 137); Ibn Isfandiyār, I, 174; cf. Daniel, *Khurasan*, 148, n. 13.

48 E.g. Tab. iii, 119f.; YT, II, 441f.; Fasawī, *Ma'rifa*, I, 6; MM, VI, 188f. (IV, §2400); IA, V, 481f.

49 Tab. iii, 119; MM, IV, §2400 (VI, 188f.), placing the revolt in 136; Maqdisī, VI, 82f.; IA, V, 481; *SN*, ch. 45:1 (279f. = 212).

impossible,[50] but he would hardly have marched all the way to Rayy in order to seize this money. Niẓām al-Mulk, Ibn al-Athīr, and Mīrkhwānd claim that he intended to destroy the Kaʿba,[51] implying that this was why he had marched westwards; but the idea that he should have rushed off in anger from Nīshāpūr in order singlehandedly to bring down the caliphate and Islam is absurd. Besides, he rebelled two months, or some months, after Abū Muslim was killed[52] and held out for a mere seventy days, which gives him some five months or so in which to await the news in Nīshāpūr, prepare for revolt and conquer Nīshāpūr and Qūmis on his way to Rayy,[53] conquer Rayy as well, and flee to Ṭabaristān to be killed. It simply is not possible.[54]

Secondly, several later sources present the revolt as Muslimī in the sense of inspired by belief that Abū Muslim was the imam and the mahdi and in some sense divine. Al-Masʿūdī envisages the Muslimīs as existing before the revolt and makes Sunbādh himself a member of their ranks.[55] Abū Ḥātim al-Rāzī implies that Sunbādh claimed to be a prophet.[56] And according to Niẓām al-Mulk (followed by Mīrkhwānd) Sunbādh denied Abū Muslim's death and claimed to be his messenger, pretending to have letters from him, while at the same time seeking vengeance for him. Sunbādh supposedly said that Abū Muslim had escaped death by reciting the greatest name of God and turning into a white dove, and that he was now residing in a fortress of brass with the mahdi and Mazdak, from which all three would one day come forth, Abū Muslim first, with Mazdak as his vizier.[57]

All this is clearly garbled, for it was in response to Abū Muslim's death that the groups called Muslimiyya emerged, and there is no reason to believe that Sunbādh was prone to deification of his friend. Abū Muslim's death dashed his hopes of recovering prominence and put him on the caliph's blacklist, making his own downfall a likely outcome. That he should have rebelled with the avowed aim of expelling the Arabs/Muslims makes eminently good sense, since restoration of the order destroyed by the Arabs was

50 It was where he had left his treasury on his previous journey (Tab. iii, 87.1; IA, V, 481). But in BA, III, 246, Sunbādh carries his own money to Rayy, as he must in fact have done if he was paying for his own troops.

51 *SN*, ch. 45:2 (280 = 213); IA, V, 481; Mīrkhwānd, III, 2559.

52 Two months according to *TN*, II, 1093; some months according to MM, VI, 189/iv, §2400.

53 Tab. iii, 119; MM, VI, 188/iv, §2400; IA, V, 481.

54 It did strike Sadighi as problematic (*Mouvements*, 148/184).

55 MM, VI, 188/IV, §2400.

56 Abū Ḥātim al-Rāzī, *Iṣlāḥ*, 160.9; cited in Stern, 'Abū Ḥātim al-Rāzī on Persian Religion', 41.

57 *SN*, ch. 45:1 (280 = 212); Mīrkhwānd, III, 2559.

now his only chance. By contrast, the beliefs that Niẓām al-Mulk imputes to him do not sit well with his aristocratic status. They may very well have been current among Abū Muslim's troops, however, and also later in the countryside of Rayy and other Muslimī strongholds. They suggest that Abū Muslim came to be cast in the image of Pišyōtan, an immortal hero who was awaiting the end of times in the fortress of Kangdiz, a stronghold with walls of steel, silver, gold, ruby, and so on, from which he and his companions would come forth to assist Sōšyans, the Zoroastrian mahdi.[58]

Niẓām al-Mulk further claims that Sunbādh would preach to Rāfiḍīs, who accepted his message when they heard mention of the mahdi, to Mazdakites, who did the same when they heard mention of Mazdak, and to Khurramīs, who would join the Shīʿites when they heard that Mazdak was a Shīʿite; he also persuaded the Zoroastrians to join by telling them in confidence that Arab rule was finished according to a prediction in a Sasanian book, and that he would destroy the Kaʿba and restore the sun to its former position as the *qibla*.[59] All this sounds quite hilarious to a modern reader, but it rests on two correct perceptions, namely that such Muslim doctrines as Khurramism contained tended to be drawn from Shīʿism, and that the Khurramīs would use these Shīʿite doctrines to opt out of the religious community formed by the conquerors, not to join them. Whether it was as imam, God, the mahdi, or the associate of the mahdi that the Khurramīs of a particular area cast Abū Muslim, they were appropriating Islam in much the same fashion that African Christians were appropriating Christianity when they elevated figures of their own to the role of black Christ, predicting that they would return to liberate their people.[60] In both cases a population under colonial rule has internalised the key religious concepts of their colonisers without feeling accepted by the conquerors themselves, and in both cases they react by nativising these concepts so as to use them against the colonists, from whose religious community they break away to form sectarian groups and dissident churches of their own.

Niẓām al-Mulk's account is hilarious because it expresses this insight as a story about a single individual consciously picking and mixing cultural ingredients without apparently having any convictions himself, to produce a devilish brew which everyone except the narrator and his readers is sufficiently stupid to accept. Niẓām al-Mulk's thinking here is

[58] Boyce, 'Antiquity of Zoroastrian Apocalyptic', 59ff.; Hultgård, 'Persian Apocalypticism', 51.

[59] *SN*, ch. 45:2 (280 = 213).

[60] Lanternari, *Religions of the Oppressed*, 15f., 19; cf. Sundkler, *Bantu Prophets*, 281ff., cf. 290f.

that characteristic of conspiracy theory, for although there is no conspiracy in his story, just one malicious individual, the essence of conspiracy theory is that it expresses the unforeseeable outcome of immensely complicated long-term developments as the result of deliberate planning by nefarious people who somehow have a grip on all the threads that elude the rest of us so that their plots always work out just as planned, without any hitch at all.

LOCAL REBELS

Whether the inhabitants of the Jibāl participated in Sunbādh's revolt or not, they soon took to rebelling on their own. If we trust a late source they started doing so at Iṣfahān in 162/778f., perhaps inspired by the Jurjānīs.[61] They certainly rebelled in 192/807f., the year in which Hārūn al-Rashīd went to Khurāsān, dying on the way: a number of villages of Spāhān (Arabic Iṣbahān/Iṣfahān) took to arms in tandem with other parts of the Jibāl, including Rayy, Hamadhān, Karaj, and Dastabā;[62] and there were also Khurramī revolts in Azerbaijan, where 30,000 men are said to have been killed, and their women and children enslaved.[63] They must have used Hārūn's departure as their cue, and it is hard to avoid the impression of large-scale coordination.

Niẓām al-Mulk knows of a third revolt in Jibāl in 212/827f., involving several districts of Spāhān/Iṣfahān, at least one of which had been involved on the previous occasion too according to him. This time, he says, the rebels went to Azerbaijan and made common cause with Bābak, the famous insurgent there who is discussed in the next chapter. Al-Ma'mūn reacted by sending Muḥammad b. Ḥumayd al-Ṭā'ī (alias al-Ṭūsī) to Azerbaijan, and when this man fell in action against Bābak the Khurramīs from Spāhān/Iṣfahān went back again.[64] Muḥammad b. Ḥumayd was in fact sent to Azerbaijan in 212/827f. according to al-Ṭabarī, to fall in battle against Bābak in 214/829f.,[65] and Niẓām al-Mulk seems to be relying on a good, local source for his information about the revolts in the Jibāl, probably Ḥamza al-Iṣfahānī's history of Iṣfahān.[66]

61 Khwāfī, *Mujmal*, I, 230.ult.; cf. Chapter 4.

62 *SN*, ch. 47:1 (312f. = 239); Dīnawarī, 387 (where it is the first Khurramī revolt in the Jibāl).

63 Tab. iii, 732.9; Maqdisī, VI, 103; Azdī, 313 (Azerbaijan and *Snbs*).

64 *SN*, ch. 47:3 (313f. = 239f.).

65 Tab. iii, 1099, 1101; YT, II, 565.

66 Cf. *SN*, ch. 47:13 (319 = 244), where he refers the reader to a *Tārīkh-i Iṣfāhān*; *EI*², s.v. 'Ḥamza al-Iṣfahānī'.

The Khurramīs of the Jibāl rebelled for the fourth time in 218/833, the year in which al-Ma'mūn died on the Byzantine frontier, once again striking at a time when the capital was denuded of caliphal troops. This time the whole of the Jibāl was involved, including Iṣfahān, Hamadhān, Māsabadhān, Mihrijānqadhaq, and the two Māhs (Nihāwand and Dīnawar).[67] According to Niẓām al-Mulk the Khurramīs of Fārs also joined and, as on the previous occasion, the rebels were coordinating their activities with Bābak (who had been in a state of revolt for some seventeen years by then). They killed tax collectors, plundered travellers, slaughtered Muslims, and took their children as slaves. In Fārs they were defeated by the local forces, but at Iṣfahān, where they were led by one ʿAlī b. Mazdak, they captured Karaj, the centre of the local ruler Abū Dulaf al-ʿIjlī, who was away with most of his troops at the time. Niẓām al-Mulk has them join forces with Bābak on the border between the Jibāl and Azerbaijan; the *Tārīkhnāma* says that Bābak sent reinforcements to the Jibāl, and al-Yaʿqūbī knows them to have defeated the first army that al-Muʿtaṣim sent against them, led by Hāshim b. Bātijūr.[68] But when al-Muʿtaṣim sent the Ṭāhirid Isḥāq b. Ibrāhīm b. Muṣʿab against them from Baghdad the revolt was ruthlessly suppressed: 60,000 or 100,000 rebels are said to have been killed, and the rest, said to number 14,000, fled to Byzantium,[69] where they were converted to Christianity and enrolled in the imperial army, with mixed success.[70] The leader of the refugees was a man called Naṣr, Nuṣayr or Barsīs, who claimed membership of the Iranian aristocracy.[71] Because these Khurramīs fled to Byzantium rather than to Azerbaijan, Niẓām al-Mulk's claim that they collaborated with Bābak has been doubted.[72] He does add some incredible details, but there are hints of coordination with activities in Azerbaijan as far back as 192/807f., as we have seen; and it is by no means implausible that Bābak should have been involved in both the planning and the execution of the great revolt of 218/833: his own fate depended on its

[67] Tab. iii, 1165; Azdī, 415; Masʿūdī, *Tanbīh*, 355.

[68] *SN*, ch. 47:4–5 (314f. = 240f.); *TN*, II, 1254; YT, II, 575f.

[69] In addition to the sources already cited see Maqdisī, VI, 114; Gardīzī (where they flee to Armenia and Azerbaijan), 175; Michael Syr., IV, 529, 531 = III, 84, 88.

[70] *EIr.*, s.v. 'Ḵorramis in Byzantium' (Venetis); add Cosentino, 'Iranian Contingents', 256f.; Letsios, 'Theophilus and his "Khurramite" Policy'. The emperor's subsequent problems with these troops is attributed to Muslim cunning by Iskāfī, *Luṭf al-tadbīr*, 56f. (where they are called Muḥammira).

[71] Venetis, 'Ḵorramis in Byzantium'.

[72] Cf. Rekaya, 'Théophobe et l'alliance de Bâbek', 51f.

outcome. When he was defeated four years later another 16,000 Khurramīs fled to Byzantium.[73]

ʿAlī b. Mazdak and Naṣr/Nuṣayr/Barsīs are the only leaders named, and the first name looks almost too good to be true (Sunbādh told the Shīʿites that Mazdak was a Shīʿite, as Niẓām al-Mulk informs us). We are not given any information about their beliefs, and beyond the fact that the rebels killed Muslims we have no information as to what drove them into action. A good guess, however, would be that they were responding to much the same developments as their counterparts in Azerbaijan, to be treated in the next chapter, for much of what we are told about that province applies to the Jibāl as well.

MUSLIMIYYA

Both the Jibāl and Azerbaijan came to count as the bastion of (Abū) Muslimī Khurramism, a religion centring on the murdered Abū Muslim much as Christianity centres on the crucified Jesus. It was among the Khurāsānīs that this religion began. Some Khurāsānīs continued to revere Abū Muslim as a hero or holy figure of some kind after his death while remaining in ʿAbbāsid service, somehow figuring out ways of reconciling continued loyalty to the ʿAbbāsids with their devotion to him. They did not question that he had died. The heresiographers sometimes call them Rizāmiyya, with reference now to their overt loyalty to the ʿAbbāsids,[74] now to their acceptance of the fact that Abū Muslim had died,[75] but others use the term Rizāmiyya quite differently.[76] In any case, continued devotion to Abū Muslim must have been extremely common in the ʿAbbāsid army. There were also Khurāsānīs who rejected the ʿAbbāsids for their killing of Abū Muslim, however – first and foremost among Abū Muslim's own disbanded troops, but probably also others. They often denied that Abū Muslim had died, claiming that he would come back;[77] this is the message that Niẓām al-Mulk imputes to Sunbādh, as has been seen. It does not

[73] Venetis, 'Ḵorramis in Byzantium'.

[74] Nawbakhtī, 32.

[75] Ashʿarī, 21f.

[76] To Baghdādī, *Farq*, 242f., they are a specific group in Marw which held the imamate to have passed from al-Saffāḥ to Abū Muslim while at the same time accepting the reality of the latter's death, except for a subgroup. In Shahrastānī, I, 114 = I, 453, they hold the imamate to have passed from Ibrāhīm al-Imām to Abū Muslim.

[77] Nāshiʾ, §48; Nawbakhtī, 41f.; Ashʿarī, 22; Ibn al-Nadīm, 408 = II, 822; MM, IV, 2398 (VII, 186).

necessarily mean that they deified him, but al-Baghdādī reserves the name of Abū Muslimiyya for those who did. He knew of people in Marw and Herat who held that Abū Muslim had become divine by God's spirit dwelling in him, so that he was better than Michael and Gabriel and all the angels, and who also insisted that al-Manṣūr had not killed him: a demon (*shayṭān*) had assumed his form (*ṣūra*). They were awaiting his return. The local name for them was Barkūkiyya.[78] Other Muslimīs identified Abū Muslim as the imam, meaning the successor to the Prophet's position as political leader and ultimate religious authority of the Muslim community. In fact, al-Baghdādī notwithstanding, belief in the imamate of Abū Muslim seems to be what the term Muslimī normally stands for. It was certainly in that form that Muslimism spread to the Jibāl and Azerbaijan. But there is nothing to suggest that Abū Muslim had acquired any religious significance in these regions before the third/ninth century. The first to identify the Khurramīs of the Jibāl as Muslimīs is Ja'far b. Ḥarb (d. 236/850).[79] The first to connect Bābak with Abū Muslim is al-Dīnawarī (d. 282/895).[80] Thereafter the Muslimī character of Khurramism in the Jibāl and Azerbaijan is well attested.[81]

Like many other Shī'ites the Muslimiyya said that the rightful occupant of the Prophet's position after the latter's death was 'Alī. They were Rāfiḍīs, meaning that they rejected Muḥammad's actual successors, Abū Bakr, 'Umar, and the caliphs thereafter, as usurpers. From 'Alī the true imamate had in their view passed to his two sons Ḥasan and Ḥusayn, and from them to a third son of his, Muḥammad b. al-Ḥanafiyya, whose mother was a slave-girl; some held the position to have passed directly from 'Alī to Ibn al-Ḥanafiyya.[82] Casting the son of a slave-girl as the rightful leader of the community was extreme. Holding him to overrule the rights of 'Alī's offspring by the daughter of the Prophet was utterly outrageous: were the sons of captives fit to lead their captors? Was it to non-Arabs enslaved by the conquests that the Prophet's guidance had passed, leaving behind the Prophet's own flesh and blood? Those who dared to say yes to both propositions were duly included under the label of extremists (*ghulāt*).

[78] Baghdādī, *Farq*, 242f.
[79] Ps.-Nāshi', §52.
[80] Dīnawarī, 397.
[81] Cf. MM, IV, §2398; Maqdisī, IV, 31; *SN*, ch. 47:14 (319 = 244); Dihkhudā in Kāshānī, *Zubda*, 187, 189; in Rashīd al-Dīn, 150, 153 (cf. 151, where the Khurramīs are explicitly placed in Azerbaijan).
[82] Shahrastānī, I, 114 = I, 453.

Like other extremists the Khurramīs claimed that Ibn al-Ḥanafiyya had bequeathed the imamate to his son, Abū Hāshim, and that the latter had bequeathed it to a man who was not a descendant of ʿAlī. The Muslimiyya identified this man as an ʿAbbāsid: a member of the Hāshimite family, certainly, but not a descendant of ʿAlī, let alone by Fāṭima. The recipient in their view was ʿAlī b. ʿAbdallāh b. al-ʿAbbās, or alternatively his son, Muḥammad b. ʿAlī, and from him the imamate had passed to Ibrāhīm b. Muḥammad, also known as Ibrāhīm al-Imām, the man who was held to have sent Abū Muslim to Khurāsān; and from him it passed to Abū Muslim. Or it had passed from Ibrāhīm to his brother Abū 'l-ʿAbbās, the first ʿAbbāsid caliph, and from him to Abū Muslim; or from Abū 'l-ʿAbbās it had passed to al-Manṣūr, who forfeited the imamate to Abū Muslim when he killed him.[83] One way or the other the Muslimīs defined themselves out of ʿAbbāsid Shīʿism too: no member of the Hāshimite family now had any right to the imamate in their view. The true leadership had passed to Abū Muslim, to remain among the non-Arabs for good.

The Khurramīs deemed practically all other Muslims to be in error. The compact majority had gone astray by following Abū Bakr and ʿUmar rather than ʿAlī; the party of ʿAlī had gone wrong by continuing to follow the ʿAlids when the latter's rights passed to the ʿAbbāsids; and the party of the ʿAbbāsids had gone wrong by staying loyal to them when they lost their rights to Abū Muslim. Only the Muslimiyya preserved the true succession to the Prophet: only they were the Muslim community, only their understanding of Islam captured the true meaning of the Prophet's message. In other words, the Muslimiyya accepted Islam merely to opt out of it again with Muslim credentials: they wanted to count as Muslims, but Islam in their view was not what anyone else took it to be. This is why they were generally held to hide behind Islam. The sources are quite right that they had not really converted. Rather, they had changed the definition of Islam to stand for their own beliefs.

Like other Khurramīs the Muslimīs used the sequence of imams from ʿAlī onwards as a mere bridge between Muḥammad and their own local authorities. Their own imams were usually Iranians (*ʿajam*), rarely Arabs, and never Hāshimites, as we are told with reference to the Muslimiyya and Khidāshiyya.[84] Those who accepted the reality of Abū Muslim's death

[83] Ps.-Nāshiʾ, §49; Baghdādī, *Farq*, 242; Shahrastānī, I, 114 = I, 453; Dihkhudā in Kāshānī, *Zubda*, 187; cf. also Ashʿarī, 21f.

[84] Ps.-Nāshiʾ, §52.

held the imamate to have passed to his descendants via his daughter Fāṭima.[85] Like the Prophet's daughter, this Fāṭima was the ancestress not just of the imams, but also of the future mahdi, whose name would be Mahdī b. Fīrūz, and whom they called 'the knowing boy' (*kūdak-i dānā*).[86] This seems to have become the common form of Muslimism in the Jibāl.

[85] For this daughter see Baghdādī, *Ta'rīkh Baghdād*, X, 207.–2 (where she dies without descendants).

[86] MM, IV, §2398; Maqdisī, IV, 31, VI, 95; *SN*, ch. 47:14 (319 = 244); Dihkhudā in Kāshānī, *Zubda*, 187, 189; in Rashīd al-Dīn, 150, 153 For the *kūdak-i dānā* (mentioned by Niẓām al-Mulk) see further Chapter 15, pp. 341f.

3

Azerbaijan

Bābak

Lesser Media or Azerbaijan is the eastern half of the Caucasus region. Today it is divided between the Iranian province of Azerbaijan and the Republic of Azerbaijan (formerly part of the Soviet Union), and both are Turkic speaking. In the past the entire region formed part of Iran, and Azeri (*ādharī*) then stood for an Iranian language grouped together with that of the Jibāl as 'Pahlavi', as we have seen.[1] It would probably be more correct to say that many different forms of Azeri were spoken, for as in so many mountainous regions there were marked differences from one valley to the next: 'seventy languages' were spoken around Ardabīl, as al-Muqaddasī roundly puts it.[2]

The Arab invasion of Azerbaijan began under ʿUmar, in whose reign (13–23/634–44) the Arabs made a treaty with a local governor (*marzbān*) based at Ardabīl.[3] There was little Arab colonisation for about a century thereafter, however, for having eliminated the Sasanian regime in the region, the Arabs found themselves confronted with the Khazars, a Turkic, tribal people in the south Russian steppe, with whom they vied for control of the region for most of the Umayyad period. Such settlement as there was in that period was overwhelmingly military. A garrison was established at Ardabīl and soldiers were settled in unidentified places under ʿUthmān and ʿAlī;[4] in the second half of the Umayyad period another military centre was established further north, at Bardhaʿa in Arrān (Albania), and Maslama settled 24,000 Syrians even further north, at Bāb al-abwāb (Derbend), for campaigns against the Khazars.[5] But the

[1] Cf. *EIr.*, s.v. 'Azerbaijan, vii' (Yarshater); Chapter. 2, p. 31.
[2] Muqaddasī, 375.3.
[3] BF, 325f.
[4] BF, 328.-5, 329.8.
[5] BF, 205, 207; *EI*², s.vv. 'Bāb al-Abwāb', 'Bardhaʿa'.

only Arabs who acquired land in Azerbaijan under the Umayyads seem to have been the Umayyads themselves, more precisely Marwān b. Muḥammad, the last Umayyad governor of the province (later Marwān II), to whom the locals would surrender land in return for protection.[6] There is admittedly a report of an influx of Arab colonists in the time of ʿUthmān or ʿAlī, but it almost certainly reflects confusion with the later influx in the ʿAbbāsid period, as will be seen.[7] It was not until 119/737 that the backbone of the Khazars was broken by Marwān b. Muḥammad[8] and, though sporadic invasions continued into the ʿAbbāsid period, this was when the Muslim colonisation of the region began. Some fifty years later the region was in a state of unrest, to flare into open revolt under Bābak.[9]

BĀBAK'S LIFE UNTIL THE REVOLT

Of Bābak's early life we have a vivid account by a certain Wāqid b. ʿAmr al-Tamīmī, who wrote an *Akhbār Bābak*[10] and who appears to have flourished at Ardabīl around the time of the revolt, or not long after.[11] According to him Bābak's mother was a village woman called Māhrū from the district of Mīmadh in the Ardabīl region; he does not identify her religious affiliation, but she is described as a member of the indigenous non-Muslim population (*ʿulūj*) in another source, in which her name is indecipherable.[12] Wāqid tells us that she was one-eyed, presumably because there

[6] BF, 329.15, 330.6; cf. *EI*², s.v. 'Marwān II b. Muḥammad'.

[7] See p. 52. Cf. the equally anachronistic report that when ʿAlī's governor arrived in Azerbaijan he found that most of the local population 'had converted and recited the Qur'ān' (BF, 329.7f).

[8] Cf. *EI*², s.v. 'Khazars'.

[9] For earlier syntheses see Sadighi, *Mouvements*, ch. 7; Nafīsī, *Bābak-i Khurramdīn*; Bahrāmiyān, 'Bābak-i Khurramdīn'.

[10] It is cited in Ibn al-Nadīm, 406f. = II, 818ff., summarised in Maqdisī, VI, 114ff., and must also be the ultimate source of the account from Abū 'l-Ḥasan b. Sahl preserved in Persian in Abū 'l-Maʿālī, 61ff., which diverges on some points and has some additional information. (Mélikoff, *Abū Muslim*, 59, gives Wāqid's work the title *Bābaknāma*, wrongly implying that it was in Persian.)

[11] He is presumably identical with the Wāqid al-Ardabīlī who is cited as an authority on the conquest of Azerbaijan in BF, 325.-5, 329.10 and who must have flourished around the middle of the third/ninth century. Iskāfī, *Luṭf al-tadbīr*, 36, tells a story about Bābak on the authority of one ʿAmr b. Wāqid al-Dimashqī, perhaps a son (or confused version) of the same man.

[12] Abū 'l-Maʿālī, 61; Tab. iii, 1232. The indecipherable name is read as Barūmand by Rekaya, 'Ḫurram-Dīn', 40, and as *rūmiyya* by Laurent, *Arménie*, 637. Yūsofī, 'Bābak', takes Māhrū (moonface, 'belle') to be sarcastic.

had to be something repugnant about the mother of so terrible a rebel: al-Muqannaʿ, Bābak's counterpart in the east, was also said to be one-eyed. Bābak's father, according to Wāqid, was an Aramaean peddlar from lower Iraq, more precisely Madāʾin, who sold ointment (*duhn*), carrying his meagre supplies in a container on his back. His name was ʿAbdallah, or ʿĀmir b. ʿAbdallāh, or ʿĀmir b. Aḥad (*sic*), so apparently he was a Muslim. He and Māhrū allegedly conducted an affair which was discovered during an outing they made to a wooded area near a spring: they were sitting on their own drinking wine, and he was singing to her, when some village women who had gone for water chanced upon them. ʿĀmir fled while Māhrū was dragged back by her hair and publicly disgraced. This is presumably meant to sling mud at Bābak via his mother: it went without saying that the enemy of Islam was the son of a whore. In a similarly disparaging vein, another story has a mercenary boast of having seduced or raped the one-eyed girl and left her pregnant.[13] But even the mud-slinging Wāqid admits that Bābak's parents were married at the time of his birth, and he tells us that they had a second son. Later Bābak's itinerant father was killed on the road to Mount Sabalān (now Savalān, the third-highest mountain of Iran). The widow remarried, and it was perhaps by her second husband that she had yet another son.[14] Bābak's given name was al-Ḥasan, his brothers were ʿAbdallāh and Muʿāwiya,[15] and there also seems to have been one called Isḥāq.[16] All four sons, then, were given names identifying them as Muslims.

Māhrū, who lived long enough to be captured by the caliph's troops at the end of her son's revolt,[17] eked out a living as a wet-nurse; al-Ḥasan was sent to work as a cowherd. Later he entered the service of an Arab magnate in the district of Sarāb, on the road from Tabrīz to Ardabīl,[18] whose animals he tended and from whose unfree servants (*ghilmān*) he learnt to play the lute (*ṭunbūr*); he could also declaim poetry, presumably in the local dialect. From there he went on to work for another Arab magnate, Muḥammad b. al-Rawwād al-Azdī, in Tabrīz, but he left after about two years, when he was eighteen years old, to return to his native village, Bilālābād in the Mīmadh district. There he met a certain Jāvīdhān b. Shahrak, a wealthy man who was passing through the village after

[13] Tab. iii, 1232 (Maṭar the *ṣuʿlūk*).
[14] Only Abū 'l-Maʿālī, 61, mentions the second son and the widow's remarriage.
[15] MM, IV, §§2812 (VII, 130); Tab. iii, 1221f., 1228, 1231.
[16] Baghdādī, *Farq*, 268.-2.
[17] Tab. iii, 1222.
[18] Cf. Le Strange, *Lands*, 163. Ibn al-Nadīm has Sarāt.

selling 2,000 sheep at Zanjān. According to Abū 'l-Ma'ālī's slightly different account Bābak stopped working for the first magnate because local hostilities of an unidentified kind forced him and his family to leave, so he took to selling watermelons and other fruit, as well as entertaining with poetry and lute-playing, until he and his family came to a village belonging to Muḥammad b. al-Rawwād al-Azdī, the Arab magnate who controlled Tabrīz, and there he got to know Jāvīdhān b. Shahrak in the course of delivering melons to him.[19] Either way, Jāvīdhān took a liking to the young man and appointed him manager of his estates and other property. This event was the turning-point in his life.

So far the picture we are given is of a boy from the landless, footloose sector of village society who supplied manual labour to the Arab warlords of the area, but Jāvīdhān was an employer of a new type. Neither an Arab nor a Muslim, he was the head of a local Khurramī organisation, which Wāqid locates at Badhdh in the Karadagh mountains some 145 kilometres north-east of Ardabīl, on the border between Azerbaijan and Arrān (Albania).[20] One wonders if Wāqid is not doing some telescoping here, for Badhdh is where Bābak was ensconced during his revolt, and one would assume him to have moved to the impregnable castle on the frontier for the purpose of rebelling. But even Badhdh was within the region controlled by the Azdī Rawwādids,[21] so Wāqid's account is not impossible.

Wherever Jāvīdhān was based, there were two Khurramī societies in the region, his own and another led by a certain Abū 'Imrān. Both leaders were wealthy and powerful men, and they were rivals. Pacifists in principle, in practice the Khurramīs were feuding. The two leaders would fight during the summer months (during the winter they were immobilised by snow), and Jāvīdhān was killed in one of these battles some time after al-Ḥasan had entered his service. Al-Ḥasan, who must have been a convert to Khurramism by then, was accepted as Jāvīdhān's successor and married his widow, of whom, needless to say, we are told that she had been conducting an affair with Bābak, or even that she poisoned her husband in order to marry him:[22] it went without saying that all women in Bābak's life were utterly depraved. Jāvīdhān seems to have had a son of his own,

[19] Abū 'l-Ma'ālī, 61 (where the magnate has turned into Muḥammad b. Dāwūd al-Azdarī and Jāvīdhān b. Shahrak into Ḥādān b. Sha'rak).
[20] See Laurent, *Arménie*, 161, n. 131.
[21] See p. 53.
[22] For this claim see Abū 'l-Ma'ālī, 61.

but he was perhaps too young to succeed him.[23] At all events, the widow gathered her late husband's followers and told them that he had predicted his own death, declaring that his spirit would pass into Bābak and that the latter would 'possess the earth, slay the tyrants, restore Mazdakism, make the humble among you mighty and the lowly high'. Jāvīdhān's followers then paid allegiance to Bābak in the course of a ritual meal: the widow broke a loaf and put the pieces around a bowl of wine which she had placed on the skin of a freshly slaughtered cow; the men dipped the bread in the wine and swore allegiance to Bābak, doing obeisance to him thereafter. Then they shared a meal, presumably prepared from the cow, and Jāvīdhān's widow gave Bābak a sprig of fragrant herbs (*rayḥān*), signifying that they were married.[24] Perhaps it was on this occasion that al-Ḥasan assumed his Persian name.[25]

After Bābak's elevation to the leadership he and his followers set out to kill a group of Yemeni Arabs in the neighbourhood and mount campaigns against Muslims; or alternatively they dispersed in their villages to mount an attack on the local Muslims on an appointed day, killing Arabs and *mawālī* alike.[26] This probably happened in 201/816f., the date usually given for the beginning of Bābak's revolt, though other dates, such as 200/815f. and 204/819f., are also offered.[27]

What kind of Muslims had Bābak and his brothers been? Unlike Ibn Ḥafṣūn, the tenth-century Andalusian who declared himself a Christian in the course of his revolt, Bābak emerged into the limelight as the leader of a non-Muslim movement, so the sources do not think of him as an apostate

[23] This Ibn Jawīdān is mentioned twenty years later: Bughā had captured him and wished to exchange him for a captive taken by Bābak (Tab. iii, 1192). It is taken for granted that Bābak would want him back. Khalʿatbarī and Mihrwarz, *Junbish-i Bābak*, 58f., make Bābak himself a son of Jāvīdhān on the grounds that Bābak's father and Jāvīdhān are described as dying in ways so similar that they were probably the same.

[24] For all this see Ibn al-Nadīm, 406f. = II, 819ff.

[25] He could have adopted it when he became a member of the sect, but his brothers continued to be known by their Muslim names (see the references given in n. 15 of this chapter), so he probably did too until his elevation.

[26] Abū 'l-Maʿālī, 61f.; Maqdisī, VI, 116, and the disjointed words in Ibn al-Nadīm, 'the Muslims, both the Arabs and the *mawālī* among them'. The translations of Ibn al-Nadīm in Dodge, II, 822, and Laurent, *Arménie*, 367, incorporate the disjointed words into the account of the wedding, where they clearly do not belong.

[27] Ṭab. iii, 1015 (repeated 1171); similarly Azdī, 342. The date was 200 or 201 according to Masʿūdī, *Tanbīh*, 353.6, but 204 according to MM, IV, §2749 (VII, 62).

and rarely comment on his change of heart.[28] From the little we are told one would guess that his parents had called their children al-Ḥasan, Muʿāwiya, ʿAbdallāh, and Isḥāq largely because these were names current among the people who controlled their village and dominated local life, that is the Arab warlords, of whom more will be said below. Being a Muslim was to make oneself visible to those who mattered in the region. How far it translated into religious practice is another question. Did al-Ḥasan's parents and neighbours attend Friday prayers or fast in Ramaḍān? We do not know. Bābak may have picked up some Arabic from his time in Arab employment, for Wāqid explains that Jāvīdhān found him to be clever despite *taʿaqqud lisānihi bi'l-aʿjamiyya*, his tongue being tied by the fact that he normally spoke an Iranian language. Of course, Jāvīdhān would not have addressed Bābak in Arabic; he would not even have addressed him in Persian, but rather in the local Azeri dialect. But Wāqid is probably forgetting about verisimilitude here, for he was writing for readers of Arabic and it was for them that the reference to Bābak's barbarous language was meant: Bābak spoke Arabic badly.[29] If Bābak had picked up some Arabic one would assume him to have learnt some basic Muslim beliefs and practices too, as his parents no doubt intended when they gave him an Arab name. One could admittedly use an Arab name without meaning to signal adhesion to Islam, but those who did so were usually men who needed to move freely in Muslim society by virtue of their high position in their own community, such as the Armenian princes[30] or the above-mentioned Abū ʿImrān, the Khurramī leader who was Jāvīdhān's rival.[31] Bābak's parents, mere landless villagers, were not in that league. More probably they realised that the future of their children lay with the Arab warlords, and so brought them up to think of themselves as Muslims. Whatever exactly it may have entailed, it was a way of adapting to the standards of the new world in which the locals now found themselves. Al-Ḥasan looked all set to make a modest life for himself in the lower echelons of that world until he lost his job with the second Arab magnate and met Jāvīdhān.

[28] The closest we get to a charge of apostasy is in ʿAbd al-Jabbār, *Tathbīt*, II, 340, where Bābak is said to have presented himself as a Muslim and an adherent of the mahdi from the Prophet's family until he was strong enough to come clean about his convictions.

[29] Ibn al-Nadīm, 407.4 = II, 820.

[30] Cf. the lords of Arrān, n. 84 of this chapter; Sahl b. Sunbāṭ had a son called Muʿāwiya (Tab. iii, 1232).

[31] Ibn al-Nadīm, 406.-3 = II, 819. He is ʿImrān in Maqdisī, VI, 115.-3.

ARAB WARLORDS AND BRIGANDS

Warlords

The world that al-Ḥasan spurned after meeting Jāvīdhān was the outcome of the Arab colonisation of Azerbaijan. As mentioned already, there is a report presenting the colonists as having come a long time before. In fact, it is by Wāqid himself: he speaks of Arabs moving to Azerbaijan from 'the two garrison cities and the two Syrias' (i.e., Kufa, Basra, Syria proper, and Mesopotamia) in a context suggesting that they did so under ʿUthmān or ʿAlī.[32] But there is a better context for Wāqid's information in the time of Yazīd b. Ḥātim al-Muhallabī, governor of Azerbaijan for al-Manṣūr (136–58/754–75). This man transferred Yemenis from Basra, as the first to do so, according to al-Yaʿqūbī;[33] in fact, he distributed Yemeni tribes in Azerbaijan with such consistency during his sixteen years in office that al-Yaʿqūbī believed there to be only two Nizārī magnates in the entire province.[34] But it was not just from Basra that the colonists came: two of the men mentioned by al-Yaʿqūbī came from, or via, Mosul, and others came from either Mosul or Kufa;[35] many people also left Mosul for Azerbaijan in response to the fiscal oppression of Yaḥyā b. Saʿīd al-Ḥarashī in the years 180–2/796–8.[36] Wāqid continues that when people came to Azerbaijan 'everyone took control of what they could; some of them bought land from the non-Arabs and villages were handed over for protection [to others?] so that their inhabitants became sharecroppers for them'.[37] There was a general land-grab, in other words. This was how the colonists of the early ʿAbbāsid period became the magnates of Bābak's world.

The magnate who controlled the region in which Bābak lived his entire life, Muḥammad b. al-Rawwād al-Azdī, was the son of a man transferred

[32] BF, 329.11 (where only one Syria is mentioned); Ibn al-Faqīh, 284.9/581.6 (*al-Shāmayn*).

[33] YT, II, 446. It was also in the second half of the second/eighth century that the colonisation of Armenia began (cf. Laurent, *Arménie*, 197f.).

[34] YT, II, 446. On the Yemeni preponderance see also Azdī, 384.

[35] Murr b. ʿAlī al-Ṭāʾī, settled at Nīz, according to YT, II, 446, elsewhere appears as Murr b. ʿAmr al-Ṭāʾī al-Mawṣilī, settled at Narīr/Narīz (BF, 331.9; Ibn al-Faqīh, 285.9/582.4). The Rawwād family (on which more below) went to Azerbaijan from Mosul (Azdī, 92). The Hamdānids (below, notes 43f.) must have come from either Mosul or Kufa.

[36] Azdī, 287.

[37] BF, 329.11f.; cf. Ibn al-Faqīh, 284/581. It is not clear to me whether one or two methods are described. *Taljiʾa* could be a fictitious sale used to avoid confiscation of one's land by the authorities (cf. Cahen in *EI*², s.v. '*ildjāʾ*', and the reference given there). But there was nothing fictitious about the transfer of ownership here.

by Yazīd b. Ḥātim from Basra or Mosul in the reign of al-Manṣur. The father, al-Rawwād b. al-Muthannā, had settled 'in Tabrīz to Badhdh', as Ya'qūbī puts it, presumably meaning that his family appropriated estates in that entire area. The sons fortified Tabrīz, and Muḥammad b. al-Rawwād emerged as one of the dominant forces in Azerbaijan during the civil war between al-Amīn and al-Ma'mūn, when the province effectively ceased to be under caliphal rule.[38] Of another son, al-Wajnā', all we know is that he was based in Tabrīz and engaged in violent activities along with another strongman, Ṣadaqa b. 'Alī (on whom more below) under Hārūn al-Rashīd, forcing the governor to fortify Marāgha, the provincial capital at the time.[39] The magnate for whom Bābak tended animals in the Sarāb district between Tabrīz and Ardabīl seems to have been another member of the same family: his name is given as Shibl b. al-Munaqqī al-Azdī, probably a corruption of Shibl b. al-Muthannā al-Azdī.[40] At all events, the Rawwādids survived al-Ma'mūn's reassertion of central control and supported the government along with the other leading men against Bābak, whose initial massacre of Yemenis had taken place on land they controlled.[41] The family stayed on as rulers of Tabrīz and environs into Seljuq times. By then they counted as Kurds.[42]

At least two other magnate families had similar histories, that is to say they were transferred to Azerbaijan with full government backing and emerged as leading figures there during the chaos of the Fourth Civil War. One of them was the family of 'Abdallāh b. Ja'far al-Hamdānī, who settled at Mayānij and Khalbāthā,[43] and who produced the local ruler Muḥammad b. Ḥumayd al-Hamdānī.[44] The other was the family of Murr b. 'Alī/'Amr al-Ṭā'ī, who settled at Narīz: he and his descendants built it up, turning it into a town, and were eventually granted autonomy there.[45] Murr's son, 'Alī b. Murr al-Ṭā'ī, remembered as a patron of poets,[46] figures in the list of rebel rulers in Azerbaijan in the Fourth Civil

38 YT, II, 446, 540.
39 BF, 330.8, 331.4; Ibn al-Faqīh, 284.-2, 285.7/581.-5, 582.3.
40 Ibn al-Nadīm, 407 = II, 819; similarly emended by Yūsofī, 'Bābak', 300.
41 YT, II, 564. One of them, Yaḥyā b. al-Rawwād, seems to have been involved in rebellious activities under al-Mutawakkil (YT, II, 594).
42 *Ḥudūd al-'ālam*, §36, no. 18, and the commentary thereto (143, 395ff.); *EI*², s.v. 'Rawwādids'.
43 YT, II, 446; BF, 331.5.
44 YT, II, 540.
45 YT, II, 446; BF, 331.9; n. 34 of this chapter; *EI*², s.v. 'Nirīz'.
46 Minorsky, *Abū-Dulaf*, 57 = §23, cf. the commentary at 82.

War[47] and was among the magnates rounded up and sent to al-Maʾmūn by Muḥammad b. Ḥumayd,[48] but the family continued and produced a governor of Azerbaijan in 260/873; the town was later seized and destroyed by Kurds.[49] The mercenary (*ṣuʿlūk*) who claimed paternity of Bābak may have been in ʿAlī b. Murr's service: it was to him that he told the story.[50]

We get a glimpse of what seems to be a similar type of magnate in the Jibāl, where local rulers also emerged during the Fourth Civil War. One was Murra b. Abī Murra al-Rudaynī al-ʿIjlī,[51] another was Abū Dulaf al-ʿIjlī. But the Dulafid family, and perhaps those of other leading men in the Jibāl as well, had risen from less exalted origins: their founding fathers had been *ṣaʿālīk*.[52]

Brigands

Often translated 'vagabonds', *ṣaʿālīk* were men who lived off their physical prowess, working as mercenaries, bodyguards, assassins, and other strong-arms when there was a demand for the services of such people, and as brigands when there was not. They congregated in mountains and other inaccessible places, with a preference for border lands where they could escape from one governor by crossing into the territory of another.[53] One would have expected them to be smugglers too, but there is no mention of such activities. What we do hear is that they would hire themselves out indiscriminately to rebels,[54] local magnates, leading men,[55] and representatives of the government,[56] usually for military service of some kind or other. Bakr b. al-Naṭṭāḥ, for example, was a *ṣuʿlūk* who

[47] YT, II, 540.

[48] Azdī, 384.6

[49] Minorsky, *Abū-Dulaf*, 57 = §23, and the commentary at pp. 82f.

[50] Tab. iii, 1232.

[51] YT, II, 540. Murra was sent to Sīsar by al-Rashīd and seized estates in Azerbaijan from a rival who had failed to oust him; but his son was removed by al-Maʾmūn (BF, 311.1ff.; Ibn al-Faqīh, 240/496).

[52] Cf. EI^2, s.v. 'Dulafids'; *EIr.*, s.v. 'Dolafids'.

[53] The brigands and ruffians (*al-ṣaʿālīk wa'l-dhuʿʿār*) who congregated in the Sīsar region in the Jibāl in the caliphate of al-Mahdī were safe because it was on the border between Hamadhān, al-Dīnawar, and Azerbaijan (BF, 310.8ff.; Ibn al-Faqīh, 239/495).

[54] See note 66 (Mankijūr); Tab. iii, 1530 (Zaydī revolt in Ṭabaristān).

[55] Cf. pp. 56f. (Ibn al-Baʿīth); Azdī, 315.13 (where they appear to be in permanent service), 345.11 (where they are hired as assassins).

[56] Cf. nn. 62 (*thughūr*), 64 (Muḥammad b. Ḥumayd) of this chapter; Tab. ii, 1725, 1933 (years 255, 265).

practised highway robbery before enrolling in the army of Abū Dulaf, the hereditary ruler of Karaj in the Jibāl, who had started as a *ṣuʿlūk* himself and who now had a semi-private army of some 20,000 *ṣaʿālīk* and other men; enrolled in his service, Bakr received stipends from the treasury.[57] Of an Azdī from Mosul we are told that he gathered the *ṣaʿālīk al-balad* and proceeded to jail Hārūn's tax collectors and pocket the taxes himself.[58] We hear of *ṣaʿālīk* in connection with Abū 'l-ʿAbbās's attempt to pacify Armenia,[59] in the retinue of the Rawwādid magnates,[60] in a Kurdish regiment that defected from the Ṣaffārids to the Zanj,[61] in garrisons maintained by the government along the Byzantine frontier,[62] and in jail.[63] The entire mountainous region from the Byzantine frontier to Hamadhān was swarming with such men. *Ṣaʿālīk* from 'Yemen, Rabīʿa and Muḍar from the Jazīra and the districts of al-Jabal' offered their services to Muḥammad b. Ḥumayd al-Ṭūsī for the war against Bābak.[64] The Afshīn preferred to remove them by way of preparation for his campaign;[65] but when Mankijūr rebelled as governor of Azerbaijan after the suppression of Bābak's revolt, he also gathered *ṣaʿālīk*.[66] The *zawāqīl* of Syria whom al-Amīn had unsuccessfully tried to enrol against his brother in the Fourth Civil War come across as men of the same type.[67]

There were *ṣaʿālīk* by the Umayyad period,[68] and even earlier if sources are to be believed.[69] Those of the ʿAbbāsid period may have given themselves a continuous history back to the heroic *ṣaʿālīk* of Jāhilī Arabia[70]

[57] *Aghānī*, XIX, 106; Tab. iii, 1686f. For *ṣaʿālīk* and *khawārij* at Dastabā in 131 see IA, V, 397.

[58] Azdī, 279 (year 177). For an ʿAbdī who *taṣaʿlaka* near Samarra and took to robbery see Tab. iii, 2114 (year 275).

[59] YT, II, 429.

[60] See p. 57.

[61] Tab. iii, 1908ff.

[62] Ibn Khurdādhbih, 253.10, 254.13 (in contrast with regular troops).

[63] Thus the *ṣaʿālīk ahl al-Jabal* in Baghdad in 249 (Tab. iii, 1510).

[64] Azdī, 386 (year 213).

[65] Cf. n. 159 of this chapter.

[66] Tab. ii, 1301; f. YT, II, 583, where he gathers *aṣḥāb Bābak*.

[67] See YT, II, 560 (chiefs of tribes, *ṣaʿālīk*, and *zawāqīl*); Tab. iii, 1463 (where both appear in the motley troops of ʿUbaydallāh b. Yaḥyā b. Khāqān); Jāḥiẓ, *Bukhalāʾ*, 49.ult. (*ṣaʿālik al-Jabal wa-zawāqīl al-Shām* in a list of brigands). For the banditry of the *zawāqīl* see Cobb, *White Banners*, 118ff.

[68] Mūsā b. ʿAbdallāh b. Khāzim was joined by *qawm min al-ṣaʿālīk* in Khurāsān in 85/704f. (Tab. ii, 1145). Only *ṣaʿālīk* and *fityān* remained loyal to Ibn Hubayra at Wāsiṭ in 132/749f. (Tab. iii, 66).

[69] BF, 395.6 (Sīstān in the aftermath of the Battle of the Camel).

[70] Cf. ʿUrwa b. al-Ward in *Aghānī*, III, 38.

(or, when they were Persian speaking, back to the heroes of the Iranian past). Mercenaries everywhere have a tendency to romanticise themselves, disguising the mercenary or downright criminal aspect of their activities as part of a chivalric ideal, and *ṣuʿlūk* could be a term of flattery. But to most people *ṣaʿālīk* were the very opposite of nobles.[71]

It was a *ṣuʿlūk* by the name of Maṭar who boasted of having raped the one-eyed girl and thereby fathered Bābak, and his claim is not entirely inept, for the *ṣaʿālīk* undoubtedly played a major role in the erosion of the rural order to which Bābak's revolt appears to have been a response. Already in the time of Marwān b. Muḥammad we hear of villagers who responded to the chronic insecurity by surrendering their land to powerful men in return for protection, thereby reducing themselves to sharecroppers: this was how Marwān b. Muḥammad had acquired Marāgha, which later passed into ʿAbbāsid ownership to become the provincial capital of the new regime under al-Rashīd.[72] The depredations of the *ṣaʿālīk* (and government officials) similarly induced the inhabitants of Zanjān to hand over their estates to al-Qāsim b. al-Rashīd for protection, thereby reducing themselves to sharecroppers.[73] In the Jibāl, where *ṣaʿālīk* were also a major problem in the early ʿAbbāsid period, the inhabitants of one locality sought protection on the same terms from an ʿAbdī commander, whose sons later found themselves unable to cope with the local *ṣaʿālīk* and so, with the agreement of the locals, surrendered the land to al-Maʾmūn in return for protection as his sharecroppers.[74]

A steeply mountainous region, Azerbaijan and the Jibāl must always have had a fair share of such men, but they are remarkably prominent in the sources relating to the century after the ʿAbbāsid revolution, and we also see them rise to unusual power in this period; for the beneficiaries of the rural changes were not always members of the ruling house or their representatives, as opposed to *ṣaʿālīk* themselves. Indeed, the distinction between the two is often unclear, for the *ṣaʿālīk* acted as the spearheads of the central government in the countryside, where they received official recognition and where their depredations were not easily distinguished from those of governors (*ʿummāl*). In Azerbaijan we hear of one Ḥulays, Julays or Ḥalbas, a tribesman of Jadīla/Rabīʿa who settled at Marand, perhaps as a soldier or ex-soldier in Marwān II's army. His son al-Baʿīth

[71] According to one eschatological vision *ṣaʿālīk* and lowly people would have their time of dominance at the end of times (Nuʿaym b. Ḥammād, *Fitan*, 142/162, no. 661).

[72] BF, 330.6.

[73] BF, 323.11; Ibn al-Faqīh, 282.13/559f.

[74] BF, 311.

(or al-Bu'ayth) worked as a *ṣu'lūk* for Ibn al-Rawwād al-Azdī, the magnate on whose lands Bābak was to rise to leadership. In fact, al-Ba'īth and his son in turn, Muḥammad, were men rather like Bābak, except that as Arabs they enjoyed social, cultural, and linguistic advantages that Bābak lacked. Al-Ba'īth amassed enough clout to fortify Marand, originally a small village, and to emerge as a big man in Azerbaijan along with his cousin al-Layth al-'Utbī. His son Muḥammad b. al-Ba'īth dug himself deeper into Marand by building castles there.[75] At one point he was allied with Bābak, for whose troops he would supply provisions and entertainment when they passed through his area. Threatened by a caliphal army in 220/835f., however, he changed sides and declared his loyalty to the caliph, using the opportunity to complete his usurpation of Marand from the indigenous lord (*ṣāḥib*) of the region, 'Iṣma al-Kurdī, whose daughter he had married. He completed his usurpation when 'Iṣma, who was also on Bābak's side, passed by Marand with a detachment. Ibn al-Ba'īth serviced his troops in the customary manner and invited 'Iṣma to come up to his castle; there he got him and his companions drunk, killed the companions, and had 'Iṣma transported to an impregnable castle (seized from al-Wajnā' b. al-Rawwād) on Lake Urmiya, or he had them all transported there and then sent him/them on to the caliph, who squeezed 'Iṣma for information about the road system and modes of fighting in Azerbaijan.[76] Thereafter we find Ibn al-Ba'īth on the caliph's side in the war.[77] He did not succeed in regularising his position, however. After Bābak's death his ambitions clashed with those of the governor,[78] and he was taken to Samarra, where he was jailed. In 234/848f. he fled from jail and returned to Marand, where he gathered *ṣa'ālīk* or, as Ibn al-Athīr calls them, *ṭaghām*, to be defeated in 235/849f., and taken to Samarra again. An accomplished poet in both Arabic and Persian, he narrowly escaped execution by means of well-crafted poetic flattery of the caliph, but died shortly after.[79] His sons were enrolled in the Samarran regiment known as the Shākiriyya.[80]

[75] BF, 330; YT, II, 446; Tab. iii, 1172.13.

[76] Tab. iii, 1171f.; YT, II, 577f.; BF, 330; Ibn al-Jawzī, *Muntaẓam*, XI, 53; see also the garbled account in *TN*, IV, 1258 = 181, where he has become a *dihqān* and descendant of the ancient inhabitants of the land.

[77] Tab. iii, 1190, 1193.

[78] Thus YT, II, 594. Others place this after his flight from Samarra and leave his presence in jail unexplained.

[79] Tab. iii, 1379–89; BF, 330; YT, II, 594 (with the *ṣa'ālīk*); Ṣūlī, *Awrāq*, 546f. (no.90); Ibn al-Jawzī, *Muntaẓam*, XI, 206; IA, VII, 41ff. (year 234).

[80] Tab. iii, 1389. The family's story is also told in Laurent, *Arménie*, 443f.

Another *ṣuʿlūk* whose depredations helped to change the nature of rural society in the mountains of western Iran is Zurayq, a big man in Bābak's Azerbaijan. He descended from a *mawlā*, presumably freedman, of the Azd called Dīnār. Of Ṣadaqa b. ʿAlī b. Ṣadaqa b. Dīnār[81] we are told that he was a *ṣuʿlūk* who practised brigandage and took refuge in the Jibāl, where he seized estates, made himself powerful, and managed to defeat a caliphal army sent against him; he escaped further attention because al-Rashīd went to Khurāsān and died, whereupon the lawlessness of the Fourth Civil War enabled him to expand even further.[82] Ṣadaqa b. ʿAlī is sometimes said to have been known as Zurayq; alternatively, he had a son called Zurayq. In any case, Ṣadaqa/Zurayq moved north, conquered Urmiya, and wrought destruction there in the time of al-Rashīd,[83] fought against Ḥamza, the (non-Arab) lord of Arrān,[84] and divested him of mines, pasture land, and a district containing fifty estates. He also seized estates from the people of Marand, and terrorised Mosul from time to time with a private army of some 30,000 men. Zurayq became big enough to ask al-Maʾmūn for the governorship of Armenia and Azerbaijan along with the command of the war against Bābak, all of which was granted him in 208/823f.[85] He collected taxes, invited people to join up, and recruited soldiers in both Mosul and Azerbaijan, but then winter came, so he did nothing and was dismissed in favour of the governor of Mosul, al-Sayyid b. Anas al-Azdī.[86] This governor, another semi-independent ruler who had emerged in the Fourth Civil War,[87] was married to a daughter of Zurayq called Bābūnaj (Zurayq evidently had not found it necessary to give his daughter an Arabic name). For all that, Zurayq refused to vacate the post and eventually killed his son-in-law in a battle, so that it was not until 212/827f. that he was finally defeated by Muḥammad b. Ḥumayd. The ʿAbbāsids seem consistently to have pardoned the rebellious strongmen

81 This form of his name is given in BF, 331.2.

82 Azdī, 358.4ff.

83 BF, 330.8, 331.2f. Cf. also Laurent, *Arménie*, 437.

84 Ḥamza, *ṣāḥib Arrān*, was presumably a member of the house of Mihran. Varaz Tirdat, the last ruler (*baṭrīq*) of Arrān from this family, was assassinated in 821 or 822: he or a predecessor appears under the name of ʿAbd al-Raḥmān *baṭrīq Arrān* in or around 197/813 (Azdī, 358; YT, II, 562, cf. *EI*², s.v. 'Arrān'; Laurent, *Arménie*, 458, n. 55).

85 Laurent, *Arménie*, 437, with reference to Vasmer's numismatic evidence. His appointment is placed in 205 in Azdī, 356, in 209 in Tab. iii, 1072.

86 Azdī, 356ff.

87 YT, II, 540; Azdī, 371f.

of the region when they could, presumably to keep their followers quiet,[88] and Zurayq was no exception: for all his depredations he too received *amān*. His estates, castles, fortresses, and other ill-gotten gains were confiscated and given to the victor, the general Muḥammad b. Ḥumayd al-Ṭūsī, a member of an Arab family that had risen to great prominence through participation in the Hāshimite revolution. But the general magnanimously returned all this wealth to the Zurayq family:[89] he must have seen them as members of the same club. *Mawlā* and *ṣuʿlūk* though he was by origin, Zurayq had made it to the top.

THE LOSERS

All in all, Azerbaijan comes across as a violent, lawless frontier society in which Arab and Arabised colonists were amassing land at the expense of indigenous landowners, big and small alike.[90] Political control rested on the possession of castles, which seem typically to have been perched high above the villages, whose inhabitants supplied the local lord with labour, produce, and perhaps military service as well; and power seems overwhelmingly to have been of the personal rather than the institutional type, that is to say the dominant men owed their position to their own physical prowess, sons, and personal retainers, rather than to membership of, or contact with, formal institutions such as the army or bureaucracy. Male strength, apparently, was an advantage of such overriding importance that women were reduced to mere emblems of the political and moral status of their menfolk: Bābak's mother and wife were whores because Bābak was an enemy of Islam; Bābak himself reputedly denounced the mother of one of his own sons as a whore on the grounds that no genuine son of his could have behaved as he did.[91] Any women that Bābak wanted had to be handed over to him; if not, he would mount raids to capture them or alternatively rape them in the presence of their menfolk by way of display of his superior might.[92] The Armenian noble Sahl b. Sunbāṭ is said to have dishonoured Bābak's mother, sister, and wife in front of Bābak before handing them all over to the caliph on the grounds that

[88] Cf. YT, II, 563f., 566, on ʿAbd al-Malik b. Jaḥḥāf and his son Sawāda (who was even offered a governorship first), and Yazīd b. Ḥiṣn; IA, VII, 42, on the handling of Ibn al-Baʿīth's second revolt; Azdī, 429.15f., on Muḥammad b. ʿAbdallāh al-Warthānī.

[89] Azdī, 359f., 365ff., 373ff., 378–82; YT, II, 564.

[90] The chaotic conditions in which Bābak grew up are stressed by Dīnawarī, 397.

[91] Tab. iii, 1220f. 'Blame the mother' has a long history.

[92] Tab. iii, 1223; Maqdisī, VI, 117.

this was how Bābak had treated his enemies.[93] In the same spirit, al-Muʿtaṣim is depicted as praising God for allowing him to deflower the daughters of Bābak, Māzyār, and the Byzantine emperor in a single hour.[94]

We hear surprisingly little about the losers in the scramble for land and local power, probably because, like most colonists, the Arab and Arabised newcomers were more interested in themselves than in the population they were displacing. It is sheer accident that we are told about ʿIṣma al-Kurdī who was ousted by the Baʿīth family. It is not clear whether any significance should be attached to the fact that ʿIṣma was a Kurd (if his *nisba* has been correctly read), for the sources do not comment on the participation of Kurds in Bābak's revolt, though it would have been an obvious way to disparage it. Of other prominent men on Bābak's side we have little but the names: Rustam,[95] Ṭarkhān,[96] ʿĀdhīn,[97] Ḥātim b. Fīrūz,[98] and Muʿāwiya.[99] The first three were clearly non-Muslims. The last may have been Bābak's own brother, Muʿāwiya, who participated in the revolt.[100] Ḥātim b. Fīrūz may have been either a local lord who had assumed an Arab name for the purpose of dealing with his Arab counterparts or a former Muslim who had kept his Arab name, as did both of Bābak's brothers, when he turned against Islam.

Several passages show that the members of the Khurramī organisation behind Bābak's revolt lived in villages,[101] but whether they did so as landlords, landowning peasants, or landless villagers is left unclear, except in one passage: Ṭarkhān asked for permission to spend the winter in a village of his (*fī qarya lahu*), suggesting that he owned both this and other villages.[102] Apparently, ʿIṣma al-Kurdī was not the only landlord among them. Jāvīdhān himself had evidently been a landowner of some importance, as had his rival Abū ʿImrān. They were not in the league of the great aristocrats of the Sasanian period, who seem to have

[93] Ibn al-ʿIbrī, *Duwal*, 242.2.
[94] *SN*, ch.47:12 (=243f.).
[95] Movsès Kałankatuac'i in Laurent, *Arménie*, 378.
[96] Tab. iii, 1179, 1193f.
[97] Tab. iii, 1179, 1195–7, 1206, 1214–17.
[98] Azdī, 357.11.
[99] Tab. iii, 1171.
[100] Tab. iii, 1221f.
[101] 'You were dispersed in your villages', as Jāvīdhān's widow reminded Jāvīdhān's troops at the time of his death (Ibn al-Nadīm, 407.14f. = II, 821; cf. Maqdisī, VI, 116.4, where they are told to return to 'their villages and dwelling places').
[102] Tab. iii, 1193f.

disappeared from the region. The only Mihrānids we hear about are those of Arrān (Albania).[103] But though the local elite may not have formed part of the Sasanian establishment, within their own community they were big men. It is probably as a local chief of this kind that we should envisage Naṣr, the Khurramī leader who cast himself as an Iranian aristocrat in Byzantium.[104]

Mīmadh, the district in which Bābak grew up, had supplied troops to the Sasanian *marzbān* at Ardabīl in his confrontation with the Arabs.[105] It was still a theatre of war in the late Umayyad period, when Maslama encountered an unidentified enemy there while serving as governor of Armenia for Hishām;[106] and soon after it became an object of colonisation by the Rawwādids. We do not have enough information to say exactly how the constant warfare and ensuing colonisation had affected the local communities, let alone to compare its relative impact on Zoroastrians, Christians, and Khurramīs; but the overall picture as far as the Khurramīs are concerned is one of social demotion: from local elite status to social ruin and/or from status as landowning peasants to that of sharecroppers. Given that Bābak spent his entire life on lands controlled by the Rawwād family and that his followers started the revolt by massacring Yemeni Arabs on the estates of this family, it is hard not to infer that he and his followers saw the Arab/Muslim conquerors and colonists as the root of their troubles. Jāvīdhān's widow spoke of 'the wickedness of the Arabs' (*shirrat al-ʿarab*),[107] while Bābak called himself 'the avenging guide' (*al-hādī al-muntaqim*).[108] In a slightly different vein, he contemptuously referred to the Muslims as 'Jews' (a habit shared by his followers): 'you have sold me to the Jews for a trifling amount', as he complained when he was betrayed by the Armenian prince Ibn Sunbāṭ, casting the latter as Judas.[109] The movement was both anti-Arab and anti-Islamic because Islam was the religion of the Arab and Arabised magnates who were transforming the countryside: the locals had never encountered it in any other form.

103 Minorsky, 'Caucasia IV', 505f.
104 See Chapter 2, p. 41.
105 BF, 325f.
106 BF, 206f.; also in Yāqūt, IV, 717f., s.v. 'Mīmadh'.
107 Ibn al-Nadīm, 407.15 = II 821 ('hostility of the Arabs').
108 Abū 'l-Maʿālī, 62.4.
109 Tab. iii, 1226, cf. 1195 ('Ādhīn).

KHURRAMĪ CULT SOCIETIES

Bābak was the leader of a religious organisation of which we would have liked to know more. He had joined it as a disciple, for Jāvīdhān is identified as his *ustādh*, his religious instructor. There were *ōstāds* in the Zoroastrian priesthood too.[110] What doctrines the organisation stood for we are not told. All we hear is that Bābak succeeded Jāvīdhān on the grounds that the latter's spirit had passed into him, and that he claimed to be the 'the spirit of the prophets' and divine (*ilāh*).[111] The implication is that Jāvīdhān had been divine as well, presumably because the prophetic spirit had been in him too. Precisely how this should be understood will be examined in another chapter.[112] Wāqid envisages the organisation as consisting of headquarters at Badhdh and a network in the villages around it. It was apparently only the members of the local constituency at Badhdh who had participated in Jāvīdhān's feuds with the rival organisation in the area, for when this feuding led to Jāvīdhān's death, his widow had to summon his supporters from their own villages in order to settle the succession. The account of how she described her husband's last wishes to them is also based on the assumption that they had not been present at the time.[113] We should perhaps envisage the men she summoned from their villages as leaders of subordinate organisations who would come together at the headquarters at certain times of the year for ritual activitities, religious instruction, the exchange of news, the settlement of disputes, and, as in this case, the regulation of the succession. It is in any case clear that the cult society was separate from, and wider than, the organisation of the village itself. This suggests that there were rituals of initiation, but we hear nothing about them. Nor are we told whether women were members. Jāvīdhān's widow is depicted as playing a leading role in his succession and as sitting openly together with the men (*ẓāhiran lahum*) when she wedded Bābak, but Bābak's own treatment of women is more suggestive of an all-male network.

The network appears to have been quite extensive. Marand, the domicile of ʿIṣma al-Kurdī, was a long way from Badhdh (if this was really where Jāvīdhān had his lodge). We do not know exactly where Abū ʿImrān, the leader of the rival organisation, was based, or whether his followers

110 Ibn al-Nadīm, 407.14f. = II, 821; *Dd*, 44 in Shaked, 'Esoteric Trends', 204 (without comment on the term).
111 Cf. Chapter 11, nn. 25f.
112 See Chapter 11.
113 Ibn al-Nadīm, 406.-2 = II, 819.ult.

came to be enrolled in Bābak's movement (as one would expect); but we do hear of a Khurramī community more distant than Marand which did eventually join.

The source for this is the Christian Dionysius of Tell Mahré (d. 848), as preserved in three later Christian sources.[114] Dionysius is speaking of people he calls Khurdanaye, which seems to be some kind of conflation of Kurds (Khurdaye) and Khurramdīnīs.[115] In Michael the Syrian's version they are introduced as 'Arab' Khurdanaye, apparently meaning those under Muslim as opposed to Byzantine rule. We are told that they included Persians and pagan Armenians and constituted 'a race of their own'. They were pagans (*ḥanpe*),[116] but their cult was Magian, presumably meaning that they had fire rituals. They had long had an oracle predicting the coming of a king called mahdi. They spoke of this king as God and said that his kingdom would pass on from one to the other in perpetuity, and, not long before Dionysius wrote, this king had actually come. He was veiled and called himself now Christ and now the Holy Spirit, or 'divine prophet'.[117] Huge crowds, including Persians (Zoroastrians?), Arabs (Muslims?), and pagans, gathered around him for pillage and booty, for the Khurdanaye were brigands. Their mahdi took up residence in the steep mountains of Beth Qardwaye (between the Tigris and Lake Urmiya), where he started terrorising the Jazīra, Armenia, Beth Zabde, and Ṭur ʿAbdin. Al-Maʿmūn 'trembled before him' and sent Ḥasan against them (probably al-Ḥasan b. ʿAlī al-Maʾmūnī, a native of Bādghīs who had defeated Abū 'l-Sarāyā in 200/815f. and was later appointed governor of Armenia).[118] The Khurdanaye treated anyone who did not acknowledge the divinity of their mahdi as an enemy. This mahdi was killed by the Armenian prince Isaac, son of Ashot, after pillaging the monastery of Qarṭmin; he was succeeded by one Hārūn, who was killed by ʿAlī (probably ʿAlī b. Hishām, another eastern Iranian who was governor of Azerbaijan and neighbouring provinces with responsibility for operations

[114] Michael Syr., III, 50–2; Bar Hebraeus, *Chronography*, 131f.; *Chron. ad 1234*, II, no. 214 (25ff. = 17ff.).

[115] The chronicle of 1234 simply replaces Khurdanaye with Khurdaye.

[116] Translated 'Muslims' by Budge, which is clearly wrong here.

[117] Thus *Chron. ad 1234*, II, 26 = 18.

[118] His appointment to Armenia under al-Maʾmūn is mentioned by YT, II, 566. Others only know him to have governed it for al-Mutaṣim (e.g. BF, 211.3; hence presumably his absence from Laurent, *Arménie*, 435f.). For his defeat of Abū 'l-Sarāyā see Tab. iii, 985.

against Bābak in, probably, 214–17/829–32);[119] and after him their leader was Bābak, the cattle-herder. When the Khurdanaye no longer had any leaders, they became Muslims.[120]

Here as in Bābak's Azerbaijan we are in a lawless mountainous region in which the members of a religious organisation terrorise their neighbours, fired by expectations of a great political change. They too were led by a divine figure, but their leader was a long-expected redeemer and apparently divine in a fuller sense than Bābak, who did not wear a veil. The veiled mahdi operated at the same time as Bābak, and his followers must surely have known about the latter's activities well before they joined him. But it was only when several of their own leaders had been killed that they placed themselves under Bābak's command. Bābak's relations with the Khurramīs of the Jibāl come across as similar. They knew about each other, helped each other, and coordinated some of their activities, but they had separate leadership and never quite fused as a single movement.

We should probably envisage the entire mountain range from Azerbaijan to Fārs as dotted with such Khurramī cult societies. Wherever there were Khurramīs there will have been a local leader in whose house the villagers met for social and ritual purposes on a regular basis. Some leaders will have received recognition beyond their local villages, drawing followers from far afield after the fashion of Jāvīdhān. It will have been through these networks that the news of Sunbādh's revolt and risings elsewhere in Iran spread to the Jibāl, causing Khurramīs to rise up in revolt there as well. But connected though they were, the rebels never managed truly to join forces.

THE REVOLT

Bābak's revolt is usually said to have started in 201/816f., nine years after the first Khurramī disturbances reported for Azerbaijan.[121] The timing seems to be connected with the fact that in that year the governor of Azerbaijan, Ḥātim b. Harthama, received the news that his father had been killed in disgrace by al-Ma'mūn in Khurāsān. Ḥātim responded by preparing a revolt, apparently inferring that he was next on al-Ma'mūn's list, and wrote to the local princes and aristocrats, encouraging them to

[119] He replaced 'Abdallāh b. Ṭāhir when the latter took over as governor of Khurāsān in 213 or 214 (Tab. iii, 1065, 1102; placed in 215 by Khalīfa, II, 778), and was dismissed and executed in 217 (Tab. iii, 1107f.; Khalīfa, II, 780).

[120] Thus *Chron. ad 1234*, II, 25 = 17.

[121] See Chapter 2, n. 63.

join, but died before anything had come of it.[122] Some sources claim that Ḥātim wrote to Bābak too, but this is implausible, for Bābak can hardly have been known to the authorities before he came out in revolt against them. He does seem to have used Ḥātim's preparation for revolt and/or death as his cue to strike, however. The death of a governor was a good time to rebel because it meant that no action would be taken for quite a while: the news had to travel to Baghdad, a new man had to be chosen, the man chosen had to be informed and allowed time first to get an army together and next to march from wherever he was at the time to his new post; and once he had arrived he also needed time to familiarise himself with the situation on the ground before deciding on a course of action. All this could take the better part of a year. Meanwhile, the province would be looked after by a deputy governor, who was not likely to organise major campaigns while he was waiting for his replacement. Several other Khurramīs also timed their revolts to the death or absence of a governor or caliph.

Bābak stayed in power from 201/816f. to 222/837, when the Afshīn stormed his fortress at al-Badhdh. Of all the revolts in the aftermath of the Hāshimite revolution, his was the longest. He operated in a mountainous territory far away from the capital and had the additional advantage of being on a frontier. His Muslim enemies were practically all to the south, with their centre at Marāgha, the provincial capital. In principle there were Muslim garrisons to the north of him as well, at Bāb al-abwāb, modern Derbend, and at Bardhaʿa in Arrān; but although one governor wintered at Bardhaʿa,[123] no armies seem to have been permanently stationed there, and of Bāb al-abwāb there is no mention at all. At his height Bābak controlled the region from the Mūqān plain in the north to Marand in the south.[124] To the east he destroyed villages and fortresses connecting Azerbaijan with the central lands, to as far south as Zanjān;[125] to the west and north his neighbours were Armenian princes, flanked by the Byzantine empire. This gave him relative freedom to act. But he did not use that freedom to establish new political structures, let alone to attempt conquest outside Azerbaijan.

Bābak's only politically organised body apart from the Khurramī cult society seems to have been his army. It included cavalry, not just

[122] Ibn Qutayba, *Maʿārif*, 389.
[123] Azdī, 357.
[124] For his safety in the Mūqān steppe see Tab. iii, 1174, 1178.
[125] Dīnawarī, 397; Tab. iii, 1171.

foot-soldiers;[126] it was sufficiently organised to have officers known as *iṣbahbadhs*;[127] and part of it was standing – Ṭarkhān needed permission to absent himself from Badhdh during the winter months.[128] Stories circulated about the tricks that Bābak used to keep his men in awe of him.[129] A late Armenian copyist claims that he called his troops 'the Army of the Immortals',[130] a name given by the Achaemenids to their elite troops and said to have been used by the Sasanids as well.[131] This could be taken to suggest Sasanian legitimism. So too could the fact that he assumed the name of Bābak (Pābag), perhaps meant to evoke the father of Ardaṣhir. But though he may have sought inspiration in the little he knew of the Sasanians, there is no sign that he was planning to move against Baghdad so as to bring down the caliphate.[132] His ambitions appear to have remained purely local.

Whether graced with the name of Immortals or not, his troops seem to have operated much like the Khurdanaye. Dionysius describes the latter as religious brigands who would ravage, pillage, and terrorise their neighbours. Bābak's followers also operated by raiding and pillaging. They would waylay caravans, occasionally ambush whole armies too, and immediately withdraw to their inaccessible fortresses and mountain lairs, without any systematic attempt to occupy or hold territory.[133] We never hear of any administrative structures being established, implying that Bābak relied on plunder and booty rather than taxes throughout his twenty-year revolt and that he did not take it upon himself to direct the administration of justice. What he practised was basically guerrilla warfare.

Bābak underused the fact that he was on a frontier in the sense that he did not ally himself with neighbouring enemies of the caliphate. Unlike Sunbādh he does not seem to have solicited the collaboration of the Iranian princes of the Caspian coast. There were rumours to the contrary. When Māzyār, the prince of Ṭabaristān to the east of Bābak, rebelled in 224/839 it was said that he had written to Bābak and promised him help,[134] or even

[126] Azdī, 357.11.
[127] Tab. iii, 1172, 1178.
[128] See n. 102 of this chapter.
[129] Iskāfī, *Luṭf al-tadbīr*, 167.
[130] Outmazian, 'Bābek et les princes de Siwnie', 208, citing a comment inserted in the margin of a manuscript of Vardan (d. 1271).
[131] Cf. Frye, 'Achaemenid Echoes', 247f.
[132] Noted by Rekaya, 'Ḫurram-dīn', 43.
[133] E.g. Tab. iii, 1171, 1174ff. (where they fail), 1178f.; Azdī, 357.
[134] Tab. iii, 1269.

that he had adopted Bābak's religion and joined 'the Red-clothed ones', i.e. the Khurramīs.[135] One source goes so far as to credit Bābak, Māzyār, and the Afshīn with a conspiracy to destroy the Arab state and restore the Sasanian royal family.[136] This may well have been a widespread fear at the time, but it can hardly be true, for Bābak's castle was stormed in 222/837, two years before Māzyār's revolt. What does seem to have happened is that a brother of Bābak's by the name of Isḥāq was captured, where we are not told, about the same time as Māzyār, so that they were crucified together (after execution) in Baghdad in 225/840.[137] This will have lent credence to the fears (probably fanned by the caliph) of an Iranian plot against Islam. Only a conspiracy theorist could believe that the Afshīn, the general who defeated Bābak, was actually in league with him.

Bābak did benefit from his Armenian neighbours, participating now as an ally and now as an enemy in their internal power struggles. But he was better at terrorising them than at cooperating with them, and Armenian sources are as hostile to him as are Muslim ones.[138] Dionysius' Khurdanaye had displayed a similar inability to cooperate with the Armenians: far from allying themselves with the aristocratic Isaac, son of Ashot, they invaded his castle, so that in the end it was by Isaac that their mahdi was killed. It was also an Armenian prince, Sahl b. Sunbāṭ, who betrayed Bābak, using the opportunity to put himself back in favour with the caliph.[139] As regards the more distant Byzantines, Bābak is said to have written to Theophilus to stave off defeat, encouraging him to take action against the 'king of the Arabs' – i.e., al-Muʿtaṣim; this was reputedly why Theophilus attacked Zibaṭra in 222/836f., causing al-Muʿtaṣim to invade Amorium in the following year.[140] But whether this is true or not it came too late. Some sources envisage Bābak and Theophilus as regular allies, but this seems to be mere embellishment.

What Bābak lacked in political skills he made up for by utter ruthlessness. Christians and Muslims alike remembered him as a killer, a

135 Gardīzī, 351.

136 Ibn Isfandiyār, I, 220; cf. also Rekaya, 'Māzyār', 159ff.; Rekaya, 'Provinces sud-caspiennes', 146ff.

137 Baghdādī, *Farq*, 268.-2. Isḥāq had probably joined the revolt of Mankijūr in Azerbaijan (cf. YT, II, 583: *jamaʿa ilayhi aṣḥāb Bābak*). We are not told how he was executed, but Māzyār was flogged to death (Tab. iii, 1303).

138 Rekaya, 'Ḫurram-dīn', 42f.; Outmazian, 'Bābek et les princes de Siwnie'; Movsēs Kałankatuac'i in Laurent, *Arménie*, 377–9.

139 Cf. YB, II, 579; Tab. iii, 1223; Azdī, 425; Minorsky, 'Caucasica IV', 508ff.

140 Tab. iii, 1234f. (placing Zibaṭra in 223); Azdī, 424; Abū 'l-Maʿālī, 62.10; Michael Syr., IV, 509 = III, 52; Treadgold, *Byzantine Revival*, 292ff.

'murderous, ravaging, bloodthirsty beast', as one Armenian put it.[141] He killed 30,000,[142] more than 100,000,[143] 255,500, counting Muslims only,[144] a million,[145] or 500,000 according to low estimates, uncountable numbers according to high ones.[146] Clearly nobody knew. It probably was not for the sheer number of his victims that Bābak was remembered as so bloodthirsty, but rather because he would slaughter anyone when he struck: he and his followers would kill men and women, adults and children, Muslims and *dhimmī*s, Arabs and clients alike.[147] It was with such an indiscriminate massacre that the revolt began, and the sheer randomness of the attacks induced fear and dread. The sources do not routinely ascribe this kind of behaviour to any anti-Islamic rebel, so it is difficult to doubt the veracity of their claims.

One may well wonder why Bābak behaved in so chilling a fashion. The explanation evidently does not lie in religious doctrine, since he was acting in the name of a supposedly pacifist religion and is said, like his predecessor Mazdak, to have had to introduce doctrinal changes to legitimise the shedding of blood.[148] No doubt his ruthlessness is related both to the sheer violence of the society in which he had grown up and to the apocalyptic sense, triggered by Hāshimite revolution, of the tables being turned, allowing former losers to seek vengeance for long years of oppression and humiliation by the high and mighty. But the Hāshimite avengers, who were animated by the same apocalypticism, did not kill women, children, or *dhimmī*s, in so far as we know. They were also directed by men with far greater political skills than Bābak, and the two facts could be related.

The reason why Bābak would kill women and children, burn monasteries full of people, dishonour the womenfolk of his enemies, and terrorise even his allies and men may be that fear was the only effective weapon he had. Though the Armenian princes sometimes had interests in common

141 Movsēs Kałankatuac'i in Laurent, *Arménie*, 379.

142 Muyldermans, *Domination*, 119 (Vardan).

143 Michael Syr., IV, 533 = III, 90.

144 Wāqid in Abū 'l-Ma'ālī, 62; Maqdisī, VI, 117 (repeated in Ibn al-'Ibrī, *Ta'rīkh*, 241); Tab. iii, 1233.

145 Maqdisī, VI, 116f. The figure has reached 1.5 million in Dhahabī, *Ta'rīkh*, yy 221–30, year 222 (p. 14).

146 Mas'ūdī, *Tanbīh*, 353. Abū Muslim killed 2 million, Bābak 1.5 million (Dhahabī, *Ta'rīkh*, ṭbq xxiii, 13).

147 Abū 'l-Ma'ālī and the disconnected words in Ibn al-Nadīm, cited in n. 26; Maqdisī, VI, 116.6, 11; repeated in Ibn al-'Ibrī, *Ta'rīkh*, 241; Movsēs Kałankatuac'i in Laurent, *Arménie*, 377 (women and children).

148 Ibn al-Nadīm, 406.11 = II, 818. For Mazdak see Chapter 13, p. 254.

with his, he had nothing to offer that might secure their permanent cooperation, so he relied on their fear of reprisals to keep them in tow. Fear may also have been the decisive factor in ensuring that the peasantry stayed on his side whenever a caliphal army moved in. His hope will have been that all would eventually be so scared of him that they would either submit or leave. He is said to have attracted highwaymen, brigands, and other troublemakers,[149] and one can well believe it: he occupied the twilight zone between private and public warfare, criminal and political activities, familiar from some guerrilla warriors and terrorists today.

In short, Bābak comes across as no more sophisticated than his counterparts in the Jibāl. They all knew how to kill government agents and ambush armies without being caught, and their religious networks made them better informed and connected than one might have expected of mountaineers. But for the rest they simply struck out indiscriminately on the principle that everyone who was not with them was against them. The very localism that made mountaineers so resistant to absorption into larger political units also made them incapable of organising themselves for effective action against them. They could make a terrible nuisance of themselves from time to time and reduce Muslim control of their mountains to nominal status for extended periods. But they could not secede. Whether they ever considered the possibility that they might inflict enough strategic damage on the Muslim state apparatus to force the caliphs to negotiate a settlement is not recorded. The caliphs were usually willing to grant *amān* to rebellious magnates in the region, and they paid Bābak the compliment of offering it to him too;[150] but that was a personal grant of safety to him and some followers, not a political settlement regulating his status as local ruler and vassal of the caliph.

The main reason why Bābak's revolt lasted so long seems to be that there was constant disarray at the centre. The Arab colonisation of Azerbaijan began in earnest in the reign of al-Manṣūr. Fifty years later caliphal control of the province was disrupted by the Fourth Civil War (195–8/811–13), with further disarray when al-Ma'mūn chose to remain in Khurāsān (until 204/819) and to appoint ʿAlī al-Riḍā as his successor. It was during these years that the magnates, robber-barons, brigands, and

[149] Maqdisī, VI, 116.12f.; Ibn al-ʿIbrī, *Duwal*, 241.

[150] He asked for, and was offered, *amān* shortly before Badhdh fell, but it fell through because he just wanted to buy time. We are also told that after Badhdh had been stormed a letter of *amān* arrived from the caliph and that Bābak angrily refused the offer (YT, II, 578f.; Tab. iii, 1217f., 1220). It is not clear whether these episodes should be read as consecutive or as two versions of the same event.

other strongmen rose to their apogee, and it was also then that Bābak struck. Al-Ma'mūn seems to have done nothing until he returned to Baghdad, but in 204/819 he appointed Yaḥyā b. Mu'ādh, a Khurāsānī of Iranian origin, to direct the war; he fought Bābak without major results.[151] The next appointee, 'Īsā b. Muḥammad b. Abī Khālid, another Khurāsānī of Iranian origin, was ignominiously defeated.[152] Al-Ma'mūn then tried to co-opt one of the robber-barons, Zurayq, but this backfired when Zurayq did nothing and then refused to vacate his post. The governorship of his successor, Ibrāhīm b. al-Layth b. al-Faḍl, yet another Khurāsānī of Iranian origin, seems to have remained purely nominal.[153] The governor and general who succeeded in removing Zurayq (in 212/827f.), Muḥammad b. Ḥumayd al-Ṭūsī, a Khurāsānī of Arab descent, preferred also to remove as many magnates as he could lay hands on. He invited them to Marāgha, and twenty-six of them came; they included descendants of the Yemenis transferred by the Muhallabids,[154] and every one of them was the owner of 'a land (*balad*), a mountain, a region and a district (*rustāq*)' endowed with 'followers, might and leadership'. The governor had all of them clapped in chains and transported to Baghdad. It helped to clear the decks, but Muḥammad b. Ḥumayd proceeded to be caught by Bābak in a narrow pass, where he and most of his men lost their lives.[155] This was in 214/829. Thereafter 'Alī b. Hishām succeeded in defeating Hārūn, the leader of the Khurdanaye in the upper Mesopotamia–Armenia region, probably between 214/829 and 217/832, only to consider joining Bābak when he fell out of favour with al-Ma'mūn himself.[156] Al-Ma'mūn got the better of him, but Bābak took over as the leader of the Khurdanaye, al-Ma'mūn was by then campaigning against the Byzantines, and in 218/833 he died in Anatolia, leaving a disputed succession. The Khurramīs of the Jibāl took

[151] Tab. iii, 1039; YT, II, 563; Azdī, 353.

[152] Tab. iii, 1045, 1233; YT, II, 563f.; cf. Crone, "Abbāsid Abnā'", n. 67 for his origins.

[153] Tab. iii, 1072; Azdī, 366.ult. This man, whose illegible *nisba* is conjecturally given as al-Tujībī in Ṭabarī, was clearly a member of the Bassām family, clients of the Layth, who had been staunch supporters of Naṣr b. Sayyār, but who defected to Abū Muslim (cf. Crone, 'Qays and Yemen', 35, nn. 195–7; Agha, *Revolution*, 344, no. 144). Another member of the Bassām family by the name of Manṣūr was governor of Mosul under al-Ma'mūn or al-Mu'taṣim (Azdī, 417). The *nisba* was probably al-Tarjumānī (Ibn Sa'd, VII/2, 95/VII, 358).

[154] Azdī, 383f. They included a *mawlā* of the Muhallabids, the Banū Ḥibbān (not mentioned elsewhere), and 'Alī b. Murr al-Ṭā'ī (on whom see p. 53).

[155] Tab. iii, 1101; YT, II, 565; Azdī, 386ff.

[156] Tab. 1107ff. (year 217).

the opportunity to rebel, so it was two years before al-Muʿtaṣim could put his mind to Bābak.

Once al-Muʿtaṣim was ready for a systematic assault on Bābak, however, it only took him two years to crush the revolt.[157] In 220/835 he appointed his best general, the Afshīn, to the war against Bābak, at the same time sending Muḥammad b. Yūsuf al-Thaghrī to Ardabīl with instructions to secure safe passage for provisions to Ardabīl by rebuilding the fortresses between Zanjān and Ardabīl and setting up garrisons along the road.[158] The Afshīn started his part of the operations by clearing the Jibāl of *ṣaʿālīk* and other local lords (*wujūh*),[159] and he proceeded to repair fortresses and establish garrisons between Ardabīl and Barzand, surrounding them with protective trenches to ensure that caravans would travel under military escort on that road.[160] Ensconced at Barzand, he engaged in systematic gathering of intelligence. By Nawrūz (March) 221/836 he was encamped a mere six miles from al-Badhdh.[161] Though he scored several victories over Bābak, he also suffered several reverses, and he would only move his camp forward by four miles a day, still insisting on digging trenches or scattering iron spikes around it to avoid surprise attacks, and putting much effort into his spy system. His slow pace provoked impatience among his troops and accusations of connivance with Bābak, but he avoided ambushes and successfully lured Bābak into the open, storming al-Badhdh in 222/837.[162] If the caliphs had taken systematic action against Bābak at an earlier stage he would presumably soon have been defeated, however difficult the terrain in which he operated. The caliphs' trouble was that too many things were going on, both at the centre and in the provinces, and they could not deal properly with all of them at the same time.

When al-Badhdh fell Bābak and a small band of relatives and followers fled westwards. Invited to seek shelter with Sahl b. Sunbāṭ, Bābak insisted that his brother be put up by another Armenian noble, but his precautions were in vain: both were handed over to the caliphal troops and sent on to the caliph. Bābak was gruesomely executed in Samarra in 223/838, his brother in Baghdad in the same year.[163] Al-Muʿtaṣim took one of Bābak's daughters as his concubine and treated his sons, or some of

157 See the chronological survey in Masʿūdī, *Tanbīh*, 352f.
158 Tab. iii, 1170f.
159 YT, II, 578.
160 Tab. iii, 1172f.; Dīnawarī, 398.
161 Tab. iii, 1187.
162 Tab. iii, 1197f., 1209f.
163 Tab. iii, 1221–31.

them, much as he had those of Ibn al-Baʿīth: he enrolled them in his army.[164]

BĀBAK'S OBJECTIVES

According to Wāqid it was predicted that Bābak would 'possess the earth, slay the tyrants, restore Mazdakism, make the humble among you mighty and the lowly high'.[165] One suspects that Mazdakism here simply means Khurramism, for we never see Bābak do or say anything suggestive of Mazdakite convictions. He and his followers are accused of large-scale killing, but not of seizing women and land to hold in common or distribute among themselves. On the contrary, Bābak is said to have accumulated large numbers of women for himself.[166] In any case, the Arab settlers were not aristocrats lording it over a rural proletariat eager for redistribution of land, but rather rivals of a local elite which they were demoting to subordinate status.

If we trust the anonymous account of Bābak's last days used by al-Ṭabarī and al-Masʿūdī, what Bābak craved for himself was status as a local king on the model of the local princes. According to that account Bābak lived like an Iranian aristocrat, hunting with falcons and accumulating women when he was not conducting war: it was during a hunting trip on Sahl b. Sunbāṭ's estates that he was caught.[167] 'One day as king is better than forty years as an abject slave,' he is reported as telling one of his sons, angrily disowning him for having brought him an offer of *amān*; what mattered was not whether he lived or not, he said, but that 'wherever I am or wherever I am spoken of, it will be as king'.[168] When his brother ʿAbdallāh faced execution in Baghdad and thought that he was going to be killed by the king of Ṭabaristān, he praised God that he would be killed by a nobleman (*rajul min al-dahāqīn*), asked for a last meal of *falūdhaj*, a sweet dish much liked by the Persian emperors, and wine, and told the king of Ṭabaristān that 'tomorrow morning you will know that I am a

[164] Ibn Ḥazm, *Jamhara*, 25.4f., spotted by Rekaya, 'Ḫurram-dīn', 46, along with the Ibn Bābak who appears in the caliphal troops in 251 (Tab. iii, 1577).

[165] Ibn al-Nadīm, 407 = II, 821.

[166] Tab. iii, 1223, cf. 1227.

[167] Tab. iii, 1125f. We are told what he wore when he was caught with his hawks (also in Azdī, 387), but the significance of the details escapes me.

[168] Tab. iii, 1221.

nobleman (*dihqān*), God willing'. The next morning he endured having his hands and feet cut off without uttering a sound.[169]

All this has been taken to mean that Bābak and his brothers were really local lords and aristocrats,[170] and that they rebelled because the caliphs were doing away with their traditional independence.[171] But this is most unlikely. For one thing, the local lords of the region were Arab and Arabised immigrants such as the Rawwādids, Ibn al-Baʿīth, and their clients,[172] who had arrived as the vanguard of the caliphal regime. They were hacking their way through a difficult land, replacing native institutions with Islamic ones wherever they settled, and thereby opening up the region to the central government; and they had established themselves so recently that one can hardly speak of their autonomy as traditional. It is certainly true that their individual interests often clashed with those of the caliphs, but as a class they benefited from caliphal backing, and the only one of them known to have supported Bābak for a while is Muḥammad b. al-Baʿīth. It was not the caliphs' attempts to keep these local lords under control that had triggered the revolt, but rather the relentless pressure of the lords in question on the indigenous inhabitants.[173]

For another thing, the dramatic impact of the account of Bābak's end turns on the assumption that Bābak and his brother were nobodies: their make-believe was over, their illusions had been exposed; in fact, Bābak's brother was killed by the executioner Nudnud, not by a nobleman; and Bābak himself was betrayed by a nobleman, not saved by him. 'You are just a herder of cows and sheep. What have you got to do with the management of kingship, political decisions, or armies?', as Sahl b. Sunbāṭ exclaims to Bābak after betraying him, finally relieved of the irksome obligation to kiss his hand and indulge the whim of a mere upstart.[174] The author was undoubtedly right about Bābak's lowly origins, for aristocrats do not claim to be the spirit of the prophets when they rebel, nor do they raise their troops by means of a religious organisation: they are entitled to obedience by virtue of their status, and they have their own

169 Tab. iii, 1231; cf. also MM, VII, 125f. (IV, §2808).

170 Sadighi, *Mouvements*, 240f./287f.; Widengren, 'Bābakīyah and the Mithraic Mysteries', 676, 677n. (and cf. app. 2); Yūsofī, 'Bābak', 301; Amabe, *Emergence*, 120f.

171 Kennedy, *Early Abbasid Caliphate*, 16; Amabe, *Emergence*, 107f., 121.

172 Similarly Kennedy, *Early Abbasid Caliphate*, 170f.; Amabe, *Emergence*, 110f., though it hardly fits their thesis.

173 Similarly Khalʿatbarī and Mihrwarz, *Junbish-i Bābak*, 57.

174 MM, IV, §2808 (VII, 126f.), where Sahl has ostentatiously addressed Bābak as king, eventually with open sarcasm. The account of Bābak's end goes so well with that of the beginning that one suspects the author is Wāqid again.

chains of command. But mere villagers have no organisation above village level beyond that provided by religion, and why should anyone listen to an illiterate soldier or a former cowherd *unless* he has special gifts, imparted to him by God through dreams, communication with spirits, or, as in Bābak's case, by Jāvīdhān's spirit dwelling in him? It is the special access to the divine that singles out people of common origin as authoritative. What the account of Bābak's last days suggests is that the former cowherd and his brother had embraced the world-view of the Iranian nobility: one lived for power and heroic deeds, ostentatious consumption of wine, women and song, and immortality in the renown one left behind. The Arab warlords that Bābak was trying to oust and the Armenian princes who were their Iranian counterparts represented the pinnacle of the social world in which he had grown up. One takes it that he wanted to be one of them, just bigger and better.

Whatever Bābak may have hoped to achieve for himself, there cannot be much doubt that the politically relevant doctrine in his revolt was the prediction of a drastic change to be inaugurated by himself in his role of avenger: the mighty would be laid low and the humble exalted. Differently put, the foreigners would be expelled: this was what galvanised his followers. It has caused many modern readers to envisage Bābak as an Iranian nationalist trying to free the Iranians from Arab rule, a view which predominates in the older literature, including that written in Iran before the revolution.[175] (Bābak has also been dragooned into service by communists on the basis of his supposed Mazdakism and by Azeri – i.e., Turkish – nationalists on the basis of his being in Azerbaijan. But it is only as an Iranian nationalist that he has made it into the academic literature.) I shall come back to all this in Chapter 8, but one point needs to be established straightaway, namely that Bābak's hostility was not directed against the Arabs as an ethnic group, but rather as a political one.

'Arab' was a word with many meanings. One meaning certainly had to do with descent: a genuine Arab (*aṣīl*, *min anfusihim*) was a person who descended from an Arab tribesman on his or her father's side. But the word was rarely used to indicate descent alone. To the Khurāsānī revolutionaries an Arab was a bigoted member of the Umayyad establishment who ascribed religious and political significance to his descent; they did not

[175] See for example Widengren, 'Bābakīyah and the Mithraic Mysteries', 677; Nafīsī, *Bābak Khurramdīn*, 9–12; Bahrāmī, *Tārīkh-i Īrān*, 215ff. (a textbook for undergraduates); cf. also Bahrāmiyān, 'Bābak-i Khurramdīn', 26 (more cautiously). Khalʿatbarī and Mihrwaz argue against it (*Junbish-i Bābak*, 51f., 59).

include themselves in the label, whatever their descent.[176] More commonly, an Arab was a member of the political and religious community founded by the Arabs, again regardless of descent: people became Arabs when they converted.[177] This usage is reflected in the modern literature, in which historians will often speak of the governors and troops sent by the caliphs as Arabs even when the governors in question were Iranians by origin:[178] an Arab was someone who professed Islam, spoke Arabic (well or badly), and saw himself as a member of the polity ruled by the caliph. It was Arabs in this sense that Bābak was opposing. As it happened, most of the colonists in Azerbaijan were also Arabs in the ethnic sense (patrilineally speaking), so initially one cannot tell the difference; but once the caliph took action against Bābak a large number of the 'Arabs' sent against him were 'Arabs' of the type who were Iranians by descent. This goes for Yaḥyā b. Mu'ādh,[179] 'Īsā b. Muḥammad b. Abī Khālid,[180] Ibrāhīm b. al-Layth b. al-Faḍl,[181] al-Ḥasan b. 'Alī al-Ma'mūnī,[182] Ḥātim b. Harthama,[183] Muḥammad b. Yūsuf al-Thaghrī,[184] and probably also Zurayq, the *mawlā* robber-baron turned governor, who had a daughter called Bābūnaj.[185] Many of these men had been Muslims for several generations and did at least speak Arabic. By contrast, al-Ma'mūnī and al-Thaghrī were fresh recruits of al-Ma'mūn's, and the former had come to Baghdad with Ṭāhir in an army contemptuously described as consisting of mere *'ajam* in the sense of raw Iranians/mere barbarians.[186] The man who actually defeated Bābak, moreover, was Ḥaydar b. Kā'ūs, the Afshīn, a

[176] See Crone, 'Wooden Weapons', 183ff.
[177] E.g. Tab. iii, 1508.
[178] See for example Ḥabībī, *Afghānistān*, I, 318, identifying as Arab an army of Khurāsānīs including Turārkhudā; *EIr.*, s.v. 'Azerbaijan, iv' (Bosworth), where Ḥātim b. Ḥarthama b. A'yan, whose grandfather was a *mawlā* from Khurāsān, is identified as the local 'Arab governor'. The usage is deliberately adopted by Arazi and El'ad, 'l'Épître', I, 70, who declare the Ṭāhirids Arabs, though foreign born.
[179] His father came from Khuttal or Rayy (YB, 253), and they were clients of Banū Dhuhl (YT, II, 563). On the family see Crone, *Slaves*, 183f.; further information on the father in Arazi and El'ad, 'l'Épître', I, 59n.
[180] See Crone, '"Abbāsid Abnā"', n. 67.
[181] See n. 153 of this chapter.
[182] He was from Bādghīs, Persian speaking, and is first encountered in Ṭāhir's troops (Tab. iii, 852f., 918, 985).
[183] His father was a *mawlā* of Banū Ḍabba (Azdī, 252.2f.) from Khurāsān (Tab. iii, 371), who was to be honoured with the title *mawlā amīr al-mu'minīn* (Tab. iii, 716, 927).
[184] He was a Marwazī and a *mawlā* of Ṭayyi', who is first mentioned as a general of al-Ma'mūn's (Tab. iii, 1093, 1407).
[185] See p. 58 of this book.
[186] Crone, '"Abbāsid Abnā"', 14.

Transoxanian prince who was a first-generation Muslim and whose officers included the Bukhārkhudā[187] and others bearing names such as Būzbāra and Abū Saʿīd Dīvdād.[188]

In short, Bābak's main enemies once the conflict escalated were Iranians who had decided to throw in their fortunes with Islam, seeing their future as lying in the new society that had formed in the lands once ruled by the *shāhānshāh*. In 842, five years after Bābak's defeat, 15,000 Iranians who had opted for the new order are reported to have perished during the campaigns against a rebel called Mūsā, chief of the Khurdanaye who had once been Bābak's allies in upper Mesopotamia; the Iranians formed part of the troops who were wintering in the mountains while the Khurdanaye were sitting comfortably in their villages, watching them freeze to death.[189] What we see in Bābak's revolt, in short, is first local Azeris fighting Arab colonists and thereafter what one might have called an Iranian civil war if the participants had had a stronger sense of a shared Iranian identity: it pitched inhabitants of the Iranian culture region who clung to the world in which they had grown up against others from the same region who had opted for the new regime.

[187] Tab. iii, 1197, 1203, 1205, 1207, 1215. Dīnawarī, 398, gives his personal name as Muḥammad b. Khālid.

[188] Tab. iii, 1226, 1228, and *passim*.

[189] Michael Syr., IV, 542f. = III, 109.

B. Eastern Iran

4

Khurāsān

Muḥammira, Khidāshiyya, Rāwandiyya, Ḥārithiyya

The route from Rayy to Khurāsān went via the Elburz mountains to Jurjān and passed from there via Nīshāpūr to Marw. In 162/778f., some twenty-five years after the suppression of Sunbādh's revolt at Rayy, the so-called 'Red-clothed ones' (Muḥammira, Surkhjāmagān) rebelled in Jurjān, led by one 'Abd al-Qahhār/Qāhir.[1] Like the 'White-clothed ones' (Mubayyiḍa, Sapīdjāmagān) the wearers of red were sectarians of the type that the medieval sources label Khurramiyya/Khurramdīniyya. We do not know on what basis the Khurramīs were divided into these groups, for no mention is made of different doctrines or practices, and we do not hear of any rivalry or hostility between the two branches either. All we can say for certain is that the Red-clothed ones are reported for Jurjān, the Jibāl, and Azerbaijan,[2] the White-clothed ones for Transoxania.[3]

Jurjān, on the south-eastern side of the Caspian coast, had been conquered by the Arabs under Yazīd b. al-Muhallab al-Azdī in 98/716f. We know next to nothing about its history thereafter beyond the fact that it had been heavily involved in the Hāshimite revolution, to which it supplied numerous recruits.[4] It was presumably former members of the revolutionary movement who rose in revolt in 162/778f., for Niẓām al-Mulk says that they were led by a son of Abū Muslim called

[1] Tab. iii, 493 ('Abd al-Qahhār), followed by IA, VI, 58; YT, II, 479 ('Abd al-Qāhir); Khalīfa, 686 (without details); Daniel, *Khurasan*, 147, with further references.

[2] E.g. Ibn al-Nadīm, 405f. = II, 817; Tab. iii, 1235; Minorsky, *Abū-Dulaf*, §15 (also in Yāqūt, I, 529).

[3] See Chapter 6.

[4] Notably Abū 'Awn al-Jurjānī (Crone, *Slaves*, 174); also Khufāf al-Jurjānī (Tab. iii, 93), Marwān al-Jurjānī, Abū 'l-Mutawakkil al-Jurjānī (Tab. iii, 55); Yazīd b. Nuhayd and his brother Bishr (*AA*. 201f., cf. 199.2); Miḥṣan b. Hānī' and his brother Yazīd b. Hānī' *min ahl Jurjān* (Kindī, *Governors*, 98.10, 102.11). cf. also *AA*, 198.8, 215.1, 293f.

Abū 'l-Gharā. In Darke's second edition of the *Siyāsatnāma* he is a son of Abū 'l-Maʿarā, a descendant/grandson (*nawāsa*) of Abū Muslim, which does not make chronological sense unless he was a small child,[5] and Abū 'l-Gharā/Maʿarā is presumably a garbled version of the ʿAbd al-Qahhār who leads the revolt in other sources and whose name also appears as ʿAbd al-Wahhāb.[6] We are not given any explanation of why the Jurjānīs rebelled in the name of Abū Muslim some twenty-five years after his death, and the little we are told about the revolt itself reflects confusion with that of Sunbādh. According to Niẓām al-Mulk the rebels declared Abū Muslim alive and wanted to restore power to him, which is close to the message that he imputes to Sunbādh; he also claims that the rebels marched to Rayy, to be stopped by ʿUmar b. al-ʿAlāʾ, the famous former butcher who had fought against Sunbādh and who had risen to become governor of Ṭabaristān.[7] No other source knows of a march to Rayy, though it was indeed ʿUmar b. al-ʿAlāʾ who suppressed the revolt: he attacked them from Ṭabaristān (suggesting that they were close to the border).[8] Rayy was where Sunbādh had rebelled. It is probably thanks to the same confusion of the two revolts that the *Tārīkhnāma* has Sunbādh flee to Jurjān.[9] All we can say about the uprising in Jurjān is that it seems to have lasted for at least two years. Muhalhil b. Ṣafwān, the client of the ʿAbbāsid family who governed Jurjān in 162/778f., must have been unable to cope with it, for he was dismissed in 163/779f.,[10] when the rebellion was still in progress; it was in that year that ʿUmar b. al-ʿAlāʾ became governor of Ṭabaristān,[11] and so in or after 163 that he defeated them.

The Muḥammira rebelled again in Jurjān in 180/796f., stirred up by a heretic (*zindīq*) called ʿAmr b. Muḥammad al-ʿAmrakī.[12] *Zandaqa* was a loose term for dissent of an Iranian, dualist kind, often Manichaean, but here presumably meaning Khurramī, since the Manichaeans are never called wearers of red. Though the *zindīq* was captured the revolt continued, or alternatively the Muḥammira rebelled again, for a revolt is

[5] *SN*, ch. 47:2 (312 = 238).
[6] Maqdisī, VI, 98.
[7] Cf. Chapter 2, p. 36.
[8] Thus Tab. iii, 493.
[9] *TN*, IV, 1093.
[10] Tab. iii, 494, 501. For his *walāʾ* see BF, 296.7; Tab. iii, 120, cf. also iii, 43f.
[11] Tab. iii, 500; cf. Ibn Isfandiyār, I, 182 (without the year).
[12] Tab. iii, 645.

also reported in 181/797f.[13] But this time we are not given any details at all, and thereafter the Muḥammira of Jurjān disappear from view.

Much later we are told by al-Baghdādī that there were Muḥammira in the mountains of Ṭabaristān adjoining the countryside of Jurjān, which is precisely where we would expect them to have been. He identifies them as descendants of the followers of the rebel Ṭabarī king Māzyār (d. 225/840): those followers were Muḥammira, he says, and 'today' they are rural labourers (*akara*) in those mountains and Muslims only on the surface.[14] The existence of such communities is eminently plausible, but their link with the history of Māzyār is doubtful. This king did set the rural labourers of the region against the landowners he was squeezing for wealth and otherwise brutalising; he allowed the labourers to seize the estates and womenfolk of their former masters, telling them to go and kill the latter in the jail in which he had gathered them.[15] But Māzyār did not do so in the name of Muḥammirī tenets. The sources do not present him as trying to legitimise his measures in terms of justice, equality, the shared nature of property, or any ideological consideration at all. He was simply engaging in the practice of transferring the assets of one set of people to another in the hope of securing their support.[16] The assets included women because women were seen as part of a man's disposable property, to be shared along with other booty when he was defeated: Māzyār reserved the pretty girls for himself.[17] In short, the unusual nature of his policies seems to lie entirely in the lowly nature of the men to whom he was transferring the assets (and who did not actually have the courage to execute his directives), not in any religious commitment. The lowly recipients could have been Muḥammira, but there is not actually any evidence that they were.

Another fifth/eleventh-century author, Kay Kā'ūs, tells us of a village he had visited in Jurjān that the women there would fetch water from a well at some distance from the village and that they would carefully watch their steps on the way to avoid treading on the worms that might have crawled on to the road from the fields: if they killed a worm the water would turn fetid and would have to be replaced.[18] Kay Kā'ūs does not tell us precisely where this village was, or whether its inhabitants were Manichaeans or

[13] Tab. iii, 646.
[14] Baghdādī, *Farq*, 251f.
[15] Tab. iii, 1269, 1278f.; cf. 1275, on the involvement of Ṭarmīs, modern Tammīsha, on the border with Jurjān; *EI*[2], s.v. 'Ḳārinids' (Rekaya) and the literature cited there.
[16] Cf. Rekaya, 'Māzyār', 171f.; Rekaya, 'Provinces sud-caspiennes', 144ff.
[17] Tab. iii, 1278.17.
[18] Kay Kā'ūs, *Qābūsnāma*, 28f. = 36.

Khurramīs: he had no interest in the reason for their behaviour, which he reports only because it was something implausible which happened to be true. Given the earlier presence of Muḥammira in Jurjān, however, the behavioural pattern is likely to be Khurramī.

MARW AND THE KHIDĀSHIYYA

Marw was the epicentre of the seismic waves that were travelling through the Iranian countryside. This was where the revolution had been planned and begun, and as one would expect there were devotees of Abū Muslim there, including one who was to raise a major revolt in Sogdia.[19] It was a centre of ʿAbbāsid power, however, and nobody rebelled in Marw itself in response to his death, or for that matter anywhere else in Khurāsān proper apart from Jurjān. But several Khurramī groups had been formed in Khurāsān before the revolution, and to these we may now turn. One of them was the Khidāshiyya.

Khidāsh is the missionary in connection with whom we first hear about Khurramism. He came to Khurāsān in, perhaps, 109/727f. to lead the mission there,[20] having formerly worked as a potter in Ḥīra and/or a schoolteacher (*muʿallim*) in Kufa, and he is said originally to have been a Christian called ʿAmmār b. Yazdād or the like.[21] As a missionary he became notorious for having permitted people to sleep with one another's wives (*rakhkhaṣa li-baʿḍihim fī nisāʾ baʿḍ*): it was in that sense that he preached Khurramism.[22] Ibn al-Athīr claims that he also denied the need to pray, fast, and go on pilgrimage, interpreting the precepts allegorically, but Pseudo-Nāshiʾ only mentions antinomianism in connection with the Khidāshiyya, not Khidāsh himself, so one suspects that Ibn al-Athīr is padding al-Ṭabarī's account with information gleaned from later heresiographers.[23] In any case, Khidāsh was denounced by his colleagues and executed in 118/736 at the order of the governor of Khurāsān, Asad b. ʿAbdallāh, together with a certain Ḥazawwar, a client who had presumably worked with him. Most of the Hāshimite *shīʿa* reverted to the proper ways, we are told. Some, however, reacted to Khidāsh's death much as

[19] See Chapter 2, p. 43; al-Muqannaʿ, Chapter 6.

[20] Tab. ii, 1503; cf. ii, 1588, where he is somewhat implausibly sent to Khurāsān in the same year in which he is executed; see further Agha, *Revolution*, 16f.

[21] BA, III, 116f.; Abū Tammām, 104 = 98; Agha, *Revolution*, 16.

[22] Tab. ii, 1588; cf. BA, III, 117: he changed the imam's *sunna*, altered the *sīra* and *ḥakama bi-aḥkām munkara makrūha*.

[23] IA, V, 196, year 118; Ps.-Nāshiʾ, §48.

later Khurāsānīs were to react to Abū Muslim's: they broke with the Hāshimiyya, declared its members to be infidels, elevated the executed man to the status of true imam, and denied that he had died, claiming that he had been raised to heaven after the fashion of Christ, who had only seemed to die when the Jews crucified him (cf. Q 4:157). This, at least, is what they were taken to believe in the mid-third/ninth century.[24]

Sharon has suggested that actually Khidāsh was denounced for preaching ʿAlid Shīʿism, but there is nothing to suggest that Khidāsh was in favour of the ʿAlids, and in any case ʿAlid sympathies could not account for the charge that he allowed people to share wives.[25] He must have done something to accommodate Khurramism. What is more, he must have done so with the backing of other members of the Hāshimite organisation at the time. Of one of these, Mālik b. Haytham al-Khuzāʿī, we are told that he was said to be a Khurramī who believed in *ibāḥat al-nisāʾ*, for all that this missionary and *naqīb* went on to serve as a pillar of the ʿAbbāsid regime and founded a distinguished family of Abnāʾ in Baghdad.[26] Of al-Ḥarīsh b. Sulaym or Sulaymān, a local potentate (*ʿaẓīm*) in Nasā who worked as a missionary in his native region, we are similarly told that he 'followed this doctrine', and others unspecified are said to have done the same; yet Ḥarīsh was a loyal member of the Hāshimiyya when the revolution broke out.[27] The son of the *naqīb* Sulaymān b. Kathīr, the leader of the Khurāsānī organisation until the arrival of Abū Muslim, is also said to have been a Khidāshite.[28] None of these people can have been converts to the doctrine that women ought to be held in common. What is more, al-Ṭabarī does not formulaically say that Khidāsh *abāḥa 'l-nisāʾ*, 'declared women to be lawful (for anyone to sleep with)', but rather uses the juristic expression *rakhkhaṣa*, to permit in the sense of granting a dispensation (*rukhṣa*) from the normal rules. This suggests that Khidāsh had been dealing with the question of what stance to take on native marital practices that ran counter to Islamic law.

Greater Khurāsān included regions known to have practised fraternal polyandry, a system in which brothers share a single wife. More will be said about this in a later chapter. Here it will suffice to note that from the earliest times until the nineteenth century outsiders have reported on such

[24] Ps.-Nāshiʾ, §§49, 51f.

[25] Cf. Agha, *Revolution*, 18f., against Sharon, *Black Banners*, 165ff.; Sharon, 'Khidāsh'; cf. further Appendix 1.

[26] IA, V, 196, year 118; Dhahabī, *Taʾrīkh*, ṭbq xvii, 413; Crone, *Slaves*, 181f., for the family.

[27] IA, V, 196; *AA*, 218.13; Dīnawarī, 341, 359.

[28] BA, III, 168.7.

marriages in scandalised tones, deeming the union of a woman with several men (as opposed to a man with several women) to be rank promiscuity. This, of course, will also have been the Muslim reaction, as we know it to have been in Tibet in later times: abstemious wife-sharing is always reported as if it were a merry free-for-all. But there is nothing particularly scandalous about the system, and men born and bred in Khurāsān will have got used to it. They will not have approved of it, of course, but high principle is one thing, practicality quite another. The Hāshimiyya were in search of converts, they were active in the polyandrous regions, and if the converts there had to renounce the marital system on which the social and economic life of their communities rested, converts were not going to be made. Converts could not simply get up and go when they converted, for the Hāshimiyya were not in charge anywhere. Those who joined the movement had to stay where they were until the revolution broke out, continuing in their old occupations, usually meaning agriculture; and a man who refused to share a wife with his brothers would not have access to the shared land. If he persuaded his brothers to let him live and work with them without being a co-husband he could not sire children; and if he sired them with a wife outside the household they would not be heirs to the family property. The question of what to do with polyandrous practices must indeed have been pressing. It makes sense that it should have come up for debate in Marw, where Khidāsh and other missionaries would seem to have been in favour of allowing them to contract such marriages, or at least to stay in them, for the time being.[29]

According to Jaʿfar b. Ḥarb, Khidāsh was executed in Kābul:[30] if so, he had been serving in a well-known polyandrous region, and Hāshimite missionaries were certainly active there.[31] But according to al-Ṭabarī, Khidāsh was executed in Āmul (on the Oxus, not the capital of Ṭabaristān) and the circumstantial details show this to be right.[32] We know nothing about marriage patterns in the Āmul region, or for that matter Nasā, where the local *ʿaẓīm* endorsed Khidāsh's position; but the issue will have come up for decision by the central organisation whether it was pressing in these particular regions or not. One of Khidāsh's

[29] For details and references see Chapter 17.

[30] Ps.-Nāshiʾ, §51.

[31] The *kābulshāh* and his troops were among the Iranians settled in the Ḥarbiyya quarter in Baghdad (YB, 248).

[32] Tab. ii, 1589. It fits the movements reported for Asad and the name of the sub-governor in charge of the execution (Yaḥyā b. Nuʿaym al-Shaybānī, appointed to Āmul in 116, Tab. ii, 1583).

supporters, Sulaymān b. Kathīr's son Muḥammad, is said later to have opposed his father's transfer of the command to Abū Muslim. Many were opposed to Abū Muslim, an unknown outsider who came to make the water flow in a canal dug by others, as some members of the movement put it. But Muḥammad b. Sulaymān's opposition is linked to his being a Khidāshite.[33] This suggests that the central organisation had continued to be divided over the question and that Muḥammad was fearful of interference by an outsider bound to judge on the basis of principle rather than experience. There can in any case be little doubt that Khidāsh was sacrificed for making concessions to local beliefs and practices. Since the Hāshimiyya did not have the authority to execute people they had to get the Umayyad governor to do it, so they denounced their former colleague as a slanderer of Abū Bakr and ʿUmar (and thus someone who held the Umayyads to be illegitimate). All or most of them were Rāfiḍīs guilty of the same crime, but this will not have been clear to the governor, who ordered Khidāsh to be blinded and his tongue cut out for the terrible things he had said about Abū Bakr and ʿUmar before having him killed.[34]

The people who broke away from the Hāshimiyya when Khidāsh was killed are likely to have included the very converts to whom he had made concessions; they were certainly Khurramīs. They were also numerous according to Jaʿfar b. Ḥarb, who identifies all the Khurramīs of Khurāsān as Khidāshiyya, distinguishing them from the Muslimiyya of the Jibāl.[35] This is clearly an oversimplification, but if there were many Khidāshiyya in Khurāsān, there will also have been many different beliefs. Unfortunately, Jaʿfar b. Ḥarb only gives us a general overview. According to him the Khidāshiyya held the imamate to have passed to the ʿAbbāsid Muḥammad b. ʿAlī, identifying him as the man who had sent Khidāsh; but since this ʿAbbāsid was responsible for Khidāsh's death in their view, the imamate had passed from him to Khidāsh, so that in practice there had never been an ʿAbbāsid imam and never would be. They found proof of Muḥammad b. ʿAlī's perfidy in the Qurʾān itself (7:175).[36] They held Khidāsh to be the imam and denied his death, claiming that he had been raised to heaven, and taking the Qurʾānic words about Jesus' seeming crucifixion to apply to him (4:157). Accordingly, they stopped with the

33 BA, III, 168.7: *kāna khidāshīyan fa-kariha taslīm abīhi al-amr ilā Abī Muslim.*

34 Tab. ii, 1589.

35 Ps.-Nāshiʾ, §52.

36 Ps.-Nāshiʾ, §§49, 52. (In §49 he oddly writes here as if both the Muslimiyya and the Khidāshiyya believed the ʿAbbāsids to have inherited the imamate from al-ʿAbbās rather than received it by bequest from Abū Hāshim).

imamate of Khidāsh (*waqafa ʿalā imāmatihi*), though Jaʿfar b. Ḥarb seems to imply that they still had imams in his time; perhaps they called them something different.[37] Absent or present, the imam was of central importance to them: whoever knew the imam no longer had to live by (the literal meaning of) the law, they said; fasting meant keeping the imam's secret; prayer meant cultivating one's relationship with him (*ṣilat al-imām*); pilgrimage meant setting out for him (in one's mind?); and holy war (*jihād*) was killing opponents by any means available, giving a fifth to the imam; they also interpreted Q 5:93 allegorically, suggesting that they did not observe Islamic dietary law.[38] It was apparently on the basis of beliefs of this kind that the Khurramīs in Khurāsān came to be known as Bāṭiniyya, adherents of the inner meaning of things. Al-Maqdisī informs us that Khidāsh was the first to institute Bāṭinism on earth, and al-Masʿūdī tells us that the Khurramīs were known as Bāṭinīs in Khurāsān and elsewhere.[39] In addition, the Khidāshiyya are reported to have believed in *qalb*, manifestation of the deity in different forms, and reincarnation.[40] I shall come back to all these points in Part II. Jaʿfar b. Ḥarb says nothing about their sharing women.

THE RĀWANDIYYA

The Khidāshiyya and Muslimiyya of second/eighth-century Khurāsān were converts to Islam who walked out of Muslim society again, and some of the Rāwandiyya were of the same type; but most of them stayed in Muslim society as extreme devotees of the ʿAbbāsids. Of the ʿAbbāsid loyalists we are told that they were Khurāsānīs and associates (*aṣḥāb*) of Abū Muslim's,[41] meaning that they had served under him in the revolution. They owed their name to ʿAbdallāh al-Rāwandī, a Hāshimite missionary who had perhaps recruited them.[42] He in his turn may have owed his *nisba* to the village of Rāwand near Nīshāpūr, but more probably he came from Balkh.[43] We first hear about the Rāwandiyya before the

37 Ps.-Nāshi', §§51f.
38 Ps.-Nāshi', §49; Abū Tammām, 104 = 98; IA, V, 196 (year 118).
39 Maqdisī, VI, 60f.; MM, IV, §2398 (VI, 188).
40 Ps.-Nāshi', §49; IA, V, 196; cf. Abū Tammām, 75, 104 = 74, 98, on the doctrines they shared with the Minhāliyya.
41 BA, III, 235; Tab. iii, 129.
42 *AA*, 222.ult. An alternative tradition gives his name as al-Qāsim b. Rāwand (Khwārizmī, 30; Abū Tammām, 104 = 98).
43 Balādhurī identifies ʿAbdallāh's son as al-Balkhī (BF, 295.ult.).

outbreak of the revolution when the governor Asad b. ʿAbdallāh (117–20/735–8) executed one of them, an 'extremist' by the name of Ablaq, meaning leper. (The tradition often equips heretics with physical deformities.) This Ablaq said that the spirit that had been in Jesus had passed into the imams, of whom the first was ʿAlī and the last Ibrāhīm b. Muḥammad, that is the ʿAbbāsid Ibrāhīm al-Imām; or rather, he was the latest, for the imams would follow one another without interruption. In addition, Ablaq and his followers were accused of wife-sharing.[44] Ablaq must in fact have been a contemporary of Ibrāhīm al-Imām, but it seems unlikely that the informant (al-Madāʾinī from his father) would have remembered that if Ablaq's followers had continued the line of imams in the ʿAbbāsids thereafter. More probably he knew Ablaq's imam to be Ibrāhīm al-Imām because Ablaq's Rāwandiyya broke away from the Hāshimiyya when Ablaq was killed (or when Ibrāhīm died): Ibrāhīm was the last ʿAbbāsid they recognized, thereafter the imamate continued in others. Two years after the accession of the ʿAbbāsids, in 135/752f., we meet a group of such Rāwandiyya who had broken away from the Hāshimiyya at Tirmidh, where they killed an officer sent to take precautions against a rebel against Abū Muslim.[45] They were led by a man called Abū Isḥāq and hailed from Ṭālaqān, probably the Ṭālaqān due east of Balkh.

The rest of the Rāwandiyya participated in the revolution and moved west with the Hāshimite troops, presumably led by ʿAbdallāh al-Rāwandī, if he was still alive, or by his son Ḥarb, who rose to prominence as a commander in ʿAbbāsid service. This Ḥarb was a noted devotee of the ʿAbbāsid family and the eponymous ancestor of the Ḥarbiyya quarter, famed for its extremist sentiments.[46] Four to ten years after the proclamation of the first ʿAbbāsid caliph, in 136 or 137, 139 or 140, 141 or 142, the Rāwandiyya shot to notoriety in Iraq and Syria. In that year, whichever year it was, they declared the caliph al-Manṣūr to be the one who nourished them, fed them, and gave them food and drink: he was their Lord, they said; if he wanted them to pray with their backs to the *qibla*, they would; and if he wanted to make the mountains move, they would do so too.[47] They also held the spirit of Adam to reside in one of the caliph's officers, ʿUthmān b. Nahīk, and declared another, al-Haytham b.

[44] Tab. iii, 418; discussed in chapter 13, p. 265.

[45] Tab. iii, 82.

[46] BF, 295.ult.; Tab. iii, 328; Crone, "Abbāsid Abnāʾ", 4, 10.

[47] BA, III, 235; Tab. iii, 129f.; cf. *EI*², s.v. 'al-Rāwandiyya' (Kohlberg), noting Ibn al-Muqaffaʿ's use of the same formula in his warning against extremist sentiments among the troops in his *Risāla fīʾl-ṣaḥāba*.

Mu'āwiya, to be a manifestation of Gabriel. We do not know why they singled out those two officers, but both had served as missionaries in Khurāsān.

These Rāwandiyya presumably also held the spirit of Jesus to have been in the imams from 'Alī onwards. Unlike Ablaq, however, they will have seen it as continuing in the 'Abbāsids after Ibrāhīm al-Imām, to culminate in al-Manṣūr. They must have held al-Manṣūr to be God in a fuller sense than his predecessors, for they are said to have circumambulated his palace, and they threw themselves from the palace walls in Hāshimiyya near Kufa, the capital at the time,[48] and from other high places in Syria. In Syria they are reported to have sold their possessions and jumped naked from the city walls, thinking that they could fly, or to have put on silken clothes and then jumped from a hill, thinking that they had become angels.[49] The silken clothes are the clothes of the people of paradise that we shall meet again in connection with al-Muqanna' and Bihāfarīdh, and the sale of possessions is characteristic of those who hold the end of the world to be at hand, as is the idea of being able to fly. ('And the spirit that they have put on shall cause them to fly, and they shall inherit the kingdom that was prepared for them from the beginning', as the fourth-century Aphrahat (Farhād) said of the resurrection.)[50] What it amounts to is that al-Manṣūr was the messiah, the last and fullest manifestation of God on earth who would inaugurate the paradisical era.

The dates proposed for the Rāwandiyya incident seem to reflect the fact that the Rāwandiyya ran wild on more than one occasion. The first incident may well have taken place in 136/754, the year of al-Manṣūr's accession, as some sources say. Ibn al-Jawzī tells us that the Rāwandiyya operated with the idea of seven eras or cycles (*adwār*).[51] Each of these cycles was associated with an imam, not with a new messenger, so they were very short; they went from al-'Abbās via Ibrāhīm al-Imām to al-Manṣūr, who would preside over the last. If the Rāwandiyya were waiting for a seventh and last imam, al-Manṣūr's accession would indeed have marked the end of earthly existence. But Ibn al-Jawzī is a late source. He classifies the Rāwandiyya as a species of Bāṭinīs, clearly in the sense of

[48] Tab. iii, 418, where Madā'inī's father has them jump off the roof of Khaḍrā', i.e. Baghdad, which had not been built yet, apparently by unconscious updating (cf. the tradition in Tab. iii, 365, which locates the disturbances at Bāb al-dhahab, also in Baghdad).

[49] Azdī, 173; Ibn al-'Adīm, *Zubda*, I, 59f.; Theophanes, AM 6250.

[50] Shchuryk, '*Lebēš pagrā*' in the *Demonstrations* of Aphrahat', 425. For Jewish expectations of flying to Jerusalem see Friedländer, 'Jewish–Arabic Studies, I', 504ff.

[51] Ibn al-Jawzī, *Muntaẓam*, ed. 'Aṭā' and 'Aṭā', VIII, 29f. (year 141).

Ismailis, with reference to their belief in seven eras, and his information also sounds anachronistic when he has them trace the imamate directly from the Prophet to the ʿAbbāsids (the doctrine of *wirātha*), not via ʿAlī and his grandson Abū Hāshim (the doctrine of *waṣiyya*). The doctrine of *wirātha* is normally said to have been formulated by a Rāwandī by the name of Abū Hurayra, probably Muḥammad b. Farrūkh, a Khurāsānī commander,[52] and to have been taken up by the caliph al-Mahdī.[53] But it is possible that the Rāwandiyya adopted the doctrine well before al-Mahdī endorsed it, and the focus on seven eras is sufficiently well attested among other Khurramī groups for Ibn al-Jawzī's claim to be credible. So the possibility that something happened in 136 cannot be ruled out.

The year 137 was a more fateful one, however, because that was the year in which al-Manṣūr killed Abū Muslim (and 139 is probably a mere mistake for 137).[54] The Khurāsānī recruits now had to make sense of an event that seemed to undermine everything they had fought for. Those who were members of Abū Muslim's own army lost their stake in the ʿAbbāsid caliphate along with him and so responded by rejecting the ʿAbbāsids, as we have seen; there were also Rāwandiyya who mutinied in Basra, demanding vengeance for Abū Muslim (though not in 137).[55] But most of the Rāwandiyya in Iraq apparently responded by casting al-Manṣūr's act as an apocalyptic test of their faith. When al-Manṣūr asked some of them to repent of their extremist beliefs they replied that he was their Lord and could kill them as he had killed his prophets, by drowning some, setting wild animals on others, and suddenly seizing the spirits of yet others; God could do as he liked, they said, one could not hold him to account.[56] The last example seems to refer to Abū Muslim, held by the Rāwandiyya to be a prophet (*nabī mursal*);[57] the spirit of God was in him,

52 His *kunya* is regularly identified as Abū Hurayra. He first appears in connection with the elevation of Abū 'l-ʿAbbās in 132 (Tab. iii, 36), thereafter in the service of al-Mahdī and as governor of the Jazīra until 171, when Hārūn had him executed, undoubtedly for having advocated Hārūn's removal from the succession (Tab. iii, 606; Azdī, 236, 252, 267; YT, II, 490; Khalīfa, 707, 724, where he is still alive in 180). He was a *mawlā* of Tamīm according to Azdī, but an Azdī according to YT, and had a *qaṭīʿa* in Baghdad (YB, 253.3). The *wirātha* doctrine is all that Abū Tammām (104 = 98f.) associates with the name Rāwandiyya.

53 Ps.-Nāshiʾ, §47; Nawbakhtī, 43ff.; Ashʿarī, 21.9–13.

54 The confusion of *sabʿa* and *tisʿa* is extremely common, and Ibn al-ʿAdīm gives 139 rather than 137 as the year in which Abū Muslim was killed (*Zubda*, I, 59.1).

55 Cf. Dīnawarī, 380 (year 142); Theophanes, AM 6252 (= AH 141–2), where they come to Basra from Syria.

56 Nawbakhtī, 47.

57 Nawbakhtī, 47.1.

as some Rāwandiyya said.[58] God in the form of al-Manṣūr had suddenly seized his spirit. The hostility between the two was only apparent, then: God was just behaving in one of his unaccountable ways. The Rāwandiyya stuck to this view 'until today', al-Nawbakhtī says, the today in question being that of the source he is quoting, probably Hisham b. al-Ḥakam (d. 179/795).[59]

Something must have happened in 141 or 142 as well, however, for this is where most sources place the incident. Theophanes, who places it in AM 6250, corresponding to AH 140, reports a second incident in AM 6252, corresponding to AH 141–2: in that year the black-clothed ones rose up at Dābiq, proclaiming the caliph's *son* to be God inasmuch as he was their provider. It was in 141–2 that al-Manṣūr appointed al-Mahdī as his heir apparent and sent him to Khurāsān as governor, with headquarters in Rayy, or so al-Dhahabī says;[60] in fact, the official heir apparent was still 'Īsā b. Mūsā, and it is not until 145 that the *laqab* al-Mahdī appears on al-Mahdī's coins.[61] But al-Manṣūr may have issued different information to different circles, and in any case the Rāwandiyya seem to have found it deeply significant that an 'Abbāsid prince was appointed to Khurāsān, which had never happened before: apparently they inferred that the son rather than the father was the mahdi who would inaugurate the heavenly era. Indeed, it may have been thanks to them that al-Manṣūr bestowed the *laqab* of al-Mahdī on his son, just as it was apparently from the Rāwandī troops that al-Mahdī was later to adopt the *wirātha* doctrine. We should probably envisage the Rāwandiyya in a permanent state of excitement from the time of al-Manṣūr's accession, fully convinced that the most climactic moment of universal history was about to occur in their own lifetime.[62]

The eastern heresiographical tradition associates the name Rāwandiyya with belief in the continuing validity of the books that had come down from heaven to the prophets, and a late text mentions as examples of such books the Scrolls (*ṣuḥuf*) of Adam, Seth, Enoch (Idrīs), and Abraham, the

58 Baghdādī, *Farq*, 255.5.
59 Bayhom-Daou, 'Second-Century Šī'ite Ġulāt', 30.
60 Dhahabī, *Ta'rīkh*, VI, 2; cf. Tab. iii, 133f.
61 Bates, 'Khurāsānī Revolutionaries', esp. 288ff.
62 My formulation is indebted to a paper by D.F. Lindenfield. Compare Christopher Hitchens with reference to the events of 1968: 'If you have never yourself had the experience of feeling that you are yoked to the great steam engine of history, then allow me to inform you that the conviction is a very intoxicating one' (quoted in the *New York Times* book review, 20 June 2010, 8).

Torah of Moses and the Gospel of Jesus.[63] Of these works the Torah, Gospels, and Scrolls of Abraham are mentioned in the Qur'ān, but the list is not based on the Qur'ān, for it omits the Scrolls of Moses mentioned there (53:36, 87:19) and includes those of Adam, Seth, and Enoch instead. Adherents of esoteric religions would sometimes make up mysterious-sounding titles, but works attributed to Abraham, Adam, Seth, and Enoch were well known in late antiquity; many are extant to this day.[64] Most of the works in question were apocalypses of the type involving heavenly journeys, angelification, visions of heaven and hell, often including instruction in the scientific mysteries of the universe and predictions of drastic reversals of fortune to come at the (invariably imminent) end of times. Produced, adapted, and revised by Jews, Christians, Manichaeans, and other Gnostics, these and other pseudepigraphic works often convey the impression of having been more widely read and revered in the Near East than the Hebrew or Christian Bible from which they drew their inspiration,[65] and they were read in the Iranian culture area too. The Jews of Parthian Mesopotamia read Enoch apocalypses,[66] and apparently produced them too: 2 Enoch, written by an unclassifiable Jew and extant only in late Slavonic (Christian) recensions, displays signs of interaction with an Iranian environment, especially in its concept of time and its attitude to animals.[67] The Rāwandiyya who hoped to fly to heaven as angels when the mahdi came show us the same interaction from the Iranian angle.

[63] Abū Muṭī', '*Radd*', 92, where their name is given as Zuwaydiyya; Mashkūr, *Haftād u sih millat*, 37f. (no. 28), where their name is Rāwandiyya and the books are listed. This text dates from the eighth/fourteenth century.

[64] For a helpful survey see Reeves, *Heralds of that Good Realm*, ch. 2; see also Reeves, 'Jewish Pseudepigrapha in Manichaean Literature'. What the Rāwandiyya read was not necessarily the same works, of course. For a critical approach which makes my acceptance of the information on the Rāwandiyya look positively naive see Frankfurter, 'Apocalypses Real and Alleged', arguing that Mani's quotations from (or rather references to) apocalyptic works are invented because they do not match the known works of the same or similar titles, even though the impact of such works on Mani's thinking is not in doubt.

[65] See Reeves, 'Exploring the Afterlife', esp. 157 and n. 39 (the Mesopotamian Audians read the Apocalypse of Abraham); Crone, 'Book of Watchers'.

[66] See Chapter 14, n. 10. Cf. also the polemical reference to a theme from Enoch's Dream Visions in the *Škand-Gūmānīk Vičār*, XIV, 39, discussed by Halperin and Newby, 'Two Castrated Bulls', 633f.

[67] Pines, 'Eschatology and the Concept of Time in the Slavonic Book of Enoch'.

THE FOLLOWERS OF ʿABDALLĀH B. MUʿĀWIYA

The followers of ʿAbdallāh b. Muʿāwiya originated in the Jibāl, not in Khurāsān, but they came to Khurāsān when their master fled to Abū Muslim, and their history is best told in tandem with that of the Rāwandiyya.

ʿAbdallāh b. Muʿāwiya was an ʿAlid who rebelled in western Iran in 127/744. Like the missionaries in Khurāsān before Ibrāhīm al-Imām he seems to have preached Hāshimite (big-tent) Shīʿism. He held the Hāshimites to have a better right to the caliphate than the Marwānids,[68] called people to *al-riḍā min āl Muḥammad*,[69] and played on the Qurʾānic theme of love of the close kin (*mawadda fī 'l-qurba*), as his coins show;[70] all the Hāshimites assembled around him, including ʿAbbāsids such as the future al-Manṣūr, and even some Umayyad nobles.[71] In so far as he had unorthodox views they were of the eternalist and materialist variety which the impious Umayyad caliph al-Walīd II (743–4), is also said to have espoused.[72] He was not a Shīʿite extremist. Like Abū Muslim, however, he came to be held responsible for the extremist views current among his recruits.[73]

Ibn Muʿāwiya started his revolt in Kufa with the help of Shīʿites from Kufa and al-Madāʾin, but they were quickly subdued by the Umayyad governor of Iraq, and after a couple of days he received a safe conduct and left Kufa with his followers, supervised by government agents.[74] He proceeded to conquer the Māhs of Kufa and Basra (Dīnawar and Nihāwand), Hamadhān, Qumm, Rayy, Qūmis, Iṣfahān, and Fārs,[75] all areas in which there were dense Khurramī populations. He could not have conquered these places with his inept band of Shīʿite devotees, supplemented by Kufan slaves who ran away to join him;[76] and the above-mentioned Hāshimites had no armies of their own. The only way he could have conquered western Iran is by recruiting locals as he went along. Like Abū Muslim, in short, he must quickly have accumulated a large army of Iranians who converted

[68] Tab. ii, 1880.2f.
[69] *Maqātil*, 165.-4, 167.8.
[70] Bernheimer, 'Revolt of ʿAbdallāh b. Muʿāwiya', 382ff.
[71] *Maqātil*, 167.
[72] *Maqātil*, 162.
[73] For Abū Muslim as a believer in reincarnation see Chapter 12, n. 7.
[74] Tab. ii, 1879ff.
[75] Tab. ii, 1880.ult., 1976.11; *Maqātil*, 166f.
[76] Tab. ii, 1880f., 1976.

to Islam when they signed up, probably as full of zeal for their new faith and the new life it represented as their equivalents in Khurāsān, but inevitably taking their own religious universe with them. Some of them presumably remained in the area in which they had been recruited, but others went east with Ibn Muʿāwiya when he was defeated. He fled to Khurāsān, doubtless hoping for cooperation with Abū Muslim, but Abū Muslim had him jailed and killed at Herat, probably in 131/148f.[77] We are not told what orders were given for his army, but as will be seen there is reason to believe that Abū Muslim simply took them over.

Like Bābak and the Rāwandiyya, the followers of Ibn Muʿāwiya believed in divine indwelling (*ḥulūl*). ʿAbdallāh b. Muʿāwiya had supposedly said that the spirit of God was in Adam (and Seth, if al-Baghdādī is to be trusted), and that thereafter it migrated (*tanāsakhat*) until it passed into him, so that he was divine (*rabb*) and a prophet (*nabī*).[78] Other versions of their beliefs concentrate on the imams rather than the prophets: ʿAlī and his descendants were gods; God's spirit had passed (*dārat*) from the Prophet to ʿAlī and his descendants, and then to ʿAbdallāh b. Muʿāwiya; God was light and dwelt in him, his followers said. Or they said that the holy spirit (*rūḥ al-qudus*) had been in Muḥammad and passed (*intaqalat*) from him to the ʿAlīd holders of the imamate, who were gods, and that the holy spirit was eternal and would never cease to be.[79] The doctrine of divine imams is credited to a certain ʿAbdallāh b. Ḥarb or al-Ḥārith al-Kindī, of whom we are told that he was the son of a *zindīq* (heretic of some dualist or Gnostic kind) from Madāʾin, i.e. Ctesiphon.[80] As Halm surmises ʿAbdallāh was probably a Kindī by *walāʾ*, i.e. a non-Arab. This man took over the leadership of some of Ibn Muʿāwiya's followers after Ibn Muʿāwiya's death.[81] He is also said to have claimed that Ibn Muʿāwiya was still alive at Iṣfahān and would return as the mahdi, and that he himself was administering his followers as the latter's attorney (*waṣī*); but according to others he did so as the imam in his own right.[82] It was after him that the followers of ʿAbdallāh b. Muʿāwiya, or perhaps just a section of them,

77 *Maqātil*, 168f., with other versions; cf. Wellhausen, 'Oppositionsparteien', 98f.

78 Ashʿarī, 6; Baghdādī, *Farq*, 236.

79 Ps.-Nāshiʾ, §56 (tr. Halm, 'Schatten, II', 22); Nawbakhtī, 29; Qummī, no. 80; Baghdādī, *Farq*, 242.

80 Ps.-Nāshiʾ, §55; Nawbakhtī, 29, 31; Ashʿarī, 6, 22f.; Halm, 'Schatten, II', 16f. and 17n.

81 An alternative tradition has Ibn Muʿāwiya take over from him; see Tucker, *Mahdis and Millenarians*, 100; add Abū Tammām, 101 = 96.

82 Ps.-Nāshiʾ, §55 (ʿAbdallāh b. Ḥarb); Nawbakhtī, 29 (ʿAbdallāh b. al-Ḥārith); Ashʿarī, 6 (ʿAbdallāh b. ʿAmr b. Ḥarb); cf. also Qummī, nos. 74, 82, 87 (ʿAbdallāh b. ʿAmr b. al-Ḥarb; ʿAmr b. Ḥarb al-Kindī al-Shāmī).

came to be known as Ḥārithiyya or Ḥarbiyya. They were also called Janāḥiyya and Muʿāwiyya.[83]

The sources link Ibn Muʿāwiya's imamate with the Testament of Abū Hāshim: Abū Hāshim bequeathed the imamate to him, or to Ibn Ḥarb. To heresiographers the Testament of Abū Hāshim conjures up al-Mukhtār and the Kaysāniyya; to a historian it conjures up circles connected with the Hāshimiyya and the ʿAbbāsids. The impression that we are in ʿAbbāsid circles is reinforced by the claim that Abū Hāshim had given the testament (*waṣiyya*) to a certain Ṣāliḥ b. Mudrik because Ibn Muʿāwiya was still a minor at the time, and that this Ṣāliḥ held it until Ibn Muʿāwiya became the omniscient imam;[84] for this matches a claim by the Rāwandiyya that Abū Hāshim had passed the testament to ʿAlī b. ʿAbdallāh, who held it on behalf of his minor son Muḥammad b. ʿAlī until the latter became the omniscient imam and divine.[85] Where would the Ḥārithiyya and Rāwandiyya have been competitors? The answer has to be in the army. What is more, we are told that when the Ḥārithiyya and Rāwandiyya disputed with one another, they agreed to accept the verdict of a certain Abū Riyāḥ: he swore that Abū Hāshim had given the testament to the ʿAbbāsids, not to Ibn Muʿāwiya, and both sides accepted his verdict; as a result, the adherents of Ibn Muʿāwiya joined the Rāwandiyya.[86] In other words, the Ḥārithiyya embraced the cause of the ʿAbbāsids, acknowledging the superiority of their claim over that of ʿAbdallāh b. Muʿāwiya. One would infer that when Abū Muslim liquidated Ibn Muʿāwiya he incorporated the army that was now going spare into that of the Hāshimiyya: like the Rāwandiyya these troops ended up in Iraq. Once it was clear that the beneficiaries of the revolution were going to be the ʿAbbāsids to the exclusion of all other Hāshimites the erstwhile followers of Ibn Muʿāwiya had to decide where they belonged: the story of Abū Riyāḥ's arbitration gives us the grounds on which they justified their switch of allegiance to the ʿAbbāsids. It was presumably by confusion with Ḥarb b. ʿAbdallāh al-Rāwandī, the leader of the notoriously pro-ʿAbbāsid Ḥarbiyya, that their old leader came to be remembered now as Ibn al-Ḥārith and now as Ibn Ḥarb. The Ḥārithiyya had become Ḥarbiyya, one could say.

[83] Muʿāwiyya seems only to be attested in Qummī, 42 (no. 86).
[84] Nawbakhtī, 29; Qummī, no. 80.
[85] Nawbakhtī, 29f.
[86] Nawbakhtī, 30.

By Abū Tammām's time some adherents of ʿAbdallāh b. Muʿāwiya had renounced both Ibn Muʿāwiya and Ibn Ḥarb and joined the Imāmīs. Others held the imamate to continue in Ibn Muʿāwiya's clan, the descendants of Jaʿfar b. Abī Ṭālib, and the rest were those who awaited his return from the mountains of Iṣfahān.[87] Where they were we are not told.

87 Abū Tammām, 102 = 97.

5

Sogdia and Turkestan

Isḥāq

Sogdia is part of the region between the Oxus (Jayḥūn, Amu Darya) and the Jaxartes (Sayḥūn, Syr Darya), more precisely the part around the Zarafshān valley. The Zarafshān valley is a 740-kilometre-long oasis formed by the Zarafshān river, along which there was a string of famed cities, notably Bukhārā at the western end and Samarqand at the eastern. Going south from Samarqand one arrives at a smaller river running parallel with the Zarafshān, the Kashka Daryā; along this river there were two major settlements, Kish at the eastern end, due south of Samarqand, and Nasaf (Nakhshab) further west. To the south of Kish were steep mountains through which one had to travel by the pass known as the 'Iron Gate' and from which one would eventually get to Tirmidh on the Oxus, which marked the boundary between Sogdia and Ṭukhāristān (Bactria to the Greeks). Today most of Sogdia is in Uzbekistan and Bactria in Afghanistan. The language of Sogdia was Sogdian, a member of the eastern Iranian language group which had come to be written in a script derived from Aramaic by the fourth century AD. It still survives in the form of Yaghnobi, spoken by a small community in that part of the Zarafshān valley which is now in Tajikistan.

Sogdia is first attested as an Achaemenid satrapy in the fifth century BC, but it did not form part of the second Persian empire, that of the Sasanians. It was divided into principalities ruled by princes of Turkish origin and Iranian culture, all apparently members of the same family, and the entire region was under the hegemony of the Türgesh, a Turkish confederacy which had its centre further east, in what was vaguely referred to as Turkestan, and which in its turn was under the hegemony of the Chinese. The Arabs invaded Sogdia under Qutayba (86–96/705–15), who occupied Bukhārā and Samarqand and established Muslim sovereignty over the entire region, without removing its local rulers. After Qutayba's death most of Sogdia was repeatedly lost and recovered down to 739 (AH 122f.), when the Türgesh confederacy fell apart.

In religious terms the Sogdians are hard to classify. At Panjikant (Būnjikath), nine farsakhs to the east of Samarqand, the population had fire-altars and placed the bones of their dead in ossuaries in the familiar Zoroastrian style, but their last king (d. 104/722) was nonetheless called Dēvāstīč, 'dēv-like', showing that *daiva*s were divine beings to him, as also in Indian religion.[1] In Zoroastrianism the *daiva*s, perhaps once worshipped by the Iranians too, had been demoted to the status of demons.[2] The city temple, in which the main cult was of fire, had a room devoted to the originally Mesopotamian goddess Nana (Nanai, Nanaia), who was one of the most popular deities in eastern Iran and who was 'queen of Panjikant'. The cult of Tammuz, also a Mesopotamian import, was closely associated with hers.[3] Another room contained a group of sculptures depicting Śiva and his wife Pārvatī, probably made between the end of the first/seventh century and 740.[4] But it is probably Ohrmazd who is represented under the name of Adbag, 'supreme god', though Sogdian Buddhist texts equate Adbag with Indra (rejected by the Zoroastrians).[5] One of the few Sogdian Zoroastrian texts to have come to light, dating from the eighth or ninth century, mentions that at the time when the 'king of the gods' (*βγ'n MLK'*), also identified as the 'supreme god' (*''δδβγ*), was in the fragrant paradise in (of?) good thought, the perfect, righteous Zoroaster came and paid homage to him, addressing him as beneficent lawmaker and justly deciding judge.[6] Here too the supreme god seems to be Ohrmazd, though the 'king of the gods' is Zurvān (Brahma) in

1 *EIr.*, s.v. 'Panjikant' (Marshak); Grenet and de la Vaissière, 'The Last Days of Panjikent'.

2 For the *dēv*s in old Iranian religion see *EIr.*, s.v. 'daiva' (Herrenschmidt and Kellens). All attestations of the *dēv*s as divine beings among Zoroastrians come from a region familiar with the Indian *daeva*s, inter alia thanks to the presence of Buddhism.

3 Grenet and Marshak, 'Mythe de Nana', 6; Azarpay, 'Nanā'; Tremblay, 'Ostiran *vs* Westiran', 223, 224f.

4 *EIr.*, s.v. 'Panjikant'; Škoda, 'Culte du feu de Pendžikent', esp. 71f.; Škoda, 'Śiva-Heiligtum in Pendžikent'.

5 Grenet, 'The Second of Three Encounters', 44.

6 Sims-Williams, 'Sogdian Fragments of the British Library', 46ff., favouring a Manichaean attribution; cf. Sims-Williams, 'Some Reflections', 8, for the date; but cf. also Grenet, 'The Second of Three Encounters', 50, 54, n. 43. That the god should be 'in good thought' is slightly puzzling; it would make more sense that he had come down to the paradise of good thought, the lowest heaven (that of the stars, cf. *Mēnōg ī Khrad*, ch. 7, 12; *Ardā Vīrāfnāmag*, ch. 7): while he was there, Zoroaster ascended to visit him.

Buddhist and Manichaean texts,[7] for the reference is surely to Zoroaster's encounter with Ohrmazd, a well-known theme in the Zoroastrian books.[8] The Pahlavi books do not envisage Ohrmazd, or for that matter Zurvān, as a lawgiver or judge, however (they ascribe the function of judge to Mithra/Mihr),[9] so it is a somewhat different Ohrmazd that we meet here. The Chinese identified the god(s) of the Hu (Westerners, especially Sogdians) as *xian* (*hsien*), using a character that had first been adopted for the Buddhist *devas*.[10] It is usually translated as Heaven-God or, when the reference is to the religion, as Zoroastrianism. This is certainly correct at times. A Chinese historical work holds that the various Hu had learnt the cult of *xian* by going to Persia – or, as another historical work puts it, the various Hu had received the rules for sacrificing to *xian* from Persia.[11] But the Heaven-God worshipped at Turfan does not seem to have been associated with either fire-worship or Zoroastrian funerary customs,[12] and the rituals associated with the Heaven-God in Chinese sources are quite different from those of official Zoroastrianism (see p. 100). Henning thought it wisest simply to translate *xian* as *baga*, god.[13]

In addition to Zoroastrianism (of sorts), Christianity, Manichaeism, and some Buddhism were found in Sogdia. In Parthian times there was Buddhism as far west as Marw, and Sogdians had been active as translators of Buddhist texts in China.[14] But though Buddhism was still the dominant religion in Chaghāniyān and Ṭukhāristān when the Arabs arrived, it was no longer found in Khurāsān, and barely in Sogdia. The *Wei-shu*, compiled in the 550s, says of the kingdom of Samarqand that 'they honour the Buddha in Iranian (*Hu*) books', but the numerous fragments of Buddhist books in Sogdian that have been recovered all come

[7] Sims-Williams, 'Sogdian Fragments of the British Library', 47.

[8] Cf. Molé, *Culte*, 313ff. Tremblay's suggestion ('Ostiran *vs* Westiran', 229) that it is a Sogdian *zand* of a lost Avestan text is attractive, but I do not see the relevance of Yt, 17, 21f.

[9] See Chapter 10, pp. 202f.

[10] For all this see Dien, 'A Note on *Hsien*', 284ff. For the contrary view that the character *xian* was specially invented to designate Zoroastrianism see de la Vaissère and Riboud, 'Livres des Sogdiens', 130 (crediting it to Dien); Lin Wushu, 'The Heaven-God in the Qočo Kingdom', 11.

[11] Daffinà, 'La Persia sassanide secondo le fonti cinesi', 162f., where *hsien* is translated as fire god, following an etymology proposed by Bailey, *Indo-Scythian Studies*, 11n.

[12] Lin Wushu, 'The Heaven-God in the Qočo Kingdom'.

[13] Cf. Waley, 'Some References to Iranian Temples', 123n., explaining that at the suggestion of Henning he uses *baga* to translate *hsien*.

[14] For a brief survey and key literature, see Sundermann, 'Bedeutung des Parthischen', 99f.; see also *EIr.*, s.v. 'Buddhism'.

from the Sogdian colonies in Central Asia rather than from Sogdia itself;[15] and though in itself this may not be of great significance, given that almost all the Sogdian texts we have are from the colonies, archaeological excavations in Sogdia still have not revealed any Buddhist buildings. According to the biography of Xuan Zang (Hsüan-tsang), the Chinese pilgrim who travelled between 629 and 645, there were only two Buddhist temples in Samarqand when he passed through, and the locals would burn the monks who visited them. He claimed to have converted the king and many others,[16] perhaps with some truth, for another Chinese pilgrim, Yiqing (I-tsing), who travelled between 671 and 695, had heard of differences between the customs of the Buddhists in Tukhāra (Ṭukhāristān) and Sūli (Sogdia).[17] But Yiqing did not visit Sogdia himself and his information could be dated, or it could refer to Sogdians outside Sogdia, or at Tirmidh, where Buddhism was still strong.[18] By around 700 the king of Samarqand seems to have turned hostile to Buddhism, for an ambassador from Chaghāniyān to Samarqand at that time reassured him that he had no need to be suspicious of him 'concerning the deities of Samarqand', perhaps meaning that the king need not fear that he would disseminate Buddhism while he was there.[19] The Korean pilgrim Hye Ch'o, who passed through around 727, only found one monastery and one ignorant monk in Samarqand.[20]

Though the Sogdians were not Buddhists when they were at home they had certainly been influenced by Buddhism, in terms of religious vocabulary, deities, and iconography alike.[21] A house at Panjikant built around 700 had a reception room with huge images of the owner's main deities as well as smaller figures of other gods and goddesses, and it also had a modest Buddha equipped with the halo and tongues of flames characteristic of the local deities.[22] The owner of this house was apparently a

[15] De la Vaissière and Riboud, 'Livres des Sogdiens', 129; Walter, 'Sogdians and Buddhism', 2.5, 2.6; other Chinese notices in Daffinà, 'La Persia sassanide secondo le fonte cinesi', 163.

[16] Walter, 'Sogdians and Buddhism', 2.5 (pp. 33f.). Hsüan-tsang does not say anything about Buddhism in Samarqand in his travel account.

[17] Scott, 'Iranian Face of Buddhism', 63.

[18] Cf. Hsüan-tsang in Beal, *Buddhist Records*, I, 38f.; see also Leriche and Pidaev, 'Termez in Antiquity', 189f.

[19] Albaum, *Zhivopic' Afrasiaba*, 55f. (my thanks to Kazim Abdullaev for this reference and a translation).

[20] Yang *et al.*, *Hye Ch'o Diary*, 54 (my thanks to Kevin van Bladel for drawing this work to my attention).

[21] Belenitskii and Marshak in Azarpay, *Sogdian Painting*, 28ff.; Naymark, 'Returning to Varakhsha' (pp. 11f. of my printout).

[22] Marshak and Raspopova, 'Wall Paintings', 151ff.

non-Buddhist who had added the Buddha to his local pantheon. A terra-cotta Buddha figure, dating from the fifth/early sixth century or later, has also been found at Panjikant, made by a local artist who may have seen images of the Maitreya Buddha, but who did not follow any Buddhist prototype. The mould was made for serial production, so there were many Sogdians who liked to call upon the Buddha even though they were not what one could call Buddhists.[23] Buddhist objects have also been found in Samarqand and southern Sogdia, near Kish and Nasaf.[24] Buddhism and the semi-Zoroastrian cults of Transoxania blended so imperceptibly into each other that they came to be subsumed under the same label of *Sumaniyya* in Muslim times and jointly identified as the pre-Zoroastrian religion of Iran.[25]

The Sogdians had colonies in Central Asia, as well as in Mongolia and China, because they were famous traders who dominated the traffic along the Silk Route both before and after the coming of the Arabs: Sogdian was the *lingua franca* of the roads in Central Asia, just as Persian was the *lingua franca* of the southern seas. The Sogdians also served as political advisers and soldiers to the Turks, on whom their influence was enormous.[26] One Sogdian who served in the army of the northern Turks lost his favoured position there in 713 and fled to China, where his son by a Turkish woman enrolled as a soldier. This son, Rokhshan the Bukharan, better known as An-Lushan, raised a revolt in 755–63 that did much more damage to the Tang dynasty, and thus to Chinese ambitions in Central Asia, than did the Arabs by defeating the Chinese at Talas in 751.[27]

There were numerous Iranian places of worship in China in the seventh and eighth centuries.[28] Some of them were served by Magi (Mu-hu), i.e. Zoroastrian priests, and others by personnel in charge of *xian* (*hsien*) cults.[29] The Hu (Westerners), as the Chinese called them, were associated with spirit possession and illusion tricks, and in Tang tales the Hu trader is often an alchemist and magician.[30] As early as the first century BC a

[23] Marshak and Raspopova, 'Buddha Icon from Panjikent'.

[24] Abdullaev, 'Image bouddhique découverte à Samarkand'; Abdullaev, *Buddhist Iconography of Northern Bactria*; Compareti, 'Traces of Buddhist Art', 16f.

[25] Cf. Crone, 'Buddhism as Ancient Iranian Paganism' (summarised in Chapter 16, pp. 386f.).

[26] Golden, *History of the Turkic Peoples*, 145; Pulleyblank, *Rebellion of An Lu-Shan*, 18f.

[27] Pulleyblank, *Rebellion of An Lu-Shan*, 7ff.

[28] Leslie, 'Persian Temples in T'ang China'.

[29] Waley, 'Some References to Iranian Temples', 123; cf. also Leslie, 'Persian Temples in T'ang China', 276f.

[30] Schafer, 'Iranian Merchants in T'ang Dynasty Tales', 414f.

Chinese observer had noted that the people of the far west, that is, Transoxania, were experts at conjuring.[31] We get some colourful descriptions. Some time before 640 the leader of worshippers at an Iranian temple in the Tung Huang region, the westernmost limit of Chinese settlement along the Silk Route, visited the Chinese court. Here he called down the *baga* spirit (in Waley's translation of *xian*), pierced himself with a knife, took out his entrails, cut off the ends, tied up the rest with his hair, and, holding both ends of his knife, turned it round and round while declaring the grandiose projects of the government to be in accordance with Heaven's will; then the divine spirit departed from him and he fell down and lay gasping for seven days, whereupon he recovered. The emperor was most impressed.[32] We are also told that the Hu traders had an annual feast at which they would ask for blessing: 'They cook pork and mutton, sing and dance in an intoxicated state to the accompaniment of guitar, drums and flute music'. After having brought a wine offering to the god(s), they would make someone come to be *xianzhu* (*hsien-chu*), Heaven-God host, and collect money for him, and he would then take an exceedingly sharp knife. 'With this knife he stabs himself in the belly so that the tip comes out of his back, turn it around in his entrails and spill blood; after a while he spits out water and recites an incantation, and then he is as well as before. This is one of the illusion tricks of the people of the western countries.'[33] Another Hu would put a nail through his head on feast days and run as fast as he could to another temple, where he would perform a dance and run back again; then he would pull out the nail and be fine, though he did need ten days to recover.[34] Some of the leaders of *xian* temples were healers, at least in later times, and their cult attracted Chinese customers as well, Buddhists included.[35]

When Qutayba began the conquest of Transoxania Islam was added to the religious repertoire of the region. We hear of natives converting en masse in Sogdia in response to promises of freedom from taxation;[36] and

[31] Hulsewé and Loewe, *China in Central Asia*, 114, cf. 117 (conjurer). I owe this reference to Michael Cook.

[32] Waley, 'Some References to Iranian Temples', 125.

[33] Eichhorn, 'Materialen', 536. (I owe my awareness of the Chinese sources on Iranian religion to references given to me, many years ago, by Michael Cook and think this was one of them.) Belly-ripping is also reported for Indian magicians in 646, again as an illusion trick (Waley, 'Some References to Iranian Temples', 126).

[34] Eichhorn, 'Materialen', 536, n. 9.

[35] Waley, 'Some References to Iranian Temples', 126; also in Eichhorn, 'Materialen', 540 (AD 1093).

[36] See Introduction, p. 14.

the Hāshimiyya also did a great deal of recruiting in Sogdia.[37] Among their recruits was a certain Isḥāq.

ISḤĀQ

Of Isḥāq we only know what Ibn al-Nadīm tells us on the basis of a number of different sources.[38] His main source was a history of Transoxania which appears to have reached him in an anonymous state and which cited, among other things, a certain Ibrāhīm b. Muḥammad. According to this Ibrāhīm, who was 'learned about the Muslimiyya' and who may also be the main source of our information on al-Muqanna''s beliefs,[39] Isḥāq was an illiterate Transoxanian who received communications from the spirits (*jinn*): if one consulted him the answer would come after a night. Isḥāq was apparently a fresh convert to Islam, and one takes it that he served as a 'Heaven-God host' who would call down the *baga* spirit for purposes of answering questions, though Ibrāhīm says nothing about belly-ripping or illusion tricks of other kinds: in fact, he contrives to make spirit possession sound almost like an office routine. We do hear of illusion tricks again later: in 322/933f. a Sogdian would-be prophet created endless supplies of food for his followers by means of magic in Bāsand near the Iron Gate in Chaghāniyān; he was a master of tricks and sleights of hand who would put his hand in a basin of water and take it out filled with dinars, and do other tricks, until he was captured on the mountain on which he had ensconced himself and was killed; for a long time people in the region continued to believe that he would return.[40] His miracles are not linked to spirit possession, but in 636/1238f. we hear of a sieve-maker from the village of Tārāb near Bukhārā who claimed that the spirits (*jinn*) had conversations with him and informed him of the hidden, and that he had powers of magic, 'for in Transoxania and Turkestan many persons, especially women, claim to have magical powers'; when people fell ill they would be

[37] For contingents from Kish and Nasaf see Dīnawarī, 360. There was a *qaṭī'at al-sughd* in Baghdad, where we also find Kharfāsh al-Ṣughdī (YB, 249.1). Other Sogdian recruits known by name include Jīlan b. al-Ṣughdī (Tab. ii, 1957; cf. Justi, *Namenbuch*, 115); Ḥammād b. 'Amr al-Ṣughdī (Tab. iii, 354, cf. ii, 1773; IA, V, 397, 591); Zuwāra al-Bukhārī, and al-Ishtākhanj (Crone, "Abbāsid Abnā'", 17).

[38] Ibn al-Nadīm, 408 = II, 822ff. According to Sadighi, *Mouvements*, 150/186, n. 2, Isḥāq is also mentioned in the Cambridge manuscript of Gardīzī (King's College Library, fol. 73a), but this is not correct.

[39] Cf. Crone, 'Abū Tammām on the Mubayyiḍa', 172f.

[40] Gardīzī, 347 (drawn to my attention by Luke Treadwell); IA, VIII, 289f., both presumably drawing on Sallāmī. Bāsand could be modern Boysun.

visited by such magicians and summon the exorcist (*parikhwān*), perform dances, and thus convince 'the ignorant and the vulgar', as Juwaynī disapprovingly explains.[41] Isḥāq formed part of a long and venerable tradition in Transoxania.

Ibrāhīm adds that when Abū Muslim was killed, Isḥāq 'called people to him. He claimed that he was a prophet (*nabī*) sent by Zoroaster, alleging that Zoroaster was alive and had not died; his companions (*aṣḥābuhu*) believe that he is alive and did not die and that he will come forth to establish this religion for them; this is one of the secrets of the Muslimiyya.' The formulation is somewhat ambiguous. One takes Isḥāq to have summoned people to the cause of Abū Muslim, claiming that the latter (not he himself) was a prophet of Zoroaster, who was still alive, but thereafter it is hard to be sure: is it that his (i.e. Abū Muslim's?) companions believed that he (Abū Muslim?) was alive and scheduled to come back to restore the religion for them? That would be one reading, but the reference could also be to Zoroaster again, or to Isḥāq.

Ibn al-Nadīm also cites another account from the anonymous history of Transoxania. Here we are told that a number of men who made propaganda for Abū Muslim fled to a variety of places when he was killed. Among them was a certain Isḥāq who came to the land of the Turks in Transoxania; he claimed that Abū Muslim was imprisoned (*maḥṣūr*) in the mountains of Rayy and would come forth from there at a specified time known to them. The anonymous author added that he had asked some people why Isḥāq was known as *al-turk*; their reply was that it was because he had gone to the land of the Turks and 'called them with [*sic*] the messengership of Abū Muslim' (*yadʿūhum bi-risālat Abī Muslim*)'. Here the text is corrupt, and there is no reference to Zoroaster, but the two accounts are otherwise compatible.

In this account Isḥāq preaches a message surprisingly close to that imputed by Niẓām al-Mulk to Sunbādh, the rebel at Rayy. As the reader may remember, Niẓām al-Mulk depicts Sunbādh as claiming that Abū Muslim had not died and that he was now in a brazen fortress (*ḥiṣārī*), whence he would come forth with the mahdi and Mazdak. Isḥāq is similarly depicted as claiming that Abū Muslim was alive and imprisoned (*maḥṣūr*) at Rayy, from where he would come forth. According to Niẓām al-Mulk, moreover, Sunbādh presented himself as the messenger (*rasūl*) of Abū Muslim, claiming that 'a letter/the letter of Abū Muslim has come to me' (*nāma ba-man āmada ast/nāma-yi Abū Muslim ba-man āmad*). This

[41] Juwaynī, *Tarikh-i Jahāngushā*, I, 85 = I, 109.

shows that the corrupt passage in Ibn al-Nadīm should be emended by the insertion of some missing words, along the lines of Isḥāq 'called them ... *and brought* the letter of Abū Muslim' (*atā bi-risālat Abī Muslim*)'. The two accounts must be rooted in a shared source, probably Ibrāhīm b. Muḥammad's on Isḥāq.

Niẓām al-Mulk may not be guilty of simply transferring information from one context to another, for Isḥāq does seem to have participated in Sunbādh's revolt. He and others like him are said to have fled (*haraba*) after Abū Muslim's death, which does not otherwise make any sense; and there is no obvious reason why Isḥāq should have placed Abū Muslim in the mountains of Rayy if he had not had an apocalyptic experience there. Sunbādh had repudiated Islam in favour of his native Zoroastrianism. If we trust the first account Isḥāq did the same, apparently identifying Abū Muslim with Pišyōtan, the messianic figure awaiting the end-time in the fortress of Kangdiz, from where he would come forth with his retinue to defeat the enemy.[42]

Ibn al-Nadīm adds, perhaps on the basis of the same history of Transoxania, that some people held Isḥāq to have been a descendant of Yaḥyā b. Zayd, the ʿAlid killed by the Umayyad governor of Khurāsān in 125/743; he had allegedly fled from the Umayyads to Turkish Transoxania and later adopted Muslimī beliefs by way of camouflage. This is obviously implausible. It probably reflects the fact that Yaḥyā b. Zayd was a hero to many of those who venerated Abū Muslim, for Yaḥyā was a member of the same holy family that Abū Muslim had worked for, and both had been victimised by the 'Arabs' who did not understand what their own prophet had preached. Al-Muqannaʿ was also said to have had a stance on Yaḥyā's death.[43] Still others knew of a sect by the name of Isḥāqiyya, named after a certain Isḥāq b. ʿAmr who traced the imamate via Muḥammad b. al-Ḥanafiyya: this suggests that the eponymous founder had been a member of the Hāshimiyya. One sub-group of the Isḥāqiyya claimed that their imam had fled from the Umayyads and the ʿAbbāsids to the land of the Turks, where he was now staying and whence the mahdi would come forth, speaking only Turkish.[44] Their Isḥāq sounds like our refugee from Sunbādh's army mixed up with Yaḥyā b. Zayd, the refugee from the Umayyads.

[42] See Chapter 2, pp. 38f.

[43] IA, VI, 39.

[44] Khwārizmī, 30; Abū Tammām, 100 = 95 (with the details).

None of the reports say that Isḥāq rebelled, or even that he preached against the Arabs/Muslims. Modern scholars sometimes connect him with the White-clothed ones (*sapīdjāmagān*, Arabic *mubayyiḍa*) whom some held responsible for the death of Abū Dāwūd, Abū Muslim's deputy in Marw and successor as governor of Khurāsān: though some attributed his sudden death in 140/757f. to machinations by the caliph, others held that he was killed by the White-clothed ones from among the group (*qawm*) of Saʿīd the Weaver (*julāh*).[45] No source says or implies that Isḥāq had dealings with the White-clothed ones, however, let alone that he founded them or played a role in the death of Abū Dāwūd, so the suggestion is gratuitous. Isḥāq was just one out of many Khurāsānīs who turned Abū Muslim into a religious hero, and we should not elevate him to special importance merely because we happen to hear about him. All we can say is that we are lucky to get a glimpse of one of the soldiers whose world collapsed when Abū Muslim was killed.

[45] Sadighi, *Mouvements*, ch. 3; *DMBI*, s.v. 'Isḥāq-i Turk' (Langarūdī); Daniel, *Khurasan*, 132, 159.

6

Sogdia

al-Muqanna' and the Mubayyiḍa

Among the devotees of Abū Muslim who remained in 'Abbāsid service in Marw after the murder of their hero was the man who was to go down in history as al-Muqanna', 'the veiled one'. His real name is usually given as Hāshim b. Ḥakīm; al-Jāḥiẓ, followed by some later authors, claimed that he was called 'Aṭā'.[1] No Iranian name is recorded for him, and not for his father either.[2] All our information about their background comes from the *Tārīkh-i Bukhārā*, composed by Narshakhī in Arabic in 332/943f. and translated into Persian with revisions by Qubāvī in 522/1128f. According to this work al-Muqanna''s father was called Ḥakīm and 'he' was a captain (*sarhang*) in the Khurāsānī army in the reign of al-Manṣūr, originally from Balkh, the capital of Ṭukhāristān.[3] The antecedent of 'he' is unclear. Most modern scholars read it as referring to al-Muqanna''s father,[4] but Daniel takes it to refer to al-Muqanna' himself,[5] and he is probably right; for a couple of lines later Narshakhī says of al-Muqanna' himself that he was an officer in the Khurāsānī army during the revolution and served as adviser to 'Abd al-Jabbār b. 'Abd al-Raḥmān al-Azdī, i.e. in the reign of al-Manṣūr. It sounds like the same information in a different formulation.

[1] Jāḥiẓ, *Bayān*, III, 103; followed by Ibn Khallikān, III, 263 (no. 420); Dhahabī, *Siyar*, 306.

[2] *Pace* Amoretti, 'Sects and Heresies', 498 (followed by Tābān, 'Qiyām-i Muqanna'', 541), who erroneously claims that Ibn Khallikān gives his father's name as Dādawayh. It is to Ibn al-Muqaffa''s father that he gives this name: see Ibn Khallikān, II, 146, 155 (no. 189, on al-Ḥallāj, in a discussion of a confusion of al-Muqanna' and Ibn al-Muqaffa' in a text by al-Juwaynī). In his biography of al-Muqanna', Ibn Khallikān explicitly says that the name of al-Muqanna''s father was unknown, though some claimed it was Ḥakīm (III, 263).

[3] *TB*, 64 S; 90 R = 65f.

[4] Thus Sadighi, *Mouvements*, 168/214; Ḥabībī, *Afghānistān*, I, 323; *TB*, tr. Frye 65f. Zaryāb Khū'ī, 'Nukātī', 89, and Langarūdī, *Junbishhā*, 79, observe that it does not make sense without noticing the ambivalence of the pronoun.

[5] Daniel, *Khurasan*, 138.

Most probably two slightly different accounts of al-Muqanna''s career have been taken from different sources and pasted into the same account.[6]

If Hāshim's father did serve in the army in the reign of al-Manṣūr he will have participated in the revolution along with his son. One would in that case assume that the father was recruited by a missionary of the Hāshimite movement in Balkh, that he called his son Hāshim in honour of the movement, and that he lived a civilian life for some fifteen or twenty years until the revolution broke out, whereupon both he and his now adult son joined the revolutionary army and came to Marw with it. All this is chronologically possible and compatible with the information that the son worked as a fuller at some point;[7] it would have the interesting implication that al-Muqanna' was a second-generation Muslim. But unfortunately it seems more likely that we know nothing about the father. Even his name is uncertain, for some sources give Ḥakīm as the name of al-Muqanna' himself,[8] reflecting uncertainty over whether Hāshim-i Ḥakīm meant Hāshim, the son of Ḥakīm, or Hāshim the Ḥakīm, i.e. the wise one (as in al-Ḥakīm al-Tirmidhī). One source credits al-Muqanna' with a brother by the non-Muslim name of *qyrm*, with the *kunya* Khūsh(n?)ām, who was killed in the revolt.[9] It may well have been al-Muqanna' himself who adopted the name of Hāshim on joining the revolutionary movement.[10] If so, it was probably also then that he became a Muslim.

It is slightly odd that al-Muqanna' should have come from Balkh, given that it was in Sogdia that he rebelled, but he could of course have been a Sogdian who had gone to Balkh. However this may be, by the time he rebelled he was living in Marw, the capital of Khurāsān. When some sources say that al-Muqanna' came from Marw, or from the village of Kāva/Kāza, they do not mean that he was born or grew up there, merely that this is where he emerged as a rebel.[11] We do not know where he grew up. He is most likely to have come to Marw with the revolutionary troops,

[6] Cf. Crone and Jafari Jazi, II, 411.

[7] *TB*, 64/90 = 65; Gardīzī, 278; also in Jāḥiẓ, *Bayān*, III, 103 (*kāna qaṣṣāran min ahl al-Marw*), from whom it passed to later Arabic sources (e.g. Ibn Khallikān, III, 263); sometimes turned into *kāna* ... *qaṣīran* (e.g. Maqdisī, VI, 97; Dhahabī, *Siyar*, 307). Langarūdī, *Junbishhā*, 80f., takes *qaṣīran* to be primary on the basis of Ibn al-Athīr.

[8] Tab. iii, 484; Maqdisī, VI, 97; IA, VI, 38 (year 159); YB, 304; Gardīzī, 278.3.

[9] Crone and Jafari Jazi, I, §19.

[10] Gardīzī, who calls him Ḥakīm, does in fact say that he adopted the name of Hāshim himself (278.-4), but his claim is probably rooted in heresiographical confusion (cf. Crone, 'Abū Tammām on the Mubayyiḍa', 180).

[11] See Bīrūnī, *Āthār*, 211, where this is explicit. Differently Langarūdī, *Junbishhā*, 78f.

to be settled, like other soldiers, in the villages around the city, more precisely in that called Kāza.[12]

Late sources identify Hāshim as a member of Abū Muslim's own army.[13] Whatever the truth of this, after the revolution he appears in the service of Khālid b. Ibrāhīm al-Dhuhlī, better known as Abū Dāwūd, a close associate of Abū Muslim who had taken over as governor when the latter was murdered and who held office from 137/755 to 140/757.[14] According to Abū 'l-Ma'ālī, Hāshim worked as his secretary (*dabīr*), or more precisely as a soldier-secretary, for he is envisaged as participating in battles too: it was in Abū Dāwūd's battle with the rebel Ḥarb b. Ziyād al-Ṭālāqānī that he supposedly lost an eye.[15] After Abū Dāwūd's death he continued in service under the next governor of Khurāsān, 'Abd al-Jabbār b. 'Abd b. 'Abd al-Raḥmān al-Azdī, another veteran of the revolution, who held office from 140/757 to 141/758.[16] Narshakhī or Qubāvī, whose language sounds overblown already when he gives al-Muqanna' the position of officer (*sarhang*) in the revolution, now goes so far as to describe al-Muqanna' as chief adviser (*wazīr*) to 'Abd al-Jabbār. In fact, 'Abd al-Jabbār's chief secretary and adviser was a man called Mu'āwiya whom he had brought with him to Khurāsān,[17] and Abū 'l-Ma'ālī more credibly describes al-Muqanna' as a simple secretary (*dabīr*) yet again.[18] But both clearly envisage him as literate – probably in Persian, the language spoken by the troops. He did speak Arabic, if we may trust the report that he was *alkan* (spoke incorrectly with an accent);[19] but literary command, required for service as a professional bureaucrat, was probably beyond him.

With or without Arabic, Hāshim was evidently a man of some education. This may have been what earned him the sobriquet of Ḥakīm, or, if it

[12] The village is called Kāza in *TB*, 64/90 = 65; Abū 'l-Ma'ālī, 57. This village was known to Sam'ānī, *Ansāb*, II, 17f., s.v. 'Kazaqī', who spells out its name and locates it in the district of Qarnābad; see also Yāqūt, IV, 226, s.v. 'Kāza' (neither Yāqūt nor Sam'ānī connects it with al-Muqanna'). Bīrūnī, *Āthār*, 211, has Kāva Kaymardān, also given in different versions in later sources. For all the variants see Sadighi, *Mouvements*, 168n/214n.; Langarūdī, *Junbishhā*, 78f.

[13] Fakhr al-Dīn al-Rāzī, *Firaq*, 109 (ch. 9) makes him one of Abū Muslim's *aṣḥāb*, and Mustawfī makes him a secretary in Abū Muslim's army (*Tārīkh-i Guzīda*, 299).

[14] Ḥamza al-Iṣfahānī, 219f./163; Gardīzī, 273.

[15] Abū 'l-Ma'ālī, 58 (where Ḥarb has turned into Ḍarb). Cf. A'yan, a *mawlā* of Naṣr b. Sayyār who served as both the latter's *ṣāḥib dawāt* and as a soldier in his army with his own armed retinue (Tab. ii, 1928).

[16] Ḥamza al-Iṣfahānī, 219f./163; Gardīzī, 273–6; cf. Crone, *Slaves*, 173.

[17] Gardīzī, 274.1, 275.-6.

[18] Abū 'l-Ma'ālī, 58 (for Azdarī read Azdī).

[19] Jāḥiẓ, *Bayān*, III, 103, and sources dependent on him (e.g. Dhahabī, *Siyar*, 307).

referred to his father, his father may have been a man of some learning too. Of Hāshim himself we are told that he had studied sleights of hand and incantations (*sha'badha wa nīranjāt*).[20] This may be a mere inference from his later career, but however he had acquired the skill he certainly shared the Sogdian ability to work illusion tricks.

All in all, Hāshim seems to have come from a less impoverished milieu than Bābak. Recruited into the revolutionary army, he proceeded to do extremely well for himself. He was not directly affected by Abū Muslim's death, but remained in service under Abū Dāwūd, and though Abū Dāwūd was eventually eliminated too,[21] he weathered that storm as well, continuing to thrive under his successor, 'Abd al-Jabbār. Domiciled in the provincial capital and serving the top governor of the province, he will have been in a position to issue orders to men of both Arab and Iranian origin in his own language, whereas Bābak always experienced Arabs as superiors. Yet Hāshim too turned his back on Islam. What went wrong?

The answer seems to lie in the downfall of his employer. 'Abd al-Jabbār was one of the many victims of the growing hostility between the 'Abbāsid and 'Alid branches of the Hāshimite family which spelt the end of the 'big-tent' (Hāshimite) Shī'ism.[22] Instructed by the caliph al-Manṣūr to eliminate commanders suspected of 'Alid sympathies, 'Abd al-Jabbār initially obeyed, but suddenly switched to the 'Alid side himself.[23] He then produced a man whom he presented as (the Ḥasanid) Ibrāhīm b. 'Abdallāh, but who was actually a *mawlā* of Bajīla by the name of Yazīd according to al-Balādhurī, or a man called Barāzbanda b. Bamrūn (or the like) according to Gardīzī; he put a black turban on this man's head while he himself dressed in white and/or adopted white banners. According to Gardīzī he paid allegiance to the pretender – i.e., as caliph – and ordered others to do the same; according to al-Balādhurī he merely had the pretender deliver the Friday oration, in which he cursed al-Manṣūr, as well as another oration in which he gave a stirring account of the caliph's killing of 'Alids that reduced people to tears. A number of officers who refused to go along with 'Abd al-Jabbār's plans were killed.[24]

Precisely what 'Abd al-Jabbār hoped to achieve with all this is unclear. Al-Manṣūr had been searching for the Ḥasanid Muḥammad b. 'Abdallāh

[20] Abū 'l-Ma'ālī, 57f. (here already from childhood); *TB*, 64/90 = 65 (where he works as a fuller first); and later sources.

[21] Exactly how he died is hard to make out: see Daniel, *Khurasan*, 158f.

[22] Cf. Crone, *Medieval Islamic Political Thought*, 71ff., 89.

[23] Tab. iii, 128, 135.

[24] BA, III, 228f.; Gardīzī, 274f.

(al-Nafs al-Zakiyya), of whom it was said that he had been singled out as the future mahdi before the revolution in a meeting of the Hāshimite family at al-Abwā', an occasion on which al-Manṣūr was rumoured to have paid allegiance to him himself. In 140/757 al-Manṣūr seized Muḥammad's father, but Muḥammad himself had gone into hiding together with his brother Ibrāhīm; and according to al-Balādhurī, 'Abd al-Jabbār tried to make Ibrāhīm come to Khurāsān before producing his pretender.[25] Why did he want Ibrāhīm to come when it was Muḥammad who was the future mahdi? The answer could be that Ibrāhīm was meant to evoke Ibrāhīm al-Imām, the 'Abbāsid whom many had expected to be the beneficiary of the revolution, but who had died in Marwān II's jail.[26] The black turban that 'Abd al-Jabbār put on the pretender's head could be taken to identify him as the true Hāshimite imam. 'Abd al-Jabbār himself adopted white. This need not mean more than that he rejected the 'Abbāsids who had in fact taken power, but Gardīzī clearly takes his change of colour to signal alignment with the White-clothed ones,[27] who rejected the 'Abbāsids with a creed of their own. Of the beliefs of the White-clothed ones we know next to nothing because they later allied themselves with al-Muqanna', so that their beliefs were automatically assumed to be identical with his, but 'Abd al-Jabbār may have tried to build bridges between those Khurāsānīs who rejected the 'Abbāsids in favour of the 'Alids and those who rejected them in favour of Abū Muslim. In any case, 'Abd al-Jabbār was soon defeated, taken to Iraq, and ignominiously killed by al-Manṣūr in 141/758.[28]

We do not know where Hāshim stood in all this. There is no sign in his later preaching that he assigned doctrinal importance to either Ibrāhīm al-Imām or the 'Alids, or for that matter to the imamate. But if he had been close to 'Abd al-Jabbār he is unlikely to have escaped scot free. At the very least he will have been dismissed. More probably he was taken to Iraq along with 'Abd al-Jabbār and jailed as a member of his party,[29] though this is not quite how the *Tārīkh-i Bukhārā* tells the story. According to this

[25] BA, III, 229.1; for the meeting at al-Abwā' and al-Manṣūr's search for the brothers see *EI*[2], s.v. 'Ibrāhīm b. 'Abd Allāh' (Veccia Vaglieri).

[26] Gardīzī actually gives 'Abd al-Jabbār's Ibrāhīm the *nisna* al-Hāshimī, more suggestive of the 'Abbāsid than the 'Alid.

[27] Gardīzī, 274.-3, has *'alam sapīd kard* for Balādhurī's *labisa 'l-bayāḍ* and uses the phrase again in connection with al-Muqanna' (278.3).

[28] BA, I, 229; Gardīzī, 275.

[29] Thus Zaryāb Khū'ī, 'Nukātī', 84f.; Sadighi, *Mouvements*, 168/215; Ḥabībī, *Afghānistān*, III, 322f.

source he claimed prophethood for a while, whereupon al-Manṣūr had him jailed in Baghdad.[30] If 'Baghdad' is correctly remembered (as opposed to simply a term for 'the capital, whatever it was at the time') the imprisonment must have taken place after 146/763, at least five years after 'Abd al-Jabbār's fall.[31] But it does seem a little improbable. A local claimant to prophecy of no great importance would hardly have been sent to Iraq for jail, and this first episode of prophecy sounds like a doublet of the second, caused by pasting from different sources again.

At all events, Hāshim was eventually released and went back to his village, now unemployed. This may be when he had to make a living as a fuller. By then he was a new man. He married the daughter of a local Arab in Marw who believed in his cause and became his chief missionary in Sogdia.[32] He was no longer a Muslim, but rather a new messenger of God.

THE REVOLT

In 151/768f. Ḥumayd b. Qaḥṭaba became governor of Khurāsān. At some point this governor tried to arrest Hāshim, who went into hiding and stayed out of sight until his followers in Sogdia had 'brought his religion into the open'.[33] They did so by taking to violence and seizing fortresses in Sogdia, including two called Nawākit and Sanjarda. Hāshim – or, as we may call him now, al-Muqanna' – crossed the Oxus with thirty-six followers and ensconced himself in one of these fortresses, Nawākit in the Sanām, Sinām or Siyām mountains in the region of Kish. It consisted of an outer fortress in which his commanders and their troops were accommodated and an inner fortress in which he himself and his wives and close associates were ensconced.[34] In 157/773f. (not 159, as the *Tārīkh-i Bukhārā* says) his followers invaded the Bukharan village of Būmijkath, where they killed the muezzin and many of the inhabitants. Their leader here was one Ḥakīm-i Aḥmad, also known as Ḥakīm-i Bukhārā. They also took over a number of other villages in Sogdia, including Narshakh near Bukhārā, Niyāza near Samarqand, Sūbakh in Kish, and unnamed villages

30 *TB*, 64/90 = 66.
31 Al-Manṣūr completed the building of this city in 146 (Tab. iii, 319).
32 *TB*, 65/92 = 67.
33 *TB*, 65f/92f. = 67; Abū 'l-Ma'ālī, 58.
34 IA, VI, 39; Gardīzī, 279.4; *TB*, 66, 72/93, 101 = 67, 74; Abū 'l-Ma'ālī, 59; Crone and Jafari Jazi, I, §15 and commentary.

in Nasaf. We have the names of several commanders who were sent against them at this stage, but no details of the fighting.[35]

Ḥumayd died as governor of Khurāsān in 158/774f. or 159/775f., either shortly before or shortly after al-Manṣūr's death, and his son took over as interim governor pending the arrival of the new appointee, Abū ʿAwn ʿAbd al-Malik b. Yazīd. It seems to have been in the hiatus between the death of Ḥumayd and the arrival of Abū ʿAwn, and/or that between al-Manṣūr and al-Mahdī, that al-Muqannaʿ made the move that brought him to the attention of the central government: the conquest of Samarqand, achieved with the help of the Turks he enrolled.[36] The *khāqān*, or perhaps al-Muqannaʿ, adopted the title 'king of Sogdia' traditionally borne by the ruler of Samarqand,[37] and it must have been in Samarqand that undated coins were struck in al-Muqannaʿ's name: he appears on them as Hāshim, avenger (*walī*) of Abū Muslim.[38]

The caliph responded by appointing a Khurāsānī commander, Jibraʾīl b. Yaḥyā, to Samarqand as governor in 159/775f.[39] Jibraʾīl was diverted on the way by the governor of Bukhārā, who was desperate for help and who persuaded him to spend the next four months suppressing the rebels there. After much fighting, and two attempts at a peaceful resolution, Ḥakīm-i Aḥmad and other leaders were killed and the rebels routed.[40] Jibraʾīl then moved on to Samarqand and reconquered the city, whereupon al-Muqannaʿ engaged in a protracted struggle to reconquer it. In 160/776f. he seems to have succeeded. Meanwhile his forces also succeeded in defeating a coalition of government troops from Balkh, Chaghāniyān, and at Tirmidh, on the southern border of Sogdia, and he tried to conquer the cities of Chaghāniyān and Nasaf too. We are not told whether he followed up the victory at Tirmidh by occupying that city or whether his siege of Chaghāniyān was successful, but he failed to take Nasaf. Even so, these were alarming moves. Tirmidh controlled the route running from Balkh through the Iron Gate to Kish and Samarqand in the north; Chaghāniyān controlled access to the Iron Gate from the east. Control of Nasaf and Bukhārā would have blocked access from the west, and despite al-Muqannaʿ's setbacks there he still had support

[35] Gardīzī, 279; *TB*, 67/93f. = 68; IA, VI, 39; Crone and Jafari Jazi, II, 399.
[36] Khalīfa, 676f., 696; Tab. iii, 459 (year 159); Crone and Jafari Jazi, II, 399ff.
[37] Crone and Jafari Jazi, I, §§1.5, 4.1 and commentary.
[38] Kochnev, 'Monnaies de Muqannaʿ'; Crone and Jafari Jazi, II, 400. Naymark and Treadwell, 'Arab-Sogdian Coin', 361, read al-Muqannaʿ as identifying himself on his coins as *waṣī Abi Muslim* rather than as his *walī*.
[39] Tab. iii, 459.
[40] *TB*, 67f./95f. = 69f.; IA, VI, 39; Gardīzī, 279.

in both regions. For a moment it looked as if the whole of Sogdia might fall to him.[41]

Al-Mahdī responded in 160/776f. by dismissing Abū 'Awn in favour of another Khurāsānī, Mu'ādh b. Muslim, who had participated in the suppression of the revolts of Ustādhsīs.[42] Mu'ādh arrived in Marw in 161/777f. and marched to Bukhārā, where he spent some time fighting the Turks, who now seem to have represented the main danger. From Bukhārā he proceeded to Samarqand and reconquered the city together with Jibra'īl b. Yaḥyā. From there he moved on to al-Muqanna''s fortress.[43] At some point the command of the war was transferred to Sa'īd al-Ḥarashī, perhaps in 163/779f., when Mu'ādh b. Muslim was dismissed from the governorship of Khurāsān, reportedly at his own request.[44] The new governor was al-Musayyab b. Zuhayr al-Ḍabbī, who held office from 163/779f. to 166/782f. or the beginning of 167/783f.,[45] and it was during his tenure that Sa'īd al-Ḥarashī succeeded in occupying al-Muqanna''s fortress.[46] Unlike Mu'ādh, he did not break the siege during the winter,[47] so the rebels were starved out and gradually surrendered, leaving al-Muqanna' with his wives, servants, and other close confidants (including his Arab father-in-law) in the inner fortress. When the outer fortress fell he committed suicide.[48]

The sources usually give 163/779f. as the date of al-Muqanna''s death,[49] but Sallāmī places it in 166/782f.,[50] others in 167/783f.,[51] or even in 169/785f. (but this is simply a scribal mistake for 167).[52] The first date is usually accepted as correct, but a good case can be made for 166 as well.[53]

[41] Crone and Jafari Jazi, I, §§1–8 and commentary, II, 401–5.
[42] Tab. iii, 477; cf. Chapter 7.
[43] *TB*, 69f./98f. = 71f.; Crone and Jafari Jazi, I, §§11ff., esp. §14.
[44] Tab iii, 484; *TB*, 70/99 = 72; Crone and Jafari Jazi, I, §§11ff.
[45] Khalīfa, 696; Tab. iii, 500, 517; Ḥamza al-Iṣfahānī, 222/164 (here Zuhayr b. al-Musayyab); Gardīzī, 282f. (where he holds office 166–7).
[46] This is explicit in the *Tārīkhnāma* (Crone and Jafari Jazi, I, §24) and also clear in Gardīzī, 155, 282; *TB*, 70/99 = 72.
[47] Crone and Jafari Jazi, I, §§17, 20.1.
[48] Crone and Jafari Jazi, I, §19ff. and commentary.
[49] Khalīfa, 687; Tab. iii, 494; Azdī, 244.1; Abū 'l-Ma'ālī, 60.
[50] Cited in Nasafī, *Qand*, no. 287. The same date or early 167 is implied in Gardīzī, 282f., and Mustawfī, *Tārīkh-i Guzīda*, 299, also has 166.
[51] *TB*, 64/90 = 65.
[52] Bīrūnī, *Āthār*, 211.
[53] See Sadighi, *Mouvements*, 179/223f.; Tābān, 'Qiyām-i Muqanna'', 549; *EIr.*, 'Moqanna'' (Crone).

A DISTURBED REGION

Like Bābak's Azerbaijan, Khurāsān and Transoxania in al-Muqanna''s time were regions racked by violence, but in a different way. In Azerbaijan the violence was generated by Arab colonists, warlords, and brigands, and semi-private in both nature and aim. In Transoxania we do not hear of any colonists or warlords, and though we do hear of brigands the most salient form of violence here was warfare generated by the activities of the Muslim state.

The revolts

Khurāsān has a history of constant revolt from the late Umayyad period to the rise of the Ṭāhirids. In 116/734 al-Ḥārith b. Surayj rebelled against the Umayyad governor and allied himself with the Turks, calling for justice of some kind until he died in 120/738. Six years later, in 126/744, the Muslims were plunged into civil war, whereupon the Hāshimiyya came out in revolt, captured Marw, and set off to conquer the western parts of the caliphate while Abū Muslim stayed behind to complete the subjection of Khurāsān. In 132/750, the year in which the first ʿAbbāsid caliph was enthroned, or in the year thereafter, two Arab members of the Hāshimite movement, Sharīk b. Shaykh al-Mahrī and an Azdī who was governor of Bukhārā at the time, rebelled at Bukhārā in the hope of replacing the newly enthroned ʿAbbāsid with an ʿAlid. 'It was not for this that we followed the family of Muḥammad, to shed blood and act unjustly,' as Sharīk said, with reference to Abū Muslim's ruthless extermination of real and alleged enemies of the revolution in Khurāsān.[54] This revolt was suppressed by Ziyād b. Ṣāliḥ, another Arab member of the Hāshimiyya.

In 133/751 this Ziyād b. Ṣāliḥ moved on to defeat the Chinese at Talas. In 134/751f. Abū Dāwūd, al-Muqanna''s employer, marched into Kish, where he killed the local king along with a number of his *dihqān*s and replaced him with a brother;[55] about the same time the *bukhārkhudā*, the king of Bukhārā, who had assisted Ziyād b. Ṣāliḥ in his suppression of Sharīk al-Mahrī, was also killed and replaced with a brother;[56] and the king (*ikhshīd*) of Samarqand may have suffered the same fate. Apparently

[54] Tab. iii, 74 (year 133); BA, III, 171; Maqdisī, VI, 74; *TB*, 60ff./86ff. = 62ff.; Gardīzī, 268f. (132 AH); Karev, 'Politique d'Abū Muslim', 8ff.

[55] Tab. iii, 79f.; Karev, 'Politique d'Abū Muslim', 18f.

[56] *TB*, 9/14f. = 10f.

they had rebelled or engaged in other subversive activity: an appeal for help from the ruler of Bukhārā and others was received by the Chinese in 752 (the princes had not apparently seen the Chinese defeat at Talas as decisive).[57] Abū Dāwūd carried away Chinese goods from Kish and took them to Abū Muslim at Samarqand, where Ziyād b. Ṣāliḥ was left in charge.[58] In 135/752f., however, Ziyād b. Ṣāliḥ himself rebelled.[59] It was as a member of Abū Dāwūd's forces against this rebel that al-Muqanna' was said to have lost an eye.[60]

In 137/755 Abū Muslim was killed by the second 'Abbāsid caliph in Iraq and his troops rebelled at Rayy under Sunbādh, as we have seen. They were suppressed by Jahwar b. Marār al-'Ijlī, an Arab veteran of the revolution, but Jahwar proceeded to rebel in his turn along with a number of top Iranian horsemen in his army, including two Sogdian commanders in Iraq, Zuwāra al-Bukhārī and al-Ishtākhanj.[61] Al-Ishtākhanj was presumably a member of the dynasty that used to rule Samarqand: they had moved their residence to Ishtākhanj, a town 60 kilometres north-west of Samarqand, when Samarqand was occupied by the Arabs.[62] As late as 745 the ruler of Ishtākhanj had asked for incorporation into the Chinese realm.[63] Now a member of his family was a (rebellious) general in the service of the Muslims along with the *ahl Ishtākhanj*, troops from this region who were lodged in the Ḥarbiyya quarter when Baghdad was built.[64] By 756–7 the upheavals in eastern Iran had uprooted enough people for the Chinese to have 'Arab' (i.e., Muslim) troops in their armies against An-Lushan.[65]

In 141/758f. the governor of Khurāsān, 'Abd al-Jabbār al-Azdī, rebelled in favour of the 'Alids. 'Abd al-Jabbār, another veteran of the revolution, was the man who caused our Hāshim to be sent to jail in Iraq. Among the governors who reacted to his revolt by rebelling against him was

57 For the view that this battle was in fact an accidental encounter of no great importance for later events in Central Asia see S. Maejima quoted in Inaba, 'Arab Soldiers in China', 40. (My thanks to Debbie Tor for sending me this article.)

58 Tab. iii, 79; Dhahabī, *Ta'rīkh*, V, 211; IA, V, 453, all claiming that the king of Kish was killed in a state of obedience (*wa-huwa sāmi' muṭī'*); Karev, 'Politique d'Abū Muslim', 17, 19.

59 Tab. iii, 81f.; Karev, 'Politique d'Abū Muslim', 25f.

60 See n. 15 of this chapter.

61 Tab. iii, 122, cf. n. d; BA, III, 247.15; Justi, *Namenbuch*, 337, 388 (Uzwārak).

62 *EI*[2], s.v. 'Ikhshīd'; cf. also Tab. ii, 1598.

63 Chavannes, *Notes additionelles*, 75f., cf. also 72.

64 YB, 248.17.

65 Inaba, 'Arab Soldiers in China', 36–9.

al-Ashʿath b. Yaḥyā al-Ṭāʾī, a distinguished participant in the revolution. He rose up at Ishtākhanj and proceeded to occupy Bukhārā and Samarqand, where he struck coins bearing the *tamgha* of the *ikhshīd* of Sogdia (then lodged at Ishtākanj)[66] in 143/760f. and again in 144/761f. as the representative of the future caliph al-Mahdī, then at Rayy as the titular governor of Khurāsān.[67] Meanwhile a massive revolt broke out in what is now south-eastern Iran and Afghanistan, led by Ustādhsīs: by the 140s/760s Sīstān, Bust, Herat, and Bādghīs were under his control.[68]

By 151/768f. Hāshim b. Ḥakīm was back in Marw to remake himself as al-Muqannaʿ, and some years later his followers were rebelling in Samarqand, Kish, Nasaf, and Bukhārā: the *bukhārkhudā* lent his support to the rebels, to be assassinated at the order of the caliph after the suppression of al-Muqannaʿ's movement.[69] The *ikhshīd* may also have found it useful to support al-Muqannaʿ, for he is said to have accepted obedience to al-Mahdī, implying that he had been in a state of disobedience before.[70] Al-Muqannaʿ must admittedly have come across to him as a rival, for as noted, he or the *khāqān* who conquered Samarqand for him had adopted the title of 'king of Sogdia'; but one could use one rival to defeat another and hope to come out as the winner in the end. At all events, while al-Muqannaʿ was threatening to take control of Sogdia, another non-Arab by the name of Yūsuf al-Barm rebelled in Ṭukhāristan in 160/776f. in the name of an uncertain religious message, possibly Khārijite, to take control of Būshanj (where he expelled Ṭāhir's grandfather), as well as Marw al-Rūdh, Ṭālaqān, and Jūzjān.[71] In 163/779f. or 166/782f. al-Muqannaʿ was defeated, but in 190/805f. Samarqand rebelled under Rāfiʿ b. Layth,[72] a grandson of the last Umayyad governor who had participated in the suppression of al-Muqannaʿ's revolt.[73] His ideological aegis remains unclear as well, but his supporters included sons of the participants in the Hāshimite revolution (*abnāʾ al-shīʿa*),[74] Ṭāhir among them.[75] He also

[66] Karev, 'Politique d'Abū Muslim', 20n.

[67] BA, III, 229, where the patronymic is wrong; Bates, 'Khurāsānī Revolutionaries', 300. For his position in the *daʿwa* see *AA*, 221.-5.

[68] See Chapter 7.

[69] *TB*, 9/14f. = 10f.

[70] YT, II, 479.

[71] See Chapter 7, n. 87.

[72] Tab. iii, 707f.

[73] Gardīzī, 279; IA, VI, 39; Crone and Jaʿfari Jazi, I, commentary to §9.6.

[74] Tab. iii, 732.

[75] Ibn Ḥazm, *Jamhara*, 184.4 (claiming that Rāfiʿ had called to the Umayyads); cf. Kaabi, *Ṭāhirides*, I, 66.

received support from Nasaf,[76] and took Bukhārā;[77] and, like al-Muqanna', he allied himself with the Turks.[78] The ruler of Shāsh and unspecified inhabitants of Farghāna joined the revolt as well,[79] and this time it spread into Ṭukhāristan, apparently including Balkh.[80] Even Marw looked in danger of falling to him.[81] In 192/807f. Hārūn al-Rashīd set out for Khurāsān together with his son al-Ma'mūn to deal with the problem (whereupon the Khurramīs of Jibāl rebelled).[82]

The arrival of al-Ma'mūn was a turning-point, however. The *abnā' al-shī'a* in Rāfi''s camp, or some of them, deserted to the 'Abbāsid side in 192/807f., and Rāfi' himself surrendered in 194/809f. in return for *amān*, which was duly honoured.[83] Now closely allied with the Ṭāhirids,[84] al-Ma'mūn proceeded to secure the allegiance of the local rulers and recruit them and their followers into his army; they included sons of the *bukhārkhudā*, who followed Ṭāhir to Baghdad.[85] In 205/821 al-Ma'mūn appointed Ṭāhir, whose son 'Abdallāh he adopted and brought up (*tabannāhu wa-rabāhu*),[86] to a position amounting to viceroy of the east; and though Ṭāhir was apparently becoming rebellious in his turn shortly before his death in 207/822, eastern Iran continued to be governed by a Ṭāhirid viceroy thereafter. Transoxania was now firmly integrated in the Muslim world as part of an autonomous region.[87] When the men who had been sent to cope with the crisis of Ṭāhir's death returned to Iraq they brought with them a number of princes from eastern Iran, including the prince of Ushrūsana, Khaydhār b. Kā'ūs, better known as the Afshīn.[88] The king of Ushrūsana had been among those who appealed to the Chinese for help against the Arabs in 752;[89] now he joined the

76 Tab. iii, 712; Barthold, *Turkestan*, 205.
77 Tab. iii, 734, where it is reconquered from his brother Bashīr.
78 Tab. iii, 712, 775.
79 Tab. iii, 712, 724.
80 Tab. iii, 729, cf. 724, 727.
81 Tab. iii, 713.
82 Tab. iii, 730f.
83 Tab. iii, 732, 777.
84 Cf. Azdī, 318.1.
85 Tab. iii, 852, 1203, 1215; Dīnawarī, 398.
86 Shābushtī, *Diyārāt*, 132 (fol. 56a).
87 *EI*², s.v. 'Ṭāhir b. al-Ḥusayn', 'Ṭāhirids'; Kaabi, *Ṭāhirides*, I, 139ff.
88 YT, II, 557. The Barmakid Faḍl b. Yaḥyā is credited with a similar policy in the east in 178/794f. (Tab. iii, 631).
89 Karev, 'Politique d'Abū Muslim', 17.

Muslims, and it was Haydhar b. Kāʾūs who suppressed Bābak's revolt for al-Muʿtaṣim, assisted by a descendant of the *bukhārkhudā*.[90]

The fundamental changes

It is nothing if not a confusing picture, but two fundamental changes are discernible behind the endless violence: the traditional Sogdian elite was being replaced by a Muslim one, and at the same time the Umayyad elite was being replaced by a Hāshimite one. One might have thought it impossible for the Hāshimites to effect two such fundamental changes at the same time, but despite the chaos caused by the civil war, revolution, and post-revolutionary struggles the Muslims were clearly tightening their grip on Sogdia at the expense of the local princes, the Turks, and the Chinese alike. It was as a general in the caliphal army that the ruler of Ishtākhanj rebelled in 138/755f., while the man who rose up at Ishtākhan, three years later, using the the *tamgha* of the *ikhshīd* of Sogdia, was an Arab long settled in Khurāsān: the Arab and the Sogdian have changed places. It was in defence of his own position at Bukhārā that the *bukhārkhudā* cooperated with the pro-ʿAbbāsid Muslims against the pro-ʿAlid rebels led by Sharīk al-Mahrī; but it was in defence of the same position that he 'apostatised' soon thereafter along with other Sogdian princes, and that his successor sided with al-Muqannaʿ, as perhaps the Samarqandī equivalent did as well; but like al-Ishtākhanj the *bukhārkhudā*'s relatives ended up as officers in the caliphal army, and so eventually did the Afshīn. It goes without saying that the removal of the old Sogdian elite must have been highly disruptive. The traditional channels of authority in the region will have been destroyed as local rulers of the region were reduced to mere stooges or departed to join the Hāshimite army, sometimes with substantial sectors of their populations in tow, leaving behind non-Muslim populations without leaders of the type they knew, or without trust in such leaders as remained.

Trust also appears to have been a prime casualty of the replacement of the Umayyad by the Hāshimite elite. In the Umayyad period there had typically been close personal connections, often kinship ties, between the caliph and the governor of Khurāsān: it was on the trust between those two men that Umayyad control of the province rested. But the revolution introduced an element of suspicion between caliph and the Khurāsānīs which lasted until the Ṭāhirids were put in charge. It was the Khurāsānīs who had enthroned the new dynasty, and the caliphs were naturally keen

[90] See Chapter 3, n. 189.

to break their ties of dependence on the men to whom they owed their position. The second ʿAbbāsid caliph, al-Manṣūr, was in the particularly galling position of owing his throne to Abū Muslim twice over, for his succession had been disputed, and Abū Muslim had obligingly come from Khurāsān to defeat the other claimant, ʿAbdallāh b. ʿAlī. Where would al-Manṣūr have been if Abū Muslim had decided to withdraw his support from him? Worse still, the entire army back in Khurāsān was dangerous to him. There were Khurāsānīs who had expected an ʿAlid to succeed, at least after the death of Ibrāhīm al-Imām, and there were others who came out in favour of the ʿAlids, disillusioned, like Sharīk al-Mahrī, by the harshness of the post-revolutionary regime. As a result, al-Manṣūr harboured deep suspicions about the loyalty of both the ʿAlids, whom he began to persecute on a scale unprecedented in the days of the Umayyads, and his own army in Khurāsān. Rightly or wrongly, they in their turn believed him to be intriguing against them. Rumour credited al-Ṣaffāḥ with a role in the sudden revolt of Ziyād b. Ṣāliḥ, who had supposedly been enlisted for a plot against Abū Muslim; many believed al-Manṣūr to have engineered the death of Abū Muslim's successor as governor, Abū Dāwūd, though other stories were current as well;[91] and he was certainly responsible for the assassination of Abū Muslim.

It must have been the mutual fear between the caliph and Khurāsān that triggered the surprisingly numerous revolts by apparent pillars of the regime who made sudden changes of allegiance. Ziyād b. Ṣāliḥ apart, Jahwar b. Marār, Zuwāra al-Bukhārī, al-Ishtākhanj, ʿAbd al-Jabbār, and Rāfiʿ b. Layth are all in that category.[92] There is a later example in Ḥātim b. Harthama, the governor of Azerbaijan who had hitherto been a pillar of the regime along with his father, who planned to rebel when he heard that his father had been executed: he must have assumed (undoubtedly correctly) that he was next on the list. The only reasonable explanation of the behaviour of the earlier Khurāsānīs is that, like Ḥātim, they suspected that they had fallen out of favour. Of ʿAbd al-Jabbār, who had faithfully been purging the army of pro-ʿAlid commanders for the caliph when he suddenly went over to the ʿAlid side himself, we are told that the caliph had

91 Daniel, *Khurasan*, 111f., 159.

92 According to Balādhurī, al-Ḥasan b. Ḥumrān, a *mawlā* veteran of the revolution who took action against the rebellious ʿAbd al-Jabbār, also changed sides and was killed by the governor sent by al-Mahdī (BA, III, 229.4). But according to Gardīzī, 275.ult., 276.4f., he was a loyalist who lived into the governorship of Abū ʿAwn ʿAbd al-Malik b. Yazīd (143–9), when he and his brother were killed in an army mutiny, and this fits the numismatic evidence (Bates, 'Khurāsānī Revolutionaries', 300f.).

tested his loyalty in diverse ways in reponse to rumours that he was turning unreliable. It was the Iraqi bureaucrats who had come up with the tests, and quite possibly with the rumours too, for reasons that may not have had anything to do with events in Khurāsān: ʿAbd al-Jabbār's family held powerful positions back in Iraq, and of intrigues at the court there was no shortage. It must at all events have been clear to ʿAbd al-Jabbār that the caliph no longer trusted him. The caliph was distant, imperfectly informed, suspicious, and all too prone to making up for his weak position by using intrigues and assassination as his means of control; nobody was safe; rumours abounded. Things may have improved under al-Manṣūr's successors, but that was too late to prevent the disaffection of al-Muqannaʿ, a small cog in the wheel to whom al-Manṣūr is unlikely to have devoted much attention.

We have a situation in which all structures of authority, rural or urban, local or central, have been shaken, leaving a highly unstable political landscape; and for all the success of the Hāshimiyya in hanging on to the state apparatus, subjecting local rulers, and even bringing new areas under its control, their efficacy on the ground was clearly limited. Leaving aside the difficulty of replacing traditional channels of authority, the endless succession of revolts will have paralysed such ability as the cities retained to impose control. Bukhārā was involved in no less than five major revolts in the fifty years after the revolution, not counting the revolution itself: one in favour of the ʿAlids under Sharīk, one for the recovery of princely autonomy under the *bukhārkhudā*, one against a rebellious governor under al-Ashʿath al-Ṭāʾī, one in favour of a divine manifestation on earth in the form of al-Muqannaʿ, and one for justice of some kind under Rāfiʿ b. Layth. It had been through a revolution and three revolts of a quite different nature by the time al-Muqannaʿ began; and all will have involved purges, the disbanding of defeated armies, the burning of villages, the stringing up of people on gallows, the flight of peasants from their land, and increased taxation for the survivors. Greater Khurāsān was a region teeming with displaced people, ruled by new men who were still sorting out power relations among themselves, in an atmosphere in which nobody knew who was going to be on whose side next, and in which one might be better off as a rebel than as a passive victim.

All this is what modern scholars have in mind when they speak of Khurāsānī 'disappointment' with the revolution. It is a dreadfully simplistic expression. It casts the Khurāsānīs as an undifferentiated set of powerless people oppressed by an undifferentiated set of rulers, the former identified as Iranians and the latter as Arabs, and it rests on the assumption that 'justice' was all the new rulers had to dispense to their passive subjects in order for everyone to return to business as usual. There was no business as usual to return to: this was what the new regime had to create. The revolution involved a fundamental redistribution and reorganisation of power; and inevitably this was a protracted affair involving the liquidation of most of the original leaders, the disillusionment of its once bright-eyed participants, and the killing of countless real and alleged opponents. There were winners and losers at all points: who was disappointed and who pleased depends on where we look and which particular time and place. Al-Muqanna' was one of the winners for a while. He made his career and lost it again at a time when power was being established and dismantled at dizzying speed, and the same unstable conditions were still prevalent when he came out of jail. He could have tried to keep his head down. Instead he made his own bid for power, setting out to establish a separate community in which he would be in control.

THE WHITE-CLOTHED ONES AND COLOUR-CODING

Al-Muqanna' did not rebel as the leader of an existing cult society, as Bābak was to do, but rather created his own organisation, drawing on his experience as a member of the Hāshimiyya: he sent missionaries from Marw[93] and had *naqīb*s (though the name of the one we hear about is spurious).[94] But he did target a particular religious group, the White-clothed ones, so we need to look more closely at them.

As mentioned already, we do not know on what basis the Khurramīs were divided into White-clothed ones (*mubayyiḍa*, *sapīdjāmagān*) and Red-clothed ones (*muḥammira*, *surkhjāmagān*). We do not even know why it was in terms of colour that they were identified. There are some scraps of evidence, however, to suggest that colour-coding was associated with apocalyptic expectations and that it had spread from China.

The Khurramī use of colour-coding is normally explained as a reflection of the fact that the Hāshimiyya adopted black clothing and banners when they rebelled, and so came to be known as the Black-clothed ones (*musawwida*). The new dynasty retained black as its emblem, and the opponents of the 'Abbāsids supposedly used a different colour to signal their rejection of the 'Abbāsid regime.[95] This explanation is found already in the medieval

93 *TB*, 65/91f. = 66f.; Abū 'l-Ma'ālī, 58.9; cf. Maqdisī, VI, 97 (where he sends them from his fortress).

94 *TB*, 69.-4/98.2 = 71; cf. Crone and Jafari Jazi, II, 283, *ad* I, §4.4 (on Sa'diyān/Sughdiyān).

95 Thus Barthold, *Turkestan*, 201; Sadighi, *Mouvements*, 170n./217n.; cf. also Daniel, *Khurasan*, 132.

sources.[96] But there must be more to it, for we hear of Red-clothed ones in eastern Iran before the Hāshimite revolution.

In 119/737 the Turkish *khāqān* marched against the Arab governor Asad in Transoxania surrounded by four hundred horsemen dressed in red. We would not have been told about the red clothes if they did not carry special significance and, since the *khāqān* was trying to oust the Arabs from Transoxania, one takes his red-clothed horsemen to have signalled that the end of the Arab regime was nigh.[97] Red-clothed ones are also expected to destroy the Arabs and Islam in Zoroastrian apocalyptic.[98] In 132/749f. Marwān II had 3,000 red-clothed ones (*muḥammira*) along with other special troops in his army.[99] He must have recruited them in Armenia–Azerbaijan, where he had served as governor until he made his bid for the throne and where we later hear of Khurramīs classified as Muḥammira. Once again, the wearers of red were indigenous people, but this time they were probably converts who paraded their apocalyptic colours by way of antidote to the *musawwida* from Khurāsān. Thereafter the symbolic language appears in Syria as a fully domesticated expression of local apocalyptic hopes in 133/750f.: in that year an Umayyad dressed himself and his troops in red to rebel as the Sufyānī against the black-clothed ones at Aleppo.[100] In some sense, then, it is quite true that the use of red was meant as a rejection of Hāshimite/ʿAbbāsid claims, but it did not owe its existence to mere inversion of the latter's idiom.

The use of white is not attested before the Hāshimite revolution. It is in Syria that we first encounter it, again as a fully domesticated expression of apocalyptic hopes, in connection with a series of rebellions against the Hāshimites in the Ḥawrān, Damascus, Qinnasrīn, and Mesopotamia in 132/749f.[101] It reappears in connection with ʿAlid revolts against the ʿAbbāsids: the followers of Ibrāhīm and Muḥammad b. ʿAbdallāh al-Nafs al-Zakiyya's revolt in Arabia and Iraq in 145/162 are called *mubayyiḍa* in some sources,[102] and sundry ʿAlid rebels thereafter are

96 Khwārizmī, 28; Samʿānī, *Ansāb*, s.v. 'mubayyiḍī'.

97 Tab. ii, 1610.

98 *GrBd*, 33:24; *Zand ī Wahman Yasn*, 6:3 (red hats, armour, banners), 5 (red banners), with the comments of Cereti at 199; Daryaee, 'Historical Episode', 67ff., adding *Zardūštnāma* 94.1448, and taking the reference to be to Khurramīs.

99 Tab. iii, 40.2.

100 Azdī, 142; Maqdisī, VI, 73 (where he wears white); Ibn al-ʿAdīm, *Zubda*, I, 56 (where his name is garbled); Cobb, *White Banners*, 47, 49.

101 Tab. iii, 51.ult-54, 55–8; Ps.-Dionysius, tr. Hespel, 150; Cobb, *White Banners*, 47ff., 76ff.

102 Baghdādī, *Taʾrīkh Baghdād*, XIII, 386.4.

said to have put on white (*bayyaḍū*).[103] In Khurāsān we first hear of white-clothed ones in 140/757, when members of a group directed by the weaver Saʿīd reputedly assassinated the governor Abū Dāwūd.[104]

It is perhaps because the adoption of white is first attested in connection with Umayyad revolts against the Hāshimiyya that it has been explained as a simple inversion of their adoption of black (the use of red is less frequently discussed). But the weaver Saʿīd takes us to a completely different setting from that encountered in Syria and Iraq. The Umayyads and 'Alids who adopted white clothing and/or banners against the 'Abbāsids were princely contenders for the caliphate who were not normally known as White-clothed ones. In Transoxania, by contrast, the White-clothed ones were humble people who owed their name to their membership of a religious organisation and who were known by that name whether they were in a state of revolt or not. The killers of Abū Dāwūd were 'from among the people (*qawm*) of Saʿīd the Weaver', as Gardīzī specifies, implying that there were several such groups. The killers were seized, 'and Saʿīd the Weaver, who was the leader of those people, was also arrested': Saʿīd had not participated in the action, then; he was arrested because the killers belonged to his constituency. One year later the next governor of Khurāsān, 'Abd al-Jabbār, rebelled and, as has been seen, he too adopted white clothing and/or banners, which Gardīzī took to mean that he made joint cause with the religious groups called *sapīdjāmagān*.[105] This is also how it is taken by modern scholars.[106] In eastern Iran, in other words, the white clothes were associated with membership of a religious organisation. This is why Niẓām al-Mulk casts the Umayyad users of white in Syria as Shīʿites and Bāṭinīs in his chapter on how Khurramīs, Shīʿites, and Bāṭinīs were really all the same![107] Like the Red-clothed ones, the users of white probably existed before the Hāshimite revolution.

This suggests that the Hāshimiyya owed their colour-coding to the Khurramīs rather than the other way round. They were active in Khurāsān for some twenty or thirty years before they took to arms, and Khurramīs were among the indigenous people that they sought to enrol, as has been seen. They presided over a religious organisation much like Jāvīdhān's in Azerbaijan: it took the form of headquarters (in Marw) and a network of remoter communities, whose leaders were in constant touch with the headquarters. The Hāshimite organisation

103 Maqdisī, VI, 109f.; MM, V, §§3145, 3278, 3517 (VIII, 33, 140, 353).
104 Gardīzī, 273.
105 BA, III, 229.11; Gardīzī, 274.-3; cf. above, p. 110.
106 Thus Barthold, *Turkestan*, 203; Daniel, *Khurasan*, 133, 160.
107 *SN*, ch. 46:39 (311 = 238).

was much tighter and maintained over much larger distances than Bābak's, for unlike their Iranian counterparts the Hāshimites were working towards a single aim from the start. When the members of Khurramī groups such as Jāvīdhān's came together one assumes that they did so to participate in shared rituals, exchange news, perhaps also to resolve doctrinal and other disputes, and to listen to songs or stories about the age of bliss to come when the redeemer manifested himself. When the members of Hāshimite communities came together we may take it that they too shared meals, news, prayers, gossip, and daydreams about the time ahead, but they were under a single political direction from Marw and had a political agenda to go through as well. Their organisation had been created for the sake of a clearly defined political objective, not simply to further a particular way of life, and it ceased to exist once the aim had been accomplished. This difference notwithstanding, it makes good sense to assume that the Hāshimiyya modelled their organisation on those of the people they wished to convert: they practised mimicry, so to speak, disseminating Islam through cult societies of a type familiar to the locals so as to persuade them that their religion was not alien, merely better. It will have been in that context that they adopted the colour language too.

What, then, can we say about the colour language of the Khurramīs? One way to pursue that question is to go to China, for there were white-clothed ones in China too. Originally they were laymen who observed some or all the rules for Buddhist monks without becoming monks themselves, as opposed to red-clothed Buddhists who were monks with shaven heads. In China, however, the white clothes developed into a distinctive feature of the sects associated with Maitreya, the Buddha who would come at a time of great evil to restore the pure *dharma* and inaugurate an age of bliss. Maitreya societies were formed to prepare for his coming. They were not necessarily rebellious, but some took to arms, led by men who claimed to be incarnations of Maitreya or of the righteous ruler who would welcome him,[108] and the colour white is prominent in their revolts. White-clothed rebels are mentioned as far back as 524, without being further identified. They reappear in an insurrection of 610, this time explicitly identified as Maitreya followers.[109] In 629 and 715 the government prohibited seditious societies of people with 'white dress and long hair who falsely claim that Maitreya has descended and been

[108] Ch'en, *Buddhism in China*, 427ff.
[109] Seiwert and Ma, *Popular Religious Movements*, 152f.

reborn'.[110] The emperor Tien-pao (742–56) prohibited the martial arts on the grounds that the imperial troops and guards 'were all white-clothed fellows from the market place'.[111] After a revolt of 1047 the authorities banned Maitreya societies, and as late as 1257 they found it necessary to ban a white-clothed society.[112] Much later the devotees of Maitreya used red or white cloth sashes to identify themselves during the time of violence preceding the messianic era.[113] Colour-coding went a long way back in China: the Red Eyebrows who rebelled in 18 AD painted their eyebrows red; the Yellow Turbans, who rebelled in 184, donned yellow headgear. The colour served as a uniform which made them recognisable to each other and heightened the religious significance of the fighting. That this was also its function in eastern Iran is suggested by the fact that the monochrome clothing was donned when the warfare began.

It may have been in interaction between Zoroastrianism and Buddhism that the Maitreya figure developed,[114] and he was certainly popular among the Iranians and Turks of Central Asia. Prophecies about him and the wonderful future he would inaugurate are preserved in Sogdian, Uighur, Tokharian, and Khotanese;[115] he was depicted with Sasanian royal features at Bāmiyān and in the Tarim basin,[116] and he appears together with other Buddhas in Bactrian protective amulets.[117] It is possible, then, that the idea of colour-coding travelled from China to Transoxania, carried by Sogdian merchants who had returned as devotees of this Buddha. From Sogdian Buddhists it could have passed to Sogdian Zoroastrians, who will have associated the white colour with their own messianic heroes, white being the colour of the clothes of their priests. Sogdian Manichaeans certainly adopted Maitreya, sometimes identifying him with Mani, and the colour will have been meaningful to them too, their Elect being depicted in Central Asian paintings as

110 Seiwert and Ma, *Popular Religious Movements*, 151; for the prohibition of 629 see Chu, *Introductory Study of the White Lotus Sect*, 26f.

111 Pulleyblank, *Rebellion of An Lu-Shan*, 67.

112 Seiwert and Ma, *Popular Religious Movements*, 154; Ch'en, *Buddhism in China*, 428f. The prohibition of 1257 is elsewhere placed in 1259.

113 Naquin, *Shantung Rebellion*, 60.

114 Basham, *The Wonder that was India*, 276.

115 MacKenzie, '*Sūtra of Causes and Effects*', lines 214f.; Emmerick, *Book of Zambasta*, 22:113–335; Abegg, *Buddha Maitreya*, 24.

116 Scott, 'Iranian Face of Buddhism', 51f.

117 Sims-Williams, *Bactrian Documents*, II, doc. Za, 7.

wearing white robes and hats.[118] In short, devotion to a messianic figure will have come to be associated with a colour, initially white, to be used as a distinguishing feature in the apocalyptic wars when they broke out.

The Hāshimiyya replaced white with black, perhaps inspired by Pišyōtan (also known as Čitromēsan), the legendary figure waiting in the fortress of Kangdiz: he was expected to emerge from it with companions dressed in black sables.[119] He would also carry a club (*vazr* = *varz*, *gorz*), and wooden clubs were of great religious significance to the black-clothed revolutionaries, who called them 'infidel-bashers' (*kāfirkūbāt*).[120] When Khurāsānī revolutionaries turned against the 'Abbāsid mahdi, replacing him with Abū Muslim, they sometimes envisaged the latter along the lines of Pišyōtan, as has been seen;[121] this also suggests that the Hāshimiyya had modelled their messianic imagery on him. How some came to replace white with red is more difficult to say. It seems unlikely that the Buddhist distinction between red-clothed monks and white-clothed laymen should have had anything to do with it. Some modern scholars hold red to have been the colour of the warrior class in Iran, which would obviously make it suitable for use in apocalyptic battle, but the evidence is poor.[122] Whom the Red-clothed ones envisaged as the messiah before their adoption of Abū Muslim is unknown.

To sum up, the colour-coded groups that we meet in Iran from the late Umayyad period onwards seem to have been members of societies awaiting the coming of the messiah, originally the Buddhist Maitreya, later probably Manichaean and Zoroastrian saviours too, and eventually the

118 Klimkeit, *Manichaean Art*, 24, 29. For the Manichaean adoption of Maitreya see below, p. 132. Cf. also Drijvers, *Bardaisan*, 106f.

119 Boyce, 'Antiquity of Zoroastrian Apocalyptic', 65, citing *Dk*, IX, 15.11 (16, 15 in West, *SBE*, XXXVII, 203), on the lost *Sūdgar Nask*, where Pišyōtan's followers wear black sables and have 10,000 banners; cf. *Dk*, VII, 8, 45f. (West, *SBE* XLVII, 104); *PRDd*, 49:12; *Zand i Wahman Yasn*, 7:22, 24, 8:7 (3:27, 29, 42, in West, *SBE*, V, 226f., 238), where the followers only number 150; Abegg, *Messiasglaube*, 221, takes the *Dk* to refer to black felt.

120 The club only figures in *Dk*, VII, 8, 45, 49 (West, *SBE*, XLVII, 104f.); cf. Crone, 'Wooden Weapons', 177, 180ff. (dismissive of the Iranian association as then proposed).

121 See above, pp. 38f., 104.

122 Widengren, 'Bābakīyah and the Mithraic Mysteries', 684, 685n., invoking Dumézil; Rossi, 'Perception et symbologie des couleurs' (drawn to my attention by Etienne de la Vaissière). In *DkM*, 203, ed. and tr. in Zaehner, 'Zurvanica, I', 305 = 307, the garments of warriorhood are red and water-blue (also Zaehner, *Zurvan*, 375 = 378, where they are red and wine-coloured), adorned with all kinds of ornament, with silver, gold, chalcedony, and ruby; cf. *GrBd* 3:4, tr. Zaehner, *Zurvan*, 333, where it is of gold and silver, *aryavān* (uncertain, translated purple with reference to *DkM*; cf. Zaehner, *Zurvan*, 326 *ad* line 15), and multi-coloured.

Muslim mahdi. The only time we see them in a completely non-Islamic (Buddhist?) form is in the Red-clothed ones accompanying the *khāqān*. The Reds recruited by Marwān II were probably converts of sorts, but we do not actually know. Saʿīd the Weaver was sufficiently within the penumbra of Muslim society to bear an Arab name. His beliefs could still have been as un-Islamic as those of Jāvīdhān's followers, who also included men bearing Muslim names, but the White-clothed ones to whom ʿAbd al-Jabbār appealed were probably recruits of the Hāshimiyya who had expected the mahdi to be or enthrone Ibrāhīm al-Imām. The Red-clothed ones of Jurjān who rebelled after the revolution were devotees of Abū Muslim, as was probably true of many other Reds and Whites by then. But red and white had also come to be used as a simple sign of dissent in revolts against the Black-clothed ones, who were now saddled with the task of coping with the messianic expectations that had carried them to power.

It was the White-clothed ones who seized the fortresses in Sogdia for al-Muqannaʿ, who gathered around him when he moved from Marw to Sogdia, and who are consistently named as his followers in the sources. Most of them were clearly Sogdian non-Muslims: they bear names such as *Krdk*, *Ḥjmy*, *Khshwī*, and *Srjmy*.[123] But ʿUmar Sūbakhī, who started the uprisings at Kish, was or had presumably been some sort of Muslim,[124] and the same is true of Ḥakīm-i Aḥmad, the sage Aḥmad or Ḥakīm, the son of Aḥmad, who also appears as Ḥakīm-i Bukhārī and who was the leader of the rebels at Bukhārā.[125] They were not all devotees of Abū Muslim, however. We hear of a woman who was headman of the village of Narshakh in Bukhārā and whose husband, from whom she had presumably inherited the position, had been an officer in Abū Muslim's army: Abū Muslim had executed him. She was now among the White-clothed ones that Jibraʾīl b. Yaḥyā fought against at Narshakh, where she and a cousin of hers were captured and put to death; she had refused to pardon Abū Muslim on the grounds that a man who had killed her husband could not be the father of the Muslims.[126] Apparently she counted herself as a Muslim. This story has evoked surprise because Abū Muslim was a hero to al-Muqannaʿ, but it was the same target that Abū Muslim was being directed against whether he was being elevated or denigrated, namely the

[123] See Crone and Jafari Jazi, II, 406.
[124] *TB*, 65/92 = 67; Abū ʾl-Maʿālī, 58 (Farrūkhī).
[125] *TB*, 66, 69/94, 97 = 68, 70; Gardīzī, 279.-3.
[126] *TB*, 69/97 = 71.

Muslim society over which the caliph presided and of which the rebels no longer wished to be members.

It is noteworthy that a Ḥakīm appears as leader of the Sapīdjāmagān at Bukhārā and that al-Muqanna' was himself known as Ḥakīm, or as the son of one. The sobriquet was also bestowed on Būdhāsaf *al-ḥakım*,[127] the Transoxanian Buddha (from *bodhisattva*), and later on Sufis in eastern Iran (but not apparently elsewhere). The earliest example seems to be the Transoxanian al-Ḥakīm al-Tirmidhī, a Sufi accused (and acquitted) in around 261/874 of the charge, among other things, of claiming the gift of prophecy.[128] Whatever Sogdian or Bactrian word the Arabic word may translate, the local understanding of a *ḥakīm* seems to have been a leader of the spiritual type, a man with direct access to the divine world, whether by spirit possession, dreams, divine indwelling, or other gifts enabling him to see and/or do things denied to normal human beings. It was probably such men who were leaders of the White-clothed ones, and it is tempting to speculate that several such leaders had joined the Hāshimiyya along with their constituencies, persuaded that the mahdi promised by the Hāshimiyya was their own expected redeemer. Al-Muqanna' would in that case have been one of them. It would explain why he found it so easy to address the White-clothed ones when he realised that the promised redeemer was actually himself.

AL-MUQANNA''S MESSAGE

The earliest account of al-Muqanna''s message is preserved by the Ismaili missionary Abū Tammām, whose information may go back to the Ibrāhīm we encountered in connection with Isḥāq the Turk. According to him al-Muqanna''s followers held that God would every now and again enter the body of a man whom God wished to act as his messenger; the messenger was charged with informing other human beings of how God wished them to behave – or, differently put, he brought them a law. God would only incarnate himself at long intervals. God had entered Adam, Noah, Abraham, Moses, Jesus, Muḥammad, and Abū Muslim, returning to his throne in between each incarnation, and it was now incarnate in al-Muqanna', who was the mahdi and thus by implication the last of them (or perhaps just the last in the present cycle: we do not know whether he

[127] E.g. Ibn al-Nadīm, 411.5 = II, 831.
[128] EI^2, s.v. 'al-Tirmidhī'.

operated with more than one). The same can be read in shortened form in other sources.[129]

For 'God' in this account we should undoubtedly understand his spirit.[130] What al-Muqannaʿ's followers subscribed to was a doctrine of periodic manifestation of the divine spirit in man (*ḥulūl*), often called *tanāsukh*, though it was not a doctrine of reincarnation (sometimes distinguished from it as *tanāsukh al-arwāḥ*).[131] Its un-Islamic character lay in the fact that it violated the dividing-line between the divine and human realms and further in that it reduced Muḥammad to a figure of the past whose message has been abrogated by the appearance of a new messenger. One would have expected the messenger after Muḥammad to be al-Muqannaʿ. Instead it is Abū Muslim, who appears in all versions of the list of messengers. But all seem to go back to Ibrāhīm (who is explicitly quoted in the *Tārīkh-i Bukhārā*), and it is hard to see why al-Muqannaʿ should have cast Abū Muslim as the bringer of a new revelation if he was going to bring a new one straightaway himself. We are explicitly told that God only manifested himself at long intervals. As the mahdi, moreover, al-Muqannaʿ was surely meant to be the seventh rather than the eighth. The division of history into seven eras, of which the last would culminate in the coming of the saviour, was extremely widespread at the time. We find it in Christianity;[132] in the beliefs of the Rāwandiyya; in those of ʿAbdallāh b. Muʿāwiya;[133] in the Middle Persian fragment M28, found at Turfan and directed against Sabbath-observing Christians who 'call the son of Mary the seventh son of Adonay';[134] and even among the Manichaeans of

[129] Abū Tammām, 76 = 74ff.; cf. Abū 'l-Maʿālī, 58; *TB*, 64f./91 = 66; for Maqdisī, Baghdādī, and others see Crone, 'Abū Tammām on the Mubayyiḍa'.

[130] The formulation is polemical: see Crone, 'Abū Tammām on the Mubayyiḍa', 171.

[131] See for example Jāḥiẓ, *Bayān*, III, 102f.; Tab. iii, 484; cf. Freitag, *Seelewanderung*, 38f.

[132] Cf. Luneau, *Histoire du salut* (drawn to my attention by Peter Brown); Witakowski, 'The Idea of *Septimana Mundi*'. God had created the world in six days and rested on the seventh, each day of the Lord was 1,000 years (Psalms 90:4, 2 Peter 3:8), and a week was the total age of the world. Augustine has the first period run from Adam to Noah, the second from Noah to Abraham, the third from Abraham to David, the fourth from David to the captivity in Babylon, the fifth from the captivity to the advent of Christ, and the sixth from the advent of Christ to his return at the end of the world (Augustine, *Contra Faustum* XII, 8). His scheme oddly omits Moses, who would have saved him from the awkward division between David and Jesus. Luneau's discussion of Augustine in his *Histoire du salut*, 286ff., does not deal with this problem.

[133] See above, pp. 88f.; below, p. 209.

[134] The whole fragment is transliterated and translated by Skjaervø, 'Manichaean Polemical Hymns', a review of Sundermann, *Iranian Manichaean Turfan Texts*; de Blois, reviewing the same publication, devotes most of it to correction of Skjaervø. The passage cited is at p. 483 in de Blois.

Central Asia, though the normal number of eras in Manichaeism was five: a Manichaean tale of five brothers preserved in Sogdian fragments speaks of the five Buddhas (i.e., divine incarnations) and apostles who guided the souls to paradise during the *seven* periods.[135] Obviously al-Muqanna' is likely to have deified Abū Muslim, if only in order to win over existing constituencies, but it was as an imam or prophet that the Muslimīs held Abū Muslim to be divine, not as a messenger. In connection with the standard list of al-Muqanna''s messengers al-Tha'ālibī tells us that al-Muqanna' held the divine spirit to manifest itself in prophets and kings alike.[136] That al-Muqanna' should have deified Abū Muslim in one or the other capacity is eminently plausible. Of course, the theological systems of rebels can be highly inconsistent, and maybe al-Muqanna''s was too, but it seems more likely that Abū Muslim's inclusion in the list is simply a mistake.

God manifested himself in human bodies, according to al-Muqanna', because he was beyond human vision: his servants could not see him in his original form.[137] Even in human form, however, the divine element in al-Muqanna' was more than human eyes could bear. This was why he wore a veil (though needless to say his opponents claimed that he was simply hiding his own indescribable ugliness: he was one-eyed, leprous, bald, and more besides). His veil was not a *padām*, as the Zoroastrians called the white veil that their priests placed over their mouths so as not to defile the fire,[138] for it covered his entire face, including his eyes (to hide that he was one-eyed, as his opponents said); and it was not white, but rather of green silk,[139] or golden.[140] Its appearance was clearly inspired by the Qur'ān, which says that the dwellers in the garden of Eden will be wearing garments of green silk and heavy brocade (*thiyāban khuḍran min sundusin wa-stabraqin*, Q 18:31). When Bihāfarīdh claimed to have visited heaven, his proof consisted of a shirt of green silk, which is here explicitly characterised as the clothing of paradise.[141] Al-Muqanna''s veil similarly demonstrated his link with the paradise that his followers would be living in when the world had been transfigured at his hands. (It was probably for

[135] Reck, 'Snatches', 245 (So. 18058 and So. 18197), 249f.
[136] Tha'ālibī, *Ādab al-mulūk*, 37, no. 14 (drawn to my attention by Hasan Ansari).
[137] Bīrūnī, *Āthār*, 211; Baghdādī, *Farq*, 244; repeated in Isfarā'inī, *Tabṣīr*, 76.
[138] For an illustration see Lerner, 'Central Asians in Sixth-Century China', 188.
[139] Bīrūnī, *Āthār*, 211; *TB*, 64, 71/90, 100 = 66, 73.
[140] Gardīzī, 278.5; IA, VI, 38 (year 159); Tha'ālibī, *Thimār al-qulūb*, no. 1100; Mīrkhwānd, III, 2573, presumably all from Sallāmī.
[141] See Chapter 7.

the same reason that the seventh ʿAbbāsid caliph, al-Maʾmūn, adopted green for his rerun of the Hāshimite revolution.)

Some sources connect al-Muqannaʿ's veil with the story of Moses. In Exodus Moses is said to have put a veil on his face when he descended from Sinai because his face was shining as a result of his having talked to God.[142] 'A man when he ascended on high, a god when he descended', as a rabbinic midrash says, one out of several texts in which Moses' ascent is regarded as in some sense a deification.[143] Al-Muqannaʿ was also shielding his followers from his divine radiance, though it was by incarnation rather than conversation with God that he had acquired it. When his followers asked him to remove his veil so that they could see his divine countenance he is said to have replied that Moses had also asked for this, but that Moses had not been able to bear the sight, and/or that Moses' people had also asked for a sight of God, to be hit by a thunderbolt (*ṣāʿiqa*) which struck them dead.[144] Both parallels are drawn from the story of Moses as told in the Qurʾān, and both are a bit strained because the Qurʾān does not speak of Moses himself as either veiled or deified, but rather casts him and his followers as equally unable to withstand the sight of God (see Q 2:55, 7:43). The Islamic traditon often speaks of God as veiled, and the transmitters probably took al-Muqannaʿ to be referring himself as the Godhead in person. But this is polemical exaggeration, and the idea of God veiling himself has nothing to do with Moses, a deified messenger like al-Muqannaʿ himself. If al-Muqannaʿ and/or his followers connected his veil with Moses they must have been drawing on Jewish or Christian traditions, for it was the deified face of Moses/al-Muqannaʿ himself that was too brilliant for his followers to behold: he did eventually remove his veil and his followers duly fell down on the ground, not because they were hit by a thunderbolt, but because the radiance of his face overwhelmed them, and in some cases even killed them. (He had produced the effect by means of sunlight reflected in mirrors, we are told.)[145]

Judaism and/or Christianity are not the only non-Islamic traditions to be discernible in his message, however. Manichaeism of the Central Asian type permeated by Buddhism clearly lurks in the background too.

142 Exodus 34:29–35.

143 Meeks, 'Moses as God and King', 361, citing *Pesiqta de Rav Kahaha* f. 198b; see also Gieschen, *Angelomorphic Christology*, 163ff.

144 *TB*, 71/99 = 72; Abū 'l-Maʿālī, 59; Isfarāʾinī, *Tabṣīr*, 76.

145 *TB*, 71f./101f. = 73; Abū 'l-Maʿālī, 59f. (admixed with the story of how he poisoned his followers before killing himself).

The Buddhists operated with a plurality of Buddhas,[146] among them the above-mentioned Maitreya, the saviour still to come, who would appear at a time when things had gone from bad to worse and inaugurate a period on bliss on earth. A Buddhist text in Sogdian promised that 'they who believe the words of the Buddha, when Maitreya Buddha shall go out in the world, will at once find salvation'.[147] Mani operated with repeated incarnations of the same divine figure, as will be seen,[148] and the Manichaeans of Central Asia identified these incarnations as Buddhas, sometimes equating Mani with Maitreya. Thus a lady writing in Sogdian asks Mani for forgiveness, saying that she has been waiting for 'the paraclete [i.e., holy spirit] of the Buddhas of the different periods and for the apostle' (apparently meaning Mani, expecting his return).[149] A queen of Argi writing in Sogdian to a Manichaean teacher politely says that 'we pay homage to you as one pays homage to the Buddhas of the various periods', envisaging the Buddhas as divine: she is using a phrase which appears in almost identical form in the Sogdian 'Ancient Letters', except that the Ancient Letters have 'gods' (*by'nw*) where this one has 'Buddhas'.[150] A Manichaean text in Parthian tells of how the Buddha (presumably Jesus) entered Nirvana, ordering his followers to await Maitreya;[151] and a Manichaean liturgy in Middle Persian and Parthian announces that 'Buddha Maitreya has come', identifying him as 'Mar Mani, the Apostle' who 'has come from paradise'; it also addresses him as God Mani, God Christ, Lord Maitreya, the Lord, Holy Spirit, and more besides.[152] Al-Muqanna' operated with a similar sequence of incarnations of the same divine being; but as he saw it, the Maitreya figure was himself.

The Maitreya Buddha was envisaged as enormously big and glittering, and he was often compared with the sun.[153] In the Khotanese *Book of Zambasta* he appears as Buddha-Urmaysde, 'the Sun Buddha'.[154] (Urmaysde – i.e., Ahura Mazda – meant the sun in Khotanese.)[155]

146 Abegg, *Messiasglaube*, 147ff.; Abegg, *Buddha Maitreya*, 1ff., 26.

147 MacKenzie, '*Sūtra of the Causes and Effects*', lines 214f.

148 See Chapter 14, pp. 300f.

149 Reck, 'Snatches', 249 (So. 14187 and So. 14190).

150 Sims-Williams, 'Sogdian Fragments of Leningrad', 235 (L44), explicitly noting that *by'nw* is used to mean gods, not 'His royal majesty'. On Mani's divinity, see also Klimkeit, 'Gestalt, Ungestalt, Gewaltwandel', 67.

151 Klimkeit, 'Buddhistische Übernahmen', 62; Skjaervø, 'Venus and the Buddha', 242.

152 Klimkeit, *Gnosis on the Silk Road*, 134, 162f.; cf. Klimkeit, 'Buddhistische Übernahmen', 64, 66.

153 Abegg, *Buddha Maitreya*, 15, 24.

154 Emmerick, *Book of Zambasta*, 22:261, 24:236.

155 Bailey, *Indo-Scythian Studies*, 12.

When al-Muqanna' cast himself as a divine being who had come from paradise and who was veiling his face to protect his followers from its unbearable brilliance, it will not just have been in circles familiar with the veils of Moses that his claim was meaningful: it will have resonated with devotees of Maitreya too.

That the Maitreya Buddha played a role in al-Muqanna''s conception of himself as a god and mahdi is suggested by his manner of death. He is usually said to have burned himself,[156] by jumping into a hearth in which, according to some, he had poured tar (or melted copper) and sugar so that he disappeared without a trace: not even any ashes were found, with the result that his followers thought that he had gone to heaven.[157] According to the *Tārīkh-i Bukhārā* he had promised his followers to bring angels to assist them, or alternatively to punish them for their lack of faith.[158] Al-Bīrūnī more convincingly explains that his disappearance was meant to prove his divine status.[159] Accordingly, many accounts go out of their way to deny that he disappeared, claiming that he failed to burn properly, or that he did not burn himself but rather poisoned everyone in the fortress, including himself, and that in any case his body was found and his head was cut off and sent to al-Mahdī at Aleppo or Mosul.[160] 'If a man tells you, 'I am God', he is a liar; 'I am the son of Man', he will regret it; 'I go up to the heavens', he promises, but he will not perform', as a rabbi said with oblique reference to Jesus:[161] this is exactly the message that the accounts of al-Muqanna' are conveying. Unlike Jesus and many others, he ascended to heaven by burning, however, and this is what suggests that he had Maitreya in mind. The latter would enter Parinirvāṇa with fire emanating from his body when his mission was over: he would disappear in flames as a cone of fire, surrounded by pupils, and be extinguished as a flame for lack of fuel.[162] This, apparently, was how al-Muqanna' wanted to disappear. His opponents duly denied, not just that he had disappeared without a

[156] Bīrūnī, *Āthār*, 211; Abū 'l-Ma'ālī, 60; Crone and Jafari Jazi, I, §22.5; cf. IA, VI, 52, where his wives and followers also burn themselves.

[157] Baghdādī, *Farq*, 244; Isfarā'inī, *Tabṣīr*, 77; Gardīzī, 131f.; Mīrkhwānd, III, 2574 (where he burns the bodies of the people he has poisoned and throws himself into a vat of acid).

[158] *TB*, 73/102 = 74f.; cf. 'Awfi, *Jawāmi'*, ed. Muṣaffā', III/1, 229f., where it is the disobedient people of the earth he wants to punish, not his followers.

[159] Bīrūnī, *Āthār*, 211.

[160] Tab. iii, 494; Maqdisī, IV, 97; Bīrūnī, *Āthār*, 211 (where a sentence starting *wa-qīla* ... or the like seems to be missing in line 13); Gardīzī, 155, 282; Dhahabī, *Siyar*, 308; Mīrkhwānd, III, 2573f.

[161] R. Abbahu in Smith, *Jesus the Magician*, 49f.

[162] Abegg, *Buddha Maitreya*, 15, 25.

trace, but also that he had done so in front of his followers: he had killed everyone else in the castle first, they said, except for a slave-girl who had feigned death and lived to tell the tale.[163] But Khwāfī does have him disappear in front of his followers;[164] Ibn Khallikān has the victorious Muslims kill such followers and adherents of his as remained in the fortress;[165] and the *Tārīkhnāma* envisages his Arab father-in-law outliving him for execution after his death.[166]

Al-Muqanna''s other miracles included a famous moon, which rose and sank at his behest, and which he is said to have produced by means of quicksilver in a well. That too must link up with something familiar from the religious traditions of the region. Maybe the point is simply that al-Muqanna' was a magician. In the Greek world magicians were famed for their ability to make the moon and stars appear, among other things by placing a jar of water on the floor, a candle higher up, and a mirror in the ceiling.[167] The method used by al-Muqanna', a master of illusion tricks, was comparable. But one wonders if his miracle did not have a religious meaning to his followers. On the Buddhist side we find that Mahāyāna Buddhists would compare all things, even the Buddha's career, to a mirage, dream, reflected image, or magical illusion in illustration of the doctrine of *sūnyatā*, 'emptiness' (to the effect that all things lack inherent existence);[168] the Khotanese *Book of Zambasta* compares it to 'a moon reflected in water'.[169] This raises the possibility that al-Muqanna''s moon was meant to evoke a well-known metaphor. If this is the case, the fact that the moon was illusory would have been an intrinsic part of the message.

Al-Muqanna''s unbearable brilliance and the 'moon of Nakhshab' are the only two miracles routinely reported for him, but al-Maqdisī says that he also claimed to revive the dead and to have knowledge of the unknown (*ghayb*), presumably meaning the apocalyptic future.[170] The veiled Christ

[163] She only figures in the Persian tradition (*TB*, 72/102 = 74f.; Abū 'l-Ma'ālī, 60; Mīrkhwānd, III, 2573; *Mujmal al-tawārikh*, 335; Crone and Jafari Jazi, I, §22).
[164] Khwāfī, *Rawḍa*, 281: he told his followers that he would go to heaven *va az miyān-i ān qawm bīrūn raft.*
[165] Ibn Khallikān, III, 264 (*fa-qatalū man fīhā min ashyā'ihi wa-atbā'ihi*).
[166] Crone and Jafari Jazi, I, §23 and commentary.
[167] Hippolytus, IV, 37.1.
[168] These are standard images in the Prajñāpāramitā literature attributed to the Buddha himself (cf. Conze, 'Ontology of the Prajñāpāramitā', 124); cf. also Williams and Tribe, *Buddhist Thought*, ch. 5.
[169] Emmerick, *Book of Zambasta*, 6:52.
[170] Maqdisī, VI, 97.

of the Khurdanaye described by Dionysius is also said to have promised to revive believers, though only for a period of forty days: then he would take them away to a secret place.[171] But one wonders whether al-Maqdisī is right when he has al-Muqanna' claim something similar. In the Sogdian account of the first Manichaean missionary sent to 'the land of the Parthians' (Khurāsān) Mani tells the missionary to follow the example of the 'Buddhas of the past, wakers of the dead' by constantly sending out missionaries.[172] If this is the tradition in which al-Muqanna' was expressing himself he was claiming to awaken the dead in the sense of bringing enlightenment to the spiritually dead by sending his missionaries to them, not to revive them after the fashion of Jesus.

All in all, al-Muqanna' seems to have lived in an environment in which people were readily putting together similar-sounding doctrines from different religious traditions in much the same way that modern seekers of spiritual satisfaction will mix doctrines of Western, Buddhist, Sufi, and other origin. But the syncretic nature of al-Muqanna''s preaching notwithstanding, his message comes through loud and clear: the veiled prophet was a divine being who had come to wreak vengeance on the tyrants, the killers of Abū Muslim, and to inaugurate an era of paradisiacal bliss for the Sogdians and Turks. His removal of his veil was a climactic event, a theophany which abolished all restraints in the relations between his followers and everyone else: 'I grant you all the districts, and the lives and the possessions and children of anyone who does not join me are lawful to you', al-Muqanna' declared after showing his face.[173] Like Dionysius' Khurdanaye, his followers treated all those who refused to believe in their divine mahdi as their enemies. Transformed by their glimpse of God into denizens of paradise, they were the only saved.

THE AIM

The inauguration of paradise on earth required the destruction of the caliphal regime in Sogdia and the elimination of its supporters, meaning the local Muslims. To the extent that Islam meant subjection to a foreign regime, al-Muqanna''s message was anti-Islamic. But, like the woman who denounced Abū Muslim as a killer unworthy of his name, he probably saw himself as a true Muslim: what he rejected was merely what everybody else

[171] Michael Syr., IV, 508 = III, 50.
[172] Tardieu, 'Diffusion du bouddhisme', 180.
[173] *TB*, 72/101 = 73.

took to be Islam (just as anti-Western nations today will claim that true democracy is what they practise themselves). We are not told what he called his Muslim opponents, but the chances are that he dismissed them as 'Arabs'. The *Tārīkh-i Bukhārā* stresses that the amir killed by the rebels at Sūbakh was a pious Arab and that the first man to attack the rebels on another occasion was an Arab called Nu'aym b. Sahl.[174] Yet al-Muqanna''s own father-in-law, 'Abdallāh b. 'Amr, was an Arab from Marw, showing that here, as so often, the term 'Arab' stood for religious and political orientation, not – or not just – for ethnic origins.[175] Al-Muqanna''s ethnically Arab father-in-law was the founder of the community in Kish and Nasaf: he was a complete renegade from a Muslim point of view. The *Tārīkhnāma* registers this by calling him 'Abdallāh b. 'Āmir b. Kurayz al-Qurashī, thereby casting him as (a descendant of) a famous opponent of the Prophet's family, 'Abdallāh b. 'Āmir al-Qurashī: this man was an Umayyad who fought against 'Alī in the Battle of the Camel and later served as governor of Basra for Mu'āwiya.[176] The *Tārīkhnāma* tells us that Sa'īd al-Ḥarashī spat in the face of this alleged descendant, telling him that 'your ancestors were enemies of the family of Muḥammad, you have become more accursed and turned wholly infidel'.[177] This is evidently embroidery, but it shows how shocking it felt that a member of Muḥammad's own people should have participated on al-Muqanna''s side.

Al-Muqanna' seems to have severed his connection with Marw after he left that city, and no source remembers him as having operated outside Sogdia, let alone as having planned to bring down the caliphate. There are no hints of Sasanian restorationism in what we are told about his message either. According to the *Tārīkh-i Bukhārā* the caliph al-Mahdī feared that his revolt would cause Islam to be lost 'in the whole world',[178] but the language in this source is often overblown. It is not impossible that al-Muqanna' talked in grandiose terms about eradicating Muslims from the earth, bringing down their polity, and conquering the entire world. But in practice his concern was with Sogdia alone.

In social terms he does not come across as having had any programme at all. Modern scholars sometimes see him as a champion of equality, without it being entirely clear who was meant to be equal to whom.[179] The idea

174 *TB*, 65, 67/92, 95 = 67, 69.
175 *TB*, 65/92 = 67; Chapter 3, p. 74.
176 Cf. *EI*², s.v. "Abd Allāh b. 'Āmir'.
177 Crone and Jafari Jazi, I, §23.
178 *TB*, 66/93 = 68.
179 Thus most recently Langarūdī, *Junbishhā*, 88, 96.

that he was a social reformer is rooted in al-Bīrūnī's claim that he 'declared women and property to be lawful' to his followers, meaning that he adopted the Mazdakite doctrine that women and property were joint possessions and should be equally shared; he 'prescribed everything that Mazdak had laid down', as al-Bīrūnī himself rephrases it.[180] But this should be dismissed. The full passage in al-Bīrūnī runs that 'the Mubayyiḍa and the Turks gathered around him, so he declared women and property to be lawful to them (*fa-abāḥa lahum al-amwāl wa'l-furūj*), killed those who disagreed with him, and prescribed for them everything that Mazdak had brought'. The parallel passage in the *Tārīkh-i Bukhārā* says that 'al-Muqanna' called in the Turks and declared the blood and property of the Muslims lawful for them (*va-khūn u māl-i muslimīn bar īshān mubāḥ gardānīd*)',[181] in other words he allowed them to kill and despoliate their Muslim opponents as they wished. What al-Muqanna' is telling the Turks here is what he is also presented as telling his followers after the epiphany: 'I grant you all the districts ... and the lives and the possessions and children of anyone who does not join me are lawful to you'.[182] It was the right of the people of paradise to take whatever they could of the property of others, as some Ḥurūfīs were later to declare.[183] Back in the Umayyad period the Khārijite extremists had similarly argued that they could take the wives, children, and property of their opponents on the grounds that the latter were infidels and polytheists, whereas they themselves were the only Muslims.[184] In all three cases the sectarians see themselves as the only legitimate inhabitants on earth. Because the Muqanna'iyya were believed to be Mazdakites, however, al-Bīrūnī or his source understood the free hand that al-Muqanna' allowed his followers in their dealing with their enemies as a doctrine of free use of women and property among the followers themselves. The claim that al-Muqanna' prescribed everything that Mazdak had prescribed is simply al-Bīrūnī's learned reformulation of this misunderstanding.

Al-Muqanna''s realised eschatology was political, not social. As the mahdi he was ridding Sogdia of the regime of which he and his followers saw themselves as the victims. If the mahdic role he was assuming was modelled on that of the Maitreya Buddha, the Turkish *khāqān* with whom

[180] Bīrūnī, *Āthār*, 211; cf. Baghdādī, *Farq*, 243.-7.
[181] *TB*, 66/93 =68. For the relationship between *TB* and Bīrūnī see Crone and Jafari Jazi, analysis, 6.
[182] *TB*, 72/101 = 73.
[183] Browne, 'Some Notes', 75f.
[184] Crone and Zimmermann, *Epistle*, text, part III, summarised 203f., 206.

he collaborated may have been cast as the righteous king who would welcome him:[185] restored to Turkish overlordship, Sogdia would enter a period of paradisiacal bliss, a heavenly return of the glorious past that it was assumed to have enjoyed until the arrival of the Muslims.

THE FOLLOWERS

Al-Muqannaʿ's followers were Sogdians and Turks, and the Sogdians among them came from villages: it was in villages that the message had spread, and it was also villages that the rebels took over.[186] The rebels included *dihqāns*, though we also hear of *dihqāns* who opposed them.[187] The little we are told suggests that either way, the *dihqāns* were village squires: they lived in the villages themselves, not in manor houses outside them, led the defence of their villages at times of attack, and functioned as their spokesmen in their dealings with the government.[188] It is hard to tell how, if at all, they differed from village headmen. A village headman, or rather head woman, participated in the revolt, as we have seen.[189] If the *dihqān* or headman supported al-Muqannaʿ, the entire village probably did, willy-nilly, but why some village leaders should have opted for him and others against him we do not know.

Villagers were not necessarily peasants, however. They included men like al-Muqannaʿ himself, an ex-soldier who is also said to have worked as a fuller, bleaching cloth for a living. The White-clothed ones active before al-Muqannaʿ at Ṭālaqān were led by a weaver.[190] Ḥakīm-i Aḥmad had three officers with him at Bukhārā described as *ʿayyār*, *ṭarrār*, *mubāriz*, and *dāvanda*:[191] *ʿayyārs* were armed men of no fixed abode, sometimes chivalric, here clearly thugs, strongmen, or brigands, the equivalent of *ṣaʿālīk*;[192] a *ṭarrār* was a pickpocket; a

[185] See Ch'en, *Buddhism in China*, 428.

[186] *TB*, 65, 67ff./92, 94ff. = 67, 68ff.

[187] Crone and Jafari Jazi, I, §§8.3, 9.1, 10, 1, and commentary; cf. *TB*, 70/98 = 71, where the meaning of the word is unclear: the statement could be read as saying that the *dihqāns* brought 570,000 (*sic*) men together, implying that the *dihqāns* were village squires, or alternatively that 570,000 *dihqāns* and warriors were brought together, implying that the *dihqāns* were peasants. Daniel, *Khurasan*, 142, opts for the former construction.

[188] Crone and Jafari Jazi, I, §§8, 9.

[189] *TB*, 69/97 = 71.

[190] Gardīzī, 273.

[191] *TB*, 66f./94 = 68.

[192] But for *ʿayyārs* as volunteer holy warriors and practitioners of chivalric ideals see Tor, *Violent Order*.

mubāriz was a 'fighter' who distinguished himself in single combat, usually as a soldier in battle, but probably also in competitions staged for entertainment; the *dāvanda*, or runner, could similarly have been either a postal runner or a runner in competitions inviting betting and other disreputable entertainment, or both.[193] The identification of the rebels as men of this kind is meant to disparage them, but there is nothing implausible about it. Many are likely to have been ex-soldiers uprooted from their villages by the revolution and later revolts.

The Turks were pastoralist tribesmen led by a *khāqān* who is further identified, in connection with the second conquest of Samarqand, as Khalluq Khāqān and said in connection with the first conquest to have been 'king of the Turks and of Farghāna'. His name could also be read as Khalaj Khāqān, but al-Muqanna''s Turkish allies came from Turkestan, not from south-eastern Iran, where the Khalaj were found, so he was almost certainly a Khalluq, that is Qarluq. Since the chief of the main body of Qarluqs had not yet adopted the imperial title of *khāqān*, the conqueror of Samarqand was perhaps the leader of a splinter group who had adopted the title by way of claiming the Türgesh heritage in Transoxania.[194] We also meet a Turkish commander called Kūlār Tekin, active at Bukhārā, and another Turkish chief by the name of Kayyāk Ghūrī, who was perhaps a Ghuzz.[195] All the Turks are presented as joining al-Muqanna' for opportunistic reasons, their interest being in plunder. This is likely to have been true of the Qarluq and the Ghuzz, but not of all the Turks. There were White-clothed ones in Īlāq and Farghāna, at least at a later stage,[196] and Isḥāq al-Turk had preached among the Turks, seemingly finding them receptive. The Turks in question must have been Türgesh, then squeezed between the Muslims advancing from the west and the Qarluqs coming from the east. Having lost their hegemony in Transoxania, the Turks who had been members of the Türgesh confederacy are likely to have joined al-Muqanna' under the new *khāqān* in the hope of restoring it.

[193] Cf. Silverstein, *Postal Systems*, 24, 68, 78.
[194] For all this see Crone and Jafari Jazi, II, 406–8.
[195] *TB*, 70/99 = 72; Crone and Jafari Jazi, I, §§6.2, 10.2, 12.1–3.
[196] Baghdādī, *Farq*, 243.9 (wrongly Ablaq); *SN*, ch. 46:22 (300 =228).

THE DEFEAT

Al-Muqanna''s revolt went down in history as lasting fourteen years, not quite as long as Bābak's, but certainly a long time.[197] Like Bābak he was on a frontier, and he certainly profited from this fact, not only in the sense that he had no enemies in his rear, but also in that he could draw on the Turks, whose assistance was crucial. Rural fighting was focused on fortresses, whether attached to villages or free-standing, and the Sogdian rebels were clearly capable of taking both types, at least if they had inside help. Once ensconced in their fortresses they would supply themselves by robbing caravans, stealing harvests, and pillaging villages; they would raid at night and then withdraw to their fortresses.[198] They had trouble taking villages when the population was united against them, however, and it is not clear that they ever took a city without Turkish help. The villagers would seek refuge in the village fortress and make sorties from there; and if the rebels could not defeat them they had to starve them out, or use trickery, for they had no siege equipment. The trouble was that they might run out of food themselves first. This was even more of a problem when they laid siege to cities. They would provision themselves by pillaging neighbouring villages, raiding one or two a day, as they did during their siege of Chaghāniyān; but they broke off the siege of Chaghāniyān after a month, presumably because all villages within a reasonable radius had been depleted. They also abandoned their siege of the city of Nasaf, where the population was united in its determination to resist, because the rich had opened their stores of grain so that everyone within the city had enough to eat, we are told.[199] There is no suggestion that al-Muqanna''s followers were perceived as Robin Hoods or bandits celebrated for upholding traditional values against an intrusive government, or that they were fed and protected by the peasantry in villages other than those they controlled.

Their Turkish allies were also raiders: they pillaged sheep and carried off women and children as captives.[200] But the Turks were capable of winning open battles. They participated against government troops in the battle at Tirmidh, which al-Muqanna' won, and it seems unlikely that

[197] See Crone and Jafari Jazi, II, 394f. (*ad* §24.1).

[198] *TB*, 65, 67/92, 95 = 67, 69.

[199] Crone and Jafari Jazi, I, §§7–8.

[200] *TB*, 66/93 = 68; Crone and Jafari Jazi, I, §§9.3, 5, 10.5, 12.1, 13, 14.3.

al-Muqanna' would have been able twice to conquer Samarqand without their help.[201] Samarqand is the only city we know for sure that he conquered. But the Turks were outsiders, however committed to al-Muqanna''s cause some of them may have been. When things went badly they could simply leave, as they seem to have done when the Muslims moved against Samarqand for the second time.

There were no other power-holders in the region with an interest in getting the Muslims out. This was al-Muqanna''s basic problem. Unlike Bābak he comes across as aware of the fact that he needed to enrol other enemies of the caliphate, for the *bukhārkhudā* sympathised with him: there must have been negotiations between them. The *ikhshīd* of Samarqand may also have decided that al-Muqanna' was a good man to back.[202] But neither was a significant power any more, and we hear nothing of the kings of Kish and Nasaf, or, if they were identical, of the king of these two areas.[203] The Chinese had also ceased to be a presence. The only power-holders in the region were Muslims, supported by the caliphate, and the Turks. Muslim adherents of the caliphal regime dominated the cities, whose inhabitants had no wish to be ruled by either al-Muqanna' or the Turks, seeing both of them as rank infidels. So basically al-Muqanna' was on his own. One does wonder why there was no rapprochement between him and Yūsuf al-Barm, who rebelled in Bādghīs and Jūzjān in (probably) 160/776f., for Yūsuf was also a non-Arab, and perhaps an apostate like al-Muqanna' himself, and he was sufficiently dangerous for the caliph to offer him *amān*, much as he did to Bābak and other warlords in Azerbaijan.[204] He was far away from Sogdia, but still within the jurisdiction of the Khurāsānī governor who had to cope with al-Muqanna', so al-Muqanna' presumably knew of him. Whatever the reason, without significant political allies in greater Khurāsān al-Muqanna' was bound to fail.

If the revolt lasted a long time it was again because it took a long time before the central government concentrated on the task. For the first two

[201] Crone and Jafari Jazi, I, §§2, 6, 10.
[202] See the reference given in n. 70 of this chapter.
[203] The king of Kish is last mentioned in Chinese sources in 746 (Chavannes, *Notes Additionelles*, 76), in Muslim sources in 134/751f. (see the references given in nn. 55, 58 of this chapter). For his identity with the king of Nasaf, last encountered as a supporter of al-Ḥārith b. Surayj's revolt, see Gibb, *Arab Conquests in Central Asia*, 86, n. 25. Nasaf is a dependence of Kish in the *Tang chou* in Chavannes, *Documents*, 147.
[204] Ibn 'Abd Rabbih, *'Iqd*, IV, 213.8, cited in Bahrāmiyān, 'Yūsuf-i Barm', 88.

years the revolt was treated as a local disturbance, handled by local commanders. It came to the attention of the central government when the rebels took Samarqand, probably shortly before al-Manṣūr's death in 158/775, but what with the change of ruler it was not till 159 that troops were sent. Jibra'īl assisted the governor of Bukhārā and reconquered Samarqand, but the new governor was preoccupied with the rebellion of Yūsuf al-Barm, so al-Muqanna' took Samarqand again in 160.[205] There were no diversions thereafter. The new governor, Mu'ādh b. Muslim, dealt with the situation at Bukhārā, moved on to reconquer Samarqand in 161, and started the siege of al-Muqanna''s fortress. It probably fell two years later, though it may have held out for as many as five.

Some of al-Muqanna''s followers may have ended up in Iraq. In 248/862f. and again in 251/865f., when al-Musta'īn and al-Mu'tazz were at war, we hear of Mubayyiḍa in the 'Abbāsid troops in Baghdad, and a few in Samarra as well.[206] No explanation is offered for their name, and they are mentioned as just one of the many military units involved in that war, though perhaps of a somewhat lowly kind: they are associated with the mob (*ghawghā'*), riffraff (*sūqa*), and strongmen (*'ayyārūn*). Were they Transoxanian sectarians who had been recruited after al-Muqanna''s defeat, or perhaps White-clothed ones from a quite different part of eastern Iran recruited by the Ṭāhirids, then in charge of Baghdad? It is in the same war that we meet descendants of Bābak and Yūsuf al-Barm in the 'Abbāsid army.[207]

What can be said is that, like Bābak, al-Muqanna' has been interpreted as an Iranian nationalist, and that again the interpretation is unpersuasive. His interests, too, were local and he too was defeated as much by Iranians as by Arabs in the ethnic sense of the word: Abū 'Awn 'Abd al-Malik b. Yazīd, the governor of Khurāsān under whom Samarqand was first reconquered, was a native of Jurjān and a client of the Azd; his successor Mu'ādh b. Muslim, who reconquered Samarqand, was a *mawlā* of the Banū Dhuhl and a native of Khuttal or Rayy; he was undoubtedly a brother of Ḥusayn b. Muslim, the governor of Bukhārā who fought against the White-clothed ones there together with Jibra'īl b. Yaḥyā al-Bajalī (an ethnic Arab).[208] Al-Muqanna' does however seem to have had a greater notion of Sogdia as a political unit than Bābak did

205 For all this see Crone and Jafari Jazi, analysis, 2.
206 Tab. iii, 1504.1, 1561.2, 1563, 1564, 1589, 1639.
207 See Chapter 3, n. 164; Chapter 8, p. 158.
208 See Crone, *Slaves*, 174, 179, 183.

of Azerbaijan in that role, probably because Sogdia had in fact had a single political overlord in the form of the king of Samarqand before the coming of the Arabs. But it was precisely because there now was a new, Islamic Iran both inside and outside Sogdia that al-Muqanna''s rural representatives of old Iran were unsuccessful.

7

South-Eastern Iran

Bihāfarīdh, Ustādhsīs, and Yūsuf al-Barm

Travelling in a south-westerly direction from Marw one reaches Nīshāpūr, the city in which Sunbādh had joined Abū Muslim. Abū Muslim had come to Nīshāpūr as the new ruler of Khurāsān, and before setting off again together with Sunbādh he did the locals a favour by ridding them of a man called Bihāfarīdh.

BIHĀFARĪDH

Like Sunbādh, Bihāfarīdh b. Māhfarvardīn was a Zoroastrian. He came from Zūzan, some 200 kilometres south-east of the city of Nīshāpūr in (or adjoining) the district of Khwāf, a region endowed with 124 villages and a Zoroastrian fire-temple.[1] He worked as a trader: in that capacity, we are told, he spent seven years in China.[2] It was Sogdians rather than Parthians (Khurāsānīs) and Persians who dominated the overland China trade, but there is nothing implausible about Parthians, including Bihāfarīdh, participating too.[3] When Bihāfarīdh came back from his seven years in China he began preaching. According to al-Bīrūnī he went up a sepulchral monument (*nāwūs*) one night and came down the next morning, dressed in a green shirt he had brought back from China, made of fabric so fine that it could be squeezed into a fist; he told a peasant who was ploughing some land that he had been to heaven, that he had seen paradise and hell and received revelations from God, and that God had dressed him in that shirt and restored him to the earth in that very moment; the peasant

[1] Bīrūnī, *Āthār*, 210, followed by Khwārizmī, 38; Gardīzī, 266; Ibn al-Nadīm, 407 = II, 822; cf. Yāqūt, II, 486, 958, s.vv. 'Khwāf', 'Zūzan'.

[2] Bīrūnī, *Āthār*, 210; al-Tha'ālibī in Houtsma, 'Bih'afrid', 34 = 32; 'Awfī, *Jawāmi'*, ed. Muṣaffā, III/1, 227; echoed in Khwāfī, *Rawḍa*, 280.

[3] Cf. de la Vaissière, *Marchands sogdiens*, 164ff. (with Bihāfārīdh in n. 92).

believed him and told others that he had seen Bihāfarīdh come down from heaven.[4] Al-Tha'ālibī tells the story slightly differently. According to him, Bihāfarīdh feigned mortal illness and had a sepulchral monument built for himself; there he spent a year, seemingly dead, feeding on rainwater and concentrated foodstuff that he had secretly prepared; and when people assembled around his monument at the time of the harvest he stood up, dressed in a green silken shirt and an undergarment with the properties described by al-Bīrūnī, and said, 'I am Bihāfarīdh, the messenger of God to you,' explaining that God had revived him, dressed him in the clothes of paradise, and told him what to say.[5] Abū Ḥātim al-Rāzī has him lie unconscious for three days.[6]

What all this amounts to is that Bihāfarīdh claimed to have been on a heavenly journey. The idea of going on such a journey was extremely popular in the Near East and Mediterranean in late antiquity – among pagans, Jews, Christians, Manichaeans, and Zoroastrians alike. Bihāfarīdh embarked on it by seemingly dying. He went up a *nāwūs*, al-Bīrunī says: a *nāwūs* (from Greek *naos*) was a non-Muslim funerary structure,[7] such as a mausoleum or the tower or hilltop enclosure in which Zoroastrians would expose their dead for dogs or wild animals to eat their flesh,[8] or the ossuary in which they would put their bones thereafter.[9] Here it seems to be a tower; one account even says that it had no path or stairs by which one could climb it, which was true of the old *dakhma*s or 'towers of silence', as they are popularly known today.[10] Other accounts replace the *nāwūs* with a mountain,[11] and in al-Tha'ālibī's version it is a mausoleum, a roomy vault in which Bihāfarīdh is placed along with his two sacks of provisions and where his wife regularly comes to visit him for a year as an ostensible mourner.

[4] Bīrūnī, *Āthār*, 210. The peasant appears as the *dihqān* called Khudādād in Khwāfī, *Rawḍa*, 281; Khwāfī is presumably using the term *dihqān* in its modern sense of peasant (differently Daniel, *Khurasan*, 98, n. 96).

[5] Abū Ḥātim al-Rāzī, *Iṣlāḥ*, 161.6; also in Stern, *Studies*, 41f.

[6] In Houtsma, 'Bih'afrid', 34 = 32f. For the foodstuffs he secretly consumed with the help of his wife cf. the story of the impostor in Ḥimṣ in Tanūkhī, *Nishwār*, II, 351ff. (no. 187) = *Table-Talk*, 289ff.

[7] Dozy, *Supplément*, s.v. *nws*; Henning, 'Two Central Asian Words', 157ff.

[8] Cf. Ḥamza al-Iṣfahani, 46/43 (*al-dahamāt wa'l-nawawīs*); 'Histoire Nestorienne', VII, 130 (*nā'ūs*, translated sarcophagus, but the dead are thrown there); Inostrantsev, 'Ancient Iranian Burial Customs', 7f.; Boyce, 'Old Village *Dakhma*', 3f.; Grenet, *Pratiques funéraires*, 227; Bahrāmiyān, 'Bih Āfarīd'.

[9] See Grenet, 'Pahlavi Text', 167 (§11).

[10] Houtsma, 'Bih'afrid', 31; *Haft kishwar*, 91; Boyce, 'Old Village *Dakhma*', 4f.

[11] 'Awfī, *Jawāmi'*, ed. Muṣaffā, III/1, 227; Khwāfī, *Rawḍa*, 280.ult.; Marwazī in Bahrāmiyān, 'Bih Āfarīd'.

This also accords with Zoroastrian funerary practice,[12] but al-Thaʿālibī's heavy stage management, designed to expose Bihāfarīdh as a fraud, makes the special properties of the Chinese shirt superfluous. The importance of its suppleness lies in the fact that Bihāfarīdh could hold it in his fist without anybody noticing while he was being prepared for exposure. The shock to the peasant will have lain in the sight of a silk-clad man rising from among the corpses on the platform.

While Bihāfarīdh lay dead his spirit ascended to heaven and visited paradise and hell, as al-Bīrūnī's version tells us. Some five centuries earlier the Zoroastrian high priest Kerdīr had 'prayed towards the gods . . . that [if you] gods are able, then show me the nature of heaven and hell '. His prayer was answered: 'I made a kind of death', he says (in MacKenzie's translation), and proceeds to give us an account of what he saw.[13] In the Zoroastrian Book of Ardā Vīrāf (or Vīrāz), the priest Ardā Vīrāf is chosen for a mission to the other world and takes a drug which makes him fall asleep and lie as if dead for seven days, mourned by his sisters, while his spirit visits heaven and hell.[14] Zoroaster's patron, Vištāsp, was similarly envisaged as having been drugged (on Ohrmazd's orders) and to have been transported to paradise while he lay unconscious: when he woke up he was a convert to Zoroaster's religion.[15] This is the tradition that Bihāfarīdh is standing in. We find it in Manichaeism too: when Mihrshāh, the brother of Shapur, derided Mani's preaching about paradise, Mani took him on a tour of heaven for three days during which the prince lay unconscious until Mani put his hand on his head;[16] and/or it was Shapur himself that he raised to heaven, and Mani accompanied him; Mani would be seized by the spirit from time to time, and should presumably be envisaged as lying unconscious for the duration too.[17] Much later we hear that an Iranian Sufi in Bahrabad lay as if dead for thirteen days, his spirit having left his body.[18] In all these

[12] Cf. Inostrantsev, 'Ancient Iranian Burial Customs', 11ff.

[13] MacKenzie, 'Kerdir's Inscription', §§22, 24; tr. Skjaervø, 'Kirdir's Vision', §§5, 9; see also Gignoux, 'Kirdār und seine Reise in das Jenseits' and other works by Gignoux on this topic (listed in his entry on Shamanism in *EIr.*). It is his heavenly counterpart, here called *hangerb*, that sees everything, presumably united with Kerdīr's earthly soul; not being truly dead, his earthly soul can return with the experiences.

[14] *Ardā Vīrāfnāmag*, esp. chs. 2–3; cf. Shaked, 'Quests and Visionary Journeys', 72f.

[15] *PRDd*, 47:15–17 (47:27–31 in Molé, *Légende*, 121); cf. also *Dk*, VII, 4, 85–86, in Molé, *Légende*, 59.

[16] Reeves, 'Jewish Pseudepigrapha in Manichaean Literature', 180.

[17] Abū Ḥātim al-Rāzī, *Aʿlām*, 70.14ff.; Bīrūnī, *Āthār*, 209.5.

[18] Elias, 'Sufi Lords of Bahrabad', 60.

accounts people fall into a trance, as we would say. They were not possessed, and they did not writhe, wriggle, or utter prophecies after the fashion of the Sogdians in China. Their souls simply left them to roam the celestial world. A villager in the Zagros mountains in the 1970s told an anthropologist of a similar experience he had had, and also that he had been ordered to assemble people and tell them about it: 'Oh woe! I didn't do it. God is great! I couldn't. I didn't have the courage.'[19] It probably was not easy for Bihāfarīdh either.

The green shirt that Bihāfarīdh was wearing when he rose from his trance proved the reality of his journey, for green silk was what the dwellers in the garden of Eden would be wearing according to the Qur'ān (Q 18:31), and Bihāfarīdh explicitly declares himself to be dressed in the honorary robes (*khila'*) of paradise in al-Tha'ālibī's account.[20] Al-Muqanna' similarly wore a veil of green silk, or of gold, as we have seen. Bihāfarīdh's message thus had celestial authority. The message was that Zoroaster was a true prophet and that 'what he had brought' was binding, except that a certain amount of ritual and law had to be changed. The Zoroastrian mumbling of prayers (*zamzama*) at mealtimes had to be replaced with a fixed number of ritual prayers in a specified direction. Some say that Bihāfarīdh introduced five daily prayers without prostration, praying to the left of the (Muslim) *qibla*;[21] others say that he prescribed seven prayers for which one should get down on one's knees (in the Christian style?), praying in the direction of the sun, wherever it was.[22] Either way, the prayers were modelled on those of the Muslims and at the same time carefully distinguished from them. The first of the seven prayers was in praise of the unity of God, perhaps meaning that Bihāfarīdh adopted monotheism, but more probably that one had to praise the unity of Ohrmazd without thereby making him the creator of the evil realm, so that one highlighted the monotheist aspect of Zoroastrianism without actually abandoning belief in two eternal powers. If he had gone so far as to declare Ohrmazd to be the one and only power in the universe it

[19] Loeffler, *Islam in Practice*, 150f. He was lying ill in bed and transported by a strange old man, not by an angel; he experienced hell as a terrible pain instead of simply visiting it as a tourist, and he was cured by a cup of tea with a piece of sugar offered him by 'Alī in paradise.

[20] Houtsma, 'Bih'afrid', 34 = 33. Pourshariati, *Decline*, 432, understands the green as 'the quintessential color of Mithra'.

[21] Ibn al-Nadīm, 407 = II, 822 (left, taken by Dodge to mean lax); Abū Ḥātim al-Rāzī, *Iṣlāḥ*, 161.8 (also *mutayāsiran 'an al-qibla*, though Stern, *Studies*, 42, says 'towards the right-hand side').

[22] Bīrūnī, *Āthār*, 210; Gardīzī, 266.

would hardly have been mentioned in so indirect a fashion. The rest of the prayers were about the creation of heaven and earth, the creation of animals and their nourishment, death, the resurrection and last judgement, and those who dwell in heaven and hell – the last being in praise of the people of paradise. (They are easily reduced to five.) He also abolished close-kin marriages, forbade the consumption of carrion and wine, and introduced Muslim-style ritual purification; perhaps he abolished fire worship too. To all these features calqued on Islam he added one Zoroastrian recommendation, transformed into a command, namely that one should not sacrifice cattle unless already of a specified age or in a bad state, plus several other rules of his own making: dowries were not to exceed 400 dirhams, hair was to be left loose (*irsāl al-shuʿūr wa'l-jumam*), and one should spend a seventh of one's property on the charitable purpose of keeping roads and bridges in good repair. He composed a book for his followers in Persian, clearly modelled on the Qur'ān and presumably containing all this supplementary legislation. Whether it was written in New rather than Middle Persian (or for that matter Parthian) is impossible to say.

Bihāfarīdh had evidently been sufficiently exposed to Islam to internalise its model of a true religion as consisting of monotheism, prophethood, revealed scripture, ritual prayer, and *qibla*. Yet he remained convinced that Zoroastrianism was true. He was suffering from what in modern jargon is known as cognitive dissonance, the uncomfortable feeling of being committed to contradictory positions, and he coped with it by revising his ancestral religion in the light of the model he no longer found himself able to dismiss. It was the same psychological tension that lay behind the emergence of Reform Judaism in nineteenth-century Europe and America, when assimilated Jews had absorbed a number of fundamental assumptions about religion from the non-Jewish society around them. In their case as in Bihāfarīdh's, the response took the form of 'modernisation', meaning 'change in any aspect of culture toward the model of the most successful societies at the time', as Curtin neatly defines it.[23] Reform Jews rejected all aspects of Judaism that were not adapted to 'the views and habits of modern civilization', the Pittsburgh Platform declared in 1885. 'We hold that all such Mosaic and Rabbinical laws as regulate diet, priestly purity and dress originated in ages and under the influence of ideas altogether foreign to our present mental and spiritual state', the declaration continued, adding that Judaism was a progressive religion ever

[23] Cf. Curtin, *The World and the West*, xiii.

striving 'to be in accord with the postulates of reason'.[24] Modern civilisation and reason in Bihāfarīdh's time was represented by Islam. Like the Reform Jews he was jettisoning traditional features of his own religion in order to accommodate key aspects of the dominant belief system, while at the same time stressing the differences between the two so as not to lose his sense of his own religious identity: Zoroastrianism now had a prophet, a scripture, ritual prayer, and *qibla*, but it was still Zoroaster's religion, not that of Islam.

Some Islamicists take Bihāfarīdh's reforms to have been made in a spirit of reconciliation with Islam,[25] but this does not follow. Reform Judaism was indeed motivated by a desire to participate in the civic and social life of the gentiles, but their ability to do so turned on the fact that the gentiles had secularised these spheres. Islam was a rival religion, not a religiously neutral sphere, and reshaping Zoroastrianism in its image was not going to allow Bihāfarīdh to blend in. What he was doing was rather refurbishing his native religion so as to make it better able to survive under the new conditions introduced by Islam, which was luring Iranians into its fold all over Khurāsān at the time. He may even have used his creed as an aegis of revolt: some sources say that he 'went out', which would normally mean that he rebelled.[26] Modernisation, whether concerned with arms, technology, economic growth, or religious ideas, and whether consciously undertaken or not, is in essence an attempt to adopt the thinking held to lie behind the strength of the most successful society of the time so as to be able to overtake that society, or at least to hold out against it. A common response is appropriation of some features of the dominant society accompanied by strident affirmation of the superiority of the native tradition: appropriation does not imply friendly feelings, nor does hostility preclude borrowing. (Muslim fundamentalists avail themselves of the internet, and so on.) This is surely the light in which Bihāfarīdh's activities should be seen. He was acting in a spirit of loyalty to his native tradition. Nor do we need to assume that he held Zoroaster to have gone wrong, or that he considered himself above him, as suggested by Sadighi and Yūsofī:[27] presumably he saw himself as the restorer of Zoroaster's original message (close-kin marriages were corruptions that had crept into it, monotheism was what Zoroaster had in mind, and so on – more or less what the Zoroastrians say today). The beliefs

[24] Steinberg, 'Reform Judaism', 125.

[25] Thus for example Daniel, *Khurasan*, 91.

[26] Thus Bīrūnī, *Āthār*, 210, followed by Khwārizmī, 38; Gardīzī, 266 (*bīrūn āmad*), and others. Poursharīati, *Decline*, 427, has him incubate a revolt to rival Abū Muslim's.

[27] Sadighi, *Mouvements*, 123/158; *EIr.*, s.v. 'Behāfarīd'.

of the Zoroastrian priests were also changing, but too slowly for them to be aware of it. Bihāfarīdh offended them by introducing massive changes for anyone to see, as a layman devoid of authority in their eyes, a mere trespasser on the domain of the priests, and one acting entirely on his own. This is why they took action against him.

Abū Muslim came to Nīshāpūr in 131/748f. to take control of the region and eliminate opponents.[28] The Zoroastrian clergy treated him as the representative of the Muslim government in the region and complained to him about Bihāfarīdh, pointing out he was corrupting Islam as well as Zoroastrianism. Whether or not Bihāfarīdh had actually taken up arms, he was important enough for Abū Muslim to think it prudent to squash him. He sent ʿAbdallāh b. Shuʿba against him, and the latter caught him along with a number of his followers in the mountains of Bādghīs, now part of the province of Herat in north-western Afghanistan, or he caught them in Bihāfarīdh's village of Zūzan; they were brought to Abū Muslim, who had them executed.[29] According to another version Bihāfarīdh saved his life by converting to Islam and enrolling in Abū Muslim's army, but was later killed for continuing to propagate his own beliefs. In this version Abū Muslim sends Qaḥṭaba against him and Salama b. Muḥammad al-Ṭāʾī executes him,[30] or he sends Shabīb b. Wāj and ʿAbdallāh b. Saʿīd.[31]

As so often, we are told that the sectarians survived and expected their founder to come back to wreak vengeance on their enemies. Al-Shahrastānī connects their hopes with Zoroastrian expectations of two saviour figures (the third, Sōšyans, is missing from his account), and also mentions their veneration for the ancient kings of Iran.[32] The messianism seems to be a later development, for there is no reference to it in the earlier accounts of Bihāfarīdh's message. Later developments also seem to be reflected in al-Thaʿālibī's statement that Bihāfarīdh's followers belonged partly to the Khusrawiyya and partly to the Khurramiyya,[33] for there is

[28] Dhahabī, *Taʾrīkh*, V, 199. It was here that he eliminated the sons of al-Kirmānī, the leader of the Yemeni faction with which he had briefly been allied (*AA*, 337.10, 354.5; Dhahabī, *Taʾrīkh*, 201), and Jabala b. Abī Rawwād al-ʿAtakī, a Marwazī *mawlā* of the Muhallabids who had worked for the Umayyad regime: see Ibn Ḥibbān, 195, no. 1570; cf. Tab. ii, 1564, 1605; *AA*, 289f. (Duʾād for Rawwād); BA, III, 116; and the biographical dictionaries s.vv. his brother ʿAbd al-ʿAzīz and son ʿUthmān.

[29] Bīrūnī, *Āthār*, 211; Thaʿālibī in Houtsma, 'Bih'Afrid', 35 = 33; Khwāfī, *Rawḍa*, 281; ʿAwfī, *Jawāmiʿ*, ed. Muṣaffā, III/1, 228.

[30] Abū Ḥātim al-Rāzī, *Iṣlāḥ*, 161.

[31] Ibn al-Nadīm, 407 = II, 822 (Shabīb b. Dāḥ).

[32] Shahrastānī, I, 187 = I, 646, with helpful comments.

[33] Houtsma, 'Bih'Afrid', 35 = 33.

nothing to suggest Khurramism in the account of Bihāfarīdh himself. Perhaps he had been appropriated by Khurramīs in some mountainous communities of the region, much as Sunbādh seems to have been.

USTĀDHSĪS (141–51/758–68)

There is no sign of Khurramism yet when, some twenty years later, we encounter Bihāfarīdh's followers in Bādghīs and adjacent regions led by one Ustādhsīs (or, as he also appears, Ustāsīs, Ashnāshīsh, Asnās).[34] Ustādhsīs was Bihāfarīdh's successor, we are told; he 'adopted the way of Bihāfarīdh'.[35] According to al-Shahrastānī, Bihāfarīdh's followers were Zoroastrians known as the Bihāfarīdhiyya and Sīsāniyya, the second a name which Houtsma recognised as derived from that of Ustādhsīs.[36] They were also known by a different name, however. Abū Ḥātim says that when Bihāfarīdh was on his way to execution he turned to one of his followers and said, in Stern's reading of the manuscript, 'this baldhead (*laghsarī*) shall be your leader', so Ustādhsīs replaced him and his followers were known as Laghsariyya.[37] In the printed edition Bihāfarīdh says 'this Oghuz' (*hādhā 'l-ughuzī*) and Ustādhsīs's followers are called al-Ughuziyya, presumably understood by the editor as referring to the Oghuz Turks. Since Abū Ḥātim himself explains the leader's name as meaning *al-aṣlaʿ*, the bald one, Stern's reading makes better sense, but what the manuscripts actually have, according to the notes in the printed edition, are *ʾl-lghʾzy*, *llghʾzy*, and *ʾl-lghʾzyh*. The name must have started with a *lam* and contained a *rāʾ* or *zāʾ*, but there is no sign of a *sīn*. It appears as Laghāriyya in Ḥamza al-Iṣfahānī,[38] Laghīriyyān in *Tārīkh-i Harāt*, Laghariyyān in Isfizārī citing that work,[39] as Laghiriyya or the like in al-Maqdisī (once read al-Ghuzziyya by the editor),[40] and as something similar in *Tārīkh-i Sīstān* and al-Ījī.[41] Ḥabībī tentatively connects the name with that of the Baluchi Laghāriyyān.[42]

[34] For a discussion of his name see Langarūdī, 'Ustādhsīs', 143.
[35] Abū Ḥātim al-Rāzī, *Iṣlāḥ*, 161; Gardīzī, 276.
[36] Shahrastānī, I, 187 = I, 645; Houtsma, 'Bih'afrid', 36.
[37] Stern, *Studies*, 42.
[38] Ḥamza al-Iṣfahānī, 221/163.
[39] *Tārīkh-i Harāt*, fol. 58r; Isfizārī, *Rawḍāt*, II, 49.
[40] Maqdisī, IV, 26, VI, 86.
[41] *TS*, 142 = 113; Ījī in Stern, *Studies*, 45, n. 41.
[42] Ḥabībī, *Afghānistān*, I, 316, 319. See also the discussion in Daniel, *Khurasan*, 151, n. 64.

The story of these followers is set in two different places, Bādghīs and Sīstān. According to Gardīzī the followers of Bihāfarīdh in Bādghīs accepted Islam at the hands of al-Mahdī and asked him for an allowance, so he sent them on a campaign to Kābul with Muḥammad b. Saʿīd; there they got their payment in the form of a share of the booty, but when they got back they apostatised and Ustādhsīs rebelled.[43] This episode is presumably set during the sojourn of the future al-Mahdī at Nīshāpūr. He came there twice during his time as governor of Khurāsān, in 141/758f. and 150/767f.;[44] and since his second journey was occasioned by Ustādhsīs's revolt the reference here must be to the first. The Muslims did in fact campaign in Hind in 141/758f. The expedition was organised by the governor of Sīstān, Zuhayr b. Muḥammad al-Azdī, and commanded by Shujāʿ b. ʿAṭāʾ,[45] and it did apparently target Kābul, for Michael the Syrian mentions that the 'Arabs' conquered Kābul about this time.[46] The participants in this expedition did rebel when they returned after acquiring much booty and elephants,[47] so this must be the expedition to which Gardīzī refers. The Muḥammad b. Saʿīd he mentions will have been sent by al-Mahdī to join the Sīstānī expedition as commander of the contingent from Bādghīs. In line with this we later find Muḥammad b. Saʿīd as governor of Sind.[48]

When the troops returned from Kābul with much booty and elephants it was to Sīstān that they went, and also here that they rebelled. Their revolt lasted until 144/761f., when they accepted Zuhayr b. Muḥammad al-Azdī as governor again, but some of them later came to Bust (between Zaranj and Qandahār) as part of an army led by a certain ʿUtayba b. Mūsā, and this army once more rebelled against Zuhayr. By 145/762f. order had been restored, but in 150/767f. a certain Muḥammad b. Shaddād from the Laghīriyān (or the like) rebelled in Bust along with two Zoroastrians called Ādharwayh al-Majūsī and Marzbān al-Majūsī.[49] The Laghīriyān were followers of Bihāfarīdh, and since Muḥammad b. Shaddād bore a Muslim name he was presumably one of the converts who participated in the expedition to Kābul. Whether his Zoroastrian collaborators were

[43] Gardīzī, 276f.
[44] Tab. iii, 135.1, 355.3f.
[45] *TS*, 141 = 112.
[46] Michael Syr., IV, 474 = II, 522.
[47] *TS*, 141 = 112.
[48] Khalīfa, 678.
[49] *TS*, 142/161 = 113.

also followers of Bihāfarīdh or local Zoroastrians one cannot tell. There is no mention of Ustādhsīs in connection with these events.

Back in Bādghīs, however, there was also unrest. We are told by Agapius that there was a mountain in Bādghīs[50] from which much silver was extracted and which employed some 30,000 workers, all of them Zoroastrians who had been granted a monopoly on its exploitation. When another rich mine was discovered there the ruler (*al-sulṭān*), presumably meaning the governor of Sīstān or Khurāsān, wanted to remove the mountain from their control, which they resisted, and when he struck one of them they mutinied and killed many of his soldiers. It is clear from the account of the suppression of this revolt that the reference is to that led by Ustādhsīs.[51] The rebels are also Zoroastrians in Michael the Syrian, who tells us that they established a kingdom;[52] and that Ustādhsīs was the leader of this revolt is confirmed by al-Yaʿqūbī, who mentions that his revolt prevented allegiance from being taken to the future al-Mahdī in Bādghīs.[53]

Bihāfarīdh's followers were thus involved in two rebellions of a different nature in two different regions. Bādghīs, the region of the silver mine, formed part of the district of Herat in which Bihāfarīdh had been active. Sīstān and Bust, the regions in which the troops from Kābul rebelled, lie several hundred kilometres to the south and south-east respectively. At some point, however, the two rebellions merged. Bādghīs, Herat, and Sīstān were the three regions involved in Ustādhsīs's revolt, as we are explicitly told.[54] It was in 150 that Ustādhsīs laid siege to Herat, and also in 150 that the Laghīrīs rebelled at Bust;[55] Ustādhsīs's chief organiser was a Sīstānī called Ḥarīsh,[56] and another rebel in his movement bore the Muslim name of ʿAbdallāh al-Sanjawī or the like.[57]

As regards the chronology of these revolts, the Laghīriyya campaigned with the Sīstānīs in Sind in 141/758f. and rebelled when they returned, presumably in the following year; submitted to the governor of Sīstān in 144/761f.; engaged in further disturbances at

[50] Written Fārʿīs.

[51] Agapius in *PO*, VIII, 544f.

[52] Michael Syr., IV, 475 = II, 522f.

[53] YT, II, 457.

[54] E.g. Tab. iii, 354; Maqdisī, VI, 86; IA, V, 591; *TN*, IV, 1143.

[55] *Tārīkh-i Harāt*, fol. 58r, 10; see n. 48 of this chapter.

[56] Tab. iii, 357.4.

[57] Daniel, *Khurasan*, 134, citing (al-Thaʿālibī?), *Ghurar*, fol. 192b, from a manuscript which does not seem to be listed in his bibliography.

Bust, where they had been suppressed by 145/762f.; and rebelled again in 150/767f. under the Laghīrī Muḥammad b. Shaddād. If we go by al-Ya'qūbī the revolt of Ustādhsīs in Bādghīs was in progress by 147/764f., when it obstructed the payment of allegiance to al-Mahdī as al-Manṣūr's heir apparent.[58] This is hard to square with the fact that a coin was struck in *Jabal al-fiḍḍa* by a certain Ma'bad 'in the *wilāya* of al-Mahdī, *walī 'ahd al-muslimīn*' in 148/765f., for *Jabal al-fiḍḍa* is undoubtedly the silver mountain involved in the revolt.[59] Perhaps the rebels had taken it some time before 147 and lost it again in 148; alternatively, the news of al-Mahdī's succession had gone out at the end of 147, the coin was struck in 148, but the formal allegiance was never sent because by then Ustādhsīs had taken over. Thereafter we learn from a source shared by al-Ṭabarī, al-Fasawī, and al-Maqdisī that Ustādhsīs and his 300,000-strong army conquered most of Khurāsān and reached Marw al-Rūdh, where al-Ajtham (alias al-Akhyam b. 'Abd al-'Azīz) al-Marwarrūdhī was sent against him with people from Marw al-Rūdh; Ustādhsīs defeated al-Ajtham/Akhyam and occupied Marw al-Rūdh, slaughtering a large number there.[60] No date is given. The narrative continues by listing a number of commanders that Ustādhsīs defeated: they included Mu'ādh b. Muslim, Jibra'īl b. Yaḥyā (al-Bajalī), Ḥammād b. 'Amr (al-Sughdī), Abū 'l-Najm ('Imrān b. Ismā'īl) al-Sijistānī, and Dāwūd b. Karrār/Karrāz/Kazzāz (al-Bāhilī). Khalīfa places the defeat of the first two commanders in 149.[61] The third commander, Dāwūd b. Karrār al-Bāhilī, was governor of Herat (where he is attested on a coin as early as 147), and Ustādhsīs laid siege to him there in Sha'bān, Ramaḍān, Shawwāl, and Dhū 'l-Qa'da of 150. Al-Mahdī, who was still at Rayy, responded by sending someone to Mu'ādh b. Muslim, who was at Nīshāpūr, while also sending Ḥammād b. 'Amr to assist 'him', presumably meaning Dāwūd b. Karrār.[62] Agapius confirms that the first army sent by al-Mahdī was defeated, adding that it had come close to the mountains containing the mine, which he clearly envisages as being under rebel control; winter then came, and when the

[58] YT, II, 457 (cf. Tab. iii, 331).

[59] Bates, 'Khurāsānī Revolutionaries', 301, 306, cf. 317n.

[60] Tab. iii, 354; IA, V, 591 (Ajsham); Fasawī, *Ma'rifa* I, 18 (year 150); Maqdisī, VI, 86f. (omits all details). For Akhyam b. 'Abd al-'Azīz see *AA*, 219.2, 222.1.

[61] Khalīfa, 656.

[62] *Tārīkh-i Harāt*, fol. 58r; cited in Isfizārī, *Rawḍāt*, II, 49; Bates, 'Khurāsānī Revolutionaries', 301.

campaigning resumed, Khāzim b. Khuzayma defeated Ustādhsīs, killing over 20,000 or 30,000 of the rebels.[63] Most sources place this in 150, but al-Wāqidī and Ḥamza place it in 151 in agreement with the *Tārīkh-i Harāt*.[64] It was also in 151 that Maʿn b. Zāʾida came to Sīstān to impose order in Bust, where the Laghīriyya had defeated the governor, Yazīd b. Manṣūr.[65] In short, the revolt led by Ustādhsīs seems to have lasted from at least 147 to 151 (764f. to 768f.), not just the two years that some assign it,[66] let alone the one year suggested by the many who only mention the year in which it was suppressed. The disturbances in Sīstān had started in 143, however, and Ustādhsīs's revolt was perhaps just the most visible part of a protracted tug of war between the caliphal authorities and the locals in Bādghīs: the rebels may have taken the silver mine in 147 and lost it again in 148; they clearly controlled it in 149 or 150 and lost it again on their defeat in 150 or 151; but perhaps they recovered it thereafter, for Elias Bar Shinaya (who used al-Khwārizmī's lost *Taʾrīkh*) places al-Mahdī's despatch against 'the Zoroastrians' (*al-majūs*) in 153.[67] Though that could simply be a mistake, a coin struck at *Jabal al-fiḍḍa* by a *mawlā* of al-Mahdī in 155 lends support to the claim that there had been further operations.[68] All in all, then, the region seems to have been in a state of unrest from 147 to 155 (764f. to 771f.).

Of Ustādhsīs himself we know nothing beyond what Abū Ḥātim tells us. If we trust his claim that he was Bihāfarīdh's successor, he was the leader of the reformed Zoroastrian organisation. Some say that he claimed prophethood.[69] His message was *kufr*, we are told; but then it would be if it was some form of Zoroastrianism.[70] He can hardly have been a Khārijite, as the *Tārīkhnāma* has it,[71] though Khārijites were also active in Sīstān at the time. Two late sources cast Ustādhsīs as a wielder of political power in the

[63] Agapius in *PO*, VIII, 545; *Tārīkh-i Harāt*, fol. 58r–p; cited in Isfizārī, *Rawḍāt*, II, 49. In *TN*, IV, 1143, Ḥumayd b. Qaḥṭaba takes the place of Khāzim b. Khuzayma.

[64] Muḥammad b. ʿUmar (al-Wāqidī, i.e. his *Taʾrīkh*?) in Tab. iii, 358; Ḥamza al-Iṣfahānī, 221/163.

[65] *TS*, 143f./162 = 113f.

[66] *TN*, IV, 1143; *Mujmal al-tawārikh*, 332.

[67] Elias Bar Shinaya, 180f.; cf. *Tārīkh-i Harāt*, fol. 58p (with extreme vagueness).

[68] Bates, 'Khurāsānī Revolutionaries', 302, 306. He was *ʿāmil* of ʿAbbād, presumably the governor.

[69] YT, II, 457; Gardīzī, 276.-3.

[70] Faḍl b. Sahl in Tab. iii, 773; cf. iii, 358, where his followers are distinguished from Muslims.

[71] *TN*, IV, 1143.

region: both al-Dhahabī and al-Suyūṭī identify him as governor (*al-amīr*) and say that he rebelled with the Khurāsānī troops (*al-juyūsh al-khurāsāniyya*), and al-Dhahabī calls him king (*malik*) as well.[72] This idea has gained currency in the modern literature because al-Ya'qūbī says that the *bay'a* to the future al-Mahdī did not come in from Bādghīs due to Ustādhsīs's revolt; some have taken this to mean that Ustādhsīs was asked to swear allegiance to al-Mahdī and refused.[73] But non-Muslims such as Ustādhsīs were not appointed to governorships with command of Muslim troops, nor were local kings asked to swear allegiance to Muslim heirs apparent. What al-Ya'qūbī means is simply that no *bay'a* came from Bādghīs because the province was in disarray: there was no Muslim authority in the region.

After his defeat Ustādhsīs fled into the mountains, where he eventually surrendered. Khāzim had him and the members of his family clapped into chains for transport to Baghdad and let the rest go free. His daughter or daughters were apparently taken to Baghdad, where one of them passed into Hārūn al-Rashīd's harem, for according to al-Sallāmī the slave-girl called Marājil by whom Hārūn al-Rashīd sired al-Ma'mūn was Ustādhsīs's daughter. Most scholars reject this information.[74] But the daughter of Bābak was similarly to pass into al-Mu'taṣim's harem when Bābak was defeated. Al-Mu'taṣim also enrolled Bābak's sons in his army, and al-Manṣūr seems to have done the same to the son or sons of Ustādhsīs, for Ghālib, who later assassinated al-Faḍl b. Sahl for al-Ma'mūn, was said to have been a son of the rebel.[75] It is only when each case is read in isolation that it sounds implausible. Taken together the cases form a pattern, attested again in connection with Yūsuf al-Barm: the caliph would use the reproductive capacities of the daughters of defeated rebels for the procreation of children for his own family, and the muscle power of their sons for the killing of his own enemies. It comes across as the ultimate humiliation that one could inflict on an enemy.

Of the social background of Ustādhsīs's followers we know next to nothing. Gardīzī mentions a *qāḍī* among the men who were put in chains when Ustādhsīs surrendered;[76] if Agapius is right a large number of the rest

72 Dhahabī, *Duwal*, I, 78 (differently his *Ta'rīkh al-islām*, VI, 32, where he cites the same tradition as Fasawī); Suyūṭī, *Khulafā'*, 280.

73 Thus Kennedy, *Early Abbasid Caliphate*, 90, 183f.; Daniel, *Khurasan*, 133; Langarūdī, 'Ustādhsīs'.

74 E.g. Daniel, *Khurasan*, 136; others in Madelung, 'Was the Caliph al-Ma'mūn a Grandson of . . . Ustādhsīs?', who shows that the doubts are unwarranted.

75 Gardīzī, 277; IA, 593V, (i.e. this comes from Sallāmī).

76 Gardīzī, 277. We are expected to know who he is, but he has not been mentioned before.

were silver miners. Like al-Muqanna''s followers they must have been mountaineers, and most of them were foot-soldiers.[77] They have been cast as peasants because one passage describes them as equipped with spades, axes, and baskets, but they brought these implements in order to fill a trench dug by Khāzim b. Khuzayma, not because their only weapons were agricultural tools.[78] They were remembered as numerous. Ustādhsīs is said to have brought 300,000 fighting men together,[79] and large numbers are said to have been killed and captured: the lowest casualty figure is 20,000.[80]

YŪSUF AL-BARM

Of Yūsuf al-Barm we know even less than of Ustādhsīs.[81] His father's name is given as Ibrāhīm:[82] he could have been a Jew, a Christian, a Muslim, or an ex-Muslim. The meaning of al-Barm is unknown. In another context we hear of a Yūsuf al-Barm, *mawlā* of the Ḥasanids, who was in the entourage of al-Ḥusayn b. ʿAlī (the later rebel at Fakhkh) when he visited the court of al-Mahdī.[83] If this took place during al-Mahdī's return from Khurāsān to Baghdad in 151/768f., when many Hāshimites are said to have come to see him,[84] it would be tempting to identify this man with the future rebel. But the *mawlā* of the Ḥasanids was still alive at the time of Ḥusayn b. ʿAlī's revolt in 169/786, nine years after the execution of our Yūsuf al-Barm;[85] according to al-Yaʿqūbī our rebel was a *mawlā* of Thaqīf in Bukhārā, not of the Ḥasanids,[86] and there is no suggestion that he was a Shīʿite.

Yūsuf's revolt is placed in 160/776f.,[87] meaning that this was the year in which it was suppressed; it had begun in the governorship of Ḥumayd b. Qaḥṭaba (appointed in 151/768f.) and may well have broken out before

[77] Tab. iii, 356.
[78] Tab. iii, 356; Maqdisī, VI, 86.ult.; cf. Daniel, *Khurasan*, 134 and n. 63 thereto; repeated by Langarūdī, 'Ustādhsīs', 143.
[79] Tab. iii, 354; IA, V, 591; Fasawī, *Maʿrifa*, I, 18; Maqdisī, VI, 86f.; *Tārīkh-i Harāt*, fol. 58r.
[80] Elias Bar Shinaya, 181.1; cf. the sources given in n. 62 of this chapter.
[81] All the information has been collected and examined by Bahrāmiyān, 'Shūrish-i Yūsuf-i Barm'.
[82] Tab. iii, 470.
[83] Tab. iii, 563.
[84] Tab. iii, 364.
[85] Bahrāmiyān, 'Shūrish-i Yūsuf-i Barm', 93f.
[86] YT, II, 478.
[87] Khalīfa, 670; Tab. iii, 470f.; IA, VI, 43.

al-Muqanna''s, with which it certainly overlapped.[88] But he operated in a different region and does not seem to have had any dealings with al-Muqanna'. His conquests included Būshanj, to the west of Herat, as well as Marw al-Rūdh, Ṭālaqān, and Jūzjān,[89] and the *nisba*s of two of his associates, Ḥakam Ṭālaqānī and Abū Mu'ādh Faryābī,[90] suggest that they came from the region between Herat and Balkh. As regards his message, we are told that he disapproved of al-Mahdī's conduct,[91] commanded good and prohibited wrong,[92] and was a Ḥarūrī, an archaic term for a Khārijite:[93] these three claims are compatible. But he is also said to have been an infidel (*kāfir*),[94] and to have claimed to be a prophet.[95]

According to Gardīzī, he was defeated by the Hāshimites of Balkh, who captured Abū Mu'ādh Faryābī and sent him to al-Mahdī.[96] This was not apparently the end of the revolt, but he says no more about it. The final defeat was inflicted on Yūsuf by Sa'īd b. Salm b. Qutayba according to Khalīfa, by Yazīd b. Mazyad according to others,[97] and Yūsuf was taken to Iraq, where he was executed at Ruṣāfa by Harthama b. A'yan, whose brother he had killed.[98] He had been sufficiently important for the caliph to promise him *amān* if he would surrender.[99] His sons, or one of them, apparently suffered the usual fate of being enrolled in the caliph's army, for a century later we hear of one Yūsuf b. Manṣūr b. Yūsuf al-Barm,[100] a commander on the Ṭāhirid side in the war between al-Mu'tazz and al-Musta'īn in Baghdad in 251/865f. along with Ḥusayn b. Yūsuf al-Barm, presumably a grandson and son of the rebel respectively.[101] Another grandson, Manṣūr b. 'Abdallāh b. Yūsuf al-Barm, had been killed

[88] Gardīzī, 280.5. A much-cited statement of Faḍl b. Sahl enumerates al-Muqanna', Yūsuf al-Barm, and Ustādhsīs as rebels in that order (Tab. iii, 773; Jahshiyārī, 277f.; IA, VI, 224), but the order was if anything the reverse. Ustādhsīs (omitted by IA) was certainly the first.

[89] Gardīzī, 280; IA, VI, 43 (this comes from Sallāmī).

[90] Gardīzī, 280.

[91] Tab. iii, 470.

[92] YT, II, 478.

[93] YB, 303, ult.

[94] Tab. iii, 773; Jahshiyārī, 278.1; IA, VI, 224.

[95] Maqdisī, VI, 97.

[96] Gardīzī, 280.

[97] Khalīfa, 670; Tab. iii, 470; YT, II, 478f.

[98] Tab. iii, 471.

[99] Bahrāmiyān, 'Shūrish-i Yūsuf-i Barm', 88, citing Ibn 'Abd Rabbih, *'Iqd*, IV, 212f.

[100] Tab. iii, 1603.

[101] Tab. iii, 1614, following Ibrāhīm rather than the Leiden edition, where the son of Yūsuf is anonymous. Bahrāmiyān, 'Shūrish-i Yūsuf-i Barm', 92ff.; Bahrāmiyān, who unearthed this material, thinks that these soldiers must be descendants of the Shī'ite Yūsuf al-Barm.

in Khurāsān, where he had rebelled in the reign of al-Ma'mūn, but whether as the member of the local army or otherwise we do not know.[102]

OVERALL

Bihāfarīdh, Ustādhsīs, and Yūsuf al-Barm belong in a different category from the other rebels considered in this book. They were active in the region stretching southwards and eastwards from Khwāf, mostly in what is now Afghanistan, rather than in Sogdia, Marw, Jurjān, or western Iran, and they were not responding to the death of Abū Muslim or any other person connected with the Hāshimiyya. Nor is there any sign of Khurramism in them until al-Thaʿālibī's report on the Khurramiyya and Khusrawiyya. But the activities of the Hāshimiyya formed part of the background to Bihāfarīdh, and all the revolts testify to the growing presence of Islam in the Iranian countryside. The disturbances started a mere century after the coming of the Arabs, and though we hear very little about Iran in that century, it is clear from the proliferation of Muslim names and other Muslim elements in the revolts that a great deal had happened in those years. Islam had made its impact felt outside the cities immeasurably faster than did the religion and culture of the Greeks in Hellenistic times.

[102] YT, II, 546.ult.

8

The Nature of the Revolts

In the course of the preceding chapters we have encountered two main interpretations of the Iranian revolts of the early ʿAbbāsid period, one that casts the rebels as nationalists trying to liberate Iran from the Arabs, and another that construes them as local rulers uniting followers of diverse ethnic origin in defence of their local autonomy against caliphal centralisation. As we have seen, neither interpretation holds up against the evidence. Yet there is something intuitively right about both of them: movements dedicated to the overthrow of foreign rulers do sound 'nationalist', and at the same time the revolts were clearly local rather than 'national' in nature. We can reconcile the two seemingly contradictory features by remembering that although it is usually difficult to speak of nationalism in pre-modern times, the same is not true of nativism.

NATIONALISM

Nationalism is an ideology rooted in the sense that the state is – or should be – an integral part of a person's identity, as opposed to simply a protective institution under which he gets on with his life. It casts the state as the organisation entitled to one's primary loyalties above the family level on the grounds that it is, or should be, the guardian of the most important community above that level, namely the nation – a people with a shared language, culture, and past assumed to be of common descent. Loyalty to the nation is deemed more important than to the church or comparable organisation of believers, though the two may coincide. If their interests clash the nationalist holds those of the nation to take priority over those of religion. Nationalism is a secular ideology, but it often assumes a religious character, sometimes by borrowing from or blending with the religion of the people it is mobilising for the nation-state, and sometimes by trying to trump it.

It is probably safe to say that in strongly hierarchical societies the only people to whom something approaching nationalist sentiments can be attributed in pre-modern times is the ruling elite, and then only at times. Members of the ruling elite, such as aristocrats and priests, might well have seen the kingdom or empire that defined their roles in life as central to their identity; and the kingdom or empire in its turn might have been identified with reference to something that sounds like a nation. The first Sasanian emperor, Ardashir I, for example, was king of kings of *Ērān*, the Iranians, and the number of military and administrative titles containing the word *Ērān* (*Ērān-spahbedh*, *Ērān-dibīrbed*, etc.) in the Sasanian period is quite striking.[1] Ardashir's successors were kings of both *Ērān* and *Anērān*, the Iranians and the non-Iranians, but the Iranians remained the politically dominant group in *Ērānshahr*, a term which sometimes stands for the entire Sasanian empire rather than just its Iranian parts;[2] and at elite level they were typically united by religion (Zoroastrianism), culture, and language (Pārsīg, known as Darī[g] in its courtly form). The members of the Sasanian ruling elite were thus in a position to see the Sasanian kingdom as the political embodiment of a nation, the Iranians.

If they did so, 'the Iranians' to them meant primarily the politically and culturally important segment to which they themselves belonged. *Ēr* sometimes translates as 'noble'.[3] When modern scholars loosely speak of 'nationalist' sentiments in Iran it is on the basis of elite statements. The masses lived by local cultures, followed partly or wholly different religions or cults, and had no particular interest in the identity of the kings as long as customary ways remained unchanged. Their prime loyalties above the level of family will have been to their villages or tribes and/or their religious community. What the hypothetical, quasi-nationalist sentiments of the elite will have lacked, in other words, is the populist character of nationalism.

Nationalism is populist because it reflects a radical political reorganisation whereby the masses are affiliated directly to the state, rather than through aristocrats, local notables, tribal chiefs, religious leaders, or the like. The aristocrats themselves are deprived of their hereditary rights, ousted or demoted to mere citizens in tandem with the elevation of the former subjects to that status; all are endowed with identical rights and duties rather than with those deemed appropriate to their particular estate, caste, or other social stratum; all are schooled in the same language and

[1] Ardashir in Christensen, *Iran*, 92; Gnoli, 'Ēr Mazdēsn', 89f.
[2] Chaumont, 'Inscription de Kartīr', 360.
[3] Gnoli, 'Ēr Mazdēsn', 92.

high culture, formerly current at elite level alone, now identified as 'national' and seen as shared since time immemorial; and all, not just the military aristocracy or other warrior class, are expected to participate in the defence of the state, and often in its government as well. In short, the horizontal loyalties uniting elites spread out over huge distances in pre-modern kingdoms and empires are replaced by the vertical loyalties uniting everyone from president to postman within the same nation-state. Nationalism is associated with the emergence, demand for, and defence of polities of this type, and it is uniquely modern because modern means of communication are a precondition for their appearance. This is why attempts to cast pre-modern rebels as nationalists strike most historians as anachronistic.

When members of the ruling elite took up arms against foreign invaders who had destroyed their kingdom or empire in pre-modern times their response was typically restorationist: what they wanted back was the political organisation in which they had been men of power and authority endowed with wealth, prestige, and a shared outlook on life; they did not give much thought to other members of the nation. We do not see much restorationism in the aftermath of the Arab conquests, except for the attempt of the royal family to stage a comeback and the revolt of Sunbādh. It is true that fourth/tenth-century Zoroastrian priests were still dreaming of the day when the Arabs would be expelled and the good religion restored to political dominance, and perhaps there were still descendants of the former aristocracy who shared their dreams; there were certainly political adventurers in north-western Iran who played with such ideas. But more commonly the memory of Sasanian Iran displayed itself in the use of Sasanian titles and genealogies for the legitimisation of upstart Muslim dynasties and, with the exception of Sunbādh, it was not the Iranian aristocracy who led the revolts in the aftermath of the Hāshimite revolution.

NATIVISM

Nativism is a different type of reaction to foreign rule. The word usually stands for opposition to immigration and other forms of xenophobia among members of a hegemonic society, but it is also used of hostility to hegemonic foreigners in societies that have been subjected to colonial rule, and that is the meaning of relevance here. Nativism in this second sense is attested with great frequency in Asia, Africa, the Americas, and Oceania in the wake of the European expansion, especially in the nineteenth and early twentieth centuries. All these movements presuppose modern means of communication and other technology in the sense that without them the Europeans would not have been able to incorporate such distant places in their empires, or to exploit them without formal incorporation; but there was nothing modern about the responses. On the contrary, they were what is sometimes called 'pre-political', meaning that they were movements by people who had not previously been organised for political action at the level of kingdom or empire. Sometimes there had never been a political elite above the local level: many revolts occurred in previously stateless societies. At other times the state had been destroyed. Like the members of the political elite the rural rebels might then talk about restoring it, but what they had in mind was not a concrete polity with a specific distribution of power and authority, as opposed to a nebulous concept of 'the good old days': things were assumed to have been fine until the coming of the invaders. The movements were always messianic and/or millenarian: the expulsion of the invaders would be followed by paradise on earth, usually inaugurated by a redeemer figure. Because the rebels came from strata that had not enjoyed the supra-local organisation that the aristocracy and religious leaders had possessed (if there had been a kingdom in the region) their revolts were often small-scale uprisings of a local nature. It is to the nativist pattern that the Iranian revolts conform.

The leaders of the revolts against the Europeans were typically men – occasionally also women – of rural origin who claimed to have special knowledge of the divine, conveyed to them by revelation, dreams, inspiration, out-of-body experiences, divination, and the like; some claimed to be reincarnations of earlier prophets and saints, such as Moses or St Anthony; others claimed to be St John the Baptist, Jesus Christ, or the Chakravartin.[4] They often invoked figures from the religious repertoire of the invaders and expressed themselves in an odd mixture of native and foreign religious idiom, for both they and other participants had often been converts. Like the Muslims the Europeans were wealthy and powerful, and one response to their arrival was to join them by espousing their religion. This was a common reaction to the coming of the Europeans in non-literate societies in which the missionaries were among the most accessible representatives of the privileged newcomers. It was not in the name of religion that the Europeans had expanded, and a more common reaction elsewhere – above all in the cities – was the adoption of that packet of secular values

[4] Lanternari, *Religions of the Oppressed*, 8, 13, 240; Adas, *Prophets of Rebellion*, 101, 206, n. 32.

(including nationalism) that we subsume under the label of modernity. This required literacy, however, as well as education and job opportunities of a type that were not usually available in the countryside.

As in Iran, the rural leaders were typically men with a wider experience than the villagers to whom they addressed themselves. Some had been trained as clergy; others had served in the army; still others had drifted from one occupation to another in different places. All were transformed into authoritative figures by their supernatural powers. 'Do you know who I am?', the founder of a nativist sect in Tahiti around 1828 reputedly asked a child who had refused to get him some sugar cane. 'Do I know who you are? You are Teau!', the child replied. 'No', he said, 'I am Jesus Christ.'[5] 'Do you know who I am?', al-Muqanna' reputedly asked when he returned to Marw after his spell in jail. 'You are Hāshim b. Ḥakīm,' people replied. 'You are wrong', he said, 'I am your Lord and the Lord of all the world.'[6] Like Teau he had turned into a superior being entitled to unquestioned obedience.

The hostile response to the foreigners usually came when the European presence began to affect the livelihoods of the rural population adversely, that is to say when the newcomers were not simply a small minority concentrated in garrison cities, ports, or other special foundations of theirs, but were spreading out in the land, directly or indirectly, through colonisation, missionary activity, education, or, in the European case, incorporation of the region in question into a world market which exposed the locals to economic forces they could neither understand nor control. The most common trigger was seizure of native land. 'At first we had the land and you had the Bible. Now we have the Bible and you have the land,' as agitators in South Africa so memorably put it in 1913.[7] 'Bishop, many years ago we received the faith from you. Now we return it to you, for there has been found a new and precious thing by which we shall keep our land,' as a member of the Maori Hau-Hau movement in New Zealand, founded in 1826, explained,[8] articulating feelings that Bābak's followers are likely to have shared. This Maori sounds polite, but the 'new and precious thing' was typically (and also in his case) an apocalyptic vision: the Day of Judgement was close; the foreigners would be expelled, or a flood would engulf the world and swallow up everybody except the

5 Moerenhout, *Voyages aux îles du Grand Océan*, I, 502.
6 *TB*, 64/90f. = 66.
7 Sundkler, *Bantu Prophets*, 33.
8 Burridge, *New Heaven, New Earth*, 19.

believers, who would be saved like Noah in the ark; or past heroes would return to establish a native kingdom; and/or an age of millenarian bliss would ensue.[9]

The movements always took a religious form because religion was the only available source of what was needed for political action: organisation above the level of family, neighbourhood, village, or tribe, legitimisation of the new political leadership, shared concepts in terms of which grievances and aims could be articulated, and authoritative experience to draw on (in the form of the story of Moses, for example). In short, religion could create a community. It also provided the assurance that what the rebels hoped to achieve could in fact be done, in the form of prophecies of the redeemer figure at whose hands the apocalyptic reversal of fortune would come: it is above all in their reliance on a messianic *deus ex machina* that the rebels' lack of political experience shows.

Where the religious idiom of the rebels was partly or wholly borrowed from the foreigners the foreign religion was always nativised. Congolese preachers claimed that Christ was a French god and that the real Christ was a Congolese by the name of André Matswa, martyred in 1942 (who thus became the Congolese Abū Muslim).[10] A preacher in the Fiji Islands claimed that the Europeans had changed the name of the deity in the Bible so as to claim it as their own: in reality the Bible belonged to the Fijians.[11] Africans mined the Old Testament for monotheist genealogies and vindications of polygamy.[12] The founder of the Maori Hau-Hau hit on the stratagem of Judaising: the Maoris and Jews were children of the same father, he himself was a prophet who had been taught ritual and sacred dances by Gabriel, and all the Jews would come to New Zealand when the British had been expelled.[13] One way or the other, all these preachers were appropriating the religious armoury of the foreigners to use it against them and, in the somewhat old-fashioned terminology of Wallace, to 'revitalise' their own tradition.[14]

[9] Lanternari, *Religions of the Oppressed*, 8, 12, 19, 204f., 255f. Participants in such revolts often believed that they would be immune to European bullets having drunk a magic potion, recited a sacred incantation, or received a special tattoo; there is no parallel to this belief among the Iranian rebels, who did not suffer from a comparable disparity of weaponry.

[10] Lanternari, *Religions of the Opressed*, 15f.

[11] Burridge, *New Heaven, New Earth*, 51; Worsley, *The Trumpet Shall Sound*, 51.

[12] Lanternari, *Religions of the Opressed*, 29, 42, 55, 62.

[13] Lanternari, *Religions of the Opressed*, 248ff.

[14] Wallace, 'Revitalization Movements'.

Islamicists confronted with similar reactions to the arrival of the Arabs react with surprise to the fact that people hostile to Islam should borrow from Islam, or they infer from the borrowing that the movements cannot have been anti-Islamic.[15] But, as observed before, it is a mistake to think that borrowing other people's ideas or arms or styles of dress is necessarily done in a spirit of friendship. (The whole world has long been getting to be more like the West without becoming noticeably friendlier to it.) Of such use of the foreigners' cultural repertoire, however, there is actually less in the case of the Iranian rebels than the habit of labelling them 'syncretic prophets' leads one to expect. More precisely, most of their syncretism dates back to before the coming of Islam. The only prophet we see engaged in the task of 'revitalising' his native faith in confrontation with Islam is Bihāfarīdh, who was a reformist rather than a nativist leader (unless we widen the rubric of 'nativism' to include any response to foreign intrusion involving defence of the native tradition). Bābak is not on record as having used any Islamic idiom at all, but then our information on his preaching is exiguous. Al-Muqannaʿ sought vengeance for Abū Muslim, alluded to the clothes of paradise as described in the Qurʾān, listed the messengers who had preceded him under Islamic names (or at least his followers did), and claimed to be the mahdi. The veiled Christ was also called the mahdi. But the use of Islamic language in the last two cases comes across as less a matter of 'revitalisation' than of simple translation. Al-Muqannaʿ in particular operated in an environment in which the Manichaeans were routinely reformulating their own religious concepts in the idiom of other religious communities, and in which everybody else seems to have done the same without giving a thought to it. If the Christians, Manichaeans, or Buddhists had left us descriptions of al-Muqannaʿ's message they would perhaps have shown him using their religious language as freely as he did that of Islam. Of course, translation of the local religious idiom into that of the Muslims was a form of revitalisation in the sense that it amounted to appropriation of powerful concepts from the hegemonic community and enabled the locals to argue back, by supplying the shared language in which to put their case. But it was not revitalisation in the sense of providing conceptual resources for supra-local action that would otherwise be lacking. Long familiar with supra-local religions and endowed with cult societies in touch with one another, the Iranian rebels did have such resources of their own.

[15] It similarly used to be regarded as impossible for the Byzantines to have been influenced by Muslim iconoclasm because they and the Muslims were enemies.

Nativist revolts were a form of peasant revolts in the broad sense of that word. Both mobilised rural people, not just or even primarily peasants in the sense of those who tilled the land, but rather landless villagers such as weavers, potters, ox-drivers, muleteers and other hired hands, runners, smugglers, and brigands, or even miners, as in the case of Ustādhsīs's revolt; and both pitched such villagers against a political elite. The elite merely happened to be foreign in some cases and not in others.[16] The two types of rural revolt are often treated together under the heading of millenarian rebellion in the modern literature, and the dividing-line between them could be thin: it was a rural revolt that culminated in the expulsion of the Mongols from China in 1368, for example, at a time when the foreign origin of this dynasty was no longer readily apparent. This revolt is also the one example of a nativist revolt/peasant revolt that succeeded. It began as rural uprisings by lowly people inspired by a mish-mash of Buddhist and Manichaean ideas comparable to al-Muqannaʿ's: the so-called White Lotus society started the uprisings in 1351, proclaiming the descent of Maitreya to be imminent. But the Chinese revolts differed from their Iranian counterparts in at least three major respects. First, they were directed against an ageing regime rather than a recently installed one. Secondly, there were several revolts at the same time – in the heartland of China, not just the borderlands. And thirdly, some of the rebel leaders, including the future winner, changed tactics. Having initially directed their violence against the landed gentry, they later dropped their messianic programmes and took to recruiting the gentry in order to build up imperial regimes of the traditional kind. Well before the Ming dynasty was enthroned the aspirations of the original rebels had been abandoned.[17] On their own rural people could not acquire political organisation, experience, and skill, let alone respectability, fast enough to defeat those who already possessed it, and who often had superior weaponry too.

Nativist rebellion does not seem to represent a common pattern in the history of the expansion of Islam. The Iranian revolts are the only (relatively) well-documented examples. There are also two poorly documented movements that conform to the description in what is now Morocco, that of Ṣāliḥ and his successors among the Barghawāṭa from perhaps 131/748f., certainly the 220s/840s, to the mid-fifth/eleventh century, and that of Ḥāʾ-Mīm among the Ghumāra which only lasted two years

[16] For a classic analysis see Worsley, *The Trumpet Shall Sound*, 227ff.

[17] See Dardess, 'Transformations of Messianic Revolt'; further references in Mote, 'Rise of the Ming', 47f.

(from 313/925f. to 315/927f.).[18] There may well have been more which went unrecorded, or which were recorded too laconically for their nativist character to be apparent; many of the nativist uprisings against the Europeans were too minor to have merited a mention in a medieval chronicle. But as the record stands there are no signs of the response in the countryside of Syria, Egypt, or Iraq.

THE *ÉVOLUÉS* WHO WALK OUT

Of the Iranian rebels three were former Muslims: Sunbādh, al-Muqannaʿ, and Bābak. Many leaders of nativist revolts against the European conquerors had been Christians. All belong in the category of natives who take up arms against the foreign rulers in whose society they have lived and whose culture they have absorbed to a greater or lesser extent. This is a well-known pattern in history, by no means limited to nativist villagers. There is a famous example in Moses, an Israelite brought up at Pharaoh's court. The Bible envisages him as an Egyptian by culture, but not by identity, and tells us that at some point he had an experience that made him realise that he did not belong with the Egyptians, the hegemonic people, but rather with the Israelites, the oppressed slaves: he proceeded to organise them for revolt. A less well-known example is Douketios, a Hellenised native of Sicily who led the Sikels in revolt against the Greeks in about 450 BC, forming a federation of all the cities of the same *ethnos* and building his capital city at the sacred precinct of the Sikel gods, at a time when archaeology shows the Hellenisation of the local population to have been well in progress.[19] Yet another example is Arminius, a tribal noble who rose high in Roman society as commander of a Germanic unit in the Roman army, obtaining both citizenship and equestrian rank before turning against the Romans and inflicting a famous defeat on them in 9 AD.[20] Nowadays there are Muslims who have grown up or studied in the post-imperial but still hegemonic West and who proceed to organise movements against it.

More relevant here, however, are the nationalists who dynamited the French and the British empires. They were often what the French called *évolués*, or what the British called 'wogs' (Westernised Oriental gentlemen),

[18] Cf. *EI*^{2}, s.vv. 'Barghawāṭa', Ḥāʾ-Mīm'.
[19] Diodorus Siculus, XI, 76, 88; Domínguez, 'Greek Cities of Sicily and the Natives'.
[20] All scholarship on this man seems to focus on military matters rather than his political *volte-face*, though it is hardly unproblematic (thus most recently Wells, *The Battle that Stopped Rome*).

that is to say natives who had absorbed the culture of their imperial rulers, who spoke their language, followed their ways, and lived in cities, where they usually worked as clerks. They were French or British by culture (to varying degrees), but not by identity, and they too had experiences that made them realise that they belonged with the 'slaves'. Like Moses they reacted by organising them for revolt.

The Arab equivalent of the *évolué* was the *mawlā*, a native conversant with Arabic and Arab ways, usually also a Muslim, who lived in a city and often worked as a clerk (*kātib*). Both Sunbādh and al-Muqanna' could perhaps be classified as *évolués*, the former as a local ruler (also represented in the ranks of the nationalists), the latter as a clerk; but their Muslim education seems to have been limited. Many *évolués* were far more acculturated, sometimes wholly 'Arab' by language and culture. Of them it can be said that like their counterparts in the French and British empires they were often angry. Their response was very different from that of the nationalists, however. Some of them did proceed to organise their people for revolt; the Berber Ibāḍīs who repeatedly established imamates of their own in North Africa from the end of the Umayyad period onwards are an obvious example.[21] But the Ibāḍīs did not tailor their message specifically to non-Arabs; they set up imamates in Oman and Ḥaḍramawt about the same time as well, working among Arabs. In principle, moreover, they did not mean to secede at all. What they wanted was rather to unite all Muslims under a ruler they considered the true imam – as their competitors, the Hāshimiyya, had done. In other words they did not intend to break up the political house established by the Arabs, but rather to take it over.

Other *mawālī* turned Shu'ūbī, that is to say they took to strident affirmation of their own superiority with reference to their glorious descent, history, or cultural achievements, in terms that are sometimes suggestive of nationalist sentiments. But these *évolués* did not organise their people for revolt. There is admittedly something of an exception in a third/ninth-century clerk by the name of Ibn Māmshādh, for although he did not take political action he did credit Ya'qūb the Coppersmith, the Iranian rebel he worked for, with a poem telling the caliph to go back to Arabia.[22] If an Indian nationalist had told Queen Victoria to go back to Britain (or rather, since she never left it, to withdraw her troops and other representatives from India), he would have meant it as a call for Indian independence; but Ibn

[21] Crone and Zimmermann, *Epistle*, 303f.

[22] Stern, 'Ya'qūb the Coppersmith and Persian National Sentiment'.

Māmshādh was not calling for an independent Iran. What he meant was that Ya'qūb the Coppersmith should *replace* the caliph – not as caliph, but rather as Persian emperor. To Ibn Māmshādh the Sasanian empire and the caliphal polity were one and the same unit: he depicted Ya'qūb as avenging the kings of Persia, claiming their inheritance, reviving their glory, and taking back the kingdom that the Persians had allowed the caliphs to have for so long, i.e., ever since enthroning them in the Hāshimite revolution ('Our fathers gave you your kingdom, but you showed no gratitude for our benefactions'). Again the assumption is that Arabs and non-Arabs will continue to share a political house; the question is only who should rule it. The reason that Ibn Māmshādh is so famous, morever, is that he is unique. Ordinarily the concern of the Shu'ūbīs was not with the government of the shared political house but rather with the relative distribution of cultural and social prestige within it, or in other words with their own position in the shared polity. They were not trying to destroy the empire that the Arabs had built. On the contrary, being comfortably ensconced in high positions within it, often in the capital itself, they had a strong interest in its survival.[23]

Why did the Arab and European expansions have such different effects on the conquered peoples? Both provoked nativist revolts, but the frequency seems to have been greater on the European than the Muslim side. Both also had to cope with angry *évolués*, but it was only on the European side that these *évolués* aimed at secession with reference to their own separate identity, unless we count Sunbādh, al-Muqanna', and Bābak as *évolués* as well. The vast majority of non-Arab Muslims who rebelled did so without reference to their non-Arab identity, their demands being rather for legitimate Islamic leadership, a true imamate. Conversely, when they did stress their own non-Arab identity their concern was with the terms of coexistence within the political house that the Arab conquerors had built. Either way, the *évolués* accepted Islam and the political unity it had brought. By contrast, those of the European empires accepted the secular culture brought by the Europeans, but not the political unity they had established.

There are evidently many reasons for this difference, but two stand out as central. The first concerns the difference between the idea of the imamate and that of the nation-state. Both are concepts drawn from the hegemonic culture of the time; it was from the Arabs that the Berbers and Iranians learnt to think in terms of the imamate, just as it was from the

[23] Cf. Goldziher, *Muhammedanische Studien* (ed. and tr. Stern, *Muslim Studies*), I, chs. 4–5; *EI*², s.v. 'Shu'ūbiyya' (Enderwitz); Crone, 'Post-Colonialism', 14ff.

French and English that they later learned to think in terms of the nation-state. But nationalism is an ideology that links political organisation with people's separate identities, making a virtue of the ethnic or racial origins that divide them; by contrast, the imamate links political organisation with shared convictions, making a virtue of the faith that transcends such distinctions. Like the Europeans the Arabs had their own ethnic identity, and their exhilaration at having come together in a single polity at the time of the conquests imparts a nationalist (in the sense of ethnic chauvinist) overtone to their early history as Muslims. Since tribes are defined by genealogy their sense of superiority sometimes comes across as racist too, and initially Islam heightened their ethnic chauvinism: God had chosen the Arabs above everyone else, all others were inferior in terms of truth, power, and genealogy alike. But, ethnic chauvinists though they were, it was in the name of Islam that they had founded a new political society and, as we have seen, they proceeded to open the floodgates to their own initially select ranks by making the bar to membership of Muslim society extraordinarily low.[24] Converts came in droves, as freedmen and voluntary immigrants alike.

This brings us to the second difference. Unlike the converts to the secular culture of the Europeans the many who converted to Islam became members of the same political and moral community as the conquerors: a *mawlā* in the sense of a non-Arab Muslim was not just an *évolué* but also a citizen. Islam differed radically from both the Christian church and the nation-state in that the community the *mawlā* joined was both a community of believers and a polity – indeed, a far-flung empire ruled by the Commander of the Believers, the caliph. The initial members of this community were the empire-bearing people, and what is so unusual about the century after the conquests is that, thanks to the fusion of the religious and the political communities, conversion admitted defeated natives to the ranks of the imperial elite more or less at will. Converts were considered inferior to the Arabs, of course, but the fact that the community was based on belief in a universalist God meant that non-Arab Muslims could 'beat the Arabs at religion', as a *ḥadīth* puts it, that is to say they could excel in religious matters to the point of eclipsing the original bearers of Islam. The Hāshimiyya beat the Arabs at religion by uniting all Muslims under an imam from the Prophet's house. Many other rebels, both Khārijite and Shīʿite, entertained comparable hopes.

[24] See Chapter 1, p. 16.

By contrast, excelling at Christianity did not help the subjects of the European empires because it was not in the name of Christianity that these empires had been formed. Excelling at the modern secular values did not help either, because Westernisation did not confer membership of the conquerors' polity. Nehru may have been the last Englishman to rule India, as he told Galbraith with reference to his thoroughly English culture; but he ruled India precisely because he had participated in the eviction of the British, not because he had received British citizenship or appointment as viceroy of India from them. Westernisation never amounted to membership of the imperial elite. Rather, it served to generate a large number of people who had been defined out of their traditional communities by their Western education without becoming either formal or informal members of the community to which their education assigned them. They did not belong anywhere; they were politically homeless and, like Nehru, they reacted by trying to establish a political home of their own. If the Muslims could be said to have made the barrier to membership absurdly low, the Europeans made it impossibly high. The only way to get respect on nationalist premises was to form a nation of one's own. In short, where Islamisation drew people into the imperial polity Westernisation set them against it.

The Arab and the European expansions differed in so many other ways, however, that even if the Europeans had expanded in Asia in the name of Christianity it is unlikely that it would have functioned in the same way as Islam. (It certainly did not in the Americas.) For one thing the church was never identical with political society, whether that of kingdom, empire, or nation-state. For another thing it was not simply by converting that the natives of the Near East succeeded in taking over the empire, but rather by rapidly becoming the majority in the conquerors' own society and taking over as the main interpreters of the ideas that the conquerors had brought with them. They could do so because the Arabs who had settled in the conquered lands were a small minority there. There were more of them in Arabia, of course, but Arabia was a sparsely populated region of limited resources, and both parties to the First Civil War moved their capital to the conquered lands. They thereby reduced the Peninsula to a mere appendix to the empire. The Arabs who dominate the textbooks on the Umayyad and early ʿAbbāsid periods are those who had left their Arabian homeland to settle in the conquered lands, not those who had stayed at home. Arabia was an appendix of enormous religious and ideological importance to the settlers, but it was not of much practical significance after it had ceased to be the metropole: the imperial revenues did not go there any more, administrators were not sent from there, nor did they go back there after fulfilment of their duties, or send their children back to be educated there; on the contrary, it was in the conquered lands that literacy, know-how, and other sophistications were available. And after the Second Civil War emigration from Arabia seems to have dried up.

By contrast, the French and the British did not have to move their capital to Algiers, Cairo, or Delhi, because they were not tribesmen from an impoverished periphery in search of power, taxes, and slaves, but rather wealthy capitalists in search of markets and raw materials. The French and the British who dominate the textbooks on the European empires are those back in the homeland, not those who had settled in the conquered lands: it was the empire that was an appendix to the metropole, not the other way round. Unlike the Arabs, in fact, the Europeans rarely settled in large numbers in colonies in which the natives had highly developed literary traditions and political organisation of their own, as opposed to colonies in which the natives could easily be brushed aside. Algeria is the main exception, and a conspicuous failure. The Europeans did recruit native administrators and soldiers but, unlike the Arabs, they did not have to use them in the top positions, let alone in the metropole itself, because they could keep sending new men from France and Britain for such posts. On top of that the French and British were not always sure that they really wanted an empire, since formal control was expensive and not always necessary for purposes of securing markets and raw materials; and they did not always envisage those colonies in which they did not settle as permanent possessions. In short, even if the Europeans had expanded in Asia as bearers of churches rather than nations the conquered peoples could not have penetrated their ranks.

Accordingly, the history of the French and British empires abounds in examples of secession by acculturated natives: they walked out as members of separatist churches, as leaders of nativist revolts, and above all as modern nationalists. By contrast, the dominant trend in the Arab caliphate is centripetal. The political house established by the Arabs did break up from the mid-third/ninth century onwards, but it continued as a post-imperial commonwealth of greater historical significance than that of the British. The long and the short of it is that Islam was vastly better than modern secular culture for the creation of fellowship on an imperial scale, and correspondingly worse for the maintenance of an ethnically distinct conquest elite.

THE GENTILES WHO SPLIT OFF

It is not simply because Islam was a religion that it created a fellowship at the cost of the conquest elite. It could not have done so if it had been indissolubly tied to Arab ethnicity. The sheer fact that one could convert to it is important, self-evident though it may look to us. Conversion was not a feature of the religions of the Near East and Mediterranean in antiquity before the rise of Christianity, for religion back then did not take the form of an abstract set of propositions that one could embrace or reject. It was philosophy that took this form. Religion, by contrast, was a set of ritual practices (above all sacrifice) designed to secure the favour of the gods of the ethnic or civic community to which one belonged. One worshipped these deities because the welfare of one's people or city was held to depend on their benevolence, and forswearing them in favour of the gods of another people made no sense at all. One could add other cults to one's traditional repertoire, and one might be expected (or simply choose) to add one signalling loyalty to the empire in which one had been incorporated. But one did not become an Assyrian by rendering homage to Ashur, nor could one become a Greek or Roman citizen by adopting Greek or Roman deities. Citizenship was acquired by birth or grant, not by a change of mind regarding the ultimate nature of this world, and cultic practice followed from one's citizenship, not the other way round.

Accordingly, nobody in the Near East and Mediterranean in antiquity expected incorporation into empires to be followed by adoption of the gods of the conquerors. The Assyrians famously campaigned in the name of religion, but only in the sense that they saw themselves as fulfilling a divine command to subject their neighbours, not in the sense of seeing themselves as called upon to convert them. The Achaemenids similarly cast themselves as agents of Ahura Mazda without conceiving of their empire as an instrument of proselytisation, and Greek and Roman religion was also too closely tied to civic identity and institutions to be exported to outsiders. The Greeks readily identified foreign deities with their own, but this was simply a way of rendering foreign cults intelligible; underneath their shared names the deities and cults remained different. It was the assimilation of Greek culture, above all philosophy, that produced the Hellenised Oriental gentlemen of the Graeco-Roman period, and Hellenisation shared with Westernisation the feature of not amounting to citizenship. The long coexistence of Greeks and non-Greeks under the same (eventually Roman) political roof in the Mediterranean and Near East did gradually serve to erode political and cultural differences, but it took an extraordinarily long time by Muslim standards.[25] In short, a plurality of religions tied to local identity coexisted under a single political

[25] For a lighthearted comparison of the speeds see Crone, 'Imperial Trauma'.

roof. This was good for the maintenance of an ethnically and culturally distinct conquest elite, and correspondingly bad for the creation of fellowship on an imperial scale. When the fellowship finally came to the Roman empire it was not supplied by Greek or Roman religion at all, but rather by Christianity.

The Arab conquerors initially seemed to be following the ancient model, for they too had their own religion and allowed all others to practise their own. The particularist concept of Islam reinforced their sense of Arab fellowship, and it also made them tolerant – except in connection with Arab Christians, whom they sometimes tried to convert by force. Non-Arabs could adhere to whatever religion they liked. (Modern historians usually disapprove of Arab exclusivism while applauding their tolerant ways, but the one was the obverse of the other.) All those who had a strong interest in the preservation of the conquest elite would have liked Islam to remain particularist. They did not deny that it was a universal truth, nor did they close their ranks to converts. What they did was rather to insist that anyone who accepted the truth of this religion had to form part of the people to whom it had been revealed; access to the Arab God presupposed membership of an Arab tribe, whether by birth or affiliation to a patron. This was the obvious way of combining a particularist concept of the religion with belief in its universal truth, and it is the solution familiar from rabbinic and later Judaism: the convert here becomes a *ger* (Arabic *jār*, protégé); the tie is with the people, not with a religious community separate from it, for the simple reason that there is not any: the religion is embodied in the ethnic group. When the Arabs instituted clientage (*walā'*) for the affiliation of converts they were adopting the same solution. But the massive influx of converts undermined it, and by the end of the Umayyad period the religious scholars had rejected it. Affiliation was with the community of believers alone in their view, not to the Arabs as a people.

The scholars could reject clientage for converts because there *was* a religious community separate from the Arabs. This is crucial for the explanation of how they successfully withstood another risk to which modern scholars rarely pay attention, namely that the Islam of the Arabs and that of their non-Arab converts would part ways. When those Jews of the Roman empire who believed the messiah to have come started preaching to the gentiles they initiated a development that eventually burst the confines of Judaism; its gentile wing split off from the mother religion, as Christians declaring ethnicity to be irrelevant to faith. Identifying themselves as the true Israel, the Christians saw their Israelite genealogy as purely spiritual and interpreted all the features that had defined the ancestral community, including the law, in an allegorical vein. The same did in fact happen to Islam in Iran, just not on a scale sufficiently large to reduce the mother religion to a minority. Like the Christians the Khurramīs saw themselves as the true Muslims, declared Arab ethnicity to be irrelevant to the correct understanding of Muḥammad's message, and interpreted the law allegorically to make room for their own traditions.[26] And just as a Jew who converted to Christianity stopped being a 'Jew', meaning someone who attached importance to his literal descent and observance of the law, so an Arab who joined the Khurramīs stopped being an 'Arab', meaning much the same. Already in the parlance of the Hāshimiyya 'Arab' has all the contemptuous overtones of 'Jew' in parts of the New Testament. But the Hāshimiyya conquered the 'Arabs' and came to terms with them (and vice versa) in Iraq; unlike the Christians and the Khurramīs, moreover, they never seem to have attacked the law. The bearers of the mother religion thus remained members of the community even after it had become overwhelmingly gentile; indeed, they continued to enjoy special respect. Just as there was no decolonisation, so there was no schism, only a revolution. The Islam that developed after the revolution was very different from what had prevailed before it, but it was still the same religion.

The rise of Ismailism could be said to represent a second round, a concerted attempt to secure acceptance for a grand vision of a gentile Islam in which the messiah would replace the law in favour of spirituality as the road to salvation. It was deeply attractive to many Iranians. But though the Old Ismailis (Qarmaṭīs) did part ways with the mother religion by abolishing the law in Baḥrayn, the Ismailis at large, both in Iran and elsewhere, preferred to stay in their ancestral community, postponing the abrogation of the law to the distant future.

The crucial point here is that Islam had never been an ethnic religion on a par with those of antiquity. Judaism was, and still is, both conceptually and terminologically indistinguishable from the Jewish people; there is no faith separate from it, just as there is no separate community of believers. But Islam was born after the rise of Christianity, and it had always taken the form of a set of propositions detachable from the ethnic context in which they were first formulated. This was true not just of the faith but also of the law; the two together formed a religion bearing a different name, embodied in a different community, from the Arabs as a people. Certainly, the initially hostile attitude of the Ismailis to the law had something to do

[26] See further Chapter 13, pp. 261ff.

with the fact that it stood in the way of their gentile heritage, and the law did yoke Islam to its Arab past in some respects, most obviously by locating the central sanctuary in Arabia and tying the legitimisation of legal rules to the lives of the Prophet and his Arabian Companions. The claim that Islam is an 'Arab' religion has reverberated down the ages and is still being heard in Iran today. Even so, the key problem posed by the law was not its Arab links, but rather the fact that it laid down a rigorous framework within which everything else had to be accommodated and which left no room for the religious conceptions that many inhabitants of Iran and Mesopotamia wished to retain. The issue was the nature of the religion itself, not its ethnic identification. This does much to explain why converts to Islam did not usually feel impelled to reject the law, however much they might resent the Arabs; on the contrary, it was mostly non-Arabs who elaborated it.

In short, the development of the Arab empire is without parallel in antiquity and modern times alike. The religious community created by Muḥammad was separate from that of the Arabs as a people *and yet* it was fused with political society. This unusual combination is a precondition for everything that followed, and it could only come about because Muḥammad operated in a stateless environment. A people and its political organisation are not normally separable, and in a sense they were not in Muḥammad's case either; but political organisation in his Arabia took the form of tribes rather than a state, and for purposes of religious unity the tribes had to be transcended, by incorporation in a wider unit which was entirely new. It was this new unit that rolled together religious and political society. In the last resort, then, the fact that the Arabs hailed from a resource-poor environment is not a contingent factor in the unusual development of the conquest society, but rather a precondition for it. Whether considered as nativists, as *évolués* who walked out, or as gentiles who seceded, the most striking feature of the Khurramīs is that they did not set the trend. This might have been different if Iran had been all that the Arabs conquered, but then so many other factors would have been different too that it is difficult to engage in counterfactual history at this point. In any case, Iran was only one among many conquered lands, and fairly peripheral in the crucial period before the revolution. By the time the Khurramīs walked out there was no question of all the Iranian converts following suit, let alone all non-Arab Muslims.

9

The Aftermath

The nativist revolts failed. What happened to the communities involved? The answer is that those of the Jibāl continued to rebel for another century or so, if never again on the same scale, and that all of them are reported still to have been awaiting the return of a messianic figure in the fourth/tenth and fifth/eleventh centuries, to which most of the information about them pertains. They were well known not to have been real Muslims: they professed Islam externally, but had their own religion in secret, as al-Bīrūnī said;[1] they would pretend to follow whatever faith was dominant while continuing to adhere to their own beliefs in secret, as Dihkhudā put it.[2] But there were no crusades against them, so they survived down to at least the sixth/twelfth century. What follows documents these points, starting with the communities in the east.

KHURĀSĀN, TRANSOXANIA

There were Red-clothed ones on the border between Ṭabaristān and Jurjān,[3] Muslimiyya, also called Khurramdīniyya, near Balkh,[4] and White-clothed ones in the rural areas of the Hephtalites, where their religion was close to *zandaqa*.[5] Abū Tammām, an Ismaili missionary active in the early fourth/tenth century, came across such people in an unidentified part of Khurāsān. He calls them followers of al-Muqannaʿ and some of

[1] Bīrūnī, *Āthār*, 211.

[2] Kāshānī, *Zubda*, 187.

[3] See Chapter 4, p. 81.

[4] Ibn al-Nadīm, 408.13 = II, 824, citing al-Balkhī.

[5] Muqaddasī, 323.14. The claim that Bihāfarīdh's followers belonged partly to the Khusrawiyya and partly to the Khurramiyya must relate to roughly the same area (Thaʿālibī in Houtsma, 'Bih'afrid', 35 = 33).

what he says does relate to them, but it comes from literary sources;[6] the rest relates to people he had met personally and disputed with, probably in the course of trying to convert them to Ismailism, and except for the learned they knew nothing about al-Muqannaʿ, probably for the simple reason that they had never had anything to do with him. They only married among themselves and, quite apart from knowing nothing about al-Muqannaʿ, in Abū Tammām's opinion they were ignorant: 'none of them has much understanding of the principles of their faith'.[7] From the point of view of a *mutakallim* this was probably quite true. The Yezidis of northern Mesopotamia have left a similar impression on modern Western observers, for as Kreyenbroek explains there is virtually no official body of doctrines and no particular virtue attaches to having this kind of knowledge either ('mere talk', as the Ahl-i Ḥaqq call it).[8] Even a shaykh may look blank if asked to expound Yezidi doctrine on a particular point, and some subscribe to mutually exclusive beliefs without giving much thought to it, for what most Yezidis seek in religion is not a coherent set of propositions about the nature of reality, but rather a deeper sense of the mysteries behind it. Religious learning is (or was) for specialists, and lay Yezidis feel no greater need for it than most Westerners feel for knowledge of biochemistry or electro-engineering. A son of Shaykh ʿAdī b. Musāfir, the founder of the Yezidis, is said to have asked a companion what he would tell the angels Munkar and Nakīr when they came to question him about his Lord in the grave: 'I shall tell them, "Shaykh ʿAdī b. Musāfir will tell you who my Lord is"', was the reply. Having a shaykh to follow was crucial, mastering his learning was not.[9] This is likely also to have been the attitude of Abū Tammām's Mubayyiḍa.

Of al-Muqannaʿ's followers Abū Tammām says that they were awaiting a new incarnation of God. Elsewhere it is al-Muqannaʿ himself that they are waiting for: according to al-Maqdisī he had promised his followers that he would come back in the shape (*qālab*) of a man with greying hair (*ashmaṭ*) on a grey (*ashhab*) horse and possess the earth.[10] Al-Thaʿālibī (d. 429/1038) says that they still survived in Kish and Nasaf, and that the Mubayyiḍa of Transoxania paid heavy taxes to their rulers.[11] Gardīzī (*c.* 442f./1050–2) and al-Isfarāʾinī (d. 471/1078f.) also mention that

6 Abū Tammām, 77 = 76; cf. Crone, 'Abū Tammām on the Mubayyiḍa'.
7 Abū Tammām, 77 = 76.
8 Mir-Hosseini, 'Breaking the Seal', 184.
9 Kreyenbroek, *Yezidism*, 17–19, 33.
10 Maqdisī, VI, 98; repeated in Ibn al-ʿIbrī, *Duwal*, 218.
11 Thaʿālibī, *Thimār al-qulūb*, no. 1100; Thaʿālibī, *Ādāb al-mulūk*, 38, no. 14.

there were still followers of al-Muqanna',[12] and Qubāvī (wr. 522/1128f.) knew of their presence in the villages of Bukhārā, several of which he mentions by name. He knew some of them personally and says that they had forgotten about al-Muqanna', but this claim is copied from Abū Tammām's report.[13]

In Īlāq White-clothed ones are mentioned by al-Baghdādī, who credits their presence to al-Muqanna'.[14] They had mosques in their villages and hired muezzins, but did not pray in these mosques, he says, which is also what he says about the Bābakiyya; they held it lawful to eat carrion and pork, every one of them slept with somebody else's wife, and Muslims were not safe among them.[15] (For this and other claims relating to wife-sharing the reader is referred to Chapter 17.) Their presence in Īlāq is beyond doubt, for an 'Alid by the name of Maḥmūd al-Īlāqī was executed there in 472/1079f., in the reign of Malikshāh, for preaching *ḥulūl*, and was said to have had bits and pieces of writings by the White-clothed ones and Khurramīs (*nubadh min maqālāt al-mubayyiḍa wa-maqālāt al-Khurramiyya*).[16] Assuming that the *Kitāb al-Khurramiyya* mentioned by al-Maqdisī (see pp. 186, 358) was a book about the Khurramiyya rather than by them, this is our only reference to literature they wrote themselves.

According to al-Shahrastānī there were also White-clothed ones in Shāsh, but he gives no details.[17] Niẓām al-Mulk mentions them in Khujand, Kāsān, and Farghāna, saying that those in Farghāna rebelled and killed all the Muslims they could find in alliance with the Ismailis in the fifteenth year of the reign of the Sāmānid Manṣūr I, i.e., 365/975f., though the correct date is probably 348–50/959–61f. and the alliance may be fictitious.[18] These White-clothed communities are most unlikely to have had anything to do with al-Muqanna' and one would very much like to know exactly what they believed, but Niẓām al-Mulk merely repeats his stereotyped list of Khurramī sins: they do not accept the duty to pray, fast, give alms, go on pilgrimage, and wage holy war; they drink wine, and are

[12] Gardīzī, 283.1; Isfarā'inī, *Tabṣīr*, 77.

[13] *TB*, 73/103 = 75; cf. Abū Tammām, 77 = 76; Crone, 'Abū Tammām on the Mubayyiḍa', 174f. Their presence in the environs of Bukhārā is also mentioned in Sam'ānī, *Ansāb*, s.v. 'mubayyiḍī' (from Qubāvī?).

[14] Baghdādī, *Farq*, 243.9, 244.-3; also Shahrastānī, I, 194 = I, 666.

[15] Baghdādī, *Farq*, 244f.

[16] Iskandar, 'Marwazī's Ṭabā'i' al-Ḥaywawān', 298 = 279; repeated in 'Awfī, *Jawāmi'*, III/1, 231f.

[17] Shahrastānī, I, 194 = I, 666.

[18] *SN*, ch. 46:22, 26 (299, 302f. = 228, 230); cf. Crone and Treadwell, 'Ismailism at the Samanid Court', 48–52.

promiscuous; they even sleep with their mothers and sisters. He does include a detail about a defloration ritual which is probably genuine, though it does not belong in Farghāna.[19]

Niẓām al-Mulk equates the White-clothed ones of Sogdia and Farghāna with Qarmaṭīs (i.e. Old Ismailis), later saying that this is the name they were known by in Transoxania and Ghaznayn, and he also places Qarmaṭīs at Ṭālaqān, the old stronghold of the anti-ʿAbbāsid Rāwandiyya; he saw Ismailis everywhere, of course,[20] but al-Masʿūdī says that the Khurramīs were called Bāṭinīs in Khurāsān and elsewhere,[21] and there are in fact obvious doctrinal similarities between them. What is more, the Ismailis must also have preached among Khurramīs, as we see in the case of Abū Tammām; it would have been hard to avoid doing so in the countryside of Rayy, where their first mission in Khurāsān was based.[22] Al-Baghdādī explicitly says that the Ismailis recruited the Kurds of the Jibāl and the Khurramīs of Bābak's region,[23] and the Nizārīs too had former Khurramīs among their adherents in Azerbaijān (see p. 184).[24] So Niẓām al-Mulk is probably right that there was much overlap between Khurramīs and Ismailis on the ground.

ʿAwfī (wr. 625/1228) seems to be the last to record the presence of White-clothed ones in the east. 'Today in the land of Transoxania there are a group of followers of his [al-Muqannaʿ's] who practise agriculture and husbandry (*dahqanat va kishāvarzī*) and call themselves White-clothed ones. They hide their customs and beliefs and nobody knows the truth about them,' he says.[25] He may be copying from an earlier source. In a different recension he says that they survive at Bukhārā and Samarqand, and here he adds that they call themselves Muslims and teach their children the Qurʾān, but that nobody knows what they really believe:[26] this is what al-Iṣṭakhrī says of the Khurramīs in the Jibāl and al-Baghdādī of the Bābakiyya in Azerbaijan. Information relating to the Khurramdīnīs is disconcertingly mobile. All Khurramīs were assumed to have the same beliefs so that information collected in the Jibāl could be cited in accounts of communities in Khurāsān or Transoxania, much as 'primitive peoples'

19 *SN*, ch. 46:28 (304 = 232); cf. Chapter 17, p. 434.
20 *SN*, ch. 46:26, 39 (302, 311/230, 238).
21 MM, IV, §2399 (VI, 188).
22 Cf. Crone and Treadwell, 'Ismailism at the Samanid Court', 64f.
23 Baghdādī, *Farq*, 266, 268, cf. 285.-3.
24 Cf. note 41.
25 ʿAwfi, *Jawāmiʿ*, ed. Sheʿar, 274f.
26 ʿAwfi, *Jawāmiʿ*, ed. Muṣaffā, III/1, 231.

were once assumed to be more or less the same everywhere, so that information pertaining to Borneo, Africa, and Alaska could be used for the reconstruction of the same picture.

JIBĀL, AZERBAIJAN, RAYY

Though the Khurdanaye became Muslims when Bābak's death left them leaderless[27] they had by no means finished with revolt. In 227/842 (1153 AS), a mere four years after Bābak's gruesome execution, they were at it again according to Dionysius, this time in Beth Qardu, the mountainous region to the north of Mosul between the Tigris and the Zāb, where their leader was a certain Mūsā. The troops sent against them were 'Persians' who were billeted in private homes, where they ate the food of the locals without accomplishing anything; then winter came and 15,000 of the troops died in the cold.[28] Muslim sources report that a Kurdish leader by the name of Ja'far b. Mihrijīsh/Faharjīs or the like rebelled in 227/841f. in the mountainous area of Mosul, presumably as part of the same revolt, though he is not identified as a Khurramī.[29] The Khurramīs of Iṣfahān also rebelled again in the reign of al-Wāthiq (227–32/842–7), pillaging Karaj,[30] so it is hard to avoid the impression of yet another spate of linked revolts, which did not become serious enough for proper coverage. They appear to have been triggered by the death of al-Mu'taṣim.[31] In the Iṣfahān region the revolts that started under al-Wāthiq continued until 300/912. Then a certain Bāryazdshāh (or the like) ensconced himself in the mountains near Iṣfahān, attacking villages and plundering caravans: like Bābak he was accused of indiscriminate cruelty, killing young and old alike. He and his followers kept it up for some thirty years, whereupon he was captured and his head displayed at Iṣfahān.[32] This was probably in 321/933, when 'Alī b. Būya is reported to have stormed some Khurramī fortresses in the Karaj region,[33] and it seems to be the end of the revolts. It is true that a general of 'Aḍud al-Dawla's is reported to have subdued Khurramīs along with

[27] See Chapter 3, n. 122.
[28] Michael Syr., IV, 542f. = III, 109.
[29] Tab. iii, 1322; Mas'ūdī, *Tanbīh*, 355; Azdī, 430; IA, VI, 506f. (year 224).
[30] *SN*, ch. 47:13 (319 = 244). For Khurramīs in jail in Baghdad in 250/864f. see Tab. iii, 1521.
[31] Ibn al-Faqīh, 53/111, 375, nonetheless credits the defeat of Ja'far al-Kurdī (as also that of a certain al-Ḥasan b. Khaylawayh) to al-Mu'taṣim.
[32] *SN*, ch. 47:13 (319 = 244). The name is missing in the translation, based on Darke's first edition.
[33] Miskawayh, *Tajārib*, I, 278 = IV, 316; IA, VIII, 269.

Jāshakiyya/Khāshakiyya, who had been infesting the roads by land and sea, probably in southern Fārs, in 360/971;[34] but these Khurramiyya are apparently a misreading of Jurūmiyya.[35]

The Khurramīs of the Jibāl still had political dreams, though. Some awaited the return of Abū Muslim as the mahdi (or along with the mahdi, as in Niẓām al-Mulk's account of Sunbādh): Abū Muslim had not died and would not die, they said; he would return to fill the earth with justice.[36] Others expected a mahdi from Abū Muslim's family, a descendant of his daughter Fāṭima who would come from Byzantium, perhaps reflecting the Khurramī rebel from the Jibāl who had escaped with several thousand followers and enrolled in the Byzantine army. They were in a state of permanent readiness to rebel, eagerly awaiting the *ẓuhūr*, and expecting power (*mulk*) to return to them, and they would start all meetings by crying over the death of Abū Muslim, cursing al-Manṣūr, and praying for al-Mahdī Fīrūz, the son of Abū Muslim's daughter Fāṭima. According to Niẓām al-Mulk they referred to this mahdi as the *kūdak-i dānā*, translated as *(al-)fatā al-ʿālim*, 'the knowing/learned boy', of whom more is said below (p. 341).[37]

According to al-Masʿūdī those who held the imamate to have passed from Abū Muslim to his daughter Fāṭima and her descendants were known as Fāṭimids: Bābak's followers were of this type.[38] Neither Jāvīdhān nor Bābak is credited with any views on Abū Muslim in Wāqid's account, but al-Dīnawarī, who died a mere sixty (lunar) years after Bābak, held the latter to have been a descendant of Muṭahhar b. Fāṭima bint Abī Muslim, clearly assuming him to have been an imam of the Fāṭimid Khurramī type.[39] They must have adopted Muslimism soon after their defeat; perhaps this was the sense in which they had become Muslims. Abū Dulaf confirms that the Khurramīs at Badhdh were waiting

34 Miskawayh, *Tajārib*, II, 299 = V, 321; cf. 300f. = 323, on the Jāshakīs (thus the Arabic text) or Khāshakīs (thus the translation).

35 See IA, VIII, 613 (year 360); *EI*², s.v. 'Khurramiyya', 65 (Madelung), with further references.

36 MM, IV, §2398 (VI, 186); see Chapter 2, p. 42.

37 MM, IV, §2398 (VI, 186f.); cf. Masʿūdī, *Tanbīh*, 354.1; Maqdisī, IV, 31 (similarly Abū Tammām, 78 = 77, here wrongly of the Muqannaʿiyya), VI, 95; *SN*, ch. 47:14 (319f. = 244), cf. 13, where he mentions the *Tārīkh-i Iṣfahān* (of Ḥamza al-Iṣfahānī) as a source on Khurramī beliefs. The article is missing in *al-fatā*, but no significance can be attached to this. For the refugee in Byzantium see Chapter 2, p. 41; for the mahdi as a child see Chapter 15, pp. 341f.

38 MM, IV, §2398 (VI, 186). The sentence is in disorder and could be differently construed.

39 Dīnawarī, 397. Muṭahhar is sometimes given as the name of the future mahdi (cf. Kāshānī, *Zubda*, 187, n. 12).

for the mahdi, without telling us who the mahdi was.[40] By al-Baghdādī's time the Khurramīs in Azerbaijan had come to trace their origin to a pre-Islamic prince named Sharwīn whose mother was a Persian princess and whose father was *min al-zanj*, which sounds like a corruption of some local name, and whom they held to be more meritorious than all the prophets, Muḥammad included.[41] By 513/1119f. some of them had converted to Nizārī Ismailism, to repudiate it in favour of their own faith. When they came to the notice of the Ismaili authorities they were led by two locals, Abū 'l-ʿAlāʾ and Yūsuf, who had served as Ismaili missionaries, and by a weaver called Budayl. They now called themselves Pārsīs. The weaver Budayl said that truth was with the Pārsīs, that the two former Ismaili missionaries were in the position of Muḥammad and ʿAlī, and that Muḥammad and ʿAlī in their turn, as well as Salmān (al-Fārisī), were gods: 'the light sometimes appears in one person and sometimes in two and sometimes in three'. They had become ʿAlid Shīʿites in other words, of a trinitarian kind recalling their former beliefs in God, Christ, and the holy spirit. But if Dihkhudā is to be trusted, they were still Muslimīs as well: the imamate had been in the Persian kings from Jamshīd onwards, then it passed to Muḥammad and ʿAlī, and from there via Ibrāhīm al-Imām to Abū Muslim, whose son in Rūm would be the mahdi. The three leaders were executed in 537/1142.[42]

Al-Masʿūdī, who wrote in 323/934f., two years after ʿAlī b. Būya's operation at Karaj, and who had engaged in disputations with Khurramīs,[43] tells us that the Khurramīs of his own time were divided into Kūdhakiyya (or Kardakiyya) and Kūdhshāhiyya (or Lūdhshāhiyya) and that he had dealt with the doctrinal differences and contention between them in other books of his – now unfortunately lost. He places them in the mountainous regions of western Iran, listing a wealth of place-names and cursorily mentioning that they were also found in Khurāsān and the rest of Iran.[44] The Kūdhakiyya and Kūdhshāhiyya sound like tribal moieties, but he does not link the Khurramīs with the Kurds, whom he covers in the preceding section. The Kūdhakiyya could be the devotees of the *kūdak-i dānā*, the knowing boy, but one might also link the

[40] Minorsky, *Abu-Dulaf*, §15; cited in Yāqūt, I, 529.

[41] Baghdādī, *Farq*, 252. In Abū 'l-Maʿālī, 451.1, based on Baghdādī, the father is also *az Zangiyān*.

[42] Dihkhudā in Kāshānī, *Zubda*, 186–90; shorter version in Rashīd al-Dīn, 149–53, where they are explicitly placed in Azerbaijan; cf. Madelung, *Religious Trends*, 9f.

[43] Masʿūdī, *Tanbīh*, 353f.

[44] MM, IV, §2398 (VI, 187); Masʿūdī, *Tanbīh*, 353.

name with *Kwtk* or *Krtk*, a heretic mentioned in the *Dēnkard*.[45] All we are told about him is that he failed the molten metal ordeal, to which heretics and polemicists had to be submitted before being declared guilty,[46] but he is placed after Mazdak, and Abū Ḥātim al-Rāzī mentions a certain Kūdak or Kūdal among other extremist Zoroastrians (*ghulāt al-majūs*).[47] The Kūdhakiyya could have been his followers.

Thereafter al-Masʿūdī lists a cluster of further subdivisions, apparently distinct from the first two: 'Muḥammira, Mazdaqiyya, Māhāniyya, and others'.[48] Muḥammira and Mazdaqiyya, normally synonymous with Khurramiyya, or at least with all those from Jurjān westwards, are here subdivisions of them along with the Māhāniyya, elsewhere identified as a branch of (Iranianised) Marcionites.[49] Abū Ḥātim al-Rāzī, on the other hand, links the labels with regions: the heretics were called Kūdhakiyya (or Kūdhaliyya) and Khurramiyya in the Iṣfahān region, Mazdakites and Sunbādhites at Rayy and elsewhere in the Jibāl, Muḥammira in Dīnawar and Nihāwand (al-Māhayn), and Dhaqūliyya (or Dafūliyya) in Azerbaijan.[50] Yet another mysterious name is provided by Ibn al-Nadīm, who says that the Muḥammira (here all the western Khurramīs before Bābak) were known as al-Laqaṭa.[51]

Al-Muqaddasī tells us that the Khurramdīniyya lived in impenetrable mountains in the Jibāl and that they were 'Murjiʾites', here apparently meaning Muslims who held observance of the law to be unnecessary: they did not perform ablutions after major ritual impurity (*janāba*), and he had not seen any mosques in their villages. He had engaged in disputation with them and asked them whether the 'Muslims' would not conduct military campaigns against them: their answer was, 'aren't we monotheists?' When al-Muqaddasī asked how they could be monotheists when they denied God's precepts and ignored the *sharīʿa* they replied that they paid an

[45] *Dk*, III, no. 345 (*DkM*, 355, *DkB*, 256); de Menasce, 'Kartak the Heretic', adding *DkM*, 181.

[46] *Dk*, III, no.169 (*DkM*, 181, *DkB*, 140), with de Menasce's comments; cf. also Molé, 'Une histoire du mazdéisme', 210, citing *DkM*, 428.7–10.

[47] Abū Ḥātim al-Rāzī, *Iṣlāḥ*, 160.9 (Kūdal); read Kūdak in Stern, 'Abū Ḥātim al-Rāzī on Persian Religion', 41.

[48] Masʿūdī, *Tanbīh*, 353.

[49] Thus Ibn al-Nadīm, 402 = II, 807; ʿAbd al-Jabbār, *Mughnī*, 18 = 168f. They are Khurramīs (or rather Mazdakites) again in Shahrastānī, I, 194 = I, 665, probably on the basis of al-Masʿūdī.

[50] Abū Ḥātim al-Rāzī, *Zīna*, 306 (cf. the readings in Madelung, 'Khurramiyya'); repeated, slightly differently, in Shahrastānī, I, 132 = I, 508.

[51] Ibn al-Nadīm, 406.2 = II, 817.

annual sum to the government.[52] Al-Iṣṭakhrī, writing about the middle of the fourth/tenth century, also says that the Khurramīs lived in the impenetrable mountains of the Jibāl, but according to him there were mosques in their villages and they recited the Qur'ān too; but inwardly they were said to believe in nothing but *ibāḥa*.[53] Unlike al-Muqaddasī he is probably citing a written source here, for al-Baghdādī says much the same in a less truncated form, with reference to the Bābakiyya of Azerbaijan rather than the Khurramīs in the Jibāl: they built mosques for Muslims (i.e., not for themselves) in their mountains, and got Muslims to make the *ādhān* in them, and they also taught their children the Qur'ān, but they did not pray in private, nor did they fast in Ramaḍān or believe in *jihād* against infidels.[54] That they knew the Qur'ān is amply clear from the specimens of allegorical interpretation we are given in other sources.[55] That they did not believe in *jihād* accords with their views on non-violence, though there are other ways of interpreting the information. Niẓām al-Mulk gives a longer, but stereotyped, list of their sins against the *sharīʿa*: they rejected ritual prayer, fasting (in Ramaḍān), pilgrimage (to Mecca), *jihād*, and ritual ablution; they regarded wine-drinking as lawful, and they shared their women and property.[56]

Al-Maqdisī, who wrote in the mid-fourth/tenth century, was one of the few who took an interest in what the Khurramīs actually believed rather than the many ways in which they failed to be proper Muslims. He had visited them in Māsabadhān and Mihrijānqadhaq,[57] but he reports on them on the basis of written sources too, including a *Kitāb al-Khurramiyya* – a book about them, or conceivably by them, that he expects the reader to know.[58] He describes them as dualists who believed in divine incarnation in human beings, continuous prophecy, and *rajʿa*, left unexplained, but probably meaning reincarnation; they held all communities to be right as long as they believed in reward and punishment after death; they believed in not harming any living being and not shedding blood except at times of revolt, nourished messianic hopes, and were extremely clean, tidy, and kind people. He also asked them about *ibāḥa*, reporting their answer with tantalising brevity: some allowed it, with the

[52] Muqaddasī, 398f.
[53] Iṣṭakhrī, 203.
[54] Baghdādī, *Farq*, 252.
[55] See esp. Chapters 12, 13.
[56] *SN*, ch. 47:14 (319 = 244).
[57] Maqdisī, IV, 31.
[58] Maqdisī, II, 20. It is not mentioned in Ibn al-Nadīm's *Fihrist*.

women's consent. Their leaders were imams to whom they would submit questions of law, and they also had religious personnel who would tour the local villages and whom they called angels.[59] All this will be discussed in detail in later chapters.

So far all the information has pertained to the Jibāl and Azerbaijan, but we hear a little about the Khurramīs at Rayy as well. Al-Mas'ūdī had seen 'a kind of Zoroastrians, Mazdakites' (*naw' min al-majūs mazdakiyya*), who lived in a village outside Rayy inhabited entirely by them and who made a living removing dead cattle from Rayy and Qazwīn; both they and their animals would feed on the cattle they removed.[60] In 420/1029 Maḥmūd of Ghazna conquered Rayy, purging it of 'unbelieving Bāṭinīs and sinful innovators', many of them Daylamīs. Their leader, Rustum b. 'Alī al-Daylamī, was interrogated and admitted to having over fifty wives. He explained that this had been the custom among his ancestors and that he had not wished to depart from it, and at some point he also mentioned that the countryside of Rayy was full of Mazdakites who claimed to be Muslims in terms of the *shahāda*, but who did not pray, pay *zakāh*, perform ablution, or abstain from eating carrion.[61] Perhaps his intention was to show that there was nothing particularly odd about his marital situation by local standards: Rayy was a region where the *sharī'a* was often ignored; he was not the only 'Murji'ite' there. In any case Maḥmūd does not seem to have made any attempt to round up the Mazdakites in the countryside or to convert them by force.

After the fourth/tenth century the information dwindles. Abū 'l-Baqā' claims that the Seljuq Ismā'īl b. Arslānjaq (d. 499/1105f.), governor of Basra, was a Khurramī, which is probably pure slander, but which could be taken to suggest that already then the Turks were known for Muslimī beliefs.[62] We also hear of Khurramīs (Pārsīs) in sixth/twelfth-century Azerbaijan, as mentioned already, and the vizier Anūshirwān b. Khālid (d. 532/1137f.) says that the inhabitants of Dargazīn and Ansābadh were all Khurramī Mazdakites.[63] Finally the Chronicle *ad* 1234 mentions that the Khurdanaye (or, as he calls them, Kurdaye) still existed, presumably in the compiler's own time, since this is not mentioned in the other summaries

59 Maqdisī, IV, 30f.

60 MM, II, §868 (III, 27f.); cf. Chapter 13, p. 259.

61 Ibn al-Jawzī, *Muntaẓam*, VIII, 39f.

62 Abū 'l-Baqā', *Manāqib*, II, 495; cf. IA, X, 402ff., year 499. (Ismā'īl is already a figure in the past, which makes it difficult to agree with the editors, I, 25, that Abū 'l-Baqā' wrote in the late fifth century.)

63 Bundārī, *Mukhtaṣar*, 124; Yāqūt, II, 568f., s.v. 'Darkazīn' (here *Mazdakiyya malāḥida*).

of Dionysius' report.[64] Yūsofī says that the Khurramīs rebelled again under the Mongols, but he does not say where or give a reference.[65]

A few related groups were brought out of their mountains in the Seljuq period, notably the Armenian Arewordi, 'sons of the sun', who lived in villages of Mardīn, Āmid and other parts of upper Mesopotamia. Some were recruited into the army of the amir of Damascus, where a group of them was executed in 1138.[66] Their Arabic name was Shamsiyya, 'sun-worshippers'. Timur destroyed some of their villages after destroying Mardīn, but they came back. They had no literary culture, but taught their children oral tradition going back to Zoroaster; they worshipped the sun, identifying it with Christ, and they and/or others also revered the moon and the stars, praying in the direction of the sun. They are sometimes said to have had idols, and they also venerated the poplar, claiming that Christ's cross had been made of it. Some of them denied the resurrection: humans were like plants that did not come back, but whose roots survived, probably meaning that they believed in reincarnation. They survived in Mardīn and Diyarbekir down to the nineteenth century.[67] In some sense so too did the Khurramīs; indeed, they still survive. But they do so under new names and in different forms that will be briefly considered in the last chapter. As Khurramīs they disappeared in the massive political and demographic upheavals of the Turco-Mongol invasions.

[64] *Chron. ad 1234*, no. 214 (II, 25 = 17); cf. Chapter 3, p. 63.
[65] *EIr.*, s.v. 'Bābak', 306.
[66] Canard, 'Une mention des Arewordik''.
[67] Bartikian, 'Arewordi en Arménie et Mesopotamie'; Cahen, 'Simples interrogations', 31f.; Garsoian, *Paulician Heresy*, 191f.; Müller, *Kulturhistorische Studien*, 73f.

II

THE RELIGION

A. Reconstituting the Beliefs

10

God, Cosmology, Eschatology

Of the God of the Khurramīs we hear next to nothing. Like everyone else they claimed to be monotheists,[1] and on their own terms they probably were. But they did not envisage God the way that Muslims did.

There is general agreement that the Khurramīs were dualists who identified God with light and evil with darkness. Unlike the Zoroastrians they seem barely to have distinguished God from the light he represented. Of al-Muqanna''s followers we are admittedly told that they held God to be a subtle body with length, breadth, and depth, suggesting that he was an actual person to them;[2] but the report may not be correct, and to others God was simply the great light (*al-nūr al-aʿẓam*),[3] the source of all the light there was. According to al-Malaṭī, certain believers in reincarnation held that God was light over bodies and places (*ʿalā 'l-abdān wa'l-amākin*) and that their spirits were born of the pre-eternal God (*mutawallida min allāh al-qadīm*). This pre-existing God was presumably also the source of the divinity that was light over bodies and places.[4] God is light, as the followers of ʿAbdallāh b. Muʿāwiya said with reference to his presence in the imams; the light sometimes appeared in two persons and sometimes in three, as the Pārsīs explained.[5] Al-Malaṭī's reincarnationists seem to be the followers of ʿAbdallāh b. Muʿāwiya, but he casts them as a subgroup of the 'Qarāmiṭa and Daylam' and tells us of the overall group that they held God to be a 'supreme light' (*nūr ʿulwī*). The supreme light was unlike any other lights in that it was uncontaminated by any darkness, and from it

[1] Muqaddasī, 399.1 ('Aren't we monotheists?').
[2] Abū Tammām, 76 = 75; cf. the discussion in Crone, 'Abū Tammām on the Mubayyiḍa', 169.
[3] Ibn al-Malāḥimī, 583. The passage is discussed below, pp. 195f.
[4] Malaṭī, 17. Cf. Chapter 12, p. 242, on reincarnation.
[5] See Chapter 9, n. 42.

had emerged another glittering light which was in the prophets and imams, whose nature was unlike that of ordinary human beings: they knew the unknown (*al-ghayb*), could do anything, were invincible, and worked miracles both before and after their public appearance. From this light in its turn emerged a shadowy light (*nūr ẓulāmī*), which is the light seen in the sun, moon, stars, fire, and precious stones (*jawhar*); being mixed with darkness it was open to defects, disease (*āfāt*), pain, lapses (*sahw*), forgetfulness, inattention, evils, passions, and wrongful things, but mankind was nonetheless born of the pre-eternal creator (*al-qadīm al-bārī'*). These sectarians would reel off impeccably monotheist descriptions of God, but they still thought of him as light. They held that ritual worship was optional, since God had no need of it, and that there was no paradise or hell: people's spirits would return to the light from which they had sprung. They believed in 'humanity in divinity' (*al-nāsūt fī 'l-lāhūt*) after the fashion of the Christians, and some of them believed in reincarnation.[6]

Al-Malaṭī's 'Qarāmiṭa and Daylam' were probably Iranians from the Caspian coast who had been exposed to Old Ismailism, often called Qarmaṭism: if so, they were ʿAlid Shīʿites rather than Khurramīs. We also hear of Kufan Ghulāt who spoke of *allāh al-qadīm*, *al-qadīm al-azalī*, and *al-wāḥid al-azalī* ('the pre-eternal God/God the pre-eternal', 'the pre-eternal eternal (one)', 'the eternal one');[7] and al-Shahrastānī reports the comparison of (partial) *ḥulūl* to light in crystal after a discussion of the Kāmiliyya, who envisaged the imamate as a light passing from the one to the other, turning now into imamate and now into prophecy.[8] But whether they were ʿAlid Shīʿites or Khurramīs, the fundamental doctrine of all those who believed in divine indwelling (*ḥulūl*) and reincarnation (*tanāsukh*) was that 'God is found in every place, speaks every language, and appears in every person', as al-Shahrastānī observes.[9] They would not separate God from the world. As light he was present in everything: in bodies and over bodies; in the heavenly luminaries, prophets, and imams; in human spirits; in the animals; and in all other beings into which human spirits would pass, in different degrees of purity.

As light God was everywhere, but as its ultimate source, the highest light, he was far removed from this world and utterly beyond human experience. He showed himself in human form because he could not otherwise be seen,

6 Malaṭī, 15f.

7 Qummī, 60f. (nos. 115, 118).

8 Shahrastānī, I, 133 = I, 511f. For the followers of ʿAbdallāh b. Muʿāwiya see Chapter 4.

9 See the preceding note.

as al-Muqanna' said.[10] He had 'delegated' (*fawwaḍa*) matters to Muḥammad and the imams after him, as some 'Alid Shī'ites put it.[11] All Ghulāt filled up the space between God and man with intermediary beings in the celestial realm and the human world alike, often envisaging the figures on earth as counterparts or incarnations or other manifestations of the ones in the celestial realm. The highest light did not engage with this world directly, and the reason we hear so little about the Khurramī conception of God is doubtless that, like other Ghulāt, they focused their worship on the celestial and human beings in whom he manifested himself. There was no need to engage in ritual worship of God, as al-Malaṭī's Qarāmiṭa and Daylamīs said. There was not even any obligation to know him, according to the believers in 'delegation' (*tafwīḍ*): what one did need to know according to them was the divinity to whom *al-qadīm al-azalī* had delegated matters and who was actually five. To al-Qummī all this was rank Zoroastrianism.[12]

To a modern reader the pentads of the Mufawwiḍa sound more Manichaean than Zoroastrian, but even so al-Qummī has a point. The Zoroastrians did not normally worship Ohrmazd directly either, at least not in official Zoroastrianism: temples were not normally devoted to him, but rather to fire, his 'son', or to a lesser deity such as Anahita or Mithra. One worshipped the highest deity, the source of all goodness and light, in the lesser forms in which he manifested himself. The lesser objects of worship included the sun, the moon, and other luminous bodies, and also the elements, as well as the deities associated with these things: on this all Iranian dualists seem to have agreed. The Khurramīs and 'Alid Ghulāt held that the objects of worship included some human beings too. How far this was in line with Zoroastrianism will be considered in Chapter 15.

COSMOLOGY AND ESCHATOLOGY

Khurramī cosmology has so far been known primarily from al-Shahrastānī and 'Abd al-Jabbār, both of whom drew on the lost work of the third/ninth-century Abū 'Īsā al-Warrāq as quoted in a later source, now also lost.[13] Al-Shahrastānī actually has three cosmologies, two shared with 'Abd al-Jabbār and a third unique to him. He attributes all three to Mazdak,

[10] See Isfarā'inī, *Tabṣīr*, 76.
[11] Qummī, 60f. (no. 118).
[12] Qummī, 61 (nos. 118–21).
[13] Their direct source was the *Kitāb al-ārā' wa'l-diyānāt* by al-Ḥasan b. Mūsā al-Nawbakhtī (d. between 300/900 and 310/912).

though they do not agree, and all three are traditionally presented as Mazdak's in a harmonised form in the modern literature.[14] We now have Abū ʿĪsā in the much fuller excerpts of Ibn al-Malāḥimī, who seems to have used Abū ʿĪsā's own book, and all accounts must henceforth start with him.[15] He allows us to see that the three cosmologies should not be harmonised. One is dualist, another trinitarian, and the third focuses on a single God with many emanations.

Dualist

Ibn al-Malāḥimī's information comes in his section on Zoroastrians.[16] Here Abū ʿĪsā tells us that the Zoroastrians (*majūs*) had diverse doctrines regarding the origins of light and darkness. Some subscribed to the myth to the effect that light and darkness were twins born of Zurwān. (Al-Shahrastānī calls them Zurwāniyya.)[17] Others held that originally the world was pure light, some of which had later metamorphosed (*inmaskha*) into darkness. (Al-Shahrastānī calls them Maskhiyya.)[18] Still others held that light and darkness had always existed and that between them there was a space or void (*khalāʾ*), which they did not count as a third principle but in which they held light and darkness to have mixed. The third view is that espoused in the Pahlavi books.[19] According to Abū ʿĪsā, adherents of the third view would adduce much the same arguments as the Manichaeans, and 'it is said that the Khurramdīnīs [also] subscribe to this doctrine'. In other words the Khurramdīnīs known to Abū ʿĪsā were dualists in the strict sense of postulating two pre-eternal beings or principles from which everything else derived.

Al-Maqdisī also notes that the beliefs of the Khurramīs were based on the doctrine of light and darkness, undoubtedly on the basis of Abū ʿĪsā, but he has them agree with Abū ʿĪsā's second group (al-Shahrastānī's

[14] Yarshater, 'Mazdakism', 1006f.; Shaki, 'Cosmogonical and Cosmological Teachings', 528f.; Shaked, *Dualism*, 127ff.; Sundermann, 'Cosmogony and Cosmology', iv, 315.

[15] Cf. Madelung, 'Abū ʿĪsā al-Warrāq', 210f. Ibn al-Malāḥimī's *Muʿtamad*, still in manuscript when Madelung wrote this article, was published by MacDemott and Madelung in 1991. Since then the missing part has come to light and the entire work has now been re-edited by Madelung, but it is still forthcoming and I have only used it for information not found in the first edition. (If the page number referred to is higher than 599 the reference is to the second edition, but I also distinguish between the two by citing the first as Ibn al-Malāḥimī and the second as Ibn al-Malāḥimī, *Muʿtamad*.) My thanks to Prof. Madelung and Sabine Schmidtke for making the new edition available to me.

[16] Ibn al-Malāḥimī, 597f.

[17] Shahrastānī, I, 183 = I, 638f.

[18] Shahrastānī, I, 185 = I, 641.

[19] See *GrBd*, ch. 1:2–5, tr. Zaehner, *Zurvan*, 312f.

Maskhiyya) rather than the third: the Khurramīs, he says, hold the origin of the world to lie in light, some of which turned into (*istiḥāla*) darkness.[20] Al-Shahrastānī also mentions the Khurramīs immediately after the Maskhiyya and seemingly has the two agree. He none the less says that the Khurramīs believed in two principles (*aṣlayn*), i.e., two pre-eternal ones, and ʿAbd al-Jabbār says the same (*kawnayn*).[21] So al-Maqdisī's claim should be dismissed. It was with the third group, the dualists in the strict sense of the term, that Abū ʿĪsā aligned them.

At the end of his account of Manichaeism Abū ʿĪsā says that there were dualists before Mani, and that Mani had taken many of his doctrines from them. These pre-Manichaean dualists held that light and darkness were both eternal and living entities. Light, however, was sentient and knowing, whereas darkness was ignorant and blind, and moved in a rough way, like a violent, self-seeking madman who does not know what he is doing. Due to its rough and uncontrolled movements some of its *humāma*, elsewhere explained as a Manichaean term for the spirit of darkness or smoke,[22] had unintentionally come into contact with the light and swallowed part of it, so that this light had ended up in its belly; by way of response the great light (*al-nūr al-aʿẓam*) had built the world for the extraction (*istikhrāj*) of the swallowed light, this being the only way the damage could be repaired. 'These people (*hāʾulāʾi*) and the Manichaeans (*Mānawiyya*) agree in many of their doctrines and claims', Abū ʿĪsā says. He then adds, 'it has reached me that the Mazdaqiyya of today, or most of them, hold fast to this [pre-Manichaean] doctrine'.[23]

Who were Abū ʿĪsā's pre-Manichaean dualists? The answer seems to be the third group of *majūs*, or a set of people within it. As we have seen, Abū ʿĪsā observed of the third group of *majūs* that they would adduce much the same arguments as the Manichaeans, and that the Khurramdīnīs were said also to subscribe to their position; here he observes of unidentified dualists that the Manichaeans borrowed ideas from them and that the Mazdaqiyya – or most of them – were said to adhere to their doctrine. It sounds like the same comment in a different formulation. This must also be how ʿAbd al-Jabbār and al-Shahrastānī understood it, for it is the dualist view of the third group that they summarise as Mazdak's dualist

[20] Maqdisī, I, 143, cf. IV, 26, 31. This cosmology is accepted for them by Madelung, 'Khurramiyya', col. 65a, and for the Mazdakites by Yarshater, 'Mazdakism', 1011.

[21] Shahrastānī, I, 185 = I, 641; ʿAbd al-Jabbār, *Mughnī*, 16 = 164.

[22] Ibn al-Malāḥimī, 562.-7; cf. Vajda, 'Témoignage d'al-Māturīdī', 18ff.

[23] Ibn al-Malāḥimī, 583f. The same report is quoted anonymously in Shahrastānī, I, 196 = I, 670, without mention of its relationship to Manichaeism and Mazdakism.

cosmology.[24] In the present state of the evidence this is the nearest we can get to a Khurramī account of how the world arose.

The Mazdaqiyya who held fast to the pre-Manichaean doctrine according to Abū ʿĪsā were almost certainly a specific group, not the Khurramīs in general, let alone Mazdak himself. They held Mazdak to be a prophet, and al-Masʿūdī lists them as a subdivision of the Khurramīs, while al-Shahrastānī places them in Iraq, where we do not otherwise hear of Khurramīs.[25] One suspects that they were learned men who had come to Baghdad and adopted Mazdak as a prophet to identify themselves. Their presence in Baghdad would explain why Abū ʿĪsā was so well informed about them. Though their pre-Manichaean doctrine could in principle go back to Mazdak himself there is no particular reason to think that it did. People simply assumed that whatever a community believed went back to its founder. This is why it is Mazdak, rather than the Mazdaqiyya, who is credited with the doctrine in ʿAbd al-Jabbār and al-Shahrastānī's version of Abū ʿĪsā.

In sum, the Mazdaqiyya (as I shall spell the name of this particular group) postulated that light and darkness had always coexisted, but stressed the superiority of light: darkness (and thus evil) was neither intelligent nor sentient, but nor was it evil, just ignorant and stupid; its collision with light had been accidental, not the outcome of malicious intent. The world had been set up for the extraction of the light it had accidentally swallowed. According to al-Shahrastānī's summary of Abū ʿĪsā they held that the liberation (*khalāṣ*) would be as accidental as the beginning.[26] This set them apart both from the Zoroastrians, who held a time to have been set for the end, and from the Manichaeans, who stressed the role of humans in bringing it about. Abū ʿĪsā further remarks that the Mazdaqiyya inclined towards Manichaeism, but he does not say in what respect.[27]

Trinitarian

After summarising Abū ʿĪsā's account of the Mazdaqiyya al-Shahrastānī credits Mazdak with the view that there were three elementary constituents (*al-uṣūl wa'l-arkān*), namely water, earth, and fire, and that the ruler of good (*mudabbir al-khayr*) and the ruler of evil (*mudabbir al-sharr*) had

[24] ʿAbd al-Jabbār, *Mughnī*, 16, cf. 64f. = 165, 237; Shahrastānī, I, 192f. = I, 663.
[25] Masʿūdī, *Tanbīh*, I, 353.ult.; Shahrastānī, I 113 = I, 449 and n. 77 thereto.
[26] Shahrastānī, I, 193 = I, 663.
[27] Ibn al-Malāḥimī, 584.1.

emerged from their mixture, the former from the pure parts and the latter from the impure ones.[28] This is obviously a quite different cosmology: light and darkness as the two primordial principles have disappeared, and everything starts with three elements, from which two divine figures emerge. (There is no mention of how the world would come to an end.)

This cosmology is well known from other sources, but not as Mazdak's. Abū ʿĪsā, who is the first to report it, credits it to the Kanthaeans and the Māhāniyya: both sects believed in three principles, and of the Kanthaeans he further observes that they held the *mudabbir*s of good and evil to have emerged from water, earth, and fire.[29] All later sources owe their information on these sects to Abū ʿĪsā.[30] Al-Shahrastānī himself tells us that the Kanthaeans held all things to have originated from three principles: fire, water, and earth. He adds that they held fire to be good (luminous, exalted, and subtle), water to be the opposite (evil, dark, and so on), and earth to be in between (*mutawassiṭa*). The life-giving principle in their view was fire (*lā wujūd illā bihā*).[31] How al-Shahrastānī came to attribute this cosmology to Mazdak is something of a mystery. The Kanthaeans of whom he correctly reports it were ascetics who rejected marriage and sacrifice. Known as 'the fasters' (*al-ṣiyāmiyya*) and variously classified as Christians, Sabians, and dualists, they were closely related to the Mandaeans, but apparently diverged from them by adopting fire worship in the time of Peroz (459–84) in order to avoid persecution.[32] We also have an account of their cosmology by Theodore Bar Koni (wrote 790s?), but it is very different. According to him they believed in a single deity who divided himself into two, from which good and evil emerged; the former assembled the light, the latter the darkness, and then darkness attacked, leading to the creation of the world (by the forces of darkness).[33] This makes them a species of what al-Shahrastānī would call Maskhiyya. Theodore and Abū ʿĪsā may not be speaking of the same groups, for the Kanthaeans were probably as diverse as the Khurramīs.

28 Shahrastānī, I, 193 = I, 663.

29 Ibn al-Malāḥimī, 589 (Kanthāniyya). For these sects see Madelung, 'Abū ʿĪsā al-Warrāq', 221ff.; and, more briefly, Madelung, *Religious Trends*, 5; *EIr.*, s.v. 'Baṭṭai yazdānī' (Madelung).

30 Maqdisī, I, 143 (Kannān); Nashwān, *Ḥūr al-ʿin*, 141f. (Kanāniyya). For Kaynān or Kīnān as their alleged founder see Madelung, 'Abū ʿĪsā al-Warrāq', 222.

31 Shahrastānī, I, 196 = I, 671 (Kaynawiyya).

32 Ibn al-Malāḥimī, 589; Theodore Bar Koni, *Scolies*, mimra xi, 85 (II, 343 = 256); *EIr.*, s.v. 'Baṭṭai Yazdānī' (Madelung).

33 Theodore Bar Koni, *Scolies*, mimra xi, 84f. (II, 344 = 256f.); English tr. in Kruisheer, 'Theodore', 165; cf. Madelung, 'Abū ʿĪsā al-Warrāq', 221ff.

The Māhāniyya mentioned together with the Kanthaeans in Abū ʿĪsā's account of the trinitarian cosmology were dissident Marcionites; unlike other Marcionites and the Kanthaeans they accepted both marriage and animal slaughter.[34] Possibly for this reason al-Masʿūdī classifies them as a subdivision of the Khurramīs. Al-Shahrastānī follows suit, placing them in Transoxania.[35] Unlike Abū ʿĪsā, al-Shahrastānī does not report the trinitarian cosmology for the Māhāniyya themselves; instead he reports it for Mazdak. Apparently he had taken their Khurrami classification to mean that they were Mazdakites, meaning that their views could be attributed to Mazdak himself.

Though the trinitarian cosmology has nothing to do with Mazdak it is of great interest for the religious milieu of late antique Mesopotamia and Iran, of which the Khurramīs formed part. To appreciate this we first need to look at the Marcionites known to Abū ʿĪsā. According to him they believed in three original beings or principles, namely God (replaced by light in sources after Abū ʿĪsā),[36] the devil, Marcion's Old Testament God recast as Ahriman (darkness in later works), and, in between the two, a third principle of a mild and meek nature. The third principle had been attacked by the devil, who mixed his own nature in it and built the world out of the mixture, setting up his own *humūm* and powers to manage and regulate it.[37] The twelve constellations and seven planets were his spirits; animals that ate one another were also his work, as were fruiting and non-fruiting trees, the division of livelihoods into four groups (presumably the four estates of the Zoroastrians),[38] and the alternation of day and night. The devil had also divided property among his troops, with the result that they fought one another over it, and it was his forces that sent false messengers and religions. When the highest exalted (*al-ʿalī al-aʿlā*) saw that the third being had become a captive in the devil's hand he took pity on it and sent a spirit of his, infusing it in this world: this was Jesus, the spirit and son of God, and whoever followed Jesus' ways, abstaining from killing, marriage, intoxicating drinks, and fetid things, would escape from the devil's net.[39]

[34] Abū ʿĪsā in Ibn al-Malāḥimī, 589; Ibn al-Nadīm, 402 = II, 807.

[35] Masʿūdī, *Tanbīh*, 353.ult; Shahrastānī, I, 194 = I, 665.

[36] See Madelung, 'Abū ʿĪsā al-Warrāq', 218; Frenschkowski, 'Marcion in arabischen Quellen'.

[37] The *humūm* is presumably a variation on the Manichaean (and, according to Abū ʿĪsā, pre-Manichaean) term *humāma*, the smoke of darkness (see n. 22 in this chapter).

[38] Cf. Marlow, *Hierarchy and Egalitarianism*, 68ff.

[39] Ibn al-Malāḥimī, 586f.

What is so striking about this account is that Marcion's three deities have been arranged in spatial terms: God/light occupies the space above; the devil/darkness occupies the space below; and a third principle comes in between. Jesus seems to be a separate figure in this account, since he arrives as the saviour of the third principle, apparently without playing any demiurgic role. But some Marcionite *mutakallim*s identified the third principle as 'the feeling, perceiving man who has always been' and 'the life in this body',[40] and as life it was taken by others to be Jesus. The Māhāniyya were in that category: the third principle was Christ (*al-masīḥ*) in their view. Still others credited Jesus with a demiurgic role, as a messenger of the third principle rather than the principle itself.[41]

It should be clear from all this that the term 'trinitarian' used so far is actually misleading: what we have here is dualism with a third, intermediate, principle. The third principle is located between light and darkness in the Marcionite account, and between fire and dark water in the description of the Kanthaeans, who identified it with earth. (Their three principles reappear in early Ismaili cosmology, but no longer as primordial.)[42] The Marcionites explained that the two contradictory principles needed a third to hold them together; without it they would not have been able to combine to form this world. It was the third principle that served to mix light and darkness in a balanced manner (*ʿalā taʿdīl baynahumā*)[43] or, as other reports put it, it served as *al-muʿaddil*, the one who balances or adjusts, the moderator.[44] The Māhāniyya who identified the third principle with Christ (*al-masīḥ*) duly called him *al-muʿaddil*.[45]

Dualism with intermediary goes a long way back in the Near East and seems to have been common in Mesopotamia. The Marcionites and Kanthaeans apart, it is attested for Bar Daiṣan (d. 222), in two Gnostic works likely to have Mesopotamian roots,[46] and in a third-century Greek

[40] Ibn al-Malāḥimī, 588f.; Madelung, 'Abū ʿĪsā al-Warrāq', 217, 219f.; cf. also Māturīdī, *Tawḥīd*, 171; Vajda, 'Témoignage d'al-Māturīdī', 31ff.

[41] Ibn al-Malāḥimī, 589; Madelung, 'Abū ʿĪsā al-Warrāq', 217, 219f.; also in ʿAbd al-Jabbār, *Mughnī*, 18 = 168f.; Ibn al-Nadīm, 402 = I, 807.

[42] Cf. Halm, 'Die Sieben und die Zwölf', 173.

[43] Ibn al-Malāḥimī, 588f.; Madelung, 'Abū ʿĪsā al-Warrāq', 217, 219f.; cf. also Māturīdī, *Tawḥīd*, 171; Vajda, 'Témoignage d'al-Māturīdī', 31ff.

[44] Maqdisī, IV, 24f.; Nāshiʾ, §3 (where *muʿaddil bi-hayʾatihi* is presumably to be read as *muʿaddil baynahumā* and the missing sentence about the *dhāt* probably explained that its essence was different from that of the other two); Vajda, 'Témoignage d'al-Māturīdī', 35, 37 (where *al-muʿaddil* is translated as 'le facteur d'équilibre').

[45] Ibn al-Malāḥimī, 589; Madelung, 'Abū ʿĪsā al-Warrāq', 217, 219f.; also in ʿAbd al-Jabbār, *Mughnī*, 18 = 168f.

[46] Cf. Casadio, 'Abendteuer des Dualismus', 68ff.

report about an 'Assyrian' Marcionite. In the system of Bar Daiṣan, a 'Parthian' active in Edessa, it is the four elements (light, wind, fire, and water) that occupy the space between God and darkness; according to Muḥammad b. Shabīb (d. 230s/840s) the Dayṣāniyya also used the term *al-muʿaddil*, but with reference to man on the grounds that he was neither pure light nor pure darkness.[47] In the *Paraphrase of Shem*, a treatise recovered at Nag Hammadi, it is spirit that is in between light and darkness.[48] Light was intelligent or, as the *Paraphrase* puts it, 'full of hearing and word', and knew of the existence of darkness, whereas darkness lacked perception and so did not know of the existence of light. This is also the situation in the Zoroastrian books and in Mandaean and Manichaean writings.[49] The *Paraphrase of Shem* interprets the difference in a Gnostic vein by linking the ignorance of darkness with the superbia theme: darkness thought there was no deity above him. Darkness is associated with water, a most un-Zoroastrian idea shared by the *Paraphrase* with the Kanthaeans and Mandaeans,[50] and the spirit was 'a gentle, humble light', just as the third principle was of a mild and meek nature according to Abū ʿĪsā's Marcionites.[51] A similar cosmology is described by Hippolytus (d. *c.* 236) in his account of sectarians he calls Sethians: there were three principles endowed with infinite powers – light, darkness ('a terrible water'), and spirit in between; light was above, darkness below, and spirit in the middle, a point repeatedly emphasised. This spatial arrangement of the three principles aligns the treatise with the Kanthaeans and Abū ʿĪsā's Iranianised Marcionites, and so also with Zoroastrianism, and sets it apart from Platonist works operating with three principles, for Platonists saw the three as successive emanations. That its roots are Mesopotamian is also suggested by the observation in Hippolytus' summary that all things that had been mixed would eventually be separated into their proper places, as could be seen in the city of Ampa or Ama near

47 *EIr.*, s.v. 'Bardesanes' (Skjaervø); cf. Casadio, 'Abendteuer des Dualismus', 68f.; Ibn Shabīb in Shahrastānī, I, 196 = I, 670. For the Platonist context to which the Dayṣānī *muʿaddil* should be related see Ramelli, *Bardaisan*, 348ff.

48 For a readable summary see Doresse, *Secret Books*, 146–53. Its affinity with Bardesanite and Manichaean cosmology is noted along with other features pointing to an Aramaic origin in *Paraphrase of Shem*, tr. Roberge, 59n., 113f., though he is more interested in its affinities with Stoicism and Middle Platonism. The name of the saviour (Derdekeas) also points to a Mesopotamian origin: see Chapter 15, p. 341.

49 Cf. Bennett, 'Primordial Space', 77n.

50 Cf. n. 31 in this chapter; Rudolph, *Gnosis*, 357.

51 *Paraphrase of Shem*, 1f. A spirit endowed with such characteristics is not very Stoic. For the dark water of the Mandaeans see Rudolph, *Gnosis*, 357.

the Tigris: here a well among the Persians separated the substance it drew up into three parts – black oil, asphalt, and something salty. For further information about their doctrines Hippolytus refers the reader to the 'Paraphrase of Seth', a lost treatise clearly related to the extant *Paraphrase of Shem*.[52]

It is also Hippolytus who tells us that an Assyrian by the name of Prepōn, a follower of Marcion 'in our time', wrote a book against Bardesanes (Bar Daiṣan, a famous enemy of Marcionism) in which he alleged that what is just constituted a third principle and that it occupied an intermediate position between the good and the bad; this intermediate principle was 'just reason' (*dikaios logos*), which brought together the antagonistic entities (that would not otherwise be able to mix).[53] Unfortunately Hippolytus does not say whether Prepōn identified this 'just reason' with Marcion's Old Testament God or with Christ. A similar cosmology appears in the *Letter to Flora* attributed by Epiphanius to the Gnostic Ptolemy (*fl.* later second century), a Valentinian rather than a Marcionite. The letter postulates the existence of a perfect God (the only unbegotten deity), a devil, and a demiurge between the two who was of a different essence from both of them. The third deity was neither good nor evil, but rather just and might 'rightly be awarded the title of intermediate (*mesōtēs*)'.[54] Here as in Prepōn (as not in Plato) intermediate status and justice go together.

Dualism with intermediary is also attested for Zoroastrianism. Plutarch (d. 120), a Platonist fascinated by eastern religion,[55] reports the Magi as saying that midway between Ōromazēs, who was comparable to light, and Areimanios, who was comparable to darkness and ignorance, there was Mithras, who was known as the *mesitēs*, the mediator. In the course of the creation Ōromazēs had enlarged himself to three times his former size and removed himself as far distant from the sun as the sun is distant from the earth: in other words Mithras, a solar god or simply the sun itself, was midway between Ōromazēs and the earth.[56] Unfortunately there is no account of the creation itself, and Ahriman's whereabouts are unclear.

[52] Hippolytus, V, 19 and 21, X, 11 (V, 14 and 16, X, 7, in the tr.); cf. Pearson, 'Figure of Seth', and the references given there; *Paraphrase of Shem*, tr. Roberge, 104ff. (minimising the similarity between the two Paraphrases).

[53] Hippolytus, VII, 31, 1, where Hippolytus goes to great lengths to identify the doctrine as Empedoclean.

[54] Epiphanius, 33:7.3 = I, 198ff.; cf. Dillon, 'Platonizing of Mithra', 80; Plato, *Timaeus*, 32B. Ptolemy's name is not mentioned in the letter.

[55] Plutarch, *Isis and Osiris*, 369 E, 370 A (also in Fox and Pemberton, 'Passages in Greek and Latin Literature', 52).

[56] For different explanations of Mithra's midway position see de Jong, *Traditions*, 189ff.

He could be under the earth, as in the Pahlavi books, or in it, and he could even be identified with it. But Ohrmazd is far above it, wholly uncontaminated by what is going on in the world of mixture: he is the pre-existing God and creator (*Allāh al-qadīm, al-qadīm al-bāri'*) of al-Malaṭī's heretics. Mithra, the sun, is the god who is light over bodies and places: he marks the upper limit of the intermediate realm of mixture, the world in which we live.

Plutarch's (undoubtedly literary) source for this account is unknown, but the author clearly knew something about Zoroastrianism. Ohrmazd is correctly associated with light, Ahriman with both darkness and ignorance, and, though the author may be Platonising the relationship between Ahriman and the earth by identifying them, he had genuine information about Mithra too. As the all-seeing sun Mithra was associated with justice, and in Pahlavi literature he is sometimes known as *miyāncīg*, intermediary or judge (syn. *dādwar*).[57] It is probably an earlier form of the word *miyāncīg* that Plutarch is translating as *mesitēs*.[58] Mithra was a judge in the sense of umpire in a duel: he would see to it that the rules were obeyed and that the fighting would stop when the time set for it was up. The fifth-century Armenian Eznik knew a myth according to which the sun had been created to act as judge between Ohrmazd and Ahriman.[59] The Pahlavi books envisage Mithra as charged with ensuring observance of the contract between Ohrmazd and Ahriman, who had agreed to limit their battle to a specified period. Abū ʿĪsā relates a version in which Mithra (Mihr) is one of four deities, or 'angels', as Abū ʿĪsā calls them, who broker this agreement and to whom the two parties hand over their swords with the pledge that if either of them breaks the terms he is to be killed with his own sword.[60] In all these accounts Mithra/the sun is a judge in the sense of intermediary or umpire, not in the sense that he would sit in judgement on

[57] Shaked, 'Mihr the Judge'. See also Turcan, *Mithras Platonicus*, 14ff; de Jong, *Traditions*, 173ff.

[58] Thus Shaked, though he also suggests that *miyāncīg* may be derived from *miyān* in the sense of 'dispute' rather than 'between', so that it would mean 'the man who sits in a trial, judge', without having anything to do with being in the middle or mediation ('Mihr the Judge', 7, 14f., 19).

[59] Eznik, 190:3–4 (where Ahriman seems to participate in its creation); cf. Russell, *Zoroastrianism in Armenia*, 266. The Armenian word is *datawor*, translated 'Schiedsrichter' by Zeilfelder.

[60] Ibn al-Malāḥimī, *Muʿtamad*, 639. Srōš (Sorūsh) also appears among the brokers, as perhaps already in the Avesta (cf. *EIr.*, s.v. 'Cosmogony and Cosmology', i); cf. also Shahrastānī, I, 183f. = I, 639, reproducing Abū ʿĪsa's account, but assigning it to the Zurwāniyya (whence its inclusion in Zaehner, *Zurvan*, 433f.).

anyone. There is no need to assume with Mansfeld that Plutarch is simply Platonising Mithra.[61] On the contrary, as Dillon suggests, it is more likely that Plutarch was stimulated by a study of Persian religion when he interpreted Plato in a dualist vein.[62]

Zoroastrians of the strictly dualist type represented in the Pahlavi books did not have a third principle. What they did have was an entity between light and darkness, namely space or void, which some called Vāy and which was the place in which the mixture of Ohrmazd and Ahriman had taken place.[63] It is in this space that we should locate the earth in Plutarch's myth. It is explicitly identified as the material world in the *Dēnkard*: here Ohrmazd divides the sky into three thirds, putting the highest heaven in the top third, relegating the powers of evil to the bottom third, and creating this world as a battlefield in between, with the sun, moon, and stars at its summit.[64] All that is missing to give us a Pahlavi version of Plutarch's account is a statement that Ohrmazd had enlarged himself to three times his former size and removed himself as far distant from the sun as the sun is distant from the earth. But as Abū ʿĪsā explicitly informs us, the Zoroastrians did not count the space between light and darkness as a third principle.[65] It is not associated with Mithra or any other deity either in the Pahlavi books. Some did call it Vāy, giving it the name of the old wind god, but *Wāy i wēh* (the good Vayu) had come to be little more than a common noun for air, atmosphere, or space in Pahlavi.[66]

The Pahlavi books only give us the teachings of one Zoroastrian school, however, and the intermediary deity remained alive in other types of Zoroastrianism. According to Eznik the Zoroastrians were divided into sects and some of them admitted three principles: the good, the evil, and the *just*:[67] justice is the quality with which Prepōn, Ptolemy, and the stories of Mithra the judge alike associate the intermediate deity or principle, as we

[61] Cf. Mansfeld, *Heresiography*, 281f., declaring all earlier translations of the passage to be wrong (in the note): Plutarch is saying that 'the Mediator' is called Mithras among the Persians, not that the Persians gave Mithras this name, i.e., he is speaking about a Greek figure and how it was handled by others. But Plutarch has not discussed any such figure in the preceding, and though *mesitēs* may well be a common Greek word it did not stand for a Greek deity or principle that anyone could be presumed to know.

[62] Dillon, *Middle Platonists*, 203, adding that the same could be true of Plato himself in the passage that Plutarch seized on (*Laws*, 896Dff.).

[63] *GrBd*, 1:5, in Zaehner, *Zurvan*, 313.

[64] *Dd*, 36:16–21.

[65] Ibn al-Malāḥimī, 598.

[66] Boyce, 'Some Reflections on Zurvanism', 311.

[67] Eznik, 144; cited in Zaehner, *Zurvan*, 29, understood in a Zurvanite vein.

have seen. Apparently there were still Zoroastrians who operated with a third principle and identified it with justice in al-Shahrastānī's time. He reports that the Marcionites believed in a third principle, namely 'the moderator who unites' (*al-muʿaddil al-jāmiʿ*), and that they held this *muʿaddil*, who was located below the light and above the darkness, to be the cause of the mixture. He objects that the Marcionite concept was contrary to Manichaeism, Zoroastrianism, and reason alike. Exactly how it contradicted Manichaeism is unclear, since all al-Shahrastānī says about it is that Mani took his doctrine from Bardesanes while disagreeing with him about the *muʿaddil*. As regards Zoroastrianism and reason, however, al-Shahrastānī explains that Zoroaster also affirmed that light and darkness were contradictory principles, but that the *muʿaddil* in Zoroaster's view was like a judge (*ḥākim*) over two disputing parties, not like the one who kept them together. Nor would it be in accordance with reason to cast the *muʿaddil* in that role, for nothing that issued from the two contradictory principles themselves could serve to hold them together: what held them together was God.[68] (Gimaret and Monnot understand the passage differently, but this is its *prima facie* meaning and the only one that makes sense.)[69] The fact that al-Shahrastānī feels moved to argue against these Marcionites suggests that they were still a live presence in eastern Iran, but what is so remarkable about his reaction is that he was familiar with Zoroastrianism as dualism with intermediary. Indeed, he mentions Zoroaster's view on the *muʿaddil* and judge in a tone so casual that he must have envisaged it as standard Zoroastrianism. Most remarkably of all he recognises the equivalence between the Marcionite *muʿaddil* and the Zoroastrian equivalent, Mihr the judge.

In short, dualism with a third, intermediate principle is attested from the third century onwards among Zoroastrians, Marcionites, Bardesanites, and Mesopotamian Gnostics such as the Kanthaeans and the circles

[68] Shahrastānī, I, 195f. = I, 669f.

[69] The text has 'wa-huwa ayḍan khilāf ʿalā mā qāla zardusht, fa-innahu yuthbitu al-taḍādd bayna 'l-nūr wa'l-ẓulma wa-yuthbitu al-muʿaddil ka'l-ḥākim ʿalā 'l-khaṣmayn [wa] al-jāmiʿ bayna a'l-mutaḍādayn lā yajūzu an yakūna ṭabʿuhu wa-jawharuhu min aḥadi 'l-ḍiddayn'. Gimaret and Monnot do not insert the missing *wa-* and so take it to mean that Zoroaster affirmed the contradictory nature of light and darkness and that Marcion held the *muʿaddil* to be like a judge who unites the two parties. But there is nothing to suggest a change of subject; the result does not yield a contradiction between Zoroaster and the Marcionites; the question regarding what holds the contradictory elements together is obscured; and the reading leaves the sentence from *lā yajūzū* onwards stranded (forcing Gimaret and Monnot to fall back on a colon). Vajda, 'Témoignage d'al-Māturīdī', 35n., discusses the passage, but unfortunately does not translate it.

reflected in the Paraphrases of Seth and Shem. As one would expect, there are signs of it in Manichaeism too. The Manichaeans also postulated a void between light and darkness, at least at times,[70] and both Mithra and Vayu appear as intermediate deities among them. Mithra, called Mihr Yazad in Manichaean Middle Persian,[71] and Vayu, called Wēšparkar (*wyšprkr*) in Sogdian,[72] both stand for the Living Spirit, a divine emanation sent to put things right after the forces of evil had attacked Primal Man and devoured his light: Mithra/Vayu, the Living Spirit, built the world out of the resulting mixture of light and darkness, 'like an architect [who] constructs [a building and] has hired workers', as a Middle Persian text says.[73] This suggests that there were versions of Zoroastrianism in which the intermediate deity, whether Mithra or Vayu, played a role in the creation, as has in fact been argued on the basis of quite different evidence.[74] If there were forms of Zoroastrianism in which Mithra, the go-between, played a role in the creation this would do something to explain why it was so easy to fit him into Middle Platonism, equated with the demiurge of the *Timaeus*, the sun of the *Republic* (book VI) and/or the *logos* of the Stoicising Platonists.[75]

All in all, we should probably be less dismissive than is currently the case of the possibility that Greek authors on Zoroastrianism actually knew something about that religion. 'It is indeed a complex operation to unravel the reciprocal influences of the Pythagorean–Platonic and the Persian traditions', as Dillon notes.[76] It is complex because some ideas passed backwards and forwards several times in ever-changing formulations, and also because foreign ideas were taken up and adapted with particular alacrity when they spoke to something already present in the native traditions.[77] Domesticating other people's thought related to one's own

[70] Bennett, 'Primordial Space', 75, citing Augustine, with the Zoroastrian parallel at 77n. Most sources on Manichaeism omit the void, making light and darkness contiguous.

[71] He also appears in Manichaean Parthian, but here he is the Third Messenger, not the Living Spirit (see Sundermann, 'Some More Remarks on Mithra', 486).

[72] Humbach, 'Vayu, Śiva und der Spiritus Vivens', 404.

[73] M 100 cited in Koenen, 'How Dualistic', 14.

[74] See Kreyenbroek, 'Mithra and Ahreman in Iranian Cosmogonies'; Kreyenbroek, 'Mithra and Ahreman, Binyamīn and Malak Ṭāwūs'.

[75] Cf. Dillon, 'Platonizing of Mithra', 80, where he seems to think that Plutarch attributed this Platonised Mithras to the Zoroastrians.

[76] Dillon, 'Platonizing of Mithra', 84f.

[77] Note Jacob of Sarug's reaction to the New Testament description of Jesus as the mediator (*mesitēs*) of a better covenant (Hebrews 8:6): as mediator he brought peace and reconciliation between the warring sides (Thekeparampil, 'Malkizedeq according to Jacob of Sarug', 130).

reduced chaotic multiplicity to order, endowed one's own system with an air of universality, or with exotic colour, and made it possible to formulate one's own views in terms that the others could understand, whether for purposes of converting or refuting them. The outcome was a set of shared ideas attested in a profusion of ever-different forms because it was in terms of those ideas that radically opposed groups would vindicate their own particular conception of the world. There will have been many more such sets of shared ideas in Mesopotamia and Iran, where a multiplicity of religious groups coexisted and argued with each other without a shared authority to decide what they should or should not believe.[78] It was in a religious world of this nature, utterly different from that of Byzantine Christianity, that the Khurramīs were at home.

Monotheist, with emanations

Al-Shahrastānī proceeds to a famous account, which he also credits to Mazdak, in which God, or rather Mazdak's object of worship (*maʿbūd*), is seated on his throne in the upper world like Khusraw in the lower one. God is surrounded by four powers – discrimination, understanding, memory/preservation, and joy – corresponding to the chief *mobedh*, chief *herbadh*, the *ispabadh*, and the *rāmishkar* around Khusraw, and these four powers are said to rule (*yudabbirūna*) the world with the assistance of another seven, who are identified only in terms of the equivalents on Khusraw's side: the commander (*sālār*), chamberlain (*pīshkār*), someone unidentified (*bʾlwn*), the messenger (?, *brwʾn*, *parwān(ag)*), the expert (*kārdān*), the minister (*dastūr*), and the page (*kūdak*). These seven in their turn had twelve spiritual beings around them, all given names in the form of Persian present participles: the one who calls (*khānanda*), the one who gives and receives (*dihanda wa-sitānanda*), the one who cuts (*buranda*), and so on.[79] Anyone for whom those four, seven, and twelve powers came together (*ijtamaʿat lahu*) would become divine in the lower world (*ṣāra rabbānīyan fī ʾl-ʿālam al-suflā*) and would cease to be bound by the law (*irtafaʿa ʿanhu al-taklīf*); and whoever could imagine something of the letters with which God ruled the world and the sum total of which was his greatest name would have access to the greatest secret (*man taṣawwra min tilkaʾl-ḥurūf shayʾan infataḥa lahu al-sirr al-akbar*); by

[78] For another example see Crone, 'Pre-existence in Iran'.
[79] Shahrastānī, I, 193 = I, 663ff., with discussion of the Persian titles; see also Sundermann, 'Cosmogony and Cosmology', 316.

contrast, whoever could not do so would remain in blind ignorance, forgetfulness, stupidity, and sorrow – the four opposites of the four great powers. There is no reference to how the world had originated or to eschatology.

Here we have a completely different account. There is no mention of light, darkness, the three elements, the two *mudabbir*s, the primordial light, or the mixture. Instead there is a single God and numerous lesser divine powers, four of them ruling this world through another seven and the twelve – clearly the seven planets and twelve constellations. This account cannot go back to Mazdak, though the ascription seems to be universally accepted in the secondary literature, occasional doubts notwithstanding.[80] Mazdak rebelled on Khusraw I's accession and was killed by him: he could not have envisaged God as Khusraw. Nor could he have used the name Khusraw in the generic sense of Persian emperor, since the Khusraw who killed him was the first. For this reason Altheim held the Khusraw here to be an obscure king of Khwārizm, while Shaki suggested that the word is a later paraphrase of the original term.[81] But why should we go to such lengths to save the ascription? Mazdak devoted his life to a utopian reform of the social order, and such a man is hardly likely to have pursued ideas of individual liberation from the shackles of the law by means of esoteric knowledge. His conviction that women and property were common to all had nothing to do with the idea of perfected individuals achieving such god-like status that they were exempt from the law.[82] He saw women and property as the key source of strife, induced by Āz, the demon of avarice: sharing them was the best way to combat this demon, and thus to secure social harmony; everyone, not just the enlightened few, could take the surplus held by anyone else.[83] The idea that deified individuals could avail themselves of other people's women or property whether they were going spare or not is an altogether different thought.

Although the author of this fragment cannot be Mazdak he could still be a Khurramī. He does share with Zoroastrians the habit of envisaging abstract entities such as thinking or joy as spiritual beings, and he thinks of the seven and twelve as rulers representing God rather than the demonic

80 Cf. Halm, 'Die Sieben und die Zwölf', 171, on Klíma, and his own doubts at 175.

81 Shaki, 'Cosmogonical and Cosmological Teachings', 532f., and the reference to Altheim given there.

82 *Pace* Bausani, 'Passo di Šahrastānī sulla dottrina mazdakita', 75f. (in a note representing a major step forward at the time).

83 See Crone, 'Kavād's Heresy', 23, 28; Crone, 'Zoroastrian Communism', 454f. This is in fact the general understanding, even of those who accept the authenticity of the fragment.

world. But there is nothing distinctly Khurramī about it either: not only is it monotheist rather than dualist, it also envisages God as a king rather than as light, and it says nothing about prophets, imams, mahdis, or divine incarnations, but on the contrary casts deification as the outcome of the individual's own efforts. Its focus is on the law, the magic properties of the alphabet and God's name, and the esoteric knowledge that can serve as a short cut to exalted status. In short, religion is conceived as the key to all the secrets of the universe and the power that the possessor of these secrets would enjoy. It was presumably by adjuration that one could unite the four, seven, and twelve powers in oneself and get them to do one's will; for access to the greatest secret one needed to be able to form an image in one's mind of something of the letters of which the (numerical?) sum was God's highest name. These are all ideas familiar from magic.

Differently put, the author of this fragment belongs in circles of the kind that surface in Sasanian Iraq in the Jewish *hekhalot* literature and the Jewish, Mandaean, Christian, and pagan magic bowls; in Shaked's words, his affinities are with theurgic mystics.[84] After the coming of Islam we meet such ideas again in diverse forms of *ghuluww*, such as the heresies of Mughīra b. Saʿīd al-ʿIjlī and some Ismaili works.[85] Halm toys with the idea that the Mazdak fragment is actually Ismaili, more precisely Old Ismaili or Qarmaṭī, but he accepts the ascription on the grounds that the author models the divine world on the Sasanian court and gives the seven and the twelve Persian names.[86] Is this a sufficient reason? The document must certainly have been composed in a Persian-speaking environment for people familiar with the *shāhānshāh* and some of his dignitaries, but no great knowledge of the Sasanian court is implied; and if Khusraw is used in the generic sense of Persian emperor, the fragment is most likely to have been composed after the Arab conquest, for a Persian-speaking audience loyal to the memory of the Sasanians. There must have been many of those in Iraq and Iran alike.

THE FOLLOWERS OF ʿABDALLĀH B. MUʿĀWIYA

We may now leave Abū ʿĪsā and al-Shahrastānī on Mazdak for Jaʿfar b. Ḥarb on the followers of ʿAbdallāh b. Muʿāwiya, here called Ḥarbiyya.

[84] Shaked, *Dualism*, 130 (still accepting the author as Mazdak).

[85] Cf. Wasserstrom, 'The Moving Finger Writes', esp. 12; Halm, *Kosmologie und Heilslehre*, esp. 38ff.

[86] Halm, 'Die Sieben und die Zwölf', 175.

Jaʿfar b. Ḥarb (whose name is not connected with the Ḥarbiyya he is writing about) says nothing about their views on the primordial elements of the world, but instead he has much on their eschatology, both individual and collective. So do other authors, and it is clear that many different views coexisted among them. All will be treated in the chapter on reincarnation, but one of them also has to be considered here.

Jaʿfar b. Ḥarb mentions that the Ḥarbiyya talked about 'shadows and cycles' (*al-aẓilla wa'l-adwār*).[87] As regards the cycles, he explains that they held God to have created seven Adams, each one of whom presided over an era of 50,000 years on earth. People would be reincarnated until the end of each cycle, whereupon they would be either raised to heaven or placed below the earth. Those released from earthly existence at the end of the first cycle would vacate their places at the end of the second, moving up to the second heaven or down to the second layer below the earth as newcomers from the earth took up their previous abodes, and so it would go on until the end of the seventh cycle, whereupon ritual worship would come to an end.[88]

This account takes us a long way away from Zoroastrianism, in which the total duration of the world is 9,000 or 12,000 years, divided into three or four eras,[89] with the same humanity persisting through all of them and just one life for every human being. It seemingly takes us even further away from Judaism, Christianity, and Islam as well, for here the duration of the world was traditionally held to be shorter still. God created the world in seven days, and a day of the Lord was believed to last for 1,000 years (Psalms 90:4; 2 Peter 3:8; Q 32:5); since the duration of the world was held to be one week of the Lord, it would last 7,000 years, or 6,000 years followed by the millennium, corresponding to the day of rest.[90] Their much larger figures notwithstanding, Ibn Muʿāwiya's followers were undoubtedly also operating with the 'world week', however. Sura 70:4 says that 'the angels and the spirit ascend to him in a day, the measure thereof is 50,000 years'. They must have taken this to mean that a divine day was 50,000 years long, divided into shorter periods of 1,000 years to

[87] Ps.-Nāshiʾ, §55; similarly Qummī, 31.

[88] Ps.-Nāshiʾ, §58. We are only given the duration of the first cycle, but we are told that this amount of time was required to separate the obedient from the disobedient (reading *wa-dhālika miqdāru mā yutamayyazu fīhi ahlu 'l-ṭāʿa min ahl al-maʿṣiya*; it makes little sense in its unemended state: cf. Halm's translation in his 'Schatten', II, 23). The length of the second cycle too is given as 50,000 years in *Tabṣira* (cf. Chapter 12).

[89] Hultgård, 'Persian Apocalypticism', 47.

[90] Tab. i, 8, 15ff.; cf. Witakowski, 'The Idea of *Septimana Mundi*'.

accommodate Q 32:5, though there is no reference to shorter periods in Ja'far b. Ḥarb's account. Since there were still seven days in a week the total duration of the world, or perhaps just of the mega-cycle, would be 350,000 years.

Cycles of 50,000 years reappear in Ismailism, where they are also inaugurated by Adam and involve a transfer at the end.[91] In a tribal village in the southern Zagros mountains studied in the 1970s there were still people who believed the duration of the world to be 50,000 years; others dismissed this as an erroneous idea of the mullahs (*sic*), claiming that it was the Day of Judgement that would last 50,000 years, a well-known popular view in Iran.[92] Among the adherents of the erroneous idea of the mullahs was an old trader, who said that there were 50,000 years from Adam to the Day of Judgement, of which 11,380 years had already elapsed; but there had been another kind of men before Adam, and before that as well, for the world had never been empty and never would be; after the day of judgement God would make another creation. The cycles postulated by this man, a devout person who served as the model of orthodoxy in the village, were not limited to seven, and he was not a believer in reincarnation, but apart from that he was unwittingly perpetuating a tradition first attested for the followers of 'Abdallāh b. Mu'āwiya.[93]

Ja'far b. Ḥarb does not explain what the Ḥarbiyya meant by shadows, but the doctrine he presents is related to that of the *Kitāb al-haft wa'l-aẓilla*, 'The book of the seven and the shadows', a Nuṣayrī work with a half Arabic and half Persian title attributed to al-Mufaḍḍal b. 'Umar al-Ju'fī. The latter was a contemporary of Ja'far al-Ṣādiq (d. 148/765) and Mūsā al-Kāẓim (d. 183/799), but Halm holds the book to be the work of al-Mufaḍḍal's pupil Muḥammad b. Sinān (d. 220/835), an older contemporary of Ja'far b. Ḥarb (d. 236/850).[94]

In the *Kitāb al-haft wa'l-aẓilla* the shadows are dark only in the sense of being less luminous than their source: actually they are light. They emerge from the eternal light that God has created, as ignorant beings that have to be taught who God was. God praises himself and his praise is hypostatized as veils *(ḥijāb)* and phantoms (*ashbāḥ*). The latter eventually become spirits and bodies, leading to the creation of the first Adam, and thereupon the

[91] Corbin, *Cyclical Time*, 80.

[92] Loeffler, *Islam in Practice*, 74, 98, 149, 180. My thanks to Michael Cook for drawing this book to my attention and to Hossein Modarresi for the information that the Day of Judgement is popularly known as *rūz-i panjāh hazār sāl* in Iran today.

[93] Loeffler, *Islam in Practice*, 37, 39.

[94] Halm, 'Schatten', part I, 239.

entire creation disobeys, forgetting what it has learnt. This leads to the creation of a lower heaven separated from the first by a veil and inhabited by the shadows, phantoms, and a second Adam. They too sin, and so it goes on until there are seven heavens or paradises, each inhabited by an Adam with shadows and phantoms. God reveals himself in every heaven, but the phantoms and shadows nonetheless forget what they have learnt again. Eventually they land on earth, where they are imprisoned in bodies and repent until God sends Muḥammad and ʿAlī with redeeming knowledge.[95]

Halm is undoubtedly right that Jaʿfar b. Ḥarb's account takes us to the source from which the Kufan Mufaḍḍal tradition is derived,[96] and it is tempting to postulate that the cosmology missing in Jaʿfar b. Ḥarb is that preserved in the Nuṣayrī book. If so, the Nuṣayrī book describes the fall of the seven Adams while Jaʿfar b. Ḥarb tells us of the journey back to the heavenly home. But it seems unlikely. Both the *Kitāb al-haft wa'l-aẓilla* and the related *Umm al-kitāb* have accounts of the creation of the seven Adams and the seven heavens, but neither tells us of the return journey through the heavens, let alone one accomplished in seven eras with collective judgements at the end of each one of them. Jaʿfar b. Ḥarb, on the other hand, only tells us about the seven eras, not about the manner in which humans came to be on the earth. If the two accounts had once formed part of the same story one would have expected some signs of it. The *Umm al-kitāb* does mention the possibility of sinners falling below the earth, but they fall in the course of a cycle of reincarnations that will eventually gain them release, not by way of eternal damnation after their cycle of reincarnation is over.[97] In addition, the *Kitāb al-haft wa'l-aẓilla* and the *Umm al-kitāb* are ʿAlid Shīʿite works of a Gnostic nature. In the *Kitāb al-haft wa'l-aẓilla* the shadows keep forgetting; this is why they are expelled from paradise seven times, to land on earth. Oblivion lies at the root of the human condition, salvation lies in redeeming knowledge. In the *Umm al-kitāb* they sink first because they forget and next because they are seduced by sexual desire.[98] But there is no trace of Gnosticism, or even of Shīʿism, in Jaʿfar b. Ḥarb's account, which makes no mention of ignorance or oblivion and in which salvation is by obedience (to whom or what we are not told). This makes it unlikely that the Ḥarbiyya operated with a Gnostic cosmology, as opposed to one that could also be reworked in a Gnostic vein.

95 Halm, 'Schatten', part I, 220.
96 Halm, 'Schatten', part II, 25.
97 Halm, 'Schatten', part II, 53.
98 Halm, 'Schatten', part II, 53.

The shadows and phantoms are attested in other Shīʿite thought as well. According to al-Mughīra b. Saʿīd al-ʿIjlī God created the shadows of men (*ẓilāl al-nās*), including those of Muḥammad and ʿAlī (or Jesus); here as in the *Kitāb al-haft wa'l-aẓilla* the shadows are the believers in pre-existence.[99] In Imāmī Ḥadīth the shadows and phantoms are only those of the holy family, not humanity at large. One tradition explains that Muḥammad and his family were the first thing that God created and that they were phantoms (*ashbāḥ*) of light in front of God. What are *ashbāḥ*? Jābir asks, to be told that they are a shadow of the light (*ẓill al-nūr*) and luminous bodies (*ʿabdān nūrāniyya*) without spirits (of their own), because all were supported by the holy spirit.[100] According to the Mukhammisa, on the other hand, Muḥammad was God, who appeared in five *ashbāḥ* or forms (*ṣūra*s), those of Muḥammad, ʿAlī, Fāṭima, Ḥasan, and Ḥusayn; but four of them had no reality (*lā ḥaqīqa lahā*), the divine essence (*al-maʿnā*) was the person Muḥammad.[101] This is closer to the meaning of 'phantoms' given in the dictionaries for *ashbāḥ*, but it is clearly not what the Imāmīs have in mind. To them the *ashbāḥ* are phantoms only in the sense of being ethereal. When God wanted to create forms (*ṣuwar*, i.e., bodies) for them he transformed them into a column of light and put them in Adam's loins, from where they were transmitted from one generation to the next as a unit until they reached ʿAbd al-Muṭṭalib, Muḥammad's grandfather. There the column divided into two, to pass into ʿAbdallāh and Abū Ṭālib, who passed them to their wives, and from their wives they passed to Muḥammad and ʿAlī. When ʿAlī married Fāṭima the column was reunited, and ʿAlī's half passed to al-Ḥasan and his offspring, Muḥammad's to al-Ḥusayn and his offspring; in al-Ḥusayn's line it would move from one imam to the next until the day of judgement.[102]

What are all these entities? They are identified as phantoms in the sense of luminous bodies without spirits, or light in the sense of a spirit without bodies,[103] or a shadow of the light, or lights in shadows,[104] or shadows of light or spirits of light.[105] The terminology comes across as chaotic. This

[99] Shahrastānī, I, 135 = I, 516f.

[100] Kulīnī, *Kāfī*, I, 442, no. 10, cited in Halm, 'Schatten', part I, 233f.

[101] Qummī, 56, no. 111. Compare the Nuṣayrīs and Isḥāqīs in Shahrastānī, I, 144 = I, 544, where all the shadows and forms are ʿAlī (*ḥaqīqatuhu*).

[102] Ibn Bābawayh, *ʿIlal*, 209 (bāb 156, 11); quoted in Amir-Moezzi, *Religion discrète*, 127, see also 114f., 312; Rubin, 'Pre-existence and Light', 99ff., for similar traditions.

[103] Kulīnī, *Kāfī*, I, 440, no. 3, of Muḥammad and ʿAlī.

[104] For this last see Rubin, 'Pre-existence and Light', 99n.; cf. Kulīnī, *Kāfī*, I, 441, no. 7: 'I said to Abū ʿAbdallāh: what were you like when you were in the shadows?'

[105] Amir-Moezzi, *Religion discrète*, 114.

suggests that the transmitters were operating with free-floating concepts originating in earlier systems of thought which they were now adapting to express their own convictions. The shadows could have their roots in Platonism, for, inspired by Plato's famous allegory about the shadows on the wall of the cave, Platonists of all stripes used shadows as a metaphor for a diminution of divine reality.[106] The *logos* was a mere image and shadow of God, as Philo said;[107] the *logos* made flesh in its turn was a mere shadow of the *logos* in its full reality, as Origen observed;[108] Plotinus characterised matter as a mere shadow upon a shadow;[109] the Valentinians and other Gnostics also used the shadow metaphor for the derived and only seemingly real existence of the material principle that has been cut off from the divine Pleroma: this last takes us close to the shadows of the Mukhammisa and Nuṣayrīs.[110] But the term *shabaḥ* elsewhere figures as a translation of Pahlavi *tan gōhr*, body substance, a poorly known Zoroastrian concept attested in the story of how Zoroaster was created in the material world after 6,000 years of pre-existence. It was one out of three ingredients that came down from on high, the other two being his *fravahr*, translated as *rūḥ*, and his *khwarra* or luminous quality, unfortunately omitted in the Arabic version.[111] Celestial body substance, spirit, and luminosity seem to be precisely the concepts in terms of which the Imāmī traditions are trying to describe the pre-existing imams. That the *ashbāḥ* were the imam's fine body substance also goes well with Rubin's understanding of them as the primordial 'spermatic substance' of the holy family, a term chosen on the basis of the traditions in which it is transmitted from the loins of Adam down to the time of their birth.[112] The correspondence is not perfect, for in the story of Zoroaster's creation it is Zoroaster's *khwarra*, not his body substance, that is transmitted by sexual reproduction, and over a much shorter period: the *khwarra* passes straight from above to Zoroaster's grandmother at the time when she was giving birth to

106 Plato, *Republic*, VII, 515a.

107 Philo, *Legum allegoriae*, III, 96.

108 *SCM Press Origen*, s.v. 'atonement' (citing *Commentary of John*, ii, 49).

109 Plotinus, *Enneads*, 6.3.8, 36f.

110 Thomassen, 'Derivation of Matter in Monistic Gnosticism', 13, cf. 2f.

111 For the Pahlavi accounts see Darrow, 'Zoroaster Amalgamated'. For the Arabic rendition see Shahrastānī, I, 186 = I, 642f., where *rūḥ* renders *fravahr* and *shabaḥ* (to be restored from n. 46) *tan gōhr*. Both discussed in Crone, 'Pre-existence in Iran'.

112 Rubin, 'Pre-existence and Light', 98ff. Rubin believes this concept to be Arabian, with reference to a pre-Islamic poem in which al-Samaw'al boasts of how 'we' are pure, the women (of the tribe) having kept 'our *sirr*' (translated 'hidden essence') pure/unmixed (p. 72). For further discussion see below, pp. 248f., 485f.

her daughter, Dugdav, whose birth illuminated the whole house; when Dugdav united with Zoroaster's father the *khwarra* passed to their son along with the body substance and the spirit, which the two of them had imbibed in the form of milk mixed with *hōm*. In the Imāmī traditions the three ingredients have become largely synonymous and combined with the idea of an unbroken succession of imams and prophets from Adam to Muḥammad's own time.

In short, we have here another idea found in different versions among Platonists, Gnostics, and Zoroastrians, and now also Muslims. This time the idea concerns pre-existence, with reference now to the imams and now to mankind at large. Ja'far b. Ḥarb belongs in the second group. There are no *ashbāḥ* in his account of the Ḥarbiyya, only shadows, undoubtedly in the sense of mankind in pre-existence: originally people had lived as spiritual beings endowed with fine bodies of light in the presence of God, and eventually the virtuous among them would return to that state again. What is not at all clear is how the Ḥarbiyya held the shadows to have come into the material world. Even if we assume his shadows to be Platonic we do not get very far, given the profusion of uses to which Plato's ideas had been put. Perhaps the shadows had sinned by oblivion and grown increasingly dense and fleshy, as in the *Kitāb al-haft wa'l-aẓilla*, implying a Gnostic view of the world. But it is only in the *Kitāb al-haft wa'l-aẓilla* that the term is used in the negative sense of an ignorant (if still spiritual) being cut off from God. In the Imāmī traditions it stands for the highest and purest state in which a human being can find itself. If this is how the Ḥarbiyya used the term they would have seen the shadows as having come into the material world in a different way. They could have held the shadows to have been impelled downwards by some natural impulse, as in Neoplatonism, but this is somewhat unlikely. They could also have seen them as guilty of some act of disobedience, as in Origen's myth of pre-existence, which was available to eastern Syrian Christians in Evagrius' formulation and which surfaced in several Mu'tazilite versions.[113] Or they could have held the bodies to have gone into the material world in agreement with God in order to be tested, as they do in one of the Mu'tazilite versions of the Origenist myth, or in order to fight evil, as they do in a Zoroastrian myth about the pre-existence of mankind. This last is perhaps the most likely, given that the Zoroastrian account in question seems to have originated in western Iran or Mesopotamia, and that it still survives in

[113] Cf. Crone, 'Pre-existence in Iran'.

this region in an account by the Ahl-i Ḥaqq.[114] But it is impossible to tell. All the different explanations imply different views of the human condition, and on this crucial point the account of the seven Adams is silent.

GNOSTICISM

The little we are told about Khurramī cosmology and eschatology suggests that we should beware of classifying the Khurramīs as Gnostics. Most scholars probably envisage them as such, since this is how all Shīʿite Ghulāt tend to be seen. But even ʿAlid Shīʿite Ghulāt were not necessarily always Gnostics, and the obvious similarities between them and the Khurramīs notwithstanding, they should not be conflated.

Gnosticism is a term commonly used for a form of religion that appeared in the Graeco-Roman Near East and Mediterranean about the same time as Christianity, usually or always within Christianity, as one of the many rival understandings of what Jesus represented. It manifested itself in a bewildering variety of different forms known from the Church Fathers, the library recovered at Nag Hammadi, and Manichaean texts, and it is traditionally identified with reference to a bundle of characteristics, not all of which are present in every single case. Prominent among these characteristics is a cosmological myth to the effect that the world owes its existence to an error or disaster in the divine realm (usually envisaged as consisting of light), whereby part of the divine came to undergo a downward movement resulting in its imprisonment in matter (usually envisaged as darkness); in al-Shahrastānī's terminology most Gnostics belong with the Maskhiyya. Matter is viewed in a negative light, sometimes as positively evil. The creation of this world is often credited to a bungling demiurge, a lesser deity of whom it is sometimes said that he mistook himself for God under the illusion that there was no one above him (the so-called superbia motif); and a host of lesser divine and demonic beings typically populate the cosmos. In short, the key characteristic of Gnosticism is a sense of cosmic alienation: the world was not meant to exist, humans were not meant to be here, they are fallen sparks of the divine held captive in gross matter, from which they must seek to escape. Sunk in deep oblivion of their true origin,

[114] For the Zoroastrian account see Bailey, *Zoroastrian Problems*, 108, citing *Gr Bd*, Anklesaria edn, 38.12ff.; in Zaehner, *Zurvan*, 324 = 336); *Dd*, 36:27; *PRDd*, 17d:13–14 (I, 94f. = II, 35); Abū ʿĪsā in Ibn al-Malāḥimī, *Muʿtamad*, 640; also reflected in Shahrastānī, I, 183 = I, 637; for the Ahl-i Ḥaqq version see Mokri, 'Kalām gourani', 241 (cf. Chapter 19, p. 477); for all of them, including the Muʿtazilite versions, see Crone, 'Pre-existence in Iran'.

they need to be awakened so that they can seek to liberate themselves from this world and return to the heavenly realm from which they have come. Liberation was possible thanks to the intervention of divine forces in the story of the creation and/or its aftermath.[115] It may be intermediaries emanating from the highest God rather than an arrogant demiurge who build the world as a machinery of salvation after the cosmic disaster (as in Manichaeism). When the devil is the builder of the world it may be the assurance of divine providence that induces the believer to strive for a return instead of simply giving up (as in the case of the Iranianised Marcionites);[116] and it is always the highest God who sends the saviour (by emanation, incarnation, or other means) who brings the saving knowledge that will allow the lost parts of the divine realm to return: one way or the other, there was a guiding hand that could lead people back.

Platonists, including Christian ones, typically also took a negative view of matter, but the Gnostics (who were often indebted to Plato) had the additional characteristic of formulating themselves in what struck many at the time, and certainly also a modern reader, as a very strange idiom. The main themes are usually biblical, but they are treated in an extravagantly mythological style which none the less often betrays familiarity with the scientific thinking of the day. All the systems are eclectic, mixing elements from all known religious traditions of the ancient world, often deliberately, with a strong preference for exotic-sounding names. The authors present their writings as esoteric, address a spiritual elite, and sometimes engage in value reversal: Judas, the serpent, and other villains may be revered as heroes, the normal heroes of the Jews and Christians may be rejected, and so on.[117] Salvation typically lies in the cultivation of spirituality, as opposed to the observance of religious law, and in detachment from this world through asceticism – sometimes extreme – though this obviously cannot have been true of everyone within the communities formed by bearers of such ideas. The heresiographers also credit many Gnostics with libertine behaviour, not always in ways that can be easily dismissed, but there is no sign of this in the Nag Hammadi literature.

115 Brakke, *Gnostics*, 53, treats cosmic alienation and the conviction that God had acted to save people as mutually exclusive in his attack on the concept of Gnosticism accepted here, but the dichotomy is hardly correct. (My thanks to Lance Jenott for drawing my attention to this work.)

116 Cf. Ibn al-Malāḥimī, 587, where they stress the self-evident presence in the world of a *mudabbir*.

117 For the frequency and distribution of the attestations see the table in Williams, *Rethinking 'Gnosticism'*, 61.

The description given here reflects the classic understanding of Gnosticism, and it has recently come under attack.[118] A fair number of scholars hold that the very term Gnosticism should be discarded as an inadequate category, not just because it has come to be used both for a mindset that can manifest itself in any religion and for a historically related cluster of ideas (an old source of confusion), but also because it positively obstructs understanding of the historical phenomenon. It is objected that all attempts to construe a typology of Gnosticism have failed; that the Gnostics consisted of many groups of diverse character that sometimes disagreed among themselves; that the term obscures the degree to which this type of religion was initially one form of Christianity among many others (as opposed to a 'virus' coming from outside); and that the old model simply is not helpful when it comes to understanding the texts. One can sympathise with much of this, given that all names and models are shorthands which invite perfunctory use; but it is hard to see how we can do without them. All attempts to construe universally valid typologies of indispensable categories such as civilisation, society, and tribes have also failed, and one would be hard put to come up with a universally valid typology of Christianity itself.[119] We have to think in terms of a spectrum, but there is scarcely a single historical phenomenon of which that is not the case. Mainstream Christianity was also embodied in a wide variety of different groups that quarrelled among themselves, and one can abandon the idea of the Gnostics as an alien presence among them without jettisoning the label under which they have so far been subsumed.[120] The similarity between them is such that we do need a single name for them,[121] and the term Gnosticism is so well entrenched by now that eliminating it is a hopeless task.[122] By far the

[118] Cf. Williams, *Rethinking 'Gnosticism'*, with chapters against all the major points mentioned above (but for his Gnostic sect allegedly endorsing the goodness of the creation see Chapter 18, n. 17); now also Brakke, *Gnostics*. Another well-known attack is King, *What is Gnosticism?*, a book that does not actually attempt to answer the question it poses, but rather surveys the history of the scholarship, to reject it in favour of a post-colonial approach. (The objections are coloured by theological considerations.)

[119] 'It includes under its umbrella too many peoples and texts that are far too many and far too diverse, and therefore provides no real understanding of them', as Brakke says, with reference to Gnosticism rather than Christianity (*Gnostics*, 21).

[120] Cf. the historical sketch in Markschies, *Gnosis*, 120, a defender of the old model (drawn to my attention by Lance Jenott).

[121] This is fully acknowledged by Williams, *Rethinking 'Gnosticism'*, but the term he suggests ('biblical demiurgical') is cumbersome and has not met with approval.

[122] For the same reason Brakke's attempt to limit the label to a specific group of 'Gnostics' is confusing regardless of its theoretical merits. The word keeps evoking its normal meaning to the reader.

most serious objection to the traditional model of Gnosticism is that it is actually unhelpful for understanding the texts. But all those who come fresh to these texts are so struck by their strange idiom and unfamiliar ideas that they grope around for an overall characterisation of the world-view they express and, until a new and better model has been proposed, the old one is all there is. It still has its defenders,[123] and it does seem to capture something important. All religions postulating the existence of a transcendental realm of perfection have to explain why the world in which we live is so imperfect while at the same time accounting for its attractive sides and ensuring that their followers do not simply despair. In short, all have to put in evil somewhere and take it away somewhere else. But they do not all do it in the same way, and the Gnostics differ from other streams of Christianity current at the time both in their explanation of evil and in their estimation of its extent, not to mention in their peculiar way of expressing themselves.

To some extent the issue is irrelevant in the present context, for it was in terms of the traditional model that the Shīʿite extremists (*ghulāt*) were identified as Gnostics and that the Khurramīs were assumed to be Gnostics as well. Accordingly, it is in those terms that I shall evaluate the assessment. Whether things will look different when the fuller and more nuanced picture of Gnosticism has been fully worked out I shall leave for others to decide.

The question how far Gnosticism lived on in Shīʿism (and Sufism) is usually posed with reference now to the concepts and themes known from the systems of antiquity and now to the world-view that these concepts have hitherto been assumed to express. As regards the concepts and themes, the work of Halm has conclusively demonstrated that many of the central ideas found in ʿAlid Shīʿite *ghuluww* are related to those familiar from Gnosticism in antiquity: there can be no doubt about the historical continuity.[124] What is not so clear is how we should account for this. Did Gnostics bring these ideas to Mesopotamia and Iran as they left the Roman empire in response to persecution by the victorious church there, or did the ideas originate in Mesopotamia and Iran and percolate from there to the Roman empire, or were both processes at work? There can hardly be much doubt that the overall similarities between the diverse

[123] In addition to Markschies, *Gnosis*, see Pearson, *Gnosticism and Christianity*, with arguments I would not always adopt myself (drawn to my attention by Lance Jenott).

[124] The fundamental work is his *Kosmologie und Heilslehre*, followed up by numerous other publications, mostly in article form. Bayhom-Daou, 'Second-century Šīʿite Ġulāt', denies that Gnosticism had surfaced in Islam by the second/eighth century, not that it did eventually appear.

Gnostic myths lie partly in the (often Platonised) Near Eastern traditions behind the ways the biblical material is handled, but these traditions were present on both sides of the border. The role of Iran (inclusive of Mesopotamia) in the formation of Gnosticism was vigorously advocated by the so-called *Religionsschule* which flourished in the first half of the twentieth century, represented by scholars such as Reitzenstein and Bousset; but, great scholars though they were, their basic approach was so wrongfooted that the subject has been discredited and nobody has dared to touch it since.[125] One hopes that it will eventually be taken up again.

As regards the world-view, the continuity between antiquity and Iran is less striking. Even in Shīʿite *ghuluww* the sense of cosmic alienation is not usually very pronounced, and the core of the belief system is not normally a cosmological myth either, but rather an account of the saviour figure or figures, typically ʿAlī and other members of his family, often seen as divine emanations or incarnations. When the world is filled with intermediaries it is not usually to accommodate a demiurge, or to illustrate the faulty nature of the creation, but rather to bridge the gap between the God beyond conceptualisation and the world in which we live. But true knowledge is still esoteric, its bearers still form a spiritual elite, value reversal is still attested; and, as in the case of the ancient Gnostics, the bearers are often accused of libertine behaviour – often, but not always, in ways that can be easily dismissed.

The Khurramīs seem to have less in common with the Gnostics of antiquity than do their ʿAlid Shīʿite counterparts in terms of themes and world-view alike. This will become clearer as we go along, but it is already suggested by the scanty material examined here. The Khurramīs share their dualism with Gnostics such as the Manichaeans, and one group assigned to their ranks believed in dualism with an intermediary principle, as did some Christians of a Gnostic type. But both types of dualism attested for the Khurramīs are also attested for Zoroastrianism, which is not a Gnostic religion; and of the sect that operated with the second type of dualism – i.e., the Māhāniyya – we are explicitly told that they had a life-affirming rather than an ascetic outlook. There is no mention of the superbia motif, a demiurge, Sophia/wisdom, oblivion, sleep, or evil beings such as demons and archons on the Khurramī side, only among ʿAlid Shīʿites. Khurramīs such as the Ḥarbiyya seem to have believed in pre-existence, but so too did Zoroastrians, Origenists, and others. Abū ʿĪsā's Mazdaqiyya did postulate

[125] On the *Religionsschule*, including Reitzenstein and Bousset, see King, *What is Gnosticism?*, ch. 4, acknowledging that they were scholars of impressive achievement.

that the world owed its existence to something going wrong in the heavenly realm, which is a standard Gnostic idea, but this is also how things start in Zoroastrianism. The Mazdaqiyya probably departed from Zoroastrianism by equating darkness with matter, as did the Manichaeans, but not the Zoroastrians; the Mazdaqiyya identified darkness as stupid rather than evil, however, while the Zoroastrians wanted to have it both ways.[126] Shaked tentatively interprets the Mazdaqite idea that the end would come about accidentally as evidence of a particularly pessimistic world-view: the world was probably governed by the evil power in this state of mixture, and no time had been set for the end.[127] But their position should probably be understood as a response to eternalism, also represented among the Khurramīs (as will be seen).[128] According to the eternalists the world had always existed and always would: the world had no creator, no beginning or end. Against this the Mazdaqiyya affirmed the slightly less outrageous view that the elements had been combined by accident and would be separated by accident: the world was devoid of providence, but it was not eternal. Views of this kind are well attested in early Muslim *kalām*, in which the deniers of God in the sense of provident creator were known as *dahrī*s and *zindīq*s (the latter coming from a Marcionite, Bardesanite, and Manichaean background).[129] All Khurramīs seem to have envisaged God as utterly distant and beyond reach; contact with the divine is through lesser forms of light, or incarnations. But they serve to bridge the gap, not to awaken us from oblivious slumber. Of the Mazdaqiyya we are told that they inclined to Manichaeism. No doubt other Khurramīs did too. The overall impression one gets is of Zoroastrians, ascetic Christians, and Gnostics, above all in the form of Manichaeans, living cheek by jowl and merging in countless ways of which only a tiny fraction was recorded.

[126] See for example *Dk*, V, 24:3f., in answer to questions by the Christian Bōkht-Mārē. First we are told that the Antagonist reached the light in ignorance, by an unwitting and aimless movement. This agrees with Abū ʿĪsā's pre-Manichaean cosmology. But thereafter we learn that his struggle to mix with the light was the outcome of his hatred, cupidity, concupiscence, envy, arrogance, quarrelsome nature, and more besides, which agrees with the *Bundahišn*: see esp. the beginning of ch. 1, where he is full of desire to fight (or kill) from the start and attacks the light to destroy it. In the pre-Manichaean cosmology, by contrast, he swallows light by accident, thereby causing the mixture.

[127] Shaked, *Dualism*, 127f.

[128] See Chapter 12, pp. 238, 247.

[129] See *EI*[2], s.v. 'Dahriyya'; *EIr.*, s.v. 'Dahrī'; van Ess, *TG*, IV, 451ff.; Crone, 'Dahrīs according to al-Jāḥiẓ'.

11

Divine Indwelling

On the question of divine indwelling *(ḥulūl)* the best information is provided by Abū Tammām in his account of al-Muqannaʿ's followers, identified as Mubayyiḍa. According to him they held that 'all the messengers are gods (*āliha*) whose bodies are the messengers of God while their spirits are Himself and that whenever God wants to speak to corporeal beings (*al-jismāniyyīn*), he enters the form (*ṣūra*) of one of them and makes him the messenger to them so that he may order them [to do] what he wants and forbid them [to do] what he does not want and what he is angered by'. In other words the messengers have human bodies, but their spirits are divine; God had entered them for purposes of transmitting his law to mankind. 'They claim that when God created Adam, He entered into his form, then He caused him to die and returned to His throne. Then, when He created Noah, He dwelled in his form (*ḥalla fī ṣūratihi*), then He caused Him to die and returned to His throne.' This is repeated in connection with Abraham, Moses, Jesus, Muḥammad, Abū Muslim, and al-Muqannaʿ. As seen already, Abū Muslim should probably be removed.[1]

Humans here consist of two components, form/body and spirit (presumably *fravahr*),[2] and divine indwelling comes about when the human spirit is replaced or complemented by 'God', as Abū Tammām somewhat crassly puts it: we are hardly to take it that the Mubayyiḍa envisaged the Godhead as moving into the messenger, so that thenceforth all divinity in the universe was concentrated in him. Centuries later Ibn Qayyim al-Jawziyya used the same crass formulation to parody the

[1] Abū Tammām, 76 = 75f.; Chapter 6, pp. 129f.; cf. Crone, 'Abū Tammām on the Mubayyiḍa'.

[2] For the translation of Zoroaster's *fravahr* as *rūḥ* see Shahrastānī, I, 186 = I, 642f. (cf. above, p. 213). For the similar translation of the *fravahr*s of humans in general see Abū ʿĪsā in Ibn al-Malāḥimī, *Muʿtamad*, 640. For further discussion see Crone, 'Pre-existence in Iran'.

Christian doctrine of divine incarnation.[3] One takes it that it was God's spirit, or some comparable hypostasis or emanation, that passed into the chosen messenger. It did not move from one human body to another, but rather went directly from its divine abode to the chosen human being and back again – with long periods in between the incarnations, as we are explicitly told. In between there were probably divine leaders of other kinds, but all we are told (by another source) is that al-Muqannaʿ deified prophets and kings.[4]

The Mubayyiḍa found support for their conviction in the Qur'ān. Sura 53 describes a vision of a divine being, sometimes taken to be an angel and sometimes God, and according to the Mubayyiḍa it described the very act of incarnation: when the Qur'ān says that the one 'terrible in power and very strong' stood poised, then drew near and 'let himself down' to stand 'two bows' length away', the meaning was that the divine being came to be closer to Muḥammad than his own brain and heart; and when the sura continues that the divine being 'revealed to him what he revealed', it meant that the divine being inspired (*alhama*) Muḥammad to the point of entering his form (*dakhala fī ṣūratihi*).[5] They did not envisage a messenger as born divine, in other words: Muḥammad's encounter with the divine being took place when he was an adult, as is clear from the Qur'ān itself. Al-Muqannaʿ became divine on his return to Marw after his spell in jail. The divine being entered him in the sense of transforming his very nature, for his veil was meant to protect his followers from his divine radiance.

The *Tārīkh-i Bukhārā*, which reports the same list of divine incarnations as Abū Tammām (probably from the same source), has an obscure passage on al-Muqannaʿ's claim to divinity which does not appear elsewhere. People objected to al-Muqannaʿ that others had merely claimed to be prophets, so why did he claim to be God? Al-Muqannaʿ replied: 'Īshān nafsānī būdand man rūḥānī am kih andar īshān būdam va-marā īn qudrat hast kih khwadrā bih har ṣūrat kih khāham binamāyam'[6] (they were endowed with appetitive souls, I am spiritual such that (*kih*) I was in them, for I have the power to manifest myself in any form I like).[7] This does not answer the question, for, if God's spirit was in all of the

[3] Lazarus-Yafeh, 'Some Neglected Aspects', 81, with reference to Ibn Qayyim al-Jawziyya, *Hidāyat al-ḥayārā*, 191.

[4] Cf. Thaʿālibī, *Ādāb al-mulūk*, 37.

[5] Abū Tammām, 76 = 75.

[6] *TB*, 65.2/91.8 = 66.

[7] This understanding of *kih* was suggested to me by Maria Subtelny. Frye has 'they were corporeal, I am the soul which was in them. I have the power to manifest myself in any form

prophets, they too could have called themselves God. The reply is followed by an obviously invented letter in which al-Muqannaʿ once more speaks as God, and the entire passage is meant to illustrate the preposterous nature of his claims;[8] but even preposterous claims have to make sense. Al-Muqannaʿ seems to be saying that he was divine in a fuller sense than his predecessors: they still had appetitive souls whereas he was *entirely* filled with God's spirit.[9] As we have seen, he also differed from them in being the mahdi.

No comparable sequence of messengers is reported for any other group, but it is clear that the followers of ʿAbdallāh b. Muʿāwiya postulated something similar. Their interest was in the transfer of the divine spirit (here explicitly mentioned) to an imam rather than a messenger, so we do not get to see the details, but according to one report Ibn Muʿāwiya preached that the spirit of God was in Adam (and Seth according to al-Baghdādī) and that thereafter it was transferred (*tanāsakhat*) or moved (*taḥawwalat*), presumably meaning from one messenger to another, until it passed into Ibn Muʿāwiya, who was divine (*rabb*) and a prophet (*nabī*); al-Qummī adds Jesus in between Adam and Ibn Muʿāwiya, without meaning the list to be exhaustive.[10] But the messengers or prophets of the past simply form the background to the imams, as also in the report on the Rāwandiyya.[11] God's spirit passed (*dārat*) to ʿAlī and his descendants, and then, via the Testament of Abū Hāshim, to ʿAbdallāh b. Muʿāwiya, as the latter's followers said; God was light and dwelling in Ibn Muʿāwiya.[12] Or the holy spirit (*rūḥ al-qudus*) had been in Muḥammad and passed (*intaqalat*) from him to the ʿAlīd imams, who were gods, and the holy spirit was eternal and would never cease to be: they spoke like the Christians, as we are told.[13]

Al-Qummī reports one version in which the widely spaced prophets (here synonymous with or inclusive of messengers) and the imams who

I like.' Apparently, he emends *rūḥānī*, 'spiritual', to *rūḥī*, 'the spirit which', and by some slip translates *rūḥ* as 'soul' rather than 'spirit'.

8 Zaryāb, 'Nukātī', 90, noting that it has al-Muqannaʿ refer to himself by that name, though it was obviously not a self-designation. The entire tone is parodying.

9 Compare Aphrahat on the resurrection: the animal spirit (*rūḥā nafshanīthā*) will be swallowed up by the heavenly spirit, 'and the whole man shall become spiritual, since his body is possessed by it [the Spirit]' (cited in Shchuryk, '*Lᵉbēš pagrā'* in the *Demonstrations* of Aphrahat', 426).

10 Ashʿarī, 6; Baghdādī, *Farq*, 236; Qummī, 41, no. 83.

11 The same spirit was in Jesus and the imams, who were all divine, as Ablaq said (Tab. iii, 418).

12 Nawbakhtī, 29; Qummī, 39, no. 80; Baghdādī, *Farq*, 242.

13 Ps.-Nāshiʾ, §56.

follow one another without interruption are combined, as they later were to be in Ismailism: God's spirit was in Adam, and all the prophets were gods whose spirit passed from the one to the other until it passed into Muḥammad, *and* from him it had passed to ʿAlī, Ibn al-Ḥanafiyya, Abū Hāshim, and then to Ibn Muʿāwiya.[14] But the combination could be due to al-Qummī himself. Like the Rāwandiyya, however, the followers of ʿAbdallāh b. Muʿāwiya saw the imamic chain as culminating in the mahdi.

Ibn Muʿāwiya's followers supported their belief in the divinity of the imams with reference to a *ḥadīth* in which ʿĀʾisha says that the Prophet's spirit – or, as the transmitter adds, 'perhaps his soul' – came out of him once and that ʿAlī (the future imam) put it in his mouth: what ʿAlī had put in his mouth, they said, was the divinity (*lāhūtiyya*) that had been in the Prophet and which had enabled him to work miracles and know the unseen; it was the holy spirit (*rūḥ al-qudus*).[15] Here, then, the holy spirit does not return to the throne to await another messenger (though it may have been envisaged as doing so in connection with the widely spaced messengers); rather, it stays on earth and passes directly from the messenger to a younger successor, the first imam, to pass from one generation to the next in uninterrupted succession thereafter. The body in which the spirit takes up abode is once again that of an adult. The same is true of a report in which both the donor and the recipient are imams: Abū Hāshim's (divine) spirit passed to his successor, here Ibn Ḥarb/al-Ḥārith, by bequest.[16]

QALB

Of the Khidāshiyya we are told that they believed in *qalb* and *tanāsukh al-arwāḥ*. *Qalb* is explained as the belief that God can change (*yaqliba*) himself from one shape (*ṣūra*) to another and appear to his servants in different manifestations (*manāẓir*);[17] and in favour of this doctrine the Khidāshiyya would adduce stories about Gabriel appearing in the shape now of Diḥya al-Kalbī, now of a bedouin, and now of a horseman at the battle of Badr. They argued that if Gabriel could do so without

[14] Qummī, 42, no. 86 (cf. 41, no. 83).

[15] Ps.-Nāshiʾ, §56. Compare *Zand ī Wahman Yasn*, 3:6f., where Ohrmazd puts his wisdom of omniscience on Zoroaster's hand in the form of water, which Zoroaster drinks.

[16] Qummī, 35, no. 74.

[17] In *kalām*, by contrast, *qalb* was the term for God's ability to change humans (Jāḥiẓ, *Ḥayawān*, IV, 73).

changing his essence (*dhāt*) or substance (*jawhar*), it went without saying that the eternal creator could do so too.[18] According to Abū Tammām, they said that if God were not able to change his own essence (*taṣrīf dhātihi*) into diverse forms he would not be able to change that of others either, a view he also reports at greater length for a certain Minhāliyya, perhaps a Khurāsānī group subsumed by others under the name of Khidāshiyya.[19] The Minhāliyya claimed that God could change himself into solids, plants, animals, reptiles, insects, grass-eating animals, predators, stinging things, humans, *jinn*, angels, and other created things; they would adduce a story about God descending from heaven and riding a donkey to visit the sick Companion Abū Hurayra, and they seem to have invoked Diḥya al-Kalbī too. The accounts suggests that they envisaged God and Gabriel as assuming different – ultimately illusory – guises, not as taking up abode in existing objects, animals, or human beings: Gabriel appeared as Diḥya al-Kalbī, i.e., he assumed the likeness of Diḥya, but Diḥya himself was not transformed into Gabriel.[20] By contrast, when the Rāwandiyya in Iraq declared al-Haytham b. Muʿāwiya to be Gabriel, one takes them to have meant that Gabriel had taken up abode in the body of this officer, turning him into a celestial being.[21] It may be that the Khidāshiyya did not believe in *ḥulūl* – divine indwelling in human beings – but rather in avatars or metamorphoses, the appearance of God in human or animal or other forms which have no separate existence.

More probably, however, they believed in both, for the two beliefs were easily combined. Thus the divine spirit that took up abode in Christ also caused Christ to assume different appearances, according to some eastern Christian works, and Mani too appeared in many forms.[22] When the Khidāshiyya are said to have believed in *qalb* and *tanāsukh al-arwāḥ* we are perhaps to take it to mean that they believed in metamorphosis and

[18] Ps.-Nāshiʾ, §49. Compare Shahrastānī, I, 79 = I, 346, where some anthropomorphists with *ḥulūlī* inclinations also invoke Gabriel's appearance to Muḥammad in the guise of a bedouin as proof that God could appear in human form, adducing his appearance as an angel to Mary as well (Q 19:17). Shahrastānī cites the *ḥadīth* about Diḥya at I, 27 = I, 171.

[19] Abū Tammām names the founder as al-Minhāl b. Maymūn al-ʿIjlī. Nothing is known about him or his sect, but his father's name suggests servile origin.

[20] Abū Tammām, 74f., 104 = 73f., 98. Diḥya is mentioned in the poem against the Minhāliyya, where the verb *taqlubu* is also used.

[21] Tab. iii, 129.

[22] Cartlidge, 'Transfiguration of Metamorphosis Traditions'; McGuckin, 'The Changing Forms of Jesus'; cf. Klimkeit, 'Gestalt, Ungestalt, Gestaltwandel', 62ff., on the Manichaeans (where some of the examples should probably be understood as references to periodic incarnation rather than metamorphosis).

repeated divine incarnation, for *tanāsukh al-arwāḥ* does sometimes have the latter meaning; more commonly, though, the addition of *al-arwāḥ* turns *tanāsukh* into a term for human reincarnation.[23]

CHRISTIAN PROPHETS

The Khurramīs of Azerbaijan and Mesopotamia/Armenia had not participated in either ʿAbdallāh b. Muʿāwiya's revolt or the Hāshimite revolution, and there are practically no Islamic elements in the first reports on them. Instead, there is a great deal of Christian language, and this should help us understand some of what they said.

Of the Khurdanaye who eventually joined Bābak we are told that they 'had a tradition, according to an oracle from their ancestors, that a king called mahdi would come forth from them and lead people to faith in him, and they proclaimed him God'; when the awaited mahdi appeared 'a veil was thrown over his face; sometimes he called himself Christ, sometimes the Holy Spirit'.[24] One takes it that the pre-existing Christ or the holy spirit had taken up abode in this man, as it did in Jesus. Here, as in Sogdia, the divine being incarnated itself in an adult, and here as there the deified person had to wear a veil.

We do not know anything about this mahdi's predecessors and we only have the names of his successors, but it goes without saying that the leaders of his community before or after him cannot have been messiahs as well. What were they then? One of them was Bābak, the leader of a cult organisation of his own. He did not claim to be the mahdi, nor did he wear a veil; what he did claim was that the spirit of his predecessor – i.e., Jāvīdhān – had passed into him,[25] that he was 'the spirit of the prophets', and that he was divine.[26] Since it was his possession of Jāvīdhān's spirit that legitimised his position as the latter's successor, all leaders of the cult organisation were presumably seen as endowed with the same divine spirit, that is, the 'spirit of the prophets'. In short, it would

[23] See Chapter 12, p. 233, on the Rāwandiyya.
[24] Dionysius (unnamed) in Michael Syr., IV, 508 = III, 50 (the fullest account, cited here); Bar Hebraeus, *Chronography*, 144; *Chron. ad 1234*, II, 25 = 17f., cf. II, ixf.
[25] Ibn al-Nadīm, 407.11 = II, 820f.; Maqdisī, VI, 115.ult.; Tab. iii, 1015.
[26] Bābak 'used to say to those whom he seduced that he was a god (*annahu ilāh*)' (Ibn al-Nadīm, 406.10); he called himself 'the avenging guide' and 'the spirit of the prophets', and claimed that he was divine (*khwadrā al-hādī al-muntaqim [va] rūḥ al-anbiyāʾ nām kard va daʿvī-yi khudāʾī namūd*) (Abū 'l-Maʿālī, 62.4).

seem that the cult organisation had been led by prophets in something close to the Christian sense of the word.

To the Christians a prophet was a man inspired by the holy spirit to make oracular statements. Of such prophets there had been many in the past, not just those of the Bible, for the early Christians held prophecy to continue into their own time. Among them the spirit would move people to stand up in the congregation to propose inspired interpretations of the scriptures, resolve disputes by oracular intervention, or make prognostications. The angel of the prophetic spirit filled a man and the man would speak, 'filled with the holy spirit', as the first- or second-century *Shepherd of Hermas* says.[27] The reference is to ecstatic prophecy, a phenomenon attested in many parts of the world, but the Christians were the only bearers of a major religion in the Near East to accept it as a contemporary source of authority. Even among the Christians its history as a generally accepted phenomenon was short. Christian prophets seem to have disappeared from the mainstream church with the emergence of a formal, ecclesiastical hierarchy. We see the transition in Ignatius of Antioch (d. *c.* 110), a bishop who used his gift of prophecy to strengthen this hierarchy: 'I spoke with a great voice, the voice of God: 'To the bishop give heed, and to the presbytery and to the deacons'', he told a congregation after a visit; 'I learned nothing from any human being, but the spirit was speaking in this manner, 'Apart from the bishop do nothing ....''[28] In the third century, however, there was a burst of prophetic activity, known as the New Prophecy, in Asia Minor led by Montanus, and several oracular statements by him and other prophets (notably female ones) in the movement have been preserved. Montanus would say seemingly outrageous things such as 'I am the Father, I am the Son, and I am the holy spirit [or the Spirit, or the Paraclete]', very much as the mahdi of the Khurdanaye seems to have spoken. The prophetess Maximilla would utter words such as 'I am word and spirit and power.' They did not mean to cast themselves as God, Christ, or the holy spirit (or Paraclete): it was God, Christ, and/or the spirit who was speaking through them. 'Do not listen to me, listen to Christ,' as Maximilla would say. The inspired person was like a harp through which the wind was moving, a passive instrument through which the divine spirit produced the sounds that emerged from the human mouth. The possibly third-century author of the Syriac Odes of Solomon saw himself as a prophet in this sense. Montanism was still

[27] *Shepherd of Hermas*, Mandates, 11.9 (tr. Holmes, 407).

[28] Aune, *Christian Prophecy*, 291f., citing Ignatius' letter to the Philadelphians, 7:1–2.

flourishing in Asia Minor in the sixth century, when Justinian did his best to eradicate it.[29]

If the veiled mahdi, Jāvīdhān, and Bābak were all prophets in the Christian sense, should we dismiss the claims of divinity attributed to them as possibly wilful misunderstanding by their contemporaries? It seems unlikely. The veil worn by Dionysius' mahdi leaves no doubt that the divine being had entered and transformed him, and all three figures differ from Christian prophets in other ways too. The spirit entered them on a permanent basis, whereas it only filled Christian prophets from time to time; it passed from one Khurramī leader to another on the latter's death, whereas it entered Christian prophets at any time from on high; there was only one leader at a time at Badhdh, whereas the spirit could fill many Christians at a time, and did so among the Montanists; and there is no sign that any of the Khurramī leaders spoke in a state of ecstasy.

Though prophets disappeared from mainstream Christianity, even mainstream Christians continued to operate with a notion of a 'bearer of the spirit' (*pneumatophoros*), or of a 'spiritual' (*pneumatikos*) or 'divine man' (*theios anēr*),[30] meaning a person endowed by the spirit with gifts such as the ability to heal, predict, and solve disputes – in short, what modern scholars call a holy man. Christians would still refer to such men as prophets.[31] This takes us closer to Jāvīdhān and Bābak, divine men in whom the spirit was innate. But Christian bearers of the spirit would hardly speak of themselves as actually being 'the spirit of the prophets', let alone as divine; and they are not on record as having thought of the spirit they bore as a physical entity which moved from them into another body when they died. In short, Jāvīdhān and Bābak seem to have operated with ideas that could be formulated with greater or lesser felicity in Christian terms, but which were not actually Christian by origin.

Abū Ḥātim al-Rāzī attributes the Khurramī understanding of Christian prophecy to Mazdak: Mazdak, he says, held prophecy (*nubuwwa*) to be a spirit that moved from one body to another, and also believed in the divinity of human beings 'like the Ghulāt in this and other communities'.[32] One wonders whether he is not inferring Mazdak's belief from those of the

[29] Aune, *Christian Prophecy*, 296ff., 314ff.; Procopius, *Secret History*, 11.23; Tabbernee, *Montanist Inscriptions and Testimonia*, 45; cf. now also the fifth- or sixth-century epitaph in Mitchell, 'An Apostle to Ankara from the New Jerusalem', 211ff.

[30] Cf. Rapp, *Holy Bishops*, 58ff., 63.

[31] Bitton-Ashkelony and Kofsky, 'Gazan Monasticism', 29; see also the examples in Bitton-Ashkelony and Kofsky, *Christian Gaza in Late Antiquity*, 119, 132, 133.

[32] Abū Ḥātim al-Rāzī, *Iṣlāḥ*, 159.

Ghulāt; but however this may be, we have a distinctive concept of divine leadership here. We find it in eastern and western Iran alike and it has five noteworthy features. First, a man is rendered divine by the presence in him of light or the divine spirit, without much difference between the two being discernible. 'All the Dualists and Manichaeans believe in Jesus and claim that he is the spirit of God, in the sense that he is part of God and the light, which is alive, sentient, and knowledgeable in their view', as al-Maqdisī reports.[33] Secondly, the divinity is present in widely spaced figures who inaugurate new cycles and bring new laws – messengers/apostles in Muslim parlance. Thus al-Maqdisī reports of the Khurramīs in the Jibāl that they 'believe in the change of the name and the body (*taghyīr al-ism wa-tabdīl al-jism*) and claim that all the messengers, with their diverse laws and religions, come into possession of a single spirit (*yaḥṣulūna 'alā rūḥ wāḥid*)'.[34] This is the doctrine that is also attested for al-Muqanna' and, in a less detailed form, the followers of 'Abdallāh b. Mu'āwiya. It reappears in a work of uncertain date attributed to Ibn Ḥanbal: here we are told that the *zanādiqa 'l-naṣārā*, translatable along the lines of 'dualist/quasi-Manichaean Christians', said that the spirit in Jesus was the spirit of God, from the essence of God (*rūḥ Allāh min dhāt Allāh*), and that when God wished to communicate something he would enter a human being and convey his commands and prohibitions in human language.[35] Thirdly, there are lesser divine figures who function as community leaders in between the divine incarnations. Al-Muqanna' is said to have deified prophets and kings, and Bābak seems to have regarded himself as both a prophet and a king.[36] What the Khurramīs of Azerbaijan expressed in terms of Christian prophecy would seem to be what the Rāwandiyya and followers of 'Abdallāh b. Mu'āwiya expressed in terms of the Islamic imamate: like the community leaders endowed with the spirit of prophecy, the imams of these two groups were men singled out by the spirit who followed one another in direct succession. Fourthly, the recipient of the spirit (and/or light) is always an adult. This is true whether the spirit passes directly from God into a messenger (as in the reports on al-Muqanna'), from a messenger into an imam, from one imam into another (as in the reports of Ibn Mu'āwiya's followers), or, in the Christian language of Azerbaijan, from one prophet to another: like the recipient of the

[33] Maqdisī, III, 122.
[34] Maqdisī, IV, 30.
[35] Ibn Ḥanbal, *Radd 'ala'l-zanādiqa wa'l-Jahmiyya*, 19.
[36] For Bābak's view of himself as king see Chapter 3, p. 72.

Testament of Abū Hāshim, Bābak was an adult when Jāvīdhān's spirit passed into him. The only exception, at least according to the Khurramīs known to al-Maqdisī, was Jesus. The learned men of the Khurramiyya said 'that Mary had intercourse and that a spirit from God was joined to that intercourse; it did not fill her without intercourse'. In other words, they denied the virgin birth, but acknowledged that Jesus was born divine in the sense that the spirit had passed into him on conception.[37] Finally, the sequence of widely spaced messengers and/or imams would culminate in the mahdi, often regarded as the seventh, and the mahdi was God incarnate in a fuller sense than the rest.

CONTINUOUS PROPHECY

According to Abū 'Īsā, the 'Mazdaqiyya of today' held that Mazdak was a prophet and that the messengers had appeared without interruption (*wa-anna'l-rusul tatrā*, cf. Q. 23:44): whenever one died, another stood up (*kullamā maḍā wāḥid qāma wāḥid*).[38] Here, as in connection with cosmology, Abū 'Īsā's Mazdaqiyya are probably a particular group of Khurramīs, and here as so often he appears to be the source of all later statements on the question. Exactly what did the Mazdaqiyya mean? Abū 'Īsā speaks of messengers, suggesting a doctrine to the effect that God would continue to send bearers of divine law in the future, but the expression is Qur'ānic and not coined with the Muslim distinction between prophets and messengers in mind. In al-Bīrūnī's paraphrase of Abū 'Īsā the Mazdaqiyya say that there will never be a time without prophets and that they are sent one after another (*'alā 'l-tawālī*), which is more suggestive of prophets in the sense of community leaders.[39]

The question whether they were prophets in the sense of messengers or in the sense of community leaders may be anachronistic, for the Khurramīs probably did not distinguish sharply between the two. To the Muslims Moses and Jesus were lawgiver prophets – i.e., messengers – whereas Jonah, Elijah, or Isaiah were prophets of other kinds, and community leaders were not prophets at all. To the Christians, all were simply prophets. To the Manichaeans, founders of 'churches' (i.e., new religions)

[37] Maqdisī, III, 122.
[38] Ibn al-Malāḥimī, 584; similarly Baghdādī, *Farq*, 332.5 (drawn to my attention by Joel Blecher).
[39] Bīrūnī in Fück, *Documenta*, 80.10; cf. also Abū Ya'lā, *Mu'tamad fī uṣūl al-dīn*, 167, where the *ahl al-tanāsukh* and Khurramīs say that there may be a prophet after Muḥammad and that prophets will never be cut off.

and those who maintained them were all apostles (*rusul*). The apostles appeared one after the other without interruption, they said; a new one was sent the moment one died.[40] What they meant was not that founders of churches such as Zoroaster, Jesus, or Mani appeared in immediate succession, but rather that there would always be somebody to uphold the truth: Jesus was followed by Paul, and when the Christians began to founder Mani appeared. The distinction between founders of churches and later leaders was present, but not highlighted. The same was probably true of the Khurramīs. As the ʿAlid Shīʿite Kāmiliyya said, there was a light which turned now into the imamate and now into prophethood (such as Muḥammad's).[41] The key distinction to the Khurramīs will not have been that between the founders of communities (messengers) and their later leaders (imams), but rather that between prophets of any kind and the last of them, the mahdi whose coming would mark the end of the material world. Whatever type of leader he used, the key point was that God would never stop communicating directly with mankind.

Al-Maqdisī elsewhere mentions that the dualists (*al-thanawiyya*) believed in the prophethood of Bardesanes (Ibn Dayṣān), Ibn Shākir, Ibn Abī 'l-ʿAwjāʾ, and Bābak al-Khurramī, and that in their view the earth would never be without a prophet (*anna'l-arḍ lā takhlū min nabī qaṭṭ*).[42] Ibn Shākir and Ibn Abī 'l-ʿAwjāʾ were *zindīq*s active as scholars and poets in Basra in the early ʿAbbāsid period, and they are supposed not to have believed in prophethood at all; yet here they have come to be accepted as prophets themselves, presumably in the quasi-Manichaean circles in which they had been active. The idea of continuous prophethood appears in ʿAlid Shīʿism as well – first, if the sources are to be trusted, among the Manṣūriyya and Mughīriyya of the mid-second/eighth century. They were the target of a refutation by Ḍirār b. ʿAmr (d. 194/809), the first to have written against the doctrine that the earth would never be devoid of a prophet.[43] In Nīshāpūr in the time of Faḍl. b. Shādhān (d. 260/874) there were Shīʿites who held that there had to be a person who knew the languages of all human beings, animals, and birds, who knew what was in people's minds, what they were doing in every land and home of theirs, whether a child was a believer or an infidel, and also who was a supporter of his and who an opponent; if he lacked the requisite knowledge God

[40] *Kephalaia*, 12.1 (tr. Gardner, 18).
[41] Shahrastānī, I, 133 = I, 511f.
[42] Maqdisī, III, 8. Ibn Shākir is normally called Abū Shakir.
[43] Ibn al-Nadīm, 215.16; cf. Ashʿarī, 9.

would supply it by revelation.[44] This was probably the kind of continuous revelation that many people hankered for, and whether one called its recipient a prophet or an imam did not really matter. One may well wonder what purpose such revelation served, however, for it was not continuous guidance that these Shīʿites were talking about. Rather, they seem to have thought that everything present in the minds of living beings, whether spoken, visible in action, or hidden as thought, had to be united in a single mind, which functioned as a kind of master switch to the mental grid of the universe. It was not enough for God to know all this: the knowledge had to be channelled through a human being here on earth. There had to be a prophet or imam who knew the unknown (*al-ghayb*), who could do anything, and who was invincible and could work miracles, as others said.[45] Without such a person the mental grid connecting the material and celestial realms could not be switched on; the world would not be connected to the light that nourished and maintained it; all would turn into darkness, as if the sun and the moon had gone extinct. In short, without a human being halfway between man and God, access to the supernatural realm would be cut off.

[44] Kashshī, *Rijāl*, 452f. (no. 416).
[45] See above, p. 192.

12

Reincarnation

There is good evidence that Mazdak believed in reincarnation, but his views are best treated in the next chapter. As regards the Khurramīs, many sources loosely say that they believed in reincarnation,[1] but we hear next to nothing about those in the east. We are told that the Rāwandiyya who came to Iraq believed in *tanāsukh al-arwāḥ*, which normally means reincarnation, but all the examples are of divine beings dwelling in humans: al-Manṣūr was God, the spirit of Gabriel was in al-Haytham b. Muʿāwiya, and that of Adam in ʿUthmān b. Nahīk.[2] The anonymous *ʿUyūn wa'l-ḥadā'iq* adds that the Rāwandiyya 'multiply the spirits of past people and allege that they are moved (*muntaqila*) to other bodies, and that they are so-and-so and that [the spirits] are perennially moving around in all bodies of people, being punished and rewarded in them'.[3] This accords with the evidence on other Khurramīs – but perhaps too well, in the sense that it may come from a common pool of knowledge rather than information specific to the Rāwandiyya. Al-Baghdādī says of the Rāwandiyya who held the spirit of God to be in Abū Muslim that they believed in divine incarnation (*tanāsukh rūḥ al-ilāh*) to the exclusion of reincarnation (*dūna arwāḥ al-nās*).[4] As regards the Khidāshiyya, Jaʿfar b. Ḥarb says that they believed in *al-qalb* and *tanāsukh al-arwāḥ*, which is ambivalent, though it probably does mean that they believed in reincarnation.[5] Abū Tammām says that the Mubayyiḍa believed in *rajʿa*, which

[1] Ps.-Nāshi', §57; Shahrastānī, I, 185 = I, 641.
[2] BA III, 235; *ʿUyūn*, 227.
[3] *ʿUyūn*, 227.
[4] Baghdādī, *Farq*, 255. Nawbakhtī, 37, says that the Rāwandiyya (corrupted to Zaydiyya) neither affirmed nor denied *al-rajʿa*, but the reference here is to the return before the Day of Judgement, not reincarnation.
[5] Ps.-Nāshi', §§ 49, 52.

means reincarnation in a Khurramī context (see pp. 237f.); but the information comes from a source on the Muslimiyya of western Iran.[6] In short, the information on the eastern Khurramīs is distressingly poor.

Moving to the west, we hear that Abū Muslim believed in reincarnation.[7] This reflects the views of the Muslimiyya, presumably those of the Jibāl and Azerbaijan, but we do not normally get any details, except that they involved belief in reincarnation across the species barriers.[8] Al-Baghdādī does tell us more about the views of Abū Muslim 'al-Ḥarrānī', but the context is Muʿtazilite rather than Muslimī, and the name is probably a corruption of that of al-Faḍl al-Ḥadathī (sometimes al-Ḥarrānī).[9] The only detailed information on Khurramī views on reincarnation comes from an account relating largely or wholly to the followers of ʿAbdallāh b. Muʿāwiya of which partly overlapping extracts are given by Jaʿfar b. Ḥarb with reference to the Ḥarbiyya/Ḥārithiyya (mentioning that the Khurramīs believed the same), by al-Qummī with reference to the Sabaʾiyya (also mentioning that the Khurramīs believe the same), by al-Nawbakhtī with reference to the Khurramdīniyya, by al-Malaṭī with reference to 'the Qarāmiṭa and Daylam', and by the *Tabṣirat al-ʿawāmm* with reference to the philosophers, Zoroastrians, Jews, Christians, and Sabians. The author is unknown, but he must have written before 236/850.[10] In what follows I examine all the versions in which this account survives.

JAʿFAR B. ḤARB'S ACCOUNT

Jaʿfar b. Ḥarb has two sections on the followers of ʿAbdallāh b. Muʿāwiya, here called the Ḥarbiyya. In the first section he tells us that they held the resurrection (*al-qiyāma*) to consist in the departure of the spirit for another body: obedient spirits would be moved into pure bodies of beautiful shapes (*ṣuwar*), in which they would enjoy enduring pleasures and from which they would continue to move up in the ranks of goodness, purity, and pleasure in accordance with their cleanliness (*naẓāfa*) until they became angels and acquired pure bodies of light (*abdān ṣāfiya nūriyya*).

6 See Crone, 'Abū Tammām on the Mubayyiḍa'.

7 Ibn Ḥazm, I, 90.-9, II, 115.12, cf. IV, 180.7, and the MSS in Friedlaender, 'Heterodoxies of the Shiites', (i) 36; Abū Ḥātim al-Rāzī, *Iṣlāḥ*, 161.10.

8 Ibn Ḥazm, I, 90.-9.

9 Baghdādī, *Farq*, 259; cf. van Ess, *TG*, III, 445, rightly noting that al-Ḥarrānī cannot be al-Khurāsānī here; Crone, 'Pre-existence in Iran'. For Faḍl as a Ḥarrānī see Friedlaender, 'Heretodoxies of the Shiites' (ii), 11.

10 The obvious candidate is Hishām b. al-Ḥakam, but Bayhom-Daou, 'Second-Century Šīʿite Ġulāt', has strong arguments against it, with alternative suggestions at 25n.

Disobedient spirits would move into impure bodies (*abdān najasa*), malformed shapes (*ṣuwar mushawwaha*), and despised natures such as dogs, monkeys, pigs, serpents, and scorpions. In support of this they would adduce Q 29:64 ('The next world is life/living beings (*al-ḥayawān*), if only they knew'), and 82:8 ('In whatever form He likes He puts you together'). Whether they held it possible for humans reincarnated as animals to achieve release we are not told.[11]

In the second section Jaʿfar b. Ḥarb picks up the point that the Ḥarbiyya talked about 'shadows and cycles' (*aẓilla, adwār*) and tells us what they said about the cycles.[12] As mentioned in Chapter 10, he says that according to the Ḥarbiyya God had created seven Adams, corresponding to seven eras. The first Adam and his offspring occupied the earth for the first era, which lasted 50,000 years and during which they lived, died, and followed one another, undergoing transmigration from one form to another. When the 50,000 years had passed the obedient ones were placed in the class (*jins*) of angels and raised to the heaven of the world, while the disobedient ones became people that God did not care about (cf. Q 25:77) and were placed below the earth. The ants, scarabs, and dung beetles that crawled around in people's houses were nations that God had destroyed in the past and whom he had transformed (*masakha*) by moving (*nasakha*) their spirits into these bodies. In support of this the sectarians adduced Q 32:26 ('Does it not teach them a lesson, how many generations We destroyed before them in whose dwellings they now go to and fro?'). After all this, they said, the second Adam appeared, or would appear, to preside over the second cycle, and at the end of this cycle the obedient would once more be raised to heaven and the disobedient moved down under the earth, and those of the first cycle would be moved up to the second heaven, and down to the second earth respectively. And so it would go on until all the seven eras were over and religious worship (*taʿabbud*) came to an end. By then, one takes it, the saved of the first cycle would have reached the seventh heaven and the damned the seventh earth, with the saved and the damned of the later cycles occupying the heavens and earths in between. The sectarians found support for this doctrine in the Qurʾān as well, adducing 95:4–6 ('We have created man in the fairest of stature, then we returned him to the lowest of the low, except such as believe and do righteous deeds, for they shall have a reward unfailing') and 84:19 ('You shall surely travel from stage to stage' (*ṭabaqan ʿan ṭabaqin*). They also

[11] Ps.-Nāshiʾ, §57.
[12] Ps.-Nāshiʾ, §58, cf. §55.

pressed the Qur'ānic terms *maskh* and *naskh* into service, carefully mentioning the Qur'ānic monkeys and pigs among the bad incarnations.[13]

Ja'far b. Harb's two accounts do not seem to fit together. In the first the virtuous obtain release on what appears to be an individual basis and become angels with pure bodies of light; others presumably continue to be reincarnated until they are also released, or for ever if they are not. In the second account, by contrast, the virtuous and the sinful are reincarnated for the same amount of time, whereupon the virtuous are raised to heaven together while the sinners are sent below the earth. There is no reason to doubt that both versions were current. As regards the first, the virtuous who made it to the top would acquire pure bodies of light. As we have seen there are also bodies of light (*abdān nūrāniyya*) in Imāmī Ḥadīth, in which they are the imams in pre-existence or, in Zoroastrian terms, in the *mēnōg*; and the 'shadows' of the Ḥarbiyya, like those of al-Mughīra and the *Kitāb al-haft wa'l-aẓilla*, were undoubtedly humanity at large in pre-existence.[14] What this version is saying is that humans could return to their original state. Al-Baghdādī, apparently using a different source, says that the followers of 'Abdallāh b. Mu'āwiya (here called Janāḥiyya rather than Ḥarbiyya) allege that when the individual among them reached the ultimate in his religion he would be raised to the heavenly kingdom (*al-malakūt*) without dying, and that they also claimed to be able to see those who had been raised from among them in the morning and the evening. The reference is probably to the morning and evening stars.[15]

The second account is odd in that it leaves it unclear where in the scheme we find ourselves. The narrative is in the past tense in connection with the first cycle and in the imperfect tense thereafter, suggesting that all subsequent cycles are still in the future. In line with this, only the inhabitants of the first cycle will reach the seventh heaven (arbitrary though this seems). On the other hand, it is only at the end of the seventh cycle that religious worship will come to an end, and it is normally at the end of times that people see themselves as living, but there is no indication that this is where we are. The scheme is also odd in that the last Adam is separated from the end by 50,000 years, so that there is no herald of the last apocalypse. The interest of Ja'far b. Ḥarb's source seems to have lain in the mechanistic regularity of the scheme rather than its messianic potential. The

[13] Cf. Cook, 'Ibn Qutayba and the Monkeys', 51ff.

[14] See Chapter 10, pp. 210f., 212f.

[15] Baghdādī, *Farq*, 236. Abū Tammām, 112 = 104, and Maqdisī, V, 130, report this for the Bazīghiyya.

Rāwandiyya were clearly acting on some variant version of this scheme, however, when they held al-Manṣūr to be God, thinking the seventh and last (mini-)cycle to have come.[16]

AL-NAWBAKHTĪ AND AL-QUMMĪ'S ACCOUNT

The two Imāmī works start by telling us that the Khurramdīniyya (al-Nawbakhtī) or Saba'iyya (al-Qummī) were the ones who introduced talk about shadows, reincarnation of the spirits, and cycles and rotations (*al-dawr wa'l-kawr*). Again, we hear nothing about the shadows, so there was probably nothing about them in the source on which they all depend. Initially al-Nawbakhtī and al-Qummī do not tell us anything about the cycles either. Instead we get some further information abut the manner of reincarnation.

This information also comes in two parts. In the first we are told that the sectarians denied the resurrection and the day of reckoning, claiming that there was no world other than this one (*lā dār illā 'l-dunyā*), or, as they also put it, that the resurrection consisted in the spirit leaving the body for another body or form (*qālab*, *ṣūra*) on the basis of its merits.[17] Bodies, they said, were simply the abode in which the spirits resided. They were like clothes that become worn out and replaced by others, or like houses that fall into ruin when people move away from them. The spirit left one house for another when a person died. Only the spirit was rewarded or punished. Upright spirits were rewarded by transfer to the beautiful bodies of humans blessed in life, whereas disobedient and infidel spirits were punished by transfer into the ugly (*mushawwaha*) bodies of dogs, monkeys, pigs, serpents, scorpions, or dung beetles and would be tormented in these bodies for ever and ever by way of punishment for their denial of the imams and refusal to obey them. Their good or bad rebirth was their paradise and hell, there was no day of judgement, resurrection, paradise, or hell other than this. It was the return of the spirit in another form that they had in mind when they spoke of 'the return' (*al-raj'a*). In favour of all this they would adduce Q 82:8 ('In whatever form He wills He puts you together'), as we have already learnt from Ja'far b. Ḥarb, and Q 6:38 ('No creature is there crawling on the earth, no bird flying with its wing, but they are a nation like unto yourselves') and Q 35:24 ('There never was a nation

[16] See Chapter 4, p. 88.

[17] Nawbakhtī and Qummī have *qālab*, later *ṣūra*; Ja'far b. Ḥarb (whose account is much shorter) only has *ṣūra*.

but that a warner lived among them'). In other words, they held all animals, not just the vermin in their homes, to be former nations.[18]

For the most part this tallies with what we are told by Jaʿfar b. Ḥarb, but it is much more detailed and we also learn something wholly new. First, *rajʿa* in the parlance of these sectarians meant reincarnation, a point of some importance in connection with other texts. Secondly, it is on the basis of obedience to the imams that people are punished and rewarded: in Jaʿfar b. Ḥarb's account the imams are not mentioned, so that one automatically assumes the obedience to be to God. Thirdly, the unbelievers would be punished by reincarnation as lowly animals for ever and ever. Did this mean that animals could not earn merit to rise to higher incarnations, or that they could do so in principle, but in practice never would? We do not get an answer in this section, but one appears in the second part. Fourthly, human life apparently never came to an end. There is no reference here to cycles of 50,000 years or individual release, and we are explicitly told that the unbelievers would be reincarnated as lowly animals for ever and ever (*abad al-abad*). They saw the world as eternal, then. In fact, al-Ashʿarī explicitly says that the followers of ʿAbdallāh b. Muʿāwiya were eternalists who held that the world would never perish; he also says of the extremists in general (*ahl al-ghuluww*) that they denied the resurrection and afterlife (in another world), believed in reincarnation of the spirits, and claimed that they would receive their reward and punishment in their bodies, that there was nothing else, and that the world would never come to an end.[19] The fact that the world would go on for ever does not necessarily mean that people could not be released from it, and one reacts by thinking that the spirits of the virtuous would return to the celestial realm when they had been purified.[20] But it does not seem to be the case. People's good or bad rebirth was their paradise and hell, there was no other, as we are told: if these sectarians had believed in release they would presumably have identified the higher realm to which their spirits passed as paradise rather than denied its existence.

After this the account moves on to discuss the Manṣūriyya, and thereafter we get the second part.[21] First we are told that the adherents of ʿAbdallāh b. Muʿāwiya, here explicitly named, claimed to know each other from each period to the next, not as specific individuals but rather

[18] Nawbakhtī, 32ff.; Qummī, 44ff. (nos, 93ff.).
[19] Ashʿarī, 6, 46.
[20] This is what Freitag, *Seelenwanderung*, 17, assumes.
[21] Nawbakhtī, 35ff.; Qummī, 48ff. (nos. 97ff.).

as occupants of spiritually privileged positions: they recognised each other as the people who had been with Noah in the Ark, as the followers of other prophets in their time, and as the Companions of the Prophet, whose names they would take, claiming that their spirit was in them. In support of this they would adduce a tradition from ʿAlī or the Prophet to the effect that the spirits were troops divided up in regiments (*junūd mujannada*): those who recognised each other would be in harmony whereas those who did not would be at variance.[22]

Thereafter we are told that some (but not all) adherents of Ibn Muʿāwiya believed in reincarnation for periods that had been fixed in advance (*muddatan wa-waqtan*). This sounds like a reference to the cycles of 50,000 years described by Jaʿfar b. Ḥarb, but what follows is about cycles of a completely different kind. The sectarians believed that they would be reincarnated for 10,000 years in human bodies and that this would be followed by 1,000 years in animal bodies, then they would revert to another 10,000 years in human bodies; conversely, their opponents would get 10,000 years in animal bodies, followed by 1,000 years in human bodies, and then 10,000 years as animals again. So apparently it would go on for ever: no attempt is made to arrange the periods in terms of larger cycles of 50,000 years, and again there is no reference to release from existence, whether individually or collectively. It could be to these alternating cycles as humans and animals that the sectarians referred as *al-dawr wa'l-kawr*. Al-Malaṭī had heard of *kawr* as a word for a period in miserable bodies, implying that the return to a more favoured form was *dawr*.[23] The Harranians, who are also said to have believed in reincarnation (indeed, to have originated the idea), are reported to have believed in an endless repetition of *al-akwār* and *al-adwār*, but we are not given any explanation of the terms.[24]

Whether as animals or humans, however, the believers and the unbelievers would have very different fates. During their 1,000 years as animals the believers, apparently meaning the spiritual elite, would be reincarnated into animal bodies of the nicest kind by way of reward for their obedience to the prophets and imams: they would become noble horses, fine camels, and other pleasure mounts used by kings and caliphs, so that they would lead pampered lives with plenty of fodder and beautiful gear of silk and

[22] This tradition is also related, here with an *isnād*, in Maqdisī, II, 102.

[23] Malaṭī, 18, on the Jārūdiyya, reported not to believe in the reincarnation of human souls in animals, only in more or less favoured human bodies.

[24] Shahrastānī, I, 249 = II, 169.

brocade and ornamented saddles. Middling people and the masses (*awsāṭ al-nās wa'l-ʿāmma*) would also be reincarnated in animals reflecting 'their faith, recognition of those to whom obedience is owed, and *walāya*'. No example of the type of animal they might become is given, but if we go by al-Malaṭī they might become nice oxen, for example.[25] God wanted to test their faith to ensure that they would not become vain and forget their obedience to their imams: this was why they had to have spells as animals.

By contrast, the 'unbelievers, polytheists, hypocrites, sinners and tormentors of the prophets and imams' would pass into ugly animals ranging from elephants and camels to bugs, moving from one to the other. Elephants would gradually turn into bugs, for the Qurʾān said that those who rejected his signs would not enter paradise 'until a camel will pass through the eye of a needle' (7:40), and since there was no gainsaying God this could only mean that elephants and camels had to reach the size of bugs before they could pass through the needle's eye. Then they would enter paradise, meaning that they would be reborn as humans for a thousand years. But they would become humans of the most unfortunate kind who had to labour and toil in demeaning occupations to scratch a meagre living, as dyers, cuppers, sweepers, and the like. They too were being tested during their thousand-year interval, namely for their faith in, and obedience to, the imams, prophets, and messengers; but they would never believe, so after a thousand miserable years as humans they would become animals again. The account concludes that this was what the sectarians took the resurrection, paradise, and hell to be and what *rajʿa* meant to them: there was no (physical) coming back after death; the forms in which people moved about would disintegrate and perish and never return or be restored.

Though the two parts are separated by other material, it is clear that they go together: they have the same focus on the imam, the same emphatic denial of the existence of paradise and hell, the same information that *rajʿa* meant reincarnation, the same eternalism, and the same lack of reference to release from earthly existence for anyone – even the obedient. Both accounts, then, refer to the followers of ʿAbdallāh b. Muʿāwiya, and the answer to the question regarding animals seems to be that they cannot earn merit, but that they get a chance to improve themselves as humans after periods of 10,000 years: they will, however, remain as obdurate as they were before.

[25] Malaṭī, 17.

The most striking aspect of al-Nawbakhtī and al-Qummī's account is that it so obviously does not reflect an oppressed minority community. There can be no doubt that 'we' are the elite in both spiritual and social terms. Even as animals 'we' will be favoured as richly decked-out mounts of the kind that kings and caliphs use for their pleasure: as humans we are clearly people familiar with such animals too. The sectarians do have middling people and common folk as well, but it is because they are all in danger of becoming too pleased with themselves that God thinks they must endure short spells as animals every now and again. By contrast the unbelievers, polytheists, and deniers of prophets and imams spend their short period in the human world as cuppers, dyers, sweepers, and other people who have to toil in order to survive.

We evidently do not find ourselves among villagers or lowly townsmen. A rural elite could perhaps be envisaged as speaking here, but if the speakers trust that as animals they will become mounts of the kind that kings and caliphs use, it is presumably because they are riding such mounts in the entourage of kings and caliphs as humans themselves. Most probably we are in Baghdad, and what we are encountering here are the followers of ʿAbdallāh b. Muʿāwiya who ended up in the ʿAbbāsid army – the Ḥārithiyya who became Ḥarbiyya. If so, the imams to whom one has to be obedient are the ʿAbbāsid caliphs, to whom all members of the Ḥarbiyya quarter were fanatically devoted. The tanners and sweepers, in that case, are the small people of Baghdad, the *ʿāmma* who were so attached to Muʿāwiya that al-Maʾmūn and al-Muʿtaḍid had to shelve their plans for having him cursed in 211 or 212/826f. and 284/897 respectively: their story-tellers vaunted Muʿāwiya's virtues, and their water-carriers would serve their customers with the exhortation to 'drink for the love of Muʿāwiya' or 'may God have mercy on Muʿāwiya'.[26] The sectarians are elite troops, *junūd mujannada* in a quite literal sense, to whom the benighted masses are so incapable of recognising the imam that they must be mere animals returned to human status for a test they are bound to fail. If all this is right the recruits of ʿAbdallāh b. Muʿāwiya must have retained their original patron as some kind of regimental badge even after adopting the ʿAbbāsid line on the Testament of Abū Hāshim, but this is not a problematic proposition: ʿAbdallāh b. Muʿāwiya was after all a Hāshimite who had rebelled against the Umayyads, and if Abū Muslim had killed him, the ʿAbbāsids had avenged him by killing Abū Muslim in their turn. Once the ʿAbbāsids were in power ʿAbdallāh b. Muʿāwiya

[26] Pellat, 'Culte de Muʿāwiya', 54f.

could be effortlessly seen as a righteous precursor. The supposition that this group was in Baghdad would explain why the heresiographers are so well informed about it. They loosely claim that all Khurramīs shared the beliefs about reincarnation reported for this group, but the only Khurramīs of whose beliefs they had real knowledge were those in the capital.

AL-MALAṬĪ'S ACCOUNT

Al-Malaṭī is quite brief. As we have seen in Chapter 11 he identifies the *aṣḥāb al-tanāsukh* as believers in *ḥulūl* who say that God is light over bodies and places, and who hold their spirits to be born of the eternal God (*Allāh al-qadīm*). They held the body to be mere clothing devoid of spirit, pain, or pleasure – i.e., it was the spirit that was the source of sensations. The spirit of a person who had done good would pass into a nice animal such as a horse, bird, or gentle ox, then after a while it would return to a human body; whereas an evil person's spirit would pass into a sore-backed donkey or a mangy dog for a period proportionate to his sins, then he would return to a human body. The world had always been like that and always would be.[27]

This is clearly a summary of al-Nawbakhtī and al-Qummī's second part, prefaced with some information possibly derived from the same shared source. If the sectarians held their spirits to be born of the eternal God, one would expect them also to believe that their spirits could return to him, and al-Malaṭī does affirm this of the wider group of 'Qarāmiṭa and Daylam' of which he casts the reincarnationists as a subdivision.[28] But his summary of the views of the reincarnationists does not mention any possibility of release.

TABṢIRAT AL-ʿAWĀMM

The seventh/thirteenth-century Persian *Tabṣirat al-ʿawāmm* combines the source reflected in the versions considered so far with information from al-Shahrastānī and others.[29] It tells us that the philosophers, Zoroastrians, Jews, Christians, Sabians, and many Muslim sects believe in reincarnation and that the philosophers hold reincarnation to be of four kinds, *naskh*, *maskh*, *raskh*, and *faskh*: *naskh* is reincarnation into human bodies; *maskh* into the bodies of grass-eating quadrupeds, predators, birds, and diverse animals; *faskh* into diverse forms of reptiles and creeping things on the earth

27 Malaṭī, 17.
28 Malaṭī, 16.
29 *Tabṣirat al-ʿawāmm*, 87ff.

and in the water, such as snakes, scorpions, beetles, (dung) beetles, crabs, and turtles; and *raskh* is reincarnation into diverse kinds of trees and plants.[30] Humans undergo these fourfold transformations in accordance with merit and continuously return in bodies, from one body to another, with the prophets and messengers representing the highest level. Thereafter the narrative shifts to a summary of al-Nawbakhtī and al-Qummī (or the source they used), without any indication that the discussion is no longer of the philosophers. 'They' believe in 'rotating and turning' (*davvār u girdān*, presumably meant to translate *al-dawr wa'l-kawr*); there is no mention of shadows. And 'they' deny resurrection, paradise, and hell, declaring this world to be the only one there is, and explaining resurrection (*qiyāmat*) as an expression for the departure of the spirit from one body to another. The lowest transformation is into that of a small worm of the size that can go through a needle's eye: the name of this worm is *raknā* in Ṭabaristān. They adduce Q 82:8 ('In whatever form He wills He puts you together'), Q 6:38 ('No creature is there crawling on earth, no bird flying with its wings, but they are nations like unto yourselves'), as we know, and also Q 56:61 ('We may exchange the like of you and make you grow again in a fashion you do not know') and Q 4:56 ('Every time their skins are scorched to pieces, We give them new ones').

What follows comes from another source. The *mutakallims* Aḥmad b. Ḥā'it and Faḍl-i Ḥadathī are declared to be guilty of extreme views regarding reincarnation, and 'they', now meaning the two *mutakallims*, explain the suffering of children and animals as punishment for sins committed in their first cycle (*dawr-i avval*). The text consistently speaks as if there were only two cycles. Animals that may be lawfully slaughtered are being punished for bloodshed they have caused in their first cycle.[31] By the same reversal the mule has lost its sex drive: it had been a prostitute in its first cycle, and if it had any sex drive left now they would put a ring (in his penis) to stop him.[32] The goat in this cycle jumps on his mother, sister, daughter, maternal and paternal uncle because he did not do any fornication in the previous cycle. Some of this information also appears in Ibn

[30] For these terms see Shahrastānī, I, 133 = I, 512 (on the Kāmiliyya) and the sources in the translator's notes, esp. Bīrūnī, *Hind*, 49.2/32 = 64; Kohlberg, review of Freitag, *Seelenwanderung*, 238.

[31] The text says animals that had *not* spilt blood in their first cycle, but the negation is clearly mistaken.

[32] This way of suppressing sexual urges was adopted by the Qalandars, who put rings through their own organs (see Karamustafa, *God's Unruly Friends*, 16 and figure 3 (between chs. 4 and 5).

Ḥazm, but in a distinctly less homely vein: Ibn Ḥazm cites Ibn Ḥā'it as saying that a killer (*qattāl*) would become an animal used for slaughter such as a sheep, cow, or hen, that a killer who was chaste would become a sexually potent animal such as a goat, sparrow, or ram, whereas a fornicator would become impotent like the mule, and someone tyrannical would become something lowly such as a worm or louse.[33] The author of the *Tabṣirat al-ʿawāmm* retells all this in a tone suggestive of village wisdom and with the focus on the behaviour of the animals rather than the humans. We also seem to be in village society when we are told, slightly later, that a man who has intercourse with an animal in the first cycle will become an animal of the type he had made use of in the second cycle – given that it was shepherds away for long spells in the mountains who were likely to resort to such practices on a scale sufficient to merit inclusion among the examples. We are also told that whoever was a woman in the first cycle will become a man in the second, and vice versa; if they were lawfully married in the first cycle they can lawfully sleep together in this cycle too, apparently without the need for marriage. They, whoever they may be, deem it necessary not to blame anyone who oppresses them on the grounds that oppression and punishment are requital for sins incurred in the first cycle and that someone who inflicts well-deserved damage on another should not be blamed for it, any more than the person who inflicts the *ḥadd* punishment on the fornicator, slanderer, wine-server, or thief should be blamed for it. If someone kills them it simply goes to prove that they have shed blood unlawfully in the first era.

Thereafter the account moves on to the question of mutual recognition. There is disagreement over the question, we are told. Some say people recognise each other in the second era, apparently even if some of them have become animals, and others specify that they recognise each other when they have migrated from one human body to another. The author argues against these propositions, understanding the recognition as personal rather than typological.

As regards the cycles (*advār* and *akvār*), we learn that some people give their length as 12,000 years and others 1,000 years, but for the rest the *Tabṣira* follows Jaʿfar b. Ḥarb's account rather than that of al-Nawbakhtī and al-Qummī: some say that when the spirits[34] have been purified by repeated reincarnation they will go to heaven and become angels; they call

[33] Ibn Ḥazm, IV, 198 (see also I, 90.ult.); van Ess, *TG*, VI, 215f. (with emendations), where the parallel in the *Tabṣira* is noted.

[34] Reading *arwāḥ* for *adwār* at 89.ult.

those people 'the departed (flown)' (*ṭāriya*). Others say that God created seven Adams and that each Adam lived on earth for 50,000 years, whereupon the good rose to the first heaven and the bad sank to the lowest earth, and so on. The fate of those who sink to the lowest earth is here identified with that of becoming ants, dung beetles, and other vermin, though it is on the surface of the earth that one finds them.

What is so interesting about this account is its homely tone. The author writes about believers in reincarnation on the basis of classical sources, yet conveys a strong sense of having heard arguments in its favour in real life, from people who would adduce examples that made sense in the context of their own lives (in villages or small towns?). He has freely reformulated and added to his source on this basis, and the none-too-sophisticated arguments against mutual recognition also seem to be his own. The worm that the camel has to turn into before it can go through the needle's eye is the one they call *raknā* in Ṭabaristān: presumably it was in Ṭabaristān that he wrote.

We hear of reincarnation again in connection with the Pārsīs in Azerbaijan. According to Dihkhudā the Pārsīs held that the resurrection (*baʿth*) and rising (*nushūr*), the beginning and the return, took the form of reincarnation and said that paradise and hell were here, there was no other place, and paradise was the body (*ṣūrat*). All this probably reflects the author's knowledge of classical sources. But he also reports them to have held that those who accepted the divine status of Abū 'l-ʿAlāʾ and Yūsuf, their two leaders, would return as human beings, whereas others would return as cattle and wild animals and, their denial of paradise notwithstanding, they identified it as '*garuzmān* of heaven', so it may be live reincarnationists that Dihkhudā is trying to fit into classical terms. One takes it that they believed in release from earthly existence for eternal life in *garuzmān* (MP *garōdmān*), presumably the luminous region beyond the sun and the moon to which the purified spirits would travel.[35]

THE ALTERNATING CYCLES

Five points are worth commenting on in greater detail. First, what was the provenance of the cycles of 1,000 and 10,000 years? In the *Tabṣirat al-ʿawāmm* they last 1,000 and 12,000 years, suggesting that the reference is to the day in the eyes of God, or alternatively the astrological millennium, and the Zoroastrian duration of the world respectively; but the figure

[35] Kāshānī, *Zubda*, 188f.; cf. Chapter 15, pp. 350f.

12,000 looks like a later adjustment, for cycles of 10,000 years are also attested for Abū 'l-Khaṭṭāb's Mukhammisa. According to them the spirits of unbelievers would flow into all things human and non-human, including everything endowed with spirit (*kullī dhī rūḥ*) and everything one could eat, drink, put on, or sleep with, so that no person, animal, or thing on earth would be free of them; they would even be in the heavenly bodies. After flowing through everything they would become solid rock or earth: this was their eternal hell. In favour of this the Mukhammisa adduced Q 15:50 ('Be ye stones or iron'). By contrast, every man of insight (*'ārif*) would live through seven eras, each era (*dawr*) lasting 10,000 years. In each era he would put on a different body, also known as a form (*qālab*) or shirt (*qamīṣ*). Seven such periods – i.e., 70,000 years – made a *kawr*, a mega-period, and on the completion of the *kawr* the veil would be removed for the man of insight and he would see God, who is Muḥammad.[36]

This scheme is clearly a variation on the seven-Adams scheme recorded by Ja'far b. Ḥarb for the followers of Ibn Mu'āwiya. The periods here last 10,000 years rather than 50,000, and it is the same people who live through all seven instead of a new population appearing in each of them, but the climax is much the same: at the end of the seventh era the saved would see God directly, as we are told here; ritual worship would come to an end, as Ibn Mu'āwiya's followers said. Abū 'l-Khaṭṭāb's followers and the Ḥarbiyya/Ḥārithiyya reflected in al-Nawbakhtī and al-Qummī's account were contemporaries in Baghdad, so it is probably the same 10,000 years they were talking about. The figure could be Platonic, perhaps imported via some Gnostic treatise, for in his *Phaedrus* Plato mentions 10,000 years as the period for which all except philosophers must undergo reincarnation: philosophers escape after three rounds of 1,000 years.[37] The Mukhammisa rather strikingly say that the spirits of the deniers will flow into 'everything one can eat, drink, wear, or have sexual intercourse with (*jamī' dhī 'l-ma'kūlāt wa'l-mashrūbāt wa'l-malbūsāt wa'l-mankūḥāt*).[38] This sounds like an echo of the things 'which one can touch and see and drink and eat and employ in the pleasures of love' in another work of Plato's, in which we are told that the impure soul of the one who always cared for such things would be dragged back to the visible world, flit about the monuments and tombs and eventually acquire bodily

[36] Qummī, 58f. (nos. 112f.).
[37] Plato, *Phaedrus*, 249a; also noted by Freitag, *Seelenwanderung*, 16n.
[38] Qummī, 59 (no. 112).

existence again as an ass, hawk, or something else reflecting his previous inclination.[39] Plato was doubtless available in Sasanian Iraq.[40]

ETERNALISM WITHOUT RELEASE

The second point concerns the view of some of the sectarians that reincarnation would continue for ever, without any possibility of release from existence. The possibly Platonic origin of the length of their cycles notwithstanding, these sectarians did not envisage them as the time they would have to spend in bodies before returning to their original home, merely as the time they would spend as humans and as animals. But a world in which the same human beings are doomed to be reincarnated time and time again for all eternity without any hope of release is so Sisyphean a prospect that there must have been some kind of let-out. One wonders if the eternalism of these sectarians was not coupled with materialism: humans disintegrated into their constituent elements on death, but somehow an essential part of them survived to live again. This would make the doctrine agreeable in that it would save its adherents from extinction without condemning them to endlessly living their lives over and over again. The Stoic emperor Marcus Aurelius (d. 180) found consolation in the assurance that all parts of him, whether material or formal, would survive in the sense that they would be 'reduced by change into some part of the universe, and that again will change into another part of the universe, and so on forever'. Like his ancestors and his offspring he owed his existence to such changes and, reduced to some part of the universe, he would eventually live again in others.[41] It is along these lines that our sectarians are likely to have thought.

Marcus Aurelius did not combine his materialism with reincarnation, however. In order to do so the Ḥarbiyya must have held that the parts in which their identity resided would come together in some way. What they said we do not know, but a materialist doctrine of reincarnation turns up in a 'scientific' form among the Dahrīs, the doctors, astrologers, and other so-called 'naturalists' (or physicists, *aṣḥāb al-ṭabāʾiʿ*) of whom they were contemporaries. Many Dahrīs explained the world in terms of interaction between four elements or elementary qualities (*ṭabāʾiʿ*) and sometimes

[39] Plato, *Phaedo*, 81bff.

[40] According to Masʿūdī, *Tanbīh*, 100, Ardashir I's famous priest, Tansar (here Tanshar, also called Dawshar) was a Platonist (*aflāṭūnī 'l-madhhab*).

[41] *Meditations*, V, 13.

added a fifth principle in the form of spirit (*rūḥ*), which permeated and regulated things; all things in their view were combinations of these elements or qualities, which came together and separated on their own, without any need for the postulate of a creator or providential ruler of the universe; the universe had always existed and always would in their view, there was no afterlife of any kind.[42] Their denial of the afterlife notwithstanding, they do sometimes seem to have believed in some form of reincarnation. Ibn Ḥazm mentions Dahrīs who said that since neither the soul nor the world would come to an end; the soul had to come back again and again for ever in different bodies (they must have assumed the number of souls to be finite).[43] Abū ʿĪsā tells us that the Dahrīs who believed in four elementary qualities plus an all-pervading spirit allowed for the possibility that the same particles could accidentally come together again in the same combination and so form the same living being; if the circumstances did not allow for re-creation of the same being they would come together as an animal of a different kind or a plant.[44] This sounds remarkably like a materialist doctrine of reincarnation, shorn of its moral dimensions: the particles come together accidentally, without any reward or punishment being involved, and it is not clear that any continuity of personality is postulated.

The existence of some such Dahrī doctrine was also known to al-Māturīdī. According to him the unbelievers in the Qurʾān who said that we die, live, and will not be resurrected, our life down here being all there is (Q 23:37), were dualists and Dahrīs who meant that when one person dies another lives from among the cattle, donkeys, and other animals who eat his dust or, in the words of Abū Bakr al-Samarqandī (d. c. 540/1145), who eat the herbage growing on the dust he has turned into.[45] In less laconic formulation, when a person died, the particles of which he was composed turned into dust from which plants grew; the plants were eaten by animals and so went to make other animals or, if the herbage or the animals were eaten by humans, to make other humans. The Manichaeans, who also believed in reincarnation, held that the divine particles could pass into plants and be eaten by animals;[46] from there, one assumes, the particles would (or could) pass into the semen of the human beings who drank their milk, along the lines familiar from the story of

[42] Cf. *EI*², s.v. 'Dahriyya'; *EIr.*, s.v. 'Dahrī'; Crone, 'Dahrīs according to al-Jāḥiẓ'.
[43] Ibn Ḥazm, I, 91.
[44] Abū ʿĪsā in Ibn al-Malāḥimī, 548.
[45] Māturīdī, *Taʾwīlāt*, 28, ad 23:37, with Samarqandī's commentary in n. 6.
[46] See Chapter 15, p. 359.

Zoroaster's creation in the material world: his body substance (*tan gōhr*) rained down, causing plants to sprout; the plants were eaten by his father's cow and its milk was drunk by his parents, who had absorbed other components of their future son by other means and who proceeded to beget him.[47] Al-Māturīdī and al-Samarqandī seem to take it for granted that there were Dahrīs whose views on the afterlife were similar to those of the Manichaeans. Some centuries later the Nuqṭavīs claimed that 'all things are nothing but the four elements, simple or composite, that there is no rational soul, nor any other life'; yet they too believed in reincarnation in accordance with merit: a person's knowledge and deeds adhered to the matter of which he had been composed and would come together again, also by passing into plants which were eaten by animals.[48]

Intriguingly, it is in the entourage of ʿAbdallāh b. Muʿāwiya that we encounter some of the earliest Dahrīs: one of his officers, explicitly characterised as a Dahrī, did not believe in God or an afterlife, while another was called al-Baqlī because he held humans to be like plants: whether he meant that they came back in other bodies or that there was no afterlife at all is not clear.[49] The former was an Arab from Kufa to judge by his name; nothing is known of the latter, but neither is likely to have been recruited in the Jibāl. ʿAbdallāh b. Muʿāwiya must have moved in Dahrī circles before he became a rebel (the ideas were popular with the smart set).[50] When he moved into the Zagros mountains, however, he recruited soldiers bearing religious ideas of the kind that the Dahrīs were turning into science in the cities. The irreligious reductionism of the Dahrīs and the wild religious imagination of the Khurramīs are so antithetical that they obscure the structural similarity between their cosmological ideas.[51] But they are clearly related, and this was not lost on al-Nawbakhtī and al-Qummī, or the source they used: they discerned a fundamental similarity between Shīʿite *ghuluww*, Khurramdīnism, Mazdakism *and* Zandaqa and Dahrism.[52]

[47] Molé, *Culte*, 285f.

[48] Pietro della Valle, *Viaggi*, II, 328f. (letter 16); cf. Gurney, 'Pietro della Valle', 112f.; Chapter 19, pp. 485f.

[49] *Aghānī*, XIII, 280; cf. Ibn Ḥazm, IV, 180.11 (he was *mutaṣaḥḥiban lil-Dahriyya*).

[50] Crone, 'Dahrīs according to al-Jāḥiẓ'.

[51] See van Ess, *TG*, I, 455; he thinks that only a Sunnī sensationalist could believe that a Shīʿite Gnostic such as Ibn Muʿāwiya (here assumed to have preached what his followers said) could have had dealings with a Dahrī.

[52] Nawbakhtī, 41; Qummī, 64 (no. 127).

RAJʿA

The third point concerns the Khurramī meaning of *rajʿa*. Al-Nawbakhtī and al-Qummī are the only authors to preserve it. Abū Tammām and al-Maqdisī admittedly also say that the Khurramīs believe in *rajʿa*, but they do not explain what it meant to them, and the word was used in many senses.[53] In Khurramī usage it meant reincarnation of a type in which people recognised themselves typologically from one era to the next. The followers of ʿAbdallāh b. Muʿāwiya knew themselves to be a spiritual elite, the only saved, in every era: the occupants of Noah's Ark, the followers of the prophets, the Companions of Muḥammad. According to al-Baghdādī they called themselves the Apostles (*al-ḥawāriyyūn*) among themselves.[54] The anonymous *ʿUyūn wa'l-ḥadāʾiq* observes the same of the Rāwandiyya, as we have seen: they were always saying that they were so-and-so in the past.[55] Ideas of this kind seem to have entered Muslim thought early, for we are told of the mid-Umayyad poet Kuthayyir ʿAzza that he believed in the reincarnation of spirits (*tanāsukh al-arwāḥ*) and *rajʿa*. Whether the two terms are synonymous here or not is disputed, but Kuthayyir's reincarnationism is not in doubt: he believed himself to be Jonah, and like so many other believers in reincarnation he would adduce Q 82:8 ('In whatever form He wills He puts you together').[56] Another poet, al-Sayyid al-Ḥimyarī (d. 119/795 or earlier), held *rajʿa* in the form of an animal to be possible.[57]

Kuthayyir is said to have been a Khashabī, meaning an adherent of al-Mukhtār's doctrines, and one wonders if al-Mukhtār too was not playing with such ideas: it would certainly make sense of the strong suggestion that Muḥammad b. al-Ḥanafiyya was in some sense Muḥammad, who was Moses, and that al-Mukhtār was in some sense Aaron, his *wazīr*, even though both men were well known to be themselves. The slaves and freedmen to whom al-Mukhtār was preaching were captives from the area conquered by Kufans, that is to say the Zagros mountains, the Caspian coast, Mesopotamia, and Azerbaijan, and they are said to have spoken Persian among themselves (though their 'Persian' may have been

[53] Abū Tammām, 78 = 77; Maqdisī, IV, 30; cf. *EI*², s.v. 'Radjʿa' (Kohlberg).

[54] Baghdādī, *Farq*, 236.

[55] *ʿUyūn*, 227.

[56] *Aghānī*, IX, 17–19; cf. Wellhausen, 'Oppositionsparteien', 93f.; Friedlaender, 'Heterodoxies of the Shiites' (ii), 23ff.; Friedlaender, 'Jewish–Arabic Studies, I', 481ff. I. ʿAbbās dismisses the claim that he believed in his own *rajʿa* as ludicrous on the assumption that *rajʿa* always meant the return of the imam (*EI*², s.v. 'Kuthayyir b. ʿAbd al-Raḥmān').

[57] *Aghānī*, VII, 242.

north-western Iranian languages).[58] Much later we learn that Mardāvīj, the fourth/tenth-century military adventurer from Gīlān, claimed that the spirit of Solomon dwelt in him: he too was both himself and someone else.[59]

DIVERSITY

The fourth point is that the anonymous account preserved in four different versions seems to have related entirely to the followers of ʿAbdallāh b. Muʿāwiya, yet it deals with a number of quite different views. Some sectarians were eternalists who did not operate with any kind of individual or collective release from existence: reincarnation would go on for ever, divided into rounds of 10,000 and 1,000 years. Others operated with individual release after many good reincarnations, postulating that they would become bodies of light, or even that they could escape death in the sense of being transported live to another realm, like Enoch, where they would be visible from the earth. Still others postulated that people were released for heaven or hell every 50,000 years, and that the world would come to an end after seven such rounds. The conceptions are so different that one keeps wondering whether they really do come from the same group. Since most of them are identified as those of the Ḥarbiyya one could postulate that they all come from the Ḥarbiyya quarter rather than the Ḥarbiyya in the sense of the Ḥārithiyya who emerged from ʿAbdallāh b. Muʿāwiya's troops. But even with this modification we are talking about a group in one and the same city. The variety of views among all those called Khurramīs must have been enormous, and there were still further variations among the ʿAlid Shīʿites. Those identified as followers of Abū 'l-Khaṭṭāb, for example, used the same vocabulary as the Ḥarbiyya/Ḥārithiyya (*kawr*, *dawr*, *qālab*, clothing, 10,000 years), but not to the same effect. Here, as in the case of cosmology and *ḥulūl*, the ʿAlid Shīʿite Ghulāt come across as operating with the same fundamental assumptions as the Khurramīs, but developing them along different lines.

OUTLOOK

Finally, it should be noted that the Ḥarbiyya were thoroughly attached to this world. Those of them who believed in individual release held that the

[58] Tab. ii, 724.11; Dīnawarī, 302.7; cf. Crone, *Medieval Islamic Political Thought*, 77–9.
[59] IA, VIII, 298, year 323 (drawn to my attention by Debbie Tor); Miskawayh, *Tajārib*, I, 162 = IV, 182. Mardāvīj cast the Turks as the demons.

obedient among them would move into beautiful, pure bodies in which they would enjoy enduring pleasures (*ladhdhāt dāʾima*) and from which they would continue to rise in the ranks of goodness, purity, and pleasure (*al-ladhdhāt*) until they became angels with bodies of light: obviously, a heavenly existence in an eternal, incorruptible body of light was better than life down here, but the virtuous expected to enjoy themselves while they were here. The same was true of the eternalists, who come across as positively complacent: even during their preordained spells as animals they would live in the entourage of rulers, enjoying all the trappings of a privileged life; their health, beauty, and wealth were their just reward for past obedience; if people were miserable it was because they deserved it. 'He who has been good, his spirit will depart and enter a beautiful form (*ṣūra*), to live happily and honoured in this world', as an Arabic heresiography puts it, probably on the basis of one of the above sources; 'in this way the kings, sultans, amirs, great men, and people of wealth and favourable conditions who live in ease, blessing, and comfort are enjoying the rewards for their deeds', as the Persian commentator explains.[60] There must have been as many differences in their attitude to this world as there were in their views on the afterlife, but in the information on these sectarians we could not be further from the Gnostic outlook.

[60] Mashkūr, *Haftād u sih millat*, 31 (no. 17).

13

Ethos, Organisation, and Overall Character

The Ḥarbiyya who looked forward to 'enduring pleasures' on their way to angelic existence were conforming to Khurramī norms. According to Ibn al-Nadīm the 'old Mazdak' told his followers, the Khurramīs of western Iran, to partake of the pleasures and fulfil their desires by eating and drinking, and also to practise equal sharing (*al-muwāsāt*) and togetherness (*ikhtilāṭ*) instead of keeping things for themselves: in line with this, they shared their womenfolk.[1] He sees their positive appreciation of the pleasures of life as the key to their marital practices, but he is not simply inferring it from these practices, for al-Maqdisī confirms that the Khurramīs could not see anything wrong with natural pleasures as long as they did not have any harmful effects on others. They deemed wine above all to be a source of blessing.[2] Of Bābak's Khurramiyya we are told that they would ostentatiously drink *nabīdh*, play the flute, and beat drums while the Afshīn, then a pillar of the Muslim establishment, was performing his noon prayer, thereby highlighting the contrast between their own religion and the legalist prohibitions of 'the Jews'.[3] It was apparently their positive view of the good things in life that earned them the name *khurramdīn*, adherent of the joyous religion. The heresiographers polemically relate this name to their scandalous sexual practices, but if it had been coined for purposes of abuse a more offensive term than 'joyous' would surely have been chosen. *Khurramdīn* is formed on the same model as *behdīn* (*weh-dēn*), adherent of the good religion, one of the terms the Zoroastrians used for themselves,[4] and if one

[1] Ibn al-Nadīm, 406 = II, 817.

[2] Maqdisī, IV, 31.

[3] Tab. iii, 1205. That they permit wine is one of their reprehensible practices in *SN*, ch. 47:14 (244 = 319), and wine and music duly figure in their supposed orgiastic night in Baghdādī, *Farq*, 252.

[4] Sadighi, *Mouvements*, 195/241; cf. Shaked, 'Religion in the Late Sasanian Period', 106.

had not been primed by the heresiographers to shudder at the word *khurramdīn* one might have assumed it to be simply another word for a *behdīn*, for the Zoroastrians too put a high premium on the pleasures of life. In fact, *khurramdīn* could be a self-designation. If so, it was probably a local name which spread when the Muslims needed a global term for adherents of religions of this type.

NON-VIOLENCE AND ITS LIMITS

Humans

Zardūsht of Fasā, the 'old Mazdak', must have preached a doctrine of non-violence towards humans and animals alike, for Kavadh is described as a heretic (*zindīq*) who ate no meat, who held bloodshed to be forbidden, and who dealt leniently with both his subjects and his enemies in his heretical phase, thereby gaining a reputation for weakness.[5] (He made up for it after his return to power as an orthodox Zoroastrian.) We may start by considering the evidence on non-violence to humans first.

No further details are offered regarding Zardūsht or Kavadh, but of Mazdak we are told that he forbade his followers to disagree among themselves, to have hostile feelings towards one another, and to fight.[6] Unlike his predecessor, however, he engaged in revolt, so the doctrine of non-violence did not apply to enemies; he justified the killing of opponents on the grounds that one thereby released their spirits from the bodies in which they would be harmed (namely by committing further sins). In 'Abd al-Jabbār and al-Shahrastānī's paraphrase of Abū 'Īsā his statement on this question is somewhat unclear: he here orders the killing of souls for purposes of saving them from evil and the admixture of darkness (*amara bi-qatl al-anfus li-yukhalliṣahā min al-sharr wa-mizāj al-ẓulma*).[7] This has been interpreted as an injunction to asceticism: Mazdakites should mortify their souls.[8] But in Ibn al-Malāḥimī's excerpt Abū 'Īsā says that Mazdak 'made it lawful for them to kill their opponents', adding that 'it is said that Mazdak believed in killing to release the spirits from the bodies in which they would be harmed' (*kāna yadīnu bi'l-qatl li-takhalluṣ al-arwāḥ min al-abdān allatī tuḍarru bihā*)'.[9] This shows that the injunction

[5] Crone, 'Kavād's Heresy', 26.
[6] Shahrastānī, I, 193 = I, 663.
[7] 'Abd al-Jabbār, *Mughnī*, 16, 65 = 165, 237; Shahrastānī, I, 193 = I, 663.
[8] E.g. Yarshater, 'Mazdakism', 1012; Shaked, *Dualism*, 128.
[9] Ibn al-Malāḥimī, 584.4.

concerned the literal killing of opponents, not metaphorical killing of the appetitive soul, and that bloodshed was legitimised on the grounds that it would save the opponents from further sins.

One would infer that Mazdak believed in reincarnation. It is true that the Zoroastrians may have seen the sacrifice of animals as releasing an animal's soul (or spirit or consciousness), enabling it to rise up and join the 'Soul of the Bull';[10] but this did not apply to the souls of noxious animals, which could not be offered in sacrifice, so Mazdak cannot have cast his enemies as sacrificial victims. The *Dēnkard* tells us that a short life is best for a man if he is likely to commit many sins, which is undoubtedly what Mazdak meant;[11] but the *Dēnkard* would hardly have agreed that one did the sinner a favour by killing him, however logically it may seem to have followed. The plausibility of Mazdak's claim rests on the assumption that the sinner had more than one life, so that one could be seen as helping him on by taking one of them: one released the sinner's soul or spirit for a better reincarnation than he would have achieved by remaining alive. Asahara, the Buddhist founder of the Aum Shinrikyo sect which mounted the nerve-gas attack on the Tokyo subway in 1995, justified his violence in those very terms: people enmeshed in social systems so evil that further existence would result in even greater karmic debts were better off dead, he said; killing them was an act of mercy which allowed their souls to move to a higher plane than they would otherwise have achieved.[12] 'It is written in our scriptures that in certain circumstances it can be right to kill a person, if your intention is to stop that person from committing a serious sin', a Tibertan monk who had fought the Chinese explained to the British traveller Dalrymple; 'you can choose to take upon yourself the bad karma of a violent act in order to save that person from a much worse sin.'[13] That Mazdak believed in reincarnation is explicitly stated by Abū Ḥātim al-Rāzī.[14]

In short, Zardūsht of Fasā prohibited the killing of human beings without exception, but Mazdak introduced killing, violence, and wars by distinguishing between fellow believers and enemies. Ibn al-Nadīm oddly claims that it was Bābak who 'introduced killing, violence, wars and

[10] See de Jong, 'Animal Sacrifice', 139, 146f. He does not adduce a great deal of evidence.

[11] *DkM*, 100.19 in Zaehner, 'Zervanite Apocalypse II', 616.

[12] Juergensmeyer, *Terror in the Mind of God*, 114 (my thanks to Irene Oh for this reference). He claimed to have found this doctrine in Tibetan Buddhism.

[13] Dalrymple, *Nine Lives*, 144, cf. 157f.

[14] Abū Ḥātim al-Rāzī, *Iṣlāḥ*, 159, 161. Monnot strangely deems it at odds with the notion of reincarnation (see Shahrastānī, I, 663, n. 50).

mutilation, which the Khurramīs had not known before'.[15] Ibn al-Nadīm can hardly have been ignorant of the fact that Mazdak was a rebel or that there had been Khurramī revolts in the Jibāl before Bābak, and he himself tells us of Khurramī feuding in Azerbaijan before Bābak's rise to power there. His point may simply be that Bābak introduced violence on a scale not seen before. At all events, he does not tell us how Bābak made religious sense of his violence, but both he and other fourth/tenth-century sources give us to understand that the Khurramīs of western Iran also had special rules for opponents. The (western) Khurramīs believed in acts of charity (*afʿāl al-khayr*) and in refraining from killing and inflicting harm on souls, except when they rebelled, we are told; they said that one should also refrain from speaking ill of adherents of other religions and finding fault with them as long as the latter were not trying to harm one.[16] Both physical and verbal violence was clearly allowed against opponents perceived as harmful to them. The philosopher Abū Bakr al-Rāzī, a native of a region teeming with Khurramīs, adhered to a comparable position. He held it to be self-evident on rational grounds that one should try to avoid inflicting harm on others, even animals. His doctrine regarding humans is not known, but as regards animals he said that one was only allowed to kill them for two reasons, namely that predators and vermin would inflict harm on other living beings if they were not killed, and that no animals of any kind could be liberated unless they were reincarnated as humans; killing harmful animals reduced the pain suffered by other living beings and also enabled the souls of the animals themselves to enter more suitable bodies, facilitating their (ultimate) deliverance.[17] This seems to be exactly the Khurramī position on human beings.

When the Khurramīs rebelled all restrictions were suspended, so that the sources more commonly associated them with violence than with principled opposition to bloodshed. After the defeat of their revolts, moreover, some of them apparently deemed themselves to be in a permanent state of revolt, so that their opponents were legitimate prey at all times, and by any means: according to Abū Bakr al-Rāzī the Dayṣāniyya and Muḥammira endorsed the use of deception and assassination (*ghishsh* and *ightiyāl*) in their dealings with their opponents.[18] In the same vein

[15] Ibn al-Nadīm, 406.11 = II, 818.

[16] Ibn al-Nadīm, 406.4 = II, 817; Maqdisī, IV, 30f.; Abū Tammām, 78 = 77 (with reference to the Mubayyiḍa, but this part of his account actually refers to the Muslimiyya of western Iran, cf. Crone, 'Abū Tammām on the Mubayyiḍa', 177ff.).

[17] Rāzī, *Sīra falsafiyya*, 314f. = 327ff.; tr. Butterworth, 231f.

[18] Rāzi, *al-Ṭibb al-ruḥānī*, 91 = 101 (ch. 19). Arberry's 'act treacherously' for *ightiyāl* is too conservative a translation. Baghdādī, *Farq*, 349, credits this position to practically all

the Khidāshiyya in the east interpreted *jihād* to mean killing opponents, taking their property, and passing a fifth to the imam – apparently as a duty and certainly by any means available, including assassination, suffocation, poisoning, or crushing.[19]

Animals

As we have seen, Kavadh is said to have abstained from meat, but al-Bīrūnī associates him with the ruling that allowed for some meat eating: cattle should not be slaughtered before the natural term of their life had come (*ḥatta ya'tiya 'alayhā ajaluhu*),[20] meaning either when it had died on its own or when it was about to die, or perhaps when it had reached the age when it was legally deemed to be about to do so. The last two views are attested for Zoroastrians.[21] Perhaps this ruling was meant for the general populace rather than Kavadh himself. At all events, Mazdak is also reported to have been a vegetarian. He 'forbade the slaughter of animals and said that what the earth brings forth and what is produced by animals, such as eggs, milk, butter and cheese, suffices as human food'.[22] One wonders whether he held it forbidden to kill even noxious animals, regardless of whether one could eat or otherwise use them or not. It seems unlikely, given that he permitted the killing of noxious human beings.

As regards the Khurramīs, Abū Tammām, al-Maqdisī, and Ibn al-Nadīm, who tell us that they believed in non-violence, do not say whether the principle applied to animals.[23] Bābak's marriage ceremony included the sacrifice of a cow, as we have seen, and he himself indulged in hunting;[24] but he is nonetheless presented as complaining, after his capture, that the breath and hands of his prison guard stank of meat: this literary touch is undoubtedly meant to bring out the absurdity of so bloodthirsty a man deeming it wrong to kill animals for food.[25] Perhaps Bābak's Khurramīs distinguished between wild and domestic animals, or between noxious and beneficent ones, holding the former to be legitimate prey because they harmed other

Ghulāt, including the *Muqanna'iyya mubayyiḍa* and the Muḥammira of Azerbaijan and Ṭabaristān.

19 Ps.-Nāshi', §49; Abū Tammām, 104 = 98, here credited to Khidāsh himself.

20 Bīrūnī, *Āthār*, 209 = 192.

21 See Chapter 15, p. 365.

22 IA, I, 413; similarly Mīrkhwānd, I, 914.

23 See n. 16 to this chapter.

24 Tab. iii, 1225.

25 Tab. iii, 1228; compare the Buddhist text in Benveniste, *Textes sogdiens*, 21 (text, no. 2:395): 'he who eats meat, his breath stinks'.

living beings. Abū Bakr al-Rāzī held that it was legitimate to hunt predators and exterminate vermin such as scorpions and vipers.[26] If this was the Khurramī position they will have restricted their slaughter of beneficent animals to ritual occasions and/or to animals close to death, killing with moderation; and perhaps they argued that a sacrificial death would release the spirit of the animal, not to join the 'Soul of the Bull', but rather to pass into a human body and so acquire the possibility of salvation. It is also possible that they lacked clearly articulated doctrines on the subject. The Zagros villagers studied by Loeffler uniformly held that being a good Muslim meant being good to others and not inflicting harm on other creatures. Even the mullah held animals to have souls.[27] According to an old hunter the *jinn* would appear as animals, and one could hurt them by killing them as game animals or snakes, or by bothering them as cats, if one did it without first invoking God. It was lawful to kill game, he said, but it was sinful to do so excessively, beyond what one needed. 'But why do we kill these animals?', he asked. 'They have lives too and their lives are dear to them. Why do we kill this chicken?' Again he affirmed that it was both lawful and sinful: anything that did harm to other beings was sinful.[28] Another villager said that it was impossible to live without sinning, giving as his examples having to throw a stone at an animal to keep it out of a field and hurting it thereby, or having to kill a chicken that had been hit by a stone: 'Then I shall have taken a life,' he said. Apparently it was the unintended nature of the animal's death that bothered him, for he said nothing about killing animals for food and he approved of sacrificing animals and distributing the meat to the poor to avert misfortune.[29] These villagers did not have a coherent set of principles, but their sentiments are clear enough. Whether Khurramī villagers had clearer guidelines will have depended on their religious leaders (priests, 'prophets', or imams) and varied from one locality to the next.

The leader of the sixth/twelfth-century Pārsīs in Azerbaijan is depicted as adopting a rigorous stance; according to him 'one is not allowed to harm anyone, whether animals, plants, or anything living, to the point that it is not allowed to hammer a peg into the soil lest the soil be hurt by it'.[30] This sounds practically Manichaean. So too does the view of an old teacher in the Zagros village that one should not cut down a tree, but rather hold

[26] See n. 17 to this chapter.
[27] Loeffler, *Islam in Practice*, 15, 21, 69, 146, 176, 188, 193, 197, 242.
[28] Loeffler, *Islam in Practice*, 142f., 147, 148.
[29] Loeffler, *Islam in Practice*, 188, 189.
[30] Kāshānī, *Zubda*, 189; Rashīd al-Dīn, 152.

trees in high esteem; he credited the doctrine to Zoroaster.[31] In the case of the Pārsīs agriculture must have been seen as too sinful for anyone to want to practise it, but then their leader was a weaver. Perhaps they were all craftsmen and traders, or maybe the prohibitions were only observed in full by their spiritual elite.

Moving from Azerbaijan to Rayy we encounter al-Masʿūdī's statement on the 'kind of Mazdakite Zoroastrians who have a village outside Rayy inhabited only by them'. He tells us that when cattle died in Rayy or Qazvīn one of them would come with his ox, load the dead animal on to it, and take it back to their village, where they would eat it; most of their food, and the food of their cattle too, was fresh or dried meat of such animals, and they would use their bones in the construction of buildings.[32] These Khurramīs seem to have held that one could (only?) eat animals when they had died on their own, much as Buddhists are forbidden to eat animals specially killed for them, but not those already dead (they need not have died on their own; having been slaughtered for others suffices).[33] Al-Masʿūdī's account may sound implausible, given that a diet of carrion carries a high risk of gastrointestinal disease. But the data relate to uncooked carrion.[34] Homely wisdom has it that you can eat just about anything as long as you cook it long enough, and some people these days eat road-kills if they look fresh. Scavenging accounts for some 20 per cent of the diet of the Hadza hunter-gatherers of East Africa, who eat animals killed by predators, not animals that have died of disease or old age, but who have been observed cutting out salvageable parts from a badly decomposed carcass.[35] The scavengers at Rayy were presumably equally knowledgeable about what to eat, what to feed to their animals, and when to use the carcass for the bones and hides alone. That the Mazdakites in the countryside of Rayy would eat carrion is also mentioned in Maḥmūd of Ghazna's letter to the caliph in 420/1029 and should probably be understood literally, not simply to mean meat not slaughtered ritually.[36] 'Mazdak' permitted the consumption of carrion, as Ibn al-Jawzī puts it.[37] This suggests that Khurramī priests had forbidden the killing of cattle,

[31] Loeffler, *Islam in Practice*, 62.
[32] MM, II, §868 (VI, 27f.), previously cited in Chapter 9, p. 187.
[33] Gombrich, *Precept and Practice*, 260.
[34] Ragir et al., 'Gut Morphology'.
[35] O'Connell et al., 'Hadza Scavenging', esp. 356, 357, 361.
[36] Ibn al-Jawzī, *Muntaẓam*, VIII, 39f.
[37] Ibn al-Jawzī, *Talbīs Iblīs*, 74. Manichaean auditors (but not the Elect) were also allowed to eat carrion: see the Middle Persian fragment in BeDuhn, *Manichaean Body*, 55.

but allowed the consumption of the meat of animals that had died on their own, or perhaps more broadly of animals that one had not slaughtered oneself. Being allowed to eat carrion, these Khurramīs had apparently come to fill a special occupational niche (or even become a caste) of their own.[38]

The information on Khurramī attitudes in the east is exiguous. According to Ibn al-Nadīm, Abū Zayd al-Balkhī examined Khurramīs' beliefs and practice (*madhāhibihim wa-afʿālihim*) regarding drink, pleasures, and worship in his lost *ʿUyūn al-masāʾil waʾl-jawābāt*, implying that they had unusual views on these topics.[39] Presumably this information related partly or wholly to the east, but we do not know what was in it, unless Ibn al-Nadīm's own information on Khurramī non-violence is drawn from it. Abū Tammām tells us that the Mubayyiḍa deemed it lawful to eat carrion, blood, pork, and other things,[40] but he is simply listing the Islamic categories of forbidden food, which the Khurramīs rejected on principle, not reporting on what they actually ate, so the value of his testimony is limited. A taboo on killing animals is reflected in the story told by the eleventh-century Kay Kāʾūs of the village women in Jurjān who would carefully watch their steps to avoid treading on worms, but we cannot be sure that the practice was Khurramī rather than Manichaean.[41]

Khurramī vegetarianism, such as it was, is never explained with reference to reincarnation: it is not because the animal could be one's deceased parents or friends that one should not kill it. On the contrary, the two passages in which we see reincarnation being brought to bear on the subject are both trying to justify exceptions from the rule: humans could be killed to release their spirits from the bodies in which they would commit further sins, as Mazdak is said to have argued; and animals could be lawfully slaughtered by way of punishment for bloodshed they had caused in their previous lives according to the Muʿtazilite and other reincarnationists cited in the *Tabṣirat al-ʿawāmm*.[42] The reason that it was wrong to kill animals seems simply to have been that animals were sentient beings.

[38] Cf. the *Dabistān*, I, 26.4 = I, 73f. Written by an illuminist Indian Zoroastrian in the tenth/seventeenth century, this work regards the killing of beneficent animals as abhorrent, but envisages Jamshīd as ruling that no sin was incurred if base people ate the meat of animals that had died on their own. Here, however, they are said not to do so any more because of the risk of disease.

[39] Ibn al-Nadīm, 406.7 = II, 817f.

[40] Abū Tammām, 77= 76; similarly Isfarāʾinī, *Tabṣīr*, 77.

[41] Kay Kāʾūs, *Qābūsnāma*, 28f. = 36 (ch. 7).

[42] See Chapter 12, pp. 243f.

ANTINOMIANISM

There is unanimous agreement in the sources that the Khurramīs disregarded Islamic law, above all the precepts relating to ritual observance (*ʿibādāt*) and marriage. We are given to understand that they accepted the law as authoritative, at least in so far as it was Qurʾānic, but wriggled out of it in one of two ways. One was by interpretation. Even the *Dēnkard* knows them to have interpreted the religion 'to remedy it', as it says of the 'Mazdakites' (in Shaki's translation), presumably with reference to Khurramīs who still counted as Zoroastrians.[43] The followers of ʿAbdallāh b. Muʿāwiya are reported to have held carrion, wine, and other forbidden things to be lawful with reference to Q 5:93 ('There is no fault in those who believe and do deeds of righteousness for what they ate').[44] The same is reported for the Mubayyiḍa, of whom we are also told that they explained the words for the things seemingly prohibited in the Qurʾān as the names of men with whom it was forbidden to have relations of solidarity (*walāya*); conversely, the positive commands were cover names for men with whom it is obligatory to have such relations. In support of their views on food they would adduce not just Q 5:93, but also 7:32 ('Who has forbidden the beautiful things (*zīna*) of God which He brought forth for His servants and the good things of sustenance (*al-ṭayyibāt min al-rizq*)?').[45] Much the same is said about other Ghulāt. The followers of Abū Manṣūr and Abū 'l-Khaṭṭāb, for example, also took the things forbidden and enjoined to stand for persons, the former adducing Q 5:93, the latter 4:28 ('God wants to make things light for you').[46]

The concatenation of the Khurramīs with the Manṣūriyya and Khaṭṭābiyya immediately causes the reader to envisage the sectarians as antinomians who would engage in ostentatious violation of the law in order to demonstrate its irrelevance, whether for everyone in general or for them as perfected individuals in particular. But this is probably wrong. Most Khurramīs were villagers, not members of urban coteries like their ʿAlid Shīʿite counterparts. Khurramism was the religion of everyone where

[43] *DkM*, 653.10ff. in Shaki, 'Social Doctrine', 293ff. The old translation by West (Dk, VII, 7:21–5 in his *Pahlavi Texts*, v, 88f.) is quite different, and also quite incomprehensible. Even Shaki's is so obscure that it is hard to know how much of his translation to trust, though the agreement between the two translations is somewhat greater at the end (see further p. 414).

[44] Ashʿarī, 6.

[45] Madelung and Walker, *Ismaili Heresiography*, 77 = 76.

[46] Nawbakhtī, 38; Ashʿarī, 10.

they lived, not just of a few individuals banding together in the belief that they were elect; and nobody lived by Islamic law for the simple reason that the entire community was still living by its ancestral customs. They could of course still have had collective rituals designed to illustrate their freedom from the law and to set them apart from other Muslims, but no such ritual is attributed to them until we reach al-Baghdādī and later authors, who credit them with an orgiastic night. The belief that certain heretics would assemble for a night of indiscriminate mating once a year was an ancient one in the Near East by then, and the Khurramīs came to be included among the heretics in question because they did 'share women' in some sense. But their sexual customs had nothing to do with deliberate antinomianism, and the charge that they had an orgiastic night is undoubtedly false.[47] Having come to accept the Qur'ān as their most authoritative text, they simply treated the law it contained much as the Christians had treated the law of Moses: they revered it while at the same time interpreting it away.

The second way of wriggling out of the law is reported by Ja'far b. Ḥarb for the Khidāshiyya and Muslimiyya: they too accepted the law as authoritative, but only for others. According to them, those who knew the imam were not bound by the religious precepts (*farā'iḍ*); all forbidden things, whether relating to food, drink, or sex, were lawful for them. But the exemption from the law only applied to those of insight (*'ārifūn*), as a reward for their recognition of the imam, not to those who did not know him: the latter were being punished for their ignorance by these prohibitions. It was a religious obligation to know the imam, who was God's proof (*ḥujjat Allāh*) and ambassador (*safīr*) between himself and man, and to maintain relationships of solidarity (*walāya*) with those who practised solidarity with him, dissociating from those who did not. Ja'far b. Ḥarb reports that the Ḥarbiyya/Ḥārithiyya likewise held that 'the servant who recognises his imam ceases to be obliged by the precepts'; indeed, this was the view of all the extremist adherents of the imamate, he says, however much they might disagree about the identity of the imam.[48] Other sources agree.[49]

Here the suggestion that the Khurramīs were Gnostic antinomians is stronger than in the reports on the first strategy. We now see them declare themselves above the law, not simply trying to bring the law into line with

[47] For all this see Chapter 17.
[48] Ps.-Nāshi', §§48, 59.
[49] Cf. Nawbakhtī, 41f.; Qummī, 64 (no. 128): the Muslimiyya 'believed in making things lawful and abandoning all the precepts, construing faith as recognition of the imam alone'.

their own convictions, and they call themselves *ʿārifūn*, literally translatable as 'Gnostics', conjuring up perfected individuals who are no longer bound by the restrictions imposed on lesser mortals, like the man who masters the divine secrets in the monotheist Mazdak fragment. But even if *ʿārif* is a translation of *gnōstikos*, it did not necessarily stand for a Gnostic, since *gnōstikos* was a flattering term for a spiritually advanced Christian, and remained so even after it had been appropriated by the Gnostics;[50] the *ʿārif* is similarly a spiritually advanced Muslim in Sufi parlance. Once again, the antinomianism of the Khurramīs is probably designed simply to accommodate their ancestral ways. The Muslimiyya, Khidāshiyya, and Ḥarbiyya/Ḥārithiyya were all defined by their recognition of their own particular imam: all were *ʿārifūn* liberated from the law. When they argued that the law only applied to others they were once more using a strategy pioneered by the Christians: Mosaic law remained valid, the Christians said, but only for the Jews who stubbornly refused to acknowledge Jesus as the messiah and so continued to be shackled by way of punishment; for Christians the law was abolished – or, as they more commonly put it, only its spiritual meaning now applied: it was to bring out the spiritual meaning that they resorted to interpretation. The fact that gentile Christians rejected Mosaic law does not mean that they lived wild, antinomian lives, though the Jews probably and the pagans certainly thought that they did.[51] The Khurramīs did not live lives of wild indulgence either; had they done so their communities would not have survived. The alternative to Mosaic and Islamic law was law of other kinds.

One reason that mainstream Muslims found it so easy to believe that the Khurramīs saw themselves as freed from all legal restraints is that Khurramīs did in fact see themselves as thus freed in their relations with *opponents*. They regarded themselves as the true believers, and when the mahdi came the sheep would be sorted from the goats: all the earth would be theirs. As the only saved the adherents of the mahdi or his precursor were free to kill, rob, and enslave the unbelievers as they wished. This is the behaviour reported by Dionysius of Tell Mahré for the Khurdanaye, by Muslim sources for the followers of Bābak and al-Muqannaʿ, and misrepresented as a doctrine of Mazdakite sharing in al-Bīrūnī's account of the latter. The Qarmaṭī Ismailis of Iraq similarly legalised indiscriminate killing and plundering of opponents in the expectation of the imminent return

[50] Cf. Brakke, *Gnostics*, 30, 33, 49.
[51] See Chapter 17, p. 435.

of Muḥammad b. Ismāʿīl.[52] After the suppression of the revolts there were Khurramīs who held such behaviour to be legal at all times, as has been seen. Like the rebels they saw their opponents as fair game, devoid of any kind of legal or moral protection, but they lacked the ability to rise up against them and so legitimised underhand means: one could deceive, kill, rob, and assassinate opponents in any way possible – indeed, one should; the normal restraints did not apply to noxious humans.

It has to be stressed that this kind of behaviour has nothing to do with liberated individuals seeing themselves as above the restraints of the law. Those who endorsed it would observe all the normal taboos at home, and they would not dream of killing or stealing from co-religionists. By contrast, it was in his own community that the liberated individual was freed from the restraints of the law. Moreover, it was not just antinomian heretics who would treat opponents as outlaws. The Khārijite extremists, who were the most nomian of sectarians, also legalised indiscriminate killing, initially openly, and after the suppression of their revolts by assassination and underhand means.[53] Indeed, they became the paradigmatic example of such behaviour: an anonymous poet satirised Khidāsh as both a Rāfiḍī and an Azraqī,[54] and the Khārijite extremists are also adduced as a parallel in the reporting on the Qarmaṭīs.[55] The Khārijites did not see themselves as a spiritual elite, but they did see themselves as the only Muslims, and the legalisation of killing by any means seems to have more to do with a conviction of being the only possessors of a truth threatened with extinction by a massive majority than with the nature of the truth in question. It may be, though, that devotees of esoteric, spiritualised beliefs are more likely than others to elevate such behaviour to ritual status, investing it with supreme religious merit and regarding it as emblematic of their community, as the adherents of the 'new mission' of Ḥasan-i Ṣabbāḥ, or in other words the Assassins, were to do. It goes well with the belief that the truth is never what it seems to be on the surface.

TRANSGRESSIVE SACRALITY

This brings us to the liberated individual. He did exist, and not just in the (possibly Khurramī, possibly Ismaili) Mazdak fragment. In al-Madāʾinī's

[52] Nawbakhtī, 64; Qummī, 85 (no. 161); tr. Madelung in Stern, *Studies*, 52.
[53] Crone and Zimmermann, *Epistle*, text, §118, comm., 178, and appendix 4.
[54] Ps.-Nāshiʾ, §49.
[55] Nawbakhtī, 64; Qummī, 85 (no. 161); tr. Madelung in Stern, *Studies*, 52.

account of the Rāwandiyya in Khurāsān in the 110s/730s we are told that these sectarians would make the forbidden lawful to the point that a Rāwandī would invite a group to his home, give them food and drink, and then pass them his wife.[56] What is described here does not seem to be guest prostitution (the guests are not foreign travellers), but rather a ritual meal followed by sexual union of the type in which the participants see themselves as enacting divine roles, as known for example from Tantric schools of Buddhism and Hinduism. Tantric Buddhism was a fast lane to enlightenment: just as many practitioners of *hekhalot* mysticism hoped quickly to acquire the legal knowledge associated with rabbinic status by means of heavenly journeys and/or magic, so the devotees of Tantric Buddhism hoped to escape years of hard ascetic practice by recourse to techniques inducing sudden enlightenment. In both cases, it would appear, a religious culture had been taken up by people outside the restricted circles in which it had hitherto been pursued. 'Transgressive sacrality' played a major role in bringing about the speedy achievement of enlightenment in Tantric Buddhism. One of the earliest texts of the Buddhist Vajrayana school, the Guhya-Samāja (*c.* AD 300), permitted stealing, meat eating, even cannibalism, and unrestrained ritual intercourse, even with one's own mother, sister, or daughter.[57] What the Zoroastrians regarded as the most meritorious unions are here being permitted as the most immoral that one could possibly imagine; the aim was to overcome the subject–object distinction enshrined in everyday thought and morality. Sexual intercourse is also considered an indispensable part of spiritual practice in other Buddhist texts. The same is true of Hindu Tantrism. The aim was to produce the vital fluids required to propitiate the goddesses and force them to share their miraculous powers and esoteric knowledge, or, in another form of the cult, to expand consciousness and obliterate the worshipper's desiring ego.[58] The Hindu pair might enact the roles of *puruṣa* (the seer, self) and *prakṛti* (the seen, the phenomena), or of Śiva and his consort: Śivahood was achieved when one's ego disappeared; one could now do or know everything desired.[59] Some Tantric texts allowed – or even recommended – another man's wife to be used, others condemned it. The Buddhists permitted it provided that there was no emission of sperm, or they always forbade the emission of sperm; the Hindus lacked

[56] Tab. iii, 418.
[57] Banerji, *Companion to Tantra*, 235f.
[58] Cf. Sanderson, 'Śaivism and Tantric Tradition', 671f., 680.
[59] Banerji, *Companion to Tantra*, 47ff.

this restriction.[60] There were (and apparently still are) rituals involving the consumption of sperm, excrement, corpses, and more besides as well, undertaken because the Tantric goddesses fed on such things, or because repulsive acts allowed a Tantric to demonstrate his total indifference to worldly conventions. Tantric sex is a 'booster rocket' to drive the mind out of the gravitational pull of everyday life, as a Bengali Baul recently put it.[61]

Tantrism was on the rise when the Muslims reached eastern Iran, and one suspects that it was a Tantric ritual that the Rāwandiyya were performing, presumably in the belief that they had achieved, or would achieve, what the local Buddhists called enlightenment and others called angelic or divine status. Other Muslims were engaged in similar endeavours. Khushaysh b. Aṣram (d. 253/867), a heresiographer from Nasā quoted by al-Malaṭī, mentions 'Spirituals', perhaps in eastern Iran and/or Basra, who held that if they concentrated their minds on their last destination they would reach it in their spirits, so that they would be able to see and talk to God, sleep with the houris, and enjoy all the pleasures of paradise. Presumably this required real women to play the part of their heavenly counterparts.[62] Other 'Spirituals' held that they might achieve such love of God that they could steal, drink wine, and engage in forbidden sexual relations, on the grounds that a friend (i.e., God, the owner of everything) does not withhold his property from his friend: Rabāḥ and Kulayb propagated this doctrine, we are told, being apparently expected to have heard of them before.[63] The aim is the same as in the monotheist Mazdak fragment, where it is not love of God but rather union in oneself of the four, seven, and twelve powers that causes the perfect man to be exempt from the law. Other 'Spirituals' said that one should train oneself like a race-horse which is given only just enough to eat when it is being prepared for a race; when one reached the extreme limit of spiritual

[60] Banerji, *Companion to Tantra*, 82, 128, 134, 173, cf. 84, 256, s.v. 'Bhairavī Cakra'; Tucci, 'Peculiar Image'.

[61] Dalrymple, *Nine Lives*, 247.

[62] Malaṭī, 73. Compare the mid-second/eighth-century Basrans who claimed that they entered paradise every night and enjoyed its fruits (Radtke, 'How can Man reach the Mystical Union?', 190, citing Sarrāj, *Luma'*, 429). The seventeenth-century Egyptian scholar al-Shirbīnī claimed that Sufis known as Khawāmis would hold music sessions during which they would enter a trance and be considered to have died and entered paradise, so that they would be offered handsome youths and women (El-Rouayheb, 'Heresy and Sufism', 376). Unfortunately al-Shirbīnī spoils his own credibility by adding that those who divulged these secrets would be killed, and sometimes cooked and eaten.

[63] Rabāḥ may be the Basran Rabāḥ al-Qaysī (Radtke, 'How can Man reach the Mystical Union?', 189f.).

emaciation and lost the ability to perceive the difference between nice food and refuse, honey and vinegar, or bitter aloe and sweetmeat, one could stop the training and give one's appetitive self (*nafs*) what it wanted. The propagator of this idea was a certain Ibn Ḥayyān. Still others said that asceticism was counter-productive since it caused the ascetic constantly to think about worldly pleasures and so ascribe excessive importance to them. It was much better to belittle desires by routinely fulfilling them when they presented themselves. Still others said that renunciation (*zuhd*) should only consist in abstention from forbidden things, not from things that God had permitted, such as nice food, exquisite dishes, spacious accommodation, servants, and the like. In their opinion the rich enjoyed a higher rank in God's eyes than the poor because they were in a position to give away some of their property.[64]

Khushaysh's 'Spirituals' are not called Khurramīs, but they appear to be related to them. All have a high regard for the good things of this world. Some declare such things to be legitimate, assigning religious merit to the rich, in agreement with the Ḥarbiyya/Ḥārithiyya; some think that one should cope with desire by simply fulfilling it, a view held by Zardūsht of Fasā and Mazdak too; the rest practise asceticism, but with no attempt to disguise the fact that its aim is achievement of the very things that the others openly legitimise: some see themselves as obtaining advance payment of post-mortem pleasures; others claim spiritual perfection to the point where they do what they like, somewhat like the Free Spirits of late medieval Europe. There is no reference to participation in repulsive acts to foster indifference to worldly conventions, or to display such indifference if already achieved, but there were certainly Sufis who used this method: two centuries later al-Ghazālī condemned Sufis who held ultimate purity to have been achieved by those who did not withhold their wives and children from sexual use by others and/or who would demonstrate their own perfection by their ability dispassionately to watch their own wives have intercourse with other men in their own homes.[65]

Al-Malaṭī reports another version of such attitudes for 'the Qarāmiṭa and Daylam'. As mentioned already, these sectarians believed in a supreme God who was light, who had created a brilliant light out of which imams and prophets were made, and another light which was visible in the sun, moon, and the human spirit, and which was subject to transmigration. They also believed in 'divinity in humanity' after the fashion of the

[64] Malaṭī, 74f.

[65] Ghazālī, 'Streitschrift', 2, 7 = 21, 26; cf. Ghazālī, *Makātib-i fārsī*, 76 (bāb V, iii) = *Briefe*, 212.

Christians. Al-Malaṭī further reports that they deemed all human excretions to be pure (*ṭāhir naẓīf*), whether they were urine, excrement, sweat, phlegm, semen, or other, to the point that they would sometimes eat each other's ordure, knowing it to be pure. They treated this doctrine as a hallmark of believing men and women. In other words, it was not that they had overcome the distinction between repulsive and attractive, but rather that the ability to see the true value of acts deemed repulsive by outsiders served as a mark of membership. They declared prayer, almsgiving, fasting, pilgrimage, and other precepts to be supererogatory and claimed that their women, children, and their own bodies were lawful (for sexual purposes) among themselves, without any restrictions, this being the very quintessence of faith. Anyone who resisted was an unbeliever. They also reversed normal views by declaring women and passive partners (in homosexual intercourse) to rank higher than the active partner, and they would greet them with 'bless you, O believer' after their performance. Even the husbands of such women would congratulate them. They shared their property too, in the sense that anybody could use what others had in their possession, in line with the household model of sharing enshrined in Mazdakism. They thought it fine to kill and to die in battle because they would be released, presumably for a better incarnation or for angelic existence, and they deemed all others to be infidels and polytheists who could be killed, robbed of their property, and enslaved.[66]

Here we have deliberate antinomianism, both internally and in relations with outsiders. Al-Mas'ūdī explains that the Daylamīs and Gīlīs used not to have any religion, or in other words they were pagans; thereafter the 'Alid al-Uṭrūsh had converted many of their rulers (to Zaydī Shī'ism), and thereafter their beliefs had been corrupted and turned into *ilḥād*, i.e. Ismailism.[67] The Ismailis had a centre at Rayy, and their converts along the Caspian coast included the Musāfirid ruler Wahsūdān, who struck a Qarmaṭī coin in 343/954f., as well as his brother Marzubān, and for a while also Asfār (d. 318/930f.) and Mardāvīj (d. 323/935), the Daylamī and Gīlī mercenaries who tried to establish kingdoms for themselves.[68] Al-Malaṭī's 'Qarāmiṭa and Daylam' were probably also among their converts. They appear to have been soldiers: they do not mind killing and falling in battle, they say. If so, it was probably in the armies of men such as Asfār, Mardāvīj, or the Būyids that one would find them. Ismailism

66 Malaṭī, 15–17.
67 MM V, §3581/IX, 9f.
68 Stern, 'Early Ismā'īlī Missionaries', 209ff.; Daftary, *The Ismā'īlīs*, 112, 121.

seems to have provided them with a language in which they could continue to insulate themselves from the mainstream Muslim world when they left their mountains. Their household model of sharing may have been rooted in some feature of their village organisation, taken up and adapted as a way of furthering solidarity in the foreign lands; this could be true even of their sexual rules. But their rules of purity must surely have originated by simple inversion of universal norms, and all their precepts seem to be designed to build high walls around them.

Al-Malaṭī's 'Qarāmiṭa and Daylam' were not the only recruits from the Caspian coast to be shockingly un-Islamic in their understanding of Islam, in so far as they were Muslims at all. Mardāvīj was the man who thought that Solomon's spirit was in him: he knew enough about Islam to cast himself as a king for whom all Muslims had great respect, but he did so by recourse to the doctrine of reincarnation which all good Muslims rejected. Asfār was notorious for his atrocities at Qazvīn, where he allowed his troops to capture the inhabitants and rape the women, and where he destroyed mosques, stopped ritual prayer, and had a muezzin who dared to call to prayer thrown to his death from his minaret.[69] He could hardly have done all this if his troops had not approved. Perhaps al-Malaṭī's 'Qarāmiṭa and Daylam' were among them, but there must in any case have been others of a similar type, and we have already met one in the Daylamī chief captured by Maḥmūd of Ghazna during his conquest of Rayy from the Būyids in 420/1029: he admitted to having fifty wives because this had been the custom of his ancestors.[70] The Būyids were probably more mainstream Muslims than Mardāvīj and Asfār from the start. They certainly behaved better, and soon became respectable rulers who surrounded themselves with Imāmī scholars and other literary men, so that a modern reader often has trouble understanding why Sunnīs viewed the dynasty with such horror. One forgets that it was not with the rulers that most people interacted. In 488/1095, when the Samarqandīs wished to rid themselves of their oppressive ruler, Aḥmad Khān, they used the fact that he had been jailed for some time in Būyid Iraq as a peg on which to hang a charge of apostasy: he had been led to permissiveness, godlessness, and heresy of the Iranian type (*ibāḥa*, *ilḥād*, and *zandaqa*) by his Daylamī prison guards, they said. The charge was undoubtedly false, but one can see why it sounded plausible.[71]

[69] MM V, §3582/IX, 10f. He was said not to be a Muslim (V, §3580/IX, 8).
[70] Ibn al-Jawzī, *Muntaẓam*, VIII, 39.
[71] IA, X, 243 (year 488); Haydar b. 'Alī, *Majma' al-tawārikh*, in *TB* (ed. Schefer), 236; cf. Crone, *Medieval Islamic Political Thought*, 283.

ORGANISATION AND RITUAL

How were the Khurramīs organised back home? We have only the barest scraps of information on the topic. As we have seen, Jāvīdhān is described as the leader of an organisation consisting of headquarters at Badhdh and a network in the villages around it, with some followers coming from far afield; and the information on the Hāshimiyya implies that there were similar organisations in Khurāsān.[72] It sounds like the pattern later reproduced in the Sufi lodges with far-flung rural clienteles. According to Abū Tammām, the Mubayyiḍa of the fourth/tenth century had a chief in every locality (*balad*) whom they called *farmānsālār* and with whom they met in secret – and so they could have, but this comes in the third section of his account, which actually refers to the Muslimiyya of western Iran.[73] We do learn that the communities in the Bukhārā region had priests called *tkāna* or *thkāna*, however,[74] and as noted there is also some slight evidence for religious specialists known as *ḥakīms* in Sogdia, where they would have been the leaders of the Mubayyiḍa.[75] It was probably such leaders who had authored the bits and pieces devoted to Mubayyiḍī and Khurramī doctrine that Maḥmūd al-Īlāqī was reading in Īlāq in the fifth/eleventh century.[76] Since we never hear of special religious buildings in either east or west we may take it that they officiated in private homes.

As regards western Iran, al-Maqdisī replaces Abū Tammām's *farmānsālārs* with imams consulted in matters of law (*aḥkām*), so these were probably the leaders formerly called prophets.[77] Some (or at least one) of the Khurramīs that al-Maqdisī knew were learned men.[78] Both he and Abū Tammām mention that the sectarians also had messengers (*rusul*) and ambassadors (*sufarā'*), who moved about among them and whom they called *firīshtagān*, that is to say *malā'ika*, or angels; so here as in Bābak's Azerbaijan it is clear that there was some organisation above village level.[79]

[72] See Chapter 3, p. 63; Chapter 6, pp. 123f.
[73] Abū Tammām, 78 = 77; cf. Crone, 'Abū Tammām on the Mubayyiḍa', 177ff.
[74] See Chapter 17, p. 434.
[75] See Chapter 6, p. 128.
[76] Iskandar, 'al-Marwazī's Ṭabā' 'al-Ḥaywawān', 298, English summary, 278; 'Awfī, *Jawāmi'*, III/1, 231f.; cf. Chapter 9, p. 180.
[77] Maqdisī, IV, 31.
[78] Maqdisī, I, 171f.; III, 122.6.
[79] The Zoroastrian clergy may also have included itinerant priests, see *Hērbedestān*, 4, 1–2 KK (1–11 HE) on the priest who goes forth to do *āθaurunəm*, rendered *āsrōgīh* in the Pahlavi translation. Kotwal and Kreyenbroek translate it as religious studies (clearly the purpose of the journey in the rest of the chapter, but here a different word is used);

Abū Tammām implies that the Muslimiyya would meet in secret because they were awaiting the mahdi, a descendant of Abū Muslim with whom they expected to rebel, but al-Maqdisī's imams were legal authorities rather than military leaders. Al-Maqdisī does not tell us anything about the law they dispensed, but he mentions that the Khurramīs paid inordinate attention to cleanliness and purity (*al-naẓāfa wa'l-ṭahāra*),[80] qualities that are also highly esteemed in Ja'far b. Ḥarb's account of reincarnation,[81] so the fact that they did not recognise Muslim laws of purity does not mean that they had none. When al-Maqdisī and Niẓām al-Mulk mention that they made much of Abū Muslim and would curse al-Manṣūr for having killed him, the reference is probably to ritual lamentation and cursing during the recital of stories about Abū Muslim and the mahdi to come, the Muslimī counterpart to ritual lamentation of al-Ḥusayn among the Imāmīs.[82] Whether these ceremonies were conducted indoors or in the open we do not know: there is no reference to mourning processions in which people would lash or stab themselves, lamenting that 'the heroes are destroyed, but as for me, I am left in peace',[83] or the like. But it was known, at least to Ibn al-Nadīm, that the ritual of the Khurramīs included texts sung with tunes and rhythm.[84] Wine probably also figured in their ritual, as implied by al-Maqdisī when he says that they sought blessing in it. It had certainly figured in Bābak's election ceremony. But this seems to be the sum total of the information in the Muslim sources.

According to Dionysius of Tell Mahré the Khurdanaye who later accepted Bābak as their leader were Magians in their cult, presumably meaning that they venerated fire.[85] The Khurramīs are never accused of fire-worship in the Muslim sources, merely of not having any mosques in their villages; but the information is so limited that silence does not count for much.

Humbach and Elfenbein leave it untranslated, and Hintze, 'Disseminating the Mazdayasnian Religion', 175, makes a good case that it meant performing priestly duties; similarly *EIr.*, s.v. 'āθravan' (Boyce). In *DkM*, 734f. (*Dk*, VIII, 28:2, West), reproduced in *Hērbedestān*, 21f. KK., such a priest is called an *āsrōgī frēstīdag*, a priest who is sent out. It is tempting to see the Khurramī *firīshtagān* as such priests, regarded as emissaries of God (as incarnate in their leader?).

80 Maqdisī, IV, 31.

81 Ps.-Nāshi', §57.

82 Maqdisī, IV, 31; *SN*, 47:14 (319f. = 244).

83 Cf. Theodore Bar Koni, *Scolies*, mimra xi, 84 (343 = 256) (English tr. in Kruisheer, 'Theodore', 164), on the Kanthaeans of Babylonia.

84 Ibn al-Nadīm, 403.17 = II, 809, says of another sect that they had words they would sing *mulaḥḥanan wa-mawzūnan* and that their procedure in this respect resembled that of the Khurramiyya.

85 Michael Syr., IV, 508 = III, 50; *Chron. ad 1234*, II, 26 = 18.

OVERALL

Panpsychism

The core of Khurramism would seem to lie in two features. The first is panpsychism, the conviction that everything is alive and endowed with soul, spirit, or mind. Like most dualists the Khurramīs seem to have conceived of light and darkness as the actual stuff of which the universe was made, corresponding to spirit and matter. Light was alive, sentient, and knowing *(ḥayy ḥassās ʿālim)*,[86] and it went into the making of everything. It followed that all things except for the densest matter were suffused with light or spirit, which rendered them alive, aware, and sentient. The Khurramīs shared this conviction with the Manichaeans, among whom we shall meet it in a more extreme form. All things were full of gods, as Thales had put it. 'Their doctrine is that God is found in every place, speaks every language, and appears in every person,' as al-Shahrastānī said of believers in *ḥulūl*.[87] He could have added that this conviction lay behind their belief in reincarnation and non-violence too, for it was the same spirit that went round and round, the same persons who come back time and again, sometimes as humans and sometimes as animals, or even as plants or minerals. Some humans were made of a purer light, or a more divine spirit, than others, and at all times there had to be a man quite unlike the rest. Such men had to be obeyed without question. They were living law, a lifeline to the supernatural world, the possessor of all knowledge, the key to all the mysteries, the master-switch that allowed for light, spirit, and divinity to flow into this world. Without such a man the world would collapse. Given his presence, each era would play out much like the next. Sometimes the eras continued for ever, bunched together in cycles of varying length; at other times they culminated in a grand finale, or there were grand finales at the end of each cycle with an even grander one at the end of all of them. Grand finales were inaugurated by the descent to earth of God himself, in the sense that his spirit would come down to reside in a human being. Clothed in that body, the divine became visible, and the inexpressible, unbearable mystery was unveiled.

The idea that the universe is alive and filled with soul or spirit has been current in many cultural traditions. Tylor's *Primitive Culture*, published in 1871, called it animism and made it practically synonymous with primitive

[86] Abū ʿĪsā, in Chapter 10, p. 229; Maqdisī, III, 122.9f.
[87] Shahrastānī, I, 133 = I, 512.

religion. Animism survived to receive philosophical and/or religious development in India, notably in Jainism, and also in Greece, notably at the hands of the pre-Socratics, Plato, and the Stoics; and it became prominent in late antiquity, especially in Neoplatonism, Manichaeism and other Gnostic systems. From the classical world the idea passed to Europe, where it was influential in the Renaissance and again in the nineteenth century, in forms that usually cast everything as alive in the sense of endowed with mind rather than with feeling. Panpsychism is still a serious rival to emergentism as a solution to the mind–body problem today.[88] As usual, we know how ideas developed in India and Greece, but not in Iran, and when we find similar ideas there we tend to react by assuming that the Iranians must have imported them from one or the other of their two better-documented neighbours. This appears to be a mistake – not just in connection with panpsychism, but also with reincarnation, as I hope to persuade the reader in what follows.

From the point of view of adherents of panpsychist beliefs, monotheism of the biblical type was intolerably reductionist. It concentrated the divine in one single being, with some carefully regulated exceptions – or, differently put, it walled in the sacred and threw away the key. It thereby drained the world of light and spirit, turning it into insentient, mindless, inert dark matter, like an extinct volcano. On top of that, 'the Jews', as Bābak called the Muslims, conceived of the divine as a distant judge who communicated with his world by means of written missives, issuing an endless stream of restrictive rules, like the administrators in the cities of whatever dynast happened to be in power. Their God punished people in much the same way as the power-holders in the cities too. It was an unbearably bleak and bureaucratic vision. Of course the Khurramīs held that there were rewards for the good and punishments for the wicked, but it was effected by natural processes, the movement of the spirit at times of birth and death, not by mechanisms such as those used by human kings and other authorities. From the Khurramī point of view the Christians were better than the Jews and Muslims in that they accepted the idea of God incarnating himself in human beings and also spoke much about the holy spirit. The Gnostics were even better, and best of all were the Platonists, whether pagan, Gnostic, Christian, or Muslim. It is not for nothing that Platonism became an integral part of Iranian Islam.

[88] For all this see Skrbina, *Panpsychism in the West*.

Alienation

The second major characteristic of Khurramism is alienation – but not of the cosmic type found in Gnosticism. Cosmic alienation is represented by Manichaeism, in which the presence of the divine in everything is construed as a tragedy. There was never meant to be a world for God to be immanent in: the light was trapped, awaiting liberation; virtue lay in contributing to its release and thus to the eventual collapse of the world, achieved when all the light had been withdrawn. The Khurramīs display no sign of seeing material existence as a tragedy. Of course it is hazardous to generalise, given the limited nature of the evidence and the huge variety of views that must have existed; some Khurramīs must have been more Gnostic than others. What such evidence as we have suggests, however, is that the Khurramīs did not see matter as evil, but rather as a cover, a mask over the reality of things, a façade of varying degrees of density behind which all things could be seen to be manifestations of the same divine forces. God was hidden by veils, just as the spirit in humans and animals was hidden by bodies, or in some cases even by stone. But behind the veils, the clothes, the moulds, and the forms, all was ultimately the same divine light or spirit in different manifestations.

The only sense of alienation that comes through loud and clear in the sources on the Khurramīs is political. Everybody else had followed imams of error; only they knew that the guardianship of the Prophet's message had passed to Abū Muslim or Khidāsh, who had been betrayed and killed by the powers that be. The Muslimiyya would curse the killers and weep over their martyrs, clearly identifying their dire fate with their own. Eventually they enrolled the Persian kings as imams, and so implicitly as martyrs too. The followers of ʿAbdallāh b. Muʿāwiya were also defined by loyalty to a martyred hero. So too, of course, were the many Shīʿites who were not Khurramīs and who wept over al-Ḥusayn. In all cases the evil powers were human, usually the caliph and his supporters, the 'Arabs' who called themselves Muslims, and no attempt seems to have been made to retell the story of the evil powers on a cosmic scale, as an account of the creation. In line with this, what the devotees of martyred heroes dreamed about was not escape from the world, but rather vengeance: the hero would come back, or a descendant of his would do so, and he would kill the oppressors, purify the world, and restore the oppressed minority to power.

What lay behind this sense of alienation? There cannot be a single answer to this question, least of all if the ʿAlid Shīʿites are included in it.

As far as the Khurramīs are concerned we know that the alienation began with their unhappy encounters with Muslim society in the form of colonisation, post-revolutionary violence, and ruined lives, but something more is required to explain its persistence. We know so little about the eastern Khurramīs that it is barely worth speculating, but as far as the western Khurramīs are concerned we may note that they lived in mountainous regions in which it will often have been the case that every valley was a world unto itself, with its own dialect, law, customs, beliefs, and rituals, its own face-to-face interactions and a limited sense of fellowship with outsiders. There were religious networks connecting the valleys, as we have seen, but as we have also seen they left the autonomy of each community intact. The inhabitants of these valleys are not likely to have relished integration into the wider world. To the modern Guran, the oldest group among the Ahl-i Ḥaqq and in effect Khurramīs under another name, every meaningful event that had ever occurred anywhere had also taken place in the Guran country, so that pilgrimage to distant places was unnecessary: local shrines offered everything that one could find abroad.[89] In the same spirit the Yezidis drew up a petition to the Ottoman government in 1872 requesting exemption from military service: Yezidis could not serve in the army, they said, explaining that every Yezidi must visit a local shrine three times a year; failure to do so would render him an unbeliever. Any man who went abroad and stayed for a year or more would lose his wife and his ability to take another from the community, that is to say he would no longer count as a member himself; a host of other rules also served to make social relations with Muslims, Jews, and Christians impossible.[90] It was to such inward-turned communities that the Arab colonists came in the Jibāl and Azerbaijan, bringing their new universalist religion and impersonal law, their mosques for formal worship, and their talk of pilgrimage to a place in distant Arabia. Like all forms of Shīʿite *ghuluww*, Khurramism was a religion designed to insulate people: it built religious walls around their communities when the mountains no longer sufficed. It did so both in the mountains themselves, when the Muslims began to settle there, and when the locals left the mountains of their own accord, as in the case of the Qarāmiṭa and Daylam described by al-Malaṭī, articulating their sense of distance from outsiders whose norms they disliked.

[89] Van Bruinessen, 'When Haji Bektash still bore the Name', 133ff. On the Ahl-i Ḥaqq, see further Chapter 19.

[90] Kreyenbroek, *Yezidism*, 6f., 149. On the Yezidis see further Chapter 19.

To this comes another factor. Back in the days of the Sasanians power had been located in the countryside. The pillars of the regime were landed aristocrats who lived in conditions of wealth and opulence that a common villager could barely even dream of, but they could at least be seen as highly favoured representatives of a shared culture rather than its enemies. The Muslims defeated the aristocrats, took a hostile stance on Iranian religion, and moved power to the cities, from where they issued their written communications, their condemnations of wine and music, and their literary culture exalting legalist piety and role models far removed from the kings and heroes of the Iranians. It was now a puritanical urban ideal that carried prestige. The heroic ideal that Bābak tried to live up to was no longer part of the hegemonic culture.

In short, the Muslim colonists in the Jibāl and Azerbaijan seized the land of the locals, incorporated them into a larger world in which universalist religion and impersonal law prevailed, reduced the countryside to urban subservience, and disseminated a religion that drained the world of divinity to concentrate it in a single transcendental God. Modern urbanites are beneficiaries of changes of the type that Islam represented, essentially the same type of change as that effected by the Reformation in Europe; from their point of view there can be no doubt that the coming of Islam was progress. To the mountaineers it was intolerable. They opted out in the name of the nearest they could find to their own religion in Islam, meaning Shīʿism stretched to the limits to accommodate their views. They did so as Khurramīs, as Qarmaṭīs and other kinds of Ismailis, above all Nizārīs, and eventually as members of all the quasi-Islamic communities that appeared in regions from the Jibāl to Anatolia after the Mongol invasions. But it was not until the Ṣafavid conquest of Iran that the mountaineers got their revenge, with consequences that are still with us.

B. Khurramī Beliefs and Zoroastrianism

14

Khurramī Beliefs in Pre-Islamic Sources

As Muslims the Khurramīs were Shīʿites – more precisely, Rāfiḍīs who held the imamate to have passed directly from Muḥammad to ʿAlī. They parted company with the ʿAlid Shīʿites by explaining the further transmission of the legitimate leadership in terms of the Testament of Abū Hāshim: the latter had passed it to the ʿAbbāsids (where the Rāwandiyya kept it) or to ʿAbdallāh b. Muʿāwiya, or to others such as Abū Muslim or Khidāsh and their Iranian successors. The sources, however, often claim that the Khurramīs were not Muslims at all. Rather, they were a species of Zoroastrians who hid under Islam, as al-Maqdisī says.[1] 'Most of their doctrines are those of the Zoroastrians (*majūs*)', as al-Qummī observes with reference to the Muslimiyya.[2] Even the Rāwandī troops in ʿAbbāsid service were perceived by the Syrian sources behind Theophanes as 'black-clothed Persians who were of the Magian religion'.[3] Shāfiʿite jurists classified the Khurramīs (though not those in ʿAbbāsid service) as one out of four Zoroastrian sects.[4]

As Zoroastrians the Khurramīs were further identified as Mazdakites: they had separated from the original Zoroastrians (*al-majūs al-aṣliyya*) by adopting belief in sharing women and property and the lawfulness of all pleasures, al-Baghdādī says, explaining that this was why the Shāfiʿites would not take *jizya* from them, i.e. did not regard them as eligible for

1 Maqdisī, I, 143.-4.

2 Qummī, 64 (no. 128). They are also a species of Zoroastrians in Maqdisī, IV, 26, and Ibn Rizām in Ibn al-Malāḥimī, *Muʿtamad*, 803, tells us that 'as for the villages of al-Rayy, the dominant [sect] among them is the *khurramiyyat al-majūs*'.

3 Theophanes, AM 6250.

4 Baghdādī, *Farq*, 347. The four *firaq* are Zurwāniyya, Maskhiyya, Khurramdīniyya (later Mazdakiyya), and Bihāfarīdiyya. Shahrastānī worked the first two into his reformulation of Abū ʿĪsā on Zoroastrian cosmology (see Chapter 10, p. 194).

dhimmī status; but other jurists would accept *jizya* even from idolaters, and so from Mazdakites as well.[5] According to Ibn al-Nadīm the Khurramīs had separated from the *majūs* under 'the old Mazdak', i.e., Zardūsht of Fasā.[6] Later 'the recent Mazdak' (i.e., the sixth-century rebel) had appeared, preaching the same doctrine, and his followers had come to be known as *'l-lqṭh*. Ibn al-Nadīm does not offer any explanation for this mysterious term, but it could be taken to imply a distinction between Khurramīs in general (followers of the 'old Mazdak') and Mazdakites in particular (the *lqṭh* who had followed the recent Mazdak). Between them, in any case, these two were the original Khurramīs (*al-khurramiyya al-awwalūn*), as distinct from the more recent Bābakiyya. They were also known as Muḥammira and were now found in the region stretching from Armenia, Azerbaijan, and Daylam to al-Ahwāz and Iṣfahān. Ibn al-Nadīm does not mention the existence of similar groups in eastern Iran or say anything about the Mubayyiḍa.[7] Many other sources loosely call the Khurramīs Mazdakites, or a species of Mazdakites, without indicating whether it is followers of the old or the recent Mazdak that they have in mind, and probably even without being aware of the distinction: when they give further details it is always the rebel they mention. But Ibn al-Nadīm's information is important. In tracing the ancestry of the Khurramīs to the third-century heresiarch he places their origin at the beginning of the Sasanian dynasty, when Zoroastrianism became the state religion. I shall come back to this point.[8]

If Khurramism formed the background to Mazdakism, as proposed above, it must have pre-dated Zardūsht of Fasā too.[9] That it did so is what this chapter attempts to show. It is not easy, for as everyone knows the information on pre-Islamic Iran is extremely poor. Hardly anything in the handful of Middle Persian ('Pahlavi') works to survive can be dated with certainty to the Sasanian – let alone Parthian – periods, though it is clear that much of it is old. The writings of the pagan Aramaic population of Mesopotamia are lost. What survives is Greek and Latin works written outside the Sasanian empire, Aramaic (including Syriac) works by Jews and Christians inside and outside the empire, and some Armenian works, plus inscriptions, magic bowls, and fragmentary texts, mostly Manichaean, recovered archaeologically. It is not much. Nonetheless,

[5] Baghdādī, *Farq*, 347.
[6] Cf. Chapter 1, p. 25.
[7] Ibn al-Nadīm, 405f. = II, 817f.
[8] See Chapter 16, p. 386.
[9] See Chapter 1, pp. 24–26.

there are some scraps of evidence for Khurramī conceptions before the time of Zardūsht of Fasā, and also some which, though later, cannot be credited to him.

BOOK OF ELCHASAI

There does not seem to be any direct evidence for the doctrine of periodic incarnation of the deity in man in pre-Islamic Iran, except in Manichaeism (on which more on pp. 296–301). We do have indirect evidence for it, however, in the form of a book written in Parthia and exported from there to the Roman side of the border. This book is of great importance for the Khurramīs, as also for the Manichaeans, but the reader will have to be armed with patience, for its pursuit requires a long journey into unfamiliar territory.

In AD 114–17 Trajan campaigned in Parthia. He occupied Armenia and the whole of what is now Iraq, including the Parthian capital Ctesiphon, and reached the Persian Gulf, where he lamented the fact that he was too old to repeat the feats of Alexander. Back home, the Jews of Cyrenaica, Egypt, and Cyprus rebelled, causing Trajan to suspect that those of Mesopotamia would follow suit, or perhaps they actually did. He sent his general Lusius to deport them from the province, and Lusius moved against them with great brutality at some point before Trajan died in 117. In the course of all this a Jew who was perhaps a follower of the Jesus movement wrote a book predicting that wars would break out among the impious angels, greatly troubling the impious nations, when 'three years of Emperor Trajan are completed, from the time he reduced the Parthians to his own sway'. This prediction must have been made in 116 or 117.[10] When this book was brought to Rome a century later it was entitled the Book of Elchasai. Elchasai was understood as a person, a righteous man, who had transmitted the book to one 'Sobiai', easily recognised as derived from an Aramaic word for baptists. In lower Iraq there were several baptist sects. A native of Hamadhān who had moved to Ctesiphon joined one such sect before 220, or around 215 if we trust the report that his wife was pregnant at the time with a child

[10] For all this see Luttikhuizen, *Elchasai*, 190–2; see also Alon, *Jews in their Land*, chs. 2–3. For the prediction compare the End Time scenario in 1 Enoch 56:5–7 (Book of Parables): 'In those days the angels will assemble themselves and hurl themselves towards the East against the Parthians and Medes . . . They will begin [to make] war among themselves'.

they were to call Mani.[11] The chief authority of this sect was a person whose name is rendered in a Parthian fragment as *ʾlxsʾ*,[12] in the Greek *Cologne Mani Codex* (*CMC*) as Alchasaios,[13] and in the Arabic *Fihrist* of Ibn al-Nadīm as *ʾlḥsyḥ*, *ʾlḥsḥ*, or *ʾlḥsj*.[14] Ibn al-Nadīm explicitly identifies this person as the founder of the sect and notes that it exists 'to this day'.[15]

In Rome, shortly before or shortly after the death of bishop Calixtus in 222, a new heresy appeared. It was disseminated by a Syrian from Apamea by the name of Alcibiades, who promised remission of sin by means of baptism with reference to a book by one Elchasai, which he had brought to Rome.[16] Around 240 Origen noted that the 'Helkesaites' had recently appeared in the Palestinian churches;[17] and a century later, around 337, Epiphanius reported that there were still 'Elkesaites' in Nabataea, Moabitis, and the Dead Sea region – i.e., in Roman Arabia, where they were formerly known as Osseans and now as Sampseans. The Osseans (Essenes?) had been joined by Elxai or Elxaios in the reign of Trajan; this man was a Jew who had changed the law. Not only the Osseans, but also the Nazoreans and the Ebionites had fallen under his influence: four sects in all had been bewitched by him.[18] Unlike Hippolythus and Origen, Epiphanius does not know of the Elchasaites as an indendent sect, only as a corrupting influence on others.

[11] Mani was born in 216 and initiated into the sect at the age of four (*CMC*, 11), so his father must have joined by 220. He could have done so long before, but the tradition had to explain how the father could have a child when the sect supposedly recommended abstention from sexual intercourse: this is why it presents him as joining when his wife was pregnant (Ibn al-Nadīm, 391 = II, 773f.; see also p. 312 of this chapter).

[12] Sundermann, 'Iranische Lebensbeschreibungen Manis', 130, 148.

[13] *CMC*, 94–97.

[14] Ibn al-Nadīm, 404.1 = II, 811; cf. Sundermann, 'Iranische Lebensbeschreibungen Manis', 148f., emending Ibn al-Nadīm's *ʾlḥsj* to *ʾlḥsyj*, reflecting a Manichaean west Iranian writing of **ʾlkhsyg*, pronounced **Alkhasī*.

[15] Ibn al-Nadīm, 404= II, 811.

[16] Hippolytus, IX, 13–17, X, 29. All my translations relating to Elchasai are from either Klijn and Reinink, 112–23, or Luttikhuizen, *Elchasai* 42–53; both works also give the Greek text. For a reconstruction of the book see Jones, '*Book of Elchasai*', 190ff. (drawn to my attention by A. Y. Reed).

[17] Origen in Eusebius, *Ecclesiastical History*, VI, 38.

[18] Epiphanius, 19.30.53. For the Nazoreans and Elchasai see 19.5.4–5; 53.1.5 = I, 47, II, 70. Epiphanius' passages on the Ebionites, Nazoreans, and Elchasaites are also edited and translated in Klijn and Reinink, with discussion. The fourth sect is presumably the Sampseans. The alternative is the Nasareans, but he denies their identity with the Nazoreans (Epiphanius, 19.5.5–7; 29.6.1 = I, 47, 116).

Alchasaios, Elchasai, Elxai, Elxaios, Helkasai (the form implied in Origen), Elksesai (implied in Epiphanius' Elkesaites) *'lxs'*, and *'lḥsyḥ*, *'lḥsḥ*, or *'lḥsj* are usually assumed to be different versions of the same name;[19] and the name in its turn is generally held to be an Aramaic term meaning 'hidden power' (*ḥyl ksy*: *ḥēl kĕsē*): this is how it was explained already by Epiphanius.[20] It could also be construed as 'hidden God' (*el[āh] kĕsē*), a reading Sundermann finds marginally better,[21] or as a construct meaning 'power of the hidden one'.[22] All the sources identify Elchasai as a person, perhaps by extrapolation from the title of the book, but it is in fact quite likely that its author styled himself the hidden power as well.[23] Hippolytus (wr. *c.* 230), a contemporary of Alcibiades who reports on the heresy in Rome, says that the book had been revealed to Elchasai by an angel, yet he also says that Elchasai had received it from 'Seres of Parthia' (*apo Sērōn tēs Parthias*), which does not make sense, partly because Elchasai cannot have claimed to have the book both from an angel and from *Sērōn tēs Parthias*, and partly because it is unclear precisely how *Sērōn tēs Parthias* is to be understood. It must have been Alcibiades who claimed to have the book from 'Sēres of Parthia', and the most plausible interpretation is that he claimed to have it from a town called Sēr on the Parthian bank of the Euphrates.[24] Elchasai himself received his vision in a mountainous locality, or one in which mountains were visible, probably in northern Mesopotamia.[25]

In short, a Parthian Jew, perhaps a Christian,[26] who was active around 117 and who came to be known as Elchasai, was revered in Jewish

[19] The dissenter is Luttikhuizen, whose book is fundamental, but whose nominalism goes too far, however salutary it may have been as a pruning operation at the time: see Jones, review. Luttikhuizen usefully summarises and defends his views in his 'Baptists of Mani's Youth', published as an appendix to his *Gnostic Revisions*, and again in 'Elchasaites and their Book', but the objections stand.

[20] Epiphanius, 19.2.1 = I, 45.

[21] Sundermann, 'Iranische Lebensbeschreibungen Manis', 148f.

[22] Jones, '*Book of Elchasai*', 214.

[23] Cf. the case of Mani on pp. 299f.

[24] Hippolytus, IX, 13, 1; cf. Luttikhuizen, *Elchasai*, 60. Note that the book preached remission of sins even for those guilty of (among other things) sleeping with a sister or a daughter, called Christ 'the great king', and justified what the Muslims were to call *taqiyya* with reference to a Levite who had supposedly bowed down to the image of Artemis (i.e., Anahita) at Susa (Hippolytus, IX, 15, 1; Epiphanius, 19.1.9 = I, 45).

[25] Jones, '*Book of Elchasai*', 213, cf. 194: Elchasai calculated the giant proportions of the two angels he saw from the fact that their heads extended beyond the mountains.

[26] Some deny that there were any specifically Christian elements in his book, though it was among Jewish Christians that it found its followers (e.g. Klijn, 'Alchasaios et *CMC*', 149). If so, the Christ to whom the book referred should be understood as the Jewish messiah,

Christian baptist circles in Mesopotamia, where Mani's father had joined one such group some time before 220. From Mesopotamia the book passed to Jewish Christian circles in Palestine, where it was disseminated by unknown teachers in the 220s–40s; and from there, or by some other mode of transmission from Mesopotamia to Apamea, Alcibiades took it to Rome. In Palestine the book engendered groups that still survived in Epiphanius' time, if only in retreat in the Arabian part of the Byzantine empire. In Iraq the groups revering Elchasai survived into the fourth/tenth century. The importance of this lies in the fact that all the groups in question are said to have believed in the periodic indwelling of a celestial figure in human beings.

According to Hippolytus, Alcibiades preached that 'Christ was a man like all (others), and that this is not the first time he was born of a virgin, but that already earlier and many times again, having been begotten and being born, he appeared and came into existence, thus going through several births and transmigrating (*metensōmatoumenon*) from body to body'.[27] This is not entirely clear. If Christ was a man like all others in the sense of being conceived by normal intercourse, why does Alcibiades go on to say that it was not the first time he was born of a *virgin*? If he was a man like all others in the sense of being an ordinary human until his baptism, why does Alcibiades say that Christ had gone through several *births*? Hippolytus seems to have had trouble understanding the doctrine. This is also clear from the fact that he presents it as a Pythagorean doctrine of reincarnation, though it was actually a doctrine of periodic incarnation of the divine, as Hippolytus himself proves to know. He later reports that the Elchasaites

> do not confess that there is but one Christ, but that there is one above and that he is infused (*metangizomenon*) into many bodies frequently, and is now in Jesus. And in like manner, he was begotten of God at one time and at another time he became a spirit and at another time he was born of a virgin and at another time it was not so. And he was afterwards continually infused into bodies and was manifested [or 'he appears'] in many people at different times.[28]

What Hippolytus is describing here is belief in a pre-existing heavenly being which has been repeatedly poured into different human vessels. The divine being did not pass directly from one human being to another; rather, he was infused from above. In other words, Jesus was an ordinary

though the Jewish Christian readers of the book evidently took the reference to be to Jesus Christ.

[27] Hippolytus, IX, 14, 1.

[28] Hippolytus, X, 29, 2.

human being in the sense that he was neither born of a virgin nor born divine: nothing had separated him from other human beings until the Christ, the pre-existing being, took up abode in him, as he had in others before him. But the examples are puzzling. Christ had been begotten of God on one occasion, born of a virgin on another, and he had also been a spirit: all this is what mainstream Christians said about Jesus Christ. Hippolytus (or perhaps Alcibiades himself) seems to be casting around for examples of what Elchasai could have meant: all he could come up with was different formulations of the case of the historical Christ.

According to Epiphanius the Sampseans

> confess Christ in name, but believe that he is a creature, and that he keeps appearing every now and again. He was formed for the first time in Adam, but when he chooses he takes Adam's body off and puts it on again. He is called Christ; and the holy spirit is his sister, in female form. Each of them, Christ and the holy spirit, is ninety-six miles high and twenty-four miles wide.[29]

Here we have the same doctrine with further information. The holy spirit is envisaged as female, a point also noted by Hippolytus: according to him the Book of Elchasai claimed to have been revealed by two angels of the same enormous dimensions as in Epiphanius, of whom the male was the Son of God and the female was the holy spirit, his sister.[30] The concept of the spirit as female is well attested in early Syriac works, though she is more commonly envisaged as the mother than a sister.[31] Christ is a pre-existing being who appears every now and again, but Epiphanius further informs us that he was created, not pre-eternal. He was first 'formed' in Adam, presumably meaning that it was first in Adam that the celestial Christ took up abode, and thereafter he had 'put on' Adam's body and taken it off again. 'Putting on the body' is a common expression for incarnation in early Syriac Christianity, in which it was used along with other clothing metaphors to bring out the idea that Christ, the second Adam, had put on the body of the first Adam in order to restore 'the robe of glory' that mankind had lost when Adam sinned. The expression is attested as early as the third century, and it is the only expression for the incarnation used by Aphrahat, the 'Persian sage' (wr. 337–45).[32] Epiphanius tells us that Christ 'keeps appearing every now and again ... he takes Adam's body off and puts it on again'.

[29] Epiphanius, 53.1.8f. = II, 71.

[30] Epiphanius, 19.4.1f., 30.17.7 = I, 46, 133; Hippolytus, IX, 13, 2f.

[31] See Brock, 'The Holy Spirit as Feminine', 73, 78ff.; Zandee, 'Silvanus', 518.

[32] Cf. Brock, 'Clothing Metaphors'; Shchuryk, '*L^ebēš pagrā*' in the *Demonstrations* of Aphrahat', esp. 420ff., 437ff.

Hippolytus, who probably owed all his knowledge of the Book of Elchasai to Alcibiades,[33] does not seem to have heard the latter speak about Adam: as noted, all his examples of Christ's appearances on earth are variations on the theme of Jesus Christ. But though Epiphanius mentions both Adam and Christ, it hardly suffices to illustrate a doctrine of periodic appearances. Apparently the book spoke about numerous incarnations, but mentioned only two, Adam and Jesus Christ, or so at least in the Greek translation.

According to Epiphanius, the Jewish Christians known as Ebionites had also adopted the doctrine of periodic incarnation, in his view because they had fallen under Elchasaite influence. He did not have this from Irenaeus or Hippolytus, the two main earlier sources on the Ebionites, for all they said about them was that they lived by Mosaic law, used only the Gospel of Matthew, regarded Paul as an apostate, denied the virgin birth and Jesus' divinity, and agreed with Cerinthus that Jesus was the son of Joseph and Mary rather than of God and that he only became divine when the holy spirit came down to him in the form of a dove on his baptism.[34] This last was quite a common doctrine in early Christianity, often called adoptianist, though this is an unfortunate metaphor here: Jesus did not become divine by being raised up, but rather by the holy spirit descending on him. Epiphanius, however, repeatedly says that both the Ebionites and the Nazoreans had fallen under Elchasaite influence.[35] Originally, he says, 'Ebion' held Christ to have been born by sexual intercourse between Mary and Joseph,[36] or, as he also puts it later, they believed Jesus to have been 'begotten of the seed of man and chosen, and thus named Son of God by election, after the Christ had come to him from on high in the form of a dove'.[37] This is the 'Cerinthian' doctrine that Irenaeus and Hippolytus report for them. Later, Epiphanius says, the Ebionites came within the orbit of the Elchasaites and gave conflicting accounts of Christ,

> for some of them even say that Adam is Christ – the man who was formed first and infused with God's spirit. But others among them say that Christ is from above; that he was created before all things, that he is a spirit, higher than the angels and ruler of all; and that he is called Christ, and the world here is his portion.[38]

[33] Thus Luttikhuizen, *Elchasai*, 225.

[34] Irenaeus, I, 26, 1f., III, 21, 1, V, 1, 3; Hippolytus, VII, 33, 1f. and 34, 1f., X, 21, 2f. and 22, 1 (tr. Klijn and Reinink, 103f., 107, 111f., 121); cf. Matthew 13:16f.; similarly Mark 1:10f.

[35] In addition to the next note see Epiphanius, 19.5.4f., 30.3.1, 53.1.3 = I, 47, 121, II, 70.

[36] Epiphanius, 30.2.2 and 3.1 = I, 120, 121.

[37] Epiphanius, 30.16.3 = I, 132.

[38] Epiphanius, 30.3.3–4 = I, 121.

This is the familiar Elchasaite doctrine, and it is hard to see where the contradiction lies: here as there, Christ is a pre-existing being, a spirit or angel created before all things and in effect God's deputy, 'one of the archangels ... ruler of both angels and of all the creatures of the Almighty', as Epiphanius later says;[39] and this pre-existing being had been infused into Adam, who was thus the Christ as well. Epiphanius continues that 'he comes here when he chooses, as he came in Adam and appeared to the patriarchs with Adam's body on. And in the last days the same Christ who had come to Abraham, Isaac and Jacob, came and put on Adam's body and appeared to men, was crucified, rose and ascended.'[40] This is the same as what we are told of the Sampseans: Christ kept appearing every now and again, putting on Adam's body and taking it off again: first in Adam himself, thereafter on various occasions, and most recently in Jesus Christ. To Epiphanius it did not make sense, however: 'But again, when they choose to, they say: No, the Spirit – that is, the Christ – came to him and put on the man called Jesus. They get all giddy from supposing different things about him at different times.'[41] But it is only Epiphanius who is getting giddy; we are not being told anything new: it was by the spirit or angel who is Christ coming down and clothing himself in Jesus that the man called Jesus became the Son of God and Christ. 'They say that Christ has been created in heaven, also the holy Spirit. But Christ lodged in Adam at first, and from time to time takes Adam himself off and puts him back on – for this is what they say he did during his visit in the flesh,' as the summary says, once more stressing the connection with the Elchasaites.[42] The fact that the doctrine makes perfect sense even though Epiphanius keeps finding it incoherent suggests that he is giving a faithful account of it.

The concept of a chief angel who functioned as the intermediary between God and man was common in Judaism around the time of the rise of Christianity, and many Christians saw Christ as such an angel, while casting him as a second Adam too. There is nothing remarkable about this. What is remarkable are two claims. First, it is not typologically that Christ is Adam here: he is Adam by actually residing in Adam's body – or, differently put, Adam is Christ by virtue of Christ lodging in him. A being coming from heaven inserts or, as Hippolytus said, infuses – itself

[39] Epiphanius, 30.16.4 = I, 132.
[40] Epiphanius, 30.3.5 = I, 121.
[41] Epiphanius, 30.3.6 = I, 122.
[42] Epiphanius, Proem II, 30.2 = I, 56.

into the body of a human being, putting bodies on and taking them off as if they were clothes. It is because the doctrine was about a single being taking up abode in different bodies that Hippolytus classified it as Pythagorean.

Secondly, the divine being incarnates itself time and again. The texts present us with a chain of ultimately identical prophets, as has often been noted before;[43] all are incarnations of the same divine, or at least angelic, figure. But we never get any details about all those incarnations. The divine being 'comes here when he chooses, as he came in Adam and appeared *to* (*pros*) the patriarchs with Adam's body on. And in the last days the same Christ who had come *to* Abraham, Isaac and Jacob, came and put on Adam's body and appeared to men, was crucified, rose and ascended', as the Ebionites said:[44] the heavenly Christ is incarnate in Adam and in Jesus, the first and the last, but in between he only appears *to* the patriarchs, not in them, presumably meaning that the patriarchs saw him as an angel in human form. That Christ had appeared to the patriarchs as an angel was a common Christian belief at the time.[45] The Elchasaite doctrine is formulated in a manner that promises much more than the examples deliver. Elchasai himself must have operated with more incarnations, but the Greek version of his book only mentioned the two most relevant to him (probably regarding himself as the last). It is not until we return to Mesopotamia that we see the chain of incarnations that the formulation promises.

Before returning to Mesopotamia, however, we need to consider the Pseudo-Clementine *Homilies* (*c.* 300–20) and *Recognitions* (*c.* 350),[46] two closely related Jewish Christian works composed in Greek in Syria and universally held to incorporate Ebionite material.[47] Here the pre-existing being, the True Prophet, was made man at the beginning of things in Adam and incarnated himself again in Christ. In between, Christ 'was ever present with the pious, though secretly, through all their generations, especially with those who waited for Him, to whom he frequently appeared'.[48] Or, as we are also told, the True Prophet (here identified as

43 E.g. Reeves, *Heralds of that Good Realm*, 8; Cirillo, 'Elchasaite Christology', 49.

44 See note 40. Merkelbach, 'Täufer', 118f., wrongly has them say that Christ had appeared *in* the patriarchs.

45 See Gieschen, *Angelomorphic Christology*, 188ff.

46 Estimates of their dates vary, and Gieschen puts the *Homilies* in the late third century (*Angelomorphic Christology*, 201).

47 For an introduction that treats them as works in their own right rather than just a mine from which early Jewish Christian works can be extracted see Reed, '"Jewish Christianity"'.

48 *Recognitions* I, 52. The *Rasā'il Ikhwān al-Ṣafā'* speak about the imam in strikingly similar terms.

'the gate'), 'is present with us at all times: and if at any time it is necessary, he appears and corrects us, that He may bring to eternal life those who obey Him'.[49] The son revealed himself *to* Enoch, Noah, Abraham, Isaac and Jacob, and Moses, but he appears to them, not in them. The difference is not normally stressed, with the result that many scholars, including Wellhausen in the context of *ḥulūl*[50] and others in the context of Manichaeism,[51] hold the Pseudo-Clementines to speak of a chain of prophets all of whom are incarnations of the same divine being. But Gieschen has persuasively argued that this is wrong: there are only two incarnations, the rest are just appearances.[52]

Yet one passage in the *Homilies* says of the pre-existing being that only he has the spirit, and that he 'has changed his forms and his names from the beginning of the world, and so appeared again and again in the world until, coming upon his own times, and being anointed with mercy for the works of God, he shall enjoy rest for ever'.[53] This sounds remarkably like the Elchasaite doctrine of periodic incarnation, of which we never get more than two examples. Indeed, it sounds like the doctrine reported by al-Maqdisī, according to whom the Khurramīs believed in 'the change of the name and the body and claim that all the messengers, with their diverse laws and religions, come into possession of a single spirit'.[54] The names stand for incarnations in other works as well. Thus the *Acts of Thomas*, an early third-century work composed perhaps at Edessa, tells Jesus that 'for our sake you were named with names, and are the Son and put on the body'.[55] God gave himself names to reveal himself, as Klijn explains. According to the latter he did so by allowing his name to assume a human form, so that his name here means much the same as the spirit, wisdom, or word;[56] but though this fits Valentinian usage,[57] Klijn does not explain why the names are in the plural. The *Acts of Thomas* also describe

[49] *Recognitions*, II, 22.

[50] Wellhausen, 'Oppositionsparteien', 93.

[51] E.g. van Oort, 'Mani and the Origins of a New Church', 152; Merkelbach, above, note 44; and at first sight also Luttikhuizen, *Elchasai*, index s.v. 'reincarnation Christology'. But he is sharp-eyed: cf. his n. 39 at 65.

[52] Gieschen, *Angelopmorphic Christology*, ch. 8 (with polemics against earlier views at 208).

[53] *Homilies*, III, 20.

[54] Maqdisī, IV, 30.

[55] Klijn, *Acts of Thomas*, ch. 48.

[56] Klijn, *Acts of Thomas*, ch. 27, and pp. 79, 122: cf. 11.

[57] The Valentinians held the name of God, rather than his spirit, to have descended on Jesus on his baptism, and the probably Valentinian *Gospel of Philip* describes the son as clothing himself with the name of the father. Quispel traces the thought to Jewish Christianity (Quispel, 'Gnosticism and the New Testament', 80f., with references).

Jesus as 'manifold in forms'. Klijn takes this to refer to the metamorphoses he underwent, especially his appearance in his twin Judas Thomas, and this must in fact be how the author understood the phrase, for there is only one incarnation in this work, but whether this is how it was understood in the source text is another question.[58] 'How many likenesses did Christ take on because of you?', the *Teachings of Silvanus* asks. Here too the author must be taking the many likenesses to be the different appearances that Christ assumed during his one incarnation as Jesus,[59] but again one wonders about the meaning in the source text, for the only examples given of the many likenesses are the incarnation itself and the descent into the Underworld. A Middle Persian Manichaean text similarly says of Christ that 'he changed his form and appearance', which Klimkeit understands as a reference to Christ's ability to assume different guises, but here the alternative explanation is more plausible, as will be seen.[60] In any case, in the Pseudo-Clementines the names and the forms are envisaged as a chronological chain ('in the beginning … until'), so that here as in al-Maqdisī the reference must be to successive incarnations. It may well be that the author of the *Homilies* took the passage to mean no more than it does in the version in the *Recognitions*: Christ is present with us at all times and sometimes appears to correct us.[61] But if so, this is merely to say that, like other readers of the Book of Elchasai in the Roman empire, the authors of the Pseudo-Clementines only accepted two incarnations, Adam and Christ. They assumed the rest to refer to the repeated appearances of the angel of the Lord or Wisdom or the Spirit, though on at least one occasion their own wording goes against it.[62]

The simplest explanation for this oddity is that the idea of periodic incarnation originated outside Judaism and that the Jews who picked it up mostly interpreted it conservatively: some did envisage the saviour as descending periodically, but others limited the incarnations to two, and still others to one. The three positions are usually classified as Gnostic, Jewish Christian, and Christian respectively. As far as the Jewish Christians are concerned Epiphanius tells us that those of Palestine owed

58 Klijn, *Acts of Thomas*, 7, 237; cf. Cartlidge, 'Transfigurations of Metamorphosis Traditions', 57ff. But in his comments to ch. 153 Klijn seems to think of the forms and the names as interchangeable.

59 Zandee, 'Silvanus', 542f., with reference to Silvanus, 103.32–104.1.

60 Klimkeit, 'Gestalt, Ungestalt, Gewaltwandel', 65; cf. p. 300 and n. 126 of this chapter.

61 *Recognitions*, II, 22. This is the version Gieschen quotes and also how he interprets both versions (*Angelomorphic Christology*, 203, 209).

62 Cf. Gieschen, *Angelomorphic Christology*, 205ff.

their Christology to the Book of Elchasai, composed in Parthian Mesopotamia. All Epiphanius' information on this point is remarkably coherent, and Origen's report on the earlier spread of Elchasaite ideas in the Palestinian churches lends support to it, so we may take him at his word. It does not of course follow that the Book of Elchasai was the only source of the idea. What it does suggest is that it was in Parthian Mesopotamia that the idea of successive incarnation was at home.

The passage in the Pseudo-Clementine *Homilies* gives us a glimpse of how the foreign idea of periodic descent was read into the Jewish tradition. As noted, many early Christians held Jesus to have been an ordinary human being who became divine on his baptism, an interpretation to which even the canonical Gospel of Matthew lends itself. It says that 'when Jesus had been baptised, just as he came out of the water, suddenly the heavens were opened to him and he saw the spirit of God descending like a dove and alighting on him. And a voice from heaven said, "This is my son, the Beloved, with whom I am well pleased"' (Matthew 3:16f.). (It is thanks to God's words here that the position came to be known as adoptianist.) The Ebionites and Nazoreans read Matthew in uncanonical versions in 'Hebrew' (i.e., Aramaic),[63] and in the Ebionite gospel God added, 'This day I have begotten you,' thereby stressing that Jesus had not been the son of God before.[64] The Gospel of the Hebrews read by the Nazoreans, on the other hand, rendered the passage as follows according to Jerome: 'when the Lord came up out of the water, the whole fount of the holy spirit descended upon him and rested on him and said to him, "My Son, in all the prophets I was waiting for you that you should come and I might rest in you"'.[65] Here too Jesus becomes the son of God on his baptism, but here he is also presented as the culmination of a chain of prophets in all of whom the spirit had been. The passage weaves together three biblical verses: one predicts of the Messiah that 'the spirit of the lord shall rest on him' and identifies the spirit as 'the spirit of wisdom and understanding' (Isaiah 11:2); the second says that 'in every generation she [wisdom] passes into holy souls and makes them friends of God and prophets' (Wisdom of Solomon 7:27); and the third has wisdom herself declare that she has held sway over every people and nation, adding

[63] On the complicated question of how the evidence on the Jewish Christian gospels is to be put together see Vielhauer and Strecker in Schneemelcher, *New Testament Apocrypha*, I, 134–78; Klijn, *Jewish Christian Gospel Tradition*.

[64] Thus Epiphanius, 30.13.7 = I, 130.

[65] Jerome, *In Esaiam*, 11, 1–3, in Klijn, *Jewish Christian Gospel Tradition*, 98 (text and a less idiomatic tr.). The passage is only cited in a truncated form in Klijn and Reinink, 233.

'among all these I sought a resting place; in whose territory should I abide?' (Sirach 24:7). What Jerome's passage is saying is that the spirit of God, which is the spirit of wisdom, has passed into holy souls, making them prophets and friends of God, but that the whole fount of the holy spirit descended on Jesus when he was baptised and found its final resting-place in him.[66]

Jewish and Christian readers of the Bible did not normally understand the spirit that passed into holy souls as deifying them, merely as inspiring them to utter revelations. But the wording obviously lends itself well to an incarnationist interpretation, and it is not only in the Pseudo-Clementines that we find it. 'The Word became flesh (John 1:14), not only by becoming man at his Advent [on earth], but also at the beginning ... And again he became flesh when he acted through the prophets,' as an unknown probably second-century Christian said;[67] here the divine being is incarnate in Adam and Christ, and in the prophets in between. As the editor observes, the passage considerably weakens the usual distinction between incarnation and inspiration; one has to go to the Pseudo-Clementines for a comparable formulation.[68]

If the idea of a divine being descending to take up abode in a human being was native to Parthian Mesopotamia, there will have been Parthian Jews to whom it seemed obvious that the spirit had taken up abode in all the prophets, rendering them divine: the spirit had passed through a whole chain of such prophets in the course of its wanderings, but would dwell in full in the messiah, the manifestation of God on earth in whom it would find its final resting-place. This is the idea that the passage in the Pseudo-Clementine *Homilies* reflects when it says that the True Prophet has 'changed his forms and his names from the beginning of the world, and so appeared again and again in the world until, coming upon his own times, and being anointed with mercy for the works of God, he shall enjoy rest for ever'. He has changed his forms and names since the beginning of time, meaning that he was first incarnate in Adam, and he will enjoy eternal rest when he comes into his own time, meaning as the messiah: apparently he has not come yet. The statement seems to have been made to Jews to whom the messiah was still to come, or alternatively to Christians

[66] Cf. Gieschen, *Angelomorphic Christology*, 207.

[67] Casey, *Excerpta ex Theodoto of Clement of Alexandria*, 19, 1. The excerpts are Valentinian, added by a later author to Clement's *Stromateis*, but they contain non-Valentinian comments, of which this is one. The editor takes their author to be Clement himself (cf. 9f.).

[68] Casey, *Excerpta ex Theodoto of Clement of Alexandria*, 29, 114.

to whom Jesus was not the last. If so, it must have originated outside the *Homilies* and its presumed source, the hypothetical *Kērygmata Petrou* (tentatively dated 180–220).[69] It probably came from the Book of Elchasai, but it is not the only example of Mesopotamian links in the *Homilies*, so other sources cannot be ruled out.[70]

MESOPOTAMIAN BAPTISTS AND OTHERS

We may now return to Mesopotamia. Most early converts to Christianity in Mesopotamia seem to have been Jews (by descent or conversion) who did not initially abjure their Jewish identity or beliefs and who imparted a strong Jewish streak to early Syriac Christianity.[71] All the baptist sects of southern Iraq appear to have been Jewish by origin. They included the Mandaeans, whose history is disputed but who must have been present in some form in Iraq by the later second century.[72] Among their earliest self-designations we find the name Nazoreans (*n'ṣwr'yy'*), which is still in use today – though only of their priests and initiates, as distinct from the laity.[73] The idea of a divine being seeking a final resting-place appears in their literature too: 'I wandered through generations and the worlds, through generations and worlds I wandered, until I came to the gate of Jerusalem,' the divine saviour Anōsh Uthra says in the Book of John.[74] All the Mandaean apostles/messengers are heavenly beings sent to enable the souls of humans to return to the world of light, and they too are ever-present with the believers.[75]

69 Discussed and reconstructed by Strecker in Schneemelcher, *New Testament Apocrypha*, II, 488–91, 531–41.

70 Compare their version of the story of the fallen angels (see Crone, 'Pre-existence in Iran') and the oddly Zoroastrian-sounding homily XX, 2 and 5, where God has appointed two kings – or, as restated in 5, begotten them. When the opponent objects that God cannot beget what is bad Peter affirms that 'through his inborn spirit He becomes ... whatever body He likes', later repeating that 'God is completely able to convert Himself into whatever He wishes' (section 6). Apparently both Christ and the devil (a former angel) are envisaged as begotten versions of the divine spirit here, much as both Ohrmazd and Ahriman are sons of Zurvān in the Zurvanite myth.

71 See Brock, 'Jewish Traditions'; ter Haar Romeny, 'Development of Judaism and Christianity in Syria' (with arguments against Drijvers, the main dissenter).

72 Cf. *EIr.*, s.v. 'Mandaeans'.

73 Rudolph, *Gnosis*, 343.

74 Lidzbarski, *Johannesbuch*, 274 = 243; cited in Fossum, 'Apostle Concept', 155.

75 Rudolph, *Gnosis*, 358f. Colpe denies that the apostle is an incarnation of a heavenly hypostasis in the Mandaean hymns that form the basis of the Manichaean Thomas psalms and which must therefore date back to the third century, the period of relevance here: the

Also present in Mesopotamia were baptists of the type reflected in the writings labelled 'Sethian' by modern scholars.[76] Known almost entirely from the Graeco-Roman side of the border, where their writings have been recovered at Nag Hammadi, these baptists saw themselves as a race apart, born of the divine seed of Seth (whereas Cain and Abel were the offspring of Eve and the devil), and envisaged the redeemer as a heavenly figure whom they called 'the Great Seth' or 'the Illuminator' (*phōstēr*) and who appeared repeatedly on earth, 'putting on' Jesus to save the elect.[77] In the *Apocalypse of Adam* 'a heavenly Redeemer enters history by means of a docetic union with an historical person', as Shellrude puts it,[78] though the historical figures are not actually named. The union is docetic only in the sense that there was no mixture of the divine and the human natures, not in the sense that the body is illusory: the opponents would 'punish the flesh of the man upon whom the holy spirit came', but the spirit itself would leave,[79] much as the Muslimiyya envisaged Abū Muslim to have left his body when he was killed.[80] By the time of Theodore Bar Koni it was the 'Awdians who read the *Apocryphon of John* and other Sethian works in Mesopotamia,[81] though for all we know others may have done so as well.

Another baptist sect was the community in which Mani grew up. Its members revered Elchasai as their highest authority. Whereas the Sethians of the Nag Hammadi writings come across as Platonised, the Elchasaites of Iraq appear to have been Iranianised. According to Ibn al-Nadīm, they 'agreed with Mani' as regards the two principles, or in other words they operated with a dualist cosmology that Mani retained; they also identified light and darkness as male and female respectively, correlating them with different plants.[82] More importantly, the *CMC* tells us that they had a

apostle in these hymns is just an inspired saviour 'like any Oriental mahdi' (Colpe, 'Thomaspsalmen', 87). But the material he cites does not support him, and he adduces Elchasai and the Pseudo-Clementine chain of prophets as relevant without apparent awareness that incarnation of a pre-existing being figures there as well.

[76] See Schenke, 'Gnostic Sethianism'. For the Jewish-Iranian background of the *Apocalypse of Adam* see Böhlig, 'Adamapokalypse', though this article is open to criticism on the Iranian side.

[77] Pearson, 'Figure of Seth', 477 (with reference to the *Gospel of the Egyptians*); Reeves, 'Prophecy of Zardūšt', 168f. (with reference to the *Apocalypse of Adam*).

[78] Shellrude, 'Apocalypse of Adam', 82.

[79] See *Apocalypse of Adam*, 77 in the Robinson edn (in section 6 of the Charlesworth edn).

[80] Cf. *SN*, ch. 45:1 (280 = 212); Mīrkhwānd, V, 2559.

[81] Cf. Puech, 'Fragments retrouvés', on their *Apocalypse of the Strangers*, with a tentative identification of their *Apocalypse of John* with the Coptic *Apocryphon of John* at 951n. The identification is accepted in the introduction to the *Apocryphon* in Robinson, *Nag Hammadi Library*, 104.

[82] Ibn al-Nadīm, 404 = II, 811.

prophecy from their forefathers concerning 'the rest (*anapausis*) of the garment' and that it included a prediction of the appearance of a seducer: they thought that Mani might be this seducer.[83] Merkelbach takes the 'rest of the garment' to refer to the end of the process of human reincarnation,[84] but the editors of the *CMC* are undoubtedly right to understand it as a reference to the last incarnation of the true prophet; *anapausis* is also the word used in the Pseudo-Clementine passage on the True Prophet changing forms and names until he shall enjoy rest for ever.[85] Apparently the Elchasaites among whom Mani grew up understood all the manifestations as divine beings 'clothed' in a human body, not just the first and the last. Mani himself certainly did, as will be seen.

Judging by the *Paraphrase of Shem* there were also sects opposed to baptism in Mesopotamia. We encountered this *Paraphrase*, which is extant only in Coptic, in Chapter 10, where it was observed that it has affinities with the 'Paraphrase of Seth' summarised by Hippolytus.[86] The title of the second work notwithstanding, neither work is classified as 'Sethian' in the technical sense today. Both operate with dualism and a third, intermediary principle, occasionally displaying affinities with the Mandaeans, Kanthaeans, and Mesopotamian Marcionites, all baptists of diverse stripes, but the *Paraphrase of Shem* is hostile to baptism.[87] This work is of interest here in that it presents the saviour as putting on different garments in the course of his mission, to assume his own unequalled garment when he has completed the times designated for him on earth.[88] When the saviour somewhat obscurely says that 'the repose is the mind and my garment',[89] and that he will cease to be on earth 'and withdraw up to my rest',[90] one takes the reference to be to what Mani's Elchasaites

[83] *CMC*, 86f.

[84] Merkelbach, 'Täufer', 114. In another context it might have referred to the 'rest of the redemption', i.e., release from reincarnation (M 5, cited in Klimkeit, 'Gestalt, Ungestalt, Gewaltwandel', 61), but it is hard to see how it could stand for the resurrection, as proposed by Heinrichs, 'Mani and the Babylonian Baptists', 55.

[85] See n. 2 to the passage; Koenen, 'Manichaean Apocalypticism', 287; Cirillo, 'Elchasaite Christology', 50f.

[86] See Chapter 10, pp. 200f.

[87] *Paraphrase of Shem* 36.25–38.28. Roberge assumes the polemics to be directed against the Great Church (introd. to *Paraphrase of Shem*, 341), but this was not necessarily the case before the treatise went into Greek and Coptic: cf. Koenen, 'From Baptism to the Gnosis of Manichaeism', 745ff.

[88] *Paraphrase of Shem*, 38.29–39.2; cf. Stahl, 'Derdekeas in the *Paraphrase of Shem*', 579.

[89] *Paraphrase of Shem*, 39.10f. The French version has 'L'intellect, c'est mon repos, avec mon vêtement', which is hardly less obscure.

[90] *Paraphrase of Shem*, 43.28–31.

called 'the rest of the garment', that is the end of the divine incarnations. The garments that the saviour has put on in the course of his mission in this *Paraphrase* will rest as well.[91]

Finally, a Mesopotamian Christian credited Zoroaster with a prediction of the coming of Christ. According to this prophecy, Zoroaster told his disciples Gūštasp, Sasan, and Mahman that a 'great king' would come, using the title carried by Christ in the Book of Elchasai, by the redeemer in the Oracles of Hystaspes, and by the eschatological ruler in Manichaean visions of the end.[92] This king would be born of a virgin and put to death on a tree, and later he would return with an army of light, riding on the bright clouds, for he was 'the child conceived by the word which established the natural order'. Asked by Gūštasp whether he would be greater than Zoroaster himself, Zoroaster replied: 'He shall arise from my lineage and family. I am he, and he is me; he is in me, and I in him.'[93] Whoever put this prophecy into circulation wanted Zoroaster to endorse his conversion to Christianity, it would seem, but one could surely achieve this result without going so far as to identify them. But identified they are. 'I and he are one,' Zoroaster later repeats. The author moved in circles in which historical prophets were simply different embodiments of the same divine figure. They are ultimately identical in Manichaeism too.

THE MANICHAEANS

Mani was initiated into the Elchasaite sect at the age of four, and gradually withdrew from it after receiving his decisive revelation at the age of twenty-four.[94] The divine realm he constructed for himself is somewhat complicated. God, the supreme being known as the Father of Greatness, presided over the realm of light, and from him came a series of emanations. One of these emanations was called the Third Messenger. From the Third Messenger emanated Jesus the Splendour, and from Jesus the Splendour came the Light-Nous. This Light-Nous is the 'father of all the apostles';[95] and from it emanated the Apostle of Light, who 'shall on occasion come and assume the church of the flesh, of humanity' or, as Merkelbach

91 *Paraphrase of Shem*, 39.17ff.

92 Reeves, 'Prophecy of Zardūšt', 172f.; Koenen, 'Manichaean Apocalypticism', 300, 313f.

93 Reeves, 'Prophecy of Zardūšt', 170f., citing Theodore Bar Koni and others; cf. Witakowski, 'The Magi in Syriac Tradition'.

94 For a short and clear account of Mani's life see Gardner and Lieu, *Manichaean Texts*; 3ff.; for more information see Sundermann, 'Mani'.

95 *Kephalaia*, 35.23f. (the Light Mind in Gardner's translation).

translates, 'he comes from time to time and clothes himself in the flesh of mankind in the church'.[96] This is the conception reported for the Book of Elchasai: a pre-existing divine being – here an emanation rather than a hypostasis of the highest God – periodically descends to this world, putting on a body. Like the Sethians the Manichaeans sometimes called this divine being 'the Illuminator' (*phōstēr*).[97]

As Mani saw it, all the founders of churches were such divine beings in bodily clothing. Thus an anti-Manichaean text by the name of *Seven Chapters*, probably by Zacharias of Mitylene (d. after 536), anathematises Mani and his teachers, Scythianus and Bouddas and Zarades (Zoroaster), 'who appeared before him in the likeness of a man, but without a body, among the Indians and the Persians'.[98] Scythianus has been tentatively explained as Śakyamuni, i.e., the Buddha,[99] which makes sense given that there are three names, but only two peoples, Indians and Persians. 'In the likeness of a man (*en homoiōsei*)' suggests that the Buddha and Zoroaster had simply assumed the guise of men, or in other words that they came in phantom bodies. That idea was certainly present among the Manichaeans. Augustine, for example, reports them as holding that Jesus did not come in real flesh, merely in a shape that resembled it;[100] the *Kephalaia* seemingly agrees when it says that Jesus Christ 'came without a body' and 'received a servant's form (*morphē*), an appearance (*skhēma*) as of men';[101] and the *Seven Chapters* anathematises those who say that Jesus 'was manifested to the world in appearance (only) and without a body in the likeness of a man'.[102] But though *skhēma* could mean appearance as opposed to reality, it did not have to, and van Lindt holds that it was something material that Jesus put on: it was the opposite of reality only in the sense that light is true reality.[103] In line with this the *Seven Chapters* says that when 'Jesus the

96 *Kephalaia* 36.3–5; Merkelbach, 'Täufer', 118; cf. also Koenen, 'Augustine and Manichaeism', 165 (where he invests himself in a series of bodies identified as churches). Cirillo, 'Elchasaite Christology', 51, adds *Keph.* 89.22f., on the Light-Nous assuming or 'putting on' the saints as a garment. But this passage is about the Light-Nous passing into all believers and making them new men (on which see Wiessner, 'Offenbarung im Manichäismus', 154).

97 Reeves, 'Prophecy of Zardūšt', 169.

98 Lieu, 'Formula', 236.

99 Lieu, 'Formula', citing O. Klíma, *Manis Zeit und Leben*, Prague 1962, 226f.

100 Klimkeit, 'Gestalt, Ungestalt, Gewaltwandel', 64, citing Augustine, *De Haeresibus*, c. 46; similarly *Acta Archelai*, VIII, 4.

101 *Kephalaia*, 12.24

102 Lieu, 'Formula', 242.

103 van Lindt, 'Remarks on the Use of *Skhēma*', 96, 101.

Begotten' – i.e., the son of Mary – was baptised, 'it was another one who came out of the water':[104] one takes this to mean that the divine being moved into the body of the human Jesus, without becoming identical with him. The degree to which the body he had moved into was conceived as real or illusory seems to depend on the context. The *Kephalaia* continues its passage on Jesus by describing the crucifixion without denying its reality: the Jews took hold of the son of God, they crucified him with some robbers, placed him in the grave, and after three days he rose from the dead and breathed his holy spirit into his disciples.[105] Here the pathos of Jesus' suffering is being stressed, and the body that suffered was illusory only in the sense of not his (not in the sense of being a phantom rather than fleshy); the divine being had left it when it was nailed on the cross;[106] Christ – i.e., the divine being – stood by and laughed during the crucifixion.[107] All that remained of the divine being after the crucifixion was the *skhēma*, the material shape, as the Coptic Psalm-book says.[108]

According to the *Seven Chapters* Scythianus, Bouddas, and Zarades also come without a body, as we have seen.[109] It does not say that Mani himself came without a body, but then Mani, the son of Pattikos, was born in a body like other human beings.[110] This body was distinct from Mani in the sense of the Apostle, however. The *CMC* speaks of it as something separate from him, both in the title ('Concerning the Origin of his Body') and in phrases such as 'when my body was young' or 'before I clothed myself in this instrument and began my wandering in this disgusting flesh'.[111] The message is that his body was simply a house that the holy spirit would occupy one day: Mani's father had built the house and somebody else moved into it, as Mani explained (with further similes).[112]

Mani's transformation into an Apostle of Light was due to his 'twin' or alter ego (*syzygos*), the holy spirit that Jesus had promised to send to his disciples, calling it the Paraclete (John 14:16). Mani had numerous visions even as a child, but the transformative encounter with the twin occurred

104 Lieu, 'Formula', 244.
105 *Kephalaia*, 13.1–19.
106 Pedersen, 'Early Manichaean Christology', 171, citing Allberry, *A Manichaean Psalm-book*, 196.9.20.28.
107 Lieu, 'Formula', 244.
108 van Lindt, 'Remarks on the Use of *Skhēma*', 101.
109 Lieu, 'Formula', 237: cf. 228.
110 *CMC*, 21f.; cf. Koenen, 'How Dualistic', 19f. He is also said to have been born of God (*CMC*, 66, cf. 22), but clearly in the sense applicable to all human beings.
111 *CMC*, 11, 22; cf. also Koenen, 'How Dualistic', 20; Bianchi, 'Dualisme de Mani', 14.
112 *CMC*, 115; cf. Koenen, 'How Dualistic', 21.

when he was twenty-four, in the year in which Ardashir conquered Hatra and Shapur was crowned (i.e. 240) according to the *CMC*.[113] It was after this encounter that he began to withdraw from the community in which he had grown up, to start his mission as an apostle. In that encounter the Paraclete came down to him and revealed all the mysteries to him. 'This is how everything that has happened and that will happen was unveiled to me by the Paraclete', Mani says in the *Kephalaia*, mentioning 'everything the eye shall see, and the ear hear, and the thought think', and more lost in a lacuna. 'I have understood by him everything. I have seen the totality through him. I have become *a single body with a single spirit*.'[114] He had become one with the spirit. It was not Mani who had come without a body, but rather the Paraclete that had done so: it had clothed itself in Mani's material shape.

The Paraclete continued to appear to Mani as a separate being thereafter, part of the function of an apostle's heavenly twin being to protect him.[115] But henceforth Mani was himself the Paraclete. According to al-Bīrūnī, citing his *Living Gospel*, he adopted the designation himself.[116] In the *Kephalaia* his followers testify that 'we have also believed that you are the Paraclete, this one from the Father, the unveiler of all these hidden things',[117] and he is also identified as the holy spirit, or the spirit of the truth, and as a god, in other western Manichaean works, sometimes forming the third member of the Trinity.[118] He is freely addressed as god Mani the Lord (*bg ... xwd'y*), God Christ, Lord Maitreya (the future Buddha, here seen as having come), and Jesus and the Maiden of Light in eastern Manichaean texts.[119] It was only when he died that he could shed his body and truly become one with his heavenly twin: he could now be invoked as the one 'who assumed worldly form because of [our] need'.[120] But from the moment of his revelation he had become identical with the

[113] *CMC*, 18; *Kephalaia*, 14.31–15.1. Another tradition places it in the year of Ardashir's coronation, when he was twelve: see Sundermann, 'Mani's Revelations'.

[114] *Kephalaia* 15.19–24.

[115] *Kephalaia*, 36.6ff.; cf. CMC, 125f., where it rescues Mani from a sandstorm, transporting him through the air for a heavenly vision.

[116] Bīrūnī, *Āthār*, 207.

[117] *Kephalaia*, 16.29–31.

[118] Gardner and Lieu, *Manichaean Texts*, 96f., 131n., 136, 179; de Blois, 'Manes' "Twin"', 15.

[119] Sundermann, 'Iranische Lebensbeschreibungen Manis', 131; Klimkeit, *Gnosis on the Silk Road*, 134 (=Henning, 'Bet- und Beichtbuch', 19f), 161–3; Sundermann, 'Der Paraklet in der ostmanichäischen Überlieferung'.

[120] Klimkeit, 'Gestalt, Ungestalt, Gewaltwandel', 67.

Paraclete who enlightened him. The author of the Book of Elchasai may similarly have called himself the 'Hidden Power', seeing himself as identical with it: the pre-existing Christ who was the hidden power had revealed things to him by taking up abode in him, transforming him into a divine being. Zoroaster too was a being 'whom he [Mani] alleges to be God'.[121] All the apostles are identified as gods (*b''n*) in a Middle Persian hymn.[122]

The Church Fathers angrily asked whether Mani *was* the Paraclete, implying that he was divine, or whether he only claimed that the Paraclete was *in* him, in the sense of inspiring him and speaking through his mouth.[123] But the question did not make sense from Mani's point of view: he was the Paraclete precisely because the Paraclete dwelt in him: what the Church Fathers saw as alternatives were two sides of the same coin to him. To the Christians this amounted to a claim that he was God, with a capital G. But the Manichaeans did not think in terms of a stark contrast between God and everything else after the fashion of the Christians – let alone the Muslims. God had many emanations, who had emanations in their turn, and there were numerous gradations in the world of mixture in this world as well. All those whose imprisoned light had been awakened and perfected had become divine to some extent: 'the divinity [i.e., the Light-Nous] that is planted in them came to them from the heights and dwelt in them', as the *Kephalaia* says of the Elect.[124]

Unlike the celestial beings of the Elchasaites, those of Mani were different beings even before they took up abode in human bodies, but ultimately they were all the same Apostle of Light. The seven Buddhas, the larger number of *aurentes* (*arhat*s), and the twenty-four *kebulloi* (on whom more below) who had appeared in India were all 'a single spirit', according to the Dublin *Kephalaia*.[125] 'The wise Buddhas [i.e., Apostles of Light] all ... appear, changing their name and their form, in order to liberate souls', as a Turkish text says, sounding remarkably like the Pseudo-Clementine *Homilies*.[126] The *Seven Chapters* anathemise 'those who say

[121] Lieu, 'Formula', 236.

[122] De Blois, 'Manes' "Twin"', 10.

[123] van Oort, 'Mani and the Origins of a New Church', 153; Koenen, 'Augustine and Manichaeism', 175 (with a lucid account of the relationship between Mani and his Twin at 173f.).

[124] *Kephalaia* 220.1–3; cf. Wiessner, 'Offenbarung im Manichäismus', 157.

[125] Cited in Gardner, 'Some Comments', 132; cf. p. 306 of this chapter.

[126] Klimkeit, 'Gestalt, Ungestalt, Gewaltwandel', 65, where it is taken to refer to metamorphoses rather than successive incarnations.

that Zarades and [Bouddhas and] Christ and Manichaeus and the sun are the same'.[127]

In the last statement the sun seems to be included to make up a list of five (Manichaeans liked to think in terms of pentads), but the Manichaeans did worship the sun. The *Seven Chapters* claims that Mani called Zoroaster the sun and also anathemises those who say that Jesus is the sun and who pray to it or to the moon or to the stars.[128] According to Alexander of Lycopolis, the Manichaeans honoured the sun and the moon above all else as avenues to God, not as gods themselves.[129] Mani himself said that they prostrated to the sun and moon because they formed their avenue to the world of (true) existence: it was via the sun and moon that the liberated soul ascended to heaven.[130]

SYRIAN CHRISTIANS

The conception of a divine being who puts on a body to use it as his instrument without becoming identical with it is also found in early Syriac Christianity. In fact there are two metaphors involving clothing. One appears in the New Testament, in which Paul, a Jew from Tarsus, says that the Christian convert 'puts on Christ' at baptism (Romans 13:14; Galatians 3:27). Here it is the human who puts on the divine being rather than the other way round, and this imagery continued in Syriac Christianity. East Syrian Christians sometimes equated it with putting on the garments of light in which they would be dressed in the next world: whoever puts on Christ reserves a place among the blessed in the next world, or even in some sense anticipates it. These garments of light seem to have roots going all the way back into ancient Near Eastern mythology, more precisely in the myth of Inanna/Ishtar's descent to the underworld, and they were popular among Zoroastrians as well.[131] What matters here, however, is the opposite idea of Christ himself putting on a human body – or putting on Adam, as it was also formulated.[132] According to Ephrem, God knew that Adam had desired to become a god, so he sent his son, who 'put Adam on', to give Adam his desire; the Firstborn wrapped

127 Lieu, 'Formula', 246.
128 Lieu, 'Formula', 236, 244.
129 Alexander of Lycopolis, v, in Gardner and Lieu, *Manichaean Texts*, 181.
130 Mani in Bīrūnī, *Hind*, 36, 479/23f., 283f. = I, 48, II, 169; cf. *CMC*, 128, where Mani teaches prostration to the lights of the heaven; see also Chapter 15.
131 Brock, 'Clothing Metaphors', 14; 13:45; Zādspram 35:60.
132 Cf. above, n. 32.

himself in a body, as Ephrem said, 'as a veil, to hide his glory' or, as a synod in 680 put it, 'to hide thereby the radiance of his eternal divinity'.[133] Here we have the idea of the transcendent God utterly beyond human reach manifesting himself in a lesser, human form in order to make himself accessible to mankind and save it – an idea that runs through Iranian heresy from the Manichaeans to the Bābīs. The body veils the deity, yet it is also what allows him to be seen; and even in a body he might need a further veil, as shown by the veiled Christ and al-Muqannaʿ. Philoxenus of Mabbog (wr. c. 505) complained of those who inclined to the position of Nestorius, 'who cast a body on to the Word as one does a garment on to an ordinary body, or as purple is put on the emperors'.[134] Cassian (d. 435) disliked that Nestorius saw Christ as a mere 'God-receiver' (*theodochus*);[135] this, he argued, showed that Nestorius had fundamentally confused the status of Christ with that of the saints, in whom God indwelt, for 'God was in the patriarchs and spoke through the prophets'.[136] To Cassian indwelling clearly meant something falling short of incarnation, but whatever Nestorius might have replied to this, an Elchasaite or Khurramī would have been puzzled by it: to them Christ was God precisely because God dwelt in him: if Cassian held God to have been in the patriarchs and prophets, how could he *not* see them as divine?

From the point of view of orthodoxy as defined by the Greeks the danger of the East Syrian conception of the incarnation lay in the suggestion that there was no union of the divine and human natures – or, differently put, that the incarnation was docetic. The Elchasaites, Manichaeans, Mandaeans, Khurramīs, East Syrian Christians, and *zanādiqa 'l-naṣāra* did not usually envisage the incarnation as docetic in the sense that the body was unreal (though the idea was not unknown), but rather in the sense that the divine being remained separate from its human lodging. It was an old and venerable position, called pneumatic Christology (or spirit Christology) in connection with the early church and dubbed 'naïve doceticism' by von Harnack;[137] and it would seem to

133 Brock, 'Clothing Metaphors', 20, 26.

134 Philoxenus, cited in Brock, 'Clothing Metaphors', 17, 18.

135 Casiday, 'Deification', 995, citing Cassian, *Incarn.* vii, 8, 1; cf. Nestorius, *Sermons*, IX, X (40, 52).

136 Casiday, 'Deification', 995, citing Cassian, *Incarn.* v, 3, 1.

137 Von Harnack, *History of Dogma*, I, 195f. I owe both the information and the reference to Lance Jenott, who comments that if a docetic thought lies in the assertion that the spiritual Christ only assumed the flesh, however real, then the Christologies of the Epistle of Barnabas, Shepherd of Hermas, Tertullian, Hippolytus, and others must also be deemed docetic. Cf. also Rudolph, *Gnosis*, 157ff., in effect adding Paul and the Gospel of John.

be the conception that was native to the Aramaic-speaking region. (Its origin will be taken up in the next chapter.) The many differences between the above groups notwithstanding, they all held that God or his spirit, wisdom, principal angel, or emanation put on a human body for purposes of revealing himself to mankind, taking up abode in an adult human being with an identity of its own (though the divine being could also appear in phantom bodies). The human being in question was deified and all humans were potentially saved by this union, but however much the divinity may have blended with the human body while it was in it, it remained separate from it and left it when it died. The East Syrian Christians eventually came to formulate themselves in Greek theological terms, but their early formulations conform to this description, and their preference, once they had to negotiate those perilous Greek formulations, for Antiochene Christology with its stress on the duality in Christ is hardly accidental. To a historian, as opposed to a theologian, the most conspicuous difference between Ephrem's conception of the incarnation and that of the other groups (unspeakable heretics in his view) is that Ephrem's God only incarnated himself once.

To return to the question with which this chapter started, as far as the concept of periodic incarnation of the divine is concerned, we see that it was indeed present on the Iranian side of the border before Zardūsht of Fasā. The earliest attestation takes us back to 116–17, and the later material shows the conception to have been both deeply rooted and widespread.

REINCARNATION

The Syrian Neoplatonist philosopher Porphyry (d. c. 305) wrote a treatise on abstention from meat in which he quotes a certain Pallas, who probably wrote under or after Hadrian (d. 138). Correcting what to him was a mistaken explanation of the Mithraic habit of giving animal names to initiates, Pallas declared that in fact it was an allegory for human souls, which they (the Magi) held to 'put on all kinds of bodies'. Porphyry also quotes a certain Euboulos, who may have flourished as early as the first century or as late as the mid-third, and who wrote a book on Mithras in which he claimed that the Magi practised various degrees of vegetarianism because 'it is the belief of them all that metempsychosis is of the first importance'.[138] In another work Porphyry claims that 'the Persians call

[138] Porphyry, *On Abstinence*, IV, 16, 2–4; cf. Turcan, *Mithras Platonicus*, 27ff., 34.

the place a cave where they introduce an initiate to the mysteries, revealing to him the path by which the souls descend and go back again', again citing Euboulos as an authority on Mithraism.[139] Two Greek authors writing before Zardūsht of Fasā thus credited the Persians, more precisely the Magi, with belief in reincarnation and vegetarianism. Since neither doctrine is endorsed in the Pahlavi books both authors have been charged with simply imputing Platonic and Pythagorean ideas to the Magi, inspired by the tradition that Pythagoras had learnt from them.[140] But the Pahlavi books only preserve a narrow range of the doctrines current in pre-Islamic Iran. Both doctrines were in fact current in Iran, and one reason why the Magi were often credited with Platonic and Pythagorean ideas (and vice versa) could be that there was some similarity between the systems in question which lent plausibility to the claims.

It would have helped to know who the Magi in question were. They will not have been those of Iran, but the term is not normally used for priests of Mithraic cults in the Roman empire. The Magi could have been those of Anatolia. There was a large Iranian population in Anatolia dating back to the time of the Achaemenids, who controlled this region between 546 and the 330s BC. The Iranian presence can be followed in western Anatolia up to the mid-third century AD, and in eastern Anatolia to the fourth century, and perhaps beyond.[141] It was from these Iranians that the Greeks learnt about Zoroastrianism before Alexander's conquests, and it stands to reason that they should have used them as sources for later information too, especially in connection with Mithraism, a cult said by Plutarch to have originated in Anatolia.[142] The Anatolian Magi, called Maguseans in Christian writings, represent a different tradition from that which came to be canonised in the Pahlavi books, and information relating to them cannot be dismissed as Greek interpretation or embroidery merely because the Pahlavi books fail to confirm it.

[139] Porphyry, *Cave of the Nymphs*, 6.

[140] Cf. Clark's commentary in Porphyry, *On Abstinence*, 188f.; Turcan, *Mithras Platonicus*, 30f.

[141] See Boyce and Grenet, *History of Zoroastrianism*, chs. 8–10. They could be among the Zoroastrians in Byzantium whose fire cult a Sasanian embassy accused Leo I of obstructing in 464, and those for whom Justinian promised to build fire-temples in his treaty with Khusraw I (p. 257), but in both cases the reference could also be to Zoroastrians in Armenia (cf. Russell, *Zoroastrianism in Armenia*, 140).

[142] For a survey of the question how much Mithraism owes to Zoroastrianism, see Boyce and Grenet, *History of Zoroastrianism*, 468–90, with Plutarch, *Pompey*, 24f., at p. 469. For the Anatolian ascription versus the alternative theory tracing the cult to slaves and freedmen in Rome (or Ostia) see Gordon, 'Who worshipped Mithras?', esp. 462ff., 467f.

Basil the Great, bishop of Caesarea in Cappadocia (d. 379), tells us that the Magusean nation 'is widely scattered among us throughout almost the whole country, colonists having long ago been introduced to our country from Babylon'. They stuck to themselves and were impervious to reason, he said, meaning that it was impossible to convert them.[143] The country to which Basil refers is Cappadocia, and in this connection it is interesting that Basil's younger brother, Gregory (d. after 394), who was bishop of Nyssa in Cappadocia, pays considerable attention to the doctrine of reincarnation. In one work he mentions that those 'outside our philosophy' – i.e., non-Christians – held that the soul 'puts on different bodies and keeps passing over into what pleases it, becoming either a winged or an aquatic or a terrestrial animal after the human; or again from these bodies it returns to human nature. Others, he said, extend this nonsense even to the shrubbery.' They held that souls were living without bodies in a society of their own, revolving with the rotation of the universe, and that those guilty of evil there lost their wings or grew heavy so that they were unable to keep up with the rotations and fell to the earth, where they would enter successively into human, animal, vegetative, and insensate bodies and return via the same steps; and they held one of their sages to have been born as a man, a woman, a bird, a bush, and an aquatic creature.[144] The beliefs described are Platonic, and the sage is Empedocles (d. *c.* 432 BC), who claimed to have been born as a boy, a bush, a bird, and a dumb sea fish.[145] In another work Gregory says of Origen's belief in pre-existence that it is too closely connected for comfort with the pagan doctrine of successive embodiment.[146] He may be unfair to Origen, but the question had come up in the churches, and those of his parishioners who liked the idea of pre-existence are likely to have combined it with reincarnation. The two ideas tend to go together, and there were certainly Christians after Origen who combined them.[147] None of this proves that the Maguseans believed in reincarnation, but it does at least suggest that the doctrine was prominent in their home province. Long settled in a Greek culture area,

[143] Basil of Caesarea, letter 258 in Boyce and Grenet, *History of Zoroastrianism*, 277.

[144] Gregory, *On the Soul*, 89, 92 (ch. 8). The speaker is his sister Macrina.

[145] Cf. Plato, *Phaedo*, 246a–249c; Plato, *Republic*, 614bff. (book 10, myth of Er); Empedocles, fr. 117.

[146] Gregory, 'On the Making of Man', 28:1–3; cf. Origen, *On First Principles*, I, 8 (tr. 72), where Koetschau 'restored' the lost Greek text by inserting a passage made up of Gregory's two statements, though the first is not about Christians (frag. 17a).

[147] See Chapter 19, p. 466.

they would certainly have formulated the doctrine in the prestigious terms of Platonist philosophy if they subscribed to it.

A century after Pallas reincarnation reappears as a fundamental doctrine in Manichaeism. In their migrations the souls would array themselves in every form, take the shape of any animal, and be cast in the mould of every figure, as Mani said in his *Book of Mysteries*.[148] He is not likely to owe this doctrine to either Pythagoras or Plato, though he does share with Plato the view that the number of souls liable to embodiment is fixed (because the number of light particles lost in matter was determinate).[149]

Mani is commonly assumed to have picked up the idea of reincarnation in India, a view advanced already by al-Bīrūnī, and perhaps also hinted at by Ephrem.[150] The Indian influence has usually been envisaged as Buddhist, for the obvious reason that Buddhism was present in eastern Iran in Mani's time and that he repeatedly identified the Buddha as one of his predecessors.[151] More recently (or rather once again), the possibility of Jain influence has also been aired,[152] with reference to the fact that *karma* is viewed as actual 'stuff' in both systems and that *kebellos* and the twenty-four *kebulloi* seem to transliterate the Jain term *kevala*, 'unsurpassed, perfect', or *kevalajñānin*, 'endowed with complete knowledge'.[153] Manichaeism and Jainism are indeed fundamentally alike. Both postulate that human beings are souls enmeshed in matter from which they must seek to escape by extreme asceticism and non-violence; both envisage everything, even the inorganic parts of the world, as full of life, the feature variously dubbed animist or panpsychist; both explain the human condition in physiological rather than psychological terms; and both see the unredeemed as doomed to reincarnation in any living form (even inorganic in the case of the Jains). In both cases the adherents of these ideas were also divided into a spiritual elite (monks, the elect) and laymen.[154]

148 Bīrūnī, *Hind*, 41/27 = I, 54. According to Augustine reincarnation was only into animals of a certain size (e.g. foxes, but not weasels); cf. Jackson, 'Metempsychosis in Manichaeism', 259, citing *C. Adimantum*, 12.2.

149 Cf. Plato, *Timaeus*, 41d; Plato, *Republic*, 811a; both noted by Casadio, 'Manichaean Metempsychosis', 109.

150 Bīrūnī, *Hind*, 41/27 = I, 54; cf. Ephrem's statement that 'the lie of the Hindus came to hold sway over Mani, who introduced two powers fighting each other' (cited in Sundermann, 'Mani, India', 11).

151 Cf. Bryder, 'Buddhist Elements in Manichaeism'; Bryder, 'Manichaeism, iii. Buddhist Elements', in *EIr*. It is Hindu sources that are adduced in Heinrichs, 'Thou Shalt not Kill a Tree', 99f.

152 The possibility was first raised by Baur in 1831 (see Jones, '*Book of Elchasai*', 187, n. 41).

153 Gardner, 'Some Comments'; Deeg and Gardner, 'Indian Influence'.

154 See Basham, 'Jainism'; Chapple, *Nonviolence to Animals*, 11.

Mani did travel to India, and he could have encountered Jains in north-west India (the closest securely attested Jain centre in Mani's time seems to have been Mathurā, between Agra and Delhi).[155] But structural identity does not lend itself to explanation in terms of influence. The presence of divine light in everything, extreme asceticism, non-violence, and reincarnation are the pillars of Mani's system: take one away and the system collapses. They presuppose years of hard thinking about the subject and cannot simply have been added as an embellishment during a trip abroad.[156] Mani went to India as a missionary to spread his own religious system,[157] already fully formed, and even if we assume that his ideas were still fluid at the time one cannot add load-bearing pillars to a system without completely rethinking it. This objection holds regardless of whether it is from the Jains, Buddhists, or Hindus that he is envisaged as picking up the doctrine of reincarnation. Differently put, we would have to postulate the presence of Jain (or Buddhist or Hindu) communities in Iraq itself, or close to it, on a scale so significant that they could be one of the parents of Manichaeism rather than a source of influence on it after it had been conceived. Such communities have in fact been proposed.[158] There were certainly Indians in Iraq, and it is worth noting that it is a Jain, not a Buddhist, parable that Burzoē retells in the preface to his translation of *Kalīla wa-Dimna*: he famously compares the human condition to a man in a well threatened by a raging elephant above and dragons and serpents below, hanging on to branches that a black and a white mouse are steadily nibbling away and forgetting about his predicament because some honey is dribbling into his mouth.[159] It may well have been from Buddhists that Burzoē heard it, however, in India rather than Iraq, and the idea that either Jains or Buddhists were sufficiently numerous in Iraq to play a generative role in the rise of Manichaeism is somewhat implausible. Mani did know about the Buddha, and perhaps he heard something about the Jains as well, in India or Iraq, but his knowledge does not seem to have been extensive, and in both cases it will have been in a spirit of recognition that he incorporated the little he

155 Deeg and Gardner, 'Indian Influence', 4.

156 Compare Klimkeit, 'Manichäische und buddhistische Beichtformeln', on the panpsychist element.

157 On his journey see Sundermann, 'Mani, India'.

158 Fynes, 'Plant Souls', 32ff., proposing a Jain mercantile community in the Persian Gulf; cf. Ball, 'Some Rock-cut Monuments'; Ball, 'How Far did Buddhism spread West?', proposing a Buddhist presence there.

159 Basham, 'Jainism', 263; cf. Nöldeke, 'Burzōes Einleitung', 25f., with the elephant in n. 4.

knew into his writings, delighted that people in a distant part of the world should have received the same truth as he had.

Mani did not think that the doctrine of reincarnation was Indian: in his view it was Christian. Al-Bīrūnī cites a passage from his *Book of Secrets* in which Mani says that the disciples knew that their souls would be reincarnated in every form and so asked Christ (al-Masīḥ) about the fate of souls that do not receive the truth. Jackson found the idea of Christ as the authority for reincarnation so implausible that he tried to understand al-Masīḥ as Mani himself, but the word used for the disciples is *ḥawāriyūn*, which clinches the reference to Christ.[160] Mani seems to have known a book of questions about the soul by the disciples, for al-Bīrūnī also quotes a statement by Mani in which they ask Jesus about dead and living matter, and yet another in which he credits Jesus with the doctrine that the soul, once released from existence, travels back to the realm of light via the moon and the sun, an idea common to Manichaeism and Zoroastrianism.[161] The book is assumed to be an apocryphal gospel of the Gnostic type.[162] Reincarnation is common in Gnostic writings. There is panpsychism comparable to that of the Manichaeans too: in the *Gospel of Thomas*, a compilation of sayings of which a Greek version was available in Egypt before about AD 200. Jesus declares: 'It is I who am the light who is above them all. It is I who am the all. From me did it all come forth and from me did it all extend. Split the wood and I am there. Lift up the stone and you will find me there.'[163] A Manichaean hymn similarly rhapsodises 'My God, you are a marvel to tell. You are within, you are without; you are above, you are below. Near and far, hidden and revealed, silent and speaking too: yours is all the glory.'[164] The gospel in which Jesus taught reincarnation and the ascent of the liberated soul had presumably circulated in the community in which Mani had grown up. Whether the doctrine of reincarnation it enshrined was ultimately derived from the Greeks or the

[160] Bīrūnī, *Hind*, 41f./27 = I, 54f.; Jackson, 'Metempsychosis in Manichaeism', 250, n. 15; the gloss as 'Mani himself' is retained in Casadio, 'Manichaean Metempsychosis', 114.

[161] Bīrūnī, *Hind*, 36, 479/23f., 283f. = I, 48, II, 169.

[162] Thus Browder, 'Bīrūnī's Manichaean Sources', 21f.; similarly Sundermann, 'Mani, India', 16.

[163] *Gospel of Thomas*, log. 77. Zandee, 'Silvanus', 537, comments that 'although some of the phraseology sounds pantheistic, the idea is not, because Christ as the light transcends everything'. The correct classification would be panentheist.

[164] BeDuhn, *Manichaean Body*, 78.

Iranians one cannot tell, and the question may presuppose too sharp a separation between the two.

Later evidence

A Syriac source tells us that the fifth-century Saba preached Christianity in a Kurdish village inhabited by 'Sadducees', meaning people who denied the resurrection. When the leader of these Sadducees saw that the Kurds had received the world of God he confronted Saba, insisting that there was 'no resurrection, no revival of the dead, and no judgement', much as the followers of ʿAbdallāh b. Muʿāwiya were to say.[165] He accused Saba of leading the villagers astray by making them stop revering their god, 'who is the luminary of this world', and was duly killed by the angel of the Lord; a miracle later obliterated the entire village.[166] No explanation is offered for their denial of the resurrection. One would expect them to have believed in reincarnation, but it is also possible that they denied the afterlife altogether. The Dahrīs did so, and there were many who had trouble with this doctrine in the Zagros village studied in the 1970s, finding it more likely that paradise and hell were in this world.[167] If Saba's Kurds had been Manichaeans this would undoubtedly have been mentioned, so they were probably what would later be called Khurramīs.

Bhavya (sixth century AD), an Indian Buddhist, took it for granted that the Zoroastrians believed in reincarnation. He mentions that the Maga of the Persians believe that one would go to heaven by killing oxen and standing on a pile of their horns, and that one would be born in an elevated position, the highest heaven, if one fumigated by burning the hearts of cattle.[168] The passage has been related to Mithraism, which also involved bull-slaying and a desire to reach the highest heaven, as well as reincarnation if we trust Porphyry's sources.[169] Elsewhere Bhavya says of the adherents of the Yonākadeva, the god of the 'Greeks' (i.e., foreigners), that they believe one would be liberated from *saṃsāra* by killing ants in a golden vessel by piercing them with a golden needle: anyone who did so accumulated the seeds of liberation, and killing cattle and having

[165] See p. 237.

[166] Bedjan, *Acta Martyrum*, II, 673–5; excerpted in Hoffmann, *Auszüge*, 75f. My thanks to Emmanuel Papoutsakis for a full translation of the story.

[167] Loeffler, *Islam in Practice*, 68, 82, 192, 198, 206f., 209, 222.

[168] Lindtner, 'Buddhist References', 439.

[169] The Mithraist overtones are noted by Kawasaki, 'Reference to Maga', 1100.

intercourse with one's parents was a cause of attaining heaven (*svarga*).[170] Though Bhavya wrote well after Zardūsht of Fasā, the Maga are not likely ever to have heard about either him or Mazdak. But Bhavya could of course simply have assumed that the Maga believed in reincarnation like everyone else he knew.

Abū Ḥātim al-Rāzī, who tells us that Mazdak believed in reincarnation, says the same of Bihāfarīdh, who was not a Mazdakite or a Khurramī.[171] According to al-Shahrastānī every nation had a sect that professed belief in reincarnation; among the Zoroastrians the sect in question was Mazdak's, and he would say more about the different types of reincarnation known as *naskh*, *maskh*, *faskh*, and *raskh* when he got to 'their sects among the Zoroastrians'.[172] Unfortunately he does not redeem his promise. All we can say, then, is that if we trust Porphyry reincarnation was represented in Zoroastrianism before Zardūsht of Fasā and that in later centuries it was certainly present in Iran, both inside and outside Zoroastrianism.

NON-VIOLENCE

Elchasaites and others

Once again we may start with the Book of Elchasai. He also rejected meat-eating; he even went so far as to claim that sacrifices had never been part of the law.[173] If that had been all it would not have been of great significance here, for Christians often renounced meat, wine, and procreation by way of transcending this world. This is condemned in the New Testament (1 Timothy 4:1–5), and it generated considerable controversy thereafter, Syriac Christianity being notoriously ascetic.[174] But it was distinctly unusual to reject meat-eating while celebrating the goodness of wine and marriage, as did the Khurramīs, who did not cultivate asceticism: they had scruples about meat-eating because it involved inflicting harm on living beings, but none about the pleasures of this world or the perpetuation of the human species. We do not know what Elchasai said about wine, but his book rejected meat-eating while at the same time vigorously endorsing

170 Lindtner, 'Buddhist References', 435.

171 Abū Ḥātim, *Iṣlāḥ*, 161.10.

172 Shahrastānī, I, 133 = I, 511f. (on the Kāmiliyya). For the technical terms see Bīrūnī, *Hind*, 49.2/32 = 64, and other sources in the translators' note to Shahrastānī; Abū 'l-Ma'ālī, 21; Kohlberg, review of Freitag, *Seelenwanderung*, 238.

173 Epiphanius, 19.3.6 = I, 46.

174 Perry, 'Vegetarianism', 178ff.; Brock, 'Early Syrian Asceticism'.

marriage.[175] In other words, he shared the unusual position of the Khurramīs. According to Epiphanius, the originally pre-Christian Nasoreans listed along with the Nazoreans among the sects bewitched by Elchasai also rejected meat-eating, denying that sacrifices had ever been part of the cult.[176] Among the Sampseans some would abstain from 'that which has life in it' (*ta empsycha*).[177] The Ebionites also refused to eat 'that which has life in it', explaining that it was produced by intercourse,[178] and of them we are explicitly told that they had exchanged their former pride in virginity for a categorical rejection of celibacy and continence.[179]

We find the same position in Bar Daiṣan (d. 222), who flourished about a century after Elchasai. He was reputedly a Parthian who had come to Roman Mesopotamia from 'Persia'. A skilled archer, courtier, and a well-dressed man, he did not cultivate asceticism: he held the world to be in a process of purification by conception and birth.[180] As Mani said, the Dayṣāniyya did not know that the body is an enemy of the soul and so believed that the Living Soul could be purified in this 'corpse' and ascend from it.[181] Muḥammad b. Shabīb, a mid-third/ninth-century Muʿtazilite, reported the Dayṣāniyya to 'believe in (*yarawna*) marriage and everything beneficial to his [*sic*] body and soul, and in abstaining from the slaughter of animals because of the pain it inflicts'.[182] Bar Daiṣan too seems to have been a panpsychist. He held the sun, moon, heavenly sphere, ocean, mountains, and wind to be endowed with limited freedom, for the use of which they would be held accountable on the Day of Judgement.[183]

175 Epiphanius, 19.1.7, 19.3.6 = I, 45, 46.

176 Epiphanius, 18.1.4 = I, 43; 19, 5, 5–7 = I, 47f.; see also 29.6.1. = I, 116 ('the Nasarean sect was before Christ'). His treatment of the Nasareans and Nazoreans is extremely confusing; for the latter see Luomanen, 'Nazarenes'.

177 Epiphanius 53.1.4 = II, 70 ('meat').

178 Epiphanius, 30.15.3–4 = I, 131.

179 Epiphanius, 30.2.6 = I, 121.

180 *EIr.* s.v. 'Bardesanes' (Skjaervø), with reference to Julius Africanus, Ephrem, and Moses Bar Kepha. Ephrem also refers to another cosmology incompatible with this orientation, presumably reflecting the presence of different schools among his followers. The evidence is harmonised, making Bar Daiṣan an ascetic, in Ehlers, 'Bardesanes von Edessa'.

181 Bīrūnī, *Hind*, 42/27 = I, 55, citing Mani's *Book of Mysteries*.

182 Shahrastānī, I, 196 = I, 670. The translators are clearly right to strike out the *ḥarām* that follows *yarawna* and which is found only in late manuscripts (and all modern editions), for the Dayṣāniyya could hardly deem everything beneficial to the soul to be forbidden. But their translation seems a little free.

183 Bar Daiṣan (or, more probably, his pupil Philip), *Laws of Countries*, 14, cf. 10 = 15, cf. 11.

Manichaeans

Like so many Christians Mani rejected meat, wine, and procreation alike. Allegedly the baptists among whom he grew up did so too, but Ibn al-Nadīm's passage to this effect envisages them as Manichaean *avant la lettre*.[184] They do seem to have rejected meat, for meat-eating is not mentioned in the account of Mani's disputes with them; the issues were the permissibility of ploughing, cutting trees, selling fruit, and washing in water.[185] Like other sects of the same type they probably took a dim view of women, possibly to the point of denying that they could be saved (until they were reborn as men), but extreme misogyny is no bar to marriage, and we simply do not know their view on this question.[186]

Since Mani rejected both meat-eating and marriage his position is at first sight of no relevance here, but he differed from other ascetics in that his rejection of meat-eating formed part of a doctrine of non-violence. No living things were to be harmed, he said, not even wild or noxious animals, and not trees or plants either,[187] for all things, even earth and air, were filled with light and the light was intelligent and sentient.[188] Fire and living things were seen as having a particularly high concentration of light, but 'everything is animated, even earth and water'.[189] The Manichaeans said that 'divine nature permeates all things in heaven and earth and under the earth; that it is found in all bodies, dry and moist, in all kinds of flesh, and in all seeds, herbs, men and animals ... bound, oppressed, polluted', as

184 Mani's father joined Mani's movement, with the result that he is presented as a Manichaean from the start: see Ibn al-Nadīm, 391f. = II, 773f. (reflecting a Manichaean source), where we are told that he joined the Elchasaite sect after hearing an injunction to abstain from meat, drink, and marriage at a time when his wife was pregnant with Mani (so that it was too late for him to abstain from procreation).

185 *CMC*, 94–9, where Mani credits his own views to Elchasai.

186 The Nuṣayrīs formally exclude women from religious activities and the possibility of salvation (they have to wait until they are reborn as men): see Tendler, 'Marriage, Birth, and *Bāṭinī Ta'wīl*', 60f. Compare Friedl, 'Islam and Tribal Women', 128f., on the Zagros villagers cited repeatedly in this book: the women, though not formally excluded, repeatedly declared religion to be 'made for men' and did not think there were any women in paradise (apart from the houris). Compare the Pseudo-Clementine *Homilies*, III, 27 ('The male is wholly truth, the female wholly falsehood'), and the misogyny hinted at in al-Nadīm, 404 = I, 811. The *CMC* conveys the impression that the baptist community was all male.

187 'Abd al-Jabbār, *Tathbīt*, I, 184, 187; Bīrūnī, *Āthār*, 207.-3. For many other attestations, including texts by the Manichaeans themselves, and further discussion see BeDuhn, *Manichaean Body*, 40–87.

188 Maqdisī, III, 122.

189 Michael the Syrian and Bar Hebraeus in Casadio, 'Manichaean Metempsychosis', 126.

Augustine observed. They 'say that the earth, wood, and stones have sense'.[190] Jesus hung in every fruit and suffered if it was plucked. No activity was possible without the infliction of harm. 'If a person walks on the ground, he injures the earth; and if he moves his hand, he injures the air, for the air is the soul of humans and living creatures, both fowl and fish, and creeping things', as an opponent described their view.[191] Agriculture – even plucking fruit or cutting bread – was impossible for the Elect, who would tell the bread they were about to eat that 'I did not harvest you nor grind you nor knead you nor put you in the oven; someone else made you and brought you to me; I am innocent as I eat you'.[192] The only justification for the cultivation of land, cutting of plants, plucking of fruit, and grinding of flour was that the auditors who engaged in such tasks provided food for the Elect, whose pure bodies would filter out the light they contained and so enable it to return to its source.[193] There was no light to filter out in meat, since the divine substance fled from dead or slain bodies,[194] and though auditors could eat it as long as they had not actually killed the animal, the Elect could not.[195] It is this panpsychist doctrine that the Manichaeans share with the Jains. It is much more extreme than anything attested for the Khurramīs, but they were thinking along the same lines.

Zoroastrians

Euboulos, who may have flourished before or after Elchasai, credited the Magi with vegetarianism according to Porphyry. He divided them into three groups with reference to their attitude to killing and eating animals, claiming that 'the first and most learned neither eat nor kill any animate creature, but abide by the ancient abstinence from animals' (Porphyry held humans to have originated as vegetarians). 'The second group make use of animals, but do not kill any of the tame animals; and even the third group, like the others, do not eat all animals. For it is the belief of them all that metempsychosis is of the first importance.' He goes on to discuss how this belief was reflected in the Mithraic mysteries.[196] Again Euboulos has been taken to impute Pythagorean ideas to the Magi, on the grounds that Zoroastrianism was

[190] Augustine in BeDuhn, *Manichaean Body*, 77.
[191] *Acta Archelai* X, 8, tr. BeDuhn, *Manichaean Body*, 79.
[192] *Acta Archelai*, X, 6 (also cited in BeDuhn, *Manichaean Body*, 82).
[193] BeDuhn, *Manichaean Body*, 80ff.
[194] Augustine in Beduhn, *Manichaean Body*, 47.
[195] BeDuhn, *Manichaean Body*, 55, 60.
[196] Porphyry, *On Abstinence*, IV, 16, 2.

not a religion of abstinence and that there is no ban on killing or eating animals in Zoroastrianism;[197] and again the verdict seems over-hasty.

The Magi in Cappadocia did not abstain from killing animals, according to Strabo, but they would not kill them with a knife: they used 'a kind of tree-trunk, beating them to death with a cudgel'.[198] The Magi of Fārs, represented by the *Dēnkard*, similarly held that the animals should be stunned with a log, but thereafter one should use the knife, they said.[199] Not all agreed, however. The Magi known to the fifth-century Armenian Eznik would stun the animals and then strangle them,[200] and those reflected in the originally Parthian poem on the Assyrian tree would break their necks with a club in what appears to be perfect agreement with those of Cappadocia.[201] Further east, the Scythians back in Herodotus' time also avoided use of the knife, strangling the animals with a lasso thrown from behind.[202] According to the *Dēnkard*, stunning them first was meant to ensure that they did not suffer pain, and also to prevent over-hasty killing. According to Eznik, the Magi were like Pythagoras in that they believed the animals to have a divine spirit in them and wanted it to leave the body without feeling pain;[203] Bar Ḥadbeshabba, bishop of Ḥulwān (late seventh century), similarly says that the Zoroastrians believed Hormizd (Ohrmazd) to be in the animals and did not want them to feel pain.[204]

The complete avoidance of the knife by the Cappadocian and some western Iranian Magi was probably due to a desire not to spill blood, for blood was polluting, as Strabo mentions in connection with Persian sacrifices to water.[205] Three centuries after Strabo, Basil of Caesarea says of the Maguseans that they 'reject animal sacrifice as a pollution (*miasma*),

197 See Clark's commentary in Porphyry, *On Abstinence*, 188f.; Turcan, *Mithras Platonicus*, 29, on Bidez and Cumont. Turcan himself is less dismissive.

198 Strabo XV, 3, 15.

199 *DkM*, 466.12, in Zaehner, *Zurvan*, 52n.

200 Eznik, no. 324:3, where 'sacrifice' should be emended to 'stun': cf. Benveniste, 'Terminologie iranienne', 51f. Eznik is accusing the Zoroastrians of killing the animals twice, first by stunning them and next by strangling them. For a reference to strangling in a Greek martyrdom see Gignoux, 'Dietary Laws', 21f.

201 Cf. the *Drakht ī Asūrīg* in de Jong, 'Animal Sacrifice', 138 ('They make clubs of me which break your neck', the tree boasts to the goat).

202 Herodotus, IV, 60. The Indians, said by Strabo also to strangle their victims, would do so in order to present the god with a whole victim (XV, 1, 54; both passages cited by Boyce and Grenet, *History of Zoroastrianism*, 296).

203 Eznik, no. 324: 2–6.

204 Cited in Benveniste, 'Terminologie iranienne', 55.

205 Strabo, XV, 3, 14; cf. Choksy, *Evil, Good, and Gender*, 61.

slaughtering through the hands of others the animals they need'.[206] In other words they would only eat meat slaughtered by members of other communities. Boyce and Grenet leave it open whether their practices had changed or Basil is reporting incorrectly.[207] De Jong suggests that the statement could be understood as meaning that the Maguseans would only eat meat slaughtered by their priests, but Basil would hardly have characterised their priests as outsiders (*allotrioi*).[208] Since Basil explicitly refers to the polluting nature of sacrifice it seems more likely that either several practices had coexisted or else their practice had changed: instead of avoiding or minimising bloodshed by clubbing animals to death they now left the dirty work to others. It is clear that the Maguseans would eat meat, however; but then so would two of Euboulos' three groups and all or most Khurramīs, at least under certain circumstances. What the sources describe seem to be attitudes comparable to those of the Buddhist villagers studied in twentieth-century Ceylon: they greatly admired vegetarianism, but would eat meat as long as they did not have to slaughter the animals themselves; they left the task to Muslim butchers.[209]

In short, there were Magi who would not eat animals, or who would not kill them, or who would not do so with a knife, because they believed a divine spirit to be in the animals, because they believed in reincarnation, because they did not want to inflict pain on the animals, or because blood was polluting: once again we encounter a spectrum of attitudes, precisely what we would expect. We know that in Islamic times there were many in Media and Azerbaijan who believed the same divine spirit to be in all living beings, who also believed in reincarnation, and who held it wrong to inflict pain on a living being; and the bearers of official Zoroastrianism also disliked inflicting pain on sacrificial animals, while at the same time regarding blood as polluting. In short, there is no reason to reject Euboulos' information merely because it sounds suspiciously like Pythagoreanism. It is in his section on Pythagoreanism that Eznik is reminded of the similar ways of the Magi. Zoroastrianism, or at least that of Media, clearly did have something in common with that system.

It is curious that Euboulos should associate the Mithraic mysteries with abstention from the killing of animals, given that these mysteries involved

206 Basil of Caesarea, Letter 258, quoted in Boyce and Grenet, *History of Zoroastrianism*, 277.
207 Boyce and Grenet, *History of Zoroastrianism*, 278.
208 De Jong, *Traditions*, 410.
209 Gombrich, *Precept and Practice*, 261. My thanks to Michael Cook for reminding me of these butchers.

the slaughter of a bull and that the participants in the cult were often soldiers. But he was presumably a bit of a Mithraist himself: he shows us how a philosopher might understand the cult. There is also something odd about the fact that the warlike inhabitants of the Zagros mountains and Azerbaijan should have been committed to non-violence, at least in principle. But though Euboulos' three groups are clearly over-schematised he is probably right that there were different levels of understanding. Complete abstention from animal meat, the practice of Euboulos' first group, is attested for Kavadh and Mazdak, a king and a member of the Magi in whom the Greeks saw the equivalent of philosophers. By contrast, Bābak hunted, which was acceptable to the second group, and he also ate a domestic animal during his wedding feast, so unless ritual eating counted as special, he fell into the third group, presumably where most ordinary Khurramīs belonged. (Widengren goes so far as to see Mithraic overtones in Bābak's wedding ceremony, but his argument is flimsy in the extreme.)[210]

In short, like the idea of divine incarnation, the belief that it was wrong to kill and eat animals, or at least to inflict pain on them, was present already in Parthian Iran, at least in Mesopotamia. Well before the rise of the Sasanians and the appearance of Zardūsht of Fasā Iranian religiosity would appear to have included the conviction that God was pure, eternal, and endless light; that this light was present in everything in greater or lesser concentrations, light and darkness being the stuff of which the universe was made; that this light (or spirit) circulated by passing from one form into another until it was released and ascended to the realm of light; and that every now and again a particularly potent concentration of light or spirit passed into a human being, in whom the highest god became accessible to humans. Khurramism and Manichaeism come across as different belief systems based on these fundamental assumptions. As will be seen in Chapter 18 the marital institutions that caused the Khurramīs to be seen as 'Mazdakites' also pre-date Zardūsht of Fasā. In short, there is nothing to rule out the proposition that the older and younger Mazdak came out of a milieu of the type that was later to be dubbed Khurramī. What remains to be established is how the fundamental assumptions in question relate to Zoroastrianism.

[210] See Appendix 2.

15

Regional and Official Zoroastrianism

Doctrines

By what yardstick is a historian to judge whether a particular doctrine was Zoroastrian or not? Anything found in the books of the priests active in the third/ninth century, when the Pahlavi books were compiled, must obviously count as such, but what these books preserve is Zoroastrianism in a drastically shrunken form: a fragmentary Avesta and the teaching of a single priestly school.[1] 'It is clearly wrong to identify the Zoroastrian religion exclusively with the views that reached us through the channel of the official Zoroastrian scriptures,' Shaked observes.[2] Nobody would disagree. Shaked's injunction is nonetheless more widely honoured in the breach than the observance, for the obvious reason that although we know that much is missing we do not know what. In eastern Iran archaeology has revealed the existence of religious forms that sometimes agree with the Zoroastrian books and sometimes depart drastically from them. The agreement lies primarily in the cult of fire and funerary practice, but deviant funerary practices are also in evidence, and though many gods are Avestan their interpretation is sometimes local; and a fair number of deities are of Mesopotamian, Greek, Indian, and other origin. The most important object of worship, moreover, was not usually Ahura Mazda. To many Sogdians and Bactrians the chief deity was Nana (Nanai, Nanaia), a Mesopotamian goddess who was not part of the Avestan heritage. In Bactria the 'king of the gods' was Kamird, probably to be identified with Zun, or perhaps with Mithra, but in any case not with Ohrmazd; and in Khotan Ohrmazd (Urmaysde) was no longer a god at all, but simply the name for the sun, though he is not a sun god in the

[1] Shaked, 'First Man, First King', 252.

[2] Shaked, *Dualism*, 43 and *passim*, esp. 71, 97.

Zoroastrian books.[3] To this must be added that it was not just the last king of Panjikant who bore a name testifying to devotion to the *dēvs*: a fair number of Sogdian bearers of such names are attested.[4] And there were other peculiarities. Is it missing parts of Zoroastrianism that we have recovered here or simply Zoroastrianism mixed with foreign elements? The author of *Šahrestānīhā ī Ērānšahr*, a Pahlavi text completed after al-Manṣūr's construction of Baghdad (begun in 145/762), found it impossible to accept it as Zoroastrianism. In Sogdia, he informs us, after the accursed Alexander had burnt the Avesta, Afrāsiyāb turned 'every single residence of the gods into a place of idolatry of the daivas', as Markwart translates the passage, or he 'made seats for each of the demons, and an idol-temple and a heathen temple', as Daryaee understands it.[5] To a scholar interested in historical origins of doctrines rather than their truth status things look different, however. Observing that 'one of the most notable features of the traditional East Iranian religion revealed by the discoveries of the twentieth century is the extent to which it differs from that of the Avestan and Pahlavi books', Sims-Williams asks whether a religion incorporating so many disparate elements can be regarded as a variety of Zoroastrianism at all. His answer is yes, in the sense that the substratum of the diverse religious forms seems to be Avestan. Essentially the same answer is given by de Jong and Tremblay. 'We are only just beginning to realize how much Zoroastrianism was characterised by local diversity', as de Jong observes, adding that this is something we should always have known, or at least expected.[6]

Tremblay divides Zoroastrianism into two main forms, eastern and western, the former largely or wholly independent of the Persian empires, the latter strongly affected by them.[7] But while it is undoubtedly true that political independence played a major role in the separate development of eastern Zoroastrianism, Muslim observers thought of Zoroastrianism (*majūsiyya*) in general as highly diverse, not simply as divided into eastern and western branches. They recorded no less than eight different

[3] See Chapter 5, p. 97; Sims-Williams, 'Some Reflections', 4, 6f. Ohrmazd clearly had affinities with the sun: see Jacobs, 'Sonnengott'.

[4] Tremblay, 'Ostiran *vs* Westiran', 226 (to which the attestations in *EI*², s.v. 'Sādjids', should be added).

[5] *Šahrestānīhā ī Ērānšahr*, 5–7. Markwart's rendition goes well with the idiom of Kerdīr's inscription, in which the process is reversed (cf. Chapter 16, p. 380).

[6] Sims-Williams, 'Some Reflections', 6f., 8ff.; Tremblay, 'Ostiran *vs* Westiran', 222ff.; de Jong, 'One Nation under God', 229.

[7] See the reference given in n. 4.

explanations of how there had come to be a good and an evil realm.[8] Some distinguished between a wider cluster of religions called *majūsiyya*, Magianism, and the religion of Zoroaster, *zardushtiyya*, meaning Zoroastrianism as we know it from the Pahlavi books (though most used the two terms indiscriminately).[9] Since modern scholars also have a strong tendency to equate Zoroastrianism with the variety endorsed in the Pahlavi books – as I have in fact done myself up to this point – it would perhaps be wise to follow suit. Unfortunately the English term Magianism sounds faintly silly. Iranianists have a better alternative in 'Mazdaism', worship of (Ahura) Mazda, but Ahura Mazda was not a deity of prime importance in eastern Iran, and the term also has the disadvantage, to Islamicists and other outsiders, of inviting confusion with Mazdakism. Accordingly, I shall continue to call the ensemble of divergent forms Zoroastrianism. This is hardly a radical move. Hinduism, the religion to which Zoroastrianism is most closely related, is even more diverse than Zoroastrianism ever seems to have been, yet most (though not all) scholars accept it as a single religion.

What then made a religion Zoroastrian? The answer has to be indebtedness to the Avestan tradition, i.e., the line of authoritative priestly works ultimately rooted in the Gāthās, in which Zoroaster is frequently mentioned. This tradition will not have taken the same form everywhere, let alone at all times. The Sogdians, for example, seem to have received the Avestan hymn *ašəm vohū* (and so presumably other Avestan works) at an early stage in a form independent of the extant recension of the Avesta.[10] What other parts of the Avesta they had we do not know. But even those who received the sacred texts in the same form, and continued to recite them as received, cannot all have understood them in the same way. It is different interpretations of the Avestan tradition, not lack of fidelity to it, that accounts for the eight different explanations of the two realms recorded by the Muslims. It might help to think of Zoroastrianism along the same lines as the Iranian languages. By historical times there no longer was a single Iranian language, but rather a family of them, divided by modern scholars into eastern and western sections, sometimes subdivided into northern and southern branches as well: Sogdian belongs in the north-eastern family group, Median and Parthian in the north-western,

[8] Shaked, 'Myth of Zurvan', 234; cf. also Sheffield, 'The *Wizigerd ī Dēnīg*', 185f.

[9] Maqdisī, IV, 26f. (where the majūs also include the Manichaeans and the Marcionites); Bīrūnī in Chapter 16, p. 387; Shahrastānī, I, 182, 185 = I, 635, 641; cf. also *Dabistān*, ch. 1, distinguishing between Zoroastrians and other Pārsīs.

[10] Cf. Sims-Williams, 'Some Reflections', 9.

Persian in the south-western.[11] Zoroastrianism will similarly have taken the form of a family, subdivided along much the same lines as the languages, and characterised by different 'loan-words', or in other words ideas taken over from their non-Iranian neighbours. When the Iranians were united in empires by Persians, i.e., people from Pārsa (later Pārs, Arabic Fārs), the Persian language and religion acquired normative status and so spread beyond its homeland. This happened twice, first under the Achaemenids and again under the Sasanians, the latter most relevant to us. The Sasanians made Middle Persian the language of the religious and civil administration, and thus the lingua franca of the entire empire; Middle Persian Zoroastrianism similarly became the official religion. In that sense all the lands from Mesopotamia to eastern Iran became 'Persia' (just as all the lands to the west had become 'Rome'). But the inhabitants of Persia continued to distinguish between the diverse peoples to be found within it,[12] and the regional languages did not disappear, as we know among other things from Ibn al-Muqaffaʿ.[13] There was much diversity even within each region too: 'seventy languages' were spoken around Ardabīl, as al-Muqaddasī observed.[14] Much the same will have been true of the regional forms of Zoroastrianism.

If we strip Khurramism of its Islamic elements what we are left with clearly is not Persian Zoroastrianism. Nor is it simply Mazdakism, as the Muslim sources assume, for as we have seen it pre-dates Mazdak and even Zardūsht of Fasā. What it is likely to be is local forms of the Avestan tradition as it had developed in interaction with the earlier religions of that region. Why the forms that flourished in greater Media should have been so similar to that of Sogdia is hard to say. Perhaps the mixture of Iranian and Mesopotamian ideas characteristic of the former had spread, like Nana and Tammuz (and also Jesus), along the highway to Khurāsān and Sogdia; or perhaps the Median understanding had always been closer to that of Parthian and Sogdian Zoroastrianism than to the south-western form.[15] Whatever the answer, Khurramism without its Islamic elements was probably a non-Persian form of Zoroastrianism.

[11] See *EIr.*, s.v. 'Iran vi. Iranian Languages and Scripts' (Skjaervø).

[12] Cf. Bar Daiṣan, *Laws of Countries*, 42f. = 43f.; Witakowski, 'The Magi in Syriac Tradition', 819, 832.

[13] See the references given in Chapter 2, n. 1.

[14] See the reference given in Chapter 3, n. 2.

[15] Cf. Pourshariati, *Decline*, with a strong sense of the difference between Parthian and Persian Zoroastrianism; unfortunately she identifies the Parthian form as Mithraism (see. App. 2). For other examples of Mesopotamian elements in eastern Iranian culture see Sims-Williams, 'From Babylon to China'.

There is no simple way of proving this hypothesis, for the Muslim sources never mention Avesta-reciting priests (*herbadhs* and *mobedhs*) or veneration of Zoroaster among the Khurramīs. Accordingly, it could also be postulated that Khurramism is a development of the ancient religion that prevailed among the Iranians before they were exposed to the Avestan tradition. In that case Khurramism and Zoroastrianism would represent different developments of a heritage pre-dating Zoroaster rather than different understandings of a shared Zoroastrian tradition. Given that Zoroastrianism is itself a development of ancient Iranian religion, and that it would have influenced its non-Avestan counterpart in the course of the centuries, the outcome would be so similar to that envisaged in the first hypothesis that our exiguous sources would not enable us to tell the difference between them. But the second hypothesis is somewhat implausible. It is true that there may have been isolated regions in Iran in which the Avestan tradition was never received, but Khurramism is attested all over Iran except for Kerman, Sīstān, and Makrān, and it was particularly strong in greater Media, including Iṣfāhān and Hamadhān, the latter an Achaemenid centre (Ecbatana), and Azerbaijan, where Median priests saw fit to place the Avestan Lake Čaečasta (later Šīz).[16] We can hardly postulate that the Avestan tradition failed to be received in such regions, let alone in most of the country.

To corroborate the hypothesis that Khurramism is non-Persian Zoroastrianism we still have to go to the priests of Fārs, for their religion remains the only form of Zoroastrianism of which we have substantial textual knowledge. But envisaging the religion as one out of several languages descended from a common ancestor changes the manner in which we use the yardstick: our task is no longer simply to determine whether a particular Khurramī feature is present or absent in the Persian tradition, and declaring it un-Zoroastrian in the latter case. Rather, we must try to establish whether there is sufficient common ground between the two sets of doctrines to suggest divergent development from common roots, with or without external input. It is in this vein that the Middle Persian tradition will be examined in the present chapter. The question how the bearers of Middle Persian Zoroastrianism viewed the beliefs that came to be called Khurramī will be examined in the chapter that follows.

[16] Thus Boyce and Grenet, *History of Zoroastrianism*, iii, 73f.

GOD, THE CREATION, AND PANPSYCHISM

Both the Khurramīs and the Persian Zoroastrians associated God with light, but the former did not give him a name or a personality: he was simply the great light or the highest light, the source of all the light there was. In Muslim parlance the Khurramīs were guilty of *taʿṭīl*, avoidance of anthropomorphism to the point of making God disappear as a person. It was a sin of which the Ismailis were later to be accused. By contrast, the Zoroastrians of Fārs were extreme anthropomorphists. On Ardashir I's reliefs Ohrmazd is depicted as a man, now standing and now mounted, looking practically identical with the king he is investing.[17] 'Your head and hands and feet and hair and face and tongue are visible to me even as are my own, and you have such clothes as men have,' Zoroaster tells Ohrmazd in an account establishing that Ohrmazd is nonetheless an intangible spirit (*mēnōg ī agriftār)*: 'It is not possible to take hold of my hand,' Ohrmazd replies.[18] The compilers of the Pahlavi books expected to see Ohrmazd in some such form at the end of times, for he would come down to earth to perform the sacrifice that would bring about the renovation.[19] Some envisaged him as armed. Saint Nino (d. c. 340) saw a bronze image of him in Georgia wearing a helmet with ear-flaps and holding a sharp, rotating sword;[20] and both Ohrmazd and Ahriman wear swords in Abū ʿĪsā's account of their pact.[21] Are we really to take it that this Ohrmazd who rode horses, wore arms, and looked like the king was the highest God, the absolute worshipped in the form of fire in temples devoid of images? He sounds more like an emanation or intermediate figure such as ʿAlī in Shīʿite *ghuluww* or Sultan Sahak among the Guran (the oldest group of the Ahl-i Ḥaqq). In practice ʿAlī and Sultan Sahak are also the highest God in their respective belief systems. Occasionally a distinction between them and the absolute is made, but no great interest is taken in their precise

17 *EIr.*, s.v. 'Ardašīr I'.

18 Boyce, *History of Zoroastrianism*, I, 198, citing *Šāyest nē šāyest* xv, 1–2; cf. *PRDd*, 46: 11ff. (Ohrmazd created water from his tears, plants from his hair, the ox from his right hand); Jayḥānī in de Ménasce, 'Témoignage', 52 (the souls of the just from his hair, the sun from his eyes, the moon from his nose, etc.).

19 *GrBd* 34:29 (*Bd*, 30:30 West); cf. Zādspram, 35:31, where he comes in person after the final sacrifice, he and the *amahraspand*s having previously taken up abode in the mind of Sōšyans and the six other agents of the renovation (35:17).

20 Russell, *Zoroastrianism in Armenia*, 154.

21 Ibn al-Malāḥimī, *Muʿtamad*, 639; similarly Jayḥānī in de Ménasce, 'Témoignage', 58; *Tabṣirat al-ʿawāmm*, 13.

relationship.[22] The same could have been true of the Zoroastrians until they had to explain themselves to Christians and Muslims. If there was a highest deity of whom Ohrmazd was the 'name', the deity in question could have been as nameless as the *dhāt* of the Guran, but there could also have been some who identified him with Zurvān. The Manichaeans applied the name of Zurvān to the inaccessible God, the Father of Greatness, reserving that of Ohrmazd for Primal Man, a divine emanation representing mankind in its original state (but not a human being); in line with this, Sogdian Buddhists identified Zurvān with Brahma, a deity who was not normally worshipped.[23] There were also versions in which Ohrmazd was the only pre-existing and eternal deity, even the realm of darkness emerging out of light (as postulated by al-Shahrastānī's Maskhiyya); and sometimes Mithra or Vayu was the intermediary figure, as we have seen.[24] In the Pahlavi books Ohrmazd and Ahriman have always existed and Ohrmazd creates everything, without either emanations or darkness being involved. But this does not seem to have been the only view even in Persian Zoroastrianism, and there were so many variations altogether that the Khurramī view of God and the intermediaries in whom he manifests himself is easily seen as just another.

Both the Khurramīs and the Persian Zoroastrians were dualists in the sense of explaining the world in terms of a mixture between light and darkness, and some held the two realms to have existed from the beginning, though this was not true of all Zoroastrians – and probably not of all Khurramīs either. If we go by the one Khurramī account that we have, both the Khurramīs and the Persian Zoroastrians held the mixture to have started by accident, and both held the highest deity to have created this world by way of response (as he does even in Manichaeism, acting through an emanation). In the Zoroastrian books Ohrmazd creates the material world out of fire, and Ahriman does not create anything material at all, but simply pollutes and corrupts Ohrmazd's creation, or he is even deemed not

[22] The Nuṣayrīs sometimes mention the highest God under the labels of the *ma'nā* (essence) or *ghayb* (absence): see Bar Asher and Kofsky, *Nuṣayrī–'Alawī Religion*, 16, 25. The Guran sometimes speak of the highest God as the *dhāt* (essence): see van Bruinessen, 'When Haji Bektash still bore the Name', 131, noting the absence of speculation on the subject.

[23] Grenet, 'Vaiśravaṇa in Sogdiana', 277; Sundermann, ' Göttern, Dämonen und Menschen', 101; cf. Zaehner, *Zurvan*, 21f., seeing this as proof that 'Zurvanism' was the current form of Zoroastrianism at the time. According to Abū 'Īsā al-Warrāq, some Zoroastrians regarded Zurvān as the greatest light (*al-nūr al-a'ẓam*), while Ohrmazd was the one whom common people believed the Zoroastrians to worship (Ibn al-Malāḥimī, *Mu'tamad*, 638).

[24] See Chapter 11, pp. 203f. One version said that Ohrmazd originated Ahriman when an evil thought occurred to him, i.e., the same mechanism by which others saw Zurvān as having originated Ohrmazd and Ahriman (Shaked, 'Myth of Zurvan', 234).

really to exist in the material world at all.[25] By contrast, the Khurramīs apparently and the Manichaeans certainly saw the world as a mixture of light and darkness in the sense that darkness was matter, while light was the spirit that organised and animated it. It is this view of the mixture that accounts for, or articulates, their panpsychism, as we have seen. But though the bearers of official Zoroastrianism did not see the mixture of light and darkness as one of spirit and matter they certainly regarded the sun, moon, and elements as divine, and so presumably also as alive in some sense.[26] 'It is their custom to venerate various spirits: of the heaven, earth, sun, moon, water and of fire,' as a Chinese observer noted.[27] According to Eznik, moreover, the conviction that all inanimate things are animate was one of the errors that the Manichaeans and the Zoroastrians shared,[28] and Bar Penkaye says that the Zoroastrians describe all the elements as *ityē* and alive.[29] The Pahlavi books do not convey the impression of envisaging the material world as animated, but it certainly is in *Yašt* 13, in which everything is full of gods (as Thales would have said): all righteous human beings, whether dead, living, or still to be born, have *fravašis* here,[30] as do all other living beings, whether animal or divine, and also plants and inanimate things such as the sky, the earth, the waters, and fire.[31]

Though there is no panpsychism in the Pahlavi books the divine is still immanent in the creation. Ohrmazd created the world out of his own divine substance. In the words of the *Bundahišn* he 'created the body of his creation in the form (*kerb*) of fire, bright, white, round, and seen from afar, from his own selfhood, from the substance of light'.[32] The fire was

[25] Shaked, 'Some Notes on Ahreman'. A more popular view seems to have been that Ohrmazd created all the good things and Ahriman all the evil ones (see, e.g., Eznik, 145: 15, 176: 4, 187: 2, 199), the view also attested in Plutarch and the *Vendīdād* (cf. Skjaervø, 'Zoroastrian Dualism', 61, 64). Though there is Avestan support for distinguishing between the two creations in terms of materiality, the priestly denial of the reality of evil could reflect Neoplatonist influence (cf. Schmidt, 'The Non-Existence of Ahreman', 84f.). The priest Tansar is said to have been a Platonist (Masʿūdī, *Tanbīh*, 100).

[26] See Christensen, *Iran*, 143f., 146f., 157.

[27] Cited in Eichhorn, 'Materialen', 534n.; Daffinà, 'La Persia sassanide secondo le fonte cinesi', 162.

[28] Eznik, 149.

[29] De Menasce, 'Autour d'un texte syriaque', 588f., translating *ityē* as *ousiai* (substances, essences).

[30] Yt 13:17, 21, 74, 145, 150, 154.

[31] Yt 13:74, 80–7.

[32] *GrBd* 1:44, cited in Yamamoto, 'Zoroastrian Temple Cult (II)', 83; more briefly Duchesne-Guillemin, 'Form of Fire', 14f.

drawn from Infinite Light, and out of it all creatures were fashioned.[33] Ohrmazd produced everything from 'that which is his own splendour', as the *Mēnōg ī khrad* puts it.[34] He created it out of his own all-embracing totality, as a modern scholar puts it.[35] Like the light or spirit of the Khurramīs and Manichaeans, fire pervaded everything and circulated through natural processes: it was present in the sky, water, earth, fire, plants, animals, and humans; and it came down as rain, which fell on the earth, on which grew plants, which passed into animals and men.[36] Ohrmazd had disseminated fire in all his creatures, as the *Bundahišn* says.[37] The human soul was of the same definition (*ham vimand*) as the gods in respect of substance (*khwatīkh pad gōhr*), as the *Dēnkard* says.[38] In line with this, Kotwal and Boyd observe that some commentators on the Yasna view the entire scheme of creation as the 'form' (Av. *kehrp*) of Ahura Mazda.[39] The sacred fire here on earth is not a symbol of the cosmic order or infinite light, but rather a sample of it, as they neatly put it.[40] The semi-divine Sasanian king, the Khurramī prophets, and other figures embodying divinity to greater or lesser degrees were all such samples too.

The presence of fire in the six creations does not make all things alive, sentient, or endowed with mind in the Pahlavi books: what it does make them is pure, and it is purity rather than panpsychism that is the dominant theme in Persian Zoroastrianism. If a Manichaean could not live without inflicting pain on the earth, air, plants, or animals, Zoroastrians of the official type could not do so without inflicting impurity on them: one polluted the fire by burning impure things in it, the water by washing, the earth by putting bodies in or on it, and so on. One should not do any of these things, but they were not all avoidable. Not to pollute and not to inflict pain come across as different responses to the same divine immanence. The one did not exclude the other: it was to avoid inflicting pain on the good animals that the Persian Zoroastrians insisted on stunning them first, and the Khurramīs were greatly concerned with purity too. But there is a distinct difference of emphasis and, as the absence of panpsychism leads us to

[33] *GrBd*, 1:50; tr. Zaehner, *Zurvan*, 316 (par. 29); cf. Duchesne-Guillemin, 'Form of Fire', 14f.

[34] *Mēnōg ī khrad*, 8:7; cf. also *PRDd*, 46: 11ff.; Jayhānī in de Ménasce, 'Témoignage', 51.

[35] Sundermann, 'How Zoroastrian is Mani's Dualism?', 354; cf. also Shaki, 'Some Basic Tenets', esp. 278ff. (*DkM*, 120.15ff., using philosophical formulation), 295f.

[36] Duchesne-Guillemin, 'The Six Original Creations', 8.

[37] *GrBd*, 3:8 in Zaehner, *Zurvan*, 334 (par. 8).

[38] *Dk*, III, no. 108 (*DkM*, 102; *DkB*, 75).

[39] Kotwal and Boyd, *Yasna*, 5.

[40] Kotwal and Boyd, *Yasna*, 5, 7.

expect, the Persian Zoroastrians did not share the Khurramī and Manichaean views on divine incarnation, reincarnation, or non-violence.

DIVINE INCARNATION

There is no concept of *ḥulūl* in the extant Zoroastrian literature. It does have a concept of avatars, best attested in the *Bahrām Yašt* (*Yašt* 14), in which the deity Verethragna (Vahrām, Bahrām) appears to Zoroaster in ten forms – as a wind(-god), a bull, a horse, a camel, a boar, a youth, a bird, a ram, a wild goat, and an armed man – in a manner recalling the avatars of Viṣṇu in Puranic literature. Similar metamorphoses are attributed to Tištrya (Tištar, Tīr, i.e. Sirius).[41] Verethragna is incarnated in the sense of becoming flesh, but the body in which he appears is not that of a pre-existing human or animal, merely one he assumes for the purpose of appearing, like the swan as which Zeus appears on one occasion in Greek mythology; or maybe Bahrām did not even become flesh, but rather assumed an illusory body like that in which some Manichaeans held Christ to have appeared. When the Khidāshiyya defended their doctrine of *qalb*, adducing the fact that Gabriel had assumed the appearance of diverse people, they could be envisaging their deity as behaving along the same lines. But it certainly was not along those lines that al-Muqanna', the followers of 'Abdallāh b. Mu'āwiya, and other Khurramīs envisaged *ḥulūl*.

In a quite different vein the *Dēnkard* says that man must make his body a hospitable abode to the gods: 'for as long as man thinks good deeds and righteousness, the gods remain in his body and the demons become stupefied and depart.' A man who protects and worships a god is saved by that god from evil: that god is his own soul. This sounds like *ḥulūl*, but what is meant is that the man becomes virtuous: he whose body is inhabited by Vahman will be eager to do good works, the one whose body is inhabited by Srōš will be good at listening and correcting his mistakes, and so on. As Shaked notes, the degree of identification with the gods may have been higher than the texts suggest, but there is no sense of divine indwelling here.[42] Finally, the Zoroastrian books envisage Ohrmazd himself as coming down to the earth at the time of the renovation (*frašgerd*), when all the dead have been resurrected, and Zādspram says that Ohrmazd will then mix himself with the Sōšyans and all human beings

[41] *EIr.*, s.v. 'Bahrām (1)' with reference to Yt 14 and Yt 8:13, 16, 20; Charpentier, 'Kleine Beiträge'.

[42] Shaked, 'Esoteric Trends', 195–8, citing *DkM*, 524f., 525, 487f.

to make them pure of will and knowledge, while other divinities will mix themselves in the animals, plants, fires, metals, and the earth to restore them to their proper nature.[43] Here at last we have the idea of divinity entering and transforming created beings, but it serves to deify all human beings, not just a single leader, and is relegated to the end of times.

Divine kingship

In the 1970s, when religion was often treated in a reductionist vein, it was common to dismiss the claims of Khurramī leaders to divinity as mere claims to royal status: the movements were *really* political, not religious, we were assured. Amabe perfectly exemplifies this approach though he wrote in the 1990s: according to him all the so-called 'religious' movements in early ʿAbbāsid Iran were in fact purely political, and al-Muqannaʿ was not saying anything unusual when he claimed to be an incarnation of God, for 'normally Central Asian kings were venerated as gods by their subjects'.[44] These days one winces both at the assumption that a movement must be either political or religious and at the dismissive attitude to religious modes of thought, not to mention the rough lumping together of the beliefs that the divine may acquire humanity and that humans may acquire divinity. For all that, one can agree with Amabe that the concept of divine kingship is likely to have played a role in notions of *ḥulūl*.

'Kings, wherever they have appeared in history, have been understood to mediate between, and so to partake in some way of, the human world they govern and the divine world that furnishes the ultimate authority over the created order': thus Peter Machinist, asking where on the spectrum between the divine and the human the Assyrian king stood.[45] We must ask the same question of the Sasanian kings and their eastern Iranian neighbours. It can be said straightaway that, *pace* Amabe, none of them claimed to be an incarnation of God, or even a god in the full sense of a celestial being entitled to worship with prayers, sacrifice, and hymns of praise (a *yazat*). Contrary to what Widengren claims, they did not wear veils either.[46] Unlike their Achaemenid forebears, however, the Sasanian kings did claim to be related to the gods, and in some sense to be gods

[43] Cf. the reference given in n. 19 of this chapter; Zādspram, 35:31, 39.

[44] Amabe, *Emergence*, 93, 124f. He shares his attitude with Shaban, whom he cites with approval.

[45] Machinist, 'Kingship and Divinity', 152.

[46] Widengren, 'Sacral Kingship ', 247, 256, referring to the second edition of his *Religionens Värld*, 264, where he turns out to have no evidence for it.

themselves: they were 'of the race of the gods (*yazatān*)', as they proclaim in their inscriptions ('akin to the gods', as the *Alexander Romance* says),[47] 'partner with the stars, brother of the son and moon',[48] divine, a god (*bay*), and sometimes 'son of god' (i.e., of his divine predecessor) as well.[49] In a recently published Bactrian document a certain Nakīn writes to Mir-Yazad, 'the god (*βayo*) of Ulishagan ... the renowned king of the gods', sending him a hundred greetings and saying that he looks forward to prostrating before him.[50] We also hear of Turkish *khāqāns* calling themselves *βy* in the sixth and the early eighth centuries.[51]

Bay is a tricky title, for it did not always mean very much. In Henning's words, 'The appellative *baga*- 'god', came to be applied to the great King of Kings of the Persians initially. Later it suffered social decline, which was most marked in Sogdiane. The local king adopted it, then the kinglet, then the owner of a castle, finally any gentleman laid claim to it.' The Muslims disapproved of this usage. In the Sogdian documents from Mount Mugh the Muslim governor, writing in the 720s, simply says 'you' where a native would have used the appellative *baga* a dozen times; and when the Afshīn, ruler of Ushrūsana, was put on trial, he was forced to translate his royal title into Arabic, so that it sounded as if he claimed to be the god of gods, whereas all the title actually meant was something like overlord.[52] *Baga* lives on today in the Turkish honorific *bey*.

Bay did mean god in the Sasanian inscriptions, however, for the Greek versions translate it as *theos*, and though the phrase identifying the king as being 'of the race of the gods (*yazatān*)' disappears from inscriptions and coins at the time of Bahram V (420–38), a fifth-century bishop of Ravenna mentions representations of the Sasanians as the sun and the moon, the latter with horns (an ancient sign of divinity). Menander quotes a letter in which Khusraw I is called divine and made in the image of the gods (*ek theōn charaktērizesthai*). The king was divine in the sense of standing

[47] Cf. Humbach, 'Herrscher, Gott und Gottessohn', 91ff.; de Jong, *Traditions*, 289f.; Panaino, 'The Bayān of the Fratarakas', 267ff.; cf. also de Ménasce, 'Autour d'un texte syriaque', 597, 599.

[48] Thus Shapur II in a letter to Constantius in 356 (de Jong, *Traditions*, 290, citing Ammianus Marcellinus, XVII, 5, 3, XXIII, 6, 5).

[49] Panaino, 'The Bayān of the Fratarakas', 274f., 279f.; Humbach, 'Herrscher, Gott und Gottessohn', 103f., cf. 99ff., 105, 110ff.: 'son of god', Parthian *bagpuhr*, came to be the title of the Kushan emperor (*bagapuro*) and also the Chinese emperor, with the result that the latter came to be known as *faghfūr* in Arabic and Persian.

[50] Sims-Williams, *Bactrian Documents*, II, 137= 136 (doc. jh, undated).

[51] Golden, *History of the Turkic peoples*, 115n., 139.

[52] Henning, 'Sogdian God', 249; Tab. iii, 1310f.

midway between his subjects and the heavenly realm, quasi-divine, as we might say: 'a god most manifest among men', as a Greek rendition of Khusraw II 's titulature has it, but nonetheless 'among the gods a righteous immortal man'.[53] The Sasanian kings are still routinely referred to as *bāyān* in the *Škand Gūmānīk Vičār*,[54] but the king does not seem to be even quasi-divine in the Pahlavi books, nor does the Islamic tradition taunt the Persians with deifying their kings, so it does seem that here as in Sogdia the sense of his divinity had dwindled.

This raises the question what exactly the Khurramīs meant when they cast their leaders as gods. There is no single answer to this question. Some Ghulāt unquestionably elevated past figures to fully divine status, going beyond anything explicable in terms of divine kingship. The members of the holy family were God, five in one, to the Mukhammisa; Muḥammad, ʿAlī, and Salmān al-Fārisī were God, three in one, to the Pārsīs of Azerbaijan: the five and the three occupy the same status as the divine emanations in Manichaeism and the Trinity in Christianity. But deification of the Prophet's family is a feature of ʿAlid *ghuluww*, not of Khurramism, and one does not get the sense that the Iranian counterpart to this family, Abū Muslim and his daughter Fāṭima, came even close to being treated in the same way. On the contrary, the divinity of Abū Muslim and other prophets/imams seems to be eminently comparable to that claimed in words and images for the Sasanian kings: like these kings Abū Muslim and other imams stood midway between the divine and the human realm. The same seems to be true of Jāvīdhān, Bābak, and the imams of the Rāwandiyya and Ḥarbiyya/Ḥārithiyya. Divine community leaders who followed one another in straight succession are particularly reminiscent of divine kings. This suggests that there were indeed Iranians, above all in the Jibāl and Azerbaijan, to whom the divinity claimed for the kings was deeply meaningful, at least when the kings were their own. They did not explain it in terms of descent from the gods, however, but rather in terms of transfer of the divine spirit.

Khwarra and the imams

To see how divine kingship could generate the Khurramī chains of messengers and/or prophets and imams culminating in the mahdi we need to

[53] For all this see Panaino, 'The Bayān of the Fratarakas', 278ff., quoting Petrus Chrysologus (sermo 120), Menander Protector (fragment 6, 1), and Theophylact, here translated from Whitby and Whitby, *Theophylact Simocatta*, 114 (iv, 8, 5).

[54] *Škand*, 10:69f.

look at two further concepts with which divine kingship was associated. One was *khwarra*. *Khwarra* is the Pahlavi version of an Avestan word (*khwarəna*) which appears in all other Iranian languages as *farn(a)* or *farr(a)* (cf. New Persian *farr-i īzadī*) and which stood for a great many things in the course of its long history. It is usually translated as 'glory'. In Bailey's words it could be thought of as a cosmic or divine force operating from within the invisible world whereby great deeds were accomplished and good fortune secured.[55] In *Yašt* 19 (*Zamyād Yašt*), perhaps dating from the time of the Achaemenids, it is both a deity and a force possessed by the gods, special human beings, and their lands: praises are given to the *khwarəna* of Ahura Mazda, the *aməša spəntas*, the *yazatas*, the Aryan/Iranian lands, Haošyangha, Takhma Urupi and Yima (Hōšang, Ṭahmūrath and Jamšīd), the Kayanid kings, Zoroaster, Vīštāspa, and the future saviour.[56] In the Pahlavi books *khwarra* is something possessed by all beings, not just the gods and special human beings, but every nation, social class, village, and family, and every individual within them;[57] it directs them towards fulfilment of their particular role in life; the Pahlavi books somewhat prosaically gloss it *khwēškarih* '(own) function',[58] interpreting it in a moralising manner.[59] It is not with their understanding that we shall be concerned.

Having *khwarra* meant having good luck and fortune, including all the good things in life, so luck was also among its meanings and it was often equated with fortune or fate. It is probably this term that is translated now as *doxa* (glory) and now as *tychē* (fortune) or *daimōn* (divine being) in Greek texts from the time of the Achaemenids onwards, though the Achaemenids do not mention their *khwarra* in their inscription.[60] Some now also hold it to be the king's *khwarra* that hovers above the ruler as his double in a winged disc in Achaemenid images (though this is by no means certain).[61] *Khwarra* was envisaged as both a component of the person who possessed it and a separate divine being which could be invoked and revered. It is invoked as a divine being in *Yašt* 19. The Achaemenids are

[55] Bailey, *Zoroastrian Problems*, 28. He nonetheless held its core meaning to be 'the good things in life', a suggestion which now seems to have been abandoned.
[56] Two new translations are available, one by Hintze and one by Humbach and Ichaporia.
[57] Zaehner, *Dawn*, 151.
[58] Bailey, *Zoroastrian Problems*, 35f.; Molé, *Culte*, 434ff.
[59] E.g., *DkM*, 344–5, in Molé, *Culte*, 435.
[60] Calmeyer, 'Bedingten Göttlichkeit'; Shahbazi, 'Achaemenid Symbol, II: Farnah', 129, 135, 140f.
[61] Cf. Shahbazi, 'Achaemenid Symbol', I and II (*khwarra*).

said to have had a special table on which gifts for the royal *daimōn* were placed, and guests were also invited to revere the royal *daimōn* during banquets.[62] When Nero placed the diadem on the head of Tiridates of Armenia, declaring him to be king of Armenia, Tiridates responded that he would worship Nero as he did Mithras, for 'you are my fortune (*tychē* = *farna*) and my fate (*moira* = *bakht*)'.[63] The royal *daimōn* also appears as a separate being invoked for help in an amusing Sogdian story set in the third century: a 'Caesar' was tricked into believing he was dead; as he lay in his coffin thieves broke into his tomb and one of them put on his diadem and royal garment and, now looking like the Caesar, told the latter not to be afraid because 'I am your *farn*'; 'Ah my lord . . . be you my helper', the Caesar replied.[64] The *farn* is addressed as a superior being (*βγ*), a guardian spirit as Henning describes it, yet it also was (or rather pretended to be) Caesar himself. The Sasanians too were endowed with *khwarra*, displayed as a nimbus around their heads.[65]

As a royal characteristic *khwarra* is related to the ancient Mesopotamian concept of *melammu*, an overwhelming power which often displayed itself as radiance and which was eventually identified with it.[66] First attested in Sumerian, by neo-Assyrian times it was depicted as an aureole or nimbus around its possessor.[67] Both supernatural beings and humans could possess it, as could objects such as weapons, but it was first and foremost a characteristic of gods and their representatives, kings.[68] Like *khwarra* it was so powerful that it overwhelmed all enemies; it is often associated with 'terror' (*puluḫtu*);[69] and like *khwarra* it could be lost, meaning that the status of king was also lost.[70] Oddly, few Iranianists seem to be aware of the

62 De Jong, *Traditions*, 300f., citing Plutarch and Atheneaeus.

63 Dio Cassius, LXVII, 5, cited in Shahbazi, 'Achaemenid Symbol, II: Farnah', 129n.

64 Henning, 'Sogdian Tales', 477ff.; also cited in Shahbazi, 'Achaemenid Symbol, II: Farnah', 137.

65 Abkha'i-Khavari, *Bild des Königs*, 43f.; Canepa, *The Two Eyes of the Earth*, 192ff. The gods were similarly depicted.

66 Thus Aster, 'Divine and Human Radiance', 29–79, modifying the consensus (based on Oppenheim, '*Pul(u)ḫ(t)u* and *melammu*'; Cassin, *Splendeur divine*) by means of an unusually sharp distinction between (divine) power and radiance. My thanks to Nicholas Harris for drawing this study to my attention.

67 Oppenheim, '*Pul(u)ḫ(t)u* and *melammu*', 31; Aster, 'Divine and Human Radiance', 149ff. (ninth century BC onwards, again with criticism of Oppenheim).

68 Cf. Aster, 'Divine and Human Radiance', 79ff.

69 Oppenheim,'*Pul(u)ḫ(t)u* and *melammu*', 31; Cassin, *Splendeur divine*, 76f.; Machinist, 'Kingship and Divinity', 160f. (line 12 of the poem on Tukulti-Ninurta); Aster, 'Divine and Human Radiance', 117ff.

70 Oppenheim, '*Pul(u)ḫ(t)u* and *melammu*', 31; Cassin, *Splendeur divine*, 77f.; Aster, 'Divine and Human Radiance', 46; Zaehner, *Dawn*, of Yima (in Yt 19:34).

Assyrian roots of *khwarra* as a royal attribute,[71] though Assyriologists make no secret of it and Iranianists are generally well aware of the massive role of Assyrian kingship in the development of its Iranian counterpart.[72] For our purposes it is important to note that the divine glory formed part of both the Mesopotamian and Iranian traditions.

The Assyrian king received his *melammu* (perhaps in the form of a robe, perhaps of headgear) directly from the gods on his accession, not from his predecessors.[73] Among the Iranians, however, royal *khwarra* was transmitted from one ruler to the next, from an older adult to a younger one. The *Ayātkār-e Jāmāsp* envisages it as transferred by coronation.[74] It singled out the leader from other people, his own family included: they too might be made of special stuff, but only he had the glory, only he was a god (*bay*).[75] In *Yašt* 19 the human holders of *khwarəna* include Yima, the legendary heroes, Kavian kings, Zoroaster, Kavi Vīštāspa, and the future saviours: they form a chain of quasi-divine beings running through Iranian history from the beginning to the end.[76] In Sasanian times the chain included the Sasanians, who cast themselves as successors of the Kavis rather than the Parthians. If we translate *khwarra* as holy spirit, we have here the Khurramī concept of chains of apostles, prophets, kings, or imams deified by their possession of the holy spirit and culminating in the mahdi.

It is well known that there are parallels between Mesopotamian *melammu* and biblical concepts of glory (*hod*, *hadar*, *kavod*), and that some of them reflect biblical indebtedness to the Mesopotamian tradition.[77] The

[71] For the rare exceptions see Panaino, 'Uranographia', 221 and n. 121; for the Indo-European roots of other aspects of the notion see Darrow, 'Zoroaster Amalgamated', 125.

[72] The so-called Melammu project, devoted to the intellectual heritage of Babylonia and Assyria in the east and west alike, adopted this name precisely because *melammu* was a concept that spread far beyond its original home; its logo is an Achaemenid seal in which Anahita appears to the Persian king in the same manner as Ishtar to members of the ruling class on Assyrian seals, complete with her *melammu* (cf. S. Parpola at http://www.aakkl.helsinki.fi/melammu/project/prhiname.php).

[73] Aster, 'Divine and Human Radiance', 102–6, 110 (with the robe suggested by Livingstone); Oppenheim, '*Pul(u)ḫ(t)u* and *melammu*', 31 (proposing headgear); cf. also Machinist, 'Kingship and Divinity', 170, citing the Neo-Assyrian king Adad-Nadari II (the gods 'put on my head the *melammu* of kingship').

[74] Shahbazi, 'Achaemenid Symbol, II: Farnah', 128, citing *Ayātkār-e Jāmāsp*, 44f.

[75] Cf. Panaino, 'The Bayān of the Fratarakas', 276.

[76] For Yima as part of the pantheon, so far attested only in Bactria, see Sims-Williams, 'Some Reflections', 7; for Zoroaster as a quasi-divine being that 'we' worship along with Ahura Mazda see *EIr*., s.v. 'Zoroaster, iii' (M. Hutter), with reference, among other things, to Yasna, 3.21 and 42.2.

[77] The most recent treatment is Aster, 'Divine and Human Radiance', where the list of passages reflecting indebtedness is pruned.

Jews were familiar with the Assyrian concept well before the rise of the Medes and the Persians. Their scripture said that the spirit passed into holy souls, making them friends of God and prophets, and that it would wander before finding its final resting-place. To those of them who came to live under Iranian rule, as eventually also to the Christians, it will have come naturally to think of the precursors of their own messiah as forming a chain of quasi-divine beings of the type familiar from the hegemonic culture. Glory (*khwarra*) and spirit were easily identified. Both were a divine quality that could be envisaged as a divine being in its own right and that nonetheless also formed part of the person to whom it passed; both could be personified at any level from the lowest *daimōn* to the highest angel of the Lord; at the same time, both were a life-giving force found in all human beings, or in all living things, or in everything, and which would be found in a particularly potent form in the last member of the chain, the Sōšyans or Messiah who would bring about the renovation. In short, if the Jews and/or Christians of Mesopotamia and Iran assimilated God's spirit to divine glory, they will have thought of the prophets and other holy figures as singled out by a divine quality on the model of the Assyrian and Persian kings.

Glory and spirit do in fact seem to have been identified, at least by Iranians affected by Christianity, whether Jewish, gentile, or Manichaean. Thus a Parthian account says that Mani's missionary Mar ʿAmmō was detained by 'the glory (*farrah*) and spirit (*vākhš*)' of the eastern province when he was sent to preach there: the two terms are treated as overlapping or synonymous here.[78] They are linked again in a Manichaean book (M 801) which invokes 'the great glory (*farrah*) and the God-created spirit (*vākhš*) of the diocese of the east', while other Manichaean works mention both in the plural, apparently envisaging them as guardian spirits.[79] More strikingly, book VII of the *Dēnkard* often replaces *khwarəna* by spirit (Pahlavi *vakhš*) in its retelling of the mythical past in *Yašt* 19 with the intention of recasting the bearers of luminous *khwarra* as prophets, *vakhšvar*s: it is now as bearers of spirit that they form a chain running from Gayōmard, the first man, via Zoroaster to Sōšyans.[80]

Molé, who noticed the recasting, did not hold *vakhš* to mean spirit here, however: in his view it translated Hellenistic, Christian, and Manichaean

78 M2 in Sundermann, 'Studien zur kirchengeschichtlichen Literatur, II', 245.

79 Henning, 'Bet- und Beichtbuch', 11.

80 *Dk*, VII, 1, in Molé, *Légende*, 2–13; Molé, 'Deux aspects', 306ff.; de Ménasce, *Encyclopédie*, 66. For all these figures as prophets see Maqdisī, III, 7; Ibn al-Jawzī *Talbīs Iblīs*, 73.

logos. But this is hard to accept. The word actually means spirit, not *logos*, in the Manichaean example he adduces: it speaks of the holy spirit making its grandeur known through the mouths of the prophets.[81] If Molé saw a reference to *logos* here it must be because he was deferring to the enormous authority of Bailey. He too took *vakhš* to translate *logos*, on the grounds that the Avestan meaning of the word was '(spoken) word' and that it is used to translate *logos* in Christian and Manichaean Sogdian. But the only Middle Persian example he gives of *vakhš* in the sense of 'word' is the very term *vakhšvar*; in all the other examples it means spirit.[82] Gershevitch casts doubt on Bailey's reconstruction with reference to the fact that Ossetic *uac* was used as a prefix in the names of pagan gods or spirits and Christian saints, where it did not mean 'word', but rather 'some higher "divine" force, comparable to *farnah- and arta-*', which were also used to form names. The pagan examples would pre-date the rise of Christianity, and though they are somewhat conjectural, Gershevitch is certainly right that no Christian would ever use *logos* to characterise a saint. He takes the semantic development from 'word' or 'voice' to 'spirit' to be a development inherent in the meaning of the Old Iranian word.[83] One wonders whether an example of *vakhš* in the sense of *logos* can be found in Middle Persian at all, for 'spirit' is the only meaning carried by the many examples adduced by Shaki, where they include *vakhš i yazat* to translate the Biblical 'spirit of God'.[84] Spirit is also the only meaning listed for Manichaean Middle Persian and Parthian.[85] The priests who coined the term *vakhšvar* for a prophet could of course have used the word in its archaic Avestan sense of 'word', but they will have coined it to counter rivals, and a prophet was not a bearer of *logos* in either Manichaeism (to which Molé sees them as responding) or Christianity. The Manichaeans did not in fact speak a great deal about prophets at all, their preferred term being 'apostle' (*frēstag*),[86] so unless we take the term *vakhšvar* to have been coined after the rise of Islam (which is certainly reflected in this book

[81] Molé, 'Deux aspects', 306, 308.

[82] Bailey, 'The word "But" in Iranian', 280f.; Bailey, *Zoroastrian Problems*, 118f.

[83] Gershevitch, 'Word and Spirit in Ossetic', esp. 478f., 487. The words quoted above are from Abayev, quoted by Gershevitch at 479.

[84] Shaki, 'Some Basic Tenets', 304; cf. *Škand* 13:7; Bailey, *Zoroastrian Problems*, 118. Shaki also tests the hypothesis that *vakhš* could mean *logos*, but unfortunately he does so in terms of philosophical equivalence rather than lexical meaning (the result is negative).

[85] Durkin-Meisterernst, *Dictionary of Manichaean Texts*, s.v. 'w'xš'.

[86] Cf. the entries for *fryštg* and *w'xšwr* (= Zoroastrian MP *wxšwr*) in Durkin-Meisterernst, *Dictionary of Manichaean Texts*.

of the *Dēnkard*),[87] the most likely rival to have triggered its formation is Christianity. To the Christians (and Jews) a prophet was identified by his possession of the spirit, and the same was true of a saint. It thus seems reasonable to infer that it was with spirit that the mythical kings and heroes were now seen as endowed in their capacity of bearers of *khwarra*.[88] In short, Iranianised Christians and Zoroastrians responding to Christianity seem to have come to envisage their sacred figures along the same model, as bearers of glory/spirit forming a chain culminating in the redeemer at the end of times.

Yašt 19 tells us that when Yima (Jamšīd) lost the *khwarəna* it flew away as a bird.[89] The Muslimiyya reportedly said that when Abū Muslim was killed he escaped death by reciting the greatest name of God and turning into a bird and flying away: one takes this to mean that the divine spirit flew away as a bird from the body in which it had been lodged.[90] Yima's *khwarra* flew away as a Verethragna/Bahrām bird, the bird of prey, probably a falcon, which was one of the ten incarnations of Bahrām, a bestower of *khwarra*;[91] by contrast, Abū Muslim flew away as a white dove (according to Niẓām al-Mulk; Mīrkhwānd leaves it unspecified). The Gospel of Matthew says that when Jesus was baptised the spirit of God descended on him like a dove while a voice from heaven proclaimed him the son of God; and the holy spirit is also compared to a dove in the Manichaean Psalm book.[92] This would suggest that Iranians exposed to Christianity had adapted their concept of *khwarra* by having it assume the form of the bird associated with Christ rather than a falcon. But it is still as a falcon (*bāz*) that the divine spirit descends to enter human beings in myths told by the Guran.[93]

[87] Cf. Josephson, 'Sitz im Leben' of the Seventh Book', 208ff.; it is also Islam that de Ménasce discerns behind the presentation, while acknowledging its long roots (*Encyclopédie*, 66).

[88] Compare the equation of *khwarra* with the soul (*ruvān*), or in Bailey's understanding, the intellect, in *GrBd*, 101:14, cited in Bailey, *Zoroastrian Problems*, 36f.

[89] Yt 19:34; cf. Bailey, *Zoroastrian Problems*, 23f.; Humbach, 'Yama/Yima/Jamšēd'. For the sin that caused the loss cf. also Shaked, 'First man, First king', 242ff.

[90] *SN*, ch. 45:1 (280 = 212); Mīrkhwānd, *Rawḍa*, V, 2559.

[91] Shahbazi, 'Achaemenid Symbol, II: Farnah', 138; Shahbazi, 'On vārəγna, the Royal Falcon'.

[92] Matthew 3:16; similarly Mark 1:10; Klimkeit, 'Gestalt, Ungestalt, Gewaltwandel', 59, citing the Coptic Psalm book 156, 19f.

[93] Van Bruinessen, 'When Haji Bektash still bore the Name', 130f.; cf. also the Sufis transforming themselves into doves and falcons in Birge, *Bektashi Order*, 37f.; Mélikoff, *Abū Muslim*, 118n.

The image and the mahdi

The evidence reviewed so far allows us to postulate a concept in Sasanian Iran of divine kings and/or prophets who succeed one another in straight succession, singled out by the possession of *khwarra*/spirit, and who culminate in a saviour destined to bring about the resurrection and transfiguration of the world: this would be the model to which the imams were assimilated. What has not been properly explained is the idea that the *khwarra*/spirit might descend directly from above, as it always seems to do in connection with the mahdi, instead of being handed from an older to a younger adult. It could simply be that the Assyrian concept of the king receiving his *melammu* directly from the gods was still alive: the idea that he received it from his predecessor may simply have been one among several views. But whether this was so or not, there is a more relevant factor in the making of a divine statue.

In ancient Egypt and Mesopotamia the primary function of the statue or image of a deity was to be the dwelling-place of spirit or fluid that derived from the deity whose image it was; the spirit or fluid in question was conceived as a rarified substance that could penetrate ordinary matter, so that in this form the gods could enter 'into every (kind of) wood, of every (kind of) stone, of every (kind of) clay', as an Egyptian text presents it as doing. The Old Testament prophets vigorously deny that there was any 'breath' (*rwḥ*) in such images (Jeremiah 10:14, 51:17; Habakkuk 2:19). The dwelling-place of a deity could also be a living body, usually that of a king, who was sometimes regarded as the lifelong incarnation of the god in question.[94]

In Assyria images of the gods were said to have been 'born' in heaven.[95] When the object had been manufactured here on earth its eyes and mouth had to be opened so that it could see and be offered food, and thereafter the divine image had to come down in order to take up abode in its earthly counterpart: a plea was addressed to it not to stay in heaven ('enter into the form ...'). Its entry completed the ritual animation of the statue.[96] It was not the deity itself that came down: the god stayed in heaven. What came down was rather the 'essence' of the god, as Winter calls it, the spirit or fluid, as Clines terms it, the *rwḥ*, as the Bible calls it when it denies its

[94] For all this and much of what follows see Clines, 'Humanity as the Image of God', 475ff., with the citation.

[95] Winter, 'Idols of the King', 22.

[96] Winter, 'Idols of the King', 22f., citing a tablet copied in the Neo-Babylonian or Persian period.

presence. When the king is described as the image of a god, the idea is not that he was a representation or reflection of the god in question, as the Greeks were to understand it, but rather that he functioned as a statue of this deity: his body had been animated by the essence of the god coming down and entering him. Both the statue and the royal body were terrestrial receptacles of the divine, which transformed their nature. Like the statue the king was described as born in heaven rather than on earth. [97] It would seem to be this conception that lies behind the Khurramī idea of the spirit descending to take up abode in human beings such as kings/prophets or the saviour.

In Genesis it is Adam who is created in or as the image (*ṣlm*) of God, so that he might have dominion over everything on earth (1:26; cf. also 9:6): was he too seen as a royal statue of God, animated by God blowing his own breath into him (2:7)? Needless to say there are diverse interpretations, but it does not seem likely. God is usually taken to have fashioned Adam *according to* his image, not *as* his image (though the latter interpretation also has its adherents);[98] God is also said to have made Adam in his likeness, suggesting a focus on representation (Genesis 5:1); and the animating breath comes in a different verse from that on the image. But *ṣlm* could certainly mean statue, and God's creation of Adam as his *ṣlm* is explicitly identified as a mandate to rule. Whatever Genesis 1:26 may originally have meant, there must have been Mesopotamian readers to whom the verse identified Adam as both king and divine, and it must surely have done so long before Jesus Christ came to be endowed with the same characteristics.[99] To a Mesopotamian Jew the divine 'essence' that descended on Adam as God's image will have been God's spirit, wisdom, word, or power, visible as the glory (*melammu* or *khwarra*) that allowed him to do magnificent deeds. Needless to say, evidence for the thought of Mesopotamian Jews in the relevant period is missing. The nearest we get to it is Paul, a Hellenised Jew from Tarsus who tells us that men (not women) were 'the image and glory of God', and that Christ was 'the image of the

[97] Machinist, 'Kingship and Divinity', 161ff.; similarly Pharaoh (Clines, 'Humanity as the Image of God', 479f.).

[98] Cf. *Dictionary of the Old Testament*, s.v. 'image of God', section 3.

[99] Cf. Psalms 8:5, where God is praised for having made man 'a little lower than *elohim* and crowned him with glory and honour'. It was apparently understood as a reference to Adam, and in the Dead Sea Scrolls the righteous are repeatedly assured that all the glory of Adam will be theirs (e.g. Damascus Document 3, 20; Thanksgiving Hymn 4, 15; cf. further Kugel, *Traditions of the Bible*, 115, 116f.; Gditzin, 'Recovering the 'Glory of Adam''. The translators of the Psalms render *elohim* as 'angels'). Aster takes this Psalm to be an uncertain example of Mesopotamian influence, however ('Divine and Human Radiance', 288f.).

invisible God' in whom 'all the fullness of God was pleased to dwell'.[100] The fact that the idiom he is using was part and parcel of Judaism by his time does not make it any less suggestive. Jews had long coexisted with Zoroastrians by then, both in Tarsus and elsewhere: the devout Jews from every nation under heaven who lived in Jerusalem in the time of the Apostles included Jews from Parthia, Media, Elam, and Mesopotamia (Acts 2:9).[101]

Whether they thought in terms of one, two, or several incarnations, it seems to be this idea of the descent of the divine into a human body as if it were a statue that lies behind the concept of incarnation encountered among the Elchasaites, Manichaeans, Mandaeans, *zanādiqa 'l-naṣāra*, and early East Syrian Christians. As Cassian says, Nestorius saw Christ as having God in him, not simply as being God: he spoke of Christ as the 'God-receiver' (*theodochus*) and made statements such as 'let us honour the God-receiving form ... as the single form of Godhood, as the inseparable statue of the divine will, as the image of the hidden God'.[102] To Nestorius the human being born of Mary was a temple for God to dwell in.[103] It would seem to be the same concept that is reflected in *Yašt* 13 when it says that the divine beings known as *aməša spəntas* (Pahlavi *amahraspands*) were the 'forms' in which (according to one translation) Ahura Mazda 'mingled himself'.[104] It is certainly the same concept of the human being as a mere 'God-receiver' that lies behind those Khurramī schemes in which the divine spirit descends from on high. The Khurramīs still spoke of the body as a 'form' (*ṣūra*) and 'mould' (*qālab*), though more commonly they saw it as clothing.

There was a comparable relationship between divine image and incarnation in India. 'From divine incarnation to divine icon was not a long step', as Davis observes, reversing the development postulated here for Iran. Among the Hindu theists, he notes, the Highest God (Viṣṇu or Śiva) had two primary modes of being, unmanifest and manifest, formless and embodied, and whereas the transcendent Absolute (the *brahman*) is

[100] 1 Corinthians 11:7 (*eikōn kai doxa theou*); Colossians 1:15, 19. There is no reference to Christ as the image of God in the Gospels.

[101] For Tarsus and other Cilician towns, see Boyce and Grenet, *History of Zoroastrianism*, iii, 305ff. Note also that Paul shares the Iranian (originally probably ancient Mesopotamian) idea of three heavens: cf. 2 Corinthians 12:2–4; Panaino, 'Uranographia', 219.

[102] Casiday, 'Deification ', 995, citing Cassian, *Incarn.* vii, 8, 1; cf. Nestorius, *Sermons*, IX, X (40, 52).

[103] Nestorius, *Sermons*, IX, X (29, 47).

[104] Yt 13:81, as read by Boyce, *EIr.*, s.v. 'Aməša spənta'. As read by Malandra he assumes their forms, and in the old translation of Darmesteter he clothes them in the forms.

inaccessible in the Upaniṣads, the Vaiṣṇavites postulated that Viṣṇu was the *brahman* and would nonetheless manifest himself in the world: 'I am indeed unborn. My self is imperishable. I am the lord of all beings,' Viṣṇu declares in the Bhagavadgītā (1st century AD or earlier). 'Even so, I do enter into the material world, which is mine, and take birth through my own powers of appearance ... Time after time I take birth in order to re-establish the world order.'[105] Early medieval liturgical texts postulated that the Absolute could be present in an image too. In the Vaiṣṇava Parasaṃhitā the question is posed how humans can praise and worship Viṣṇu if he is unconstrained by form, unlimited in place, time, and shape. The answer is that the deity can be worshipped only in embodied form, and that the deity actually entered the image. 'Viṣṇu descends into a stone or metal icon much as he may incarnate himself in a body of flesh and blood', Davis comments, 'in a movement of sympathy and good will, to make himself accessible to his devotees – even while retaining his supreme Otherness.'[106] This is precisely how the Khurramīs saw it. The relationship between the concepts of divine incarnation and divine presence in an image was well understood by Abū Zayd al-Balkhī (d. 322/934). 'To those who believe that the deity is a body capable of moving around and incarnating himself (*al-intiqāl wa'l-ḥulūl*) it is not an implausible idea that God can dwell in a man's person or in that of an idol' (*fī shakhṣ insān aw fī shakhṣ ṣanam*), he observed, adding that this is what lay behind deification of ʿAlī by a group of early Shīʿites.[107] Given that the avatar concept is found in the Avesta, we probably should not envisage the concept of *ḥulūl* as simply an Akkadian 'loan-word' in non-Persian Zoroastrianism, but rather as the outcome of interaction between ancient Near Eastern, eventually Aramaic, and Iranian beliefs, now untraceable for lack of source material. At all events, it is the belief in the descent of the divine into a statue that lies behind the notion of the deity descending to take up abode in a pre-existing, adult human being.

The statue imagery was also used in a slightly different sense in the centuries before the rise of Islam. 'You cannot know God through anyone except Christ, who has the image of the Father ... a king is not usually known apart from an image', we read in the *Teachings of Silvanus*.[108] As a king founding a city would put up his statue for the inhabitants to venerate,

[105] Davis, 'Indian Image-Worship', 112, citing Bhagavadgītā 4.6–8.
[106] Davis, 'Indian Image-Worship', 113.
[107] Abū Zayd al-Balkhī in Fakhr al-Dīn al-Rāzī, *Tafsīr*, XXX, 144, *ad* Q 71:24 (on the Noachite gods).
[108] Silvanus, 100, 24–32.

so God placed Adam on earth for all creation to honour God through him; and as those who had the emperor's image in their city honoured the absent emperor, so humans honoured the unseen God through Christ, Theodore of Mopsuestia said. Narsai said much the same.[109] The divine incarnation was 'an image of the hidden, or a statue of the judge', as Nestorius put it.[110] Again the role of the statue is to serve as the intermediary between the unknowable God and mankind, but here the stress is on representation and likeness, as also in Genesis 5:1. This sets it apart from the ancient Near Eastern concept, which did not require the image to look like the deity at all (it could in principle be an unhewn stone, as in Arabian stone worship). Christ was both an incarnation and a representation of God in the material world, and so he allowed mankind to know and worship the deity beyond form, time, and place. Christ was the door or gate (*thyra*) to salvation, as Silvanus said. Others said the same, all reflecting Jesus' words in John 10:9 (echoing Psalms 118:20): 'I am the gate: by me, if any man enter in, he shall be saved.'[111] This is the idea that runs through Iranian heresy from the Ghulāt to the Bābīs, who owed their name to centuries of further speculation about a human being as the gate (*bāb*).

Both the radiant glory (*khwarra*) that the kings shared with the gods and the idea of the divine spirit descending to take up abode in a human body were, at least in part, what one might call 'loan-words' in Zoroastrianism, but the former had been so completely naturalised that many modern Iranianists think of it as a uniquely Iranian concept. By contrast, it is only in regional Zoroastrianism that the latter concept seems to have been fully accepted. We encounter it from Media to Sogdia, but not in Fārs. Sōšyans, the saviour who brings about the resurrection, seems to be no more than a special human being, his virgin birth and prodigious *khwarra* notwithstanding. Nobody is deified. Eznik (d. after 450) does admittedly preserve an account in which Sōšyans is a son of God (though not an incarnation); in his rendition it is Ohrmazd rather than Zoroaster who is the progenitor of the three saviour figures of whom Sōšyans is the last.[112] This makes good

[109] McLeod, *Image*, 65f., 68, 72; Narsai, *Homélies sur la création*, IV, 1–6; cf. the introduction, 483f.

[110] Nestorius, *Sermons*, X (52f.).

[111] Silvanus, 106, 27; cf. Zandee, 'Silvanus', 534, 539, 552; *Recognitions*, II, 22; Eusebius, *Ecclesiastical History*, II, 23. 8 and 12; cf. Nestorius, *Sermons*, IX (38). The term 'gate' does not seem to be of any special interest to historians of religion on the Greek side of the fence.

[112] Eznik, 194. The translation of Blanchard and Young takes it to be the son of Ohrmazd rather than Ohrmazd himself who deposits his seed in the water, clearly because a son of Ohrmazd is mentioned later in the passage. But this son is a different figure (cf. 190) adduced to deny that Ohrmazd could keep any son alive, and Zeilfelder leaves the text

sense, but the possibility that Eznik is confusing Zoroaster and Ohrmazd here cannot be ruled out (he envisages Ohrmazd as dying). In the Pahlavi books the apocalyptic script does culminate in a theophany, but it is Ohrmazd himself who descends to earth to perform the *yasna* that will bring about the transfiguration of the world;[113] To those who conceived of God as the highest light or the absolute beyond conceptualisation this finale will have been impossible: the only way God could walk on earth was by inhabiting a human body, meaning that of the redeemer.

The mahdi as 'the knowing Boy'

It would also seem to be in terms of the Semitic tradition that we have to explain the concept of the mahdi as *kūdak-i dānā*, attested only in Niẓām al-Mulk on the Khurramīs of the Jibāl, probably on the basis of the fourth/tenth-century Ḥamza al-Iṣfahānī.[114] The idea of the saviour as a child or youth is first attested in the Manichaean Thomas Psalms, composed in the later third century, and in the Mandaean hymns on which the Thomas psalms are based.[115] The child stands for both the suffering soul and the saviour. In Manichaeism 'the boy' is Jesus the Splendour, who assumed a body as Jesus the Youth/Child/Boy and who addresses this Boy as his alter ego enduring exile below in a Parthian hymn.[116] In Mandaeism it is Mandā dḤayyī, 'Knowledge of Life', a great light-being, who is a child; and in the *Paraphrase of Shem* we encounter a saviour by the name of Derdekeas, whose name is assumed to be derived from Aramaic *dardaq*, meaning child or boy, though the saviour is not described as a child here.[117] In short, the concept takes us to much the same Mesopotamian circles as the idea of periodic divine incarnation.

The child or youth personifying the suffering soul and the suffering saviour is presumably a new version of Tammuz, the 'divine child' (as a Chinese envoy characterised him) or youth attacked by malign powers and relegated to the underworld: his fate was lamented once a year in

unemended. (Blanchard and Young also make at least the first of the three sons a figure of the past, the tense used of the next two being obscure.)

113 *GrBd*, 34:29 (*Bd*, 30:30 West); Zādspram, 35:31.

114 *SN*, ch. 47:14 (319f. = 244); cf. Chapter 9, p. 183.

115 Colpe, 'Thomaspsalmen', 90; cf. 83f. for a discussion of the work of Säve-Söderberg demonstrating the dependence of these psalms (now only extant in Coptic) on those of the Mandaeans.

116 Colpe, 'Thomaspsalmen', 90; Stahl, 'Derdekeas in the *Paraphrase of Shem*', 577, citing M42; Franzmann, *Jesus in the Manichaean Writings*, ch. 7.

117 Stahl, 'Derdekeas in the *Paraphrase of Shem*', 576f., citing *Ginza* 191 for Mandā dḤayyī; Rudolph, *Gnosis*, 85f. (treating the Paraphrases as Sethian in a loose sense).

Mesopotamia and Sogdia alike on the eve of Islam, much as that of al-Ḥusayn was to be thereafter.[118] He must have travelled to Sogdia by the same route as Nana and Jesus, so it makes sense that we should find him in Media; presumably he had been disseminated all along the route to Khurāsān. But how was he understood where he was received? In the Thomas Psalms, Mandaean hymns, and Manichaeism his descent to the underworld has been reinterpreted as a descent into this world of gross matter. It will also have been in a Gnostic vein that he came to be associated with knowledge, so it was apparently as a Gnostic figure that the Khurramīs received him. Yet they cast him as the mahdi, the victorious avenger, rather than a spiritual saviour. Did they continue to see him as a bringer of redeeming knowledge like Mandā dḤayyī?[119] We do not know. All one can say is that it is surprising that Niẓām al-Mulk translated *kūdak-i dānā* as *(al-) fatā al-ʿālim* rather than *al-ʿārif*: the reference was surely not to knowledge in the sense of learning. In Ismailism we later meet a 'perfect child' (*al-walad al-tāmm*),[120] but his precise relationship to the 'knowing child' remains to be identified.

REINCARNATION

Mainstream Zoroastrianism taught bodily resurrection, not reincarnation. In fact, one could not guess from the Zoroastrian books that the doctrine of reincarnation had ever been present in Iran, though the priests who compiled them must certainly have known about it, if only from Manichaeism. Such Zoroastrian polemics against Manichaeism as survive display little interest in conceptions of life after death, and they say nothing about reincarnation.[121] The priests must also have known that the Zagros mountains were teeming with believers in reincarnation, if only because the Muslims talked about it, yet that too is left unmentioned. As with Nana, it should teach us never to take their silence as evidence for non-existence. But how then does reincarnation relate to Persian Zoroastrianism? The short answer is that it can easily be seen as a

118 Cf. Grenet and Marshak, 'Mythe de Nana', 6f., also postulating laments for Tammuz' sister; Bar Penkaye in de Ménasce, 'Autour d'un texte syriaque', 590; Ibn al-Nadīm, 387 = II, 758; Widengren, 'Synkretismus', 55ff.

119 Cf. Rudolph, *Gnosis*, 131.

120 Corbin, *Cyclical Time*, 99.

121 *Škand*, 16:49–51, mentions that the Manichaeans deny the resurrection of the body, but not what they believe instead (xvi, 50); for other polemics see de Ménasce, *Troisème livre*, 209f., no. 200 (*DkB*, 169; *DkM*, 216).

development from the same roots as those from which the Persian doctrine grew. The long answer is very long, for first we need to familiarise ourselves with the Zoroastrian doctrines of resurrection (*ristākhēz*) and renovation (*frašgerd*).

The Pahlavi books tell us that after death the soul lingers by the body for three days, often envisaged as pleasurable for the righteous and sheer torment for the wicked, and that it moves on to the Činvad bridge on the fourth day. The righteous soul passes the bridge and meets his own *dēn* (a personification of his acts) in the form of a beautiful maiden who escorts him to paradise, or she meets him at the grave and escorts him to the bridge. From there the soul of the righteous passes via the stations of good thought, good speech, and good deeds to heaven or, according to some, it stops in one of the three corresponding heavens, that is limbo (*hamēstagān*), paradise (*vahišt*), and the realm of endless light (*garōdmān*). The wicked soul, on the other hand, meets his *dēn* as a foul woman and sinks via the stations of evil thought, evil words, and evil deeds to the presence of Ahriman and the demons in the deepest darkness.[122]

According to the Pahlavi books the souls that have passed to heaven and hell will only stay there until the renovation (*frašgerd*). At the end of time all the dead will be resurrected and reunited with their bodies, which will take fifty-seven years. After the resurrection (*ristākhēz*) the righteous will go to paradise and the wicked to hell, but only for three days and three nights. When rivers of molten metal cover the earth they will all return to the earth to go through the hot metal, which will be easy for the righteous, painful for the wicked, and which will purify all of them; or alternatively the wicked will be damned for ever in the sense of not participating in the renovation (there will be no hell after the renovation has taken place).[123] The purified will receive the *haoma* drink, which will endow them with immortality. Ahriman is then defeated, the mountains will become low and the earth is smoothed out, and humans will live happily without thirst, hunger, or death, enjoying the taste of meat in their mouths and the pleasures of love without procreation.[124]

Minor discrepancies and repetitions apart, the oddity of this combination of individual and universal eschatology lies in the fact that it reduces paradise and hell to mere interludes on the way to the renovation and

[122] Cf. *EIr.*, s.v. 'eschatology, i' (Shaked).

[123] *Dd*, 36:101.

[124] For all this, and references, see *EIr.*, s.vv. 'eschatology, i' (Shaked), 'frašokərəti' (Hintze); Hultgård, 'Persian Apocalypticism', 54ff. According to *MahFr* 44–6, all couples will have a child at the age of fifty-seven and none thereafter.

subjects all humans except those alive when the renovation comes to two judgements. This did not necessarily bother ordinary believers. The Zagros villagers studied by Loeffler in the 1970s repeatedly gave essentially the same account of eschatology without finding anything to be odd about it regardless of whether they were convinced of its truth or not. According to them the soul of the deceased would be questioned by Munkar and Nakīr in the grave, and if his record was good (all the speakers were men) a houri would come to him and say, 'I am your good deeds; God made me from your good deeds' and take him to heaven, or to some pleasant place; if he was bad he would see his evil deeds in the form of a frightful creature and be taken to hell, or to some nasty place; on the day of judgement all the dead would be resurrected and judged, to go to paradise or hell. One man compared the experience in the grave to questioning by the gendarmerie: a good person can go home thereafter until the court proceedings, but the bad one will be locked up in a bad place; their final fate will be settled later.[125] The Zoroastrian account did come across as problematic to some Zoroastrian priests, however: why submit all those who have already been assigned to paradise or hell to a second judgement? One of the most perplexing questions was that 'there is no need for a new reckoning', as Manuščihr observed, without suggesting a solution.[126] The incongruity of paradise as a mere stage on the way to a transfigured earth is softened by the doctrine that the earth will be raised to the star station and paradise come down to it, so that the two will merge: Ohrmazd, the *amahraspands*, the gods, and men will all be in the same place.[127] Even so, we are told that the blessed in paradise would be so happy there that they would wish the day would never come.[128]

A modern reader also wonders why believers transported to the realm of the gods in endless light should want their bodies back. The *Dēnkard* explains that the essence of man is the soul; the body is simply clothing required for purposes of defeating the lie (*druj*) in the material world (*gētīg*) and will be left behind when one has done one's combat duty. When the renovation comes, it adds, man will resume his *gētīg* clothing. The incongruity is startling.[129] No doubt some kind of clothing (i.e., form) was

[125] Loeffler, *Islam in Practice*, 56f., 74, 105, 177, 187, cf. also the mullah at 24f.
[126] Bailey, *Zoroastrian Problems*, 117, citing *Dd*, 30:9.
[127] *PRDd*, 48:98f.; cf. Bailey, *Zoroastrian Problems*, 116f.; similarly *MahFr* 39.
[128] *PRDd*, 25:4.
[129] *DkM*. 245f., in Molé, *Culte*, 469f. (= *Dk*. III, no. 222); cf. also the passages in Shaked, '*Mēnōg* and *gētīg*', 80, 88, 92. The incongruity is noted by Duchesne-Guillemin, *Religion de l'Iran*, 352.

necessary for existence. Even the gods, the sun, the moon, and the stars had clothing: they were immortal and their clothing was inseparable from them. By contrast, the *dēv*s and noxious animals had mortal natures and separable clothing, so that they would perish when their clothing was lost. Humans were in between, having immortal natures and separable clothing.[130] One takes that to mean that they would survive as spiritual beings with clothing of light.[131] Clothing in the sense of a form or body was required for individuation, but it did not have to be fleshy, and without their gross bodies humans were *amahraspands*:[132] why should their clothing after the renovation be the body they had worn for purposes of combat in the *gētīg* and which had been torn up and dispersed by animals after completion of its duty?

Zoroastrians were also troubled by the incongruous nature of their own funerary customs.[133] How was it possible to reassemble bodies that had been torn apart by dogs, birds, wolves, and vultures, they asked.[134] It was an old question, first posed by Greek and Roman pagans in refutation of the Christian belief in bodily resurrection;[135] but it was particularly relevant to Zoroastrians, who deliberately exposed their dead so that their bodies would not only be dispersed, but also become part of the food chain (the key problem, though it is not spelt out). The Zoroastrians gave much the same answer as the Christians: the proof of the resurrection lay in the creation; it was easier to reassemble bodies than to create them in the first place.[136] Bodily resurrection is presented as a dogma that had to be accepted: 'I must have no doubt about . . . the three nights' judgement, the resurrection, and the future body.'[137] But people still felt uneasy about the funerary customs: would it be painful to be torn up, what was the point when body and vital soul (*jān*) were to be united again? They were reassured that only the wicked would grieve at the sight of their bodies

[130] *DkM*, 42 in Molé, *Culte*, 471f. (no. 4) (= *Dk*, III, no. 51).

[131] Cf. Yt 13: 45; Zādspram, 35:60.

[132] *DkM* in Molé, *Culte*, 471f. (no. 4) (*Dk*, III, 51 in de Ménasce, whose translation runs together *amahraspand* and *amarg* in the single word 'immortels').

[133] See Shaked, *Dualism*, 40, 43; see also Bremmer, 'Resurrection between Zarathustra and Smith', 98.

[134] Zādspram, 34:3; cited along with other passages in Molé, *Culte*, 113ff.; cf. also Shaked, *Dualism*, 33.

[135] See Bynum, *Resurrection of the Body*, 32f., 42f., 55f., 61, 63, 75, 80; Barnard, 'Athanagoras', 10, 21; Theodoret of Cyrus, *On Providence*, Or. 9.34f.

[136] Cf. Molé, *Culte*, 113ff.

[137] Boyce, *History of Zoroastrianism*, I, 236, n. 32, citing Jamasp Asana, *Pahlavi Texts*, 43.18–44.6 (and holding the doctrine to go back to Zoroaster).

being torn apart;[138] yet when the animals came, the conscience (*boy*) of the deceased would cry, 'Do not eat the body which is mine (and) which Ohrmazd will return to me at the end, at the time of the future body.'[139] Disbelief in bodily resurrection seems to have flourished even in the highest circles. The Christian Catholicos Babai is presented as expounding the doctrine of bodily resurrection to King Jamasp (496–8) on the apparent assumption that the latter subscribed to a different view: 'if you do not believe what I say, consider that man is first created from a drop'.[140]

It should be obvious that the Pahlavi books combine two quite different conceptions of the afterlife, as several scholars have noted before: the doctrines relating to individual and universal eschatology simply do not go together.[141] It is not just of the Pahlavi books that this is true; it also applies to the eschatology of the Ḥarbiyya. In their account of the seven eras presided over by seven Adams they solved the problem of where to park humans who died before the collective judgement by means of reincarnation: those who died would simply be born again, and this would go on for 50,000 years, whereupon all would be moved either to heaven or below the earth. Yet they, or some of them, also said that those who succeeded in purifying themselves would become angels with bodies of light on an individual basis: those left behind would see them every morning and evening. There was no waiting for the grand judgement for them.[142] Both conceptions are old, and it is possible that the attempts to combine them also go a long way back. The view of heaven as a mere interlude to life in a new body on earth appears in Josephus (d. *c.* 100), who credits it to the Pharisees and seems to believe in it himself.[143] It is tempting to see this as reflecting a Zoroastrian conception, given the widespread (if by now somewhat embattled) idea that Zoroastrianism contributed heavily to the formation of Jewish eschatological ideas. Be that as it may,

138 *Dd*, 15 (also in Shaked, *Dualism*, 39), cf. 16:1, 17:1.

139 Zādspram, 30:32.

140 Scher, 'Histoire Nestorienne', 130. Compare *Dk*, III, no. 251 (*DkB*, 205; *DkM*, 271), referring to learned men who were disdainful of the *gētīg*, paradise, and the future body and who apparently held that most people would go to hell for ever.

141 Bailey, *Zoroastrian Problems*, 116f.; Duchesne-Guillemin, *Religion de l'Iran*, 352f.; cf. Shaked, 'Eschatology and the Goal of the Religious Life', 223f., with a defence of its coherence.

142 See Chapter 12, p. 236.

143 See Mason, *Flavius Josephus on the Pharisees*, 161–70 (drawn to my attention by Joseph Witztum). Josephus presents the doctrine in the language of reincarnation which commanded Greek respect because it was Platonist; but, as Mason shows, reincarnation is not what he had in mind.

there must have been more conceptions of the afterlife in Iran than the two we happen to hear about in the extant Zoroastrian books (no less than four are attested for the Jews in Josephus' time),[144] and the two that we do hear about are unlikely to have originated together.

Universal eschatology

To start with the collective fate of mankind, we may ignore the controversial question of precisely what the Gāthās do or do not say on the question and go straight to the younger Avesta, more precisely *Yašt* 19 (*Zamyād Yašt*). This *Yašt*, which we encountered above in connection with *khwarra*, is said to be undatable,[145] but it is certainly much older than the Pahlavi texts, and it is in this work that we first hear of the return of the dead: two passages between them state that 'we' worship the *khwarəna* of the Kavis, which is Ahura Mazda's, so that his creatures may make life excellent, without decay, everlasting, which will happen when the dead rise, when the victorious Saošyant and his helpers come.[146] There is no mention of judgement, paradise, or hell. One takes it that it is this world that will be magically transformed by the *khwarəna* so that all will live for ever, even the dead springing back to life on a transfigured earth.

According to the so-called *Fragment Westergaard*, a young Avestan commentary on the old Avestan *Airiiaman*, the dead who were raised again would have 'life with bones', which the Pahlavi translation preserved in the *Dēnkard* takes to mean that their bodies would be restored.[147] The translation may be anachronistic, but whatever exactly 'life with bones' may have meant at the time when the commentary was composed, the text does seem to operate with some concept of resurrection.[148] That the dead would be restored to life was also known to Theopompus of Chios (fourth century BC), but he did not envisage it along the lines of the much later Pahlavi books. He is cited by Diogenes Laertius as having said in his *Philippica* that 'according to the Magi, men will return to life

[144] That is, reincarnation (Philo, d. *c.* 50); resurrection (Pharisees); spiritual afterlife (Essenes); and no resurrection, perhaps meaning no afterlife at all (Sadducees).

[145] Kellens, 'L'eschatologie mazdénne ancienne', 49.

[146] Yt 19:9–11, 89.

[147] Vevaina, 'Resurrecting the Resurrection', 217f., with full details and references.

[148] Cf. the review of the attestations in Gignoux, "Corps osseux et âme osseuse" and his *Man and Cosmos*, 91–3. Gignoux interprets the evidence in the light of shamanism but does not discuss the passage in *Fragment Westergaard*.

(*anabiōsesthai*) and be immortal'.[149] Theopompus' passage in its turn was known to Aeneas of Gaza, a Christian who died in 525. According to him 'Zoroaster prophesies that there will be a time in which a resurrection of the corpses will take place. Theopompus knows what I say.'[150] It is not clear whether Aeneas is actually quoting Theopompus or just reading him as confirming information from other sources, namely that the Zoroastrians believed in bodily resurrection. But, as noted by Bremmer and de Jong, a Christian-style resurrection is not likely to be what Theopompus had in mind, for the verb he uses is that which he also employs in his notice on Epimenides, who reputedly claimed to 'have returned to life repeatedly' (*pollakis anabebiōkenai*).[151] Epimenides' many returns to life are usually called reincarnations in the modern literature, but this was not what the Magi had in mind either, as is clear from Theopompus in the rendition of Plutarch. According to Plutarch, initially quoting another source, Horomazes, born of the purest light, and Areimanios, born of darkness, were constantly at war, but Areimanios would eventually perish, whereupon the earth would become flat and level, with one government for all men, who would be happy and speak the same language. As in *Yašt* 19 the *frašgerd* is about life on a transfigured earth, as in fact it still is in the Pahlavi books. Plutarch then quotes Theopompus as saying that according to the Magi the two gods would rule successively for three thousand years, then they would fight for another three thousand years, and in the end 'Hades [i.e., Ahriman] shall pass away; then men will be happy, and neither shall they need to have food nor shall they cast any shadow'.[152] That the blessed will stop eating is also mentioned in the Pahlavi books, but not that they will stop casting shadows. Comparing Theopompus with Zoroastrian passages that do involve the absence of shadows, de Jong persuasively interprets the statement as meaning that humans will have spiritual (*mēnōg*) bodies.[153] Though this was not the official view by the time of the Pahlavi books, it was certainly represented. Zādspram has Zoroaster ask Ohrmazd whether those endowed with bodies (*tanōmandān*) will come back in bodies or whether

[149] Diogenes Laertius, I, 8f., discussed in de Jong, *Traditions*, 224f. The statement continues 'and that the world will endure through their invocations' or alternatively that 'the things which are will continue to be through their revolutions'.

[150] Aeneas of Gaza, *Theophrastus*, 64.8–10; Colonna in Bremmer, 'Resurrection between Zarathustra and Smith', 99; cf. de Jong, *Traditions*, 327f.

[151] Diogenes Laertius, I, 114.

[152] Plutarch, *Isis and Osiris*, 370, A–C.

[153] De Jong, 'Shadow and Resurrection'. As he notes, in the Pahlavi books humans stop eating even before the renovation (discussed below).

they will be 'like those who have no shadows' at the time of the renovation. In accordance with the doctrine prevalent in Zādspram's time Ohrmazd replies that they will be endowed with bodies again.[154] Yet Zādspram himself later tells us that they will have clothing (= bodies) of light.[155] Perhaps he meant clothing in the literal sense of the word.

The *mēnōg* form in which the Magi of Theopompus' time, and apparently also some in Zādspram's, and even Zādspram himself, envisaged the dead as returning was not spiritual in the sense of deprived of material reality, but rather in that of lacking the dense materiality characteristic of the physical world: a *mēnōg* body was not visible, tangible, or fleshy. It was in *mēnōg* bodies that humans had been created before they were transferred into the material world (*gētīg*). Apparently it was also in such bodies that Theopompus' Magians envisaged the dead as returning to life on the transfigured earth. One could call immortal life in *mēnōg* bodies 'bodily resurrection', of course, but it is not what is normally understood by the term which stands for restoration of our old bodies; and there is still no mention of a judgement.

Why did the representatives of official Zoroastrianism opt for resurrection in fleshy rather than luminous bodies? And why did they follow the Christians in envisaging the resurrection as a reunion of scattered body parts? There is something undignified about a deity who has to tinker with recycled material: surely he could create a new body just like the old one out of nothing, or out of fire, as in the first creation? When Paul described the resurrection he compared the future body to wheat growing from a seed, which decays in the process; this image was developed by Origen (d. 254), who credited the resurrection to a seminal force in the body, without any need for reassembly of the old parts. Neither Paul nor Origen envisaged the resurrection as one of the flesh: Paul described the resurrection body as spiritual, and Origen held it to be luminous and made of subtle matter. This was felt not to be good enough, however, and, Paul's authority notwithstanding, Origen was denounced for practically denying the resurrection of the body.[156] For a variety of reasons, including martyrdom, the resurrection had rapidly come to be understood as reanimation of the flesh. When people came to think deeply about the question it was

[154] Zādspram, 34:1–2 adduced by de Jong, 'Shadow and Resurrection', 220 (in the translation of Zaehner, 'Zervanite Apocalypse II', 606, the question is whether they will get their bodies back or be 'like unto shades').

[155] Zādspram, 35:60. The *fravašis* also have garments of light in Yt 13:45 in Darmester's translation, but in Malandra's they are merely surrounded by light.

[156] 1 Corinthians 15:37, 44; *SCM Press Origen*, s.v. 'Resurrection' (Daley).

their very own familiar bodies that they wanted back in order to feel that they would be themselves in their new life, and so the reassembly model won out.[157] Perhaps the priests charged by the Sasanians with the unification of Zoroastrianism also discovered that most people wanted their old bodies back. They certainly did not want them to believe in reincarnation, and stressing that their resurrection bodies would be the very flesh that they were inhabiting right now was perhaps the most effective way of ruling it out. It will have been for some such reasons that they adopted the reassembly model, utterly at odds with Zoroastrian burial customs though it was. That this concept of the resurrection in the Pahlavi books is late is corroborated by the fact that the term 'future body' (*tan ī pasen*) has no Avestan precursor.[158]

There were still people who preferred the alternative solution, however. The fourth/tenth-century al-Maqdisī informs us that 'many Zoroastrians' believed in the resurrection (*al-baʿth wa'l-nushūr*): evidently not all of them did. Some Zoroastrian(s) in Fārs had told him that when the reign of Ahriman came to an end there would be no more toil, disease, or death, and all human beings would become 'spiritual beings (*rūḥāniyyūn*) dwelling for ever in eternal light'.[159] It is not clear whether they would do so in the highest heaven or on a transfigured earth, but either way it is clear that they would not be in fleshy bodies. The Ḥarbiyya also hoped to become angels with bodies of light. It was presumably in polemics against such people that the third/ninth-century Zādspram had Zoroaster ask Ohrmazd to settle the question in favour of the body casting shadows.

Individual eschatology

We may now leave universal eschatology for the fate of the individual soul. This is where we find the conception of the afterlife as ascent to the realm of eternal light rather than life on a transfigured earth, and this too is attested in the younger Avesta. The *Vīdēvdād*, generally placed in or around the time of the Achaemenids, explains, much like the Pahlavi books, that the soul would be assailed by demons for three days after death, whereupon the demon Vizareša would carry off the soul of a *daeva* worshipper who had been sinful; the soul of a righteous person, by contrast, would pass via

[157] Cf. Davies, 'Resurrection of the Flesh'; Bynum, *Resurrection of the Body*, 68, and the review by Shaw, 'Out on a Limb', 45.
[158] Boyce, *History of Zoroastrianism*, I, 236, n. 32.
[159] Maqdisī, II, 143; also adduced by de Jong, 'Shadow and Resurrection', 220.

the Činvad bridge and meet a girl with dogs at her side; she would take him to the mountain Harā Bərəzaitī, where Vohu Mana would rise from his throne to greet him with the question 'Have you come to us, you holy one, from that decaying world into this undecaying one?' He would then take the soul to *garōdmān*, the seat of Ahura Mazda and all the holy beings.[160] The *Hādōkht Nask* and *Yašt* 24 are similar, except that they make no mention of the Činvad bridge and imply that there were three grades of paradise before one reached the endless light; the former also supplies three grades of hell on the way to endless darkness for the sinner. Even in the highest heaven, in the presence of Ahura Mazda, there was food.[161]

It has been suggested that Darius I (d. 486 BC) envisaged his afterlife as an ascent to the realm of endless light.[162] It was certainly how Antiochus of Commagene (d. 38 BC), the scion of a Hellenised Iranian dynasty in Anatolia, envisaged it: he tells us in his funerary inscription that he has constructed his mausoleum (on the mountain of Nimrud Dağ) near the heavenly throne so that the outer husk which is his body might rest there for countless ages after sending his soul (*psychē*), dear to the gods, up to the heavenly throne of Zeus Oromasdes.[163] He hardly expected to leave the heavenly throne for a universal judgement and resurrection. Boyce nonetheless contrives to have him believe in the Last Day with reference to another inscription. Here he concludes by threatening any man who violates the sanctuary in question with dire punishments: the unerring arrows of Apollo and Heracles shall pierce his heart, he shall suffer punishment through the anger of Hera, and both his family and his descendants will be burnt by the lightning of Zeus Oromasdes. All this, as Boyce agrees, is about the terrible things that will befall this man, his family, and his descendants in this life at the hand of gods who are conceived as Greek, not only in their names but also in the sense that they punish people (whereas in Zoroastrianism only Ahriman and demons do so). Antiochus continues, however, that those who are clean of unrighteous ways and zealous for holy works, and who maintain his (Antiochus') cult, will have a 'good life' and Zeus Oromasdes will hearken to their prayers and be their fellow fighter (*synagōnistēn*) in their good acts; other gods, including Artagnes Heracles (i.e. Verethragna/Bahrām) and Apollo Mithra, will also help them, and they shall find the images (*charakteras*, apparently here meaning

[160] *Vd*, 19:28–32.
[161] *Hādōxt Nask*, 17; Yt 24:65.
[162] West, 'Darius' Ascent to Paradise'.
[163] Boyce and Grenet, *History of Zoroastrianism*, 333.

the sculptured reproductions set up by Antiochus) of the kindly spirits to be undeceiving announcers of a happy life and fellow fighters in good undertakings.[164] Again it is in this life that the virtuous people will have Zeus Oromasdes and other gods and spirits and fellow fighters and helpers, and so become happy. But there are more Zoroastrian reminiscences in this section, not only in the names of the gods but also in the concept of the gods and humans as fellow fighters, and perhaps in the promise of a 'good life' (*bion agathon*) as well. Boyce relates this term to the Avestan *vahišta-vahu-*, meaning 'best life', eventually paradise, and further argues that the concept of fellow fighters testifies to belief in dualism, and that since Antiochus trusted his gods he must have expected them to win, meaning that he must have believed in the last day and the renovation. It is hard to take this reasoning seriously. Even if we accept that Antiochus meant paradise by the good life, the paradise in question is presumably that which he describes in his other inscription – that is, life at the throne of Zeus Oromasdes. There is no shred of evidence for belief in universal judgement, resurrection, and transfiguration here. In the first inscription, moreover, Antiochus says that 'the generations of all men whom boundless time (*chronos apeiros*) shall, through its destiny for the life of each, set in possession of this land' are commanded to keep the land in question inviolate.[165] If there would be generations of men in *boundless* time there would not be a last day. The Zoroastrians of the Pahlavi books lived in a world ruled by the limited time that Ohrmazd had instituted by setting the heavenly bodies in motion in order to prevent the conflict with Ahriman from going on for ever: the duration of the world was the time set for the contest, and it was limited time, i.e., the movement of the heavenly bodies, which determined the fates of men until then. If Antiochus held that unlimited time held sway over the generations of men, he was an eternalist. This is in fact what one would expect on the basis of his Greek culture, though there may well have been Zoroastrian eternalists too.

Some 700 years later an inscription carved between 670 and 750 in the opposite end of the Iranian culture area, Khwārizm, declares an ossuary to belong to the soul of a certain Srawyōk son of Tišyān and expresses the wish that both Srawyōk's soul and that of his father may dwell in the eternal paradise. The hope is clearly that they are in paradise now, not that they will enter it at the end of times, and paradise is identified as eternal,

[164] Boyce and Grenet, *History of Zoroastrianism*, 334.
[165] Boyce and Grenet, *History of Zoroastrianism*, 332.

not as a temporary abode that would disappear, along with hell, when the whole of mankind had been resurrected and purified.[166]

There is no evidence that those who envisaged the afterlife as a release of the individual soul to the world of endless light combined it with belief in collective purification for life on a transfigured earth until we reach the third/ninth-century evidence. In principle it could have been in response to Islam that the Zoroastrians began to combine the two ideas. More probably, however, they had begun to do so under the Sasanians, in tandem with their sponsorship of bodily resurrection. Christianity integrated elite and masses in the same moral community on a scale hitherto unknown in the ancient world. To be competitive the Zoroastrians now had to emphasise the communal nature of their own religion too: those who considered themselves righteous could not simply escape to their private world of bliss; all adherents of the good religion had to be assembled for collective purification and transformation. Since the idea of individual ascent to heaven was well entrenched in the tradition it could not simply be eradicated, so life in heaven (and hell) was accepted as a phase on the way to collective judgement – or, if the combination already existed, this was the only view that was deemed acceptable now. Though this generated some insoluble problems it was clearly a good solution, destined for a long life even among Muslims. But again there were some who resisted. The author of the *Mēnōg ī khrad* pointedly tells us that those who reached the abode of the gods would stay there for ever, dwelling in glory for all eternity; it was only the denizens of hell who would be recalled at the time of the renovation.[167] Does this mean that only the latter would get their own bodies back, or that all bodies would actually be of light? The author does not tell us.

It was in terms of individual eschatology that the Zoroastrian burial customs made sense.[168] The body was destroyed because it became impure when the soul left it, as Ādhurfarnbag explains in a debate set in the time of al-Maʾmūn. The faster the body was torn apart, the clearer it was that the soul would reach paradise, Agathias informs us.[169] Those whose bodies were quickly dragged from their biers by birds were considered fortunate, Strabo explains in connection with the funerary customs of the Caspians, whereas those taken by wild beasts or dogs were considered less fortunate, and those who were not taken by anything were held to be cursed by

166 Grenet, *Pratiques funéraires*, 252f.; also cited in Gignoux, *Man and Cosmos*, 91.

167 *Mēnōg ī khrad*, 2:157, 193 (West).

168 Cf. above, p. 345.

169 Stausberg, *Religion Zarathustras*, I, 350, citing the *Abāliš Gizistag* and Agathias II, 23, also discussed in de Jong, *Traditions*, 326.

fortune.[170] When Alexander caught Bessos, the satrap who had killed Darius after the defeat at Gaugamela, he punished him for his regicide by executing him in a deeply humiliating manner and posting guards to keep the birds away from his corpse.[171]

Individual ascent and reincarnation

What all this establishes is that until the Sasanian period, and to a lesser extent thereafter, there were Zoroastrians who envisaged the afterlife as individual ascent to heaven for the saved, without any concern for universal eschatology. It is the variations on their beliefs that are of relevance here. The followers of ʿAbdallāh b. Muʿāwiya believed in individual ascent, but also in reincarnation. Was the latter another belief of foreign origin or was it rooted in the Avestan tradition? The answer may be neither. Most probably the idea formed part of ancient Iranian religion or eventually developed out of it. Either way, it is closely related to the Avestan tradition and unlikely to have been perceived as extrinsic to it, except by its opponents.

The moon as a transfer point

The *Šāyest nē-šāyest* cites the *Dāmdād Nask*, part of the lost portion of the Avesta, as saying that 'when they sever the consciousness of men, it goes out to the nearest fire, then out to the stars, then out to the moon, and then out to the sun'.[172] In other words, when people die, the nearest fire, meaning the fire lit in the room,[173] attracts the immortal part of the soul, itself a luminous or fiery entity, and propels it upwards to its final abode in the sun, or in the infinite light beyond it. The journey is mentioned in several Pahlavi texts. They do not always mention the nearest fire, and some stop at the sun while others continue the journey to *garōdmān* or infinite light beyond it;[174] some correlate the stars, moon, and the sun with good thought, good speech, and good action. But the stars (envisaged as closest to the earth), the moon, and the sun are all identified as stations (sg. *pāyag*) or habitations (sg. *mehmānīh*), and the route was certainly

170 Strabo, XI, 11, 8.
171 Curtius Rufus, VII 5, 36ff., in Jacobs, 'Tod des Bessos', 182; cf. *EIr*., s.v. 'Bessos'.
172 *Šāyest nē šāyest*, 12.5, tr. West, *SBE*, 341f.; cited in West, 'Darius' Ascent to Paradise', 53.
173 Cf. Yamamoto, 'Zoroastrian Temple Cult, II', 96.
174 In *Sad Dar*, lxxxvii, 11, the soul travels via the fire to the star station and the moon station to the sun station and beyond, but not to the endless light: the journey here culminates in the Činvad bridge!

ancient: *Yašt* 13 is devoted to the *fravašis* who were (among other things) the deified souls of the ancestors, and it praises them (again among other things) as those 'who showed us their path to the stars, the moon, the sun, and the endless lights'.[175] *Yašt* 12 enumerates the stars, moon, sun, endless light, paradise, and *garōdemāna* in a manner also suggesting they were stations.[176] It was by the same route (here terminating at the sun) that the soul of the primal bull had travelled for divine reassurance that cattle would have a protector in the *gētīg* according to the *Bundahišn*,[177] and it was also via the stars, moon, and sun that Ardā Vīrāf reached *garōdmān* and the abode of Ohrmazd.[178] What happened to those who did not deserve to rise to infinite light or beyond? The usual answer is that they were taken by the demons after the three days in the grave, or on reaching the Činvad bridge, but the Pahlavi books also allow for a limbo for those whose good and bad deeds are equally weighty (*hamēstagān*), while the book of Ardā Vīrāf turns the star, sun, and moon stations into permanent abodes for those who had good thoughts, good words, and good deeds respectively but fell short of a place in *garōdmān*.[179] In the Upaniṣads, dating from the seventh or sixth century BC, on the other hand, all the imperfect souls are sent back for reincarnation on reaching the moon.

According to the *Bṛhadāraṇyaka Upaniṣad* those who follow the superior religious path travel from the funeral pyre (the equivalent of the fire lit in the room) to the light, 'from light to day, from day to the increasing half (of the moon), from the increasing half to the six months when the sun goes to the north, from those six months to the world of the devas, from the world of the devas to the sun, from the sun to the place of lighting'; from there they are guided to the worlds of Brahman (the equivalent of endless light). 'There is no returning for them.' Those who follow the other path go via smoke, night, and the decreasing half of the moon, where they become food and the *devas* feed on them; then they pass into space and from there to air, from air to rain, and from rain to the earth, where they become food offered to the altar fire, which is man, and born in the fire of women,

175 Yt 13:57. For other Avestan references to this sequence see *Hādōxt Nask*, 105. For the belief that the stars were closer to the earth than the sun and the moon see Henning, 'Astronomical Chapter', 230; for the origin of the conception (which also appears in some pre-Socratic philosophers) see Panaino, 'Uranographia'.

176 Yt 12:25–30.

177 Shaked, 'Moral Responsibility of Animals', 580.

178 *Ardā Vīrāfnāmag*, chs. 7–11.

179 *Ardā Vīrāfnāmag*, chs. 7–9; cf. *Mēnōg ī khrad*, 7, which does not seem to suggest that all three parts of heaven had permanent residents, however.

eventually to do the same round all over again; but those who know neither of the two paths become worms, birds, and creeping things.[180] In the *Chāndogya Upaniṣad*, which has almost the same account, those who go on the return journey turn into mist, cloud, and rain, which rains them down for rebirth as trees, herbs, grain, and other foodstuff.[181] A simpler presentation appears in the *Kauṣītaki Upaniṣad*. Here

> All who depart from this world [or this body] go to the moon. In the former, [the bright] half, the moon delights in their spirits; in the other, [the dark] half, the moon sends them on to be born again. In the first fortnight [the moon] waxes on their breath-souls, while in the latter half it prepares them to be born [again]. Verily, the moon is the door of the Svarga world [the heavenly world].

As regards the return journey, we are told that 'if a man objects to the moon [is not satisfied with life there], the moon sets him free', presumably meaning that he travels on.

> But if a man does not object, then the moon sends him down as rain upon this earth. And according to his deeds and according to his knowledge he is born again here as a worm, or as an insect, or as a fish, or as a bird, or as a lion, or as a boar, or as a serpent, or as a tiger, or as a man, or something else in different places.[182]

The moon also appears as a transfer point between heaven and earth for both upward and downward traffic in the Zoroastrian literature, again linked with its waxing and waning; but it does not distribute souls or spirits here, only the goodness, fortune, and *khwarra* from the divine world in return for the good deeds of human beings. A Pahlavi commentary on a prayer in praise of the moon (*Māh niyāyišn*) explains the Avestan words 'Fifteen [days] when the moon waxes, fifteen when the moon wanes' with the observation that 'for fifteen days it receives the good deeds of the material beings and from the spiritual ones reward and recompense; and for fifteen days it delivers the good deeds to the spiritual beings and the reward and recompense to the material ones'.[183] Here we have a clear statement of circulation between the divine and human worlds, but it is only the good deeds that are transported upwards and transmuted into things sent downwards, not the souls or spirits scheduled for good or bad reincarnations. The *Bundahišn* says that the moon waxes for fifteen days in order to distribute *khwarra* to terrestrial beings and wanes for another

[180] *Bṛhadāraṇyaka Upaniṣad*, 6.2.15f. Müller.
[181] *Chāndogya Upaniṣad*, 5.10. 1–8 Müller.
[182] *Kauṣītaki Upaniṣad*, 1.2 Müller.
[183] *Māh Ny*. 3.4, in Skjaervø, 'Iranian Elements in Manicheism', 279. A fuller extract in both transliteration and translation is given in Panaino, 'Manichaean Concepts', 464f.

fifteen days when they receive it, comparing the moon to the male organ which waxes in order to discharge semen.[184] Here it is *khwarra* that is being circulated, or at least sent down: it is not clear whether it is from above or below that the moon receives it when it is waxing. Another Zoroastrian text says that the moon brings all goodness from spiritual beings to the material beings for transmission into their bodies, for Ardwīsūr transmits the goodness (from the moon?) to the firmament and from there it is distributed to all via chance;[185] 'Sōg consigns [it] to the moon, the moon consigns it to Ardwīsūr, Ardwīsūr consigns [it] to the sphere, the sphere distributes [it] to the living beings', as the *Bundahišn* says.[186] In these two passages the link with the waxing and waning of the moon is missing, but the goodness that comes down now goes into human bodies. It is distributed from the firmament or the sphere by chance, presumably meaning astrological fate; elsewhere *khwarra* is produced by Ohrmazd and distributed in seeds/semen by time.[187] Of the semen of beneficent animals we are explicitly told that it comes from the moon.[188] An Avestan passage says that *khwarəna* is 'placed in the rains',[189] suggesting that it was rained down as in the two Upaniṣads. Fire, present in lightning, was also rained down, as water, which caused the growth of plants, which were eaten by animals and humans, and so became fiery semen.[190] It was in the form of *khwarra* that Zoroaster's semen was preserved in the lake out of which his three posthumous sons were to be born.[191] *Khwarra* was associated with semen, yet it was also identified with spirit, and there is even a Pahlavi passage identifying it with soul (*ruwān*).[192] The Persian Zoroastrians did not see spirits or souls as circulating, but their affinities with the Upaniṣads are nonetheless close.

[184] Panaino, 'Manichaean Concepts', 467, citing *GrBd*, 26:21; also cited in Duchesne-Guillemin, 'Le X^varənah', 30f., citing *Bundahišn* (Anklesaria 1908 edn), 164, 13ff.

[185] Pahlavi commentary to *Sīh Rōzag* 1.3 in Skjaervø, 'Iranian Elements in Manicheism', 279; Panaino, 'Manichaean Concepts', 466. Cf. Bīrūnī, *Āthār*, 233.1 = 219: God (i.e., Ohrmazd) created the moon for the distribution of good things in this world; water, animals, and plants increase when it waxes and decrease when it wanes.

[186] *GrBd*, 26:34, in Panaino, 'Manichaean Concepts', 466f.

[187] *DkM*, 347, in Zaehner, *Zurvan*, 369f.; in Molé, *Culte*, 436 (= *Dk*. III, no. 363 de Ménasce).

[188] *GrBd*, ch. 3:14 (ed. and tr. in Zaehner, *Zurvan*, 323 = 334, no. 12).

[189] *Tištar Yašt*, stanza 34; Panaino, cf. p. 122.

[190] Duchesne-Guillemin, 'The Six Original Creations', 8; cf. Duchesne-Guillemin, 'The Form of Fire'; Duchesne-Guillemin, 'Le X^varənah'.

[191] Hultgård, 'Persian Apocalypticism', 52.

[192] *GrBd* 101, 1–14, in Bailey, *Zoroastrian Problems*, 36f. (the invisible *khwarra* entered them, that is, the *ruwān*).

Manichaeans and Khurramīs

According to the Manichaeans, the souls liberated from earthly existence travelled back via the moon and the sun to the highest world of light: this was the doctrine that Jesus taught his disciples according to Mani.[193] The souls went via the Milky Way to the moon, which waxed until it was full and then passed them on to the sun, which delivered them to their final destination.[194] The Khurramīs envisaged the release from existence in much the same way, though they identified the immortal part of man as spirit rather than soul. Al-Maqdisī had read in *Kitāb al-Khurramiyya* (presumably a book about them rather than by them) that 'the stars are balls and holes which attract the spirits of created beings (*al-khalā'iq*) and deliver them to the moon, which waxes until it reaches its utmost point in fullness and completion, whereupon it sends those souls to the one above it, emptying itself; then it resumes receiving souls which are sent by the stars until it is full again'.[195] Both the Manichaeans and the Khurramīs thus envisaged the liberated soul as travelling back via the route also taken by the righteous soul in Persian Zoroastrianism. The route is distinctive because it goes via the stars to the moon and the sun, meaning that the stars are envisaged as closest to the earth, an idea attested already in *Yašts* 12 and 13.[196] As in the Pahlavi books, moreover, the traffic between the human and celestial worlds accounts for the waxing and waning of the moon. The difference is that there is only one ascent in Persian Zoroastrianism, so that the freight that causes the moon to wax and wane does not consist of souls. But those who held the souls to ascend and descend repeatedly are hardly departing from the Avestan tradition.

How the Khurramīs held the spirits of those destined for reincarnation to travel we are left to guess. Given that the souls are sent down from the moon in the Upaniṣads, and that the same is true of *khwarra*, fortune, and good things in the Pahlavi books, it is a reasonable guess that the Khurramīs saw the spirits as being sent down from there as well, to pass into the rain, and then to sprout as plants and be eaten by animals, whose milk and meat were consumed by humans, so that with or without going through all these steps they passed into human seed and were born again.

193 See Chapter 14, p. 308.

194 *Acta Archelai*, VIII, 5–8; Abū ʿĪsā in Ibn al-Malāḥimī, 565; cf. also Ibn al-Nadīm, 394.11–15 = II, 782; Shahrastānī, I, 191 = I, 650; ʿAbd al-Jabbār, *Mughnī*, 13 = 160; Skjaervø, 'Iranian Elements in Manicheism', 279.

195 Maqdisī, II, 20f.

196 See the references given in nn. 174f. to this chapter.

The Manichaeans, however, sent sinners to hell for punishment before they were ready for reincarnation,[197] and this may have suggested a different route to them. For just as the Zoroastrians envisaged *khwarra* as ascending from the earth every day (via the station of the stars)[198] so the Manichaeans held the divine particles dispersed in this world to be exhaled by the earth and rise towards heaven on a daily basis: on the way they were diverted into plants, and so eaten by animals, who imprisoned them in their bodies when they mated.[199] The divine parts of the souls punished in hell were perhaps envisaged as rising from the earth as well: they too would be diverted into plants and so pass into the food chain, meaning that sooner or later they would pass into humans and be born again, unless the plants were eaten by the Elect (who did not eat meat or procreate). Some such route is compatible with the *Seven Chapters*, which anathematises 'those who introduce metempsychosis, which they call transmigration (*metangismos*) and those who suppose that grass and plants and water and other things without souls in fact all have them and think that those who pluck corn or barley or grass or vegetables are transformed into them in order that they may suffer the same'.[200]

Since the evidence on the Khurramīs is late it cannot be ruled out that those cited by al-Maqdisī from the *Kitāb al-Khurramiyya* owed their conception of the ascent via the moon to the Manichaeans, but it does not seem likely. Like the Zoroastrians the Khurramīs spoke of the stars rather than the Milky Way, and their identification of the stars as 'balls and holes' (*kuran wa-thuqab*) suggests that they also shared the Zoroastrian concept of the sky as made of stone, glass, or shining metal, with windows for the heavenly bodies. The Manichaeans held the sky to be made of the skins of demons, but do not seem to mention holes in it.[201] Panaino's suggestion that the Zoroastrians themselves owed their explanation of the lunar phases to the Manichaeans is hardly plausible either. His reasoning is that the upward movement of good deeds and thoughts

[197] *Acta Archelai*, X, 5 XI, 2. Compare the Sogdian fragment in Sims-Williams, 'Christian Sogdian Texts', 293, where the soul is sometimes brought to hell, sometimes into the body of insects or birds. The text asserts this as correct doctrine, not by way of polemics against it, so *pace* Sims-Williams this cannot be a Christian text. Most probably it is Manichaean. Its repeated use of the phrase 'You say' is hardly significant, given that this is how polemics against anybody's doctrine are introduced, though it is also attested in an anti-Manichaean text (cf. 290f.).

[198] Bailey, *Zoroastrian Problems*, 41f., citing *GrBd*, 173.10ff.

[199] BeDuhn, *Manichaean Body*, 79, citing Augustine.

[200] Lieu, 'Formula', 248.

[201] See *EIr.*, s.v. 'Āsmān' (Tafazzoli).

is not attested in the older Zoroastrian tradition, and that the Pahlavi commentary on the prayer in praise of the moon may date from the Sasanian period.[202] This may be true, but leaving aside that the explanation is also found in the *Bundahišn*, the upward movement of the soul via the stars, moon, and sun to endless light is mentioned long before the Manichaeans, as Panaino himself notes; the downward movement of *khwarəna* from the moon is attested in the *Māh Yašt* (as he also notes). On top of that, the concept of the moon as a transfer point in the circulation between the divine and the human world, and the explanation of its waxing and waning with reference to this, are so similar in the Upaniṣads and the Zoroastrian texts that one would agree with Skjaervø that the Manichaeans must be indebted to the Zoroastrians here, not the other way round.[203]

The Greeks

The Mithraists in connection with whom both Pallas and Euboulos volunteered their information on the Magi are famed in the modern literature for their concept of the ascent of the soul of the saved. According to Celsus they envisaged the five planets (each associated with a deity and a metal), the sun, and the moon as a ladder with seven gates that the soul passed through, with an eighth gate at the top of the ladder, presumably the gate to the endless light beyond the sun.[204] This should perhaps be seen as a development of the Zoroastrian idea of ascent, securely attested for Anatolia in Antiochus' Nimrud Dağ inscription.[205] But the planets take the place of the Zoroastrian star station, the preoccupation with the figure seven is absent from the Zoroastrian accounts (except for a stray attempt in the *Bundahišn* to fit the four stations into a scheme of seven),[206] and the Zoroastrians do not compare the route to a ladder, so the divergence is considerable. What did the Mithraists say about the souls of those who had not been initiated, or who had failed to reach the requisite rank? No

[202] Panaino, 'Manichaean Concepts', 469–71.

[203] Skjaervø, 'Iranian Elements in Manicheism', 279.

[204] Origen, *Contra Celsum*, VI, 22. Cf. the eighth 'house' above the planets as the place where God and the holy spirit lived in Klijn, *Acts of Thomas*, ch. 27, cf. 81f.

[205] Cf. above, p. 351. One theory about the origin of Mithraism is that the cult was founded by dependants, military and civilian, of the dynasty of Commagene to which Antiochus belonged as it made the transition from client rulers to Roman aristocrats (Beck, 'Mysteries of Mithras', 121). Beck uses Antiochus' monument mainly for its iconography, without reference to the ascent to heaven, presumably thanks to his association with Boyce.

[206] Cf. Zaehner, *Zurvan*, 322 = 333f. (par. 7), citing *GrBd*, 3:7.

information appears to be available; the topic is not even discussed in the modern literature: the testimony of Pallas and Euboulos seems to be routinely rejected as information about *both* the Magi *and* Mithraism. It might be more fruitful to accept that the doctrine of reincarnation was represented on both sides.

When the soul travels to the moon in the Greek philosophical literature of the time, it is precisely in connection with reincarnation. Thus Plutarch (d. AD 120), an eclectic thinker and vegetarian with a strong interest in Persian religion who took the idea of reincarnation seriously, wrote an elaborate myth in which the souls travel to the moon. The myth involves punishment and purification between the earth and the moon and other complications reflecting its Platonic model, but the gist of it is that the imperfect do not get past the moon: sinners are sent back again in human bodies. Those who have purified their minds, however, achieve separation of their minds from their souls, which are left behind on the moon while their liberated minds travel to the sun through the lunar gates facing heaven. The sun meanwhile makes new minds, which are received by the moon, which makes new souls for which the earth provides the bodies.[207] In a work replete with references to Mithras along with Pythagoras and Plato, Porphyry observes that 'those who speak about the gods (*theologoi*) make the sun and the moon gates for the souls, and say that they ascend through the sun and descend through the moon'.[208] Here as in Plutarch, we have both upward and downward movements, and it is from the moon that the souls come down. Only the link with the waxing and waning of the moon is missing. The 'theologians' were presumably eclectic thinkers like Plutarch and Porphyry himself, another adherent of reincarnation and vegetarianism interested in Persian religion.

In short, the idea of the soul journeying via the moon and the sun and/or to the eternal light appears in the Upaniṣads, in Avestan texts and several Pahlavi works, in Greek eclectic texts, in Manichaeism, and in Khurramism. In all but the Zoroastrian material from Fārs it is associated with reincarnation for the less than perfect. In the Upaniṣads, Manichaeism, and a Khurramī text the journey of the soul is linked with the waxing and waning of the moon, a theme which also appears in the Pahlavi texts in connection with the circulation of goodness or *khwarra* rather than souls or spirits; and in the Upaniṣads, the Zoroastrian material, and two Greek texts the moon is the centre of both upward and downward movement. This suggests

[207] Cf. Hamilton, 'The Myth', 26ff., on Plutarch, 'The Face of the Moon', 943–5.
[208] Porphyry, *Cave of the Nymphs*, 29.

that we are dealing with a cluster of closely related doctrines with shared roots in Indo-Iranian religion. If so, ancient Iranian religion either included the idea of reincarnation or contained notions that made it likely to develop. Given the paucity of the evidence, and the currency of the view that the Indian idea of reincarnation is of Dravidian rather than Indo-European origin, this is perhaps a hazardous conclusion. What can be said for sure is that the doctrine is so closely in tune with Zoroastrian ideas about circulation between the divine and human worlds that we can effortlessly accept that it formed part of regional Zoroastrianism – certainly that of Media, but probably of Parthia and Sogdia too (if only because of the former presence of Buddhism there). On top of that, it is in the inaccessible mountains of western Iran that it is best attested, and also where it has survived to this day.[209] This makes it unlikely that it owed its presence to either the Greeks or the Indians: if it is of external origin it is from the pre-Iranian religion of Media that it was taken over. But whether its ultimate roots are Iranian or pre-Iranian, Pallas, Euboulos, and Bhavya seem to be right: there must indeed have been Magi who believed in reincarnation.

ETHOS, NON-VIOLENCE

Like the Khurramīs the Zoroastrians had a high regard for the good things in life. The material world had been created by Ohrmazd, not Ahriman, and the *Vīdēvdād* assigns superiority to the rich over the poor, the one who eats over the one who does not eat, and the man with children over unmarried men. The merit of having children is also vaunted in the Pahlavi books.[210] According to Abū ʿĪsā, the Zoroastrians claimed that God had 'ordered them to eat, drink and marry, forbidding them to fast'.[211] They had no fasts at all, al-Bīrūnī explains, and anyone who fasted was a sinner who had to expiate by feeding the poor.[212] Abū ʿĪsā, however, also tells us that some Zoroastrians held the spirit to come from God and the body from Ahriman, suggesting that there were Zoroastrians who 'inclined to Manichaeism', as he says about some Khurramīs (and who identified the immortal part of the human being as a spirit rather than a soul).[213]

209 See Chapter 19.

210 Molé, 'Ascétisme moral', 147, 149f., 151ff., citing *Vd* 7: 47–9; *Dd* 37:40–3 (36:29–30 Jaafari Dehaghi); *PRDd*, 36: 8–13.

211 Ibn al-Malāḥimī, *Muʿtamad*, 640.-2.

212 Bīrūnī, *Āthār*, 230 = 217.

213 Ibn al-Malāḥimī, *Muʿtamad*, 641.5; cf. Abū ʿĪsā on the Khurramīs in Chapter 10, p. 196, and Chapter 15, p. 368, on spirit and soul.

'From the middle of your body upwards you belong to Ohrmazd; from the middle downward, to Ahriman', as a Jew was told by a Zoroastrian priest according to the Babylonian Talmud.[214] The strongly anti-ascetic stance of the Zoroastrian books also implies that there were Zoroastrians who longed to escape from the material world. But there is nothing here to set them apart from the Khurramīs.

At first sight, however, the Zoroastrians and the Khurramīs do not seem to have much in common on the subject of animals. Where the Khurramīs deemed it wrong to inflict harm on any living beings, the Zoroastrians regarded it as virtuous to kill noxious animals (*khrafstra*). Herodotus (d. before 420 BC) says that the Magi took pride in personally killing animals of all kinds except humans and dogs, and vied with each other to kill ants (also mentioned by Bhavya), as well as snakes, reptiles, and other things, whether flying or creeping. Plutarch knew them to kill water-rats.[215] Vasubandhu (fourth or fifth century AD) mentions the Persian claim that snakes, scorpions, and wasps should be killed because they cause harm, and that deer, cattle, birds, and buffaloes could be killed for food.[216] Bhavya mentions their slaughter of oxen.[217] The worms that the women in Jurjān would try not to trample underfoot were classified as noxious animals by the Zoroastrians.[218]

In addition, Zoroastrian ritual included bloody sacrifice (though Zoroaster is sometimes held to condemn it in the Gāthās).[219] Yima sacrificed a hundred horses, a thousand oxen, and ten thousand sheep to Anahita, according to the *Yašts*, which present other heroes as sacrificing on an equally prodigious scale. The Achaemenid kings also sacrificed horses, bulls, and other animals to Zeus (Ohrmazd), and to other gods as well; and bloody sacrifice continued to be practised in the Sasanian period.[220] Finally, hunting was highly appreciated by the Sasanian elite.[221] Many of the animals hunted will have counted as noxious, but this can hardly have been true of all of them. In addition, the Zoroastrians prohibited the consumption of animals that fed on carrion, and so presumably also carrion

[214] De Ménasce, 'Early Evidence', citing Sanhedrin 39a.
[215] De Jong, *Traditions*, 339f.; Lindtner, 'Buddhist References', 439, cf. 435.
[216] Lindtner, 'Buddhist References', 440f.
[217] Lindtner, 'Buddhist References', 439, cf. 435; Kawasaki, 'Reference to Maga', 1102.
[218] Gignoux, 'Dietary Laws', 23f.
[219] On this question see Humbach, 'Zarathustra und die Rinderschlachtung'; de Jong, 'Animal Sacrifice', 129f.
[220] Cf. Benveniste, 'Terminologie iranienne', 46, 48; Humbach, 'Zarathustra und die Rinderschlachtung', 25ff.; de Jong, 'Animal Sacrifice', 143–5.
[221] See Gignoux, 'La chasse'.

itself; but like the Khurramīs they held it permissible to drink wine and eat blood and pork (on the condition that the animal had been fed on grass for a year).[222]

If we disregard the distinction between good and noxious animals, however, the difference between the official Zoroastrian and Khurramī positions is not great. The Zoroastrians had a great concern for the welfare of good animals,[223] especially cattle, which they revered almost as deeply as Hindus revere cows, and qualms about killing and eating animals classified as good, especially cattle, are well attested in the Zoroastrian books. (Ibn al-Jawzī even credits them with a view that it was forbidden to kill or slaughter animals, but he is probably mixing them up with the Manichaeans.)[224] Several Pahlavi texts associate Yima's sin (of which there are many explanations) with meat-eating, either in the sense that he introduced it,[225] or in the sense that, though sinful, he recommended meat-eating in moderation, a view which Humbach takes to be the correct understanding of the Avestan passage they are trying to explain (Yasna 32, 8).[226] A gloss to the Pahlavi translation of Yasna 9, 1 explains the human loss of mortality as a consequence of the eating of 'Yima's meat', perhaps meaning that they started eating meat as Yima had done – or, as Humbach prefers, that they ate meat kept by Yima for sacrifical purposes.[227] And a passage in the *Pahlavi Rivāyat* praises Jam(šid) – i.e., Yima – for having opposed the demons who told people to kill (i.e., sacrifice) beneficent animals (*gōspand*), but people acting without his permission went ahead and did so, with the result that they became mortal.[228]

The *Pahlavi Rivāyat* further says that when the cattle disputed with Ohrmazd in their *mēnōg* state about the evil that humans would inflict on them in the material world, Ohrmazd reassured them that by way of compensation no sins they committed would be debited to them: rather, all the sins committed by cattle, such as that of a camel that killed a man, would be transferred to the one who ate them, or even to one who just killed a fish, as soon as he in his turn committed a sin, even if the sin he

[222] Gignoux, 'Dietary Laws', 19, 20, 25, 29, 31ff.
[223] See Macuch, 'Treatment of Animals'.
[224] Ibn al-Jawzī, *Talbīs Iblīs*, 73; cf. 74, where he credits them with the Manichaean view that heaven is made of the skins of demons.
[225] Cf. Stausberg, *Zarathustra and Zoroastrianism*, 39.
[226] Humbach, 'Yama/Yima/Jamšēd', 72, 74, 76.
[227] Humbach, 'Yama/Yima/Jamšēd', 72f.
[228] *PRDd*, 31b1–3; cf. Humbach, 'Yama/Yima/Jamšēd', 73.

committed was minor. This certainly suggests that it might be prudent to avoid eating good animals altogether.[229] The passage continues that it was not allowed to buy any meat at all from non-Iranians, suggesting that this had been used as a way out, as it had among the Maguseans of Anatolia.[230]

If cattle, small or large, were to be killed, it had to be done lawfully: otherwise grave reckoning would ensue. Killing them unlawfully meant killing them unnecessarily (or in excess of the right measure), or when they were less than a year old, or before they had reached maturity, meaning four years in the case of bulls, sheep, and goats; thereafter they were held to go into decline.[231] Zādspram seems to think that good animals should not be killed at all: he has representatives of their five kinds assemble to accept the religion from Ohrmazd, and he (apparently Ohrmazd) ordered Zoroaster 'not to kill and not to inflict suffering on and to protect the five kinds of animals well', an order which was 'very insistent'. Later Zādspram says that one had to distinguish between killing and non-killing, such as (between) noxious animals and cattle, just as one had to distinguish between giving and not-giving, such as (between) the just and worthy (on the one hand) and the bad and unworthy (on the other): what he means seems to be that one should only kill noxious animals and only give to the just and worthy. He also mentions a subdivision of the *nask*s called *Stōrestān* which dealt with sins committed against small and large cattle and reparation for their wounds,[232] and of which the *Dēnkard* has a summary.[233] He did envisage the righteous as eating 'the form' (*kirb*) of milk and meat after death, when everything they saw and enjoyed would be the 'form' of their earthly counterparts, apparently meaning that they would be without material substance: the milk would be drawn from 'the form' of animals in such a way as not to grieve them, and the forms of animals and birds would turn into the form of meat and back again; there would be no 'form' of slaughter, then.[234] In line with this, the ritual with which Sōšyans and his assistants would awaken the dead does not seem to

[229] *PRDd*, 14:1–6; discussed by Shaked, 'Moral Responsibility of Animals', 578f.; cf. also *PRDd*, 61:2–5; Molé, *Culte*, 196ff., citing *Dk*, IX, 29.

[230] *PRDd*, 14:7, following Shaked's translation rather than Williams's; cf. Chapter 14, p. 315.

[231] Shaked, 'Moral Responsibility of Animals', 585f. citing *Dk*, III, nos. 199:8, 200:7, 287:13, 288:9; and *Rivāyat*, Unvala, i, 76:6–7.

[232] Zādspram, 23:2, 27:2, 28:4; cf. Gignoux, 'Dietary Laws', 25. For *gōspand* in the sense of good animals in general see Molé, 'Ascétisme moral', 179.

[233] Reproduced and discussed in Macuch, 'Treatment of Animals', 179f.

[234] Zādspram, 30:58.

include the sacrifice of the bull/cow (*gāv*) Hadāyōš in his account, as it does in the *Bundahišn*: in the latter work they kill the animal and mix its fat and white *hōm* to make the drink that will make people immortal.[235] In Zādspram, by contrast, we only hear of white *hōm* and the *milk* of the cow Hadāyōš.[236] The last paragraph of Zadspram's treatise, which is incomplete, nonetheless says that the blessed will be immortal and have the sweetness and fat of the cow Hadāyōš as their nourishment, so his attitude is not entirely clear. Elsewhere we learn that people who have eaten meat will be resurrected at the age of forty, those who have not at the age of fifteen, but the reference is probably to children who died before they were able to eat meat rather than to vegetarians.[237]

If cattle had to be killed then they had to be stunned with a club before they were cut or strangled, or they had to be killed outright that way, as we have seen, because good animals were sentient beings endowed with a soul and/or spirit.[238] One passage in the *Dēnkard* seems to credit the ancient sages with a recommendation of straightforward vegetarianism: 'They held this too: Be plant-eaters, you men, so that you may live long. Keep away from the body of cattle, for the reckoning is vast. Ohrmazd, the lord, created plants in great number for helping cattle.'[239] We are also told that when, towards the end of the world, the wild animals will seek refuge with the Zoroastrians, Ašvahišt will cry out from heaven, 'Do not kill these beneficent animals any more as you used to do.' It then somewhat incongruously proceeds to have Ašvahišt lay down the normal rule that cattle can only be slaughtered on reaching a certain age. The Zoroastrians will accept this, we are told; in fact, they will only kill animals so old that they beg to be killed and eaten by them rather than by reptiles and serpents.[240] According to Zādspram, on the other hand, Ašvahišt will descend to show mankind that killing cattle is a great sin of which the profit is minimal: once again, the slaughter of good animals seems to trouble him. When people stop killing them, the power of Ahriman will be diminished by a quarter and people will subsist on

[235] *GrBd*, 226, 3–6, cited in Molé, *Culte*, 87 (cow); also cited in Humbach, 'Zarathustra und die Rinderschlachtung', 27f. (bull).

[236] Zādspram, 35:15.

[237] *MahFr*, 41; cf. Shaked, *Dualism*, 43f., who links it with the previous section and understands it as a reference to vegetarianism; followed by Grenet, 'Pahlavi Text', 170, though his translation of the previous section does not support the linkage.

[238] See Chapter 14, p. 314.

[239] *Dk*, VI, 276, in Shaked, *Wisdom*, 109.

[240] *Dk*, VII, 9:9; *PRDd*, 48:20f.; Molé, 'Ascétisme moral', 178ff.; Hultgård, 'Persian Apocalypticism', 53.

milk, eventually giving that up as well.[241] The *Dēnkard* and the *Bundahišn* also have this theme, though not in connection with the episode of Ašvahišt: in their versions, people will give up meat for milk and plants, later water and plants, or just water: one way or the other, they will reverse the steps whereby their ancestors had become meat-eaters.[242] There would be no meat-eating in the regenerated world: people would have the taste of meat perpetually in their mouths.[243]

All in all, the overlap between the Khurramī and Zoroastrian views as recorded in the Pahlavi books on the topic of animals is considerable. Both held it wrong to inflict pain on at least some animals, and both held such animals to have souls or spirits similar to their own. The Khurramīs are not said to have distinguished between good and noxious animals, however. Rather, if we go by Euboulos, their distinction was between wild and domestic animals, the killing of the former being less serious than that of the latter, though it was best not to kill or eat any animals at all. If domestic animals translate as cattle, it was the same group of animals that generated the most serious scruples on both sides. Once again, Persian Zoroastrianism and the beliefs enshrined in Khurramism come across as variations on the same themes.

THE MISSING PRIESTS

If the Khurramīs were simply non-Persian Zoroastrians, they must have had priests trained in the Avesta. As noted above, the Muslim sources never mention them, but there is evidence for them elsewhere. It is Magi, i.e., priests, who believe in reincarnation and practise varying degrees of vegetarianism in Pallas and Euboulos; it is Magians – i.e., Zoroastrians – who believe that animals have a divine spirit/Ohrmazd in them in Eznik and Bar Ḥadbeshabba;[244] and there is indirect evidence for Zoroastrian priests bearing what the Muslims were to call Khurramī beliefs in the Pahlavi books as well.

Yašt 13, the by now much-cited *Yašt* which takes us to the roots of Iranian panpsychism, is devoted to praise of the *fravašis* (Pahlavi *fravahr*s), a vast army of warlike deities who include the spirits of past, present, and

[241] Zādspram, 34:38ff.

[242] Molé, 'Ascétisme moral', 171f., 180ff., quoting *GrBd*, 220, 15-221, 11; *Dk*, VII, 10:2–9, VII, 11:4.

[243] *PRDd*, 48: 103ff.; cf. Molé, 'Ascétisme moral', 167. Shaked, 'Moral Responsibility of Animals', 587.

[244] See Chapter 14, pp. 303, 313.

future human beings. Some Zoroastrians inferred from this *Yašt* that humans were *fravahr*s endowed with bodies.[245] According to them Ohrmazd asked the *fravahr*s whether they were willing to go into the material world in order to combat evil on his behalf, and they accepted; this was how human beings came to find themselves in their current condition. Slightly different versions of this myth are found in the *Bundahišn*,[246] the *Dādestān ī dēnīg*,[247] the *Pahlavi Rivāyat*,[248] the ninth/fourteenth – tenth/fifteenth-century Persian *Sad Dar-i Bundahišn*.[249] and an account by Abū ʿĪsā al-Warrāq.[250] Abū ʿĪsā translated *fravahr* as *rūḥ*, spirit. Humans are assumed to consist of a *fravahr* and a body again in another myth, this time about the creation of Zoroaster in the material world. According to the *Dēnkard* three components were required to (re)create him: his *fravahr* (spirit), his *khwarra* (glory), and his *tan gōhr* (body substance). All three were sent down from on high (like the divine image and the body of the Assyrian king, Zoroaster's fleshy form was made in heaven).[251] In the lost *Spand Nask* as summarised in the *Dēnkard* only two components were mentioned: his *fravahr* and his *khwarra*.[252] Al-Shahrastānī has a third version, presumably from Abū ʿĪsā, in which the two components are Zoroaster's *fravahr* (*rūḥ*) and his body substance (*shabaḥ*): here his glory is missing.[253] But all versions give Zoroaster a *fravahr* rather than a soul (*ruvān*). Both the myth about the *fravahr*s and that about Zoroaster were clearly formulated by priests familiar with *Yašt* 13, and that about the *fravahr*s also develops a number of ancient themes rooted in the Gāthās.[254]

The significance of this lies in the fact that the Persian Zoroastrians did not think of humans as consisting of a body and an immortal spirit (*fravahr*). The immortal element in their view was the soul (*ruvān*). The

245 What follows is a summary of Crone, 'Pre-existence in Iran', to which the reader is referred for further discussion and references.

246 *GrBd*, 38:12ff (3:23f.) in Bailey, *Zoroastrian Problems*, 108. Slightly different translations are found in Zaehner, *Zurvan*, 324 = 336, and Malandra, *'Fravaši Yašt'*, 23f.

247 *Dd*, 36:25–8.

248 *PRDd*, 17d13–14 (I, 94f. = II, 35).

249 Translated in de Jong, 'First Sin', 194f.

250 Ibn al-Malāḥimī, *Muʿtamad*, 640. It is also Abū ʿĪsā who is reflected (unnamed) in Shahrastānī, I, 183 = I, 637.

251 *Dk*, VII, 2, in Molé, *Légende*, 14ff.; Molé, *Culte*, 284ff.; cf. Darrow, 'Zoroaster Amalgamated'.

252 *Spand Nask* in *Dk*, VIII, 14, in Molé, *Culte*, 276 = 277 (no. 1); similarly Zādspram, 5–6.

253 Shahrastānī, I, 186 = I, 643. The *rūḥ* is placed in a tree, the *shabaḥ* (wrongly *rūḥ* again in some MSS, preferred by Gimaret and Gignoux) goes into the milk: this identifies them as the *fravahr* and *tan gōhr* respectively (similarly Darrow, 'Zoroaster Amalgamated', 131).

254 Crone, 'Pre-existence in Iran'.

Pahlavi books often speak about the *fravahr*, but they understand the term differently. Some explain it as a biological entity responsible for the growth and maintenance of the body,[255] others as that part of a human being that remains in Ohrmazd's presence, i.e., a person's heavenly counterpart.[256] Once they are dead humans join that counterpart and so become *fravahrs*, ancestral spirits, but they are not *fravahrs* dressed in bodies down here. The Persian concepts of the *fravahr* also rest on interpretation of *Yašt* 13.

The myths about the creation of the *fravahrs* and Zoroaster in the material world must have passed into the Pahlavi books from priests who had a different interpretation of *Yašt* 13 from their own. They sound like priestly bearers of ideas of the type later branded Khurramī, for the Khurramīs also saw humans as consisting of a body and an immortal spirit. The same view appears among a number of early Muʿtazilites.[257] What is more, the myth about the *fravahrs* survives to this day among the Ahl-i Ḥaqq.[258] In their rendition humans have to undergo reincarnation before they can return to their divine home, which tallies with the view of those Khurramīs who held release from material existence to be possible, and reincarnation also appears in several myths about pre-existence told by early Muʿtazilites (in which panpsychism is a prominent theme as well).[259] By contrast, the Pahlavi books reward the *fravahrs* with bodily resurrection. Since those who believe themselves to have originated as divine beings in subtle bodies of light are normally longing to return to that state, not to be reunited with their fleshy frames, one would assume the original bearers of this myth also to have believed in reincarnation and eventual return to the celestial realm. The Persian Zoroastrians adapted it to their own doctrinal position.

If we are willing to go by indirect evidence, the priests in question, presumably active in greater Media, had formulated the myth by the third century at the latest.[260] The myth about Zoroaster's creation in the material world could be even earlier, given that it was found in the

[255] Zādspram, 30:35. Cf. also 29:2, 30:22; Bailey, *Zoroastrian Problems*, 98ff. (citing *DkM*, 241.13ff.), 100f., 107f.; *Dk*, III, no. 123 (*DkB*, 92.3; *DkM*, 119); *Dd*, 2:13; cf. Shaki, 'Philosophical and Cosmogonical Chapters', 150; Shaked, *Dualism*, app. E; Gignoux, *Man and Cosmos*, 17ff.

[256] *GrBd* 3:13 (in Zaehner, *Zurvan*, 323 = 334; Bailey, *Zoroastrian Problems*, 112).

[257] Thus al-Naẓẓām (Ashʿarī, 229.4, 331.9; cf. also Bāqillānī in van Ess, *TG*, VI, 114), Ibn Khābiṭ and other Muʿtazilite Sufis; cf. Crone, 'Pre-existence in Iran'; cf. also Chapter 19, p. 477.

[258] Mokri, 'Kalām gourani', 240f., with further discussion in Crone, 'Pre-existence in Iran'.

[259] For all this see Crone, 'Pre-existence in Iran'; cf. also Chapter 19, p. 466.

[260] This too is discussed in Crone, 'Pre-existence in Iran'.

Avestan *Spand Nask*. With the rise of the Sasanians these priests will have been incorporated into a priestly hierarchy dominated by men from Pārs (on which more will be said in the next chapter). This may be when their myths were taken up by their Persian colleagues. It may also be their incorporation into this hierarchy, and the Persianisation of their beliefs, that account for the absence of priestly bearers of Khurramī ideas in the Muslim sources.

OVERALL

Stripped of its Islamic elements Khurramism displays considerable overlap, and occasionally complete agreement, with Persian Zoroastrianism on fundamental subjects such as dualism, divine immanence, panpsychism, *khwarra*, individual eschatology, the proper attitude to the good things in life, and the proper treatment of beneficent/domestic animals. Muslim sources consistently identify the Khurramīs as *majūs* by origin; according to Dionysius of Tell Mahré the Khurdanaye were Magians in their cult; and two myths preserved in the Pahlavi books suggest that beliefs of the type labelled Khurramī were once carried by priests trained in the Avestan tradition. In short, it may reasonably be concluded that Khurramism stripped of its Islamic accretions was Middle Zoroastrianism of a regional, above all north-western, type.

16

Regional and Official Zoroastrianism on the Ground

If the Khurramīs adhered to regional forms of Zoroastrianism, how were they perceived by the bearers of the Persian variety when that came to be hegemonic: as heretics who ought to be brought to their senses or as adherents of inoffensive, if not particularly reputable, beliefs who could be left alone to form what we might call a low church, as Madelung suggests? Unfortunately this question is more easily asked than answered, for although the Zoroastrian priests often talk about heresy (*ahramōgīh*) they tend to keep silent about its nature. They seem to have had a deliberate policy of not referring to the views of opponents in terms that made them intelligible to outsiders, and to avoid mentioning them altogether if possible.[1] One should not give a tongue to a wolf, as the *Hērbedestān* says in answer to the question whether it was allowed to teach the sacred words to unbelievers; apparently one should not do so by revealing the unholy words of heretics to the believers either.[2] Of a heretic called Rašn Rēš we are told that he adhered to ten erroneous doctrines, enumerated in contrast with those of the saintly Sēn, but all one can tell is that he seems to have preferred spirituality to involvement in the material world along quasi-Christian lines.[3] Of other heretics we are left with no information at all, and we would not recognise Manichaeism in the Pahlavi accounts if we did not know it in advance.[4]

[1] Cf. de Ménasce, *Troisième livre*, index, s.v. 'hérésie'; Shaked, 'Esoteric Trends', 190, 214f.; Shaked, 'Myth of Zurvan', 227.

[2] *Hērbedestān*, 19:6 KK; 19,7f. HE.

[3] *Dk*, III, no. 198 (*DkB*, 166; *DkM*, 213), with de Ménasce's comments at 408. Rašn Rēš is also mentioned at *Dk*, VII, 7: 11 (West).

[4] *Dk*, III, no. 200 (*DkB*, 169; *DkM*, 216). The *Škand* is something of an exception, but then it is Zoroastrian *kalām* rather than a traditional priestly work.

In so far as the Khurramīs were followers of Mazdak they were certainly regarded as heretics, for the Pahlavi books roundly denounce Mazdak as a terrible adversary of the religion who abandoned people to famine and death.[5] The *Dēnkard* condemns using religious authority to gather a hungry rabble for robbery and pillage, probably with him in mind;[6] an obscure passage in the Pahlavi commentary on the *Vendīdād* has been read as a condemnation of his vegetarianism;[7] and a late passage in the *Bundahišn* briefly mentions his communist doctrine in much the same words as Muslim sources.[8] Apart from that we learn nothing about his preaching. What we do hear about is the doctrine of his predecessor. A heretic once wanted to know why holding women and property in common was not approved, given that it was through women and property that envy, pride, and other sins attacked men and that sharing them would put an end to this and thus diminish the evil spirit in conformity with Zoroaster's teaching. The response informed him that this was a false doctrine preached by Zardūšt, son of Khrōsak, from Fasā.[9]

That still leaves us with the question of how the Zoroastrian authorities responded to belief in divine incarnation, reincarnation, and non-violence. If the *Kwtk/Krtk* who may have lent his name to the Kūdhakiyya/ Kardakiyya taught these doctrines, we are left in no doubt that they too were violently condemned, for between them Dēmak (*Dymk*, or *Smk*, whoever he may be), Mazdak, and Kardak (*Kwrtk/Krtk*) were the greatest calamity to have befallen Zoroastrianism since the time of Alexander.[10] But as usual we are left in the dark as to what their calamitous doctrines were. We do get a glimpse of the official reaction to the doctrine of non-violence, however. An unnamed heretic asked why 'you' battle with the king and judges of non-Iranians given that this cannot be done without sinning.[11] The gist of the reply is that the one can inflict harm without

[5] Cf. the passages gathered by Christensen, 'Kawādh', 20–2. For additional translations see Crone, 'Kavād's Heresy', nn. 28, 42, 65, 112, 127.

[6] *Dk*, III, no. 202 (*DkB*, 172; *DkM*, 220); cf. Shaki, 'Social Doctrine', 295ff., with a somewhat different translation.

[7] Pahlavi commentary to *Vendīdād* 4:49 in Christensen, 'Kawādh', 20; cf. Crone, 'Kavād's Heresy', n. 127.

[8] *GrBd*, 33:19, in a historical survey which includes the Arabs, the 'Abbāsid revolution, and the coming of the Turks.

[9] *DkM* 6.10–7.16, in Molé, 'Sectes', 24f.; for a different, less lucid, translation see Shaki, 'Social Doctrine', 290ff. (reading *dris-dēn* for Molé's Khrōsakān).

[10] *Dk*, III, no. 345 (*DkB*, 256; *DkM*, 355); cf. Chapter 9, pp. 184f. It could conceivably be this *Smk* who lives on in the story of Samak-i 'Ayyār (on which, see *ĒIr*, s.v.).

[11] *Dk*, III, no. 6 (*DkB*, 6; *DkM*, 7).

sinning, as Ohrmazd did when he created his creatures to combat the *druj* even though this meant exposing them to suffering, wounding, death, and other harm. The issue was the permissibility of inflicting harm on living beings, then, not the laws of purity which required Zoroastrians to keep apart from non-Zoroastrians. As the term *ahramōg* suggests, the person asking the question seems to have been a heretical Zoroastrian rather than an adherent of a rival religion such as Manichaeism, for the answer assumes the opponent to subscribe to a Zoroastrian view of the creation of man. Apparently the Khurramī doctrine of non-violence is here being condemned as heretical. A modern reader is surprised that this is the doctrine singled out for refutation, given that it seems quite innocuous, but the heretical question implies that it was associated with refusal to serve in the army. ('What are you good for since you go neither fighting nor hunting!', as the priest Kerdīr said to Mani.)[12]

No polemics against divine incarnation seem to be recorded, and if there are polemics against the doctrine of reincarnation they are tacit. The Zoroastrian literature frequently takes issue with deniers of the existence of heaven and hell, the resurrection, and the future body, and some of the passages could be directed against believers in reincarnation. The earliest evidence is probably the Avestan *Sūdgar Nask*, but it only survives in a Pahlavi summary and it is impossible to tell how far it has been updated. According to this summary, the *nask* dealt, among other things, with 'the idea of the wicked that there is no heaven, that the renovation does not occur, that the dead are not raised, and that the transformation cannot occur'.[13] The deniers here could be eternalist believers in reincarnation of the type encountered in the Jibāl.[14] A more securely dated early attestation is the proclamation of the third-century Zoroastrian priest Kerdīr (on whom more later) on three monumental inscriptions, in which he tells passers-by not to be incredulous of the things beyond, 'for they should know for certain that there is a heaven and there is a hell, and he who is virtuous goes forth to heaven and he who is sinful is cast into hell'.[15] This Kerdīr could say with certainty because he had been on a heavenly voyage and seen them for himself. But thereafter the evidence is less likely to relate to belief in reincarnation because it is associated with loss of faith in the gods, God (Ohrmazd), and/or the

[12] Henning, 'Mani's Last Journey', 951.
[13] *Dk*, IX, 11:19.
[14] See Chapter 12, p. 238.
[15] MacKenzie, 'Kerdir's Inscription', 61.

afterlife altogether. Thus the famous physician Burzoē, active under Khusraw I (531–70), tells us in his preface to *Kalīla wa-Dimna*, preserved in Arabic translation, that when he lost faith in his ancestral religion he tried not to 'deny the awakening and resurrection, reward and punishment'.[16] The courtier Vuzurjmihr is credited with a Pahlavi treatise to the same Khusraw I in which he proclaims himself free of doubts concerning the existence of the gods, the non-existence of the demons, paradise, hell, and the resurrection, lamenting the fact that the evil spirit had caused the rewards for good deeds and the punishment for sins at the end of times to be hidden from people's thoughts.[17] A Zoroastrian creed reproduced by al-Maqdisī in Pahlavi or Persian similarly says: 'I am free of doubt concerning the existence of Ohrmazd and of the Amahraspands; I am free from doubt concerning the Resurrection.'[18] In the *Ardā Virāfnāmag*, a work of Sasanian origin but later redaction, Ardā Virāf/Virāz goes on a tour of heaven and hell much like Kerdīr's and sees people in hell who 'did not believe in the spiritual world (*mēnōg*) and were ungrateful for the religion of Ohrmazd, the creator, and doubted the blessings of paradise, the evils of hell, and the coming of the resurrection and the final body'.[19] A Pahlavi advice book says that a man becomes wicked on account of five things, one of which is lack of belief 'in the (imperishableness) of the soul' and assures us in its closing statement that all will be well if we are without any doubt 'about Ohrmazd's creation of the spiritual and terrestrial worlds, the resurrection and the future body'.[20] Apparently there were deniers of the entire divine realm, the creation, and the afterlife altogether. These testimonia seem to reflect the presence in Iran of what the high priest Veh-Shāpuhr, also active under Khusraw I, calls *anastgōwišnīh*, 'saying non-existence', translatable as atheism.[21] The third/ninth-century *Škand Gūmānīk Vičār* deals with atheists who have to be persuaded of the existence of the Zoroastrian God and his rival under the label of *nēst-yazad-gōwān*, 'no-god-sayers', and refutes those atheists who deny the creation and the afterlife under the Muslim label of

[16] Nöldeke, 'Burzōes Einleitung', 18f. This preface cannot be by Ibn al-Muqaffaʿ, whose real or alleged scepticism was of an entirely different nature.

[17] Nawwābī, *Yādgār-i Buzurgmihr*, nos. 4, 42; also in Tarapore, *Pahlavi Andarz-Nāmak*, 39f., 43, where the gods and demons are replaced by good and bad beings. For the non-existence of the demons see Chapter 15, n. 25.

[18] Maqdisī, I, 62f.; tr. Shaked, *Dualism*, 32f.

[19] *Ardā Virāfnāmag*, 61:3.

[20] *Andarj ī Aōshnar i Dānak*, 18 (no. 38), 23.

[21] *MHD*, A34:12, rendered 'slander' by Perikhanian (in English translation), as 'utterance of untruth' in Macuch. For the translation as atheism see *EIr.*, s.v. 'Dahrī' (Shaki).

Dahrīs.[22] Given that most of the attestations seem to refer to what the Muslims were to call Dahrīs, it may be that the first two examples do as well.

In the absence of explicit polemics against the Khurramī beliefs to do with reincarnation and divine incarnation it could be argued that these beliefs were tolerated; and since it is mostly as humble villagers that we meet their bearers, the suggestion that – the rebellious Mazdakites apart – we should envisage the bearers of these beliefs as forming a 'low church' of Zoroastrianism is attractive. In some sense this is precisely what will be argued in what follows. It will not be argued in quite that form, however, for it is open to a major objection, namely that it is deeply misleading to think of Zoroastrians as forming a church. This requires a long explanation.

ANCESTRAL VS FAITH-BASED COMMUNITY

A church is a community based on shared faith. By way of later development, the word also stands for the priestly hierarchy in charge of this community, and in that sense there was indeed a Zoroastrian church by Sasanian times: a single priestly hierarchy developed in the course of the Sasanian period. But it presided over a completely different body from its Christian counterpart. The Christian church was formed by converts of diverse ethnic, social, and cultural origin who adopted the Christian faith on the basis of individual conviction, in defiance of their ancestral religion (Jewish or pagan), and who thereby established a religious community of a type that was entirely new at the time. Previously it was as members of ethnic and/or political communities that people had cultivated the gods, supplementing their ancestral religion with freely chosen associations of other kinds. Most religious communities were ancestral, or in other words acquired by birth, not by adoption of freely chosen beliefs; and though there were also voluntary associations, these were never alternatives to the ancestral communities, merely supplements to them. One cultivated one's ancestral gods because the collective welfare of one's city or people depended on it, and one sought private spiritual or intellectual satisfaction in other forms of devotion (such as mystery cults) and/or philosophy, without feeling obliged to renounce the one in favour of the other. The church was the first community based on freely chosen conviction to rule

[22] *Škand*, chs. 5 and 6.

out loyalty to any other religion, whether freely chosen, ancestral, or imperial.

There was no Zoroastrian church in the sense of a community based on shared faith, for Zoroastrianism was an ancestral religion of the pre-Christian type, the religion of the Iranians (*Ērān*), a religion into which one was born and which had no communal embodiment apart from whatever social and political organisation the Iranians happened to have at any given time. For most of the time their organisation took the form of petty kingdoms. The Sasanians had a new sense that all these petty jurisdictions had to be united in a single empire, which they were apparently the first to call Ērānšahr, the land of the Iranians.[23] But the religious unification of the Iranians could only be effected top down, by the creation of a hierarchy empowered over the entire empire. There was no religious community formed by the Zoroastrians themselves, only a mass of kin groups, villages, and petty kingdoms, supplemented by voluntary cult societies such as those that we meet in the history of the Khurramīs. What the emperors created on top was in the nature of a state department, the equivalent of a modern Ministry of Guidance, not a church, let alone a community of believers such as that which the Muslims were to bring.

Like most ancestral religions, moreover, Zoroastrianism consisted first and foremost in ritual and law, not in a 'philosophy', as the Greeks would have called it (and as the Christians called their own teaching, too), i.e., a set of abstract propositions about the world addressed to anyone who would listen. *Pōryōtkēšīh*, the religion of the righteous forebear, usually translated as 'orthodoxy', was overwhelmingly about being on the right side, obeying the legitimate king and the right priests, performing the proper ritual, and observing the religious law.[24] Zoroastrianism did have a creed (*fravarane*), of which the key passage is prefaced to the *Yašts* ('I profess myself a Mazda worshipper, a follower of Zoroaster, one who hates the daevas and obeys the laws of Ahura Mazda'); a longer version forms part 12 of the Yasna.[25] But of doctrinal definition such as one finds in Christian and Muslim creeds there was none. Like Judaism, a religion of the same ancestral type, Zoroastrianism changed considerably after its loss of political autonomy; and Zoroastrians – above all the priests – will of course also have pursued 'philosophy' – indeed, philosophy in the literal sense of the word. But, they will have done so by way of supplementing

[23] Gnoli, 'Basileus basileōn arianōn'; more briefly Gnoli, 'Ēr Mazdēsn', 89f.

[24] Cf. *Dk*, III, no. 338 (*DkB*, 253; *DkM*, 330); Molé, 'Sectes', 9ff.

[25] *Y* 12 is translated with a brief comment in Boyce, *Textual Sources*, 57.

their ancestral religion, for their own private satisfaction. Anyone who had the means could do so. But, some basic doctrines apart, it was not assent to abstract propositions that the Zoroastrians shared.

The fact that Zoroastrianism was a religion of the ancient type is well illustrated by the fact that it did not have a congregational service.[26] Like other religions of the pre-Christian type it was focused on temples, that is to say sacred places where the gods were present and where the service focused on their needs, their satisfaction being required for the welfare of the people or polity in question, or indeed for the maintenance of the universe altogether. 'Service' is perhaps not the best word in connection with Zoroastrianism, for the idea of *serving* the gods is an ancient Mesopotamian idea rooted in the assumption that the gods needed food, drink, and housing and that humans had been created as their servants (or slaves) charged with the task of looking after them. The Zoroastrian conception seems rather to have been that the gods were invited to festive meals, where they were treated as honoured guests expected to reciprocate with gifts of their own.[27] The gods were honoured with ritual recitations and sacrifice (*yasna*): it was by a sacrifice that the world had come into being,[28] and by a sacrifice that the renovation would be brought about.[29] It was also by sacrifice and other ritual that evil was fought and the moral order of the world upheld in between.[30] Much of the ritual was (and still is) performed by priests without the participation of laymen, and at one point it was apparently forbidden for laymen to see a fire of the highest grade (Vahrām fire).[31] The Yasna, the central ritual, was a priestly act of worship performed on behalf of the whole community, not by it.[32] Of course laymen also visited temples to participate in ritual and have it performed for them, for purification and other rituals connected with birth, initiation, marriage, and death. But they did not meet there for prayer and instruction once a week as they did in synagogues, churches, and eventually mosques.

[26] Cf. de Jong, 'Sub Specie Maiestatis', 351.

[27] See *EIr.*, s.v. 'Zoroastrianism, I: Historical Review' (Malandra).

[28] *GrBd*, 3:20 in Zaehner, *Zurvan*, 324 = 336; Molé, *Culte*, 126ff.; see also Kreyenbroek, 'Mithra and Ahreman in Iranian Cosmogonies', 175ff.

[29] Molé, *Culte*, 86ff., 132ff.; Shaked, 'Eschatology and the Goal of Religious Life', 225; Shaked, 'Yasna Ritual', 337.

[30] Cf. Kotwal and Boyd, *Yasna*, 5f. (the stress here is on the effect of the participants); Shaked, 'Yasna Ritual', 338f.

[31] Yamamoto, 'Zoroastrian Temple Cult (II)', 89, with reference to the period after the rise of Islam.

[32] Kotwal and Boyd, *Yasna*, 3.

The main role of the laity was to patronise the priests, partly by visiting the temples and partly by hiring priests for ceremonies performed in their homes. The Sasanian king and aristocracy were the most important patrons. It was they who built the fire-temples. The king would establish a fire which served as the symbol of his sovereignty, to which all other fires had to be subordinated, and which the ruler and his entourage, and possibly others too, would visit from time to time.[33] According to Yāqūt, the king would make a *ziyāra* on foot to the fire temple at Shīz in Azerbaijan on his accession;[34] the reference is probably to a temple built in the fifth century or later on the hill now called Takht-i Sulaymān.[35] This was the closest the Zoroastrians had to a central sanctuary. An Arab poet, perhaps Jarīr (d. 110/728f.), mentions *hērbadhs* going on pilgrimage to the sanctuary of Zūn *(ḥajjū bīʿata 'l-Zūn)*, perhaps in eastern Iran, or perhaps at Ubulla:[36] this deity was of non-Avestan origin and, the use of the verb *ḥajja* notwithstanding, his appeal must have been local.[37] Al-Masʿūdī mentions that the fire-temple at Jūr, built by Ardashir I, had a festival (*ʿīd*) and that it was one of the pleasure-grounds (*muntazahāt*) of Fārs.[38] Presumably there were pilgrimages to many other local shrines as well, in line with modern Zoroastrianism,[39] but they are not well attested, and we do not hear of an annual pilgrimage bringing people together from far and wide. There was, however, a shared Zoroastrian calendar, and also feasts which were observed by all Zoroastrians and which thus served to highlight their unity.[40] The most important of these was the New Year's feast (*nōg rōz*), preceded by Fravardīgān, when the spirits of the dead returned. The New Year's feast survived in Islam (*nowrūz*), suggesting that what it highlighted was the unity of the Iranians as a people rather than their shared beliefs.

All in all, Iranian religion between Alexander and the Sasanians is probably better envisaged on an Indian than a Christian model. In Iran

33 Yamamoto, 'Zoroastrian Temple Cult (II)', 67ff.; Choksy, 'Ritual Fires', 253.

34 Yāqūt, III, 356, s.v. 'Shīz' (*zārahu māshiyan*). The fire was Ādhur Gushnasp.

35 See Boyce and Grenet, *History of Zoroastrianism*, 75, referring to archaeological evidence; Ibn al-Faqīh, 246.11/504.2, identifying Anūshirwān as the king who moved this fire to Shīz; MM, II, §1400 (IV, 74), where he moves it from Shīz to the pool (*al-birka*).

36 Marquart and de Groot, 'Der Gott Žun', 283.

37 He probably owed his presence at Ubulla to Indian merchants, and Marquart and de Groot deny that Zoroastrians participated in his cult, though Jarīr is not the only one to affirm it ('Der Gott Žun', 283–7).

38 MM, II, §1404 (IV, 78).

39 See Langer, *Pīrān und Zeyāratgāh*.

40 Cf. *EIr*., s.vv. 'Calendars', 'Festivals'; Boyce and Grenet, *History of Zoroastrianism*, 279ff.

as in India the priests (Magi, Brahmins) formed an estate or caste distinguished by their monopoly on the transmission of an ancient body of texts. Here as there, training for those who wished to practise as priests consisted of memorisation of the ancient texts in question (Avesta, Vedas), composed in a language that in the Iranian case, even the priests themselves could barely understand: the value lay in the ritual power of the spoken words, not in their meaning. Both the Vedic and the Avestan priests cultivated religious wisdom of their own, sometimes apparently esoteric;[41] and here as there laymen developed their own cults, served by priests of their own, in Iran by worshipping Nanai, Zūn, the Buddha, and probably also Christ when he arrived, while continuing to seek out the Avestan priests for the performance of the traditional rituals. The priests must have competed for patrons, above all kings, but like their Indian counterparts they seem not to have used their royal patronage to impose their own beliefs on the laity; or perhaps the kings simply lacked the will or the way to cooperate before the rise of the Sasanians. It is quite possible that one priestly school dismissed the doctrines of another as heresy, and the cults of the masses as the sheerest superstition; but until the rise of the Sasanians no ruler seems to have thought that he should opt for one particular form of the religion and impose it on all his subjects, priests and laity, elite and masses alike. In short, the religious landscape of the pre-Sasanian period must have been one of enormous diversity, even at the priestly level, and this is noted in the Pahlavi books themselves. After Alexander, when the people of Ērānšahr had no lord, no ruler, no chief, and no religious authority well versed in religious matters, they fell into doubt concerning the divine beings, and numerous faiths, beliefs, heresies, doubtful views, and deviant laws appeared in this world, the Book of Ardā Vīrāf says.[42] Naturally the religion was assumed to have been one in the good old days.

With the rise of the Sasanians everything changed so much that al-Yaʿqūbī assumed Iran to have become a Zoroastrian country under their rule: according to him Ardashir was the first of the Persian kings to practise Zoroastrianism (*awallu mulūk al-furs al-mutamajjisa*).[43] We now have the creation of the state department sometimes called the Zoroastrian church. The tradition credits Ardashir with a priest called Tansar or Tōsar who is identified as the author of an epistle extant in a seventh/thirteenth-century

[41] Shaked, 'Esoteric Trends'.
[42] *Ardā Vīrāfnāmag*, 1:8–15.
[43] YT, I, 179.

Persian work. This epistle, which tells of the reign of Ardashir with details belonging to the time of later kings, presents Ardashir as centralising the cult of fire by razing all royal fire-temples apart from his own and 'reviving' the religion after a long period of decay.[44] Other sources tell of campaigns against kings and queens who were venerated as divine and whose treasuries were plundered.[45] We are on firmer ground with the priest Kerdīr, who recorded his career in monumental inscriptions. His career spanned the reigns from the second Sasanian king, Shapur I (*c.* 240–70), to Narseh (293–302), and he tells us that Shapur 'made me absolute and authoritative in (the matter of) the rites of the gods, at the court and from province to province, place to place, throughout the Magian land (*mowestān*)', as MacKenzie translates, or more probably, 'over the entire body of Magi', as others understand it.[46] Kerdīr retained this position under Hormizd I (*c.* 270–3), Bahram I (273–6) and Bahram II (276–93), and at the end of his career he was both *mōbad* and judge (*dādvar*) of the entire realm (*hāmšahr*). A single authority had now been placed over all the Avestan priests of the empire.[47]

Kerdīr used his position to embark on an extensive programme of religious reform. 'From province to province and place to place', he says, 'the rites of the gods were much increased, and many Vahrām fires were established and many priests (*mowmard*) were (made) content and prosperous'. This he tells us under each of the successive kings he served, but under Bahram II he adds that the Mazdayasnian religion and its priests became greatly honoured in the empire and that great blows fell on Ahriman and the demons, whose religion (*kēš*) departed in defeat: the Jews (*yḥwdy*), Buddhists (*šmny*), Brahmans (*blmny*), Christians of one kind (*n'ṣl'y*), Christians of another kind (*klstyd'n*), unidentified *mktky*, and Manichaeans (*zndyky*) were smitten, idols were destroyed, and the abodes of the demons turned into seats of the gods.[48] It would have been good to know who the *mktky* were, but it is impossible to tell.

Kerdīr carefully enumerates every region of the realm affected by his activities, from Mesopotamia in the west to the country of the Kushans up to Peshawar in the east. But he was active in Anērān, too, from Antioch to Anatolia and the Caucasus: there, 'wherever the horses and men of the king reached', he made arrangements 'for the priests (*mowmard*) and the fires

[44] *Tansar's Epistle*, 11f., 22 = 37, 47; cf. de Jong, 'One Nation under God', 233ff.
[45] De Jong, 'One Nation under God', 235f.
[46] MacKenzie, 'Kerdir's Inscription', §2; cf. below, n. 50.
[47] MacKenzie, 'Kerdir's Inscription', §10; cf. Gignoux, 'Die Religiöse Administration', 254ff.
[48] MacKenzie, 'Kerdir's Inscription', §11; cf. de Blois, '*Naṣrānī* and *ḥanīf*, 5ff.

which were in those lands'. Apparently there were Avestan priests not just in Cappadocia, Armenia, and the Caucasus, but also in Cilicia and Antioch; and Kerdīr clearly recognised them as fellow Zoroastrians, for he tells us that he did not allow them to be harmed and would have those of them who were taken captive sent back again.[49] He also 'made the Mazdayasnian religion and the good priests noble and honoured in the land (*šahr*), and the heretics and degenerate men in the priesthood (*mowestān*) who, as regards the Mazdayasnian religion and the rites of the gods, did not live a proper life – them I punished, and I reprimanded them until I made them better'.[50] It is not clear whether the land in question is that of Anērān or Ērān. He adds that many men who were unbelievers (*anāstawān*) became believers, and that many who held the doctrine of the demons ceased to do so, now with explicit reference to the land of Ērān.[51] There would not be enough room on the monument to enumerate all the rites he had performed in the empire, he says, moving on to an account of his journey to heaven and hell designed to persuade people of the reality of both.

In practice there cannot have been enough soldiers around for Kerdīr to have accomplished all this, and neither the Jews nor the Christians preserve any memory of persecution in this particular period. But the intention is unmistakable, and there can be no doubt that the use of force was real. There is archaeological evidence for the conversion of at least one Buddhist abode of demons into a seat of the gods in the form of a fire-altar by Sasanian troops in the land of the Kushans around this time,[52] and the Islamic tradition associates the first Zoroastrian kings with religious violence on a major scale. The first Zoroastrian kings in this narrative are not Ardashir and his successors, but rather Bishtāsb/Gushtāsb, who was converted by Zoroaster. According to Ibn al-Kalbī the newly converted king forced people to adopt Zoroastrianism, making a huge slaughter (*maqtala ʿaẓīma*) of his subjects in that connection, a claim repeated by al-Thaʿālibī.[53] Bishtāsb made Zoroastrianism victorious by military force (*qātala ʿalayhā ḥattā ẓaharat*), as al-Masʿūdī observes;[54] he imposed it on

[49] MacKenzie, 'Kerdir's Inscription', §§14f.; cf. Boyce and Grenet, *History of Zoroastrianism*, 255, 304ff., 354ff.

[50] MacKenzie, 'Kerdir's Inscription', §16, rendering *mowestān* as 'the Magian land'. I follow Boyce and Grenet, *History of Zoroastrianism*, 255; de Ménasce, 'Conquête de l'Iranisme', 2; Gignoux, *Quatre inscriptions*, 66.

[51] MacKenzie, 'Kerdir's Inscription', §17.

[52] Staviskij, *Bactriane sous le Kushans*, 198; Staviskij, 'Le problème des liens', 51; Raschke, 'New Studies', 808, 1058.

[53] Ibn al-Kalbī (Hishām) in Tab. i, 648.13; Thaʿālibī, *Ghurar*, 257.

[54] Masʿūdī, *Tanbīh*, 90.14.

his subjects, who accepted it willy nilly (*ṭaw'an wa-karhan*), as others put it;[55] he and his son Isfandiyār spread Zoroaster's religion by force and by treaty *(qahran wa-ṣulḥan)* in east and west alike, setting up fire-temples all the way from China to the Byzantine empire, according to al-Bīrūnī;[56] he removed idols from a sanctuary on a mountain at Iṣfahān, turning it into a fire-temple, Ibn al-Jawzī adds.[57] The Zoroastrian Martan Farrukh was familiar with the same tradition: according to him Spendād and Zarēr (Guštasp's son and brother) propagated the new religion all the way to the Byzantine empire and India together with other warriors.[58] The violent behaviour with which the mythical kings are credited here is that of the first Sasanians.[59]

Exactly how the Sasanians came to adopt this policy is another question. Zoroastrianism played a major role in the legitimisation of their seizure of power from the Parthians, but from there to a demand for religious uniformity there is a long way; and no model for this kind of behaviour was provided by the rival empire, for Kerdīr was active well before the conversion of Constantine. But however this may be, their rise to power marked a drastic change in the relationship between the Magi and the state. There was now an authority defining a single norm for all Zoroastrians of the empire.

THE NATURE OF CONFORMITY

The fact that this authority was in charge of an ancestral rather than a faith-based community meant that the conformity demanded was first and foremost ritual. Kerdīr boasts in his inscription of having increased the rites of the gods, established Vahrām fires (i.e., fires of the highest grade), made charters relating to the priests and fires, and made the priests content and prosperous: this is his refrain throughout the section concerned with his services to the good religion, where he also mentions that he has performed many close-kin marriages. Among the ways in which he increased the rites of the gods was his expulsion of Ahriman and the

55 Ibn al-Muqaffa' (attrib.?) citing *kutub al-'ajam* in *Nihāyat al-irab*, 82; Dīnawarī, 27.

56 Bīrūnī, *Hind*, 15f./10f. = I, 21.

57 Ibn al-Jawzī, *Talbīs Iblīs*, 59.

58 *Škand*, 10: 65–8.

59 Cf. Crone, 'Buddhism as Ancient Iranian Paganism'. Cf. *Šahrestānīhā ī Ērānšahr*, 50, where Frēdōn replaces Khusraw I as the conqueror of South Arabia; Yarshater, 'Iranian National History', 402f., on how the legendary kings are cast in a Sasanian mould and credited with Sasanian institutions.

demons as represented by Jews, Christians, Manichaeans, Buddhists, Brahmans, and others, as well as his measures against deviant priests, perhaps in the land of Anērān and perhaps everywhere, and his conversion of unbelievers and followers of demonic religion into believers in Ērānšahr. The deviant priests 'did not adhere to doctrine regarding the Mazdayasnian religion and the rites of the gods', as MacKenzie translates:[60] this could refer to disagreements over doctrines as well as rites. But in Boyce and Grenet's rendition they 'did not in their expositions further the Mazda-worshipping religion and the service of the *yazads*', which is ambivalent, and in de Ménasce's translation they led an improper life in respect of the Mazdayasnian religion and the cult of the gods, which is roughly how Gignoux renders it as well; this takes us back to ritual.[61] The converts that Kerdīr boasts of having made in Ērānšahr were presumably the forcibly converted adherents of the religions he claims to have expelled. It is only when he tells of his tour of heaven that he addresses inner conviction: passers-by who might read the inscription 'should know for certain that there is a paradise (*vahišt*) and there is a hell (*dušokh*), and he who is virtuous goes forth to paradise and he who is sinful is cast into hell'.[62]

It is clear from Kerdīr's refrain that honouring the gods with proper rites is what he sees as the core of the religion. He was not alone in this. When Peroz (459–84) outlawed all religions other than Zoroastrianism the Kanthaeans responded by adopting fire-worship, and apparently this sufficed.[63] In line with this the Christian accounts of the martyrs never mention abjuration formulas or demands for affirmation of belief in Ohrmazd and Ahriman, for example by recital of the Zoroastrian confession of faith.[64] The Christians were not in fact being asked to renounce anything, but rather to add worship of the gods, sun, moon, fire, water, or the elements to their religious repertoire. Here, as in the Roman empire, they were being told to show that they belonged, that they were loyal

60 MacKenzie, 'Kerdir's Inscription', §16.

61 Boyce and Grenet, *History of Zoroastrianism*, 255; de Ménasce, 'Conquête de l'Iranisme', 2; Gignoux, *Quatre inscriptions*, 72.

62 MacKenzie, 'Kerdir's Inscription', §37.

63 Theodore Bar Koni, mimra xi, 85 (II, 343 = 256). Cf. Michael Syr., IV, 255 = II, 151, for his reputation as an 'evil persecutor of Christians'; Wiesehöfer, 215, for his persecution of Jews.

64 E.g. Hoffmann, *Aufzüge*, 24, 29, 53, cf. also 79f. At 51 an attempt is made to make them 'deny Christ and worship fire', but this was presumably one and the same act: worship of fire amounted to denial of Christ from a Christian point of view. Cf. also Walker, *Legend of Mar Qardagh*, 57f.

citizens rather than 'atheists' who refused to honour the gods of the land and thereby threatened to destroy it. When they depict themselves as responding with utter intransigence, their message is precisely that they did *not* belong in the same community as the Zoroastrians: it was of their own church that they were members. They insisted that this was compatible with purely political obedience to the *shāhānshāh*, but the idea of a subject belonging in one community politically and another for purposes of religion was alien to the *shāhānshāh*, unless the subject was a non-Iranian in a tributary position. On top of that, the Christians lacked respect for the religious and political order that the *shāhānshāh* represented. They refused to worship fire or pray to the sun, polluted water by washing and the earth by burying their dead, belittled the *shāhānshāh*'s importance by dying for a king above him, induced members of the Iranian nobility to defect from their ancestral religion, rejected the authority of the Zoroastrian priests, and could not restrain their zealots from smashing up fire-temples and engaging in other obnoxious behaviour. On top of that their hateful doctrine came to be shared by the Romans. In practice, of course, the two parties did come to some sort of understanding. The Christians made themselves at home in the land, joined the army, penetrated the elite, adopted its culture, and Christianised the landscape around them by strategic distribution of saintly shrines.[65] But they did all this as members of the church, a community of their own, thereby threatening to take over Iran rather than to disappear in it. Kerdīr and his successors not unnaturally wanted their own Ērānšahr to prevail. If the Christians had been willing to adopt fire-rituals after the fashion of the Kanthaeans – or at least to stop proselytising – all their other convictions, however perverse, would undoubtedly have been deemed tolerable.

It follows that we should not see Kerdīr and his successors as engaging in a systematic attempt to eradicate beliefs of which they disapproved. Obviously there were some convictions that could not be tolerated, such as pacifism or disbelief in paradise and hell, but Kerdīr and his successors are not likely to have taken issue with doctrines that did not impinge on public life. This is why the regional understandings of Zoroastrianism may have been left alone as what Madelung calls a 'low church'.

We should not envisage the bearers of these local forms as peasants and pastoralists alone, however. As we have seen, there is evidence for Avestan priests voicing beliefs of the type later classified as Khurramī,[66] and educated

[65] On all this see Payne, 'Christianity and Iranian Society'.
[66] See Chapter 15, pp. 367ff.

bearers of non-Persian beliefs, perhaps priests, survived long enough for al-Bīrūnī to be familiar with them, as will be seen in the following section. It was also members of the *mowestān* that Kerdīr reformed in the land of Anērān, and it is the priestly estate that is associated with heresy in the *Dēnkard*.[67] It summarises the Avestan *Baga Nask* as mentioning 'apostates' who had been forced to hide their apostasy and teach the good religion, reluctantly calling themselves Zoroastrian priests. It also warns against seeking instruction in the Avesta or Zand from evil people and heretical people; one should not teach them either.[68] The aristocrats and gentry who came together in the Sasanian empire are not likely to have been any less diverse, but how they were handled we do not know. One would assume that those who frequented the court adjusted their beliefs to conform with those of the Persians, willingly or unwillingly; Burzoē, a court physician, mentions religious beliefs that rested on mere 'fear and compulsion'.[69] But at least some of those who spent their entire lives in the countryside kept their local beliefs along with their local languages. The members of Jāvīdhān's cult society included substantial landowners, notably Jāvīdhān himself and his rival, as well as ʿIṣma al-Kurdī and Ṭarkhān.

Further down the social scale our information runs out. Zoroastrian priests did not have any compunctions about using force against their social inferiors: a heretic who figures in a debate set in the time of al-Maʾmūn objected to their habit of thrashing sinners and cutting off their hands.[70] But even if they had fully intended to impose uniformity on everybody from priests to peasants, in terms of ritual and doctrine alike, the physical and political geography of the empire made it impossible for them to do so. A great many people lived in inaccessible mountains and remote villages where the priests are likely to have been as innocent of Persian ways as the population at large; and most rural people lived on aristocratic estates shielded from royal interference, ruled by great aristocratic families unlikely to worry about the beliefs of subjects as long as there were no disturbances. In short, the disappearance of the regional forms of Zoroastrianism from the highest echelons of Iranian society must have started under the Sasanians, but, whether tolerated or not, it lived on below them.

[67] *Dk*, III, no. 331 (*DkB*, 248; *DkM*, 325); cf. no. 338 (*DkM*, 330. 7–22, cited in Molé, 'Sectes', 10).

[68] Shaked, 'Esoteric Trends', 190 n. 40, citing *DkM*, 834.19–21; cf. *Dk*, VI, nos. C27f. (*DkM*, 558f.); also in Molé, *Culte*, 215f. For the *Baga Nask*, see *Dk* IX, 52:3.

[69] Nöldeke, 'Burzōe's Einleitung', 15. This preface cannot be by Ibn al-Muqaffaʿ, whose real or alleged scepticism was of a quite different nature.

[70] Abālish in Stausberg, *Religion Zarathustras*, I, 349.

FROM REGIONAL ZOROASTRIANISM TO ISLAM

It will have been in response to the drive towards priestly unification under the first Sasanians that Zardūsht, son of Khrōsak/Khurrak, 'the older Mazdak', formulated his creed, systematising beliefs that were now under threat. He was probably a priest and he either came from Fasā in Fārs or held office there, but the views he systematised were not those of the dominant school in Fārs. They included a utopian vision of non-violence and internal harmony achieved by shared ownership of women and property, and also, by Mazdak's time at least, a doctrine of reincarnation. He was not successful, and over the following centuries the local forms of Zoroastrianism will have suffered social decline. But educated bearers of non-Persian beliefs were still known to al-Bīrūnī.

Al-Bīrūnī tells us that one could still find pre-Sasanian forms of Zoroastrianism in his time, partly within Zoroastrianism itself (which he like so many others takes to mean that of the official Sasanian kind) and partly within Buddhism. This is the message that emerges from two somewhat complicated passages. In the first he tells us that the whole region from Khurāsān through Fārs, Iraq, and Mosul to the border of Syria had once practised the religion of the Shamaniyya; it continued to do so until Zoroaster appeared in Azerbaijan and preached in Balkh, where Gushtāsb and his son Isfandiyār adopted Zoroastrianism (*majūsiyya*) and spread it by force and by treaty in east and west alike, setting up fire-temples all the way from China to the Byzantine empire. The later kings of Fārs and Iraq, presumably meaning the Sasanians, also chose it as their religion, he says, so the Shamaniyya withdrew to Balkh.[71] Contrary to what one might think, al-Bīrūnī is not saying that the whole region from Khurāsān to the Byzantine empire had once been Buddhist. Like several other authors he is using the term Shamaniyya (elsewhere Sumaniyya) to mean Iranian paganism and Buddhism alike, the two having merged in Transoxania: what he is saying is that once upon a time the whole region in question had been pagan, but that this had changed with the imposition of Zoroastrianism so that paganism had withdrawn to Balkh, where it was still visible in the form of Buddhist remains. He credits the forcible imposition of Zoroastrianism to the Pīshdādids, but, as noted already, this must be a back-projection of the activities of the Sasanians.[72]

[71] Bīrūnī, *Hind*, 15f./10f. = I, 21.

[72] For all this see Crone, 'Buddhism as Ancient Iranian Paganism'.

In the second passage al-Bīrūnī tells us that the ancient Magians were those who existed before Zoroaster (*ammā 'l-majūs al-aqdamūn fa-hum alladhīna kānu qabla ẓuhūr Zarādusht*). Nowadays, he says, they are no longer found in a pure form (*ṣirfun sādhij*): all of them are now to be found within Zoroastrianism, except in so far as they are Shamaniyya (here meaning Buddhists).[73] He is talking about the same pre-Zoroastrian pagans as in the first passage here, now calling them Magians. In short, once upon a time the whole of what eventually became the Sasanian empire had followed a Magian religion of a pagan, pre-Zoroastrian kind which had been stamped out by the first Zoroastrian kings, but of which there were still traces in Zoroastrianism and Buddhism.

The Zoroastrians also had a tradition concerning the pre-Zoroastrian religion of Iran, but according to them it was the same religion as Zoroaster's. Spandārmad (the *amahraspand* in charge of the earth) had brought it 520 years before him, at a time when Afrāsiyāb had removed the waters from Iran.[74] The *Šahrestānīhā ī Ērānšahr* knew of two fire-temples that pre-dated Zoroaster, one apparently built by the accursed Afrāsiyāb (concatenated with Spandārmad again), but rebuilt by Kay Khusraw, son of Sīyāwakhš, who had also founded the other.[75] According to al-Mas'ūdī, eleven fire-temples pre-dated Zoroaster, having been built by Afrīdūn (Frēdōn), the first Persian king to venerate fire in his view.[76] Al-Bīrūnī does not seem to be drawing on this tradition, for he envisages the Zoroastrian kings as hostile to this earlier religion, which consisted in veneration of the elements and the heavenly bodies, not in fire-worship, and it was precisely by setting up fire-temples all the way from China to the Byzantine empire that the kings tried to suppress it. The tradition that al-Bīrūnī is drawing on is found in Ḥamza al-Iṣfahānī and al-Khwārizmī and concerns the history of paganism,[77] but he has synthesised it with information collected by himself on the ground, and this is what makes it so valuable. Of the ancient Magians who survived in Zoroastrianism he

[73] Bīrūnī, *Āthār*, 318 (for *shamsiyya* read *shamaniyya*).

[74] Zādspram, 4:4–8. Spandārmad assumed the form of a young girl in radiant clothes carrying the religion in her belt: one takes it that her intention was to seduce Afrāsiyāb to make the waters flow again. For his reaction see the following note. According to Theodore Bar Koni, mimra xi, 13, she became engaged to him. But nobody seems to tell us the rest of the myth.

[75] *Šahrestānīhā ī Ērānšahr*, 3 (Samarqand), 38 (Zarang, where Afrāsiyāb proposes to Spandārmad).

[76] MM, II, §§1399–1402 (IV, 72–5); cf. Shahrastānī, I, 197 = I, 673.

[77] See Crone, 'Buddhism as Ancient Iranian Paganism'.

further informs us that they added some ancient things to their religion which they had taken from the laws of the Shamaniyya and the ancient Harranians. What exactly did they add? Unfortunately he does not say, but reincarnation could have been one of the doctrines in question.[78]

In the seventh century Ērānšahr was conquered by the Arabs, with the result that 'the Zoroastrian church collapsed', as we were often told in the older literature. In fact, all that collapsed was the centrally upheld hierarchy that Kerdīr had taken such pride in initiating; what was left was once more a variety of regional forms, some more Persianised (and indeed Christianised) than others, and now under Muslim rule. The Muslims found it convenient to use the Persian language of the Sasanian establishment as a medium of communication with their Iranian subjects, thereby facilitating its transformation into New Persian (Fārsī); but they did not extend any comparable service to the Persian form of Zoroastrianism. It survived the longest in Fārs and Kerman, where it was at home. But by far the majority of those who became Muslims in the first centuries were carriers of regional varieties of other kinds. This is why there are many more Iranians of the type bundled together under the label of Khurramī than mainstream Zoroastrians in the revolts after the Hāshimite revolution. It is for the same reason that the Zoroastrian legacy in Islam is predominantly of the Khurramī rather than the Persian type.

[78] Bīrūnī, *Āthār*, 318. Further discussion in Crone, 'Buddhism as Ancient Iranian Paganism'.

III

WOMEN AND PROPERTY

17

'Wife-sharing'

Al-Baghdādī, a learned heresiographer much given to hostile stereotyping of his opponents, tells us that the Mazdakites, here in the sense of Khurramīs, deemed it lawful to indulge in any natural inclination, such as intercourse with close relatives and other partners, drinking wine, eating carrion, and doing anything pleasurable.[1] This was a truth universally accepted in his time. The maliciousness of the stereotype lies in the way in which it strings together a number of decontextualised practices to depict the opponents as brutes who did not believe in civilised restraints. On their own, all the practices were real. The Khurramīs did believe in the legitimacy of natural pleasures, they did drink wine, they did eat carrion in the sense of meat not slaughtered in accordance with Islamic law, and sometimes in the literal sense as well; and the Zoroastrians of Fārs did encourage close-kin marriage. It is not clear how far the Khurramīs did, however. Bar Daiṣan (d. 222), writing at the end of the Parthian period, thought of next-of-kin marriage as a custom peculiar to the Persians, who would practise it in all the countries they went to, such as for example Media, Atrapatene (Azerbaijan), and Parthia.[2] It did not apparently form part of north-western and north-eastern Zoroastrianism. Al-Baghdādī credits the Khurramīs with incestuous unions simply because they were universally assumed to believe in *ibāḥat al-nisāʾ*, literally making women lawful (for anyone to use), and intercourse with close relatives was the ultimate illustration of indiscriminate mating. It is this levelling of all historical contours that makes it so hard to tell what kind of reality lies

[1] Baghdādī, *Uṣūl*, 323.

[2] Bar Daiṣan, *Laws of Countries*, 42f., cf. 54f., 60 = 44f., cf. 55f., 61; cited from the lost Greek version in Eusebius, *Praeparatio*, VI, 10, 16f.; *Recognitions*, IX, 21, both with Phrygia and Galatia instead of Atrapatene.

behind a stereotype unless one has other evidence to view it against. But on the topic of wife-sharing we do have some evidence. What then lay behind the charge?

The answer given in this chapter is that it reflects a number of different practices, no one of which was wife-sharing in the sense that anyone could avail himself of any woman whenever he wished, as titillated upholders of the established order liked to think. The 'transgressive sacrality' discussed in an earlier chapter is the nearest we get to it.[3] The rest were marital institutions which Muslims found utterly unacceptable, and it is to them that this chapter is devoted. The reader should not expect a high-resolution picture. What follows is written on the assumption that even a blurry outline is better than no picture at all, and that widening the net to include pre-Islamic and non-Islamic information helps to give us a better sense of the types of practice that could be involved.

POLYANDRY

The best place to start is with the the Ismaili missionary Abū Tammām. He worked in Khurāsān in the first half of the fourth/tenth century and twice tells us that the Mubayyiḍa, identified as the followers of al-Muqannaʿ, believed in holding women in common. His first statement is based on a literary source, perhaps Ibrāhīm b. Muḥammad, and it simply informs us that al-Muqannaʿ's followers hold it lawful to share women among themselves (*istiḥallū fīmā baynahum al-nisāʾ*). This is too unspecific to be helpful. The second statement refers to sectarians he had met and disputed with in person, presumably in the course of his attempt to convert them to Ismailism. Here he observes that

> they say that a woman is like a fragrant herb (*rayḥāna*) which is not diminished by the one who smells it. If one of their men desires to be alone with a woman belonging to another of them, he enters that man's house and puts a marker (*ʿalāma*) on the door, showing that he is inside. When her husband comes back and recognizes the marker, he does not go in, but leaves until the other has satisfied his need.[4]

Niẓām al-Mulk had picked up some similar information, but he attributes it to the Mazdakites of the past: whenever a man went to have commerce with a woman he would put his hat on the door and go inside; another man

[3] See Chapter 13, p. 265.

[4] Abū Tammām, 77f. = 76; cited in *TB*, 73/103 = 75 (*gul* for *rayḥāna*); further discussion in Crone, 'Abū Tammām on the Mubayyiḍa'.

seized by the same desire would turn back on seeing the hat.[5] This information may not be true, but it is highly informative: stories about men leaving markers by the door when visiting a woman are widely attested in the most diverse languages from antiquity to modern times,[6] and to my knowledge there is only one exception to the rule that all refer to polyandry, the marital state in which a woman has more than one husband at a time.[7]

Fraternal and non-fraternal polyandry

Polyandry comes in two main forms, fraternal and non-fraternal, which can coexist. Fraternal (or adelphic) polyandry is a system whereby brothers inherit the property of their parents without dividing it up, cultivate it in common, and share a wife, whose sons will jointly take over the family property in their turn. The system allows the property to pass intact from one generation to the next and seems to be attested particularly where cultivation is difficult (as in hill agriculture) and/or where the men would spend long periods away from home, conscripted as labourers by the state, forced to work for feudal lords, or seeking income away from home as mercenaries or traders; the environment was usually such that it was wise to keep the population small, encouraging female infanticide. Variants such as fathers and sons sharing a household and a wife are also encountered where fraternal polyandry prevails. Non-fraternal polyandry, on the other hand, involves unrelated men who share a wife because they cannot afford a wife each (until they can afford it), or because women are scarce, or because the male population is so mobile that land is transmitted in the female line. Where land is transmitted in the female line men live with their sisters, not with their wives; the sisters are impregnated by visiting husbands or lovers (who also live with their sisters when they are not working away from home), and the males of the household are uncles and nephews, not fathers and sons. Authority is wielded by the senior male, not by the women through whom the property is traced.

Polyandry is reported for a surprisingly large number of ancient societies, both agriculturalist and pastoralist, in both the Old and New

[5] *SN*, ch. 44:4 (260f. = 198).

[6] Strabo, XVI, 4, 25 (Yemen); Herodotus, I, 216 (Massagetes), IV, 172 (Nasamones); Enoki, 'Nationality of the Ephtalites', 51 (Tokharians or Hephtalites), 53 (Bolor), 54 (Kansu); Peter, *Polyandry*, 91, 94 (Nayars), 99 (Ceylon); Parmar, *Polyandry in the Himalayas*, 91 (Himachal Pradesh); Aiyyappan, 'Fraternal Polyandry in Malabar', 270.

[7] The exception is Marco Polo, II, ch. 47, on Caindu, where it refers to guest prostitution.

Worlds; its function among nomadic tribes is often unclear, and there is much debate about the precise factors, apart from resource limitation, behind the presence of the institution elsewhere as well.[8] Non-fraternal polyandry is best known from the Malabar region of southern India and the Marquesas Islands, but it is also attested for some African societies, and has sprung up in the modern West from time to time as well without receiving legal expression: among Polish coal miners suffering from a shortage of women, for example, and in boarding-houses.[9] One would expect the male–female imbalance arising from the selective abortion of females in China and India to cause it soon to appear there as well. The fraternal version, linked with patrilineal succession, seems to have been by far the more common. In Eurasia alone it is documented, for example, for Sparta by Polybius;[10] for northern Europe in the form of mythology and Caesar on the ancient Britons;[11] for pre-Islamic Arabia by Strabo[12] and, without mention of its fraternal nature, by Agatharchides and Artemidorus,[13] and by Ḥadīth;[14] for Ceylon by a fourteenth-century

[8] Cf. Stephens, 'Half a Wife is Better than None', 355.

[9] Peter, *Polyandry*, 62; cf. also Stephens, 'Half a Wife is Better than None', with an example from Canada (Churchill, Manitoba) and the view that the institution is likely to have been much more common than the anthropological literature suggests.

[10] Polybius, XII, 6b: among the Lacedaemonians 'it was a hereditary custom and quite usual for three or four men to have one wife or even more if they were brothers, the offspring being the common property of all'. This could be taken to mean that non-fraternal and fraternal polyandry coexisted there (as it has elsewhere as well), but perhaps Polybius simply did not know that it was only brothers who shared wives.

[11] Peter, *Polyandry*, 57 (on Frigg, married to Odinn and his brothers), 59, citing Caesar, *Bellum Gallicum*, v, 14: 'Ten and even twelve have wives common to them, and particularly brothers among brothers, and parents among their children; but if there be any issue by these wives, they are reputed to be the children of those by whom respectively each was first espoused when a virgin.' Somehow this information passed to Bar Daiṣan, *Laws of Countries*, 48 = 49; cited from the lost Greek version in Eusebius, *Praeparatio*, VI, 10, 28; *Recognitions*, IX, 24 (among the Britons many men take one and the same wife).

[12] Strabo, XVI, 4, 25: 'Property is held in common by all kinsmen, though the eldest is lord of all. One woman is also wife for all' (followed by a story involving door-markers); discussed by Wellhausen, 'Ehe bei den Arabern', 462; Henninger, 'Polyandrie', 316ff.

[13] Agatharchides, §61, in Photius, *Bibliothèque*, 170 (453b); Artemidorus in Strabo, XVI, 4, 17, on the Troglodytes of the Red Sea coast who had their women in common.

[14] Bukhārī, *Ṣaḥīḥ*, *nikāḥ* 36: of the four types of marriage in pre-Islamic Arabia the third was that of a group of kinsfolk (*rahṭ*) who would share a wife; she would assign paternity to one of them after the birth of a child, and the man in question would have no way of preventing it (told in a tone suggesting that the arrangement was a form of prostitution). See further Wellhausen, 'Ehe bei den Arabern', 460ff.; Henninger, 'Polyandrie', 314. See also the *ḥadīth* in which the paternity of a child by a woman in Yemen who has slept with three men is settled by 'Alī by lot-casting (cited in Crone and Silverstein, 'The Ancient Near East and Islam', 437); here too the wording suggests that the woman was just a slut.

inscription, European travellers, British legislation against it, and modern observation;[15] for diverse parts of India, both northern and southern, in a wide array of sources from the *Mahābhārata* till the late twentieth century;[16] for diverse tribes of Central and Inner Asia,[17] and above all for Tibet and other parts of the Himalayan region, for which we have an abundance of sources,[18] and where it is still practised, if only just.[19] It is also attested for Iran. Before we turn to the Iranian case, however, we need to know more about how the systems function.

Fraternal polyandry is reported with numerous variations. The rule might be that if a woman married a man she was automatically married to his brothers too, or she might formally marry all of them. Several brothers might share one wife, or they might share several.[20] All brothers might count as the father of children born to the shared wife (if one asked a child for his father, he would reply, 'which one?');[21] or the children might be affiliated to the eldest brother, or they might be assigned to individual brothers in the order of seniority or by some other reckoning. If all brothers counted as fathers and the household split up, paternity might be assigned by lot, by information supplied by the mother, by birth order, on the basis of physical similarity, or by other means.[22] In Tibet (allowing for simplification, since there were variations within the Tibetan culture area) the brothers could marry additional wives of their own, and even bring them

[15] Peter, *Polyandry*, 98ff.; Tambiah, 'Polyandry in Ceylon'; for the inscription (in which a queen calls herself the chief consort of two brother kings) see Husayn, 'Eka-ge-kema'.

[16] Raha and Coomar, *Polyandry in India*.

[17] Enoki, 'Nationality of the Ephtalites', 51–4.

[18] Parmar, *Polyandry in the Himalayas* (reflecting the 1930s); Peter, *Polyandry* (minutely detailed fieldwork done in Tibet in 1938–9, 1949, and intermittently between 1950 and 1957, at a time when the existence of polyandry was still widely doubted).

[19] Levine, *Dynamics* (based on fieldwork in 1973, 1975, and 1983); Haviland, 'Nepal's wife-sharing custom fades', where the locals expect the institution soon to disappear; Sidner, 'Brothers share wife' (Himachal Pradesh, undated, by a CNN reporter with less sympathy for the institution); Polgreen, 'One Bride for Multiple Brothers'.

[20] One is the norm in Peter's material, except where the wife is barren; similarly Levine, *Dynamics*, 148f.; for a system where the wives are added one by one see Majumdar, *Himalayan Polyandry*, 72.

[21] Aiyyappan, 'Fraternal Polyandry in Malabar', 275. When Prince Peter asked a Tibetan woman who was the father of the young child in her arms she looked surprised and refused to answer, saying she was an honest woman who had no preference; the locals approved of this reply (Peter, *Polyandry*, 366f.; cf. also 325f.). But in the community studied by Levine, differentiated paternity was important (Levine, *Dynamics*, 167ff.).

[22] Enoki, 'Nationality of the Ephtalites', 53; Caesar, above, n. 11; 'Alī above, n. 14 (lot casting); Parmar, *Polyandry in the Himalayas*, 83 (lot casting), 92f.; Berreman, 'Himalayan Polyandry', 181f.; Levine, *Dynamics*, 167ff.

into the household with their brothers' permission; polygyny was common among the wealthy.[23] If additional wives were shared by the brothers, their children inherited the family property along with the other sons, but a brother who insisted on a separate wife might have to leave the household; he could not take any of the joint children with him, and his offspring by his new, individual wife would only inherit property he had acquired after his departure – unless the joint property was partitioned, a calamity that the parties would do their best to avoid.[24]

Though fraternal polyandry is usually associated with patrilineal succession, in Tibet succession could be matrilineal as well: if there were no sons among the children the family property would pass to the eldest daughter, who was free to take and dismiss as many husbands as she liked, presumably on the understanding that she chose them from within the normal pool of acceptable husbands; her children would inherit the property in their turn. ('It is cheaper to take an extra husband than a servant,' as a woman explained in 1938 when an anthropologist asked her why she had taken a second husband.)[25] It was a system in which in principle it did not matter who sired the future heirs as long as one of the parents was a transmitter of the family property.

It is perfectly accurate to describe fraternal polyandry as wife-sharing, but it is of course misleading too: for it was not the case that men shared each other's wives as they pleased, but rather that brothers shared one wife in accordance with custom. Nonetheless, the vast majority of outsiders have reacted to polyandrous societies by branding them as immoral, licentious, and promiscuous. In Tibet polyandry was only practised by Buddhists (apparently including the Bon-po);[26] both the Hindus and the Muslims found it disgusting. Christian missionaries usually (though not always) found it repulsive as well, and both Muslim and European colonial rulers tried to suppress it, as did the Chinese.[27] Polyandrous people living in close promixity to disapproving outsiders would become secretive, refuse to talk about the institution, or simply deny its existence.[28] By the middle of the

[23] Peter, *Polyandry*, 313, 346f., 414, 420, 460.

[24] Peter, *Polyandry*, 85; Parmar, *Polyandry in the Himalayas*, 83, 86, 92.

[25] Peter, *Polyandry*, 315f., 334, 390, 414. This rule does not seem to have obtained among the Tibetans in Nepal studied by Levine, *Dynamics*.

[26] I have not see any distinction between them in Peter, *Polyandry*, or other literature on the polyandry in Tibet.

[27] Peter, *Polyandry*, 86f., 99f., 311f., 379, 415f. Polyandry was 'contrary to the European concept of public order, morality and bad for the moral evolution of the native race', as the Belgians said in Congo (67).

[28] Peter, *Polyandry*, 85, 392.

twentieth century young Tibetans were sometimes reluctant to enter into polyandrous marriages, calling them immoral. The older generation blamed the new attitude on the influence of Indian and Turkish traders, European missionaries, and other outsiders who were 'perpetually speaking against the time-honoured custom of polyandrous matrimony'.[29]

It was not, of course, because the Tibetans and others were promiscuous that they would share a wife instead of having one (or four) each. In 1945, when an Indian high court judge of the Tehri Garhwal district in the Indian Himalayas asked the locals why they practised a custom looked down upon by other people, they said that they did it to keep the family property together.[30] The Tibetans, too, regularly said that they practised it to keep the family property together: if divided up, the shares would be too small to suffice for a living. It was practised by the wealthy too: the institution helped to keep the wealth and power of the family intact, Tibetan aristocrats said.[31] Observing that converts to Islam ceased to practise polyandry and so had to impoverish themselves by dividing up their family property, one Tibetan explained the presence of European colonies all over the world with reference to the European unfamiliarity with the institution: given their family system, the Europeans could not in his view have enough to live on at home.[32] What polyandry really was, the Indian high court judge said, was 'a sort of family communism in wives' or 'a joint family both in property and in wives'.[33]

Non-fraternal polyandry is considerably less well known, especially if we exclude societies in which it has been practised on a temporary basis. Only two systems survived long enough for descriptions by travellers and modern anthropologists, that of the Nayars of the Malabar coast in south India and that of the Marquesas Islands in formerly French Polynesia. The Nayars were a warrior caste coexisting with higher-ranking, patrilineal Nambudiri Brahmins and lower castes. Nayar men were often away, and the landowning group consisted of women and brothers or maternal uncles headed by the senior male, who would no longer be serving as a

[29] Peter, *Polyandry*, 326, 344, 361, 417.

[30] Peter, *Polyandry*, 84.

[31] Peter, *Polyandry*, 378, 453. Similar answers were given in Ceylon (Peter, *Polyandry*, 98; Tambiah, 'Polyandry in Ceylon', 298) and elsewhere (Parmar, *Polyandry in the Himalayas*, 83, 89). The Tibetans also said it was a good way of obtaining sufficient labour for the land, especially if the men were often absent (a point made in Ceylon as well), and better for domestic peace than several sisters-in-law living together. The Sinhalese added that the wife and children would be provided for even if one husband died.

[32] Peter, *Polyandry*, 361ff.

[33] Quoted in Peter, *Polyandry*, 83.

mercenary. Daughters were ritually married to a husband from whom they would immediately be divorced, and thereafter they were free to take temporary husbands, several at a time, from the same Nayar sub-caste, as well as lovers from among the Nambudiri Brahmins. Husbands and lovers would visit at night and leave in the morning without sharing any meals with the women, to whom they had no obligations and from whom they received no domestic services. The children were affiliated to the mother's line, but the fathers had to acknowledge paternity by paying the delivery expenses: without this acknowledgement (which was not onerous) the woman would be assumed to have slept with a man from a lower caste or sub-caste, with the result that she would be expelled or killed. The same is true if she had sexual relations without having been ritually married first. It did not matter who sired the future heirs as long as the progenitor came from the right sperm bank, so to speak, but this proviso was extremely important. The ritual initiation and acknowledgement of paternity ensured the children's membership of the mother's community.[34]

The Marquesas system is not nearly so well documented, but it appears to have been quite different. Women seem to have been in short supply.[35] A household typically consisted of two or three men to one woman or, in the case of chiefs, eleven or twelve men to three or four women. All male members of a household had sexual rights in all female members. According to Tautain a husband automatically acquired the right to sleep with his wife's sisters whether they were married or not, and his own brothers acquired the right to sleep with his wife, but Linton denies that there was any fraternal polyandry: according to him the eldest son inherited the household and younger brothers would leave to become lovers and husbands of other women, living with their parents or attaching themselves, married or unmarried, to a wealthy household. If the eldest child was a daughter she inherited the household and took and dismissed husbands at will, as in Tibet. If a younger brother who attached himself to

[34] Peter, *Polyandry*, 91ff., with further literature; Gough, 'The Nayars and the Definition of Marriage'; Gough., 'Female Initiation Rites', 47ff. (examining the ritual in a different vein). The earliest description is by a south Indian (Mapilla) Muslim, Shaykh Zayn al-Dīn Makhdūm, who wrote in 1579f. (Aiyyappan, 'Fraternal Polyandry in Malabar', 269f., calling him an Arab).

[35] Tautain, 'Étude', 641, relates the development of the system to the rarity of women on the canoes that brought the Polynesians to the islands. They denied that they practised female infanticide, but Linton thought they must have done so ('Marquesan Culture', 155), and Otterbein agrees ('Marquesan Polyandry', 157).

a new household was married, the head of the new household would marry his wife and become her principal husband, reducing him to a secondary husband.[36] The head of the household might also marry women who had lovers attached, incorporating them in his household too. Either way, marriage seems to have served as a way of recruiting retainers. Marrying a woman with males in tow was somewhat like hiring a female housekeeper and sleeping with her, while employing her husband or boyfriend as a gardener. But the woman was taken on for the sake of the males she brought with her, or was deemed capable of attracting, and all the young men brought into the household had sexual access to the chief's wife as well. The head of the household had to keep his underlings satisfied so that they would not wander off with other women; sexual access took the place of, or complemented, material rewards such as the bread, gold, and plunder with which faithful retainers were rewarded in other societies in which power rested on personal relations.[37] In short, the main function of polyandry seems to have been political: it served to create big and prestigious households. But it is poorly understood because the political system it served had disappeared by the time it was described.

Here too, however, the women had to undergo an initiation ceremony: all the males of the community would have intercourse with the bride, propped up on the knees of her husband. (Women would boast about how long they had lasted before passing out.) For noble women this had to be repeated every time they married, for others once was enough.[38] Herodotus describes a polyandrous society with a similar initiation ceremony in North Africa. The Nasamones were promiscuous, he says, mentioning that 'a staff is planted before the dwelling and then they have intercourse'; and 'when a man of the Nasamones first weds, on the first night the bride must by custom lie with each of the whole company in turn: and each man after intercourse gives her whatever gift he has brought from his house'.[39] One takes it that here, as among the Nayars, the bride was seen as in some sense married to all the males of the community – represented by the ritual husband among the Nayars, here literally by all of

[36] Tautain, 'Étude', 644; Linton, 'Marquesan Culture', 156, 158.

[37] For all this see Linton, 'Marquesan Culture', 152ff.

[38] Tautain, 'Étude', 642f. Linton, by contrast, says that there was no formal marriage ('Marquesan Culture', 157), which could have been true by his time, but he comes across as less reliable than Tautain (similarly Otterbein, 'Marquesan Polyandry', 159).

[39] Herodotus, IV, 172; cf. Asheri *et al.*, *Commentary*, ad loc.; Andò, 'Comunanza delle donne', 94f., takes the report to reflect pre-marital sexual freedom, which is hardly what the text suggests.

them – and that this was why she could procreate children by any one of them thereafter.[40] There does not seem to be any information on what would happen to Marquesan women (or those of the Nasamones) if they had sexual relations without having been initiated first.

There is no mention of door-markers in the Marquesas Islands, but visiting husbands among the Nayars would leave their weapons on the veranda, and in other societies we hear of spears, trousers, bows, hats, and the like being left by the door.[41] When the anthropologist Prince Peter asked the Tibetans whether they used door-markers, some thought that they might have done so in the past (perhaps because so many anthropologists had asked them about it), but others laughed uproariously at the idea, and the cramped conditions in which most of them lived certainly made the practice superfluous.[42]

Polyandry in eastern Iran

Fraternal polyandry is well known to have been practised in south-eastern Iran, where there is both literary and documentary evidence for it. The earliest reference relates to north-eastern Iran, however, and comes in Herodotus. He famously says of the Massagetes, an Iranian tribe of Central Asia ranging from the Syr Darya to the Ukraine, that 'each man marries a wife, but the wives are common to all', and that a man would signal his presence with a woman by hanging his quiver on her wagon.[43] He adds that the Greeks wrongly believed wife-sharing to be practised by the Scythians (i.e., the Sakae), another Iranian steppe people. It is not clear who the Greeks in question were,[44] but later Greeks certainly idealised the Scythians as people who, in the formulation of Ephorus (*c.* 350 BC), had 'all things in common, their wives, children, and their whole kin', or, in the formulation of Pseudo-Scymnus (*c.* 90 BC), as 'living in common, having their property and whole social life on a communal basis'; they had their wives and children in common 'after the Platonic manner', as Strabo

[40] Back in the days when scholars were looking for reflections of a stage when women had been held in common the community was seen as exercising its rights for the last time, the opposite of what is being proposed here (cf. Gsell, *Afrique du nord*, V, 30, sensibly arguing against this interpretation). For a similar custom see Diodorus Siculus, V, 18, on the Balearics.

[41] See n. 6 to this chapter.

[42] Peter, *Polyandry*, 314, 325, 375, 451.

[43] Herodotus, I, 216 (repeated by Strabo, XI, 8, 6); cf. Asheri *et al.*, *Commentary*, ad loc.

[44] Cf. Braund, 'Herodotus' Spartan Scythians', 28.

(*c.* AD 24) said.[45] One branch of the Sakae/Scythians is known to have moved into Sogdia, Bactria, and neighbouring areas, leaving their name behind in that of Sijistān/Sīstān: these are regions in which polyandry is later attested. Another branch moved into Thrace, where they were known as Agathyrsi. Of the latter, Herodotus says that they were similar to the Thracians except that 'their intercourse with women is promiscuous, so that they may be brothers and – as all are kinsfolk to each other – they may neither envy nor hate their fellows'.[46]

Herodotus is not simply describing barbarians in terms of an inversion of Greek norms, let alone condemning them. On the contrary, in the passage on the Agathyrsi he shows signs of sharing the Greek tendency to equate the absence of sexually exclusive unions with social harmony and so to idealise what others condemned as immoral. To many Greeks, communism of property and wives seemed to be the original state of nature, lost with the onset of civilisation, but preserved by some happy tribes. Herodotus is not idealising in the passage on the Massagetes, however.[47] Here he is out to correct a mistake: the Scythians in his view did not share their wives, only the Massagetes (and, as he later gives us to understand, the Agathyrsi).

Exactly what kind of wife-sharing was involved? Herodotus does not identify the wife-sharers as brothers, except (among the Agathyrsi) in the metaphorical sense, perhaps because they were not brothers or perhaps because he did not know this to be the case. The latter seems the more likely, though in principle he could be referring to non-fraternal polyandry.

Turning now to south-eastern Iran we find that here too the earliest evidence is Greek. According to Diodorus Siculus (late first century BC), citing Agatharchides of Cnidus (*fl. c.* 116 BC), the Ichthyophagi or 'Fish-eaters' of the coast from Carmania and Gedrosia to the Arabian Gulf went naked and had their women and children in common like their flocks and herds.[48] Agatharchides doubtless took the locals to have no marriage or private property at all: he saw them as innocents. But if there is any truth to his information, the institution he had heard of was presumably what the Indian judge called 'family communism', for we are explicitly told that the

[45] Ephorus (cited by Strabo, VII, 3, 9) and Pseudo-Scymnus in Lovejoy and G. Boas, *Primitivism*, 324, 327, with Strabo himself (VII, 3, 7) at 289f.

[46] Herodotus, IV, 104; cf. Asheri *et al.*, *Commentary*, ad loc.; Andò, 'Comunanza delle donne', 92, suggests that the passage reflects classificatory kinship.

[47] Cf. Lovejoy and Boas, *Primitivism*, index, s.vv. 'Communism', 'Community of wives'.

[48] Diodorus Siculus, III, 15, 2.

fish-eaters shared their property along with their wives. Flocks are not normally shared by entire tribes or clans, but rather by the families within them, so it was probably within families that wives were shared as well. His fishermen were perhaps inhabitants of what is now Baluchistan. Of course, all he may have picked up is vague rumours. But the rumours themselves would be in need of explanation.

Thereafter there is silence down to the fourth century, when the documentary evidence sets in. The earliest document is written on leather in Bactrian and dated to 110 of the Bactrian era, corresponding to AD 333, if the Bactrian era is simply that of the Sasanians, as has now been persuasively argued.[49] It takes us to the time when Bactria was ruled by the *kūshānshāhs* and records the marriage of a girl, Ralik, to two men, Bab and Piduk, sons of Bag-farn. The father requests the girl from her parents on his sons' behalf and lays down, among other things, that the brothers are not to take a second wife or free concubine without her consent (slave-girls seem to have been a different matter).[50]

For the next attestations we have to turn to Chinese sources. The *Chou-shu* (written 583–666) reports that the Hephtalites (or 'White Huns'), a possibly Iranian people who occupied Sogdia and Bactria in the mid-fifth century, were polyandrous: 'in this country, brothers jointly have one wife. If her husband has no brother, the wife wears a hat with one horn. If her husband has brothers, as many horns as they are added.'[51] A later source adds that if a man had no brothers he would secure another as a sworn brother, since he would not otherwise be able to marry. Presumably this means that local custom was against it because the household would not be viable with just a single adult male.[52]

Around 630 the Buddhist pilgrim Hsüan-tsang described the marriages of the inhabitants of Kāpiśa, now a province in Afghanistan, as 'a mere intermingling of the sexes'.[53] But Hui-chao, a Buddhist pilgrim from Korea who travelled through the region around 725, is more informative. After

49 De Blois, 'Chronologie bactrienne'. It makes the documents ten years earlier than previously assumed.

50 Sims-Williams, *Bactrian Documents*, I, doc. A; cf. Sims-Williams, *Bactrian Documents*, II, 17n., accepting de Blois' identification of the Bactrian era.

51 Enoki, 'Nationality of the Ephtalites', 51 (drawn to my attention by Kevin van Bladel); cf. the report in Miller, *Accounts of Western Nations*, 12: 'They also have a custom by which elder and younger brother both marry one wife.'

52 Enoki, 'Nationality of the Ephtalites', 51. Among the Nyinba studied by Levine a lone brother might bring a friend into the marriage, and there were other ways of 'doubling up' (Levine, *Dynamics*, 161ff.; cf. also Parmar, *Polyandry in the Himalayas*, 94).

53 Hsüan-tsang in Beal, *Buddhist Records*, I, 54.

mentioning the incestuous marriages of the Persians he says that in the country of Ṭukhāristān, as well as in Kāpiśa, Bāmiyān and Zābulistān (all now in Afghanistan), 'two, three, five or even ten brothers are jointly married to one wife. They are not allowed to marry separately as they are afraid that separate marriages would ruin their livelihood.'[54] Hui-chao does not explain how separate marriages might lead to impoverishment, and it would not have been easy to guess on the basis of his report alone, for, like so many other informants, he does not see fit to mention that the brothers shared their land as well as their wives: it was always the sexual angle that caught the attention of outsiders. But the locals must have explained their polyandrous custom to Hui-chao along the same lines as the modern Tibetans: they shared a wife so as not to split up the family property.

Thereafter we have documentary evidence again, this time in the form of a Bactrian document drawn up in 527 of the Bactrian era, that is AD 750 (133f. AH), at the time of the 'Abbāsid revolution. It records the agreement of four brothers, Kamird-far, Bab, Wahran, and Mir, sons of Bek, to settle a dispute among themselves, laying down that now that 'it is not necessary for us to quarrel and it is not necessary [for us] to destroy [our] house', all the property, which seems to have been considerable, '[shall] belong [to us] equally, and we shall live just as it is the custom [for] brother to live with brother'. Three of them agree that 'we shall possess the woman whose name (is) Zeran as a three-(some), I Kamird-far, and I, Wahran, and I, Mir', and that whichever of them acted contrary to the agreement or no longer wished to live with the others should 'go from the house without a share (of the property)'.[55] Nothing is said about the cause of the dispute, which had apparently pitched Kamird-far and Bab against the other two, but Bab is not listed among the brothers who were to share Zeran, so maybe his refusal to be a co-husband had something to do with it. No mention is made of a separate wife for him, suggesting that he had not been allowed to bring one in. Twenty-two years later, in 771–2 (549 of the Bactrian era, 155 *hijrī*), we learn that Bab had left. Mir was now asking for immunity for himself and his other brothers, as well as his sons and people, from any liability incurred by Bab, and the document is the governor's

[54] Yang *et al.*, *Hye-Ch'o Diary*, no. 29 (drawn to my attention by Kevin van Bladel); also cited in Enoki, 'Nationality of the Hephtalites', 51, where it is 'dispersion of property' that they wish to prevent.

[55] Sims-Williams, *Bactrian Documents*, I, doc. X.

grant of it.[56] The chances are that Bab had become a Muslim, though this cannot be proved.[57]

Thereafter there is silence down to al-Bīrūnī (d. after 449/1050). Immoral kinds of marriage (*al-faḍā'iḥ fī'l-ankiḥa*) still exist in our time, he says, explaining that the people inhabiting the mountains stretching from the region of Panjshīr in Afghanistan into the neighbourhood of Kashmir live under the rule that several brothers have one wife in common. A good comparativist, he notes that the same system is reported for pre-Islamic Arabia.[58]

The last reference before the Mongol invasions comes in Ibn al-Athīr and Bar Hebraeus. Ibn al-Athīr records that in 602/1205f. the Ghūrids defeated the Tīrāhiyya, who had long been harassing the Muslims in alliance with the people of Peshawar and who had no religion. According to Bar Hebraeus they were idolaters, but he identifies them as Zoroastrians and Kurds, an odd mistake. Both sources mention that when a girl was born among them she would be offered for marriage, and if nobody accepted her (for a son of theirs), she would be killed, with the result that there were very few women among them, as Bar Hebraeus explains. Accordingly, a woman had a number of husbands, as Ibn al-Athīr says; she became the wife of all the sons of a house, as Bar Hebraeus more informatively puts it. When one of them was with her he would put his shoes by the door; if another husband came and saw the shoes he would go away again. The child was affiliated to the oldest of them.[59]

This irrefutably establishes the presence of polyandry in Bactria and adjoining areas of eastern Iran at the time of relevance to us. We know that

56 Sims-Williams, *Bactrian Documents*, I, doc. Y.

57 De Blois, 'Chronologie bactrienne', 993f., has tried to do so. In 138/755 a certain Ghālib b. Nāfi' manumitted his slave woman Zeran (Khan, *Arabic Documents*, no. 29). De Blois takes this Zeran to be identical with the shared wife of the Bactrian document X, implying that one of the brothers had converted to Islam and taken the wife with him, in its turn implying that the brothers had partitioned the family property. But this is impossible. The slave-girl was freed, and thus owned, by Ghālib b. Nāfi', and living with Sa'īd, Ghālib's client and presumably a former slave of his. She was Sa'īd's *umm walad*, here apparently in the literal meaning of the mother of his children (Sa'īd cannot have owned her), and the four children she had borne him were also freed by Ghālib. The shared wife of a polyandrous household cannot be the slave of another man (or a slave at all); all the brothers in the Bactrian document were free men; and Bab, the brother most likely to have become a Muslim, cannot have taken Zeran with him when they partitioned the property, since he was not one of the co-husbands according to document X.

58 Bīrūnī, *Hind*, 83/51f. = I, 108f

59 IA, XII, 211f.; Bar Hebraeus, *Chronography*, 362.

there were Khurramīs in this region,[60] so at least some reports on Khurramī *ibāḥa* must reflect polyandrous practices, and this is confirmed by Abū Tammām's door-markers. He does not mention that the wife-sharers were brothers, nor does any other Muslim, in connection with this or any other region, except for al-Bīrūnī. But even al-Bīrūnī fails to mention that the property was also shared, and it is the absence of both points that makes the institution so hard to recognise in the scandalised Muslim reports. As we have seen, however, polyandry makes sense of the reports on Khidāsh, who 'permitted some to sleep with the wives of others (*rakhkhaṣa li-baʿḍihim fī nisāʾ baʿḍin*).[61] For all we know Bab could have been one of Khidāsh's converts. Bab tried to stay in the shared home without sleeping with the shared wife, but as one would have expected it did not work. Splitting up, on the other hand, meant alienating one's brothers, the pillars of one's social position in the community, and renouncing one's share in the family property along with such children as one had sired: it was no trivial matter. Khidāsh ruled that converts could continue in their polyandrous arrangements by way of special dispensation, and other missionaries supported him. But it was a rule that only locals could understand, so the imam (meaning the Kufan directors of the movement?) disapproved and Khidāsh was liquidated. It is probably also polyandry that lies behind al-Baghdādī's report on the alleged followers of al-Muqannaʿ in Īlāq, every one of whom enjoyed somebody else's wife, as he puts it, noting that they were intolerant of Muslim intruders.[62]

The Buddhist evidence

There is some interesting Buddhist evidence relating to the marital customs of the Maga, meaning Iranian priests in the borderland between India and Iran. The earliest appears in the *Karmaprajñāpti*, said to date from the second century BC and extant in Tibetan. It credits the 'Magas of the western Brahmins' with the view that 'we can have sexual intercourse with our own mother, with a virgin, sister, wife, elder sister-in-law and younger sister-in-law', on the grounds that women are like cooked food which must be used for eating, like utensils which must be used for their purpose, a road which must be used for coming and going, the water of a

[60] See Chapter 1, p. 25.
[61] Tab. ii, 1588; cf. Chapter 4, p. 82.
[62] Baghdādī, *Farq*, 244f.

river which must be used for bathing, and the fruit of a tree which must be used as food. 'Thus all women should be used for sexual intercourse', it adds after every example. 'They are permitted [to have] sexual intercourse with every woman without punishment.'[63]

Statements of this type frequently reappear in the Buddhist literature thereafter. The *Mahāvibhāṣā*, compiled in Sanskrit in Kashmir in the second century, but preserved only in Chinese translation, mentions that there are some barbarians called Maga to the west who have sexual relations with their mother, wife (or daughter), elder sister, younger sister, and daughter-in-law without punishment and who hold that 'enjoyment shared with other persons is natural like the sharing of ripe fruit on a tree, cooked food, the use of roads, bridges, ships, stores [or steps], and utensils [or a millstone or socket]. Due to this common enjoyment there is never punishment when they have enjoyed sexual intercourse' [or 'Just as these things are common property, so a woman may be the common object of love and enjoyment'].[64] Similar statements are found in the *Abhidharmakośa* of the fourth-century Vasubandhu and the *Abhidharma-mahāvibhāṣā-śāstra*, composed before Vasubandhu and translated into Chinese in AD 656–9.[65] The fifth- or sixth-century Buddhist Bhavya mentions in his commentary (preserved in Tibetan) to his own *Tarkajvala* that 'the Maga, and others, have a perverse behaviour', and explains that the Persians who live in a/the barbarian country say that 'all women are like a socket [or millstone or utensil], a flower, a fruit, cooked food, stairs for the landing, a road, and so forth, therefore it is not right to forbid connubiality with one's mother, sister, or daughter, and so forth'.[66]

There are several points to be made about all this. First, the main polemical target in these passages is clearly close-kin marriage, but it is not the only one. The *Karmaprajñāpti*, the earliest source, has the Maga approve of intercourse not just with relatives by blood, but also with one's elder sister-in-law and younger sister-in-law – that is, an unrelated woman married to one's older or younger brother. This is suggestive of fraternal polyandry. The *Mahāvibhāṣā* replaces the sisters-in-law with a daughter-in-law, an unrelated woman married to one's son; and father–son sharing

[63] Kasugai, 'Ancient Iranian Religion', 113f.

[64] Kasugai, 'Ancient Iranian Religion', 113; Lindtner, 'Buddhist References', 440, cf. 439, n.19 for the word translated as utensils by Kasugai, as socket by Lindtner, and as millstone by Kawasaki, 'A Reference to Maga', 1102 (in a different passage).

[65] Kawasaki, 'A Reference to Maga', 1099; Lindtner, 'Buddhist References', 439f.

[66] Lindtner, 'Buddhist References', 439; Kawasaki, 'A Reference to Maga', 1102f.

is also attested where fraternal polyandry prevails.[67] That 'the foreign-born' Brahmins would have sexual intercourse with their daughters-in-law is also mentioned by the fourteenth-century historian of Kashmir, Kalhaṇa, with reference to the Gandhāra region in which polyandry is well attested.[68] Secondly, one wonders how the analogy with cooked food, utensils, roads, rivers, and fruit justifies close-kin marriage. In the *Karmaprajñāpti* the Maga's argument seems to be that there is no qualitative difference between one woman and another: all things must be used for their purpose and, since women are meant for sexual intercourse, one can sleep with any one of them. But the analogy could also be understood as meaning that all women are eligible for sexual intercourse in the sense that one can share them, and this understanding is explicit in the *Mahāvibhāṣā*, where women are like cooked food, roads, rivers, fruit, and so on in the sense that anyone can use them. The Maga here declare 'enjoyment shared with other persons' to be normal, so that women may be the object of 'common enjoyment'. This sounds like a defence of polyandry, and what is more, it is the same argument that we have met in Abū Tammām: women are like flowers that anyone can sniff. Thirdly, both the *Karmaprajñāpti* and the *Mahāvibhāṣā* have the Magi include wives in the list of women they could sleep with. Since the list is meant to illustrate outrageous practices the reference must be to the wives of other men. Lindtner translates wife as daughter in the second work, perhaps meaning that the wife should be struck off the list in the first work as well. If we leave her in, the reference could again be to polyandry, or to some form of wife-lending. Finally, the *Karmaprajñāpti* has the Maga approve of intercourse with a virgin, again clearly not one's own bride. In short, three or four different institutions seem to be described – close-kin marriage, polyandry, perhaps wife-lending of some kind, and ritual defloration of virgins – conflated because they all involve women rather than men having more than one sexual partner, deemed deeply immoral. I shall come back to this evidence in the appropriate contexts later.

Translating back

Running together quite different institutions repugnant to the observer is common in Muslim sources too. Al-Baghdādī and Niẓām al-Mulk conflate Khurramī wife-sharing with incestuous relations; and even a

[67] Peter, *Polyandry*, 80, 390f., 419, 426, 434, 465ff.
[68] Kasugai, 'Ancient Iranian Religion', 114.

major intellect such as al-Ghazālī will tell us that the Khurramīs held intercourse with all women to be lawful to the point of deeming incestuous unions to be acceptable.[69] But polyandry and close-kin marriage do not go together. Brothers who share a wife do not marry their own sister, presumably because it would be a ruinous reproductive strategy. The sisters are given away without a share in the family property, and another woman is brought in to sire the joint sons to whom the property will pass. Conversely, a man who married his own sister did not share her with others: she brought a share of the family property with her, and the purpose of the marriage was to keep her share together with his.

There is no fraternal polyandry in official Zoroastrian law. It did recognise the practice of leaving the estate undivided on the father's death, with the sons taking the status of legal partners (*brāt-hambāy*).[70] Where brothers living together take separate wives, the danger that their partnership will dissolve is high,[71] so the Zoroastrian law of the Persians allowed the brothers to marry women who were sisters;[72] sisters who have grown up together live together more easily than unrelated sisters-in-law.[73] A father and a son left to share the land might also marry a sister each, instead of sharing one (or both), as they might do in a polyandrous society.[74] But where a brother and a sister, a father and a daughter, or a mother and a son were left together they were strongly encouraged to marry each other, thereby keeping their shares together.[75] Why some Iranians should have favoured close-kin marriages and others polyandry is impossible to say, since the development of both systems lies in

[69] Baghdādī, cited in n. 1 of this chapter; *SN*, ch. 46:28 (304 = 232); Ghazālī, *Faḍā'iḥ*, 10 (muqadd. 2, 1).

[70] Perikhanian, 642, cf. 641.

[71] This point is frequently made by members of polyandrous societies: sisters-in-law will quarrel; four men will get along well, but not four women, etc.: see Peter, *Polyandry*, 378, 562; Parmar, *Polyandry in the Himalayas*, 97f.; cf. also Aiyyappan, 'Fraternal Polyandry in Malabar', 275f.

[72] For two brothers marrying two sisters, or father and son doing so, see Timothy in Sachau, *Syrische Rechtsbücher*, II, 72f., §19, where it is forbidden as a pagan and Zoroastrian custom. But Isho'barnūn, 126f., §§25–6, could see nothing wrong with two brothers marrying two sisters, a practice attested in the Old Testament.

[73] That too was common knowledge in polyandrous societies, where second wives were often sisters of the first and the brothers of one family would sometimes marry all the sisters of another (Peter, *Polyandry*, 414; Parmar, *Polyandry in the Himalayas*, 82; Levine, *Dynamics*, 149).

[74] For fathers and sons sharing a wife see Peter, *Polyandry*, 80, 390f., 419, 426, 434, 465ff.

[75] For a brief account of close-kin marriages in Pahlavi literature see de Jong, *Traditions*, 430f.

prehistory, but the Persian system is certainly the more unusual of the two.[76] Both make perfect sense, but the practitioners of close-kin marriage had to overcome the incest taboo, whereas brothers sharing a wife had merely to cope with jealousy.[77]

It is rare for the sources to explain alien marital institutions in terms of property, however. Hui-chao did so implicitly in connection with Bactrian polyandry, as we have seen, echoing native informants.[78] Some Christian churchmen explicitly did so in connection with Zoroastrian close-kin marriage too: 'the son is not content with his share of the inheritance which is due to him by law; he also wants the shares of his sister and his mother', the Nestorian patriarch Isho'bokht (d. 780) said, echoing the sixth-century Mar Aba.[79] To him and to others, the alien practice was rooted in a moral failing, here greed rather than licentiousness, and he adds shock value by insinuating that the greedy son would marry his sister and mother alike, which does not seem to have been possible. In effect, polemics of this kind are translations: hostile sources will speak of sex rather than marriage, explain law and customary rules in terms of mere personal preference rather than socio-economic exigencies, and present institutions venerated by their practitioners (such as 'the time-honoured custom of polyandrous matrimony') as moral failings of the worst kind. We must not be led astray by the moral terms in which the sources present such institutions. Modern scholars sometimes accept the hostile evaluation (many speak of Khurramī 'promiscuity'), but more often they reject the reports as mere polemical invention or exaggeration. Either way they leave the polemical packaging of the information intact. We must seek to unpack it, or, in a different metaphor, to translate back. Perhaps the package will prove to be empty, or, in the alternative metaphor, maybe something altogether different is being translated into sexual terms so that there is nothing to be learnt about marriage. But we cannot simply presume this to be the case, not even when the charges sound too stereotyped or outrageous to be true. Hsüan-tsang's description of marriage in Kāpiśa as 'a mere intermingling of the sexes',[80] for example, is no better than

[76] Something like it seems already to have existed in Elam, where the Persians perhaps picked it up (See Hinz, *Lost World of Elam*, 46, 91, 109).

[77] For Zoroastrians struggling with the idea of close-kin marriage, see Panaino, 'Zoroastrian Incestuous Unions', 83f.; for jealousy, see Chapter 18, p. 442.

[78] See above, n. 54.

[79] Isho'bokht in Sachau, *Syrische Rechtsbücher*, III, 36f. (ch. 3); Mar Aba in Chabot, *Synodicon Orientale*, 82 = 335.

[80] Hsüan-tsang in Beal, *Buddhist Records*, I, 54.

stereotyped Muslim charges of *ibāḥat al-nisāʾ*: what he tells us is first and foremost that he was disgusted. But he does say enough for us to see that what disgusted him had to do with an absence of restraints that he regarded as intrinsic to marriage. It is not much to go by, and if his had been the only evidence we would not have been able to do much with it. But simply to dismiss it as unfounded would still have been a mistake. We also have to bear in mind that our own sense of what is plausible and implausible is severely limited by the fact that the modern world is dominated by an extremely narrow range of family arrangements. Looking in anthropology books on kinship and marriage is like opening a book on a huge variety of dead and dying languages, all victims of the inexorable homogenisation of the world that has been in progress since the dawn of civilisation.[81] The only way to compensate is to study the dead or dying systems in question.

Polyandry in western Iran

Polyandry cannot be documented for western Iran. It is true that both Xanthus and Strabo, considered below in connection with other institutions, could be taken to describe it, with reference to Anatolia and Media respectively, but this is probably not the best way to interpret their information. As regards the Sasanian period, the Christian evidence practically rules out that it existed, except perhaps in isolated pockets. There are admittedly some ambivalent passages, but they all seem to refer to the levirate. The Nestorian Catholicos Mar Aba (d. 552), a convert from Zoroastrianism, tried to harden the boundaries of the Christian community by prohibiting a large number of marital practices that converts had so far retained. Among other things he renewed the decision of the Council of Neocaesarea (*c.* AD 315) that a woman who married two brothers should be cast out. The reference is to consecutive marriages, or in other words to widows who have married their deceased husbands' brothers, not polyandry.[82] Elsewhere Mar Aba mentions two categories of sinners: one is men who marry their sisters-in-law (i.e., practise the levirate) in ignorance of the fact that this is a sin, or even thinking it meritorious; the other is 'Sons of the Covenant' who 'take the wives of

[81] The last phases of this are nicely illustrated in Cook, *Brief History*, 322ff., 339f.

[82] Fulton, *Index canonum*, 213 (Neocaesarea, canon 2); Joyce, *Christian Marriage*, 538; Braun, *Synhados*, 140f. (canon 16); cf. Chabot, *Synodicon Orientale* 550 = 561. My thanks to Yifat Monnickendam for discussions which helped to clarify matters.

their brothers'.[83] Sons of the Covenant were elite Christians living in celibacy, though they were not actually monks. One would have thought that when such men failed to remain celibate their choice of partners would be a subsidiary matter: why should sisters-in-law be singled out in connection with them? At first sight Mar Aba's regulation conjures up a situation reminiscent of that in Tibet, where Buddhist monks might be tolerated as extra husbands by their polyandrous brothers though they did not retain any rights in the family property;[84] but this reading is undoubtedly wrong. Sons of the Covenant will have found it as difficult as laymen to resist the social pressure (and perhaps also the temptation) to marry their widowed sisters-in-law, and thus provide them with male protection, and the reason they are discussed separately from laymen is simply that Mar Aba regulates their situation differently: Sons of the Covenant have to separate from their wives, whereas laymen might have to stay in the marriage and atone for their sins in other ways.[85] That Mar Aba knows nothing about polyandry is clear from his discussion of men having more than one wife: it is terrible, he says, and so is a wife having two husbands.[86] But whereas he proceeds to regulate the position of men with more than one wife he leaves the case of women with more than one husband as a purely theoretical possibility, and he does not refer to it in his discussion of women marrying brothers.

This conclusion is reinforced by a passage by the Catholicos Timothy (d. 823). 'Is it right for a man to marry two sisters, or for a woman to marry two brothers?', he asks. The question is about marriage to two women who were sisters or two men who were brothers, not to two of one's own, and he responds with a categorical denial: 'it is not right at all, but contrary to the law'.[87] Sachau takes the question to be about consecutive marriages, and he is surely right: if the reference had been to concurrent marriages the question regarding the woman would undoubtedly have been mentioned first and followed by a violent outburst against the very idea of a woman having two husbands, quite apart from the husbands being brothers. Timothy did say more than we have, for there is a lacuna in the text, but the other marriages he condemns are with a step-mother, daughter-in-law, and uncle's wife, so the issue was the type of marriage partner rather than

[83] Braun, *Synhados*, 131f.; Chabot, *Synodicon Orientale*, 83f. = 336f. (translating *bnay qiyama* as 'clercs').
[84] Peter, *Polyandry*, 414.
[85] Chabot, *Synodicon Orientale*, 83f. = 336f.
[86] Braun, *Synhados*, 130f.; more intelligibly in Chabot, *Synodicon Orientale* 82 = 335.
[87] Timothy in Sachau, *Syrische Rechtsbücher*, II, 72f., §20.

the number. Timothy could hardly have asked a question so reminiscent of fraternal polyandry without condemning it if he had known about it. One takes it that, like Mar Aba, he had not heard of it.

What we do find in western Iran is sworn brotherhoods which may sometimes have involved sharing a wife. The fifth-century Syro-Roman Lawbook lays down that 'when somebody wants to draw up a document of brotherhood with another to the effect that they shall jointly own and inherit everything they have and will have, then the law forbids it and declares their document void, for their wives and children cannot be held in common'.[88] The reference is to mutual adoption as brothers, an institution attested elsewhere in the later Roman empire and forbidden by Diocletian in a rescript probably relating to the Danube region.[89] This clause in the Syro-Roman Lawbook has generated much controversy, for although the creation of brotherhood was forbidden in Roman law, instituting shared property (*societas bonorum*) was perfectly valid and, contrary to what is often assumed, the Syro-Roman Lawbook is an originally Greek compilation of Roman law, not a Syrian compilation of mixed Roman and provincial law. In Nallino's interpretation the clause prohibits the institution of joint ownership between adopted brothers on the grounds that the property does not belong to them alone, but also to their families: since they cannot share their families as well, the family of whoever died first would be disinherited, which would be contrary to the law. If this is correct it adduces the fact that the sworn brothers cannot share their wives and children as something taken for granted, not as a prohibition.[90] It accords with the understanding in the Arabic translation, but its reasoning is wholly alien to Roman law.[91] Since all attempts to understand it in terms of Roman law have failed, it seems reasonable to postulate that a response to a local custom has crept into the translation.[92]

Robertson Smith was the first to interpret the clause as prohibiting the establishment of a polyandrous household between fictitious brothers. He adduced the brotherhood instituted by Muḥammad in Medina

[88] Syro-Roman Lawbook in Bruns and Sachau, L 86, 126 Arm Ar. 127; in Selb and Kaufhold, II, §79, cf. III, 157ff. (commentary); in Vööbus, §127.

[89] Cf. Shaw, 'Ritual Brotherhood', and the legal literature in Selb and Kaufhold, *Syrisch-römische Rechtsbuch*, III, 157ff. Diocletian had forbidden it 'even among foreigners' (CJ 6, 24, 7).

[90] Nallino, 'Intorno al divieto', 339.

[91] Thus Koschaker, 'Adoptio in fratrem', 370f.

[92] Cf. Koschaker, 'Adoptio in fratrem', 371f.; even Selb and Kaufhold admit that some local law may be reflected.

as a parallel case: according to a well-known *ḥadīth* one Medinese offered to share his property and wives with his Meccan brother, though only in the sense of ceding half of them to him.[93] Nallino objected that the Medinese was not volunteering to set up a polyandrous household with his Meccan brother and that Muḥammad's brotherhood was related to the sworn alliance known as *ḥilf*.[94] Both points are correct, but *ḥilf* might involve joint property as well as mutual inheritance,[95] and the step from shared property to shared wives was small in the Iranian culture area, in which the one was regularly held to include the other. It is hard not to suspect that the *ḥadīth* was meant to warn against joint property in the Iranian style, though in the form in which it survives it glosses the sharing as a mere partition so as not to besmirch the eminent Medinese Companion who is cast as proposing the arrangement. We see the institution again in a ruling credited to the Zoroastrian jurist Rad-Ohrmazd: 'If two men have property in common and one gains a thing and the other a woman, then the thing is to be held in common, [but] the woman by the better person.'[96] Here the two men are not identified as brothers by either blood or oath, but the reference is surely to the same sharing of property that the Syro-Roman lawbook and the *ḥadīth* reject. To Rad-Ohrmazd holding property in common is perfectly lawful, and that he deems women – or at least female slaves – to be included in the property is clear from the fact that the woman who is acquired by one of the partners does not remain his property; rather, she passes into the pool of shared property, to be awarded to whichever partner is the 'better' or (in Perikhanian's translation) the more 'pious and dutiful' because she cannot cohabit with both. That women cannot be shared sexually is a point on which all three sources agree. What the law said was one thing, however, and what people did was quite another. A century or so after Muḥammad's brotherhood two *zindīq*s, Ḥammād

[93] Robertson Smith, *Kinship and Marriage*, 160f.; cf. Wellhausen, 'Ehe bei den Arabern', 461, relating the clause to the evidence for fraternal polyandry in Arabia. For the *ḥadīth* see Bukhārī, *Ṣaḥīh* e.g., *nikāḥ* 7; Ibn Sa'd, III/1, 88f. (III, 125f.); further references in Nallino, 'Intorno al divieto', 346, nn. 56f. The Meccan brother was 'Abd al-Raḥmān b. 'Awf, the Medinese was Sa'd b. al-Rabī'a.

[94] Nallino, 'Intorno al divieto', 346, 349ff.

[95] See now Landau-Tasseron, 'Alliances among the Arabs', 155f., 161f.,

[96] *MHD*, ii, 4. 4–5; tr. Perikhanian, 253; tr. Macuch, 72; also cited by Shaki, 'Sassanian Matrimonial Relations', 338.

ʿAjrad and Ḥurayth b. Abī ʾl-Ṣalt, were accused of being partners (*sharīkayn*) who shared everything, including their wives.[97]

If allies and other partners might share everything, including their wives, one would expect fraternal polyandry to lurk somewhere in the background, not just in the sense of being found in eastern Iran, but also by being present in the mountains of the western regions. It ought to lie behind the 'family communism' of al-Malaṭī's 'Qarāmiṭa and Daylam', who claimed that their women, children, and their own bodies were lawful (for sexual purposes) among themselves and who shared their property in the sense that anybody could use what others had in their possession.[98] But it is impossible to prove it. Sworn brotherhood was still practised among the Ahl-i Ḥaqq in the 1960s, but the brothers did not share their property, let alone their wives. If one died leaving a family in straitened circumstances, the other would nevertheless have to look after it and bring up the children as if they were his own.[99]

The *Dēnkard* has an interesting passage on polyandry, but it probably refers to the eastern institution. It tells us that the heretics called Mazdakites (*mazdagīg*) neglect external worship, interpret the religion, and 'reckon the lineage through the mother', while believing in wolfishness, 'that is to say, they do a thing wolfishly: their gratification of [sexual] desire is like that of a wolf, whose progeny is reckoned through the mother. They also recognize lineage through the mother.' In addition, 'that which their offspring, sons and brothers, receive [should be held] in usufruct. They say to them: we have given you shares as communal property, you are not allowed but to hold them in common.'[100] Other accusations are made, but the passage is somewhat obscure even in Shaki's translation, and totally unintelligible in the older translation by West, where all one recognises is the wolfish gratification of desire, the lineage formed through mothers, and something to do with sons or brothers.

The Mazdakites in this passage can hardly be the Mazdakite rebels of the past, for although the continuation is about Khusraw it is practices

[97] *Aghānī*, XIV, 324, last two lines. Some Christian sources credit the Manichaeans with wife-sharing, but their testimony does not count because they are simply confusing Manichaeans and Mazdakites (who duly came to be known as *zindīq*s as well in Muslim times); cf. Crone, 'Kavād's Heresy', 30f. (Malalas, Theophanes); Bar Ḥadbeshabba, 'Cause de la fondation des écoles', 364, where both Plato and the Manichaeans hold that women should be held in common.

[98] See Chapter 13, p. 268.

[99] Edmonds, 'Beliefs and Practices', 99.

[100] *DkM*, 653.10–654.8 (B fol. 318 v. 1ff.) in Shaki, 'Social Doctrine', 293–5; *Dk*, VII, 21–5 in West, *Pahlavi Texts*, v, 88f.

under normal conditions that are being described. When we hear of Mazdakites after the revolt in Muslim sources they are always Khurramīs of some kind, and it is also Khurramīs that this passage calls to mind with the charge that they neglect ritual worship and interpret the religion (allegorically). The wolfish gratification of sexual desire is presumably a reference to their supposed licentiousness. The passage also tells us something startlingly new, however: it twice informs us that the heretics trace the offspring through the mother and explains, at least in Shaki's translation, that the family property is to be held in common by 'their offspring, sons and brothers'. It is not clear whether the reference is to sons who *are* brothers or sons *and* brothers (of the mother), but the maternal affiliation initially suggests the latter. If so, we would have here a matrilineal system of descent comparable to that of the Nayars. But it does seem a little implausible that there should have been non-fraternal polyandry somewhere in Iran without anyone else noticing it, except perhaps Herodotus (whose account of the Massagetes is compatible with it). By contrast, one would have expected at least some Zoroastrian polemic against fraternal polyandry as practised in eastern Iran, and this is probably what we have here. As noted already, affiliation was normally patrilineal in Tibet, but it was matrilineal when the only heir was a daughter; and postulating that the same was true of the border region between India and Iran is a good deal less hazardous than taking the view that non-fraternal polyandry was practised there or elsewhere in Iran. The idea of a daughter inheriting the family property, taking as many husbands as she liked, and affiliating the children to herself will have struck the exponents of official Zoroastrianism as particularly outrageous: in their view she should have been married off to a close agnate to produce a son for her deceased father. This would explain why matrilineal succession is singled out for particular attention. The rest is in perfect accordance with fraternal polyandry. The injunction in a compilation of gnomic advice (*andarz*), 'Have your own wife for yourself,' should perhaps also be read as polemical against the polyandrous easterners.[101]

OTHER REPRODUCTIVE AND POLITICAL STRATEGIES

The other main institutions to which the charges of Khurramī wife-sharing are likely to refer are temporary co-marriage and the practices subsumed under the names of guest prostitution. A third institution, overlapping with

[101] Tarapore, *Pahlavi Andarz-Nāmak*, 24 ('Andarz ī Ātrōpāt', no. 42).

the second, was ritual defloration. Unlike polyandry they all involved the sharing of women only, not of property as well.

Temporary co-marriage

Xanthus of Lydia (*fl.* mid-fifth century BC), who lived in Anatolia under Achaemenid rule, wrote a book, now lost, called *Magica* in which he reported that 'the Magi make love to their own mothers, and to their daughters and their sisters (so goes their custom); and the women belong to everyone in common, so that when a man wants to take another man's wife as his own he does so without using force or secrecy but with mutual consent and approval'.[102] The first part of the statement is the earliest Greek attestation of the Iranian close-kin marriage. Its bearers are Magi, perhaps a priestly tribe of Media in Xanthus' time,[103] in any case priests of some kind, and though the entire statement is sensationalist in tone, nobody questions the veracity of this part of it. The second part is more problematic. The alleged wife-sharing has been explained as a mistaken impression of frequent divorce, a presentation of the 'Other' by inversion of Greek norms, and, more recently, as an interpolation by Clement of Alexandria, to whom we owe the quotation.[104] Clement adduced it in connection with the Carpocratian Gnostics, who held that women and property were free for all. But the first explanation is *ad hoc*; the second is a *passepartout* which would eliminate the first part of the statement too; and as regards the third, it is hard to see why the Carpocratians should have reminded Clement of Xanthus' passage if Xanthus had not spoken about wife-sharing himself. All three explanations take it for granted that Xanthus is wrong, but as we have seen, both the *Karmaprajñāpti* (second century BC) and the *Mahāvibhāṣā* have the Maga include (other people's) wives and/or daughters in the list of women they could sleep with, and Kalhaṇa says that the foreign-born Brahmins would give their own wives to others.[105] We are hardly to take it that there was a Graeco-Indian conspiracy to defame the Iranians.

[102] Kingsley, 'Meetings with Magi', 179, quoting Xanthus as preserved in Clement, *Stromateis*, III, 2, 11, 1, with a helpful account of the treatment of Xanthus in earlier literature.

[103] Cf. Herodotus, I, 101; Asheri *et al.*, *Commentary*, ad loc.; de Jong, *Traditions*, 387ff. (arguing against it).

[104] Cf. Kingsley, 'Meetings with Magi', 180ff., adding the third explanation.

[105] Kasugai, 'Ancient Iranian Religion', 114.

Let us try to 'translate' Xanthus' account. In fact, everyone does this in connection with the first part of the statement: Xanthus says that the Magi make love to their own mothers, daughters, and sisters, and we translate this as meaning that the Magi could marry such relatives. Xanthus is clearly talking about marriage in the second statement too. Though wife-sharing suggests polyandry it is not necessarily what he had heard of. Taking another man's wife as one's own required 'consent and approval', as Kingley translates, 'an agreement', as others put it.[106] This suggests a different institution.

Zoroastrian law recognised a number of ways in which others could produce children for a man who had none. If the childless man died and left a widow of childbearing age, she could enter a so-called *stūrīh* marriage with her husband's brother or another person, preferably a close agnate or a *stūr* (guardian, substitute) designated by the deceased, otherwise someone appointed by the court; she only became the latter's *čagar* wife, as opposed to his *pādikhšāy* wife, i.e., it was not a full marriage giving him guardianship over her and incorporating her in his agnatic group; any children born of the union would be affiliated to the deceased husband, whose wife she remained. If the deceased left no widow, a daughter or sister would be called; and if no female relatives were available, a woman could be hired for the task. Part of the estate was set aside for the upkeep of the *stūr*, or both of them;[107] and if the estate was large several *stūrhīh*s could be established for the deceased. This would presumably involve hiring additional women for the task, and perhaps additional men as well, though one might suffice to impregnate all of them. Men could also act as *stūr*s (in effect studs) on behalf of several men, whereas women could only act for one at a time.[108]

According to one jurist, a daughter qualified for the *stūrih* even if she was married and her husband had not divorced her.[109] She would probably be divorced if actually called upon to act, but to an outsider it will have looked

[106] Thus for example de Jong, *Traditions*, 426 (without discussion of this part of the statement).

[107] The literature, both ancient and modern, always speaks of the *stūr* in the singular without specifying which of the two parties is intended in any particular context. This makes it hard to reconstruct the institution.

[108] Perikhanian, 649 (adducing the Indian *niyoga* and *pūtrika*, the Greek epiklerate, and the biblical levirate as parallels); Shaki, 'Sassanian Matrimonial Relations', 325ff.; Shaki, 'Obligated Successorship'; Macuch, *Sasanidische Rechtsbuch*, 115ff.; cf. also the succinct account in *Tansar's Epistle* 21f. = 46f., noting the parallel with the biblical institution and observing that the Christians forbid it. It calls the parties *abdāl*, substitutes or surrogates.

[109] *MHD*, i, 21.10–15; Shaki, 'Obligated Successorship', 232.

as if her husband was simply lending her to the inseminator, for the tie between the two was not completely severed. The Sasanian Lawbook says that 'if a man wants a *stūr*ship for his wife from a *pādikhšāyīh* marriage, then [the *pādikhšāyīh* marriage] must be dissolved'; in other words, if he wants his wife to produce a child for another man he has to divorce her. But it adds that he remained her guardian, or could have himself appointed as such. Presumably he took her back, or was free to do so, when she had produced the requisite heir.[110] There were also situations in which the husband could stay married to her and renounce the guardianship instead: 'if he declares to his wife: "I have granted you authority over your own person," he has not divorced her, but she has been authorized to take a *čagar* husband':[111] here he is clearly lending his wife to someone else on the basis of a mere 'agreement', as Xanthus said.

In the last statement it is quite unclear for whom the wife was meant to produce a child: for a deceased person or for her own husband, or for another man who was still alive? All three options were available: a man did not have to be dead in order for others to produce heirs for him. These days women with infertile husbands (or no husbands at all) will go to sperm banks, but before artificial insemination they had to sleep with the inseminator. If the husband wanted children for himself, he would hand over his *pādikhšāy* wife to another man for a specified period and any children born of the union would be his, but she would leave his home for the duration.[112] This could be what he is envisaged as doing in the statement in which he empowers her to enter a *čagar* marriage without divorcing her.[113] Much the same institution was found in India and Greece, or at least in Sparta. In the *Mahābhārata* the sonless Pandu is worried that his ancestors will perish with his body and that as a sonless man he will not be admitted to heaven (an idea also encountered in Zoroastrianism); but he is informed of Manu's rule that 'men failing to have legitimate offspring of their own may have offspring begotten upon

110 *MHD*, i, 49.3–6 (where the English version of Perikhanian's originally Russian translation has 'claims' for *xwāhēd*).

111 *MHD*, i, 3.10–11, tr. Carlsen, 'Cakar Marriage Contract', 105 (the English translation of Perikhanian unintentionally suggests that the wife is granted a right).

112 Perikhanian, 650; Shaki, 'Sassanian Matrimonial Relations', 331; cf. also Hjerrild, 'Some Aspects'. The details are complicated and often obscure.

113 Thus Carlsen, '*Cakar* Marriage Contract', 104f., without discussing *MHD*, 49.3–6. Differently Perikhanian, 650, who must have *MHD*, 49.3–6 in mind: she holds the husband to retain his guardianship over her. Shaki, 'Sassanian Matrimonial Relations', 324, 327, 331, 340, assumes both passages to be about a husband wishing to sire children for himself, with the result that he is confusing on the question of the guardianship.

their wives by others' and recites a whole list of ways it would be done (before or after the death of the beneficiary, against payment to the inseminator or by his kindness, etc.); his wife Kunti duly goes and solicits a Brahmin, by whom she has three sons.[114] As regards Sparta, Plutarch tells us that 'Lycurgus made it honourable for them, while keeping the marriage relation free from all wanton irregularities, to share with other worthy men in the begetting of children ... For example, an elderly man with a young wife, if he looked with favour and esteem on some fair and noble young man, might introduce him to her, and adopt her offspring by such a noble father as his own.' Plutarch actually calls this polyandry, but it was temporary.[115] Back in Iran, it is presumably the same temporary co-marriage that lies behind the defamatory story to the effect that Papak lent his wife to a soldier called Sasan who sired Ardashir, the founder of the Sasanian empire.[116]

A man could also lend his wife or daughter to produce children for someone else, however, and not just for someone who had died. One passage leaves it unclear whether the beneficiary is alive or dead: a father could tell his daughter, 'go and become the *stūr* for such-and-such a man'. The daughter had to obey because 'her income belongs to her father', showing that she was paid and that the father's incentive was financial; by contrast, she could refuse if her father told her to go and marry someone, but the jurist Zurvāndād i Yuvān-Yam held that she could refuse in both cases because telling her to become a *stūr* for someone was no different from telling her to become his wife.[117] A daughter might also be empowered by her father to make an agreement with someone that 'I shall be your wife for ten years'; if the father died during those ten years she could not act as surrogate for him until the ten years were over, since she was acting in that capacity for her temporary husband. One takes the latter to be alive.[118] Daughters apart, 'a man is entitled to hand over his wife from a *pādikhšāyīh* marriage, without the wife's consent, to a man bereft of wife and children, and innocent of this privation, who has legally [officially] requested [= presented a demand for] a wife'. The wife's

[114] *Mahābhārata*, Adi Parva CXX.

[115] Plutarch, *Lycurgus*, 15:6; cf. Pomeroy, *Spartan Women*, 40–2, 46f., and the sources cited there.

[116] Agathias, II, 27:1–4 (where it could also be read as guest prostitution). That Papak was not his real father is said in the *Kārnāmag ī Ardašīr* as well: see *EIr.*, s.v. 'Ardašīr I'.

[117] *MHD*, i, 36.9–16.

[118] *MHD*, i, 23.1–4; also tr. in Shaki, 'Obligated Successorship', 233; Macuch, 'Zoroastrian Principles', 241, also adducing *MHD*, i, 87.2–3.

property would remain with the lending husband.[119] Shaki interprets this as a straightforward gift of the wife rather than a temporary co-marriage on the grounds that this is what it is in the *Dēnkard* and that the *Nīrangistān* forbids her to cohabit with both men.[120] But it seems a little implausible that a man could lawfully give away his wife while keeping her property. No doubt he could *also* give her away (with her property) if he so wished, but in this particular transaction the first marriage cannot have been wholly dissolved. He may have divorced her while remaining her guardian, as in the passage considered earlier,[121] but if the tie between them had been severed it would not have been necessary to point out that she could not cohabit with both men. As Macuch says, it is probably this arrangement that resulted in the problem, considered in the Sasanian law-book, of two men claiming to be married to the same woman.[122] Once again, a similar institution was also found in Sparta. 'When a man had begotten enough children, it was honourable and quite usual for him to give his wife to one of his friends,' as Polybius says.[123] The borrower, in Plutarch's ever-so-delicate words, would be 'a worthy man who admired some woman for the fine children that she bore her husband and the modesty of her behaviour as a wife'; this man 'might enjoy her favours, if her husband would consent, thus planting, as it were, in a soil of beautiful fruitage, and begetting for himself noble sons, who would have the blood of noble men in their veins'.[124]

In short, Xanthus' statement on Magian wife-sharing appears to be eminently translatable: men did indeed pass their wives around, now lending wombs to others and now renting inseminators for themselves. The institution was no more outlandish than some that could be found among the Greeks themselves, but Xanthus had no need to handle Iranian customs with delicacy; by contrast, Plutarch goes out of his way to present the Spartan institution in the best of lights, stressing its moral character and casting it as a testimony to the Spartans' admirable freedom from the womanish passion of jealousy. As a result, Xanthus' statement is normally rejected by modern scholars whereas Plutarch's is normally accepted. Once

119 *MHD*, i, 101.4–8. The glosses are the translator's.
120 See Shaki, 'Sassanian Matrimonial Relations', 324, 337, against Bartholomae, with reference to *DkM* 715.6–7 and *Nīrangistān*, 15, 26–9.
121 See n. 110 to this chapter.
122 Macuch, 'The Use of Seals', 85.
123 Polybius, XII, 6b.
124 Plutarch, *Lycurgus*, 15:7.

again, we must learn not to judge the veracity of information on the basis of its moral packaging.

After Xanthus there is silence until we reach Strabo (d. AD 21 or later). He tells us that among the inhabitants of mountainous Media it was customary for kings to have many wives: they had to have at least five. The women of Media too, he says, took pride in having many husbands, considering less than five a misfortune.[125] The first claim is undoubtedly correct: Iranian rulers traditionally stood out from their subjects by the number of their wives and concubines.[126] The second claim is a flat assertion of polyandry in the Jibāl, again without any mention of brothers (though Strabo mentions them, along with door-markers, in his famous account of polyandry in South Arabia). The idea of less than five husbands as a misfortune does not sit well with polyandry, however, for cooking, sewing, washing, gathering firewood, and cleaning for a flock of husbands in addition to a flock of children was back-breaking work.[127] Slaves could admittedly have made a difference for those who could afford them, and the *Chou-shu* claims that Hephtalite women would display the number of their husbands on their helmets, implying that they took pride in it; but this statement has been questioned (on quite different grounds).[128] Boasting of the number of husbands goes better with a situation in which the amount reflects the women's own abilities and charms rather than the accidental number of brothers in a family. A married woman lent out to sire offspring for men who admired her for 'the fine children that she bore her husband and the modesty of her behaviour as a wife', as Plutarch puts it, might well take pride in the number of men she had served, especially if they were chiefs or other men of high social standing (who should perhaps be envisaged as able to requisition such short-term wives). Another possibility is that he was describing guest prostitution and/or the custom of requiring girls to have many partners before they could marry, both to be discussed below. But this is somewhat implausible, partly because he would hardly have upgraded lovers to husbands and partly because he does not seem to

[125] Strabo, XI, 13, 11. As the note in the Loeb edition observes, despite the unanimity of the manuscripts this claim has been considered so implausible that some have emended the text to say that the women considered less than five *wives for their husbands* to be a misfortune. This is presumably why Median polyandry is far less well known than that of the Massagetes and the Yemenis.

[126] Morris and Scheidel, *Dynamics of Ancient Empires*, 276ff.

[127] See Levine, *Dynamics*, 152. These women expressed a preference for no more than two or three husbands, which was in fact the norm (147f.).

[128] Enoki, 'Nationality of the Ephtalites', 51, 55f.

think of the five husbands as consecutive. Either he was speaking of polyandry (kings had many wives, other men shared them) or else the institution reflected is temporary co-marriage.

However this may be, Strabo had actually heard of temporary co-marriage of the 'lend-a-womb' variety in Iran as well. He mentions it in connection with the Tapyri, who lived on the Caspian coast to the west of Hyrcania (Jurjān): 'it was a custom of theirs to give their wives in marriage to other husbands as soon as they had two or three children by them', he says, adding that this was just as 'in our times, in accordance with an ancient custom of the Romans, Cato gave Marcia in marriage to Hortensius at the request of the latter'.[129] No evidence seems to be available on the ancient Roman custom in question, but the story of Cato and the orator Hortensius is well known. Hortensius, wishing to ally himself more closely with Cato, first asked for Cato's daughter, though she was married with two sons, arguing that she would either waste her fertility or burden her husband with unwanted children if she stayed in that marriage, and that if her husband was deeply attached to her he could remarry her when she had born Hortensius a son. When Cato refused, Hortensius asked for Cato's own wife, once again arguing that she had born enough children to him. Cato asked for his wife's father's permission (not, apparently, his wife's), and when the father agreed he divorced Marcia, to take her back six years later when Hortensius died.[130] Here as in Sparta two or three children are deemed to be enough, but the first marriage is fully dissolved before the second is contracted, so it was not formally an institution of temporary co-marriage. But in practice Cato took Marcia back 'as if he had merely lent her', as Appian says.[131] In social terms the main difference between the Roman and Iranian cases seems to be that the practice was not customary in Rome by Strabo's time, if it had ever existed, whereas it remained sufficiently common in Iran to be enshrined in a Sasanian collection of legal views.

In 535f. Justinian addressed a *novella* to inhabitants of Osrhoene and Mesopotamia who had entered into unlawful marriages. Exactly what the unlawful marriages were we are not told, merely that they had been contracted by the rural masses (*agroikos plēthos*), and that men of higher status and married clergy should also note the prohibition of such unions.

[129] Strabo, XI, 9, 1.

[130] Plutarch, *Cato the Younger*, 25f., 52; cf. Gordon, 'The Eternal Triangle', casting doubt on the existence of the custom (my thanks to Walter Scheidel for sending me this article); cf. also Hopkins, *Death and Renewal*, 87f., 97.

[131] Appian, *Roman History: Civil Wars*, II, 99.

The prohibition was repeated in 566 by Justin II, who had received troubling reports from Mesopotamia, Osrhoene, and the Euphratensis: the provincials had entered such marriages, from which children and grandchildren had sprung, partly through ignorance and partly through dealings with Persians and Arabs. What the marriages were is once more left unspecified.[132]

Lee, who drew this material to public attention, argued that the unlawful unions were close-kin unions. If so, it is odd that the emperors do not say so directly. Lee suggests that the emperors were too embarrassed to acknowledge the presence of such unions within their realm, but when Diocletian legislated against incestuous union in 295 he identified what he was outlawing, openly acknowledging that cases had occurred within the empire.[133] The fact that Justin II debited the unions to both Persian and Arab influence also suggests that other practices were being targeted, for only the Persians had close-kin marriage. Admittedly the Nabataeans had once practised brother–sister marriages,[134] but that was a long time ago; and though the polyandrous Yemenis are reported to have had intercourse with their mothers[135] the reference is presumably to the widows of their fathers; the Arabs are reported still to have married their fathers' widows on the eve of Islam.[136] (Taking over the father's widow along with his property is a well-known practice, and it was found in the Sasanian empire too: the Catholicos Mar Aba forbade it.)[137] If Justinian was targeting something the Arabs and the Persians had in common, the reference cannot be to close-kin marriages. Both the Persians and the Arabs were polygynous, a hotly disputed issue between Christians and Zoroastrians;[138] both practised fraternal polyandry (if we take Persians to mean Iranians), and the Arabs also shared with the Iranians the feature of recognising co-marriage and other temporary unions. The emperors would hardly have found it difficult to name polygyny or polyandry, but there was no one word for temporary co-marriage and other unions bringing in outsiders to inseminate or substitute for a wife; there still is not today. It would be reasonable to infer that the emperors had such nameless practices in mind.

[132] Lee, 'Close-Kin Marriage'.
[133] Chadwick, 'Relativity of Moral Codes', 145f.
[134] Graf, 'Nabataean Army', 291f.
[135] Strabo, XVI, 4, 25; Ibn al-Kalbī in Shahrastānī, I, 440 = II, 515f.
[136] Q 4:22; Ibn al-Kalbī in Shahrastānī, I, 440 = II, 515.
[137] Chabot, *Synodicon Orientale*, 83 = 336.
[138] Cf. Braun, *Ausgewählte Akten*, 210f., where one of the key Zoroastrian charges against Mar Aba is that he did not permit his fellow Christians to take many wives.

The practices continued because they were eminently useful, and not just for the infertile. The only grounds on which the Sasanian lawbook recognises temporary co-marriage is childlessness, meaning having no son; but it was when Spartan men wanted children by 'a noble father' that they would give their wives to other men for impregnation, or they would borrow worthy women to beget 'noble sons' for themselves; Plutarch does not mention childlessness as a motive at all. It was the same desire for noble offspring that made the pre-Islamic Arabs tolerate co-husbands. A famous *ḥadīth* told by ʿĀ'isha informs us that the pre-Islamic Arabs knew of a union called *nikāḥ al-istibḍāʿ* whereby a man would cede his wife to another with a view to securing noble offspring (*najābat al-walad*) for himself.[139] In Ammianus Marcellinus' words the Arabs had 'mercenary wives, hired under temporary contracts'; the woman would give her (temporary) husband a spear and a tent, with the right to leave him after a stipulated time. 'It is unbelievable with what ardour both sexes give themselves up to passion,' he adds, inevitably viewing the custom as immoral.[140]

Van Gelder persuasively relates the Arabian institution to endogamy, arguing that 'noble offspring' actually meant 'healthy offspring'.[141] The preferred marriage in Arabia was with the father's brother's daughter, which was socially and politically advantageous, but often resulted in stunted children, as the Arabs freely noted.[142] The preferred marriage in Zoroastrian Iran was *khwēdōdah*, endogamous unions including parent–children and sibling marriages, and stunted children were sufficiently common for Sasanian inheritance law to take account of it.[143] They were also noted by Ishoʿbokht.[144] Diverse arrangements, nowadays known as renting an inseminator or a womb, will have been a neat way of avoiding the heavy reproductive costs of the socially desirable marriages. Another solution will have been the custom condemned in the *Dēnkard*: one should

139 Bukhārī, *Ṣaḥīḥ*, III, 427 (*nikāḥ* 36); translated and discussed in van Gelder, *Close Relationships*, 19f.

140 Ammianus Marcellinus, XIV, 3, 4 (AD 354); cf. Matthews, *Roman Empire of Ammianus*, 347f.

141 Van Gelder, *Close Relationships*, 20.

142 Van Gelder, *Close Relationships*, ch.1.

143 Cf. Macuch, *Sasanidische Rechtsbuch*, 76, on double shares to sons who are blind or have crippled arms or legs; Macuch, 'Zoroastrian Principles', 236f., on the unions covered by *khwēdōdah*.

144 Ishoʿbokht in Sachau, *Syrische Rechtsbücher*, III, 36f. (ch. 3): the children of such unions were often abnormal in some way, either their eyes, hands, feet, or other limbs having some weakness or their skin having a different colour.

not say, 'you lie with my sister or daughter in order that I too may lie with yours'.[145]

If the Zoroastrians lent and exchanged wives to procure healthy or noble offspring for themselves and others, or offspring of any kind, it is not surprising that Xanthus, Buddhist sources, and eventually the Muslims accused the khurramīs of *ibāḥat al-nisāʾ*. What is more surprising is that the Muslims do not accuse the mainstream Zoroastrians of doing so as well. East Syrian Christians do stress the Zoroastrian inclination to indulge in carnal pleasures;[146] Agathias observed that although Persians could and did have any number of wives, adultery was still committed, implying that so-called adultery was practised openly;[147] and Ibn al-Jawzī knew that Zoroastrians would hire men to produce heirs for men who had died sonless.[148] Muslims taunted them with marrying their mothers etc., but they reserved their accusations of promiscuity for the Khurramīs. Perhaps the reason is simply that all educated Muslims 'knew' wife-sharing to be a Mazdakite deviation, so that they automatically classified any community known to have practised it as Mazdakite or Khurramī. The mainstream Zoroastrians are not likely to have rushed to correct the misclassification: even close-kin marriage was actually a Mazdakite deviation, as the Zoroastrians were eventually to conclude themselves.[149]

Chiefs and holy men

It was suggested above that political leaders could have used the institution of temporary co-marriage to requisition wives, but it would perhaps be more correct to say that the politically powerful would amass women by any means available. According to the *Wei shu,* Sasanian kings would take away pretty girls who had reached the age of ten or more to bring them up at the court and hand them out as rewards to their followers, presumably after taking their pick.[150] When the king of Khwārizm in the time of Qutayba (d. 96/715) lost his power to his younger brother, the latter requisitioned any goods he wanted, whether riding-animals, slave-girls, or beautiful daughters, sisters, or wives, taking the women by force if

[145] *DkM*, 714.17–19 in Shaki, 'Sassanian Matrimonial Relations', 338.
[146] Cf. Stausberg, *Religion Zarathustras*, I, 242.
[147] Agathias, II, 30:5.
[148] Ibn al-Jawzī, *Talbīs Iblīs*, 74.
[149] Cf. Christensen, *Iran*, 325.
[150] Daffinà, 'La Persia sassanide secondo le fonti cinesi', 149; also the *Chou-shu* in Miller, *Accounts of Western Nations*, 14.

necessary.[151] Of al-Muqanna' we are similarly told that when he was shown a beautiful woman he would bring her to live with him, so that he had a hundred daughters of *dihqāns* from Sogdia, Kish, and Nasaf with him in his castle.[152] When Bābak heard of a pretty daughter or sister of a *baṭrīq*, he would similarly ask for her, and if she was not sent he would go and seize her, along with the *baṭrīq*'s possessions; as a result there were children of his in all the noble families of the Christians; he also had a large number of captive women, daughters of Arabs and of *dihqāns*, in his fortress at the time of his defeat.[153] ('Whenever he went to a village, every woman he wanted had to go to him. When she wasn't willing, he had her husband beaten up and imprisoned and their household raided,' as a peasant in the southern Zagros said of a chief who was finally ousted in 1971.)[154] A Daylamī chief interrogated by Maḥmūd of Ghazna's jurists after the latter's conquest of Rayy had over fifty wives: he had not wished to depart from ancestral custom, as he explained.[155] But we are not told how he had acquired them.

Bābak and al-Muqanna' are depicted as behaving like kings rather than men in whom the divine was incarnate: they simply requisitioned women, or took them by force. If they had been full of divine power, women would have offered themselves to them, pushed by their menfolk, whether for an extended period or just for the night. Of the fourth/tenth-century Sufi leader Muḥammad b. Khafīf we are told that high-ranking women would offer themselves in marriage to him in the hope of blessing (*tabarruk*). He would marry them and send them back without consummating the marriage: he is said to have got through four hundred of them in the course of his life, keeping forty of them for longer periods, two or three at a time, and one of them for forty years, without sleeping with any of them.[156] Needless to say, Ibn Khafīf's opponents had a somewhat different impression of his behaviour.[157] In his treatise against antinomian Sufis written in Persian al-Ghazālī mentions that a husband would tell his wife not to veil herself in the presence of a Sufi leader on the grounds that it

151 Tab. ii, 1237.
152 *TB*, 71/99f. = 73.
153 Tab. iii, 1223, 1227; cf. Movsès Kałankatuac'i in Laurent, *Arménie*, 378, where he marries the daughter of Vasak of Siwnie, his ally.
154 Loeffler, *Islam in Practice*, 108.
155 Ibn al-Jawzī, *Muntaẓam*, VIII, 39.
156 Hujwīrī, *Kashf*, 318 = 247.
157 Tanūkhī, *Nishwar*, III, no. 148 = *Tabletalk*, ii, 227; quoted by Ibn al-Jawzī, *Talbīs Iblīs*, 358.

would be to their advantage if he picked her out; so she would approach him for the sake of the blessing and later boast that the great man had rested on her breast.[158] According to al-Maqrīzī, the Yazīdīs would bring their daughters to any descendant of Shaykh Ḥasan al-Bawwāb who came to them: he would be alone with them and do with them what he liked; the parents believed that 'this was a bond of kinship by which one became related to God'. The Yazīdīs declared forbidden sexual intercourse to be licit, as he also says.[159] Of the Muhājirūn, a non-Islamic sect of baptists in Iraq, we are told that they 'do not withhold their women from their chiefs and regard *zinā* as lawful'.[160] The Tahtacis, a small, endogamous community of eastern Turkey, were (perhaps still are) said to require their virgins to be deflowered by their chief and to allow their women in general to offer themselves to him: if a son was born of the union his name had to be ʿAlī.[161] The idea seems to be that the offspring of such men inherited their father's special characteristics and/or that the holy man's blessing would somehow or other rub off on the family. The belief that the special powers – such as light or *baraka* – of a holy person could be transmitted through intercourse (heterosexual or homosexual) is also attested by al-Baghdādī on al-Shalmaghānī, al-Shirbīnī on the Khawāmis, and Westermarck on early twentieth-century North Africa, and probably also by the fact that Egyptian women would allow holy fools to take any liberty with them in the public street without being considered disgraced by it among the lower orders, as Lane observed.[162] It was another way of begetting superior offspring.

'Guest prostitution'

'Guest prostitution' is an inept term for the custom of giving one's wife, daughter, or other womenfolk to strangers for the night, or for however long they might stay. The practice differs from temporary marriage in that it is of briefer duration, does not take the woman away from her home, and does not involve a formal agreement between the males, but the sources are often too brief for a modern reader to be able to tell whether one or the other is being described. The *Karmaprajñāpti*, the *Mahāvibhāṣā*, and

158 Ghazālī, 'Streitschrift', 6 = 26.
159 Maqrīzī in Kreyenbroek, *Yezidism*, 35.
160 Ibn al-Nadīm, 403 = II, 810.
161 Özbayri and Roux, 'Quelques notes', 71f.
162 Baghdādī, *Farq*, 249 (drawn to my attention by Bella Tendler); Shirbīnī, Westermarck, and Lane in El-Rouayheb, 'Heresy and Sufism', 376.

Kalhaṇa, for example, could have either or both in mind when they include wives and/or daughters in the list of women that the Maga could sleep with. The term 'guest prostitution' is inept because the practice was not a commercial transaction: the head of the household was not out to make money, the women were not paid. Whatever the best name for it, it has had more than one function in its history.

Most obviously it could serve to demonstrate the magnanimity of the host. The Meccan jurist 'Aṭā' b. Abī Rabāḥ (d. 115/733f.), a *mawlā* from al-Janad in Yemen, thought it fine for any man to lend his slave-girls to his guests.[163] Members of a tribe between Mecca and Yemen would lend visitors their own wives, according to Ibn al-Mujāwir;[164] Burckhardt mentions the custom for a tribe in Asīr, probably the region that Ibn al-Mujāwir was referring to; and according to Landberg, writing in 1905, it was current among most tribes of the mountains between Yemen and Ḥaḍramawt.[165] In many other parts of the world too, including Berber North Africa, men would lend their own womenfolk, or boys.[166]

Another function of the practice was to secure healthy offspring – or just offspring. A Sabaic votive text has been interpreted to mean that two women slept with a passing stranger and that one of them conceived, for which she gives thanks.[167] The Ḥaḍramī Humūm, who were still giving girls to guests in the mid-twentieth century, explained that they did it to increase the number of the tribe, and that it was useful to have bastards who could be killed without provoking a blood-feud if the tribe had to kill one of its own by way of expiation.[168] As regards healthy offspring, Khalīl b. Aḥmad (d. 175/791) says that when the pagans (*'ulūj*) of Kābul saw a stout and handsome Arab they would leave him alone with their women in the hope that he would impregnate one of them.[169] In isolated communities foreigners might be actively sought out. Some such custom was known to Abū Dulaf, though his report is sensationalist and based on hearsay rather than personal observation: among the Qarluqs, according to him,

[163] Ibn Khallikān, III, 262 (deeming the report implausible).

[164] Cited in van Gelder, *Close Relationships*, 21. See also Wellhausen, 'Ehe bei den Arabern', 463.

[165] Landberg, *Etudes*, 907ff., citing Ibn al-Mujāwir, Burckhardt (*Reisen*, 682), and more along with his local information (here it is Nöldeke who deems it hard to believe). For other evidence relating to Arabia, see Müller, *Kulturhistorische Studien*, 265f.

[166] See the references to Bakrī, Ibn Ḥawqal, and Idrīsī in Gsell, *Afrique du nord*, V, 33.

[167] Beeston, 'Temporary Marriage'. If Beeston's reading is correct they were (permanently) married, but childless.

[168] Serjeant, 'Zinā', 152.

[169] Cited in van Gelder, *Close Relationships*, 21.

wives, daughters, and sisters alike would display themselves to travellers and take them home for the night, or for as long as they wished to stay, with the full knowledge of their menfolk.[170] At Kamul (in Chinese Central Asia), according to Marco Polo, men would offer their wives to foreigners, considering it an honour for the latter to sleep with them; they held their welfare, including the fertility of the fields, to depend on this custom.[171] Much the same is reported for the Hazaras of the Hindukush.[172] Guest 'prostitution' is also attested for a large number of other peoples – Tibetans, Mongols, and Eskimos included – undoubtedly thanks to the same desire to avoid inbreeding.[173] The healthy offspring produced by such unions will have encouraged religious explanations of their meritorious nature. The Quqites, a Gnostic sect in the Edessa region in pre-Islamic times, deemed it virtuous to allow strangers to sleep with their wives, probably (according to Drijvers) because any stranger who happened along might be a son of God sent to save his betrothed.[174]

Sometimes women were forbidden to marry until they had slept with other men, in at least some cases meaning foreigners. Marco Polo reports that this was so in Tibet, where old women would actively solicit the cooperation of foreigners by displaying the girls where the travellers arrived. The traveller had to give the girl a ring or some other token that she could show when she wanted to get married: she needed at least twenty; and women took great pride in the number of their tokens. Once they were married nobody was allowed to meddle with them.[175] It is undoubtedly the same institution that lies behind Herodotus' report that women among the Libyan Gindans, in north-western Tripolitania, would put on an anklet of leather for every man they had slept with, and be the more highly esteemed the more anklets they had.[176] Here it is not clear that the men had to be foreigners. In Lydia, Aelian (*c.* 235) tells us, it was once the custom for women 'to live as courtesans before setting up house with

[170] Abū Dulaf's so-called 'first epistle' in Yāqūt, III, 449 (s.v. 'al-Ṣīn'); cf. Minorsky, *Abū-Dūlaf*, 11ff.; also cited in van Gelder, *Close Relationships*, 21.

[171] Marco Polo, I, ch. 41.

[172] See Yule's note to Marco Polo, II, ch. 47, citing Elphinstone, *Caubul*, I, 209, and other parallels.

[173] Hermanns, *Familie der A mdo-Tibeter*, 36.

[174] Drijvers, 'Quq and the Quqites', 116. Quq probably flourished in the mid-second century, but the relevant information about the sect seems to relate to the fourth (cf. 110f.).

[175] Marco Polo, II, ch. 45.

[176] Herodotus, IV, 176; cf. Asheri *et al.*, *Commentary*, ad loc.; Andò, 'Comunanza delle donne', 97. Though I do not always agree with Andò's article, it seems to me to engage in exactly the right kind of attempt to 'translate back'.

their husbands; once married, they behaved correctly'.[177] The reference is presumably to the indigenous Lydians, or perhaps the Iranian colonists, rather than the Greeks, and again it is not clear that the men had to be outsiders. As noted already, it could conceivably be the same custom rather than temporary co-marriage that Strabo described for Media, where the women considered less than five husbands a misfortune. A more extreme version of it is mentioned by Hung Hao (wr. 1243), who says that when the Uighurs were living at Chin-chuan (Shan-hsi and Kansu) a girl had to have several children by a Chinese before she could marry into her own tribe: the more men she had been with, the better her marriage prospects.[178] The Uighur custom may be explicable in terms of the desire for healthy offspring by men who were not available or acceptable as marriage partners. Elsewhere, however, the girls only had to collect tokens, not to produce children, and the purpose of the practice is unclear.

Guest prostitution is first attested for Iran in the Syriac author Bar Daiṣan (Bardesanes, d. 222). He claims that women among the Bactrians known as Kushans wore male clothes, rode horses, were served better than the men by their slaves and slave-girls, and slept with both their slaves and foreigners without being afraid of their husbands, who regarded their wives as their masters.[179] He says much the same about Gīlī women: they did all the agricultural work and slept with foreigners and their own slaves without anyone taking it amiss.[180] Though women probably did do the agricultural work in Gīlān[181] the rest sounds like a wandering trope, for Pseudo-Scylax says much the same about the Libyrni (in Thrace): their wives had intercourse with their slaves and men from neighbouring tribes, and they ruled their menfolk.[182] Bar Daiṣan was well versed in ancient ethnography.[183] But he may simply be using a stereotyped formulation to convey genuine information, for Khalīl b. Aḥmad's report for the people of Kābul, cited earlier, is entirely credible, and it takes us close to Bactria. If so, the report on the Gīlīs should presumably also be taken seriously.

[177] *Historical Miscellany*, IV, 1.

[178] Pelliot, *Notes on Marco Polo*,156.

[179] Bar Daiṣan, *Laws of Countries*, 46 = 47; cited from the lost Greek version by Eusebius, *Praeparatio*, VI, 10, 21 (also in the *Recognitions*, IX, 23, but here the Kushans have become Susaeans). My thanks to Kevin van Bladel for drawing this passage to my attention.

[180] Bar Daiṣan, *Laws of Countries*, 44 = 45; cited from the lost Greek version by Eusebius, *Praeparatio*, VI, 10, 18; *Recognitions*, IX, 22.

[181] Cf. *Ḥudūd al-ʿālam*, §32.25, on Gīlān: 'All the agricultural work is done by the women. The men have no other business but warfare.'

[182] Ps.-Scylax, §21 (Müller, *GGM*, I, 26f.), cited in Pembroke, 'Women in Charge', 34f.

[183] Cf. his knowledge of the ancient Britons, in n. 11 of this chapter.

There can in any case be no doubt that some of the accusations of Khurramī *ibāḥa* relate to guest prostitution. Ibn al-Nadīm tells us that the Khurramīs of western Iran 'share their women and wives (*lahum mushāraka fi'l-ḥuram wa'l-ahl*), nobody is denied anything in respect of another's womenfolk, nor does he deny it (*lā yamtaniʿ al-wāḥid minhum min ḥurmat wa-lā yamnaʿ*), and for all that they believe in acts of charity'. He adds that 'they have a custom (*madhhab*) concerning hospitality which is not found in any other nation: when they host a guest, they do not deny him anything, whatever it may be'.[184] He seems to be describing two institutions: they share their womenfolk among themselves (by way of temporary co-marriage?) *and* they do not deny (foreign) guests anything. Niẓām al-Mulk also credits them with giving their wives to guests, or rather he presents Mazdak as having instituted this custom, but what he had heard about (and grossly distorted) seems to be Tantric-style rituals such as those recorded for the eastern Rāwandiyya rather than the servicing of passing foreigners.[185] In a more reliable vein al-Maqdisī, who visited the Khurramīs at Māsabadhān and Mihrijānqadhaq before 355/966, tells us that he asked his informants whether they permitted the sharing of women (*ibāḥat al-nisāʾ*): the answer was that some of them did 'with the women's consent' (*ʿalā riḍā minhunna*).[186] This confirms that the practice was real, but was it to chiefs, religious leaders, and/or strangers that the Khurramīs would give their women, for the night or for longer periods, in the woman's or the recipient's home? Al-Maqdisī provides no details. It is a pity that a man sufficiently interested to do some fieldwork should have been so laconic.

Dihkhudā is equally tantalising. According to him, the Pārsīs who apostatised from Ismailism were strictly monogamous: Budayl the Weaver forbade polygyny, divorce, and the purchase of slaves alike. Yet he also declared that for Abū 'l-ʿAlāʾ and Yūsuf everything forbidden is permitted and allowed, and women are just pure water prepared for the thirsty, there is no need for dower or wedding ceremony (*mahr u nikāḥ*), and daughters are legitimate (marriage partners) for their fathers and brothers.[187] That Budayl forbade polygyny is plausible enough: it was (perhaps still is) forbidden among the Ahl-i Ḥaqq as well, and they too took – or take – a restrictive stance on divorce.[188] The claim that Budayl's

[184] Ibn al-Nadīm, 406 = II, 817.
[185] *SN*, ch. 44:4 (260 = 198).
[186] Maqdisī, IV, 31.
[187] Dihkhudā in Kāshānī, *Zubda*, 188f.; Rashīd al-Dīn, 151f.
[188] Edmonds, 'Beliefs and Practices', 100 (on the Ahl-i Ḥaqq in relation to the Khurramīs see further Chapter 19). Cf. Özbayri and Roux, 'Quelques notes', 74 (polygamy is rare).

followers practised close-kin marriage should probably be dismissed, however, though it is just possible that the weaver had taken it up in a defiant vein as part of his Pārsī heritage. The comparison of women with pure water is a variant on the argument that women were like flowers that anyone could smell, but what did it mean?[189] The reference is clearly to some kind of sexual freedom, underscored by the claim that there was no need for a wedding ceremony or *mahr*. Since it follows the statement that everything forbidden was lawful for Abū 'l-ʿAlāʾ and Yūsuf, the two former Ismaili missionaries whom Budayl declared to be manifestations of God, the most plausible interpretation of his statement is that the two divine incarnations could freely use the women of their community, whether by taking them away to their homes after the fashion of al-Muqannaʿ and Bābak or by sleeping with them as they passed through the villages. Everyone else had to live in lifelong monogamy.

There are suggestions of a more relaxed village attitude to sexual relations in general in the *Tabṣirat al-ʿawāmm*, however. Here we are told that the adherents of reincarnation held that everyone who had been a woman in the first *dawr* would become a man in the next, and vice versa, so that marriages made in the first *dawr* would remain valid in the second: if it had been lawful for two people to sleep together in the previous cycle it was lawful in the present cycle too, even without a marriage ceremony, while conversely it would remain unlawful for them if it had been so before.[190] This comes in the section that speaks of reincarnation in the homely tone suggestive of a village or small town environment, and it sounds like a local way of legitimising pre-marital and/or non-marital relations. In Ṭabaristān, where the *Tabṣirat al-ʿawāmm* – or at least its chapter on reincarnation – seems to have been written, there were fortnightly markets where young people would meet and amuse themselves. It was customary for a man who fell in love with a woman to carry her away, if he could persuade her, for three days of cohabitation; then he would ask her father to give her in marriage to him:[191] perhaps such couples saw themselves as having been married in the previous cycle. The concept could also have been used to avoid marriages arranged by parents, by sudden

189 Twenty years ago I took Budayl to be explaining why marriage had to be strictly monogamous: since women were common to all they had to be distributed equally so that nobody had more than others (Crone, 'Zoroastrian Communism', 454). But this hardly fits the insistence that there was no need for marriage or dowry.

190 *Tabṣirat al-ʿawāmm*, 89.

191 *Ḥudūd al-ʿālam*, §32.22. Cf. Muqaddasī, 369, on Daylam, but here the girl would reportedly be killed if they had intercourse before the marriage contract.

discovery that the union proposed had been unlawful in the previous *dawr*. Altogether, the management of sexual relations in rural Iran is likely to have been a good deal more varied than the simplistic image of Islamic propriety versus scandalous indulgence purveyed by the religious scholars is apt to convey.

Defloration rituals

Women could also be given to others for defloration. It seems to have been widely assumed in ancient times that the removal of a girl's hymen was dangerous and/or polluting (because blood was spilt), so that it was best done by priests, holy men, passing foreigners, midwives, female relatives, or others – for example, when the girl had had her first menstruation or on the eve of her marriage, as part of a collective ritual or on an individual basis. Though the practice has been receding in historical times it is still alive in, for example, South India and Tibet today (or was until quite recently).[192] The custom is attested for Herodotus' Babylonia, where every woman had to 'sit in the temple of Aphrodite and have intercourse with some stranger'. She had to accept whoever first offered her some money, and she would only sleep with one; thereafter she would go home and no amount of money could buy her.[193] She did not have to collect tokens, then, and she would not take pride in the number of men she had been with: getting rid of her maidenhead was all she wanted. Strabo mentions a similar practice in the temples of Anahita in Armenia; Ephrem documents it for fourth-century Mesopotamia;[194] and it was still alive in the sixth century, when Mar Aba enumerated ritual defloration by priests (*kumre*) and foreign travellers among the five categories of natural, i.e., uncivilised or brutish, intercourse.[195] The Maga held that one could have sexual intercourse with diverse women and also with 'a virgin', as we have seen, presumably meaning that they were charged with ritual defloration. Ḥamza al-Iṣfahānī knew of an Iranian ceremony of ritual defloration called the 'rose-picking night';[196] and Abū Tammām tells us that a certain ʿAmr b. Muḥammad had told him on the authority of a

[192] For South India, see White, *Kiss of the Yoginī*, 68 (female relatives); for Tibet, see Hermanns, *Familie der A mdo-Tibeter*, 35f., 235 (guest prostitution as defloration ritual); n. 161 of this chapter for the Tahtacis (chiefs).

[193] Herodotus, I, 199.

[194] Strabo, XI, 14, 16; Yamauchi, 'Cultic Prostitution', 219 (unfortunately without precise references). Cf. Gsell, *Afrique du nord*, V, 31.

[195] Mar Aba in Sachau, *Syrische Rechtsbücher*, III, 258f.

[196] See below, p. 436.

shaykh in Bukhārā that 'every group of these Mubayyiḍa have a chief (*ra'īs*) who is appointed to deflower their women on the night of the marriage procession'. Abū Tammām added that he had not verified this for himself. Though he is commendably cautious we need not doubt his information, for the institution still existed some two centuries later. Qubavi, who translated Narshakhī's history into Persian in 522/1128f., inserted Abū Tammām's statement into Narshakhī's text and mentioned that he, Qubāvī, had asked the elders of a Bukharan village about this institution. He formulated the question in nicely egalitarian terms: 'What was the sense of allowing such great pleasure to this one man while the rest were deprived of it?' If the Bukharan shaykh cited by Abū Tammām had invented or garbled his information, the Bukharans to whom Qubāvī put his question some two centuries later would not have known what he was talking about, but apparently they understood him perfectly well: they replied that 'every youth who reached maturity should satisfy his need with this person until he should marry a woman. His repayment for that was that the wife should stay with him for the first night.' They also supplied the local name for such a person: he was called *tkāna* (or *thkāna*), and when he grew old they would appoint a new one.[197] Presumably he was some kind of priest.

Niẓām al-Mulk had also heard of this institution, but, as so often, he or his informant corrupts the information. He tells us that when the White-clothed ones of Farghāna, identified with the followers of al-Muqanna', rebelled and killed all the Muslims they could find, the Sāmānid amir sent a commander against them accompanied by the scholar Abū Muḥammad. When the army returned to Bukhārā this scholar was asked about the religion of the rebels: he responded that they did not accept the duty to pray, fast, give alms, go on pilgrimage, or wage holy war; they drank wine, and they were promiscuous: 'when a man was married, their chief was the first to lay hands on the woman, afterwards the husband'.[198] For good measure Abū Muḥammad added that they also slept with their mothers and sisters. No doubt he imputed the defloration ritual to the White-clothed ones of Farghāna on the basis of information relating to Bukhārā.

197 *TB*, 73f./103f. =75f. Nicholas Sims-Williams kindly informs me that the word is plausible enough in Sogdian, but that there is no obvious etymology for it.

198 *SN*, ch. 46:28 (304= 231f.); cf. ch. 47:14 (319 = 244), where Niẓām al-Mulk enumerates much the same charges in connection with the Khurramīs of the Jibāl, but not the defloration ritual. The identification of the rebels as *muqanna'īyān* is only in the text, not in the translation (based on Darke's first edition), where they are 'loathsome' instead.

The orgiastic night

According to al-Baghdādī the community left behind by Bābak in Azerbaijan had a night during which their men and women would assemble for wine and song and then extinguish the lights, whereupon they would mate indiscriminately.[199] He is the first to direct this charge against the Khurramīs, but the charge itself was very old.

The first attestation seems to come in Agatharchides (*fl.* second century BC), who tells us that the apparently polyandrous Fish-eaters of south-eastern Iran had a feast in which the whole tribe came together and every man slept with whatever woman he happened to encounter: the purpose was to beget children.[200] He does not mention any extinction of lights, and he sees Fish-eaters as unperverted by civilisation rather than depraved. The extinction of lights was added by Nicolaus of Damascus, a Syrian of the Augustan age who credited the orgiastic night to the Libyans. In North Africa the feast was regularly associated with Berber tribesmen from the time of Leo Africanus down to modern times.[201]

In the eastern Mediterranean, however, the feast came to be associated with sectarians rather than tribesmen, and the depravity of which it was now seen as a symptom was underscored by the addition of the incest motif. From the second century onwards it was the Christians who were the targets: they were said to engage in nocturnal feasts in which, after much carousing, they would extinguish the lights and engage in indiscriminate intercourse, even with their own mothers or sisters.[202] Origen credited the Jews with spreading the rumour that Christians 'turn out the lights and each man has sexual intercourse with the first woman he meets'.[203] Modern scholars usually explain the charges with reference to the Christian practice of meeting at night (for safety), 'promiscuously' calling one another brother and sister, and greeting each other with a kiss; but fluid boundaries with antinomian forms of Gnostic Christianity may also have been a factor.[204]

The victory of Christianity put an end to the charge as an anti-Christian theme in the Roman empire, but not on the Persian side of the border.

199 Baghdādī, *Farq*, 252.
200 Diodorus Siculus, III, 17:1.
201 Gsell, *Afrique du nord*, V, 32f.
202 Minucius Felix in Benko, *Pagan Rome*, ch. 3; cf. Theophilus of Antioch, III, 4.
203 Origen, *Contra Celsum*, VI, 27, with further references in the note to Chadwick's translation.
204 Benko, *Pagan Rome*, ch. 3.

According to al-Bīrūnī, ignorant people credited the Christians with a feast called the night of *māshūsh* during which they would copulate with whomever they chanced upon in the dark. Al-Shābushtī believed this feast to be celebrated in the monastery of al-Khuwāt near Baghdad, where Muslims also participated. Ḥamza al-Iṣfahānī identifies the feast somewhat differently: it was celebrated by priests and monks for the deflowering of virgins, and the Persians called it *shab-i gulhirzān*, 'rose-abandoning evening', meaning a night of defloration. He adds that the Christians denied the charge.[205] Apparently the old accusation had accompanied the Christians as they moved to the Sasanian empire, where some had understood the alleged feast along the lines of a local defloration ritual by priests.[206] Even thereafter the charge lived on in the Near East, buried deep in some cultural recess normally invisible to historians, to surface again some eight hundred years later in Arabia. Here the British traveller Doughty was told by bedouin that the Christians coupled like animals: 'their lights quenched in their religious assemblies, there is a meddling among them in a strange and horrible manner, the son may be lying in savage blindness with his own mother'.[207]

Though the Christians were outraged by the charge, they happily directed it against sectarians of whom they disapproved themselves. Clement used it as ammunition against the Carpocratian Gnostics of the second century,[208] others against the Montanists.[209] The Borborian Melyonaye, who came from Persia in the time of Justinian and who were Marcionites and Manichaeans – i.e., what the Muslims would call *zindīq*s – were also held to be light-extinguishers, and indeed to kill infants for use in the eucharist, a charge once levelled at the Christians too.[210] A ninth-century Greek abjuration formula for Manichaeans anathemises those who engage in incestuous intercourse and turn out the lights for indiscriminate debauchery.[211] The Qarmaṭīs of Iraq are also credited with an orgiastic night, but as a single climactic event rather than an annual

[205] De Blois, 'Laylat al-Māšūš', 87ff.

[206] De Blois' objection that the term 'night of lost virginity' could not refer to a festival seems to rest on his conception of defloration as an individual (and private) activity rather than a coming-of-age ritual. That Ḥamza should have invented the whole story about the *laylat al-māshūsh*, as he suggests, is unlikely, especially as Ḥamza conscientiously notes that the Christians deny it (de Blois, 'Laylat al-Māšūš', 90, 93).

[207] Doughty, *Travels*, I, 341.

[208] Clement, *Stromateis*, III, 2, 10, 1.

[209] Müller, *Kulturhistorische Studien*, 267.

[210] De Blois, 'Laylat al-Māšūš', 84.

[211] Lieu, *Manichaeism*, 117 (this is not part of the two abjuration formulas published in the same volume).

feast, and without the light-extinguishing motif;[212] the standard version complete with the extinguished lights and the incest motif appears in connection with the Qarāmiṭa in Yemen.[213] After al-Baghdādī had credited it to the Khurramīs others repeated it.[214] Thereafter it was the turn of the so-called Sun-worshippers (Arewordi, Shamsiyya) of Armenia and Upper Mesopotamia,[215] as well as the Qizilbāsh, Alevis, Tahtacis, Yezidis, Ahl-i Ḥaqq, followers of Badr al-Dīn, and other sects of the same type: the charge can be followed down to the nineteenth century, and sometimes even to the twentieth.[216]

There clearly is a pattern to the charges: the targets are always sectarians of a spiritualist, Gnostic, and/or antinomian kind, who are secretive because their beliefs diverge radically from those of their neighbours. Their failure to live by the religious law of the land is equated with libertinism. The accusers were not necessarily always wrong to suspect that the antinomianism of the sectarians extended to sexual matters, but this cannot be inferred from the charge that they had a light-extinguishing feast. The Dönme of Salonica, converts to Islam from among the followers of the seventeenth-century Jewish messiah Sabbatai Zvi, were also reputed to have a light-extinguishing feast, and Scholem, who wrote sympathetically about them, was convinced that this was true, partly because there was no doubt about their radical antinomianism and partly because the nature of the feast had been revealed to outsiders by members of the younger generation. He held the Dönme to have adapted to their mystical beliefs an old bacchanalian cult of pagan origin which had supposedly lived on in Asia Minor: they also believed in the sacramental value of exchanging wives.[217] But, though they may well have exchanged wives, what had lived on in Asia Minor was only rumours of such a feast, attached now to this sect and now to that, and if the younger generation

212 Ibn al-Dawādārī, *Kanz al-durar*, 50f.; tr. from al-Nuwayrī's version in Lewis, *Islam from the Prophet*, 64f.

213 Landberg, *Etudes*, 919f. (citing 'Umāra, ed. Kay, 143f.).

214 Ghazālī, *Faḍā'iḥ*, 11 (ch. 2.1); Sam'ānī, *Ansāb*, s.v. 'Bābakī'; Ibn al-Jawzī, *Muntaẓam*, V, 114.3; Ibn al-Jawzī, *Talbīs Iblīs*, 100f.; Dhahabī, *Ta'rīkh*, ṭbq xxviii, 271 (year 278).

215 Garsoian, *Paulician Heresy*, 107, n. 95; Müller, *Kulturhistorische Studien*, 74 (where one account replaces women with a cake).

216 Landberg, *Etudes*, 920ff.; Minorsky, *Notes*, 261ff.; Mélikoff, *Sur les traces*, 9f.; Müller, *Kulturhistorische Studien*, 5, 29, 103f., 205 (cf. also 48, 61, 68, 87, 120); Eberhard, *Osmanische Polemik*, 94f.; Bumke, 'Kizilbaş-Kurden in Dersim', 540; Minorsky, 'Shaykh Bālī-Efendi on the Ṣafavids', 448; cf. also Özbayri and Roux, 'Quelques notes', 70; Morton, '*Chūb-i ṭarīq* and *Qizilbāsh* Ritual', 237ff (on a ritual that may have triggered the charge).

217 Scholem, 'Redemption through Sin', 114.

confirmed the truth of what everybody suspected, the chances are that they were simply craving acceptance as mainstream Muslims: repeating the old charges against their forebears served as a kind of abjuration formula. There is admittedly some complicating evidence in a nineteenth-century Nuṣayrī manuscript brought to light by Tendler: here the author presents the *laylat al-ibāḥa* (under this and other names) as good Nuṣayrī practice, complete with the extinction of the lamp.[218] But this account is such an odd mixture of the familiar stereotype and genuine Nuṣayrī doctrine that until Tendler has finished her work on it all one can say is that some kind of embrace of the hostile stereotype may be involved. As far as the Khurramīs are concerned, it seems safe to conclude that the stereotype is simply a cultural marker for those beyond the pale.

OVERALL

What lay behind the charges that the Khurramīs would share their womenfolk? The answer seems to be a wide range of practices relating to reproduction, the transmission of property, and the display of power. The most important institution in the east is fraternal polyandry; in the west the key institution seems to be temporary co-marriage; in east and west alike there is evidence for the lending of women to religious leaders or chiefs, as well as to passing foreigners, and for defloration rituals by priests. A fair number of the institutions were found in Arabia too. The overall impression is that in terms of management of sexual relations and the transmission of property, Iran (and to some extent the Near East in general) was a very different place in antiquity from what it is today. Just as the bedouin of Arabia were still as bare-headed and scantily clothed as the Assyrians had depicted them,[219] so they and their neighbours in mountainous Iran come across as closer to the world of the Old Testament and the *Mahābhārata* than to modern times in terms of marriage practices. The Christians had eradicated many of their traditional practices, but they had not got very far on the Sasanian side of the border, let alone in Arabia, when the Muslims arrived to complete the task. Wherever they went in the former Sasanian empire the Muslims brought with them a new marital regime, denouncing the alternative customs as so much Zoroastrian incest and Mazdakite *ibāḥa*. Their charges are often simplified, stereotyped, distorted, uninformative, and occasionally downright wrong. But very few of them are mere figments of the heresiographical imagination.

[218] Personal communication from Bella Tendler.

[219] See Crone, 'Bare foot and Naked'.

18

The Mazdakite Utopia and After

We now have sufficient information to return to the question of the relationship between Khurramism and Mazdakism. Mazdakism is one of the most striking examples of pre-modern communism, and also one of the few that were (briefly) translated into practice. It was communist in the elementary sense of postulating that property, including women, belonged to everyone, not to individuals: there could be no exclusive rights of ownership in the means of production and reproduction. A similar view had been formulated close to a millennium before Mazdak by Plato, to the perennial embarrassment of Christian admirers of Plato. But Plato only envisaged the guardians of his ideal city, not all its inhabitants, as sharing their wives and property, and as far as property is concerned it would perhaps be more correct to say that he prescribed renunciation, for what they shared was not the land itself but rather its proceeds. Their communism was of consumption, as Durkheim said, noting that this was true of most pre-modern forms of the phenomenon, the early Christians included.[1] 'All who believed were together and had all things in common', as we read in the Acts of the Apostles (2:44); Lucian of Samosate (d. after 180), no lover of Christians, also knew that they held 'all things to be common'. But what this meant was that Christians would sell their land and hand over the proceeds to the community chest for distribution among themselves, or rather among the needy. 'They would sell their possessions and goods and distribute the proceeds to all, as any had need' (Acts 2:45). They did not pool the land for joint cultivation, or even for redistribution on an equitable basis; they did not even share the proceeds equally.[2]

[1] Cf. Crone, 'Zoroastrian Communism', 455f.

[2] Dawson, *Cities of the Gods*, 273, citing Lucian, *Peregrinus* 13 (where a Christian gives away all his property); Acts of the Apostles 4:32–5.

Renunciation and sharing are closely related ideas, and there are times when it is difficult to distinguish between them (as in Plato or Christian monasteries, for example). Since entire societies cannot renounce women and property without ceasing to exist, however, renunciation can only be a solution for individuals or specific sections of the community, whereas whole societies can in principle share women and property alike. Until the nineteenth century it was mostly in accounts of distant, exotic, or wholly fictitious lands that they did so, and fairly infrequently at that until early modern times.[3] There were occasional attempts to put the fantasies into practice by participants in messianic movements (such as the early Christians, the Ismailis or the Taborites), for whom they served to express, and induce, cohesion. Usually they involved property alone, but sometimes women as well, and some revaluation of the relations between men and women invariably accompanied the rethinking of property relations: this was true even of Soviet and Maoist communism. But Zardūsht of Fasā and Mazdak are distinctly unusual in that they advocated outright sharing of both women and property, not just property, for all members of Iranian society, not just a sector of it, as a solution to the problems of the here and now, not as a way of confronting the end of times, and further in that they envisaged the land itself as shared along with the women, not just its proceeds.

The two Mazdaks were not modern communists, however. They did not contemplate vesting the means of production, let alone reproduction, in the state. More precisely, we do not know how Zardūsht of Fasā envisaged the realisation of the utopia, but Mazdak is depicted as seeing the state as a mere obstacle to the realisation of the ideal. To him communism meant equal distribution, not to be brought about by land reform, but rather by people taking what they needed from those who had a surplus. He is reported to have said that 'if someone can take what is in people's hands and obtain their women by theft, treachery, trickery or blandishment, or in any way whatever, that is allowed and permitted to him. The surplus which is in the hands of those who have more than others is forbidden to them, so that it may be distributed equally among the servants.'[4] The endorsement of theft, trickery, and treachery suggests that this report dates from after the revolt, but the sources are in agreement that during the revolt his followers put his ideas into practice by plundering the homes of the rich and powerful.

3 The literature on utopias is enormous, but the distribution of communist fantasies on a worldwide basis does not seem to have been tabulated. No book on pre-modern communism as a worldwide phenomenon seems to exist either.

4 Malaṭī, 72f.

What Mazdak preached could be seen as a simple inversion of the behaviour of the kings of the day, for Iranian kings were in the habit of taking what they wanted from their subjects, as we have seen, requisitioning girls along with taxes as if it were the most natural thing in the world: the last example was the king of Khwārizm, who would requisition anything from riding animals to beautiful daughters, sisters, or wives, taking the women by force if necessary.[5] The only difference between his behaviour and that of Mazdak's followers is that the flow of women and property went from the lowly to the exalted rather than the other way round.

In a society in which the rich and powerful routinely despoil the population beneath them people do not usually find it easy to imagine that things could be fundamentally different. There must have been something that enabled the two Mazdaks to conceive the idea of reversing the direction of the flow, and keeping things balanced thereafter. Apparently the source of inspiration was the 'household communism' of eastern Iran. No brother in a polyandrous household could or would behave like the king of Khwārizm, everyone shared the family property equally because it was a joint inheritance. 'God created the world as a single creation for a single creature, namely Adam. He gave it to him for him to eat of its food, drink of its drink, delight in its pleasures, and sleep with its wives, and when Adam died, He made his children inherit it equally; nobody has a better right than others to property or wives,' as the Mazdakites are said to have argued.[6] The shared inheritance of the sons of Adam had come to be allocated disproportionately to some at the expense of others by means of power and oppression, as Ibn al-Balkhī's summary says.[7] The formulation is Islamic, but Muslims are not in the habit of appealing to Adam to illustrate the right way of things, so some Zoroastrian myth is likely to lurk behind it. According to the mainstream Zoroastrians, mankind owed its existence to three successive close-kin unions: first between Ohrmazd and his daughter, the earth (Spəntā Ārmaiti, Spandārmad); next between Gayōmard and his mother, the earth; and thereafter between Mašya and Mašyāne, the Zoroastrian Adam and Eve.[8] There must have

[5] Tab. ii, 1237 (cited in Chapter 17, n. 151).

[6] Malaṭī, 72f.

[7] Ibn al-Balkhī, *Fārsnāma*, 84; cf. also *SN*, ch. 44:4 (260 = 197). A different version says that God had created all men equal and given them the means of sustenance to share: men had started oppressing one another (Tab. i, 885f.; Maqdisī, III, 167; other sources in Crone, 'Kavād's Heresy', n. 84).

[8] Herrenschmidt, 'Le xwêtodas', 121ff.; cf. *Dk*, III, no. 80 (*DkB*, 53; *DkM*, 73), against a Jew (= Muslim?) asking about close-kin marriage; cf. also Choksy, *Evil, Good, and Gender*, 45, citing *PRDd*, 8:2–4, for a glimpse of the domestic bliss of Ohrmazd and Spandārmad: 'my daughter, my house-mistress of paradise, and the mother of creation'.

been a polyandrous counterpart to this myth which stressed the harmony of brothers.

The Tibetans, the best-known practitioners of polyandry, insisted that polyandry was a more moral form of marriage than other types on the grounds that it was geared to the common good of the family rather than that of individuals: it was not easy to share one's property and wife, one's most precious possessions; it required fraternal solidarity; brothers had to learn to suppress their feelings of jealousy, but if they did so, the result was happy and prosperous families.[9] Similar views were voiced elsewhere.[10] It will have been this positive appreciation of 'household communism' that Zardūsht of Fasā articulated when he said that envy, pride, and other sins attacked people through women and property, who were the ultimate causes of practically all dissension among mankind, and that sharing both would put an end to this by diminishing the power of Āz, the demon personifying desire and covetousness.[11] All Iranians were to share *as if* they were brothers who formed a single household, taking what they needed and never accumulating things for themselves. The polyandrous background also explains the most unusual feature of this communist vision, namely that it involved the land itself, not just the proceeds from it.

Explaining how there came to be a communist vision in Iran has long been a problem, to which the usual reaction has been to postulate that the ideas came from Greece. Agathias and Bar Ḥadbeshabba had already noted the similarity between Plato and Kavadh's views on sharing women – without suggesting that Kavadh was influenced by Plato, however. On the contrary, Agathias opined that Kavadh had not instituted his law with a view to 'any of the utilitarian ends suggested by the hidden meaning of Socrates' words in the Platonic dialogue', but merely to facilitate licentiousness.[12] Modern scholars do not usually consider Plato a source either, but rather postulate that Zardūsht of Fasā and/or Mazdak owed their ideas to the Carpocratians.[13] This is most implausible.

[9] Peter, *Polyandry*, 344, 357, 361, 417, 451, 562.

[10] 'It keeps all the brothers together; union and cooperation gives them strength', as a Malabar informant said, stressing that this made them the best agriculturalists in their country (Aiyyappan, 'Fraternal Polyandry in Malabar', 275). Here as in Tibet brothers were deemed better at agreeing than sisters-in-law would be.

[11] Cf. the question in the *Dēnkard*, in Chapter 16, p. 372; further sources in Crone, 'Kavād's Heresy', n. 82.

[12] Agathias, IV, 7; Bar Ḥadbeshabba, 'Cause de la fondation des écoles', 364.

[13] Cf. Crone, 'Kavād's Heresy', 28 (on Klima and Caratelli); also Yarshater, 'Mazdakism', 1020.

The Carpocratians were Gnostics who claimed to have the secret doctrine of Christ and were often accused of libertine behaviour. They are first attested by Celsus, writing around 160–80, under the name of Harpocratians, suggesting that they owed their name to the Graeco-Egyptian God Harpocrates. Celsus does not know of any founder. Carpocrates first appears in Irenaeus (wr. *c.* 180), where he seems to be a construction like Ebion, the supposed founder of the Ebionites. Clement of Alexandria (d. *c.* 215) credits this Carpocrates with a son called Ephiphanes, who died at the age of seventeen and was venerated as a deity on the island of Cephallenia: this son, he says, was the author of a treatise, *On Justice*, of which he gives some extracts. It claimed that private property was an unjustifiable human convention: God had made sunshine common to all, whether human or animal, male or female; the food that the sun drew up from the ground was likewise meant for all; animals pasturing on the land did not have any laws regulating what they ate, and God had not laid down any rules regarding the production of offspring either; sexual desire was natural, and all could share a woman just as animals did; 'mine' and 'yours' only came into existence through the laws.[14] The basic idea of the treatise could be summarised in Proudhon's famous dictum that 'property is theft'. Clement's extracts do not say anything about the social or political effects of property rights (inequality, poverty, competition, strife), and we do not hear anything about how things were to be shared either, but the extracts consistently speak about food rather than the land: sharing was apparently about consumption in his conception as well.

There is no reason to think that this treatise had anything to do with either the Carpocratians or the Mazdakites. It is unlikely to be Carpocratian because there are no Christian elements in it. What is more, the Carpocratians believed this world to have been created by inferior angels led by Satan; the treatise *On Justice*, by contrast, equates nature with God and adduces natural phenomena such as the behaviour of the sun and animals as normative. The Carpocratians regarded the body as a prison and deemed Jesus to have destroyed those passions that dwelt in men by way of punishment (for their sins in pre-existence?). If they indulged in libertine behaviour it was not because they held sexual desire to be natural in the normative sense of the word.[15] But it is precisely

[14] Cf. Clement, *Stromateis*, III, 2. For Clement's explanation of Plato's all-too-similar-sounding proposals see III, 2, 10, 2 and Dawson, *Cities of the Gods*, 266.

[15] Irenaeus, I, 25, 1 and 4.

because it is natural in that sense that the treatise endorses sexuality in an unrestricted form. Carpocrates had completely misunderstood Plato's dictum that wives are to be held in common, as Clement protests.[16] (It is after this that he cites Xanthus on the promiscuous Magi.) In fact the author must have been a pagan, probably someone connected with a cult on the island of Cephallenia that did not have anything to do with the Carpocratians or any other Gnostic sect.[17]

The attempt to link *On Justice* with Zardūsht of Fasā and Mazdak have so far focused on the alleged founder of the Carpocratians on the assumption that he was the author of the ideas in the treatise and that Zardūsht and/or Mazdak were also Gnostics. In fact, neither the author of the treatise nor the two Iranians were Gnostics, so one could still link them, but they were widely separated in space: Cephallenia lies off the western coast of Greece (the irrelevant Carpocratians flourished in Alexandria and Rome). The complicated acrobatics required to get the communist ideas from the Graeco-Roman world to Iran are unsatisfactory in that they involve chance encounters between individuals rather than interaction between communities;[18] and the case for the relevance of the treatise rests entirely on the fact that it advocates sharing of women and property, not on any specific similarity with the Iranian ideas (e.g., sunlight is never invoked on the Iranian side, nor is there any appeal to nature). Obviously if the treatise had somehow been available in Iran, we can be sure that Zardūsht of Fasā would have read it with interest, but we do not actually need it to explain his utopian vision. What we do need is to abandon our tacit assumption that the Greek tradition was the only source of communist ideas in antiquity. It was after all the Scythians, an Iranian tribe, that the Greeks romanticised as the embodiment of primitive communism, just as it was Iranian priests who sprang to Clement's mind as the epitome of communist abomination. Whether as an ideal or as a nightmare, the Greeks associated the sharing of women, and sometimes property as well, with Iran. The Iranians had their source of inspiration in their own land.

[16] Clement, *Stromateis*, III, 2, 10, 2; cf. Dawson, *Cities of the Gods*, 266.

[17] For all this see Kraft, 'Gab es einen Gnostiker Karpokrates?'. Kraft's argument eliminates from the Gnostic repertoire the only source containing an unambiguous advocacy of libertinism, but by the same token it also eliminates the only evidence for Gnostics endorsing the goodness of the creation (to the detriment of Williams, *Rethinking 'Gnosticism'*, 99, 185ff.).

[18] See Crone, 'Kavād's Heresy', 28.

MAZDAK AND THE KHURRAMĪS

This leaves us with the question of the relationship between Khurramism and Mazdakism after the suppression of Mazdak's revolt. Did Mazdak leave behind communities committed to his doctrine that women and children were common property – not just in the sense that polyandrous brothers shared a wife or that others might pass their wives or daughters to guests, chiefs, or religious leaders, but rather in the sense that 'nobody has the right to more property or wives than others', as Mazdak's followers are reported to have said? The answer must surely be yes. The sect cannot have disappeared overnight; and al-Malaṭī's account of Mazdakite doctrine sounds as if it comes from later Mazdakites. It is unusually detailed and, contrary to what is often stated, there was no *Mazdaknāma* from which the information could have been drawn.[19] But it is impossible to say anything about the afterlife of this sect because the sources conflate it with the Khurramīs. Much later the illuminist Zoroastrian work called the *Dabistān-i madhāhib*, composed in eleventh/seventeenth-century India, mentions several Mazdakites of the author's own time by name and says that they lived as Muslims, but practised their religion secretly. They seem to have been neo-Mazdakites in the true sense of the word, that is to say they had rediscovered Mazdak's doctrine and revived it. The author, who writes in very positive terms about Mazdak, says that they had a book by him called the *Dīsnād*, from which he quotes several extracts: much of it is simply a translation of al-Shahrastānī's account of Mazdak, though it also contains doctrinal elaborations not found elsewhere, possibly worked out by the Neo-Mazdakites themselves. There is no sense of a continuous tradition.[20]

Whether the sect that Mazdak left behind included our rural Khurramīs is open to question. Al-Bīrūnī does claim that al-Muqannaʿ 'prescribed everything that Mazdak had prescribed', but, as seen already, this rests on a misunderstanding;[21] and when Wāqid has Jāvīdhān's widow predict that Bābak would restore Mazdakism one suspects that the reference to Mazdakism was supplied by Wāqid himself.[22] Like al-Muqannaʿ, Bābak believed in accumulating women for himself, not in making them freely available to all or distributing them equally. When Māzyār set the

[19] See Tafazzoli, 'Soi-disant Mazdak-Nāmag'.
[20] *Dabistān*, I, 118ff. = I, 372ff.
[21] See Chapter 6, p. 137.
[22] See Chapter 3, p. 72.

Muḥammira of Jurjān against the landowners of the region, allowing some of them to seize the estates and the womenfolk of their former masters, no ideology seems to have been involved at all.[23] Many villagers may have remembered Mazdak as a great hero who had stood up for them, allowing them to seize what they liked. To that extent Niẓam al-Mulk could be right that Mazdak joined the company of the mahdi in the countryside of Rayy. One Khurramī rebel in the Jibāl was known as ʿAlī b. Mazdak, if we trust Niẓām al-Mulk, who is drawing on Ḥamza al-Iṣfahānī here, and the Khurramīs known as Mazdaqiyya who venerated Mazdak as a prophet in (perhaps) Baghdad could have done so back in their villages too. But it was not as believers in the Mazdakite utopia that the Khurramīs kept their distinct identity through the centuries.

SHARING AS AN ISLAMIC IDEAL

What we can say is that visions of sharing property and/or women are extremely common in medieval Islam, especially Iran. How far it is a legacy of Mazdakism, as opposed to of Iranian practice in general, is hard to say, for Mazdak is never invoked, and the idea seems to be too widespread to be explained in terms of a single root. But however this may be, we first encounter it in a satirical vein in al-Jāḥiẓ's epistle on singing-girls. Al-Jāḥiẓ here has dealers in such girls declare that if it were not for the prohibitions laid down in the law we would have to accept the argument that nobody has any better right to women than anyone else and that 'they are simply like nosegays or apples that people pass around among themselves'.[24] The analogy is immediately recognizable: women are like flowers, fruits, cooked food, utensils, stairs for the landing, roads, ships, and other things held in common enjoyment, as the Maga had said; they were like the fragrant herbs/basil sprigs or flowers that people passed round to sniff at, as Abū Tammām and Qubāvī were later to put it, or like a well that anyone could drink from, as the Pārsīs were to say. (When Wāqid says that Jāvīdhān's widow gave Bābak a basil sprig, signifying that they were married, he may be crediting the widow with the same idea.)[25] But it is not, of course, as an argument for polyandry that al-Jāḥiẓ's slave-dealers use the comparison. What they are saying is rather that women are free for all in what Westerners call the state of nature; it is the revelation (or, in

[23] See Chapter 4, p. 81.
[24] Jāḥiẓ, 'Qiyān', 148 = *Singing Girls*, §9.
[25] Ibn al-Nadīm, 407 = II, 821.

Western terms, civilisation) that introduces restrictions: if it were not for the law, one would indeed have to accept that anyone could sleep with them; there would not be any jealousy if it were not for the legal prohibitions, they claim. They continue with the comment that if one did accept this argument, one would also have to accept that 'the man with a number of them should limit himself to one and distribute the rest to those close to him (*al-muqarrabīn*)'. In other words, sharing meant equal distribution of an informal kind: as a man would pass his nosegay to others sitting next to him, so he should hand over his spare women to them, if he had more than one. If it were not for the law this would be how people behaved. But for the law they would be Mazdakites, it would seem. Whether al-Jāḥiẓ means us to be reminded of Mazdak or not, he presents the argument as one that every educated person could be expected to know.

The idea turns up in many other reports, usually in a sectarian context. Al-Qummī reports of the ʿAlid Shīʿite Mukhammisa, adherents of Abū 'l-Khaṭṭāb, that they held all prophets, messengers, and kings, including those of the Persians, to be different manifestations of Muḥammad, who was God, and that they held marriage to be meaningless, except in the sense of solidarity with the believing brothers. In other words they devalued the family to make their sect the primary organisation of its members; the sectarian community *was* their family. Like al-Malaṭī's Daylamī Qarāmiṭa they thought of their new family as a unit within which women were shared: women were like a basil sprig (*rayḥāna*), the Mukhammisa said, one plucks it when one wants it, and after smelling it one greets one's brother with it.[26] In the east Abū Muṭīʿ al-Nasafī (d. 318/930) mentions a sect called the Ḥisbiyya who argued similarly, but only with reference to property: they held that the world is shared equally between the servants because God says that 'the believers are brothers' (Q 49:10). Since no brother received more than another of the father's inheritance, it was unlawful (*bāṭil*) to accumulate things, to regard them as private property, and to deny others a share.[27] It is not that humans are brothers, only that the believers are, but among believers everything was shared. Another sect, the Ghīriyya, held that Muḥammad was actually a sage, not a messenger from God, and that he had composed the Qurʾān to assist people's livelihoods, i.e., by establishing laws that facilitated the accumulation of private property, trade, and social life in general. That a revealed law was necessary for the proper functioning of social life was a

[26] Qummī, 58; cf. Halm, *Kosmologie und Heilslehre*, 159.
[27] Abū Muṭīʿ, '*Radd*', 104.

well-known view, and one assumes the Ghīriyya also to approve of its social utility even though they did not hold it to be revealed; but the continuation says that they held property to belong to everyone by law (*shar'an*). The text is so corrupt that one hardly dares to trust it on this point.[28] The idea that fundamentally everything is shared certainly persisted, however. The poet Niẓāmī (d. *c.* 600/1200), who came from Azerbaijan and held, like the Khurammīs, that it was wrong to inflict harm on living beings, imagined a community in which property was distributed equally and everybody would help a friend in need, being satisfied with necessities; Alexander the Great encountered them towards the end of his life.[29] Sharing with others when you do well was old Iranian religion, as a Zagros villager said in the 1970s.[30]

As far as women were concerned, the Ghīriyya only held it legitimate for men to look at them, but Abū 'l-Mu'īn al-Nasafī (d. 508/1114) mentions people who held that God had created both humans and property free for all (*mubāḥ*), and that anyone who needed property or a woman could help himself, for when Adam and Eve died their descendants inherited their property equally.[31] This is the argument that al-Malaṭī credits to Mazdak, but al-Nasafī does not suggest that these people were Mazdakites or Khurramīs. In the *Haftād u sih millat*, probably composed in eighth or ninth/fourteenth or fifteenth-century Tabrīz, a group called the Fushāriyya similarly say that the world and its property are shared among the children of Adam, nicely adding as good Muslims that men are entitled to twice the share of women.[32] The same work also mentions a group called the Shumrākhiyya, one of several sects with classical names and wholly unclassical beliefs in this work. They said that 'women are the basil sprigs of the world, nothing is wrong with anyone sleeping with them without marriage or a witness (to the contract)', explained in Persian as meaning that the world is like meadows or gardens, and beautiful women are like basil growing in it, basil is for smelling, and so you may sleep with anyone, whether relatives or not, any woman who offers herself to you is your property, and there is no need for a marriage contract.[33] It sounds like much the same view of sexual relations as that defended with reference

28 Abū Muṭī', '*Radd*', 111.
29 See the references in Crone, *Medieval Islamic Political Thought*, 329, 356.
30 Loeffler, *Islam in Practice*, 78.
31 Abū 'l-Mu'īn, *Baḥr*, 309.
32 Mashkūr, *Haftād u sih millat*, 27 (no. 9).
33 Mashkūr, *Haftād u sih millat*, 76f. (no. 72).

to marriage in an earlier life in the *Tabṣirat al-ʿawāmm*.[34] James Buckingham, who came to Baghdad in 1816, met an Afghan dervish who believed in God but not in any revealed religion and who practised what amounts to the doctrine of the Shumrākhiyya together with his friends. The women he felt free to sleep with were just for pleasure: it was boys that he truly loved, Platonically.[35]

When Sufis saw themselves as perfected to the point of no longer being bound by the law it was usually ritual worship that they saw as falling away, but we have already encountered 'Sprituals' (*rūḥāniyyūn*) to whom it was the legal barriers around women and property that vanished; they might achieve such love of God, they said, that they could steal, drink wine, and engage in forbidden sexual relations, on the grounds that a friend (i.e., God, the owner of everything) does not withhold his property from his friend. They were also known to Abū 'l-Muʿīn al-Nasafī, presumably on the basis of Khushaysh:[36] when the servant reached the utmost limit of love it became lawful for him to sleep with other people's wives and slave-girls because women were God's slave-girls and a friend does not deny his friend anything. Here they add that women are like basil sprigs that they are free to smell, which Abū 'l-Muʿīn must have imported from another context.[37] From Abū 'l-Muʿīn the argument passed to the Ottoman empire, where tenth/sixteenth-century polemicists imputed it to the Ṣafavids.[38] The *Haftād u sih millat* has a group called the Bakriyya who said that he who becomes learned is freed from the duty of ritual worship, and the more learned he becomes the greater a share he acquires in other people's property. Anybody who stopped him taking what he needed from people's property was a wrongdoer (*ẓālim*), for this was the reward for the hard slog of acquiring learning, and if he and his likes spent their lives acquiring money instead, the world would become ignorant and the legal sciences (*ʿulūm sharʿiyya*) would be lost. The scholars were the upholders of the Muḥammadan religion (*dīn-i Muḥammadī*) and it was incumbent on the community to reward them.[39] What is so interesting is that it is legal

[34] See Chapter 17, pp. 432ff.

[35] See El-Rouayheb, 'Heresy and Sufism', 377f.; Buckingham, *Travels*, I, 80, 84f., partly cited by El-Rouayheb, who drew my attention to the passage.

[36] Malaṭī, 73; Abū 'l-Muʿīn, *Baḥr*, 358.

[37] Malaṭī, 74; Abū 'l-Muʿīn, *Baḥr*, 360. A Ḥabībiyya also figures in Mashkūr, *Haftād u sih millat*, 28 (no. 12), but the reference is only to the end of ritual worship here.

[38] Eberhard, *Osmanische Polemik*, 92f. (My thanks to Michael Cook for reminding me of this work.)

[39] Mashkūr, *Haftād u sih millat*, 37 (no. 27). They have nothing in common with the classical Bakriyya.

scholars who say all this, not Sufis: they see the property they are taking as a kind of tax, collected by self-help rather than the authorities. They are not likely to have been scholars of a distinguished kind, however. The *Haftād u sih millat* shares with the *Tabṣirat al-ʿawāmm* the feature of being written by a man of limited learning, and if the former work seems to take us to a village setting in its account of reincarnation, the latter often conveys the impression of arguing against scholars and Sufis of the type who flourished in his own semi-educated circles. The Sufis in question shared some of their ideas with the Ḥurūfīs. The latter too, or some of them, held that they could help themselves to other people's property, but they did so as *ahl al-janna* in a world in which all non-believers had lost their legal protection.[40] In practice, of course, there may not have been much to distinguish between them.

[40] Browne, 'Some Notes', 75f.

IV

CONCLUSION

19

Iranian Religion versus Islam and Inside It

To most early Muslims religion of the Zoroastrian type was an abomination. This was so whether it was Persian or regional Zoroastrianism that they were confronted with. As far as the idea of sharing women and property is concerned this is hardly surprising, but why were they so opposed to the metaphysical doctrines? They were soon to be influenced by them themselves, and the result was not always deemed heretical.

There can be no doubt that the Muslims disliked Zoroastrianism for the fundamental reason that it was not monotheist. Some might object that Zoroastrianism can also be characterised as monotheist. This may well be true today;[1] in some sense it may even have been true at the time of the Muslim conquest of Iran. But there is a big difference between monotheism of the biblical type, in which a jealous God prohibits the worship of other deities, eventually denying their existence altogether, and pagan monotheism or monism, in which the many gods are seen as emanations, hypostatised attributes or manifestations of the One rather than as his rivals. (By 'pagan' here I simply mean not Jewish, Christian, or Islamic, without pejorative connotations; by 'monotheism' I henceforth mean that of the biblical type.) Pagan monists often renounce the attempt to describe the highest God, declaring the ultimate reality behind everything, the absolute (*brahman* in Indian parlance), to be so categorically different from our world that our minds lack the ability to conceptualise it. Since such a reality is also beyond worship, the believers direct their attention to lesser emanations or manifestations of God who function as intermediaries between the divine and the human worlds; it is thanks to these intermediaries that there can be communication between the two otherwise incompatible networks.

[1] When the *Bundahišn* was first published in the nineteenth century some Zoroastrians were apparently surprised by its dualist cosmogony (Sheffield, 'The *Wizigerd ī Dēnīg*', 186).

In practice the God beyond conceptualisation thus coexists with anthropomorphic deities, sometimes to the point that he himself is virtually forgotten. Regional Zoroastrianism was a religion of this type.

In addition, Zoroastrians and Muslims operated with radically different metaphysical maps. To the Zoroastrians the divine was both transcendent and immanent. God had made the world out of his own selfhood, from the substance of light; the divine fire, light, or spirit permeated the world, extending from the highest realm to the fire in the room. But it was only half of reality. The other was darkness, rising from the lowest depths to the darkness in the room. Light and darkness met in the middle, where they were locked in combat, but they were fundamentally different realities. To the Muslims, by contrast, it was God and the creation that were fundamentally different realities. God created the world out of nothing, not out of himself, and he was not present in it; the fire in the room was at best a symbol of the divine realm, not a sample of it. As Peter Berger observes, monotheism is secularising.[2] It concentrates all divinity in a being outside the cosmos and thereby drains everything else of it; it disenchants the world by removing the supernatural and all the awe that it inspires from the things around us and vesting them instead in a supra-mundane power. This power is conceived as a king who is known to us from his commands. The cosmic order or natural law that pagans would see as the highest manifestation of the true and right is brushed aside in favour of positive law, the edicts of the sovereign: just as nature ceases to be 'full of gods' (in Thales' words) so it ceases to be normative. In principle the edicts of the transcendent king are the only interface between the divine and the human worlds: God is represented by his law and nothing else, piety lies in obedience. In practice there are always exceptions. Even the Wahhābīs venerate the Black Stone and envisage the *ḥaram* as sacred. But within limits that vary from case to case strict monotheists deny that there can be divinity in any physical substance. Accordingly they reject sacred persons, places, and objects as idolatrous and take a hostile view of the rich array of images, pictures, dolls, music, wine, play-acting, and other make-believe characteristic of religions in which the sacred is allowed to leak. Strict monotheism is puritanism, a type of religion familiar from some forms of Judaism and Christianity (Syriac Christianity included), and above all from Islam.[3]

[2] Berger, *Sacred Canopy*, 113ff.

[3] The contrasting outlooks are brilliantly portrayed, in a manner hostile to puritanism, in Bergman's film *Fanny and Alexander*, in which a woman from the world of make-believe marries a bishop trying to empty the world of all but the divine command.

The confrontation between Islam and Zoroastrianism did not involve images, as did that between Islam and Christianity. Rather, the main issues were divine immanence, human reincarnation, the God beyond conceptualisation, and the problem of evil.

Immanence

To the monotheists the dividing-line between God and the world he had created was replicated in the barriers between the angelic, human, animal, vegetable, and inanimate realms of which the created world was composed. Each realm was separated from the others by ontological gulfs that nothing could cross; the divine could not become human, humans could not turn into angels or animals, nor could animals turn into gods or something else again. Christianity is a religion based on belief in a single, startling, exception to this rule, and there is also a minor exception in the Qur'ān, in which humans are transformed into monkeys and pigs. But in principle the categories were hermetically sealed.[4] The sealed categories were stacked on top of each other as parallel worlds: God and his subordinates, the angels, ruled humans and their subordinates, the animals. Humans represented God here on earth and stood in the same relationship to everything in it as God to the rest of the universe. The monotheists were nothing if not chauvinists on behalf of the human species. But humans were special as God's favourites, not by sharing in his essence. They were just his slaves.

To the Zoroastrians, by contrast, the fundamental cleavage was vertical rather than horizontal. Divinity ran through this world, aligning half of it with the realm of eternal light and the other half with demons and darkness. Like their counterparts in Greece and India the Zoroastrians were accordingly more given to seeing the categories of creation as forming a hierarchy, a great chain of being, as the Neoplatonists called it, a ladder in which divinity, light, spirit, or mind was present in increasingly diluted and/or polluted forms as one moved down the steps. They did not close the categories either. In Iranian as in Greek and Indian mythology gods may appear as animals or humans; humans may be born divine or achieve that status; they may also turn into animals, plants, or even inanimate things in diverse ways, including reincarnation.[5] Humans may still be perceived as special; in fact, it is difficult for them not to see themselves as such. But they

[4] For all this see Cook, 'Ibn Qutayba and the Monkeys', 69.
[5] Cf. Cook, 'Ibn Qutayba and the Monkeys', 70ff.

were special by virtue of their position in the spectrum of divinity, light, and spirit – the Zoroastrians saw them as having originated at the very top of the spectrum as divine beings;[6] and they formed part of a cosmos in which everything circulated by natural processes. Seeing themselves as part of the natural world rather than its rulers, all Zoroastrians had a marked concern for the purity of the elements and the welfare of the beneficent animals, and some Zoroastrians extended the concern to all living beings or even inanimate things, as we have seen. To monotheists, by contrast, the superiority of mankind entitled them to use other animals as their slaves, as they say in an Ismaili fable in which their claim is challenged.[7] On paper pagans score higher than monotheists in terms of modern environmentalism and concerns about animal rights. (Needless to say their behaviour in practice is a different matter.)

To Muslims the idea that humans might become divine violated the fundamental distinction between God and his creation which is stressed time and time again in the Qur'ān. It was also bad for public order: people who claim to be divine, or to have divine powers, expect others to obey them and so disrupt the normal distribution of power. It is probably for this reason that the Persian Zoroastrians did not endorse the idea of divine incarnation and that the Muslims themselves quickly declared Muḥammad to have been the last prophet. But something more fundamental was at stake as well.

What the Muslims were defending in their confrontation with adherents of the great chain of being was a vision of all humans as fundamentally equal, distinguished in the eyes of God by their moral efforts alone, and ruled by God alone, meaning by his command as executed by humans rather than by other humans as the latter saw fit. The conception of the divine and human worlds as parallel was fundamental to this. All humans were equal because they were all made of the same substance and sealed off from the categories above and below them. Even the head of state was no exception: God was represented by the caliph, who ruled mankind just as mankind ruled the animals, but he was made of the same stuff as all other human beings. By contrast, those who cast Adam, the ʿAlids, or the ʿAbbāsids as divine turned the parallel realms into a ladder along which humans could ascend or descend, traversing the ontological gulfs. Divinity

[6] Cf. Crone, 'Pre-existence in Iran' (summarised in Chapter 15, pp. 368f.). There are also statements about the superiority of man over all creatures in the Pahlavi books (e.g. *Dk*, IX, 24:19, IX, 29:4 in Molé, *Culte*, 197), but they sound biblically inspired.

[7] 'Case of the animals'; cf. Crone, *Medieval Islamic Political Thought*, 355f.

now flowed from God to a lower category of being, engendering humans who were different from the rest in terms of their substance, not simply obedience to the law. The ontological barrier thus appeared within the category of humans, dividing mankind into two or more radically unlike classes. The Imāmīs who held the imams to be made of special stuff (such as the light of God's greatness and special clay) usually also held that the Imāmīs themselves were different in substance from the rest of mankind.[8] The more strongly the imams were separated from the rest of mankind the more tempting it was to see divinity, light, and/or purity as running through the entire creation in increasingly diluted or polluted forms; and where humans are ranked in terms of the divinity or purity of their substance the outcome is a caste system: it is no longer the whole of mankind that forms a single egalitarian realm, but rather each caste or estate within it that does so. Zoroastrian Iran did not quite have a caste system, but it did operate with a division of mankind into three or four endogamous estates reminiscent of the Indian *varṇas*; it did accept that kings were made of different stuff from the rest of mankind; and it did have a category of unclean persons – in effect, untouchables.[9] To the early Muslims Zoroastrian inegalitarianism was deeply repugnant (though of course their attitudes changed).[10]

Reincarnation

If the leakage of the divine into the human realm engendered a caste-like hierarchy, the doctrine of reincarnation reinforced it. For just as the divinity, light, or purity running through the creation in progressively weaker forms assigned different moral worth to human beings on the basis of a substance imputed to them by outsiders, so the doctrine of reincarnation conflated moral worth and external factors such as power, health, and wealth: people were what they were thanks to their moral score in their previous lives; if they were poor, ill, and afflicted by misfortune it was because they deserved it. Reincarnation offers a better justification of

[8] Kohlberg, 'Imam and Community', 31.

[9] Those who handled funerals and mourning lived separately outside the city walls; they were known as 'unclean persons' and would ring bells to warn of their presence when they entered the city (thus the *Chou-shu* in Miller, *Accounts of Western Nations*, 15). For those who handled dead animals see al-Mas'ūdī cited earlier in Chapter 13, p. 259. For the four estates see Marlow, *Hierarchy and Egalitarianism*, 69f.

[10] Cf. Marlow, *Hierarchy and Egalitarianism*, esp. ch. 3; Crone, *Medieval Islamic Political Thought*, 334f.

evil than anything monotheism can offer, but it does so by blaming the victim and sanctifying the status quo.

The doctrine of reincarnation had the further drawback, from the Muslim point of view, of de-emphasising the great moral importance of our lives. Muslims had one single chance to secure eternal bliss or eternal damnation: the test was short and the stakes were exceedingly high. Believers in reincarnation, by contrast, could try again and again and so take a more nonchalant view of human life. This is why Mazdak could argue that he was doing sinners a favour by killing them. In principle it was wrong to kill any living being in his view, but one life was not of great consequence to those who had many, and so it was best to help them along to a better one than they could have achieved as his opponents. The Qur'ān has an account that skirts perilously close to the same idea: a mysterious companion of Moses kills a youth to prevent him from saddening his parents by the unbelief he would have adopted if he had been allowed to live (the favour is to the parents rather than the victim: Q 18:74, 80). But the killer is a supernatural figure, and the story is meant to explain the mysterious ways in which God's justice manifests itself, not to allow humans to kill real or potential sinners. It shares with the doctrine of reincarnation the feature of justifying evil by blaming the victim: those who die young are those who would have been bad and whom we would rather be rid of anyway. But it takes the sanctity of human life for granted.

The deity beyond conceptualisation

Muslims did not deny that God is utterly beyond human understanding; if he had not revealed himself to mankind it would not have been possible to say anything about him. But he *had* revealed himself to mankind, describing himself in human language in the Qur'ān, and on that basis one could indeed know him. Those who denied this were guilty of *taʿṭīl*, stripping God of all his attributes, the opposite extreme of *tajsīm* and *tashbīh*, envisaging him as endowed with the physical and psychological features of human beings. Since it was impossible to form a relationship of love or obedience with a being beyond conceptualisation, *taʿṭīl* was often used to mean something close to atheism. Most of those who were accused of it compensated for the unknowable nature of God by postulating intermediary divinities and so evidently were not atheists, but there does seem to have been some truth to the charge in connection with the Dahrīs and others who refused the intermediaries in favour of a scientific universe.

A God beyond conceptualisation goes very well with a scientific universe – that is, a universe conceived as impersonal and run by its own amoral laws rather than a providential deity. To monotheists this was unacceptable. To them the world had been created for a moral purpose and arranged for the convenience of human beings, as a small and short-lived setting for their efforts to win eternal bliss. God had created the sea so that they could sail on it, the heavenly bodies so that they could tell time, and so on; everything had been established with their welfare in mind, and everything that happened was a coded message to them, warning them, punishing them, and occasionally rewarding them. A modern reader does not quite know whether to marvel at the innocence or the arrogance of all this, but it had the advantage of making the cosmos a place in which humans could feel at home, and it also underlined the moral importance of human acts: all natural events – or at least all unusual ones – were comments on their performance.

The universe of the Persian Zoroastrians was not fundamentally different. Though it had not been created for the sake of human beings, but rather to combat evil, it certainly had a moral purpose and it was of relatively short duration too, indeed very short as far as the phase involving human beings in the material world was concerned; and a happy end was guaranteed. But other Zoroastrians were prone to eliminating the moral purpose, as we have seen, by holding the world to have been created by accident, or to be one out of many worlds, or to be destined to last for an enormously long time, with countless cycles on the way, or as without a beginning or end altogether. Some apparently even denied that salvation or release was possible.

The problem of evil

A deity beyond conceptualisation has the advantage of making it unproblematic that the world is full of evil: God is good, but the world is dominated by other powers. The Zoroastrians explained these other powers as demons from an evil realm that had always existed, or that had emerged out of the realm of goodness and light, or that had emerged together with light as its twin, the one being the obverse of the other. However they had come to exist, the mixture of the two realms explained both the beauties of this world and its all-too-obvious shortcomings. This explanation gave the Zoroastrians a trump card that monotheists had trouble matching, for there is no way of resolving (as opposed to masking) the contradiction between an all-powerful deity who is entirely good and the manifest presence of evil in the world that he alone has created. Dualism was the single most successful doctrinal export of Iran in antiquity.

Dualism endowed the Zoroastrians with a thorough dislike of the Jewish, Christian, and Muslim deity, who allowed his own creatures to be misled by evil and punished them for what he should have prevented, inflicting pain and punishment on them for ever after. They were probably the first to identify the Old Testament God with Ahriman, as we know the Marcionites later to have done. The monotheists felt the attractions of the Zoroastrian solution, but they stopped short of splitting the universe into two autonomous realms, resisting even the mitigated form in which the evil realm emerged from the divine pleroma. To mainstream Christians the devil was a subordinate being, not a power in his own right; the many Gnostics who disagreed were deemed to be beyond the pale (if not for that reason alone). Mitigated or otherwise, dualism encouraged the view that human beings were innocent victims of evil forces rather than moral agents responsible for their own fate, the view that monotheists tended to favour. It also fostered a proliferation of divine and demonic figures, the appearance of gradations of purity and light even within the human realm, and belief in divine immanence and human reincarnation. In short, it undermined the fundamental distinction between God and the world on which the monotheist outlook rested.

THE LATE ANTIQUE TREND

Monotheism had been on the rise for some six hundred years in the Near East and Mediterranean by the time the Muslims arrived, having triumphed on the Graeco-Roman side of the border and being well on the way to repeating its success on the Iranian side; but it had also been affected by paganisation, in the sense of a tendency for the divine to split into an inaccessible reality and mediator figures, and for the divine to flow into this world in other forms as well. This trend is observable in Judaism in Philo (d. AD 50) and has been postulated for the Jews of Mesopotamia as well in this book. It is certainly observable in Christianity itself, based as it is on a great violation of the ontological rules. But the trend intensified thereafter. By the third century we see it in Judaism, Christianity, Greek and Aramaic paganism, and Gnosticism, and it still had not abated by the sixth. Everywhere there was a tendency for mediator figures to appear (and also for demons to proliferate). The heavens – an elaborate multi-storeyed structure by now – had come to be filled with a huge number of angels. Many were just heavenly messengers without names, or on the contrary mere names for powers that magicians wished to invoke, but others were identified with attributes of God's such as his wisdom, spirit or reason/speech (*logos*), or with deified humans such as Enoch or Jesus, and still others with former deities such as Apollo, Shamash, Bel, Nanai, or the gods of the *mushrikūn* in the Qur'ān. The mediators in heaven generated counterparts on earth in the form of divine incarnations, emissaries, and other recipients of divine power such as messiahs, apostles, wonder-workers, spirit-bearers, and saints: these last were beginning to populate the heavens too. Angels and saints, strictly separated from God himself, were the two forms in which Christians (and eventually Muslims) found it possible to accept a whole swarm of intermediaries between God and mankind.

Intermediaries proliferated on earth because people hankered for direct contact with the divine, by touch, sight, or feeling, or by angelification or deification of themselves (magical recipes were available). Accounts of heavenly journeys were hugely popular across the entire religious spectrum. Everywhere people hoped to ascend to the celestial realm, at least for immortal life there after death, but preferably also for a visit in the here and now; and heavenly journeys usually involved face-to-face encounters not only with angels, but also with God himself. The guest in heaven would also be initiated into divine secrets such as the workings of the cosmos, past and future events, or the meaning of all things, and great power might be obtained on such journeys if one could accomplish them (but they were difficult and dangerous). The dominant mood was one of wanting out of this world. Above all, people wanted to get out of their own bodies, which kept them captive in the circumscribed world of mundane needs, chaining them to a daily treadmill with its endless demands, and holding them hostage to the powers that be, whose control depended entirely on all the physical misery they could inflict on their inferiors. If God was a supremely wise, just, and merciful king, the denizens of the demonic realm had all the characteristics of oppressive rulers: evil beings were powers and archons; evil was stupid, evil invaded, evil thought that goodness was weak, as Mani said.[11] Christians such as Origen, Evagrius, or Stephen Bar Sudaili, pagans such as Plotinus and other Neoplatonists, most Gnostics, some Jews, and many or most Zoroastrians agreed that humans had originated without bodies, or rather with subtle bodies of

[11] See Bennett, 'Primordial Space', 77n.; cf. Chapter 16, p. 373, where a member of the Sasanian establishment dismisses Mani as a useless weakling for his pacifism.

light, in the presence of God or as part of him. All shared the conviction that the human soul or spirit was consubstantial with God, so that the divine was to be found within themselves – the fundamental conviction behind the new brand of religiosity that was emerging (known to us as mysticism). All hoped to return to God, and all wanted to start the journey back to him straightaway, to partake of the life of divinity in the here and now. So they set to work on the one part of the world over which they had complete control, their own selves, embarking on asceticism, mortification of the soul, spiritual development, and contemplation with a view to purifying themselves. Or they contented themselves with seeking out those in whom the divine was present, hoping to benefit from their touch or their miracles; or they opted for mastery by magic. The interface with the divine had become very broad. God's command was only a small part of it, in so far as it figured at all.

Islam should probably be seen as a hostile response to this development, a reformation in the sense of reimposition of the puritan pattern, a closing up of the holes through which the divine had been steadily leaking for so long. Thanks to the conquests the trend was in fact reversed. Islam was also to provide a permanent counterbalance to it, for its puritan core was preserved by the traditionalists and periodically reasserted itself from time to time thereafter (as indeed it is doing today). But inevitably the Muslims came to be affected by the paganising trend themselves. Among the beliefs that resurfaced were those of regional Zoroastrianism.

The traditionalist chain

The process whereby the austere Qurʾānic universe came to be populated by a profusion of mediator figures, in heaven as on earth, is vastly too complicated for summary in a mere epilogue, involving as it does the entire legacy of antiquity and a millennium of sifting and remoulding by thinkers spread over an area from the Atlantic to the Indus. Ideas of Iranian (or Irano-Mesopotamian) origin stand out here and there, however.

'I was sent from the best generations (*min khayri qurūn*) of humans, one generation after another (*qarnan fa-qarnan*), until I was sent from the generation that I was in', Muḥammad says in a tradition cited by Ibn Saʿd (d. 230/845). Goldziher was surely right that this is a reformulation of the old doctrine of the pre-existing prophet who appears under different names in one age after the other until he 'comes upon his own time', as the

Pseudo-Clementines put it.[12] But the meaning has drastically changed. Muḥammad was sent *from* the best generation in every age, not to them: the interest is in his noble birth throughout the ages; his primordial substance (or, as we might say, his DNA) had been transmitted through noble ancestors until it emerged in him. He is not envisaged as making cyclical appearances, nor is he identified as a pre-existing or divine being. 'I was carried by the best generations (*ḥumiltu min khayri qurūn*) of mankind, generation upon generation, until I emerged from the generation I was from', as a variant version says, clarifying that Muḥammad was only born once.[13] 'One generation after another (*qarnan fa-qarnan*) they transmitted you (*tanāsakhūka*)', as the Shīʿite poet Kumayt (d. 126/734) said;[14] here only the verb *tanāsakha* hints at the different conceptions in the background. Or again, in sura 26 the Messenger is told to put his trust in God who sees *taqallubaka fī 'l-sājidīn*, 'your turning about among those prostrating themselves' (Q 26:219). A tradition attributed to Ibn ʿAbbās apparently took it to mean 'your *moving* about *in* those prostrating themselves', for it glosses the passage with the words 'from prophet to prophet until he (God) despatched you as a prophet'. Here too the reference is to the transmission of Muḥammad's primordial substance in the loins of his ancestors (those prostrating themselves). According to Fakhr al-Dīn al-Rāzī, the Rāfiḍa (presumably meaning the Imāmīs) would adduce the passage in conjunction with the tradition 'I never ceased being transmitted from the loins of pure [men] to the wombs of pure [women]' in order to prove that all Muḥammad's ancestors were believers;[15] al-Qummī identifies the ancestors as prophets.[16] The Sufi al-Sulamī also mentions the view that the Qur'ānic passage referred to Muḥammad's moving about in the loins of the prophets and messengers, and al-Suyūṭī transmits the same from the Sufi Abū Nuʿaym.[17]

In effect, then, here we see the doctrine of periodic incarnation of the same pre-existing prophet being rejected. There was no room for it in traditionalist forms of Islam.

[12] Ibn Saʿd, I/1, 5 (I, 25); Goldziher, 'Neuplatonische und gnostische Elemente', 340; Chapter 14, p. 289.

[13] Rubin, 'Pre-existence and light', 72n., with other references.

[14] Cited in Goldziher, 'Neuplatonische und gnostische Elemente', 335 (from Kumayt's *Hāshimiyyāt*, III:39f.).

[15] Rāzī, *Tafsīr*, XXIII, 174.

[16] Qummī, *Tafsīr*, II, p. 100.

[17] Sulamī, *Tafsīr*, II, 83; Suyūṭī, *Durr*, VI, 332.

Shīʿite imams and mahdis

Ideas of Iranian origin surfaced early in Shīʿism – often, but by no means always, to be rejected there too. They appear as early as the revolt of al-Mukhtār (in the form of *rajʿa*), as we have seen, thereafter in *ghuluww* of the type examined in this book, and also in the enormous contribution of *ghuluww* (whether resisted or welcomed) to the formation of Imāmism.[18] Most obviously, there is a persistent tendency for the imams to be deified.[19] But the very idea of being led by superhuman imams in the first place belongs in the Iranian thought world studied in this book, for the Shīʿite imams are not humans like any others even when they are not divine. Divinely protected against error and 'made to understand' (*mufahham*), they hold the entire cosmos together. 'The earth will never be without an imam', as numerous Imāmī traditions attributed to Jaʿfar al-Ṣādiq declare. Some versions identify the imam as simply a righteous ruler or as a scholar who can teach the law, but others say that without an imam the earth would subside as if in a landslide, or well up like the sea, and destroy mankind;[20] and this was the role that required the imam to stay alive even after he had disappeared and could neither rule nor teach any more. The imam is the man unlike all others who links the world to the divine realm that nourishes and maintains it, the man who was either a king or a prophet endowed with special *khwarra* in the past; he is the pole or axis (*quṭb*), as people said with reference to a similar idea developed in Sufism. 'If no *pīr* remained in the world, then neither the earth nor time would remain stable. The *pīr* exists even now, but has gone into hiding', as the poet ʿAṭṭār (d. 618/1221) said; 'how could the world stand firm without the pole (*quṭb*)? It is thanks to the pivot that the mill-stone stays in place. If the pole of the world were not firmly in the ground, how could the heavens turn?'[21] The philosopher al-Suhrawardī (d. 587/1191) also held that there had to be a man unlike any other: the earth could never be without a 'divine sage (*ḥakīm ilāhī*) who is deeply engaged in both divine investigation (*al-taʾalluh*) and philosophical investigation (*al-baḥth*)'.

[18] For Imamism as theosophy bordering on *ghuluww* see Amir-Moezzi, *Religion discrète* (English tr. as *Spirituality of Shiʿi Islam*) and other studies by the same author listed there.

[19] Cf. Amir-Moezzi, *Religion discrète*, ch. 3. Ashʿarī knew Twelver Shīʿites who held the holy spirit to have been in all the twelve imams by *tanāsukh* (Ashʿarī, 14), and the Shaykhīs (followed by the Bābīs) skirted perilously close to the idea (Smith, *Babi and Bahaʾi Religions*, 11).

[20] Kulīnī, *Kāfī*, I, 178f. (*Kitāb al-ḥujja*, bāb 5).

[21] Landolt, "ʿAṭṭār, Sufism and Ismailism', 4.

Ideally this *imām muta'allih* would rule openly as the *khalīfa* (of God, like Adam), receiving knowledge from God by direct instruction (*talaqqī*, the method by which Adam was taught the names); but he might also be hidden, in which case he was the person that the multitude (*kāffa*) would call the *quṭb*, he said.[22] The Ismailis of the Seljuq and Mongol periods similarly observed of the *qā'im-i qiyāmat* (lord of the resurrection) that he was eternally present, now in hiding and now manifest, and they too identified him with the *quṭb* of the multitude, more precisely the Sunnīs.[23] The *qā'im* was a manifestation (*maẓhar*) of the supreme word (*kalima-yi a'lā*) in human form, as the Nizārīs explained when the imam Muḥammad II assumed the role of *qā'im* himself at Alamūt.[24]

Ismailism, both Nizārī and other, is well known to be indebted to the religious universe of pre-Islamic Iran, above all thanks to Corbin.[25] Several examples have also been noted in the course of this book. In the Ismaili reformulation neither the prophets who appear on a cyclical basis nor the imams who maintain the community in between are divine any more, nor are the prophets different manifestations of the same pre-existing being; they merely bring different versions of the same message. But both chains still culminate in the mahdi (the 'lord of the resurrection'), and the mahdi did repeatedly prove to be divine when he came, as he did in Qarmaṭī Baḥrayn, in Fāṭimid Egypt (according to the Iranian missionaries who identified al-Ḥākim as him),[26] and again among the Nizārīs at Alamūt. Whether thanks to Ismailism or Sufism, or both (or neither, as opposed to the underlying Iranian conception), similar ideas later appeared in Bābī Imāmism. Here the prophets became manifestations of a single being once again: the Bāb claimed to have been Noah in the time of Noah, Abraham in the time of Abraham, and so forth down to Muḥammad and 'Alī, and he would be all future manifestations too.[27] He saw himself as a manifestation of the divine *logos*, as Smith comments, and as the mahdi as well.[28]

[22] Suhrawardī, *Ḥikmat al-ishrāq*, introd., 5; cf. Landolt, ''Aṭṭār, Sufism and Ismailism', 5; Landolt, 'Suhrawardī between Philosophy, Sufism and Ismailism', 17f.

[23] Landolt, ''Aṭṭār, Sufism and Ismailism', 5, citing *Haft bāb-i Bābā Sayyidnā* and Ṭūsī, *Taṣawwurāt*.

[24] Landolt, ''Aṭṭār, Sufism and Ismailism', 7 (with a parallel in 'Aṭṭār again); Hodgson, *Assassins*, 163f.

[25] See his *Cyclical Time* and other publications. I have used him less than I had hoped because his evidence on the pre-Islamic Iranian side tends to be weak even when his insights are right.

[26] Halm, *Reich*, 231ff. = 258ff.; Daftary, *The Ismā'īlīs*, 186ff.

[27] Cited in Goldziher, 'Neuplatonische und gnostische Elemente', 339.

[28] Smith, *Babi and Baha'i Religions*, 24.

SUFISM

Iranian ideas also surfaced early in Sufism, and it was here that they found their most comfortable home. We encounter them among the so-called Muʿtazilite Sufis mentioned earlier in the chapter on reincarnation. All flourished in the mid-third/ninth century. The best known of them, Aḥmad b. Khābiṭ (or Ḥā'iṭ) was actually a Christian by background, not a Zoroastrian, and this could be true of his colleagues, Ibn Mānūsh (or Bānūsh etc.), and Faḍl al-Ḥadathī as well, but the Iranian environment to which they had been exposed is clear in their teaching. Both Ibn Khābiṭ and Ibn Mānūsh believed in pre-existence along lines ultimately derived from Origen, but they departed from their Christian roots by claiming that all things were endowed with reason (*nāṭiqa*): this was true of animals, birds, stones, and mountains, and even heaven and earth. All animals formed nations much like those of humans, Ibn Khābiṭ said, and all in his view received prophets from their own kind. He allegedly held social animals such as ants, lice, elephants, monkeys, pigs, and pigeons to score high in terms of knowledge, intelligence, and prophecy, but there were mental processes in stones as well. All the 'ignorant Sufis', as al-Jāḥiẓ called them, believed animate and inanimate things alike to be endowed with minds and, needless to say, some (perhaps all) of them also believed in reincarnation. Some animal species – bats, sparrow-hawks, and frogs among them – counted as obedient and rewarded, presumably for merits in previous lives, while others, such as scorpions, snakes, kites, ravens, dogs, and the like, were being punished for disobedience. The inability of stones to speak was also punishment.[29] These Sufis operated with only one divine incarnation, however, that of Christ, or so at least in the case of Ibn Khābiṭ.

Sufis did not normally operate with the concept of divine incarnation at all. When they achieved unity with the divine they did so by self-annihilation, not through a divine being descending to take up abode in them, and the process was not normally seen as having anything to do with *ḥulūl*. In trying to annihilate their selves they were aiming to recover the original unity of God and the soul or spirit, lost in primordial existence: before the creation the soul had lived and moved in God, they said, now it was in exile pining to return, like a moaning dove that has lost its mate, like a falcon summoned by the fowler's whistle, like snow melting and rising to

[29] Van Ess, *TG*, III, 430–45; Crone, 'Jāḥiẓ on *aṣḥāb al-jahālāt*'; Crone, 'Pre-existence in Iran'.

the sky.[30] In less poetic language the aim was to eliminate the duality of subject and object, to get beyond the bondage of unreal selfhood and be reunited with the infinite being.[31] Successful Sufis might say outrageous things that sounded like self-deification: 'Is anyone here but God?', as Bāyazīd is supposed to have replied when somebody asked whether he was there; 'Only God is in the cowl', as Abū Saʿīd b. Abī 'l-Khayr is said to have declared.[32] The idea was not that the human being had been deified, however, but rather that it had lost its separate existence. As Nicholson observes, there was no infusion of the divine essence.[33]

Yet the old incarnationist model sometimes surfaces. Al-Ḥallāj, who followed the long tradition of seeing both Adam and Jesus as divine incarnations, also saw himself as filled with the divine spirit: 'Your spirit is mingled with my spirit even as wine is mingled with pure water,' he said to God, giving this as his explanation for his identity with him. 'I am he whom I love, and he whom I love is I: we are two spiriṭs dwelling in one body.'[34] He is credited with a poem praising God for revealing himself in his creation in the shape of someone who ate and drank so that the creation could see him with their own eyes;[35] and according to al-Baghdādī, he preached that whoever renounced worldly pleasures would rise in rank until he was purified of his humanity; at that point the divine spirit would take up abode in him as it did in Jesus.[36] When he exclaimed, 'I am Reality,' he did not apparently mean the same as did Bāyazīd.

Al-Ḥallāj's conception was exceptional, however, and accordingly the term *ḥulūl* came to be used with a different emphasis in connection with Sufism. Whereas before it had stood for the incarnation of the divine in a human being, now it usually meant the presence of God in anything. Al-Ashʿarī mentions Sufi ascetics (*nussāk*), presumably in Iraq, who believed in *ḥulūl*, explaining that in their view God could dwell in the bodies of living beings (*al-ashkhāṣ*), including humans and wild animals,

[30] Nicholson, *Mystics of Islam*, 116. Its age notwithstanding, this is one of the most attractive accounts of Sufi sentiments, beautifully written and studded with well-chosen examples from the poetry that Nicholson excelled at translating.

[31] Nicholson, *Mystics of Islam*, 83, 85f.

[32] Nicholson, *Mystics of Islam*, 159; Radtke, 'How can Man Reach the Mystical Union?', 165n.

[33] Nicholson, *Mystics of Islam*, 157.

[34] Nicholson, *Mystics of Islam*, 150f., cf. 154. I have slightly modernised his translation.

[35] Andrae, *Person Muhammeds*, 296, citing ʿArīb, *Ṣila*, 104. Andrae relates the conception to the Hellenistic (here meaning late antique) *theios anthrōpos*.

[36] Baghdādī, *Farq*, 248.

and that when they saw something beautiful they would say that perhaps God was dwelling in it or him.[37] Al-Bīrūnī mentions Sufi believers in *ḥulūl*, presumably in Iran, who held it possible for God to be immanent in the entire world – in animals, trees, and inanimate things alike: they called this 'the universal manifestation' (*al-ẓuhūr al-kullī*).[38] There is no sense in these passages of a divine being having descended to take up abode in these things or beings. Rather, God, though utterly transcendent, is also present in the physical world, sometimes completely hidden and sometimes almost visible – as in the case of beautiful beings. God takes the place of the light or spirit that suffused the world in the Khurramī and (in a suffering vein) the Manichaean vision, and *ḥulūl* has come to mean immanence. There is a similar combination of transcendence and immanence in Transoxania, in the theology of Jahm b. Ṣafwān and/or his followers.[39]

The idea that God was present in beautiful people was also espoused by Abū Hulmān, a Damascene of Persian descent mentioned by al-Baghdādī, who seems to have been his contemporary: it was because of Adam's beauty (*ḥusn taqwīm*, cf. Q 95:4) that God ordered Iblīs to worship him, he said.[40] Thereafter the view is widely encountered, above all in connection with the question of the legality of gazing on beautiful boys.[41] 'In the beauty of those with a beautiful face every moment I have openly seen God's essence. The beauty of God which was concealed behind the curtain appeared to me unexpectedly from the cheek of the beloved,' as a Persian poet said.[42] 'I was blamed by mankind for loving beauty, and they do not know my aim ... By means of it I attained the unbounded,' as an eleventh/seventeenth-century Damascene Sufi declared.[43] To Fakhr al-Dīn 'Iraqī (d. 686/1287), who died intoxicated by beauty, God was in every form and showed his face in a thousand mirrors in every moment, 'sometimes in the garment of Eve, sometimes in the form of Adam'.[44] God was submerged behind everything and erupted to the surface in certain types of being: 'My beloved pervades existence and appears in white and black, and in Christians and Jews, and in dogs and cats,' as an unknown poet

[37] Ash'arī, 13f. Cf. Maqdisī, V, 148, where the Sufi belief in *ḥulūl* turns out to be the conviction that he dwells between the cheeks of beardless boys.

[38] Bīrūnī, *Hind*, 44/29 = I, 57f.

[39] van Ess, *TG*, II, 501f.; cf. Crone, 'Jāḥiẓ on *aṣḥāb al-jahālāt*'.

[40] Baghdādī, *Farq*, 245f.

[41] Ritter, *Ocean*, ch. 26; cf. also El-Rouayheb, *Before Homosexuality*, 111ff.

[42] Ritter, *Ocean*, 496. The poem is attributed to Aḥmad Jām (d. 536/1142), but taken by Ritter to be much later.

[43] Ayyūb al-'Adawī al-Khalwatī (d. 1660) in El-Rouayheb, *Before Homosexuality*, 99.

[44] Ritter, *Ocean*, 498.

said.[45] But it was above all in beautiful people, in prophets, and in other captivating persons that the divine shone through.

Ḥulūl usually went with reincarnation, typically into human and animal forms alike. Both al-Sarrāj and al-Sulamī condemned the belief that the spirit migrates from body to body as an error,[46] but as al-Bīrūnī explained, it came naturally to those who believed in 'universal manifestation'.[47] In fact, the connection between divine immanence or incarnation and reincarnation was so close that sometimes it is hard to tell the difference between them. In a poem attributed to Rūmī the beloved appears in different clothes, sometimes old, sometimes young, as Noah, Abraham, Joseph, Moses, Jesus, in the form of an Arab, i.e., Muḥammad, and as the sword of 'Alī; indeed, it was he who said, 'I am the truth,' not al-Ḥallāj, as ignorant people think. 'This is not *tanāsukh*', the poet assures us.[48] It certainly sounds like *tanāsukh* in the old sense of successive incarnation of the divine, but he is probably right. Rūmī himself has a poem declaring that 'The Turk you saw that year on his raid is the one who this year rose like an Arab. That friend is the same even if the clothing has changed ... the wine is the same even though the glass has changed ... O people who imagine that those firebrands are dead ... even if the sun has gone down, in setting it has not perished, that moon of light rose up from another constellation.'[49] Rūmī is speaking of his friend, Shams-i Tabrīzī: it is he who has set as the sun and risen again as a moon of light. Here too the formulation is suggestive of *tanāsukh*, now in the sense of reincarnation, but this is not what Rūmī has in mind. His point is rather that ultimately all the special people you see are mere façades for the divine. It is the divine that keeps reappearing, not the particular person called Shams as distinct from all the others. 'Flesh and blood are simply the means that the One employs to appear to you in shadowy forms,' as Ḥāfiẓ said.[50] The old concepts of divine and human *tanāsukh* have been transposed into a higher key.

In a slightly different vein 'Abd al-Karīm al-Jīlī (d. 811–20/1408–17) tells us that the *quṭb* on whom the spheres of existence revolve appears in

45 Quoted with disapproval by al-Shirbīnī in El-Rouayheb, 'Heresy and Sufism', 377.
46 Radtke, 'How can Man Reach the Mystical Union?', 187f.
47 Bīrūnī, *Hind*, 44/29 = I, 58 (where Sachau translates *arwāḥ* as souls). Bīrūnī here refers to reincarnation as *ḥulūl al-arwāḥ bi'l-taraddud*, perhaps meant to bring out the close connection between belief in divine immanence and in reincarnation also noted by al-Shahrastānī (I, 133 = I, 511).
48 Shafī'ī Kadkanī, *Guzīda-yi ghazaliyyāt*, 573f. (mansūba, no. 1).
49 Shafī'ī Kadkanī, *Guzīda-yi ghazaliyyāt*, no. 115.
50 Ritter, *Ocean*, 502.

every age, bearing the name suitable to his 'clothes' (*libās*) and that he, al-Jīlī, had actually met him in the form of his own shaykh. 'Do not imagine that my words contain any tincture of the doctrine of metempsychosis, God forbid!' he exclaims.[51] There is in fact no hint of a spirit or soul moving from one body to another. In return, there is a strong hint of *tanāsukh* in the old sense of periodic incarnation of the divine, for the *quṭb* in al-Jīlī's work is the Perfect Man, who is both the *ḥaqīqa Muḥammadiyya* (the pre-existing, archetypal form of Muḥammad) and the angel Rūḥ, created by God from his own light and, as Nicholson remarks, essentially God regarded as the Holy Spirit or as the First Intelligence.[52] Other Sufis too identified Muḥammad's true reality (*ḥaqīqa*) with the holy spirit, or with world reason (*'aql*), and saw it as capable of manifesting itself in human beings in the here and now.[53] But al-Jīlī does not envisage the Rūḥ as descending to take up abode in a pre-existing human being, for he defends his doctrine on the grounds that 'the Prophet is able to assume whichever form he wishes, and the Sunna declares that in every age he assumes the form of the most perfect man'.[54] It sounds like a new form of *qalb*. If it was no longer quite divine incarnation, it led to the same expectation of complete surrender to another human being: 'if you perceive mystically that the *ḥaqīqa* of Muḥammad is displayed in any human form, you must ... regard its owner with no less reverence than you would show to our Lord Muḥammad'.[55]

Sufis did not usually deny the existence of heaven and hell after the fashion of the Khurramīs, but rather brushed them aside as irrelevant. 'I do not say that paradise and hell are non-existent, but I say they are nothing to me', as Abū 'l-Ḥasan Kharaqānī put it, explaining that both were created objects and there was no room for such things where he was.[56] 'Ayn al-Quḍāt al-Hamadhānī said that paradise and hell were within you.[57] Sufis still say that in India, to the disapproval of those who take their cue from the Wahhābīs.[58]

[51] Jīlī in Nicholson, *Studies*, 106.
[52] Nicholson, *Studies*, 110, 111n.; cf. also *EIr.*, s.v. 'Ensān-e kāmel' (Bowering).
[53] Cf. Andrae, *Person Muhammeds*, 322ff., 333ff.
[54] Jīlī in Nicholson, *Studies*, 106.
[55] Jīlī in Nicholson, *Studies*, 105 (I have modified the transliteration).
[56] Nicholson, *Mystics of Islam*, 87.
[57] Arberry, *A Sufi Martyr*, 15.
[58] Dalrymple, *Nine Lives*, 135, 141.

Sufi literature abounds in tales of pity shown to animals. Some Sufis were vegetarians,[59] and Sufis behaved with courtesy towards all of God's creatures, including animals, according to Abū Manṣūr al-Iṣfahānī (d.418/1027).[60] 'Universal charity is one of the fruits of pantheism', as Nicholson remarks, citing a story about Bisṭām travelling hundreds of miles to return some ants he had inadvertently removed from their home.[61] Al-Suhrawardī, who was born in Azerbaijan a mere thirteen years after the apostasy of the Pārsīs, shares with them the features of being a vegetarian, of believing in – or at least flirting with – reincarnation, and of elevating figures from the Persian past to sacred status. (The Ahl-i Ḥaqq in their turn identify him with one of the seven divine beings known as the Haftawāna.)[62] The poet Niẓāmī, also a native of Azerbaijan, disliked the use of violence against living beings of any kind.[63] Tolerance of other faiths was characteristic of Sufis too. But in so far as there is continuity with old Iranian beliefs here, the Sufis have once more transposed them into a higher key. For one thing, they did not reserve the right to hack down their enemies under conditions of revolt; and for another, their understanding that nothing but God exists meant that the diversity of positive religion was not so much tolerated as transcended. 'Not until every mosque beneath the sun lies ruined will our holy work be done; and never will true Musalmān appear till faith and infidelity are one', as Abū Saʿīd b. Abī 'l-Khayr famously said.[64] Ḥāfiẓ's poetry is full of statements of this kind. True monotheism was above communities, boundaries, and doctrinal policing; all these things belonged to the world of duality that the Sufi had left behind.

Finally, the antinomianism of which Sufis were so often accused belongs partly under the same heading, for ritual worship and conventional morality were also part of the world the Sufi had left behind, most obviously when they did so as *qalandar*s, 'ferocious-looking, extremely poor, mendicant vagrant dervishes with a conspicuous disrespect for canonical religious obligations and a strong penchant for intoxicants', as

59 Karamustafa, *Sufism*, 41, 155, 158.

60 Karamustafa, *Sufism*, 92.

61 Nicholson, *Mystics of Islam*, 108f.

62 Hodgson, *Venture of Islam*, II, 236; Landolt, 'Suhrawardī between Philosophy, Sufism and Ismailism'; Edmonds, 'Beliefs and Practices', 92f.

63 Bürgel, 'The Idea of Non-Violence'; cf. Crone, *Medieval Islamic Political Thought*, 329, for his quasi-Mazdakite utopian community in the *Iqbālnāma*.

64 Nicholson, *Mystics of Islam*, 90.

van Bruinessen nicely characterises them.[65] The flower that anyone can smell without detracting from it turns up in accounts of Sufi groups, as has been seen.[66] But even without engaging in forbidden acts Sufis were prone to antinomianism in the simple sense of regarding ritual worship as irrelevant. 'Truth lies within. If this is so, then why bother going to the mosque or the temple?', as a modern Baul puts it. The Bauls also say that the divine is everywhere, even in rocks.[67]

Iranian ideas are only one of the many materials that went into the making of Sufism: Gnosticism, Neoplatonism, and Christian mysticism are among the rest. In fact, Sufism is one of the best examples of the Muslim transformation of a confusing mass of cultural material of the most diverse origin into a high cultural edifice of orderly construction, high complexity, and great beauty. But the Iranian elements are visible in the outcome, especially in Iran itself, and the point to note here is that they come from regional forms of Zoroastrianism, not from that of Fārs.

THE NEW SECTS

Unlike Persian Zoroastrianism Islam was never a religion for the elite alone, let alone one imposed through the equivalent of a Ministry of Guidance. Whether by colonisation, missionary activity, or other means the Muslims gradually converted the countryside from the bottom up. But, as one would expect, the old beliefs died hard and in some areas they survived for a long time – in a few cases until today – reformulated in a more Islamic form as the doctrines of new sects. The sects in question appeared in the Jibāl, Mesopotamia, and Anatolia, but not, surprisingly, in eastern Iran. The explanation of this oddity seems to be that the religious tradition of eastern Iran was transplanted to Anatolia when massive numbers of eastern Iranians migrated there, uprooted by the Mongol invasions. Rūmī, born in Balkh, was one of them; so too was Hajji Bektash, a Khurāsānī, as well as numerous anonymous *qalandar*s: they appeared in Khurāsān in the late fourth/tenth or early fifth/eleventh century and expanded westwards from there to Anatolia, Syria, and Egypt.[68] As the Iranians left and the Turks moved in, the religious character of what is now Central Asia changed. There is no Turkmen version of

[65] Van Bruinessen, 'Haji Bektash', 66; cf. Karamustafa, *God's Unruly Friends*; Shafīʿī Kadkanī, *Qalandariyya*.
[66] Cf. the reference given in Chapter 18, p. 448.
[67] Dalrymple, *Nine Lives*, 237.
[68] Van Bruinessen, 'Haji Bektash', 66; cf. Karamustafa, *God's Unruly Friends*, 1–4.

Bektashism, nor any Uzbek mystical pantheism, and the nearest we get to an eastern version of the new sects that appeared in western Iran is the Rawshaniyya, an Afghan movement, not a Turkish one.[69] This makes it somewhat unlikely that Mélikoff was right in her tireless advocacy of Turkish origins for the *ghuluww* of eastern Anatolia and western Iran, the indisputable presence of numerous Turkish elements in it notwithstanding.[70]

Ahl-i Ḥaqq

Of the new groups, several had been through an ʿAlid Shīʿite phase – in some cases perhaps Ismaili – but all were the outcome of the activities of Sufis. The closest restatement of old Iranian beliefs is that of the Ahl-i Ḥaqq, also known as Ali Ilahis, Yārisān, and Kākāʾīs, whose beliefs seem to come in almost as many forms as Khurramism itself.[71] Their founder was one Isḥāq, a *sayyid* later known as Sultan (or Soltan) Sahak (or Sohak), who seems to have flourished in the ninth/fifteenth century[72] and who counts as a divine incarnation and inaugurator of a cycle. Apart from that, nothing is known about their formation. They are led by sayyids believed to descend from Sultan Sahak and his later manifestations, from whom they have inherited a divine quality that makes them greatly venerated.[73]

To the Ahl-i Ḥaqq, God is offstage. They rarely even talk about him, though he does figure in their cosmological myth as the divine essence (*dhāt al-ḥaqq*) who created a pearl at the beginning of all things, or was hidden in it; this pearl floated in the primordial ocean, and from these waters everything emerged.[74] (No Khurramī parallel to this is recorded, but ʿAbd al-Karīm al-Jīlī had a related cosmology.)[75] God is too radically unlike the bounded world in which we live for even the angels and the prophets to be able to know him. Out of pity, however, he will unite his

[69] Cf. Andreyev, 'The Rawshaniyya', esp. 311ff.

[70] E.g. Mélikofff, *Sur les traces*, esp. 21. For a more reasonable estimate see van Bruinessen, 'When Haji Bektash still bore the Name', 121.

[71] For a sense of the social and political factors underlying the differences in the sacred texts see Mir-Hosseini, 'Inner Truth and Outer History'.

[72] Mokri, 'Étude d'un titre de propriété', 314ff.

[73] Mir-Hosseini, 'Breaking the Seal', 180f.; cf. Stead, 'Ali Ilahi Sect', 186f.

[74] The story is told slightly differently in Mokri, 'Kalām gourani', 240f.; Edmonds, 'Beliefs and Practices', 90; Ivanow, *Truth-Worshippers*, 102ff.; Minorsky, *Notes*, 25; and other sources.

[75] Cf. Nicholson, *Studies*, 122.

spirit to a bodily frame in every era and cycle so that the creatures can behold him, in a pale reflection of his real being;[76] of one such incarnation, Sultan Sahak, we are told that he derived from the sun, which is a mere atom of power that has separated from the light of the self-manifestation of God.[77]

The Ahl-i Ḥaqq owe their name of Ali Ilahis to the fact that they have a history of identifying the lesser divine being that incarnates itself as ʿAlī, sometimes called 'the light of God' and sometimes simply identified with the sun.[78] Thus a poet who probably lived in the eleventh/seventeenth century or later says: 'From the time the world began ʿAlī was; from (when) the face of the earth and time existed, ʿAlī was', and affirms that 'the object of angels' worship which became Adam came from ʿAlī: Adam was like a *qibla* and the object of worship was Adam'. In other words, just as humans worship God through the Kaʿba to which they turn in prayer, so the angels were worshipping ʿAlī when they prostrated to Adam. 'Both Moses and Jesus, and also Khiḍr and Ilyās as well as Ṣāliḥ the prophet and David, were ʿAlī': all were incarnations of the same celestial being.[79] ʿAlī came in the body of the father of mankind, i.e., Adam; he was present in Noah's Ark; later he assumed the clothing of Abraham in the fire, and thereafter that of Moses when he spoke with God, as we are told in another eleventh/seventeenth-century work,[80] which here sounds like the poem attributed to Rūmī, and this time there is no ambiguity about the doctrine of *tanāsukh*: the core of Ahl-i Ḥaqq beliefs is the doctrine of successive divine incarnation that we first met in accounts of the Book of Elchasai. Like some of their predecessors the Ahl-i Ḥaqq defended their doctrine with reference to Gabriel's appearance in the body of Diḥya al-Kalbī.[81]

The Ṣafavid leader Shāh Ismāʿīl was also an Ali Ilahi. He called his devotees Ahl-i Ḥaqq and identified ʿAlī as the divine light (*nūr-i ilāhī*), a

[76] *Dabistān*, I, 265 = II, 452. Minorsky's conjecture (*Notes*, 67f.) that the ʿAlī Allāhiyān described in this work were a kind of Ismailis in the borderland between Iran and India is implausible. It is true that it locates them in the *Kūhistān-i mashriq*, an area populated by Ismailis. But it also makes them neighbours of Yezidis, likewise placed in eastern Kūhistān, and it is a little hard to believe that there were Ali Ilahis living in the neighbourhood of Yezidis in more than one place. The Yezidis cannot be explained away as Khārijites (their ruler boasts of Umayyad descent), and the beliefs described for the ʿAlī Allāhiyān are those of the Ahl-i Ḥaqq back in the days when their alternative name made sense (*Dabistān*, I, 242, 257, 265 = II, 356, 417, 451).

[77] Edmonds, 'Beliefs and Practices', 100.

[78] *Dabistān*, I., 267 = II, 458; Minorsky, *Notes*, 74, 91.

[79] Shafīʿī Kadkanī, *Qalandariyya*, 58, noting the continuity with Khurramī doctrine.

[80] *Dabistān*, I, 266 = II, 455.

[81] *Dabistān*, I, 266 = II, 453 (the translators hilariously misunderstand Diḥya's name), 455.

manifestation of God (*maẓhar-i ḥaqq*) and Reality (*ḥaqq*): God descended to show himself to men in him; one of God's names was ʿAlī, but he had thousands of them. The divine substance that manifested itself as ʿAlī was now manifest in him, Ismāʿīl; Adam had put on new clothes, his body was God's house; and people should prostrate to him.[82] Like al-Muqannaʿ and the mahdi of the Khurdanaye Ismāʿīl was veiled.[83] His followers shared their goods, presumably in the sense that anybody could use what others had in their possession, in line with the household model attested for al-Malaṭī's extremists (but without the sexual component, though Ottoman polemicists accused them of sharing women too).[84] They wore red caps (whence their name Qizilbāsh) and used red banners, perhaps by way of continuity with the Muḥammira of the region.[85] They were certainly devotees of Abū Muslim and avid listeners to the *Abū Muslimnāma*. This epic is found in both Sunnī and Shīʿite versions, and the Shīʿite versions are largely or wholly Imāmī, so the work is not a product of Muslimism, but it does have some resonances of it. There are versions in which Ibn al-Ḥanafiyya appears, and though there is no transfer of the imamate to him, or from him to the ʿAbbāsids or Abū Muslim, the latter does receive his letter of appointment (*firmān*) from Ibrāhīm al-Imām, who sprouts green wings and flies to heaven when he is executed much as Abū Muslim himself was believed to have done when he was killed.[86]

The ʿAlī-orientated religion represented by the Ṣafavids and the eleventh/seventeenth-century testimonia no longer seems to be dominant among the Ahl-i Ḥaqq, however. Stead, writing in 1932, reported that ʿAlī did not occupy as important a place in their thought as Binyāmīn (Gabriel, also identified with Christ) and Dāwūd, two angels who figure among God's seven companions in the creation myth, whereas ʿAlī is absent.[87] Van Bruinessen, writing in 1995, notes that among the Guran ʿAlī is surpassed in importance by Sultan Sahak, the last (or latest) great divine incarnation. They do not deny ʿAlī's divinity: on the contrary, they consider all sects that deify him as brothers-in-faith. But it is Sultan Sahak who has appeared time

[82] Minorsky, 'Poetry of Shāh Ismāʿīl I', 1026a; cf. also Arjomand, 'Rise of Shah Esmāʿil', 46–8.

[83] Aubin, 'L'avènement des Safavides', 39 (testimonia referring to 1504–7). His veil is visible under his turban, drawn away from his face, in the woodcut reproduced in Savory, *Iran under the Safavids*, 28.

[84] Aubin, 'L'avènement des Safavides', 43; Chapter 13, p. 268; Eberhard, *Osmanische Polemik*, 92f.

[85] Minorsky, 'Poetry of Shāh Ismāʿīl', 1027a.

[86] Mélikoff, *Abū Muslim*, 63, 116–19 (the parallel with Abū Muslim is noted at 118n.); Babayan, *Mystics*, 126f.

[87] Stead, 'The Ali Ilahi Sect', 184f.; Mokri, 'Kalām gourani', 241f.; cf. also Minorsky, *Notes*, 26.

and again, not ʿAlī, and ʿAlī just brought *sharīʿat* (law); another incarnation brought *ṭarīqat* (the Sufi way), and yet another *maʿrifat* (spiritual knowledge), but it was Sultan Sahak incarnate as himself who brought *ḥaqīqat*, the full spiritual truth.[88]

Whoever he is, the divine figure always incarnates himself together with a number of angels: four according to some, six or seven according to others. Each incarnation opens a new cycle in which the same key events will recur: the angel who was killed as Ḥusayn had previously been killed as Yaḥyā (John the Baptist), and was later killed again as Faḍl (Allāh, the founder of Ḥurūfism).[89] Traditionally the number of cycles was given as seven, capped by the appearance of the *ṣāḥib al-zamān*, the (divine) Lord of Time who would unite the world under his sway.[90] But the Guran apparently operate with four cycles, each cycle representing an improvement over its predecessor, and the deity is also said to have incarnated itself 1,001 times, or so many times that 'we cannot remember the names of all of them'.[91] According to Mokri the incarnation is always by birth to a virgin; van Bruinessen's Guran merely said that there had to be at least one virgin birth in every cycle.[92] Either way, the divinity usually enters the virgin by her mouth, as a sun ray or ash, powder, or a seed, and she mostly gives birth by her mouth too, along lines familiar from the followers of Ibn Muʿāwiya, who held ʿAlī to have taken Muḥammad's divinity from the latter's mouth and put it in his own.[93] The three posthumous sons of Zoroaster who preside over the last three millennia of human history in Persian Zoroastrianism are also born of virgins, impregnated by bathing in the lake in which Zoroaster's sperm is stored. In all three cases the virgin birth differs from that of Christianity in that the divinity enters

[88] Van Bruinessen, 'When Haji Bektash still bore the Name', 118, 123; Edmonds, 'Beliefs and Practices', 93.

[89] Van Bruinessen, 'When Haji Bektash still bore the Name', 119f., 124, 125. The divine being who incarnates himself with six or seven angels is reproducing the pattern of Ohrmazd and the *amahraspands*, who are seven along including Ohrmazd himself. One could read this as further evidence that there were Zoroastrians who saw Ohrmazd as an incarnation or manifestation of the highest deity (cf. pp. 322f.).

[90] Minorsky, *Notes*, 42f.; cf. 63, where nomadic Ahl-i Ḥaqq in Mazandarān that he met in 1902 are awaiting a new *ẓuhūr*.

[91] Edmonds, 'Beliefs and Practices', 91; Ivanow, *Truth-Worshippers*, 8; cf. Stead, 'Ali Ilahi Sect', 188, on how they will include all the great men they have ever heard of in the incarnations.

[92] Mokri, 'L'idée de l'incarnation', 497; van Bruinessen, 'When Haji Bektash still bore the Name', 125.

[93] Mokri, 'L'idée de l'incarnation', 497; van Bruinessen, 'When Haji Bektash still bore the Name', 125, 127 and n.23, 129; Chapter 11, p. 224. Differently the Ahl-i Ḥaqq known to Edmonds, 'Beliefs and Practices', 93, where the virgin dreams she is pregnant and wakes up to find a child in her arms and dies soon afterwards.

the human recipient as a physical substance, that it does so by natural processes, and that no celestial being informs the virgin of what is going on.

The child is sometimes the deity himself and sometimes one of the angels, and there are two possible ways in which it can relate to the human body. One is that the divine or angelic spirit puts on the body as one puts on a piece of clothing, by which the informants mean that the body has no independent existence: like that assumed by humans when they are reincarnated it exists only for purposes of allowing the being in question to exist on earth. This is called *ẓuhūr* (manifestation). The other way is that the spirit dwells as a guest in a body that is already endowed with a soul: this is called *ḥulūl*, and it is *ḥulūl* in the old sense in which we have encountered it time and again in this book, the indwelling of a deity in a human being endowed with independent existence. The human in question is known as the *khudā* (or *shāh*) *mihmān*, 'God-receiver/host'. This was also what Nestorius was accused of calling Jesus, and what the Chinese called the Sogdians who impressed them with their ecstatic feats in China.[94] The visit could be permanent or temporary. If the celestial being visited the host temporarily he would experience ecstacy and illumination.[95]

According to the sacred words (*kalām*) preserved in Gurani, the spirit of God created celestial companions in his image and then made a pact with them: they were to go into the material world, where they would suffer all the problems intrinsic to the human condition and where they had to put on 1,001 clothes (i.e., bodies); if they sinned they would be punished by additional incarnations, even as animals.[96] This is easily recognised as the Zoroastrian myth of the descent of the *fravahr*s which explains how humans came to find themselves in the material world: it postulated that humans had accepted embodiment in agreement with God, whereas Christian believers in pre-existence always said that they had been put in bodies for their sins.[97] The account current in Persian Zoroastrianism does not include reincarnation of course, but, as we have seen, that of the Mu'tazilite Sufis did combine belief in pre-existence with reincarnation, and, as one would expect, so do the Ahl-i Ḥaqq. Apparently there were

[94] Cf. Chapter 5, p. 101 ('heaven-god host') and Chapter 15, p. 302 ('God-receiver').

[95] Mokri, 'L'idée de l'incarnation', 497f.; van Bruinessen, 'When Haji Bektash still bore the Name', 130 (his Guran informants could not agree whether *ḥulūl* was temporary or permanent, but the stories they told illustrate both). For an ecstatic Ali Ilahi foaming at the mouth in India, immune to wounding by swords, see *Dabistān*, I, 267 = II, 458f.

[96] Mokri, 'Kalām gourani', 241, 249.

[97] Crone, 'Pre-Existence in Iran'.

versions that equated 1,001 incarnations with 50,000 years:[98] if so we have here a living form of the doctrine first attested for the followers of Ibn Muʿāwiya, according to whom God created seven Adams, each one of whom presided over a cycle of 50,000 years on earth. As will be remembered there were residues of this doctrine in an impeccably Imāmī Shīʿite village in the southern Zagros in the 1970s too.[99]

Van Bruinessen's Guran did not display much interest in the topic of reincarnation, or the afterlife altogether; but they admitted, when asked, that reincarnation as an animal was a possibility. In line with their formal acceptance of the doctrine of reincarnation they and other Ahl-i Ḥaqq denied the existence of paradise and hell, usually in the Sufi style: hell was in the heart; both paradise and hell were states of mind. Nonetheless, their texts speak of the Day of Judgement as well, and some combined the doctrines of reincarnation, Day of Judgement, and paradise and hell.[100] Finally it should be noted that some Ahl-i Ḥaqq held that it was forbidden to kill living beings: 'don't make your stomachs the cemeteries of animals', as ʿAlī had said according to them. When the Qur'ān permitted some animals to be killed it actually meant Abū Bakr, ʿUmar, ʿUthmān, and their followers.[101] To maltreat an ant, or even a mangy dog, was a sin; governments and their crimes and wars were sinful too. Nonetheless the Ahl-i Ḥaqq were not vegetarians, and animals were sacrificed. They were certainly antinomians, however, not in the sense of engaging in deliberate violation of the law or flouting sexual taboos, but rather in that of denying that the core of the religion was law. Ritual worship was not important in their view, and they interpreted the Qur'ān accordingly.[102]

The Ahl-i Ḥaqq have recently spawned a reform movement which recasts the sect as a Sufi order and brings it into closer alignment with Imāmī Shīʿism. Thanks to drastic changes wrought by modernity, the leaders of the reform movement have now presented themselves as the bearers of a universal message and seek recruits in the West. This has transformed the ancient doctrines and led to a break with the traditionalists who uphold the inherited views – Deifiers of ʿAlī and

98 Mir-Hosseini, 'Inner Truth and Outer History', 281; Mir-Hosseini, 'Breaking the Seal', 180.

99 Chapter 10, p. 210.

100 Van Bruinessen, 'When Haji Bektash still bore the Name', 132; Minorsky, *Notes*, 251ff.; id., 'Études', 98; Ivanow, *Truth-Worshippers*, 74; Edmonds, 'Beliefs and Practices', 90f.

101 *Dabistān*, I, 267.21 = II, 459; partly also in Minorsky, *Notes*, 75.

102 Edmonds, 'Beliefs and Practices', 91, 95ff.

Devil-worshippers, in the vocabulary of the second leader of the reform movement, – and this very same second leader has now been accepted as the last (or just the latest?) manifestation of the Divine Essence.[103] There may still be room for the likes of Elchasai in the modern world.

The Yezidis

The Yezidis of northern Iraq, Armenia, and Anatolia are closely related to the Ahl-i Ḥaqq, though they lack the Shīʿite element and indeed venerate the Umayyads. They were converted to Sufi Islam by Shaykh ʿAdī b. Musāfir (d. 685/1160f.), a Lebanese who settled in the Hakkari mountains after studying in Baghdad, and until quite recently they were brigands and robbers much like the Khurdanaye and Bābak's followers. Their saints include one Shaykh Bābik.[104]

Like the Ahl-i Ḥaqq they have a cosmological myth according to which the highest God created a pearl from his own pure light, from which everything emerged; they too operate with a succession of divine incarnations, though the concept is less prominent among them, and believe in human reincarnation (combining it with belief in heaven and hell); and they too think of time as cyclical, with some casting the inaugurator of each cycle as Adam.[105] Here as among the Ahl-i Ḥaqq, however, it seems more commonly to be the founder of the sect who is cast in that role. In poetry attributed to ʿAdī b. Musāfir the shaykh declares: 'I am the ʿAdī of yesterday, of the day before yesterday, of today, of the past, and of what is to come', affirming that 'I am the unique Shaykh; and it is I, myself, who created things'. He also declares that 'it is I who received a book, a book of good tidings. It came from my God, piercing the mountains' (cf. Q 7:143), i.e., he was Moses. 'I am the Syrian ʿAdī, the son of Musāfir. The compassionate God has favoured me by names,' as he also says, meaning the names under which he has incarnated himself: 'there is no God but I'.[106] He also informs us that 'all men of God have made *ṭawāf* around me, and, as for the Kaʿba, it comes to me in pilgrimage'; indeed, 'I was seated in the holy valley, on Mount Sinai ... the angels made *ṭawāf* around me'.[107]

[103] For this fascinating story see Mir-Hosseini, 'Breaking the Seal', 182ff. The author says 'the last' (191).

[104] Kreyenbroek, *Yezidism*, 2, 61, 103.

[105] Kreyenbroek, *Yezidism*, 37 (Christians only know history since the last Adam), 43, n.79, 147

[106] Kreyenbroek, *Yezidism*, 51.

[107] Kreyenbroek, *Yezidism*, 47.

In historical fact Shaykh ʿAdī may have been a perfectly orthodox Sufi, but this poetry sounds no more orthodox than that of Shāh Ismāʿīl.[108] It is true that very similar statements are made by other 'drunken' Sufis. A Bektashi poet, for example, describes the unfolding of Reality from before the creation until his own time as a journey accomplished by himself: he was alone with Reality in his oneness and he designed the world; he appeared in the material world as the elements, then as the prophets and saints, he became the rose that cried out to the nightingale (i.e., the human soul yearning for God); he rained down with the rain and grew as the grass to appear as Aḥmad, ʿAlī, and other the prophets and saints, and now praise is to God, he says, naming himself; 'I came, I went. They never knew my real self.'[109] Yet this man is probably not professing belief in divine incarnation or deifying himself. What he is describing is the unity of existence that stands revealed to the one who has overcome the self, who no longer perceives the world through the duality behind which Reality is normally veiled. His focus is on the higher being into which he has merged rather than the grandeur he has thereby acquired. It was by using the language of incarnation and reincarnation to describe the nature of ultimate reality rather than of humans that the Sufis transposed these doctrines into a higher key, much as they did with the themes of passionate love, infatuation, wine, and drunkenness. But the perspective could always be flipped back again, so that it was God who filled the human being rather than the human who disappeared in him. Shaykh ʿAdī certainly sounds as if he has flipped the perspective. In short, Sufism provided a new avenue to deification. Unlike the Ahl-i Ḥaqq, the Yezidis do not seem to think in terms of the divine spirit taking up abode in human beings, but they did not have to: Sufism allowed them to achieve the same result.

The Ḥurūfis

Shaykh ʿAdī, Hajji Bektash, Shaykh Isḥāq (later Sultan Sahak), and Shaykh Ṣafī, the founder of the Ṣafavid order, were all Sunnīs whose Sufism seems to have been perfectly orthodox by the standards of the day.[110] All four came as outsiders to the region in which they established themselves, and in all four cases the system of belief they brought was

[108] Cf. Minorsky, 'Poetry of Shāh Ismāʿīl I', esp. nos. 15, 18.
[109] Birge, *Bektashi Order*, 122ff.
[110] Kreyenbroek, *Yezidism*, 29; van Bruinessen, 'Haji Bektas', 67f.; *EI*², s.v. 'Ṣafawids', 766, col. 1.

transformed by the beliefs of the locals. The founders of the Ḥurūfī and Nuqṭavī movements, by contrast, were insiders who systematised local ideas, and their movements were heterodox from the start. The novelty of Faḍl Allāh Astarābādī (d. 796/1394), the founder of the Ḥurūfīs (who is recognised as an incarnation of Sultan Sahak by the Guran), lay in his systematic letter mysticism: everything was the word of God and the words are composed of letters, so the sum total of the letters (and their numerical value) was the total of the creative possibilities of God, and whoever mastered the science of the letters had the key to everything; in particular, man was the book of God, the living letters in which God manifested himself, being particularly present in beautiful faces; so God was within and full knowledge was deification.[111] (With the exception of the possibly Khurramī possibly Ismaili fragment attributed to Mazdak, no letter speculation is attested for the Khurramīs.) Though deification could be achieved by knowledge, however, Faḍl Allāh and/or his followers also operated with the familiar idea of an inaccessible deity (*kanz-i makhfī*, hidden treature) who incarnates himself in an adult endowed with independent existence. Thus a Ḥurūfī work composed in 810/1407f. declares that 'the being of the creation (*hast-i mawjūdāt*) through which things are maintained descended on the luminous inner self of Faḍl, lord of the universe' in 789/1387 in Tabrīz; the divine essence (*dhāt-i ḥaqq*) manifested itself (*ẓuhūr kard*) in Tabrīz, as it also said (using the word *ẓuhūr* in a sense that the Guran would have found inaccurate).[112] Faḍl Allāh was a manifestation of the deity (*maẓhar-i ulūhat*) and of the pre-eternal word (*maẓhar-i kalām-i qadīm*) as well as the mahdi, the messiah (*al-masīḥ*), the *qā'im* of the family of Muḥammad, and more besides.[113] The world – or rather the present cycle – consisted of three periods: one of prophethood, closed with Muḥammad; one of sainthood, closed by Faḍl Allāh; and one of divinity, when God was manifested in man. The third period was inaugurated by Faḍl Allāh.[114] According to a later Ḥurūfī work the number of cycles was infinite: each one was inaugurated and closed by the appearance of Adam and ended with the resurrection; and each one was absolutely identical with the next.[115] We are close to the world-view of the followers of Ibn Muʿāwiya here.

[111] Cf. Ritter, 'Anfänge der Ḥurūfisekte', 3ff.; *EI*², s. v. 'Ḥurūfiyya' (Bausani), cols. 4f.; Bashir, *Fazlallah*, ch. 4.

[112] Ritter, 'Anfänge der Ḥurūfisekte', 22, citing the *Kursīnāma*. For the hidden treasure see *EI*², s.v. 'Ḥurūfiyya'.

[113] Dihkhudā, *Lughatnāma*, s.v. 'Ḥurūfiyān' (477, col. 2).

[114] Mir-Kasimov, 'Deux textes', 204, 220ff.; Bashir, *Fazlallah*, 56.

[115] Mir-Kasimov, 'Deux textes', 219f., citing the *Maḥramnāma*.

Like the followers of ʿAbdallāh b. Muʿāwiya, the Ḥurūfīs called the eternal return *rajʿat*, but it is not clear that they believed in actual reincarnation.[116] Some of them did deny the doctrine of the resurrection, paradise, and hell. Indeed, some denied that there was any consciousness at all after death: the letters of which humans were composed would come apart as singles (*mufradāt*), and without composition there was no seeing, understanding, or pleasure.[117] Denials of life after death turn up among the Bektashis too;[118] and a small heresiography composed, probably, in Tabrīz in the eighth/fourteenth or ninth/fifteenth century also mentions heretics, simply called Malāḥida ('godless people'), who denied the afterlife on the grounds that human beings are ultimately composed of earth, wind, water, and fire: as long as their temper is balanced they are healthy, but when their temper is corrupted they perish in the ocean of nothingness and become nothing; restoring the non-existent is impossible: it will never, ever assume the form of existence again. They roundly rejected resurrection and denied the existence of paradise and hell.[119] Once again we see that divine immanence and materialism, *ghuluww* and Dahrism, went hand in hand in the mountains of western Iran. The materialism formed part of an utterly religious style of thinking. The Ḥurūfīs who denied that there was consciousness after death argued that paradise was knowledge and hell ignorance, and that since they knew the science of the letters all things were now paradise for them; further, since there were no obligations in paradise, there were no ritual duties or forbidden things for them any more; everything was now lawful to them.[120] Those who denied the existence of the afterlife and those who believed in the resurrection thus reached the same conclusion: paradise had come, the *ʿārif* was free to help himself to whatever was within reach, and he should strive to remove the rest from the hands of others. Like al-Muqannaʿ's followers they saw themselves as having inherited the earth. Though the leader of the sect at the time did his best to suppress such views they were prevalent in Rūm, Tabrīz, Shirwān, Gīlān, Luristān, Iraq, and Khurāsān.[121]

[116] Browne, 'Some Notes' 71f.
[117] Ritter, 'Anfänge der Ḥurūfīsekte', 44, 48.
[118] Birge, *Bektashi Order*, 87.
[119] Mashkūr, *Haftād u sih millat*, no. 33.
[120] Ritter, 'Anfänge der Ḥurūfīsekte', 44f.; Browne, 'Some Notes', 73f., both citing the *Istiwānāma*.
[121] Browne, 'Some Notes', 74ff., citing the *Istiwānāma*; cf. Bashir, *Fazlallah*, 94.

The Nuqṭavīs

The founder of the Nuqṭavīs was Maḥmūd Pasīkhānī (d. 831/1427f), a native of Gīlān who broke away from the Ḥurūfī movement. He retired to the borderland between Arrān and Azerbaijan, where Bābak had once had his centre. Faḍl Allāh was then residing at Shirwān, while the Ṣafavids were at Ardabīl, so the old type of religion could fairly be said to have returned to dominance in the region, though only the Ṣafavids presided over a cult organisation reminiscent of Bābak's. Later Maḥmūd's followers spread all over Iran, and when Shāh ʿAbbās turned against them many of them fled to India, where they were described by a sympathetic Zoroastrian under the name of Wāḥidiyya; in Lār, where Pietro della Valle became friendly with them in 1621, they called themselves Ahl al-Taḥqīq.[122]

Where Faḍl Allāh Astarābādī saw hidden significance in the letters of the alphabet Maḥmūd Pasīkhānī based his system on points, perhaps meaning the four points used as codes for the four elements in Nuqṭavī writings.[123] His science of points was in any case a theory about the elements, and this is where his interest lies in the present context. Unlike the other sectarians he was an outright pantheist, not a panentheist: God and the world were co-extensive, for God was the four elements, and nothing but the four elements existed. According to ʿAbd al-Karīm al-Jīlī, the physicists who worshipped the four elementary qualities – hot, cold, dry, and wet – were really worshipping the four essential attributes of God – life, knowledge, power, and will;[124] and Maḥmūd, a contemporary of his, seems to have agreed, finding proof of God's identity with the four elements in the fact that there were four letters in God's name.[125] Again, the materialism was not meant in an anti-religious vein. On the contrary, the aim of life was deification, most easily achieved by celibate males (sg. *wāḥid*), presumably by Sufi exercises. Matter was seen as having evolved thanks to a power inherent in the combination of the elements through the mineral, vegetable, animal, and human realms, producing ever greater perfection and purity and culminating first in Muḥammad and

[122] *Dabistān*, I, 273ff. = III, 12ff.; Pietro della Valle, *Viaggi*, II, 328ff, cf. Gurney, 'Pietro della Valle', 112f. Pietro wrongly makes Maḥmūd a native of Babylonia.

[123] Cf. Algar, 'Nuḳtawiyya'; Langarūdī, *Junbishhā*, 257f., both with the alternative explanation offered in the *Dabistān-i madhāhib*, I, 274, that their name referred to the point constituted by earth, from which the other three elements derived.

[124] Nicholson, *Studies*, 131, 133.

[125] Pietro della Valle, *Viaggi*, II, 328.

thereafter in Maḥmūd.[126] Both were divine: 'Whatever you are, you are Maḥmūd, and Maḥmūd is water, earth, air, and fire, and they are one (*wāḥid*), and one is Adam/human, and Adam is Muḥammad, and Muḥammad is the truth, and the truth is God, and God is one, and one is water, earth, air and fire,' as one can read in their virtually unintelligible writings.[127] Maḥmūd did not think in terms of divine beings descending to take up abode in human beings.

Time was cyclical and associated with the coming of prophets. In his *Mīzān*, Maḥmūd described a great cycle of 64,000 years, which he probably saw as endlessly repeated; he certainly had followers who held that 'the world is eternal, and that the variations and successions of it are also eternal'.[128] He divided the great cycle into four lesser ones of 16,000 years each, and the lesser cycles in their turn were divided into two periods of 8,000 years, of which the first was the age of the Arabs (*dawr-i 'arab*) and the second that of the Iranians (*dawr-i 'ajam*). The first cycle of 16,000 years ran from the *afrād*, the simple elements which were the basis of everything, to the emergence of man; the second cycle was that of Adam/man, in which the Arab period was taken up by eight perfected Arab messengers (*mursal-i mukammal-i 'arab*), the Iranian period by eight perfected Iranian expositors (*mubayyin-i mukammal-i 'ajam*); thereafter it would be the turn of the simple elements (*nawbat-i afrād*) again, and so on until the whole cycle of manifestation (*ẓuhūr*), inwardness (*buṭūn*), secrecy (*sirr*), and openness (*'alāniya*) had been completed.[129] The same archetypal events would recur in each cycle, presumably meaning each of the sixteen cycles of 1,000 years that constituted the cycle of man, but they would not be completely identical: in the time of Moses Pharaoh had drowned, but in the time of Ḥusayn he had been victorious (as Yazīd) and denied water to his victim. When the era of the Iranians came, people would worship humans, calling the human essence Reality (*ḥaqq*) and greeting one another as Allāh. When the Iranian era was over people would take the humans who had been worshipped to have been superior to themselves and so make idols of them, and this idolatry would continue till the era of the Iranians came back. This was how it would always go.[130] Maḥmūd

[126] *Dabistān*, I, 273 = III, 13.

[127] Kiyā, *Nuqṭaviyān yā Pasīkhāniyān*, 94.

[128] Pietro della Valle, *Viaggi*, II, 329. The 64,000 years are the total duration of the world in Algar, 'Nukṭawiyya', col. 2; Amanat, 'Nuqṭawī Movement', 285; Babayan, *Mystics*, 18f.

[129] *Dabistān*, I, 275 = III, 16ff. The formulation is clumsy and sometimes obscure.

[130] *Dabistān*, I, 276 = III, 21f. This does not quite fit the *Mīzān*, where the end of the Iranian era would be followed by another turn of the simple elements (*afrād*).

marked the end of an Arab period, and a transition from secrecy to openness. According to his followers, all the prophets and ancient lawgivers had really preached the same as Maḥmūd, but either they had not known this or else they had not wished to disclose it.[131] The 'Iranian soul' (*nafs-i 'ajamī*), that is Maḥmūd,[132] however, declared himself the mahdi in 800 AH (which must have corresponded to 8,000 of the cycle he was living in) and pronounced Muḥammad's religion to have been abrogated.[133] For all his materialism, then, Maḥmūd conforms to the old pattern of the mahdi who presides over the transfiguration of the world as a manifestation of God himself.

Their materialism did not prevent the Nuqṭavīs from believing in reincarnation (*raj'at*) either. Humans returned to God when they died, meaning to the four elements of which they were composed, but the knowledge and the deeds (*'ilm u 'amal*) they had accumulated in their lives survived and were re-embodied. When someone died and was buried the particles of the body (*ajzā'-i jasad*) turned into inanimate substances or plants, and the plants were eaten by animals and humans and so achieved human 'clothing', presumably by passing (via the blood) into the sperm of the animal or human that ate them. The Nuqṭavīs claimed that all the knowledge and deeds would come together in the food and be re-embodied in inorganic, vegetable, animal, or human form. How humans came back depended on their merits: the great were being rewarded for their former deeds, the abject were being punished. Paradise and hell were in this world. There was no disembodied rational soul.[134] As humans moved from inanimate to vegetable, animal or human form or vice versa, they would receive a mark from each state (*nashā'*), and this would enable people skilled in the science of *iḥṣā'* to tell what they had been in their former lives: assigning demeaning former lives to opponents seems to have been a source of much amusement.[135] It was by the pure and powerful particles of the bodies of all the prophets and saints coming together that the bodies of Muḥammad and 'Alī had been formed, and the chosen particles of their bodies in their turn came together in that of Maḥmūd, who was thus a reincarnation of both of them.[136]

[131] Pietro della Valle, *Viaggi*, II, 329.
[132] Amanat, 'Nuqṭawī Movement', 285 (without reference).
[133] *Dabistān*, I, 273.20, 276.25 = III, 12, 22 (wrongly 600 for 800).
[134] *Dabistān*, I, 276 = III, 16; Pietro della Valle, *Viaggi*, II, 328f., with amazing agreement, but only the former work explains the mechanics.
[135] *Dabistān*, I. 275.26ff = III, 19ff.
[136] *Dabistān*, I. 274.1.

Writing a millennium before the Nuqṭavīs Gregory of Nyssa had coped with the problem of bodily resurrection by explaining that some signs of our compound nature remained in our body parts even after they had dissolved into their constituent elements; these marks would enable the soul to recognise the parts to which it had earlier been joined.[137] The Nuqṭavīs seem to have operated with a similar theory, except that they omitted the soul: some kind of sign enabled the particles to be reunited in the food, one assumes, though this we are not actually told. The Nuqṭavī conception of body particles is in any case close to that of the Zoroastrian *tan gōhr*, the body substance that rains down to earth in the story of Zoroaster's creation in the material world: that too grew up as plants to be eaten by animals and pass into human beings, and it also seems to have been a carrier of personal identity, or part of it. As we saw, the Dahrī physicists of the early Islamic world likewise allowed for the same body particles to come together again – though only by accident, not by way of reward or punishment. All these ideas reflect attempts to explain the reappearance of a human being in another body in naturalist terms and even, in the case of the Dahrīs and the Nuqṭavīs, without belief in anything supernatural at all.

Unlike the Dahrīs, who did not believe in a divine realm, the Nuqṭavīs merely conflated it with that of nature; but what exactly did they take divinity to be? The answer seems to be power (*quvvat*) and purity (*ṣafvat*), more precisely the power that is inherent in the compounds and which drives the progress (*taraqqī*) of the body particles towards ever greater purity and perfection. This process has been underway since the appearance of Adam the pure *(Ādam-i ṣafī*) and results in Perfect Man (*insān-i kāmil*).[138] (The concept of Perfect Man was also at the centre of ʿAbd al-Karīm al-Jīlī's thought.) Perfected humans are God because they represent the acme of power and purity.[139] Like the Stoics the Nuqṭavīs saw God as a force (or, as the Stoics called it, spirit) built into matter, which it organised and animated. There were also Stoics who defined survival

137 Gregory of Nyssa, 'On the Making of Man', 27:2.

138 *Dabistān*, I, 273f. = III, 12.

139 Several Western authors claim that the perfected person was identified as 'the manifest compound' (*al-murakkab al-mubīn*), cf. Algar, 'Nuḳtawiyya', col. 2; Amanat, 'Nuqṭawī Movement', 288; Babayan, *Mystics*, 64, on the basis of *Dabistān*, I, 274.22 (= III, 16). But the text has *mrkb* without the definite article: 'I am *mrkb* of *al-mbyn*' (and it replaced *laysa ka-mithlihi shay*ʾ in their ritual, not, as Algar implies, in the creed). Langarūdī, *Junbishhā*, 270, reads *markab al-mubīn*, also characterising Perfect Man as *dhāt markab mubīn* without the article (271). The exact import of the expression is not clear to me.

after death as resorption into the elements, as we saw in connection with the followers of ʿAbdallāh b. Muʿāwiya and the Dahrīs;[140] and both the Stoics and the Nuqṭavīs held the world to be eternal, but destroyed and recreated at regular intervals, each time resulting in a world similar to or (according to the Stoics and some Ḥurūfīs) exactly the same as its predecessor. Given the presence of Stoicism in the region in antiquity the similarity may not be accidental: there are suggestions of Stoicism in the evidence on the Dahrīs too. If so, this is another case of Greek philosophical ideas being adopted with alacrity because they gave form and definition to notions already present on the Iranian side.

Pietro della Valle held that there were two sects in Lār, the Ahl al-Taḥqīq who are easily recognised as Nuqṭavīs, and the followers of *taric zenadeca*, 'the way of the *zanādiqa*'; the latter lead him to engage in a learned discussion of Manichaeism, but in fact they too seem to be Nuqṭavīs of some sort. They denied the resurrection and held that God was in everything, or more precisely that everything that could be seen and heard in this world actually *was* God, just as the Nuqṭavīs did. They also venerated the heavenly bodies, as did the Nuqṭavīs: the latter identified the sun as the soul of fire, and the moon as the soul of water, and called the sun 'the Kaʿba of worship and the fire-temples of obedience to the holy essence' (*dhāt-i aqdas*), presumably meaning the human essence (*dhāt-i ādamī*) that people would worship as Reality in the era of the Iranians.[141] The only significant difference between the two groups seems to be that the Zanādiqa believed in divine beings separate from the elements. One of them was an ardent worshipper of the sun, to whom he would make long and affectionate prayers every day; when Pietro objected, he responded that he was not worshipping the sun or the moon as gods, only as blessed, sublime spirits in the same way as Pietro venerated angels and saints, 'concurring with us in believing in the intercession of the saints which the heretical Christians of Europe deny', as Pietro remarks. In line with this he reports the Zanādiqa as believing that the heavenly bodies were animate and driven by intelligences, which were 'supreme and blessed angels near the God of great power' and which administered 'the lower things of this world'.[142] Pietro was also told of philosophers who said that the soul is fiery and so must go to either light (*nūr*) or fire (*nār*), suggesting belief in

140 Cf. Chapter 12, p. 247.
141 *Dabistān*, I, 274.12, 276.18, 21 = III, 14f., 22.
142 Pietro della Valle, *Viaggi*, I, 330f.

both hell and a luminous paradise, but whether these philosophers formed part of the sects in Lār is not clear.[143]

OVERALL

Birge remarks of the Bektashis that their beliefs have grown by gradual accretion, without an overall authority sitting in control of the process: layer upon layer has been added with the passing of time, so that today one is confronted with a confusing mass of often contradictory doctrines of diverse origin.[144] Hajji Bektash may have had a coherent system; ʿAdī b. Musāfir, Soltan Sahak, Faḍl Allāh Astarābādī, and Maḥmūd Pasīkhānī undoubtedly did. But their systems soon drowned in the vast ocean of beliefs that they were meant to replace – not only in the sense of turning heterodox when they had not been so from the start, but also in the sense of diversifying. The onset of diversity was immediate, as we see in the case of Ḥurūfism, which eventually disappeared as an independent sect, leaving behind a thick deposit in Bektashism.

What Birge says holds true of Khurramism too, and of the regional forms of Zoroastrianism underneath it. Here too we see a confusing mass of beliefs of diverse origin, deposited as one philosophical school and religion after another washed over the region in question. The Avestan layer was 'overlaid and obscured by accretions from the popular beliefs of Sogdiana and the surrounding regions', as Sims-Williams says of the Sogdian religion revealed by archaeology (with an implicit distinction between priestly Avestan and popular non-Avestan religion that may not be easy to defend).[145] It will have been by deposits and accretions that religion developed on the ground all over Iran until the rise of the Sasanians. No doubt the priests had systems characterised by varying degrees of coherence and similarity with one another along the lines of those of Faḍl Allāh and Maḥmūd Pasīkhānī; but in the absence of an institution empowered to declare one or other of these systems to be orthodox each system is likely to have diversified and eventually disintegrated, surviving only as residues on the ground. The terrain militated against the formation of uniform beliefs even when the Sasanians made an attempt to create them. Religion did provide some degree of unity even in the mountains, but what it united was local networks centred on prophets

[143] Pietro della Valle, *Viaggi*, I, 332.
[144] Birge, *Bektashis Order*, 87.
[145] Sims-Williams, 'Some Reflections', 12.

or holy men of one kind or another, many of them itinerant, none of them part of a grand supra-local organisation or network such as the Christian church or the scholarly establishment of the Sunnīs.

The Christians and Muslims had devised ways of organising communities across geographical and chronological divides, and in the long run this meant that the extreme localism of the mountaineers was doomed. The Christians came and went, leaving behind a deposit that we have encountered time and again in this book. But the Muslims came and stayed, and over the centuries they drew large numbers of mountaineers out of their isolation. Most Kurds and Turks today are Sunnīs, and most Iranians would have been Sunnīs too if the Ghulāt had not scored their one and only political victory by conquering Iran under the Ṣafavids. Shāh Ismāʿīl, all of fourteen years old at the time, set about imposing some form of his own beliefs on his new subjects, against the advice of his elders and betters.[146]

One may well wonder what he thought he was doing, for there was no Islamic tradition of rulers imposing their own brand of Islam on their subjects: the only precedent was Sasanian. What is more, Shāh Ismāʿīl did not have a coherent set of beliefs to impose, merely fanatically devoted followers full of the sort of Ali Ilahi beliefs that were endemic in the region. He evidently could not rule through them alone, but whether he was aware of this at the tender age at which he made his intention clear is open to debate, not least because he wanted to impose Shīʿism on the whole world; this is more suggestive of messianic fantasies than pragmatic politics.[147] As far as pragmatic politics are concerned, one would have expected him to follow the example of the Fāṭimids or the ʿAbbāsids, who also arrived with Shīʿite extremists unacceptable to the vast majority of their subjects. The Fāṭimids kept their heresy but left their subjects alone. The ʿAbbāsids modified their heresy while at the same time doing their best to cool the overheated beliefs of their troops, who would have prayed with their backs to the *qibla* if the caliph had so commanded; when the Rāwandiyya declared their belief in the divinity of al-Manṣūr they were suppressed.[148]

[146] Savory, *Iran under the Safavids*, 29 (at Tabrīz). The date is usually given as 1501. If Arjomand, 'Rise of Shah Esmā'il', 53, is right that the correct date is 907/1502, Ismāʿīl was fifteen.

[147] He declared his intention to impose Shīʿism on the whole world in a letter to the Mamluk sultan Qanṣūḥ al-Ghawrī according to Aubin, 'Politique religieuse', 237f. Unfortunately Aubin gives no reference, but cf. also Arjomand, 'Rise of Shah Esmāʿil'.

[148] Cf. Chapter 4; Crone, *Medieval Islamic Political Thought*, ch. 8. For Shāh ʿAbbās's interest in Nuqṭavism see Babayan, *Mystics*, 103ff.

By contrast, Ismāʿīl's behaviour among his troops can only be described as inflammatory. If Ottoman polemicists are to be believed there were also plans to change the *qibla* to Ardabīl (somewhat later Shāh ʿAbbās and his successors did apparently discourage the pilgrimage to Mecca, but in favour of Mashhad rather than Ardabīl).[149] What is more, it is hard to see the pragmatism of forcible conversion of an entire kingdom by the heretic who needs to rule it, and it is particularly hard when the heresy to which he converts it is not actually his own – for, Ismāʿīl's veneration of the twelve imams notwithstanding, his Ali Ilahi beliefs were far removed from Imāmism. The most plausible explanation is that he wanted to impose Shīʿism on the entire (Islamic) world in his capacity as the divine incarnation who makes the religion manifest, and simply did not know that Imāmī Shīʿism was actually a religion quite different, indeed inimical, to his own. Brilliant though he was, he was a mere child. The *kūdak-i dānā* had come with a vengeance, one could say: Iran owes its current religious identity to a delusional teenager.

One may also wonder why the religious ideas of inward-turned mountaineers should have been so prominent in the aftermath of the Turco-Mongol invasions, but this question seems to be under-researched. The sheer destruction, with extraordinary cruelty, of cities by the Mongols and Timur must play a role, as must the fact, often mentioned, that the Mongols were non-Muslims: for some fifty years the scholarly establishment in Iran was deprived of state support. Another part of the answer, however, must be that power had returned to the countryside – not in the form of Iranian aristocrats, but rather in that of Turkish confederacies. The Turks clustered together where there was pasture for their animals, and this happened to be first and foremost in the highlands running from western Iran to Anatolia. This process had begun under the Seljuqs, but the Seljuqs did not rule through their tribal followings. The subsequent dynasties did, however, so not only did power return to the countryside, but the old Khurramī heartlands now rose to the unusual position of being the political centre of Iran. This is what allowed for the harnessing of Turkish military power to Iranian religious ideas that we see in the Ṣafavid conquest of Iran. The mountaineers scored their one and only political victory because they had Turkish troops; on their own they would never have been able to get their revenge. Conversely, the Turks would hardly have conquered Iran in the name of religion (and certainly

149 Eberhard, *Osmanische Polemik*, 101f., 104; Melville, 'Pilgrimage to Mashhad', esp. 215ff.

not in that of *ghuluww*) if they had not been exposed to the mountaineers; in the long tradition of Turkish state formation and conquest the Ṣafavids represent a rare case of Turkish tribal power being yoked to a religious cause.[150]

The rise of Turkish power in the countryside also had cultural effects. Turkish rulers did not live in cities, but rather in tents. This too was true already of the Seljuqs. Even the tent-dwelling dynasties patronised cities, and the favoured city of the Ilkhanids, the Aq Qoyunlu, and the Qara Qoyunlu was Tabrīz, which rose to the status of capital. Without a permanent court it could not function as a cultural magnet after the fashion of Baghdad, however. In fact, no city could do so any more, given that the Middle East was now divided into Arabic-speaking and Persian-speaking zones: what had once been a single zone of imperial culture was now divided into two of a more parochial variety. But Tabrīz hardly achieved the cultural status of Cairo either. What with the Mongol and Timurid destruction of cities on the one hand, and the rural locus of Turkish power on the other, cultural life in Iran in the Turco-Mongol period came to be conducted in what by the standards of ʿAbbāsid Baghdad were small provincial towns. The Mongol and Timurid periods were marked by an appreciable erosion of urban high culture, as Bashir remarks.[151] There was a growing tendency towards folk Islam, as Luft says.[152] This may have been more pronounced in western than in eastern Iran, but it is precisely what the spread of Ḥurūfism and Nuqṭavism illustrates. The doctrines had wide appeal, even at the top. The Timurids had no love of Ḥurūfism, whose founder they executed, but Shāh ʿAbbās and even Akbar displayed an interest in Nuqṭavism; the devotees of both Nuqṭavism and Ḥurūfism included secretaries, physicians, poets, and itinerant dervishes; and in Lār, where Pietro della Valle met the Nuqṭavīs, several were astronomers and mathematicians of an impressive quality in Pietro's estimation.[153] Perhaps such beliefs had always appealed to craftsmen, artisans, and small-town intellectuals, topped by the occasional ruler: this was certainly true of Ismailism, which began among villagers in close contact with townsmen of the semi-educated kind, going on to recruit converts in higher social levels thereafter.

150 My thanks to Michael Cook for this point and a reminder that I have written about it myself (cf. Crone, *Slaves*, ch. 2).

151 Bashir, *Messianic Hopes*, 33.

152 *EI*², s.v. 'Mushaʿshaʿ'.

153 Gurney, 'Pietro della Valle', 112; Amanat, 'Nuqṭawī Movement', 290ff.; Babayan, *Mystics*, 94.

But their large numbers in Iran notwithstanding, the Ismailis never became the dominant voice. The unusual prominence of related beliefs in post-Mongol Iran suggests a thinning of the layer, above the small-town thinkers, of scholars and thinkers on a par with those of the fourth/tenth and fifth/eleventh centuries who had retained the ability to set the cultural tone. Or perhaps the key factor is that so many of them had become Sufis. In any case the gulf between the high culture and Khurramī-type beliefs was no longer as wide as it had been in the past.

Back in the fourth/tenth century al-Maqdisī had deemed Ismailism, or Bāṭinism, as he called it, to be rooted in the Khurramī perversion of Islam; this had started in the days of Abū Muslim, he said, and it been motivated by a desire to restore sovereignty to the Iranians (*al-ʿajam*).[154] As Ibn Ḥazm explained, the Persians had once been the masters of a large kingdom and endowed with such self-esteem that they called themselves free men/nobles and regarded others as slaves; when the revolts of Sunbādh, Ustādhsīs, al-Muqannaʿ, Bābak, and others failed, they took to subverting Islam from within by means of Shīʿism.[155] Al-Baghdādī cites anonymous historians who similarly traced the roots of Bāṭinism to the descendants of Zoroastrians who hankered for their ancestral religion without being able to profess it openly for fear of Muslim swords; they had joined up with Bābak's Khurramīs and appealed to Iranian restorationists, and they were really Dahrī *zindīqs* in his opinion.[156] To others Ismailism owed its existence to a conspiracy by Zoroastrians, Mazdakites, Dualists, and philosophers who imported their pernicious views into ʿAlid Shīʿism so as to destroy Islam from within and return power to the Iranians: adherents of this view also held them to have manifested themselves at different times in different guises.[157] Opponents of the new sects continued this storyline. According to Faḍl Allāh b. Ruzbihān Khunjī (d. 927/1521), Shāh Ismāʿīl's father, Ḥaydar, adopted the law of Bābak.[158] According to tenth/sixteenth-century Ottoman polemicists, the Ṣafavids were destroying Islam from within.[159] Afūshta'ī Naṭanzī, writing under Shāh ʿAbbās (d. 1038/1629), presented Nuqṭavism as the latest in a

[154] Maqdisī, V, 134.
[155] Ibn Ḥazm, II, 115 = Friedlaender, 'Heterodoxies of the Shiites'(i), 35f.
[156] Baghdādī, *Farq*, 268.5, 269.2, 271.2, 278.10, 285.-3.
[157] Ibn Rizām in Ibn al-Malāḥimī, *Muʿtamad*, 803; Stern, 'Abū 'l-Qāsim al-Busti', 310, 317 (where they are linked with the Barmakids); Ghazālī, *Faḍā'iḥ*, 9ff. (bāb 2, faṣl 1 and 2); *SN*, ch. 47, esp. 47:39 (311 = 238); Ibn al-Jawzī, *Talbīs Iblīs*, 103.
[158] Aubin, 'L'avènement des Safavides', 43n.
[159] Eberhard, *Osmanische Polemik*, 115f.

line of satanic brews that appeared in every age and which had previously displayed itself in Manichaeism and Mazdakism.[160] A certain Isḥāq Effendi, writing as late as 1291/1874f., similarly denounced the Bektashis as derived from the Ḥurūfīs, descended in their turn from the Qarāmiṭa and Ibāḥiyya, presumably meaning Khurramīs and/or Mazdakites.[161] Hostile, distorted, and shaped by conspiracy theory though these portraits are, it has to be conceded that they have a point. Many modern scholars too have observed that the Khurramīs, Iranian Ismailis and Sufis, the Ḥurūfīs, Nuqṭavīs, and the Bābīs form part of a persistent strand of Iranian religiosity that runs through its history from early to modern times.[162] It is the same ideas that we find at the core of all of them, worked out in countless different forms: the presence of the divinity in this world, cyclical time, reincarnation, and messianism, propounded by a male suffering from what to a modern Western reader looks like outsize megalomania. (In Bashir's kindly words, the mahdis of this period had a 'tremendous sense of self-significance'.)[163] It is in non-Persian Zoroastrianism, above all that of Media, that this vision of light, spirit, or divinity circulating in different forms and endlessly returning is rooted, and it is this vision rather than the doctrines familiar from the Pahlavi books that we meet time and again in Islamic times. It is now doomed by modernisation, though it may still survive in reformulations for urban clienteles. But this rather than official Zoroastrianism comes across as the main religion of Iran in Zoroastrian times, and until recently it remained a significant strand of religiosity in Islamic Iran as well.

[160] Babayan, *Mystics*, 47f.
[161] Browne, 'Further Notes', 535.
[162] E.g. Amanat, *Resurrection and Renewal*, 13f., 144f.; Babayan, *Mystics*, preface and *passim*; Bashir, *Fazlallah*, 110, 112; Shafiʿī Kadkanī, *Qalandariyya*, 55ff. I made a similar point myself in *Medieval Islamic Political Thought*, 330f.
[163] Bashir, *Messianic Hopes*, 37.

Appendix 1

Sharon and the Khidāshiyya

The sources agree that Khidāsh was denounced by the Hāshimiyya for preaching Khurramism. Sharon, however, holds that actually he was denounced for preaching ʿAlid Shīʿism. Sharon thinks so because the pro-ʿAbbāsid *Akhbār al-ʿAbbās* identifies a certain Abū Khālid as a follower of Khidāsh: this Abū Khālid, the *Akhbār al-ʿAbbās* tells us, led a movement in Nīshāpūr devoted to the rights of the descendants of Fāṭima in the time of Abū Muslim and al-Manṣūr, being one of those who held the imamate to have reverted to the ʿAlids when Ibrāhīm al-Imām died (*AA*, 403f.; Sharon, *Black Banners*, 169ff., 183n.). Ibrāhīm al-Imām had been the imam of the Hāshimiyya. Quite how he had got himself into that position is unknown, but he had been widely accepted as the man that the movement would enthrone, and his death in Marwān II's jail while the revolution was in progress led to disagreement over how he was to be replaced. Many members of the movement now wanted an ʿAlid candidate, Abū Khālid among them. Sharon sees Khidāsh as the founder of the pro-ʿAlid wing: this is why Abū Khālid was called a Khidāshite.

This inference is invalid. Khidāsh died in 118/736, fourteen years before the death of Ibrāhīm in 132/749. It follows that Abū Khālid had not seceded when Khidāsh was executed, but on the contrary remained loyal to the Hāshimiyya for another fourteen years. To maintain Sharon's hypothesis we would have to argue that 'Khidāshite' had become a general word of abuse for supporters of the ʿAlids whenever they appeared. But how could it have acquired this meaning when the Khidāshiyya themselves were not associated with the ʿAlids? They held the imamate to have passed to the ʿAbbāsid Muḥammad b. ʿAlī, Ibrāhīm's father: from him it passed to Khidāsh, as we have seen.

The *Akhbār al-ʿAbbās* is doubtless right that there were Shīʿites in Nīshāpūr who favoured ʿAlī's descendants by Fāṭima in the time of Abū

Muslim and al-Manṣūr, led by a certain Abū Khālid, a former member of the Hāshimiyya. According to al-Madā'inī, there were also supporters of the children of Fāṭima in Nīshāpūr back in the time when the first missionary of the Hāshimiyya (or, as he says, of the 'Abbāsids) was sent to Khurāsān, that is, in the first governorship of Asad b. 'Abdallāh, which ended in 109/727f. (the year under which al-Ṭabarī cites the report). We are told that this missionary was warned to stay away from a certain Ghālib in Nīshāpūr because he was extreme (*mufriṭan*) in his love of the children of Fāṭima (Tab ii, 1501, year 109). The *Akhbār al-'Abbās* itself tells us that this missionary was warned against Ghālib and a group of people who adhered to 'the view of the Kufans' and who were Fāṭimīs calling to the imamate of Muḥammad b. 'Alī b. al-Ḥusayn (i.e. Muḥammad al-Bāqir, the fifth imam of the Imāmīs); it also tells us that the group included a certain Abū Khālid al-Jawāliqī (AA, 204; cf. Sharon, *Black Banners*, 148, 158, 162f.). Here, then, Abū Khālid is an adherent of 'Alī's descendants by Fāṭima's before Khidāsh has even arrived. If we take the accounts at face value Abū Khālid al-Jawāliqī was a young devotee of the 'Alids in 109, but drifted to the Hāshimiyya in support of Ibrāhīm at some point, reverted to the 'Alids on Ibrāhīm's death in 132, and preached on their behalf in the time of Abū Muslim and al-Manṣūr, that is, around 137. This is not impossible, but it is hard to avoid the suspicion that the episode of 109 is back-projection. For one thing, it is too reminiscent of the situation around 137 for comfort. For another, al-Madā'inī tells us that the missionary who was warned against Ghālib engaged in a disputation with him, arguing the case of the 'Abbāsids against that of the 'Alids (or more precisely Ṭālibids). Disputations between adherents of the 'Abbāsids and the 'Alids must have been common enough after the revolution, but not back in the time of Hāshimite ('big-tent') Shī'ism, let alone back in the time when the missionaries had to work in secret. Even if we accept that the 'Abbāsids were always the leaders of the movement it would have been the height of folly for a missionary of theirs to stage disputation with a view to vindicating their rights against those of the 'Alids, represented by a missionary he had been explicitly warned against.

If Khidāsh and Abū Khālid had different views on the imamate, why does the *Akhbār al-'Abbās* say that Abū Khālid was a Khidāshite? One possibility is that Abū Khālid shared some other heresy with Khidāsh and/or the later Khidāshiyya. For example, he too could have taken a concessionary stance on native marriage customs. In Nīshāpūr the problem is more likely to have been incestuous unions than polyandrous ones, but the term would easily have been generalised. Fakhr al-Dīn al-Rāzī (*Firaq*, 95) lists a party of

Murji'ites called the Khālidiyya who held that God would place sinners in hell, but not for ever: eventually he would admit them to paradise. Van Ess connects them with our Abū Khālid (*TG*, II, 605), but unfortunately the founder of this Murji'ite group is identified as Khālid, not Abū Khālid. Another possibility is that 'Khidāshite' had come to be used as a general term of abuse for dissidents after the fashion of 'revisionist' or 'capitalist roadster'. No doubt there are still other possibilities, but whatever Abū Khālid and Khidāsh may have had in common, it does not seem to have been love of the 'Alids.

Appendix 2

Widengren on Bābak's Mithraic Wedding Ceremony

Mithraism is a cult of Iranian origin which flourished in the Roman empire in the first two centuries AD, at a time when sources for Iranian religion are scarce. It is not surprising, then, that Iranianists should try to use this cult as information for the history of Zoroastrianism. Unfortunately the cult seems to have lost most of its Iranian features in the process of transplantation to Rome, and the literary evidence on it is extremely limited; our information about it is largely based on iconography. Exploiting the Mithraic evidence for the history of Iranian religion is thus extremely difficult. One person has nonetheless succeeded in making excellent use of it. Looking at the Mithraic myth in the light of Zoroastrian cosmogony, Kreyenbroek makes a serious case for the existence of an alternative cosmogony (which he takes to be pre-Zoroastrian rather than a variant within Zoroastrianism), which is now lost, though there are residues of it in the mythology of the Yezidis and Ahl-i Ḥaqq (Kreyenbroek, 'Mithra and Ahreman in Iranian Cosmogonies'; Kreyenbroek, 'Mithra and Ahreman, Binyāmīn and Malak Ṭāwūs'). More commonly, however, the Mithraic evidence is simply moved back into Iran on the basis of superficial similarities, or none at all. This is how Widengren proceeds.

Widengren was an extremely learned and prolific scholar who left a major footprint on Iranian studies. Unfortunately he was also prone to letting himself be carried away by grand ideas, and useful though his work remains, most of it is marred by unacceptable conjectures and somewhat cavalier use of the sources. Of course nobody working in Iranian studies can avoid conjecture, and there is never going to be any agreement on where the line between good and bad conjectures runs. But Widengren's treatment of the allegedly Mithraic ritual in Bābak's wedding ceremony ('Bābakīyah and the Mithraic Mysteries') must be said to cross the line by any standard.

His best argument for the Mithraic character of Bābak's cult society is that Bābak's followers were known as the Red-clothed ones (684ff.). He claims that red was the colour of the warrior function in Iran, and it is well known that Mithraists were often soldiers. The colour of Mithra's tunic is red in all representations known to him with three exceptions. (It is on the basis of one of the three exceptions that Pourshariati, *Decline*, 432, declares green to be 'the quintessential color of Mithra' in order to cast Bihāfarīdh as a Mithraist.) Here there is at least a genuine similarity to consider. It is when Widengren turns to the ritual that things go wrong.

Widengren discerns a Mithraic element in the wedding ceremony in the fact that it involved the slaughter of a cow. It was a bull that was slaughtered in the Mithras cult. The gender of the animal mattered, for it is generally agreed that the slaughter was a re-enactment of the slaughter of the primal bull, and Widengren is aware of this; he infers that the deeper meaning of the ritual had been forgotten (694). What then identifies it as Mithraic? Widengren has several answers to this.

The first is that the cow in Bābak's ceremony was flayed and spread on the ground, and that wine was placed on it with pieces of bread around it. By way of parallel he adduces depictions in which Sol (i.e., the Sun) and Mithras sit on a couch (*klinē*) covered with a bull skin, or directly on a bull, or they are positioned behind a couch covered with bull skin (681f.): one way or another, the skin is connected with seating. In his view Bābak and his wife take the role of these two gods (693). Bābak and his wife do in fact also sit on a couch (or bed, *firāsh*), but the skin of the cow is not spread over it; it is placed on the floor to serve as a *sofre*, a tablecloth on which the food is presented. In the Mithraic reliefs the bread is placed on a small three-legged table. There is no correspondence, then.

Secondly, Widengren makes much of the fact that in Bābak's wedding ritual the food consisted of bread and wine (679f., 682ff.). The Mithraic rituals used bread and water, he says, but he notes that Sol has a drinking horn in one representation. Here there is no bread on the table, however. He also adduces a Magian, possibly Mithraic, initiation ceremony in Lucian in which the initiate has to drink milk, honey-mead, and water. But this ceremony is surely irrelevant: it is not identified as Mithraist and it gives us three drinks that do not fit. To Widengren honey-mead is wine, and he relates the three drinks to the tripartite nature of Indo-European society à la Dumézil in a learned discussion which causes the reader to feel that everything fits in some deep sense that is difficult to articulate. (Covering problems in a cloud of learned observations of dubious truth and/or relevance is a favourite tactic of his.)

Thirdly, when Bābak's followers pay allegiance to Bābak they kiss his hand. Widengren relates this to the *iunctio dextrarum* of the initiate (*mysta*) and his elder (*pater*), which repeats that of Mithras and Sol (690f.). But a *iunctio dextrarum* is a handclasp, and two men clasping hands are not engaged in the same gesture as one kissing the hand of another. In addition, if Bābak and the follower paying allegiance are re-enacting the roles of Sol and Mithras, how can it be Bābak and his wife who correspond to Mithras and Sol in another context (cf. 693)? Further, Widengren notes that 'only men were admitted as members' to the Mithras ritual (686), but Bābak's wife sat openly with the men during the ceremony, a point on which he abstains from comment.

In short, the cow was not a bull, the food was placed on the skin instead of a three-legged table, the two protagonists sat on a bed, not on the skin, the meal was of bread and wine, not bread and water, the participants kissed the hand of the leader instead of clasping it, and a woman was present where she would have been absent. As if all this were not enough, Widengren thinks that Bābak was a 'dehkan' whose followers had inherited the ideas and social customs of the Mazdakites, who had split off from *Manichaeism* (676). If the Mazdakites were a Manichaean offshoot, how could they preserve an old *Zoroastrian* cult? Widengren does not notice this problem. To Pourshariati, Widengren 'had long ago already demonstrated the Mithraic rituals of the Bābakiyya' in 'a fascinating study which was again conveniently ignored by subsequent meager scholarship on the rebel' (*Decline*, 459). One can only say that subsequent scholarship has exercised better judgement on this point than she has.

Works Cited and Abbreviations

Where references to sources are given in the form 6 = 39, the first figure refers to the text and the second to the translation. Š is treated as S for purposes of alphabetisation. Only one death date is given for authors even when several are on record.

AA = *Akhbār al-dawla al-ʿabbāsiyya wa-fīhi akhbār al-ʿAbbās*, ed. ʿA.-ʿA. al-Dūrī and ʿA.-J. al-Muṭṭalibī, Beirut 1971.

ʿAbd al-Jabbār (d. 415/1025), *al-Mughnī fī abwāb al-tawḥīd wa'l-ʿadl*, vol. V, ed. ʿA.-Ḥ. Maḥmūd and S. Dunyā, Cairo n.d.; chs. against the dualists and Zoroastrians tr. G. Monnot, *Penseurs musulmans et religions iraniennes*, Paris 1974.

Tathbīt dalāʾil al-nubuwwa, ed. ʿA.-K. ʿUthmān, 2 vols., Beirut 1966.

Abdullaev, K., *Buddhist Iconography of Northern Bactria*, forthcoming.

'Une image bouddhique découverte à Samarkand', *Arts Asiatiques* 55, 200, 173–5.

Abegg, E., *Der Buddha Maitreya*, Sankt Gallen 1946 (offprint from *Mitteilungen der Schweizerischen Gesellschaft der Freunde Ostasiasticher Kultur* 7, 1945, 7–37).

Der Messiasglaube in Inden und Iran auf Grund der Quellen dargestellt, Berlin and Leipzig 1928.

Abkhaʾi-Khavari, M., *Das Bild des Königs in der Sasanidenzeit*, Hildesheim 2000.

Abū 'l-Baqāʾ (wr. sixth/twelfth century), *Manāqib al-Mazyadiyya fī akhbār al-mulūk al-asadiyya*, ed. Ṣ. M. Darāka and M. ʿA.-Q. Khuraysāt, 2 vols., Amman 1984.

Abū Dulaf: see Minorsky.

Abū 'l-Faraj al-Iṣbahānī (d. 356/967), *Kitāb al-aghānī*, 24 vols., Cairo 1927–74.

Maqātil al-ṭālibiyyīn, ed. S. A. Ṣaqr, Cairo 1949.

Abū Ḥātim al-Rāzī (d. 322/934), *Aʿlām al-nubuwwa*, ed. Ṣ. al-Ṣāwī, Tehran 1977.

Kitāb al-iṣlāḥ, ed. Ḥ. Minūchihr and M. Muḥaqqiq, Tehran 1377/1998.

Kitāb al-zīna, section on *aṣḥāb al-ahwāʾ wa'l-madhāhib*, in ʿA. S. al-Sāmarāʾī, *al-Ghuluww wa'l-firaq al-ghāliya fī 'l-ḥaḍāra al-islāmiyya*, Baghdad 1972, 247–312.

Abū 'l-Maʿālī (wr. 485/1092f.), *Bayān al-adyān*, ed. H. Raḍī, Tehran 1342 [1964]; ed. J. Wāʿiẓī, Tehran 1387 [2008]. All references are to Raḍī's edition unless otherwise noted.

Abū 'l-Muʿīn al-Nasafī (d. 508/1114), *Baḥr al-kalām*, ed. W. M. Ṣ. al-Farfūr, Damascus 1417/1997.

Abū Muṭīʿ al-Nasafī (d. 318/930) in M. Bernand (ed.), 'Le *Kitāb al-radd ʿalā l-bidaʿ* d' Abū Muṭīʿ Makḥūl al-Nasafī', *Annales Islamologiques* 16, 1980, 39–126.

Abū Tammām = W. Madelung and P. E. Walker (ed. and tr.), *An Ismaili Heresiography: The 'Bāb al-shayṭān' from Abū Tammām's Kitāb al-shajara*, Leiden 1998.

Abū Yaʿlā Ibn al-Farrāʾ (d. 458/1066), *al-Muʿtamad fī uṣūl al-dīn*, ed. W. Z. Ḥaddād, Beirut 1974.

Abū Zurʿa (d. 281/894), *Taʾrīkh*, ed. Sh.-A. al-Qawjānī, 2 vols., Damascus 1980.

Acta Archelai: see Hegemonius.

Adas, M., *Prophets of Rebellion: Millenarian Protest Movements against the European Colonial Order*, Chapel Hill 1979.

Aelian (d. *c.* 235), *Historical Miscellany*, ed. and tr. N. G. Wilson, Cambridge, Mass., and London 1997.

Agapius (d. 330/941f.), *Kitāb al-ʿunwān*, ed. and tr. A.-A. Vasiliev, part II, fasc. 2, in R. Graffin and F. Nau (eds.), *Patrologia Orientalis*, VIII, Paris 1912.

Agathias (d. *c.* 580), *The Histories*, tr. J. D. Frendo, Berlin and New York 1975.

Agha, S. S., *The Revolution which Toppled the Umayyads: Neither Arab nor ʿAbbāsid*, Leiden 2003.

Aghānī: see Abū 'l-Faraj.

Aiyappan, A., 'Fraternal Polyandry in Malabar', in M. K. Raha and P. C. Coomar (eds.), *Polyandry in India*, Delhi 1987, 269–76.

Albaum, L. I., *Zhivopic' Afrasiaba*, Tashkent 1975.

Algar, H., 'Nuḳṭawiyya', in *EI*².

Alon, G., *The Jews in their Land in the Talmudic Age*, II, Jerusalem 1984.

Amabe, F., *The Emergence of the ʿAbbāsid Autocracy*, Kyoto 1995.

Amanat, A., 'The Nuqṭawī Movement of Maḥmūd Pisīkhānī and his Persian Cycle of Mystical-Materialism', in F. Daftary (ed.), *Mediaeval Ismaʿili History and Thought*, Cambridge 1996, 281–97.

Resurrection and Renewal: The Making of the Babi Movement in Iran, 1844–1850, Ithaca and London 1989.

Amir-Moezzi, M. A., *La religion discrète*, Paris 2006; English tr. *The Spirituality of Shiʿi Islam*, London 2011.

Ammianus Marcellinus (d. after 391), *Res Gestae*, ed. and tr. J. C. Roaf, 3 vols., Cambridge, Mass., and London 1935–9.

Amoretti, B. S., 'Sects and Heresies', in *Cambridge History of Iran*, IV, ed. R. N. Frye, Cambridge 1975, 481–519.

Andarj ī Aōshnar i Dānak, ed. and tr. B. N. Dhabhar, Bombay 1930.

Andò, V., 'La comunanza delle donne in Erodoto', in *Philias Kharin: Miscellanea di studi classici in onore di Eugenio Manni*, I, Rome 1980, 87–102.

Andrae, T., *Die Person Muhammeds in Lehre und Glauben seiner Gemeinde*, Stockholm 1918.

Andreyev, S., 'The Rawshaniyya: A Sufi Movement on the Mughal Tribal Periphery', in L. Lewisohn and D. Morgan (eds.), *The Heritage of Sufism*, III, Oxford 1999, 290–318.
Apocalypse of Adam, tr. G.W. MacRae in Charlesworth, *Pseudepigrapha*, I, 707–19; in Robinson, *Nag Hammadi Library*, 277–86.
Appian (d. *c.* 165), *Roman History*, ed. and tr. H. White, 4 vols., Cambridge, Mass., and London 1912–13.
Arazi, A., and ʿA. Elʾad, '"L'épître à l'armée": al-Maʾmūn et la seconde daʿwa', *Studia Islamica* 66, 1987, 27–70; 67, 1988, 29–73.
Arberry, A. J. (tr.), *A Sufi Martyr: The 'Apologia' of ʿAyn al-Quḍāt al-Hamadhānī*, London 1969.
Ardā Vīrāfnāmag, ed. and tr. P. Gignoux, *Le livre d'Ardā Vīrāz*, Paris 1984. For the question whether the correct form is Vīrāf or Vīrāz see the editorial introduction, 7f.
Arjomand, S., 'The Rise of Shah Esmāʿil as a Mahdist Revolution', *Studies on Persianate Societies* 3, 2005, 45–65.
al-Ashʿarī (d. 324/935f.), *Kitāb maqālāt al-islāmiyyīn*, ed. H. Ritter, Istanbul 1929–33.
Asheri, D., A. Lloyd, and A. Corcella, *A Commentary on Herodotus Books I–IV*, Oxford 2007.
Aster, S. Z., 'The Phenomenon of Divine and Human Radiance in the Hebrew Bible and in Northwest Semitic and Mesopotamian Literature: A Philological and Comparative Study', Ph.D. dissertation, University of Pennsylvania 2006.
Aubin, J., 'L'avènement des Safavides Reconsideré (Etudes Safavides III)', *Moyen Orient et Océan Indien* 5, 1988, 1–130.
'La politique religieuse des Safavides', in *Le Shîʿisme imâmite* [ed. T. Fahd], Paris 1970, 235–93.
Aune, D.E., *Christian Prophecy in Early Christianity and the Ancient Mediterranean World*, Grand Rapids, Mich., 1983.
ʿAwfī (fl. 630s/1220s), *Jawāmiʿ al-ḥikāyāt*, ed. B. Muṣaffā (Karīmī), III/1, Tehran 1352 [1973]; ed. J. Sheʿar, Tehran 1995.
Azarpay, G., 'Nanā, the Sumero-Akkadian Goddess of Transoxiana', *Journal of the American Oriental Society* 96, 1976, 536–42.
Azarpay, G. (ed.), *Sogdian Painting: The Pictorial Epic in Oriental Art*, Berkeley 1981.
al-Azdī (d. 334/946), *Taʾrīkh al-Mawṣil*, ed. ʿA. Ḥabība, Cairo 1967.
BA: see al-Balādhurī, *Ansāb*.
Babayan, K., *Mystics, Monarchs, and Messiahs: Cultural Landscapes of Early Modern Iran*, Cambridge, Mass., and London 2002.
al-Baghdādī (d. 429/1037), *al-Farq bayna 'l-firaq*, ed. M. Badr, Cairo 1910.
Uṣūl al-dīn, Istanbul 1928.
al-Baghdādī, al-Khaṭīb (d. 463/1071), *Taʾrīkh Baghdād*, 14 vols. Cairo 1931.
Bahrāmī, A., *Tārīkh-i Īrān az ẓuhūr-i Islām tā suqūṭ-i Baghdād*, [Tehran] 1350.
Bahrāmiyān, ʿA., 'Bābak-i Khurramdīn', and 'Bih Āfarīd', in *Dāʾirat al-Maʿārif-i Buzurg-i Islāmī*, ed. K.M. Bujnūrdī, Tehran 1367 [1988–].
'Barrasī va taḥlīlī dar bāra-yi shūrish-i Yūsuf-i Barm dar qarn-i duvvum-i hijrī', *Maʿārif* 18, 1380, 77–94.

Bailey, H. W., 'The Word "But" in Iranian', *Bulletin of the School of Oriental and African Studies* 6, 1931, 279–83.
Zoroastrian Problems in the Ninth-Century Books, 2nd edn, Oxford 1971.
Bailey, H. W. (ed. and tr.), *Indo-Scythian Studies, being Khotanese Texts*, IV, Cambridge 1961.
al-Balādhurī (d. 279/892), *Ansāb al-ashrāf*, III, ed. 'A.-'A. al-Dūrī, Wiesbaden 1978; IV a, ed. M. J. Kister, Jerusalem 1971; V, ed. S. D. F. Goitein, Jerusalem 1936. Abbreviated as BA.
Futūḥ al-buldān, ed. M. J. de Goeje, Leiden 1866. Abbreviated as BF.
Bal'amī: see *Tārīkhnāma*.
Ball, W., 'How Far did Buddhism Spread West?', *al-Rāfidān* 10, 1989, 1–11.
'Some Rock-Cut Monuments in Southern Iran', *Iran* 24, 1986, 95–115.
Banerji, S. C., *A Companion to Tantra*, Delhi 2007.
Bar Asher, M. M., and A. Kofsky, *The Nuṣayrī–'Alawī Religion*, Leiden 2002.
Bar Daiṣan (Bardesanes) (d. 222), *The Book of the Laws of Countries*, ed. and tr. H. J. W. Drijvers, Assen 1965.
Bar Ḥadbeshabba (fl. late sixth century), 'Cause de la fondation des écoles', ed. and tr. A. Scher in *Patrologia Orientalis*, IV, Paris 1908, 317–404.
Bar Hebraeus (d. 1286), *Chronography*, ed. (facsimile) and tr. E. A. W. Budge, London 1932.
(Ibn al-'Ibrī), *Ta'rīkh Mukhtaṣar al-duwal*, ed. A. Ṣalḥānī, Beirut 1890.
Barnard, L. W., 'Athanagoras: De Resurrectione. The Background and Theology of a Second Century Treatise on the Resurrection', *Studia Theologica* 30, 1976, 1–42.
Barthold, W., *Turkestan down to the Mongol Invasion*, 3rd edn, London 1968. References are to the original pagination given in the margin.
Bartikian, H., 'Les Arewordi (fils du soleil) en Arménie et Mésopotamie et l'épître du catholicos Nersès le gracieux', *Revue des Etudes Arméniennes* NS 5, 1968, 271–88.
Basham, A. L., 'Jainism', in R. C. Zaehner (ed.), *Living Faiths*, London 1959, 261–6.
The Wonder that was India, London 1967.
Bashear, S., *Arabs and Others in Early Islam*, Princeton 1997.
Bashir, S., *Fazlallah Astarabadi and the Hurufis*, Oxford 2005.
Messianic Hopes and Mystical Visions: The Nūrbakhshīya between Medieval and Modern Islam, Columbia, SC, 2003.
Basset, R. (ed. and tr.), *Le synaxaire arabe-jacobite (redaction copte)* in *Patrologia Orientalis*, XVI, 1922, 187–424.
Bates, M. L., 'Khurāsānī Revolutionaries and al-Mahdī's Title', in F. Daftary and J. W. Meri (eds.), *Culture and Memory in Medieval Islam: Essays in Honour of Wilferd Madelung*, London 2003, 279–317.
Bausani, A., 'A proposito di un passo di Šahrastānī sulla dottrina mazdakita', *Rivista degli Studi Orientali* 22, 1974, 74–6.
Bayhom-Daou, T., 'The Second-Century Šī'ite Ġulāt: Were they Really Gnostic?', *Journal of Arabic and Islamic Studies* 5, 2003–4, 13–61.
Bd: see *Bundahišn*.
Beal, S., (tr.), *Buddhist Records of the Western World*, London 1906.
Beck, R., 'The Mysteries of Mithras: A New Account of their Genesis', *Journal of Roman Studies* 88, 1998, 115–28.
Bedjan, P. (ed.), *Acta Martyrum et sanctorum*, 7 vols., Paris 1890–7.

BeDuhn, J. D., *The Manichaean Body*, Baltimore 2000.
Beeston, A. F. L., 'Temporary Marriage in Pre-Islamic South Arabia', *Arabian Studies* 4, 1978, 21–5.
Benko, S., *Pagan Rome and the Early Christians*, Bloomington 1986.
Bennett, B., '*Iuxta Unum Latus Erat Terra Tenebrarum*: The Division of Primordial Space in Anti-Manichaean Writers' Descriptions of the Manichaean Cosmogony', in P. Mirecki and J. BeDuhn (eds.), *The Light and the Darkness: Studies in Manichaeism and its World*, Leiden 2001, 68–78.
Benveniste, E., 'Sur la terminologie iranienne du sacrifice', *Journal Asiatique* 252, 1964, 45–58.
Benveniste, E., (ed. and tr.), *Textes Sogdiens*, Paris 1940.
Berger, P., *The Sacred Canopy: Elements of a Sociological Theory of Religion*, New York 1967.
Bernand: see Abū Muṭīʿ.
Bernheimer, T., 'The Revolt of ʿAbdallāh b. Muʿāwiya, AH 127–130: A Reconsideration through the Coinage', *Bulletin of the School of Oriental and African Studies* 69, 2006, 381–93.
Berreman, G. D., 'Himalayan Polyandry and the Domestic Cycle', in M. K. Raha and P. C. Coomar (eds.), *Polyandry in India*, Delhi 1987, 179–97.
BF: see al-Balādhurī, *Futūḥ*.
Bianchi, U., 'Sur le dualisme de Mani', in A. van Tongerloo and S. Giversen (eds.), *Manichaica Selecta: Studies Presented to Professor Julian Ries*, Louvain 1991, 9–17.
Birge, J. K., *The Bektashi Order of Dervishes*, London and Hartford, Conn., 1937.
al-Bīrūnī (d. after 442/1050), *al-Āthār al-bāqiya ʿan al-qurūn al-khāliya*, ed. C. E. Sachau, Leipzig 1878 (repr. 1923); tr. C. E. Sachau, *The Chronology of Ancient Nations*, London 1879 (repr. 1984).
Kitāb fī taḥqīq mā li'l-Hind, ed. E. Sachau, London 1887; ed. Hyderabad 1958; tr. E. C. Sachau, *Alberuni's India*, 2 vols., London 1910. References are given in the form '41/27 = I, 54', where the first figure stands for the Hyderabad edition (the edition I have actually used) and the next two to Sachau's edition and translation.
Bitton-Ashkelony, B., and A. Kofsky, 'Gazan Monasticism in the Fourth–Sixth Centuries: From Anchoritic to Cenobitic', *Proche-Orient Chrétien* 50, 2000, 14–62.
Bitton-Ashkelony, B., and A. Kofsky, (eds.), *Christian Gaza in Late Antiquity*, Leiden 2004.
Blois, F. de, 'Laylat al-Māšūš: Marginalia to al-Bayrūnī, Abū Nuwās and other Authors', *Journal of Semitic Studies* 29, 1984, 81–96.
'Manes' "Twin" in Iranian and Non-Iranian Texts', in C. G. Cereti, M. Maggi, and E. Provasi (eds.), *Religious Themes and Texts of Pre-Islamic Iran and Central Asia* (Studies in honour of G. Gnoli), Wiesbaden 2003, 7–16.
'*Naṣrānī* (*nazōraios*) and *ḥanīf* (*ethnikos*): Studies on the Religious Vocabulary of Christianity and Islam', *Bulletin of the School of Oriental and African Studies* 65, 2002, 1–30.
'Du nouveau sur la chronologie bactrienne post-hellénistique: l'ère de 223–224 ap. J.-C.', *Comptes rendus de l'Académie des Inscriptions et Belles-Lettres*, 2006 [2008], fasc. 2, 991–7.

Review of W. Sundermann (ed.), *Iranian Manichaean Turfan Texts in Early Publications*, London 1996, in *Journal of the Royal Asiatic Society*, third series, 8, 1998, 481–5.
Böhlig, A., 'Die Adamapokalypse aus Codex V von Nag Hammadi als Zeugnis jüdisch-iranischer Gnosis', *Oriens Christianus* 48, 1964, 44–9.
Bosworth, C. E., *The Ghaznavids*, Beirut 1973 [first publ. 1963].
Boyce, M., *A History of Zoroastrianism*, I, Leiden 1975; II, Leiden 1982.
'An Old Village *Dakhma* of Iran', in P. Gignoux and A. Tafazzoli (eds.), *Mémorial Jean de Menasce*, Louvain 1974, 3–9.
'On the Antiquity of Zoroastrian Apocalyptic', *Bulletin of the School of Oriental and African Studies* 47, 1984, 57–75.
'Some Reflections on Zurvanism', *Bulletin of the School of Oriental and African Studies* 19, 1957, 304–16.
Boyce, M. (tr.), *Textual Sources for the Study of Zoroastrianism*, Chicago 1990 [Manchester 1984].
Boyce, M., and F. Grenet with a contribution by R. Beck, *A History of Zoroastrianism*, III, Leiden 1991
Bradley, K., *Slavery and Society at Rome*, Cambridge 1994.
Brakke, D., *The Gnostics: Myth, Ritual, and Diversity in Early Christianity*, Cambridge, Mass., and London 2010.
Braun, O. (tr.), *Ausgewählte Akten Persischer Märtyrer*, Kempten and Munich [1917].
(tr.), *Das Buch der Synhados*, Stuttgart and Vienna 1900.
Braund, D., 'Herodotus' Spartan Scythians', in C. J. Tuplin (ed.), *Pontus and the Outside World*, Leiden 2004, 25–41.
Bremmer, J. N., 'The Resurrection between Zarathustra and Jonathan Z. Smith', *Nederlands Theologisch Tijdschruft* 50, 1996, 89–107.
Bṛhadāraṇyaka Upaniṣad: see *Upaniṣads*.
Brock, S. P., 'Clothing Metaphors as a Means of Theological Expression in Syriac Tradition', in M. Schmidt (ed.), *Typus, Symbol, Allegorie bei den östlichen Vätern und ihren Parallelen im Mittelalter*, Regensburg 1982, 11–40.
'Early Syrian Asceticism', *Numen* 20, 1973, 1–19.
'The Holy Spirit as Feminine in Early Syriac Literature', in J. Martin Soskice (ed.), *After Eve: Women, Theology and the Christian Tradition*, London 1990, 73–88.
'Jewish Traditions in Syriac Sources', *Journal of Jewish Studies* 30, 1979, 212–32.
Browder, M. H., 'al-Bīrūnī's Manichaean Sources', in P. Bryder (ed.), *Manichaean Studies*, Lund 1988, 19–28.
Browne, E. G., 'Further Notes on the Literature of the Ḥurúfís and their Connection with the Bektáshí Order of Dervishes', *Journal of the Royal Asiatic Society* 3, 1907, 533–81.
'Some Notes on the Literature and Doctrines of the Ḥurūfī Sect', *Journal of the Royal Asiatic Society*, Jan. 1898, 61–94.
Bruinessen, M. van, 'Haji Bektash, Sultan Sahak, Shah Mina Sahib and Various Avatars of a Running Wall', *Turcica* 21–3, 1991, 55–69.
'When Haji Bektash still bore the Name of Sultan Sahak: Notes on the *Ahl-i Haqq* of the Guran District', in A. Popovic and G. Veinstein (eds.),

Bektachiyya: études sur l'ordre mystique des Bektachis et les groupes relevant de Hadji Bektach, Istanbul 1995, 117–38.
Bruns and Sachau: see Syro-Roman Lawbook.
Bryder, P., 'Buddhist Elements in Manichaeism', in U. Bianchi (ed.), *The Notion of 'Religion' in Comparative Research*, Rome 1994, 487–90.
'Manichaeism, iii. Buddhist Elements', in *EIr*.
Buckingham, J., *Travels in Assyria, Media, and Persia*, London 1829.
al-Bukhārī (d. 256/870), *al-Ṣaḥīḥ*, ed. L. Krehl and T. W. Juynboll, 4 vols., Leiden 1862–1908.
Bumke, P. J., 'Kizilbaş-Kurden in Dersim (Tunceli, Türkei')', *Anthropos* 74, 1979, 530–48.
Bundahišn (abbreviated as *Bd*): Iranian or Greater *Bd* (referred to as *GrBd*), mostly cited from transliterations and translations given in monographs and articles, but I have also benefited from preliminary translations kindly given to me by P. O. Skjaervø. References in the form 3:13 are to the chapter and paragraph division of B. T. Anklesaria (translit. and tr.), *Zand-Ākāsīh*, Bombay 1956, even when the scholars I rely on use a slightly different chapter and paragraph division. References in the form 212.6 are to the pages and lines of Anklesaria's facsimile edition, taken on trust from the scholars who refer to it. Occasional reference is also made to the Indian *Bd*, tr. E. W. West in his *Pahlavi Texts* (Sacred Books of the East, ed. F. M. Müller, vol. V), Oxford 1880; repr. Delhi 1970.
al-Bundārī (d. after 639/1241f.), *Mukhtaṣar zubdat al-nuṣra*, ed. M. T. Houtsma in his *Recueil de textes relatifs à l'histoire des Seljoucides*, II, Leiden 1889.
Buren, E. D. van, 'The *ṣalmē* in Mesopotamian Art and Religion', *Orientalia* 10, 1941, 65–92.
Bürgel, J. C., 'The Idea of Non-Violence in the Epic Poetry of Niẓāmī', *Edebiyât* 9, 1998, 61–84.
Burridge, K., *New Heaven, New Earth: A Study of Millenarian Activities*, Oxford 1969.
Bynum, C. W., *The Resurrection of the Body*, New York 1995.
Cahen, C., 'Simples interrogations hérésiographiques', in R. Gramlich (ed.), *Islamwissenschaftliche Abhandlungen Fritz Meier zum sechstigen Geburtstag*, Wiesbaden 1974, 29–32.
Calmeyer, P., 'Zur Bedingten Göttlichkeit des Grosskönigs', *Archaeologische Mitteilungen aus Iran* 14, 1981, 55–60.
Canard, M., 'Une mention des Arewordik' dans un texte historique arabe', *Revue des Etudes Arméniennes* NS 3, 1966, 200–3.
Canepa, M., *The Two Eyes of the Earth: Art and Ritual of Kingship between Rome and Sasanian Iran*, Berkeley, Los Angeles, and London 2009.
Carlsen, B. H., 'The *Cakar* Marriage Contract and the *Cakar* Children's Status in *Mātiyān i Hazār Dātistān* and *Rivāyat ī Ēmēt ī Ašavahištān*', in W. Skalmowski and A. van Tongerloo (eds.), *Middle Iranian Studies*, Leuven 1984, 103–14.
Cartlidge, D. R., 'Transfigurations of Metamorphosis Traditions in the Acts of John, Thomas, and Peter', *Semeia* 38, 1986, 53–66.
Casadio, G., 'Abendteuer des Dualismus auf der Seidenstrasse', in R. E. Emmerick, W. Sundermann, and P. Zieme (eds.), *Studia Manichaica: IV. Internationaler Kongress zum Manichaïsmus, Berlin, 14.–18. Juli 1997*, Berlin 2000, 55–82.

'The Manichaean Metempsychosis: Typology and Historical Roots', in G. Wiesner and H.-J. Klimkeit (eds.), *Studia Manichaica: II. Internationaler Kongress zum Manichaïsmus, 6.–10. August 1989, St Augustin/Bonn*, Wiesbaden 1992, 105–30.

'Case of the Animals' = *Rasāʾil Ikhwān al-ṣafā*, epistle 22 (Beirut 1957, II, 198–377); tr. L.E. Goodman, *The Case of the Animals versus Man before the King of the Jinn*, Boston 1978; ed. and tr. L.E. Goodman and R. McGregor, Oxford 2009.

Casey, R.P. (ed. and tr.), *The Excerpta ex Theodoto of Clement of Alexandria*, London 1934.

Casiday, A.M.C., 'Deification in Origen, Evagrius and Cassian', in L. Perrone *et al.* (eds.), *Origeniana Octava: Origen and the Alexandrian Tradition*, Leuven 2003, II, 995–1001.

Cassin, E., *La splendeur divine*, The Hague 1969.

Cereti: see *Zand ī Wahman Yasn*.

Chabot, J.B. (ed. and tr.), *Synodicon Orientale ou Recueil de synodes nestoriens*, Paris 1902.

Chadwick, H., 'The Relativity of Moral Codes: Rome and Persia in Late Antiquity', in W.R. Schoedel and R.L. Wilken (eds.), *Early Christian Literature and the Classical Intellectual Tradition in Honorem Robert M. Grant*, Paris 1979, 135–53.

Chāndogya Upaniṣad: see *Upaniṣads*.

Chapple, C.K., *Nonviolence to Animals, Earth, and Self in Asian Traditions*, Albany 1993.

Charlesworth, J.H. (ed.), *The Old Testament Pseudepigrapha*, I (*Apocalyptic Literature and Testaments*), New York 1983.

Charpentier, J., 'Kleine Beiträge zur Indoiranischen Mythologie, II: Die Inkarnationen des Vərəθraγna', *Uppsala Universitetets Årsskrift* 1911, 25–68.

Chaumont, M.L., 'L'inscription de Kartīr à la "Kaʿbah de Zoroastre"', *Journal Asiatique* **248**, 1960, 339–80.

Chavannes, É., *Documents sur les Tou-kiue (Turcs) occidentaux*, St Petersburg 1903; 2nd edn, Paris n.d.

Notes additionelles sur les Tou-kiue (Turcs) occidentaux, printed at the end of the Paris edition of his *Documents sur les Tou-kiue*.

Ch'en, K(enneth) K.S., *Buddhism in China*, Princeton 1964.

Choksy, J.K., *Evil, Good, and Gender*, New York 2002.

'Reassessing the Material Contexts of Ritual Fires in Ancient Iran', *Iranica Antiqua* **42**, 2007, 229–69.

Christensen, A., *L'Iran sous les sassanides*, 2nd edn, Copenhagen 1944.

'Le règne du roi Kawādh I et le communisme mazdakite', *Det Kgl. Danske Videnskabernes Selskab*, Hist.-fil. Meddelelser, **9**, 1925, 3–127; offprint Copenhagen 1925.

Chronicon ad 1234, ed. J.B. Chabot, 3 vols., Paris 1916–20; tr. A. Abouna, Louvain 1974.

Chu, Y.R., 'An Introductory Study of the White Lotus Sect in Chinese History', Ph.D. dissertation, Columbia University 1967.

Cirillo, L., 'From the Elchasaite Christology to the Manichaean Apostle of Light', in A. van Tongerloo and L. Cirillo (eds.), *Il Manicheismo: nuove prospettive della ricerca*, Turnhout 2005, 47–54.

Clement of Alexandria (d. *c.* 215), *Stromateis*, books I–III, tr. J. Ferguson, Washington 1991.

Clement of Alexandria (attrib.), *The Clementine Recognitions, The Clementine Homilies* (Ante-Nicene Christian Library: Translations of the Writings of the Fathers down to AD 325, ed. A. Roberts and J. Donaldson, III, XVII), Edinburgh 1867, 1870 (repr. 2005).

Clines, D. J. A., 'Humanity as the Image of God', in his *On the Way to the Postmodern: Old Testament Essays 1967–1998*, Sheffield 1998, II, 447–97.

CMC = *Der Kölner Mani-Kodex*, ed. and tr. L. Koenen and C. Römer, Opladen 1988. The references are to the pages of the codex, which are so small that I do not include line references.

Cobb, P., *White Banners: Contention in ʿAbbasid Syria, 750–880*, Albany 2001.

Colpe, C., 'Die Thomaspsalmen als chronologischer Fixpunkt in der Geschichte der orientalischen Gnosis', *Jahrbuch für Antike und Christentum* 7, 1964, 77–93.

Compareti, M., 'The Last Sasanians in China', *Eurasian Studies* 11, 2003, 197–213.

'Traces of Buddhist Art in Sogdiana', *Sino-Platonic Papers* no. 181, August 2008 (web journal).

Conze, E., 'The Ontology of the Prajñāpāramitā', *Philosophy East and West* 3, 1953, 117–29.

Cook, M., *A Brief History of the Human Race*, New York 2003.

'Ibn Qutayba and the Monkeys', *Studia Islamica* 89, 1999, 43–74.

Corbin, H., *Cyclical Time and Ismaili Gnosis*, London 1983.

Cornu, G., *Atlas du monde arabo-islamique à l' époque classique*, Leiden 1985.

Cosentino, S., 'Iranian Contingents in the Byzantine Army', in *La Persia e Bisanzio* (Atti dei Convegni Lincei 201), Rome 2004, 245–81.

Crone, P., 'The ʿAbbāsid Abnāʾ and Sāsānid Cavalrymen', *Journal of the Royal Asiatic Society* 8, 1998, 1–19 (repr. in *From Arabian Tribes to Islamic Empire*, no. VIII).

'Abū Tammām on the Mubayyiḍa', in Omar Ali-de-Ungaza (ed.), *Fortresses of the Intellect: Ismaili and other Islamic Studies in Honour of Farhad Daftary*, London 2011, 167–88.

'"Barefoot and Naked": What Did the Bedouin of the Arab Conquests Look Like?', *Muqarnas* 25, 2008 (Festschrift for Oleg Grabar), 1–10.

'The Book of Watchers in the Qurʾān', forthcoming in H. Ben-Shammai, S. Shaked, and S. Stroumsa (eds.), *Exchange and Transmission across Cultural Boundaries: Philosophy, Mysticism and Science in the Mediterranean (Proceeding of a Workshop in memory of Prof. Shlomo Pines, the Institute for Advanced Studies, Jerusalem; 28 February–2 March 2005)*, Jerusalem.

'Buddhism as Ancient Iranian Paganism', forthcoming in T. Bernheimer and A. Silverstein (eds.), *Late Antiquity: Eastern Perspectives*, Cambridge, 25–41.

'The Dahrīs according to al-Jāḥiẓ', forthcoming in *Mélanges de l'Université de St Joseph*.

From Arabian Tribes to Islamic Empire, Aldershot 2008.

From Kavād to al-Ghazālī, Aldershot 2005.
'Imperial Trauma: The Case of the Arabs', *Common Knowledge* 12, 2006, 107–16 (repr. in *From Arabian Tribes to Islamic Empire*, no. XII).
'al-Jāḥiẓ on *aṣḥāb al-jahālāt* and the Jahmiyya', forthcoming in R. Hansberger, A. al-Akiti, and C. Burnett (eds.), *Medieval Arabic Thought: Essays in Honour of Fritz Zimmermann*, London and Turin.
'Kavād's Heresy and Mazdak's Revolt', *Iran* 29, 1991, 21–42 (repr. in *From Kavād to al-Ghazālī*, no. I).
'Mawālī and the Prophet's Family: An early Shī'ite View', in M. Bernards and J. Nawas (eds.), *Patronate and Patronage in Early and Classical Islam*, Leiden 2005, 167–94 (repr. in *From Arabian Tribes to Islamic Empire*, no. XI).
Medieval Islamic Political Thought, Edinburgh and New York 2004 (American title *God's Rule*).
'A Note on Muqātil b. Ḥayyān and Muqātil b. Sulaymān', *Der Islam* 74, 1997, 238–49 (repr. in *From Arabian Tribes to Islamic Empire*, no. V).
'The Pay of Client Soldiers in the Umayyad Period', *Der Islam* 80, 284–300 (repr. in *From Arabian Tribes to Islamic Empire*, no. X).
'Post-Colonialism in Tenth-Century Islam', *Der Islam* 83, 2006, 2–38.
'Pre-existence in Iran: Zoroastrians, Ex-Christian Mu'tazilites, and Jews on the Human Acquisition of Bodies', forthcoming in *Aram*.
'The Significance of Wooden Weapons in al-Mukhtār's Revolt and the 'Abbāsid Revolution', in I. R. Netton (ed.), *Studies in Honour of Clifford Edmund Bosworth*, I, Leiden 2000 (repr. in *From Arabian Tribes to Islamic Empire*, no. VI).
Slaves on Horses: The Evolution of the Islamic Polity, Cambridge 1980.
'Were the Qays and Yemen of the Umayyad Period Political Parties?', *Der Islam* 71, 1994, 1–57 (repr. in *From Arabian Tribes to Islamic Empire*, no. IV).
'Zoroastrian Communism', *Comparative Studies in Society and History* 36, 1994, 447–62 (repr. in *From Kavād to al-Ghazāli*, no. II).
Crone, P., and M. Jafari Jazi, 'The Muqanna' Narrative in the *Tārīkhnāma*: Part I, Introduction, Edition and Translation', *Bulletin of the School of Oriental and African Studies* 73, 2010, 157–77 (cited by the paragraphs into which both the text and the translation are divided); Part II, 'Commentary and Analysis', *ibid.*, 73, 2010, 381–413 (cited by page).
Crone, P., and A. Silverstein, 'The Ancient Near East and Islam: The Case of Lot-Casting', *Journal of Semitic Studies* 55, 2010, 423–50.
Crone, P., and L. Treadwell, 'A New Text on Ismailism at the Samanid Court', in C. F. Robinson (ed.), *Texts, Documents and Artefacts: Islamic Studies in Honour of D. S. Richards*, Leiden 2003, 37–67.
Crone, P., and F. Zimmermann (ed. and tr.), *The Epistle of Sālim b. Dhakwān*, Oxford 2001.
Curtin, P. D., *The World and the West*, Cambridge 2000.
Dabistān-i madhāhib (mid-eleventh/seventeenth century), ed. R. Riḍāzāde Malik (giving the author as Kaykhusraw Isfandiyār), 2 vols., Tehran 1363 [1983]; tr. D. Shea and A. Troyer, 3 vols., Paris 1843.
Dādestān ī Dēnīg (fourth/tenth century), part I, ed. and tr. M. Jaafari-Dehaghi, Paris 1998; complete tr. in E. W. West, *Pahlavi Texts*, part ii (Sacred Books of the East, ed. F. M. Müller, vol. XVIII), Oxford 1882; repr. Delhi 1870 (barely

usable). References are to the question (*pursišn*) numbers and their subdivisions. Abbreviated as *Dd*.

Daffinà, P., 'La Persia sassanide secondo le fonte cinesi', *Rivista degli Studi Orientali* 57, 1983, 121–70.

Daftary, F., *The Ismāʿīlīs*, 2nd edn., Cambridge 2007.

Dāʾirat al-maʿārif-i buzurg-i islāmī, ed. M. Bujnūrdī, Tehran 1367–. Abbreviated as *DMBI*.

Dalrymple, W., *Nine Lives: In Search of the Sacred in Modern India*, New York 2010.

Daniel, E. L., *The Political and Social History of Khurasan under Abbasid Rule 747–820*, Minneapolis and Chicago 1979.

Dardess, J. W., 'The Transformations of Messianic Revolt and the Founding of the Ming Dynasty', *Journal of Asian Studies* 29, 1970, 539–58.

Darmesteter: see *Yašts*.

Darrow, W. R., 'Zoroaster Amalgamated: Notes on Iranian Prophetology', *History of Religions* 27, 1987, 109–32.

Daryaee, T., 'The Collapse of the Sassanian Power in Fārs/Persis', *Nāme-ye Īrān-e Bāstān* 2, 2002, 3–18.

'A Historical Episode in the Zoroastrian Apocalyptic Tradition: The Romans, the Abbasids, and the Khorramdēns', in T. Daryaee and M. Omidsalar (eds.), *The Spirit of Wisdom: Essays in Memory of Ahmad Tafazzoli*, Costa Mesa 2004, 64–76.

Šahristānīhā: see *Šahristānīhā*.

Davies, J. G., 'Factors leading to the Emergence of Belief in the Resurrection of the Flesh', *Journal of Theological Studies*, 23, 1972, 448–55.

Davis, R. H., 'Indian Image-Worship and its Discontents', in J. Assmann and A. I. Baumgarten (eds.), *Representation in Religion: Studies in Honor of Moshe Barasch*, Leiden 2001, 107–32.

Dawson, D., *Cities of the Gods: Communist Utopias in Greek Thought*, Oxford and New York 1992.

Dd: see *Dādestān ī Dēnīg*.

Deeg, M., and I. Gardner, 'Indian Influence on Mani Reconsidered: The Case of Jainism', *International Journal of Jaina Studies* (Online) 5, 2009, 1–30.

Dēnkard (late third/ninth century), Book III, tr. J. de Ménasce, *Le troisième livre du Dēnkart*, Paris 1973; book V, ed. and tr. J. Amouzfar and A. Tafazzoli, Paris 2000; book VI, tr. S. Shaked, *The Wisdom of the Sasanian Sages*, Boulder, Colo., 1979; book VII and parts of V, ed. and tr. M. Molé, *La legende de Zoroastre selon les texts pehlevis*, Paris 1967; books V, VII, VIII, tr. E. West, *Pahlavi Texts*, parts iv and v (Sacred Books of the East, ed. F. M. Müller, vols. XXXVII, XLVII), Oxford 1892, 1897; repr. Delhi 1969 (sparingly used). There is a full edition, transliteration and English translation by P. B. Sanjana, 19 vols, Bombay 1874–1928, but I have only used it for book IX. References given in the form *Dk* III, no. 202 and *Dk* IX, 11:19 are to books and sections and books and chapters (sometimes paragraphs) respectively. All other references are to the pages and lines of Madan's edition (*DkM*) or the Bombay manuscript (*DkB*) as given in the specialist works from which the passages are taken (and which are always named).

al-Dhahabī (d. 748/1348), *al-Juzʾ al-awwal [wa'l-thānī] min Kitāb duwal al-Islām*, 2 vols. in one, Hyderabad 1337/1919.

Siyar aʿlām al-nubalāʾ, ed. S. Arnaʾūṭ *et al.*, VII, Beirut 1981.

Taʾrīkh al-islām, Maktabat al-Qudsī, Cairo 1369. References to vols. V and VI are to this edition; ed. ʿA. ʿAbd al-Sallām Tadmurī, 70 *ṭabaqas*, Beirut 1990–2000. The volumes are unnumbered, but identified by the *ṭabaqa* and years they cover (with a few exceptions the *ṭabaqas* cover a volume each).

Dictionary of the Old Testament: Pentateuch, ed. T. D. Alexander and D. W. Baker, Downers Grove, Ill., and Leicester 2003.

Dien, A. E., 'A Note on *Hsien*, "Zoroastrianism"', *Oriens* 10, 1957, 284–8.

Dietrich, A., 'Die Moscheen von Gurgān zur Omaijadenzeit', *Der Islam* 40, 1965, 1–17.

Dihkhudā (medieval): see Kāshānī.

Dihkhudā, ʿA. A., *Lughatnāma*, Tehran 1325–52. Issued in parts numbered in accordance with the date of issue, bound in 16 vols. in some libraries. Cited by entry.

Dillon, J., *The Middle Platonists*, London 1977.

'The Platonizing of Mithra', *Journal of Mithraic Studies* 2, 1977, 79–85 (repr. in his *The Golden Chain: Studies in the Development of Platonism and Christianity*, Aldershot 1990, no. XVII).

al-Dīnawarī (d. 282/895), *al-Akhbār al-ṭiwāl*, ed. V. Guirgass, Leiden 1888.

Diodorus Siculus (wr. *c.* 60–30 BC), *Library of History*, ed. and tr. C. H. Oldfather, 12 vols., Cambridge, Mass., and London 1935.

Diogenes Laertius (third century AD), *Lives of Eminent Philosophers*, ed. and tr. R. D. Hicks, 2 vols., Cambridge, Mass., and London 1925.

Dk: see *Dēnkard*.

DMBI: see *Dāʾirat al-maʿārif*.

Dodge: see Ibn al-Nadīm.

Domínguez, A. J., 'The Greek Cities of Sicily and the Natives', in G. R. Tsetskhladze (ed.), *Greek Colonisation: An Account of Greek Colonies and Other Settlements Overseas*, Leiden 2006, 324–57.

Doresse, J., *The Secret Books of the Egyptian Gnostics*, London 1960.

Doughty, C. M., *Travels in Arabia Deserta*, New York 1979 [first published 1888].

Dozy, R., *Supplément aux dictionnaires arabes*, Leiden 1881 (repr. Beirut 1968).

Drijvers, H. J. W., *Bardaisan of Edessa*, Assen 1966.

'Quq and the Quqites: An Unknown Sect in Edessa in the Second Century AD', *Numen* 14, 1967, 104–29.

Duchesne-Guillemin, J., 'The "Form of Fire"', in *Dr J. M. Unvala Memorial Volume*, Bombay [1964], 14–17.

La religion de l'Iran ancient, Paris 1962.

'The Six Original Creations', *Sir J. J. Zarthoshti Madressa Centenary Volume*, Bombay 1967, 7–8.

'Le Xᵛarənah', *Annali dell' Istituto Universitario di Napoli* 5, 1963, 19–31.

Durkin-Meisterernst, D., *Dictionary of Manichaean, Middle Persian and Parthian Texts*, III/1 (*Texts from Central Asia and China*) (Corpus Fontium Manichaeorum), Turnhout 2004.

Eberhard, E., *Osmanische Polemik gegen die Safawiden im 16. Jahrhundert nach arabischen Handschriften*, Freiburg im Breisgau 1970.
Edmonds, C. J., 'The Beliefs and Practices of the Ahl-i Ḥaqq of Iraq', *Iran* 7, 1969, 89–101.
Edwards, M. J., *Origen against Plato*, Aldershot 2002.
Ehlers, B., 'Bardesanes von Edessa: ein syrischer Gnostiker', *Zeitschrift für Kirchengeschichte* 81, 1970, 334–51.
EI[2] = *Encyclopaedia of Islam*, 2nd ed., Leiden 1960–2009.
Eichhorn, W., 'Materialen zum Auftreten iranischer Kulte in China', *Die Welt des Orients* 11, 1955, 531–41.
EIr. = *Encyclopaedia Iranica*, ed. E. Yarshater, London and Boston 1982–.
Elias, J., 'The Sufi Lords of Bahrabad: Sa'd al-Din and Sadr al-Din Hamuwayi', *Iranian Studies* 27, 1994, 53–75.
Elias Bar Shinaya (wr. 1019), *Eliae Metropolitae Nisibeni Opus chronologicum*, part i, ed. E. W. Brooks, part ii, ed. J.-B. Chabot (CSCO, Script. syri, 21, 23), Louvain 1909–10.
El-Rouayheb, K., 'Heresy and Sufism in the Arabic-Islamic World, 1550–1750: Some Preliminary Observations', *Bulletin of the School of Oriental and African Studies* 73, 2010, 357–80.
Before Homosexuality in the Arab-Islamic World, Chicago 2005.
Emmerick, R. E. (tr.), *The Book of Zambasta: A Khotanese Poem on Buddhism*, London 1968.
Enoch: 1 Enoch, tr. G. W. E. Nickelsburg and J. C. VanderKam, Minneapolis 2004; for 2 and 3 Enoch see Charlesworth.
Enoki, K., 'On the Nationality of the Ephtalites', *Memoirs of the Research Department of the Toyo Bunko* (Tokyo) 18, 1959, 1–58.
Epiphanius (d. 403), *Panarion*, tr. F. Williams, 2 vols., Leiden 1987–1994. Cited by sect number and subdivisions, followed by the volume and page of the translation in parenthesis because the translation does not have the sect number in the running heads.
Ess, J. van, *Theologie und Gesellschaft*, 6 vols., Berlin 1991–7. Abbreviated as *TG*.
Eusebius (d. 339), *Ecclesiastical History*, ed. and tr. H. J. Lawlor and J. E. L. Oulton, Cambridge, Mass., and London 1926, 1932 (repr. 2000).
Praeparatio Evangelica, ed. and tr. É. des Places *et al.*, 9 vols., Paris 1975–87.
Excerpts: See Casey, *Excerpta*.
Eznik of Kołb (alive 450), *Ełc ałandoc*[c] (Against the Sects), ed. and tr. S. Zeilfelder, Graz 2004; tr. M. J. Blanchard and R. D. Young, *On God*, Leuven 1998. Cited by section number (identical in the two translations, though only the first uses subdivision). All references are to Zeilfelder's translation unless the contrary is indicated.
Fakhr al-Dīn al-Rāzī (d. 606/1209), *I'tiqadāt firaq al-muslimīn wa 'l-mushrikīn*, ed. M. M. al-Baghdādī, Beirut 1986.
al-Tafsīr al-kabīr, 32 vols. in 16, Tehran 1413.
Fāmī: see *Tārīkh-i Harāt*.
al-Fasawī (d. 277/890f.), *al-Ma'rifa wa'l-ta'rīkh*, ed. K. al-Manṣūr, 3 vols., Beirut 1999.
Faṣīḥ-i Khwāfī: see Khwāfī.

Feissel, D., 'Bulletin épigraphique: inscriptions chrétiennes et byzantines', *Revue des Études Grecques* 100, 1987, 347–87.
Fihrist: see Ibn al-Nadīm.
Fossum, J. E., 'The Apostle Concept in the Qur'ān and Pre-Islamic Near Eastern Literature', in M. Mir (ed.), *Literary Heritage of Classical Islam: Arabic and Islamic Studies in Honor of James A. Bellamy*, Princeton 1993, 149–67.
Fox, W. S., and R. E. K. Pemberton, 'Passages in Greek and Latin Literature Relating to Zoroaster and Zoroastrianism Translated into English', *Journal of the Oriental Cama Institute* 14, 1929, 1–145.
Fragner, B., *Geschichte der Stadt Hamadān und ihrer Umgebung in den ersten sechs Jahrhunderten nach der Hiğra*, Vienna 1972.
Frankfurter, D., 'Apocalypses Real and Alleged in the Mani Codex', *Numen* 44, 1997, 60–73.
Franzmann, M., *Jesus in the Manichaean Writings*, New York and London 2003.
Freitag, R., *Seelenwanderung in der islamischen Häresie*, Berlin 1985.
Frenschkowski, M., 'Marcion in arabischen Quellen', in G. May and K. Greschat (eds.), *Marcion und seine Kirchengeschichtliche Wirkung*, Berlin 2002, 39–63.
Friedl, E., 'Islam and Tribal Women in a Village in Iran', in N. A. Falk and R. M. Gross (eds.), *Unspoken Worlds: Women's Religious Lives*, Belmont, Calif., 1989, 125–33.
Friedlaender, I., 'The Heterodoxies of the Shiites in the Presentation of Ibn Ḥazm: Commentary', *Journal of the American Oriental Society* (i) 28, 1907, 1–80; (ii) 29, 1908, 1–183.
'Jewish–Arabic Studies, I: Shiitic Elements in Jewish Sectarianism', *Jewish Quarterly Review* NS 2, 1911–12, 481–516.
Frye, R. N., 'Achaemenid Echoes in Sasanian Times', in H. Koch and D. N. MacKenzie (eds.), *Kunst, Kultur und Geschichte der Achämenidenzeit und ihr Fortleben*, Berlin 1983, 247–52.
'Parthian and Sasanian History of Iran', in J. Curtis (ed.), *Mesopotamia and Iran in the Parthian and Sasanian Periods*, London 2000, 17–22.
Fück, J., *Documenta Islamica inedita*, Berlin 1952.
Fulton, J., *Index canonum*, 2nd edn, New York 1883.
Fynes, R. C. C., 'Plant Souls in Jainism and Manichaeism: The Case for Cultural Transmission', *East and West* 46, 1996, 21–44.
Gagniers, J. de, and T. Tam Tihn (eds.), *Soloi: dix campagnes de fouilles*, I, Laval 1985.
Gardīzī (d. after 432/1041), *Tārīkh*, ed. 'A.-Ḥ. Ḥabībī, Tehran 1363 [1984].
Gardner, I., and S. N. C. Lieu (trs.), *Manichaean Texts from the Roman Empire*, Cambridge 2004.
Gardner, I., 'Some Comments on Mani and Indian Religions according to the Coptic *Kephalaia*', in A. van Tongerloo and L. Cirillo (eds.), *Il Manicheism: nuove prospettive della ricerca*, Turnhout 2005, 123–35.
Garsoian, N., *The Paulician Heresy*, The Hague and Paris 1967.
Gelder, G. J. van, *Close Relationships: Incest and Inbreeding in Classical Arabic Literature*, London 2005.
Gershevitch, I., 'Word and Spirit in Ossetic', *Bulletin of the School of Oriental and African Studies* 17, 1955, 478–89.
al-Ghazālī (d. 505/1111), *Faḍā'iḥ al-bāṭiniyya*, Amman 1993.

Makātib-i fārsi-yi Ghazāli, ed. ʿA. Iqbāl, 2nd printing, Tehran 1362 [1983]; tr. D. Krawulsky, *Briefe und Reden des Abū Ḥāmid Muḥammad al-Ghazzālī*, Freiburg 1971.

'Die Streitschrift des Ġazālī gegen die Ibāhīja', ed. and tr. O. Pretzl, *Sitzungsberichte der Bayerischen Akademie der Wissenschaften*, Phil.-Hist. Klasse, 1933, 1–52, followed by Persian *1–*28.

Gibb, H. A. R., *The Arab Conquests in Central Asia*, London 1923.

Gieschen, C. A., *Angelomorphic Christology*, Leiden 1998.

Gignoux, P., 'La chasse dans l'Iran sasanide', *Orientalia Romana*, ed. G. Gnoli, Rome 1983, 101–18.

'"Corps osseux et âme osseuse": essai sur le chamanisme dans l'Iran ancien', *Journal Asiatique* **267**, 1979, 41–79.

'Dietary Laws in Pre-Islamic and Post-Sasanian Iran', *Jerusalem Studies in Arabic and Islam* **17**, 1994, 16–42.

'Der Grossmagier Kirdīr und seine Reise in das Jenseits', in *Orientalia J. Duchesne-Guillemin emerito oblata* (Acta Iranica 23), Leiden 1984, 191–206.

Man and Cosmos in Ancient Iran, Rome 2001.

'L'organisation administrative sasanide: le cas du *marzbān*', *Jerusalem Studies in Arabic and Islam* **4**, 1984, 1–29.

'Die religiöse Administration in sasanidischer Zeit: ein Überblick', in H. Koch and D. N. MacKenzie (eds.), *Kunst, Kultur und Geschichte der Achämenidenzeit und ihr Fortleben*, Berlin 1983, 253–66.

Gignoux, P. (ed. and tr.), *Les Quatre Inscriptions du mage Kirdir*, Paris 1991.

Gnoli, G., 'Basileus basileōn arianōn', in G. Gnoli and L. Lanciotti (eds.), *Orientalia Iosephi Tucci Memoriae Dictata*, Rome 1987, 509–32.

'Ēr Mazdēsn, Zum Begriff Iran und seiner Entstehung im 3. Jahrhundert', in *Transition Periods in Iranian History (Actes du Symposium de Fribourg-en-Brisgau, 22–24 Mai 1985)*, Leuven 1987, 83–100.

Golden, P. B., *An Introduction to the History of the Turkic Peoples*, Wiesbaden 1992.

Goldziher, I., *Muhammedanische Studien*, 2 vols., Halle 1889–90 (ed. and tr. S. M. Stern, *Muslim Studies*, London 1967–71).

'Neuplatonische und gnostische Elemente im Ḥadīṯ', *Zeitschrift für Assyriologie* **22**, 1908, 317–44.

Golitzin, A., 'Recovering the 'Glory of Adam': 'Divine Light' Traditions in the Dead Sea Scrolls and the Christian Ascetical Literature of Fourth-Century Syro-Mesopotamia', at http://www.marquette/edu/maqom/Recovering.html.

Gombrich, R. F., *Precept and Practice: Traditional Buddhism in the Rural Highlands of Ceylon*, Oxford 1971.

Gordon, H. L., 'The Eternal Triangle, First Century BC', *The Classical Journal* **28**, 1933, 574–8.

Gordon, R., 'Who worshipped Mithras?', *Journal of Roman Studies* **7**, 1994, 459–74.

Gospel of the Egyptians (CG III, 2 and IV, 2), tr. A. Böhlig and F. Wisse in Robinson, *Nag Hammadi Library*, 208–19.

Gospel of Thomas (CG II, 2), tr. H. Koester and O. Lambdin in Robinson, *Nag Hammadi Library*, 124–38.

Gough, E. K., 'Female Initiation Rites on the Malabar Coast', *Journal of the Royal Anthropological Institute of Great Britain and Ireland* **85**, 1955, 45–80.

'The Nayars and the Definition of Marriage', in M. Kumar Raha and P. C. Coomar (eds.), *Polyandry in India*, Delhi 1987, 246–66.

Graf, D. F., 'The Nabataean Army and the *Cohortes Ulpiae Petraeorum*', in E. Dabrowa (ed.), *The Roman and Byzantine Army in the East*, Cracow 1994, 265–311 (repr. in his *Rome and the Arabian Frontier*, Aldershot 1997, no. V).

GrBd: see *Bundahišn*.

Gregory of Nyssa (d. after 394), 'On the Making of Man', in P. Schaff and H. Wace (eds.), *A Select Library of Nicene and Post-Nicene Fathers of the Christian Church translated into English*, V (*Gregory of Nyssa*), Edinburgh 1892 (repr. Grand Rapids, Mich., n.d.), 387–427.

On the Soul and the Resurrection, tr. C. P. Roth, New York 2002.

Grenet, F., *Les pratiques funéraires dans l'Asie centrale sédentaire: de la conquête grecque à l'islamisation*, Paris 1984.

'The Second of Three Encounters between Zoroastrianism and Hinduism: Plastic Influences in Bactria and Sogdiana (2nd–8th c. AD)', in G. Lazard and R. SarDesai (eds.), *James Darmesteter Memorial Lectures*, Bombay 1994, 41–57.

'Vaiśravaṇa in Sogdiana', *Silk Road Art and Archaeology* 4, 1995–6, 277–97.

Grenet, F. (ed. and tr.), 'The Pahlavi Text *Māh ī Frawardīn rōz i Hordād*: A Source of Some Passages of Bīrūnī's *Chronology*', in W. Sundermann, A. Hintze, and F. de Blois (eds.), *Exegisti Monumenta: Festschrift in Honour of Nicholas Sims-Williams*, Wiesbaden 2009, 161–70.

Grenet, F. and B. Marshak, 'Le mythe de Nana dans l'art de Sogdiane', *Arts Asiatiques* 53, 1998, 5–17.

Grenet, F. and E. de la Vaissière, 'The Last Days of Panjikent', *Silk Road Art and Archaeology* 8, 2002, 155–96.

Gsell, S., *Histoire ancienne de l'Afrique du nord*, 2nd edn., 8 vols., Paris 1914–30.

Gurney, J. D., 'Pietro della Valle: The Limits of Perception', *Bulletin of the School of Oriental and African Studies* 49, 1986, 103–16.

Gutas, D., *Greek Thought, Arabic Culture*, London 1998.

Haar Romeny, B. ter, 'Hypotheses on the Development of Judaism and Christianity in Syria in the Period after 70 CE', in H. van de Sandt (ed.), *Matthew and the Didache*, Minneapolis 2005, 13–33.

Ḥabībī, A.-Ḥ., *Tārīkh-i Afghānistān ba'd az Islam*, 3 vols., Kabul 1386 [2007].

Hādōxt Nask: see Piras.

Haft kishwar yā ṣuwar al-aqālīm (written in 748/1347f.), ed. M. Sutuda, Tehran 1353 [1974].

Halm, H., 'Das "Buch der Schatten": Die Mufaḍḍal Tradition der Ġulāt und die Ursprunge des Nuṣairiertums', part I, *Der Islam* 55, 1978, 219–65; part II, *Der Islam* 58, 1981, 15–85.

Kosmologie und Heilslehre der frühen Ismā'īlīya, eine Studie zur islamischen Gnosis, Wiesbaden 1978.

Das Reich des mahdi: Der Aufstieg der Fatimiden (875–973), Munich 1991; tr. M. Bonner, *The Empire of the mahdi: The Rise of the Fatimids*, Leiden 1996.

'Die Sieben und die Zwölf: Die ismā'īlitische Kosmogonie und das Mazdak-Fragment des Šahrastānī', in *XVIII: Deutscher Orientalistentag, 1–5 Oktober 1972, Lübeck*, Wiesbaden 1974, 170–7.

Halperin, D. J., and G. D. Newby, 'Two Castrated Bulls: A Study in the Haggadah of Kaʿb al-Aḥbār', *Journal of the American Oriental Society* 102, 1982, 631–8.
Hamilton, W., 'The Myth in Plutarch's *De Facie* (940F–045D)', *The Classical Quarterly* 28, 1934, 24–30.
Ḥamza al-Iṣfahānī (d. before 360/970), *Tawārīkh sinī mulūk al-arḍ wa'l-anbiyā'*, ed. and tr. (Latin) J. M. P. Gottwaldt, 2 vols., Leipzig 1844, 1848; ed. (with *Ta'rīkh* for *Tawārīkh* in the title) Beirut 1961. Cited in that order in the form 221/163.
Hansen, V., 'New Work on the Sogdians, the Most Important Traders on the Silk Road, AD 500–1000', *T'oung Pao* 89, 2003, 149–61.
Harmatta, J., 'The Middle Persian–Chinese Bilingual Inscription from Hsian and the Chinese–Sāsānian Relations', in *La Persia nel Medioevo* (Atti del Convegno), Rome 1971, 363–77.
Harnack, A. von, *History of Dogma*, 7 vols., Gloucester, Mass. 1976 [Freiburg 1888–90, 4 vols.]
Haviland, C., 'Nepal's wife-sharing custom fades', 23 November 2005, at BBC News, http://news.bbc.co.uk/2/hi/south_asia/4461196.stm.
Haydar b. ʿAlī (wr. 1020–8/1611–19), *Majmaʿ al-tawārikh*, extract in *TB*, ed. Schefer, 230–43. Schefer misleadingly calls this work *Mujmil al-tawārikh* in his introduction and lists it as the first rather than the third of the extracts which follow his edition of the *Tārīkh-i Bukhārā*, without giving an author or a date. It was identified to me by O. Otsuka.
Hegemonius (wr. 330–48), *Acta Archelai*, tr. M. Vermes, with an introduction and commentary by S. N. C. Lieu, assisted by K. Kaatz, Louvain 2001.
Heinrichs, A., 'Mani and the Babylonian Baptists', *Harvard Studies in Classical Philology* 77, 1973, 23–59.
'Thou Shalt not Kill a Tree: Greek, Manichaean and Indian Tales', *Bulletin of the American Society of Papyrologists* 16, 1979, 85–108.
Henning, W. B., 'The Ancient Language of Azerbaijan', *Transactions of the Philological Society* 53, 1954 (repr. in his *Selected Papers*, II), 157–77.
'An Astronomical Chapter of the Bundahishn', *Journal of the Royal Asiatic Society* 1942 (repr. in his *Selected Papers*, II), 229–48.
'Mani's Last Journey', *Bulletin of the School of Oriental and African Studies* 10, 1942 (repr. in his *Selected Papers*, II), 941–53.
'Mitteliranisch', in *Handbuch der Orientalistik*, IV (*Iranistik*), I (*Linguistik*), 20–130.
Selected Papers, 2 vols. (Acta Iranica 14, 15), Leiden 1977. All references are to the original pagination.
'A Sogdian God', *Bulletin of the School of Oriental and African Studies* 28, 1965 (repr. in his *Selected Papers*, II), 242–54.
'Sogdian Tales', *Bulletin of the School of Oriental and African Studies* 11, 1945 (repr. in his *Selected Papers*, II), 465–87.
'Two Central Asian Words', *Transactions of the Philological Society*, 1945 (repr. in his *Selected Papers*, II), 150–62.
Henning, W. B. (ed. and tr.), 'Ein manichäisches Bet- und Beichtbuch', *Abhandlungen der Preussischen Akademie der Wissenschaften*, Phil.-Hist. Klasse, 1936 (repr. in his *Selected Papers*, I), 3–143.

Henninger, J., 'Polyandrie im vorislamischen Arabien', *Anthropos* 49, 1954, 314–22.

Hērbedestān, ed. and tr. F. M. Kotwal and P. G. Kreyenbroek, *The Hērbedestān and Nērangestān*, vol. I, Paris 1992; ed. and tr. H. Humbach and J. Elfenbein, Munich 1990. The two editions are distinguished as KK and HE.

Hermanns, M., *Die Familie der A mdo-Tibeter*, Freiburg and Munich 1959.

Herodotus (d. *c.* 425 BC), *Histories*, ed. and tr. A. D. Godley, 4 vols., Cambridge, Mass., and London 1920–5.

Herrenschmidt, C., 'Le xwêtodas ou mariage "incestueux" en Iran ancien', in P. Bonté (ed.), *Epouser au plus proche*, Paris 1994, 113–25.

Hinds, M., 'The First Arab Conquests in Fārs', *Iran* 22, 1984 (repr. in his *Studies in Early Islamic History*, Princeton 1996, no. 8), 49–53.

Hintze, A., 'Disseminating the Mazdayasnian Religion: An Edition of the Avestan Hērbedestān Chapter 5', in W. Sundermann, A. Hintze, and F. de Blois (eds.), *Exegisti Monumenta: Festschrift for Nicholas Sims-Williams*, Wiesbaden 2009, 171–90.

Zamyād Yašt: see *Yašts*.

Hinz, W., *The Lost World of Elam*, London 1972.

Hippolytus (wr. *c.* 230), *Refutation of all Heresies*, ed. M. Marcovich, Berlin and New York 1986; tr. J. H. MacMahon (Ante-Nicene Christian Library, ed. A. Roberts and J. Donaldson), Edinburgh 1868, where the chapter divisions are somewhat different; section on Elchasai, ed. and tr. Klijn and Reinink, *Patristic Evidence*, 112–23; ed. and tr. Luttikhuizen, *Elchasai*, 42–53.

'Histoire Nestorienne': see Scher.

Hjerrild, B., 'Some Aspects of the Institution of *Stūrīh*', in F. Vahman and C. V. Pedersen (eds.), *Religious Texts in Iranian Languages*, Copenhagen 2007, 165–74.

Hodgson, M. G. S., *The Order of the Assassins*, The Hague 1955.

The Venture of Islam, 2 vols., Chicago 1974.

Hoffmann, G., *Auszüge aus syrischen Akten persischer Märtyrer* (= *Abhandlungen für die Kunde des Morgenlandes* 7, 1880).

Homilies: see Clement (attrib.).

Hopkins, K., *Death and Renewal*, Cambridge 1983.

Houtsma, M. T., 'Bih'afrid', *Vienna Oriental Journal* 3, 1889, 30–7.

Ḥudūd al-ʿālam, tr. V. Minorsky, ed. C. E. Bosworth, London 1970.

Hujwīrī (d. after 465/1072), *Kashf al-maḥjūb*, ed. V. Zhukovski, Leningrad 1926; tr. R. A. Nicholson, London 1911.

Hulsewé, A. F. P., and M. A. N. Loewe (trs.), *China in Central Asia: The Early Stage, 125 BC–AD 23*, Leiden 1979.

Hultgård, A., 'Persian Apocalypticism', in J. J. Collins (ed.), *The Encyclopedia of Apocalypticism*, I, New York 1998, 39–83.

Humbach, H., 'Herrscher, Gott und Gottessohn in Iran und in angrenzenden Ländern', in D. Zeller (ed.), *Menschwerdung Gottes: Vergöttlichung von Menschen*, Freiburg and Göttingen 1988, 91–114.

'Die Pahlavi–Chinesischen Bilingue von Xi'an', in W. Sundermann *et al.* (eds.), *A Green Leaf: Papers in Honour of Professor Jes P. Asmussen* (Acta Iranica 28), Leiden 1988, 73–82.

'Vayu, Śiva und der Spiritus Vivens im ostiranischen Synkretismus', in *Monumentum H. S. Nyberg*, I (Acta Iranica 4), Leiden 1975, 397–408.
'Yama/Yima/Jamšēd, King of Paradise and the Iranians', at http://www.azargoshnasp.net/Din/jamshidkingparadisehelmut.pdf.
'Zarathustra und die Rinderschlachtung', in B. Benzing, O. Böcher, and G. Mayer (eds.), *Wort und Wirklichkeit: Studien zur Afrikanistik und Orientalistik*, Meisenheim am Glan 1977, II, 17–29.
Husayn, A., 'Eka-ge-kema': Fraternal Polyandry among the Olden-Day Sinhalese', at http://www.lankalibrary.com/rit/ekage.htm.
IA: see Ibn al-Athīr.
Ibn ʿAbd al-Ḥakam (d. 257/871), *Futūḥ Miṣr*, ed. C. C. Torrey, New Haven 1922.
Ibn al-ʿAdīm (d. 660/1262), *Zubdat al-ḥalab min taʾrīkh Ḥalab*, ed. S. al-Dahhān, 3 vols., Damascus 1951–68.
Ibn al-Athīr (d. 630/1233), *al-Kāmil fī ʾl-taʾrīkh*, ed. C. J. Tornberg, Leiden 1851–76 (repr. (with different pagination) Beirut, 12 vols., 1965–67). References are to the Beirut reprint unless otherwise specified. Abbreviated as IA.
Ibn Bābawayh (d. 381/991), *ʿIlal al-sharāʾiʿ* [Najaf 1966].
Ibn al-Balkhī (wr. early sixth/twelfth century), *Fārsnāma*, ed. G. Le Strange and R. A. Nicholson, London 1921.
Ibn al-Dawādārī (d. 713/1313), *Kanz al-durar wa-jāmiʿ al-ghurar*, VI, ed. Ṣ.-D. al-Munajjid, Cairo 1961.
Ibn al-Faqīh (third/ninth century), *Kitāb al-buldān*, ed. M. J. de Goeje, Leiden 1885; ed. Y. al-Hādī (second part based on a fuller Mashhad manuscript), Beirut 1430/2009. Cited in that order, separated by a slash or with indication of editor.
Ibn Ḥajar al-ʿAsqalānī (d. 852/1449), *Tahdhīb al-tahdhīb*, 12 vols., Hyderabad 1325–27 [1907–9].
Ibn Ḥanbal, Aḥmad (d. 241/855) (attrib.), *al-Radd ʿalā ʾl-zanādiqa waʾl-Jahmiyya*, Cairo 1393 [1973f.].
Ibn Ḥazm (d. 456/1064), *Jamharat ansāb al-ʿarab*, ed. ʿA.-S. M. Hārun, Cairo 1962.
Kitāb al-faṣl fī ʾl-milal waʾl-ahwāʾ waʾl-niḥal, 5 vols. in 2, Cairo 1317–21 [1899–1903f.]. (Normally transliterated as *K. al-fiṣal*, but *fiṣal* does not seem to be a real word.)
Ibn Ḥibbān al-Bustī (d. 354/965), *Kitāb mashāhīr ʿulamāʾ al-amṣār*, ed. M. Fleischhammer, Cairo and Wiesbaden 1359/1959.
Ibn Isfandiyār (wr. 613/1216f.), *Tārīkh-i Ṭabaristān*, ed. ʿA. Iqbāl, 2 vols., Tehran 1320 [1941f.].
Ibn al-Jawzī (d. 597/1200), *al-Muntaẓam*, vols. V–X, Hyderabad 1357–9 [1938–40f.] (the edition used for those volumes unless otherwise indicated); ed. Muḥammad and Muṣṭafā al-Qādir ʿAṭā, 18 vols., Beirut 1992–3 (used for the rest).
Talbīs Iblīs, ed. M. M. al-Dimashqī [Cairo 1928].
Ibn Khaldūn (d. 808/1406), *Muqaddima*, ed. Beirut n.d.; tr. F. Rosenthal, 3 vols., Princeton 1967; tr. A. Cheddadi, Paris 2002.
Ibn Khallikān (d. 681/1282), *Wafayāt al-aʿyān*, ed. I. ʿAbbās, 8 vols., Beirut 1977–8.
Ibn Khurdādhbih (d. *c.* 300/911), *al-Masālik waʾl-mamālik*, ed. M. J. de Goeje, Leiden 1889.

Ibn al-Malāḥimī (d. 536/1141), *Kitāb al-muʿtamad fī uṣūl al-dīn*, ed. M. McDermott and W. Madelung, London 1991 (referred to as Ibn al-Malāḥimī); enlarged edition by Wilferd Madelung. Tehran: Iranian Institute of Philosophy and Institute of Islamic Studies, Free University of Berlin, forthcoming 2012 (all page numbers higher than 599 are to this edition, referred to as Ibn al-Malāḥimī, *Muʿtamad*).

Ibn al-Nadīm (d. 380/990), *al-Fihrist*, ed. R. Tajaddud, Tehran 1971; tr. B. Dodge, *The Fihrist of al-Nadīm*, 2 vols., New York and London 1970.

Ibn Qutayba (d. 276/889) (attrib.), *al-Imāma wa'l-siyāsa*, 2 vols. in 1, Cairo 1969.

al-Maʿārif, ed. T. ʿUkāsha, Cairo 1969.

Ibn Saʿd (d. 230/845), *al-Ṭabaqāt*, ed. E. Sachau *et al.*, 9 vols., Leiden 1904–40; ed. Beirut, 5 vols., 1957–60. References are given to both editions in that order.

al-ʿIbrī: see Bar Hebraeus.

al-Imāma wa'l-siyāsa: see Ibn Qutayba.

Inaba, M., 'Arab Soldiers in China at the Time of the An-Shi Rebellion', *Memoirs of the Research Department of the Toyo Bunko* (Tokyo) 86, 2010, 35–61.

Inostrantsev, K. A., 'On the Ancient Iranian Burial Customs and Buildings', *Journal of the K. R. Cama Oriental Institute* 3, 1923, 1–28.

Irenaeus (d. *c.* 202), *Contre les hérésies*, ed. and tr. F. Sagnard *et al.*, 10 vols., Paris 1952–74.

al-Isfarā'inī, *al-Tabṣīr fī 'l-dīn*, ed. M. Z. al-Kawtharī, n.p. 1940.

Isfizārī, Muʿīn al-Dīn (wr. 899/1493f.), *Rawḍāt al-jannāt fī awṣāf-i madīnah-yi Harāt*, ed. M. K. Imām, 2 vols., Tehran 1338 [1959].

al-Iskāfī (d. 421/1030), *Kitāb luṭf al-tadbīr*, ed. A. ʿAbd al-Bāqī, Cairo and Baghdad 1964.

Iskandar, A. Z., 'A Doctor's Book on Zoology: al-Marwazī's Ṭabā'iʿ al-Ḥaywawān (Nature of Animals) Re-Assessed', *Oriens* 27, 1981, 266–310.

al-Iṣṭakhrī (wr. *c.* 340/951), *Masālik al-mamālik*, ed. M. J. de Goeje, Leiden 1870.

Ivanow, W., *The Truth-Worshippers of Kurdistan: Ahl-i Haqq Texts Edited in the Original Persian and Analysed by W. Ivanow*, Leiden 1953.

Jackson, V. W., 'The Doctrine of Metempsychosis in Manichaeism', *Journal of the American Oriental Society* 45, 1925, 246–68.

Jacobs, B., 'Der Sonnengott im Pantheon der Achämeniden', in J. Kellens (ed.), *La religion iranienne à l'époque achéménide*, Ghent 1991, 58–80.

'Der Tod des Bessos: Ein Beitrag zur Frage des Verhältnisses der Achämeniden zur Lehre des Zoroastres', *Acta Praehistorica et Archaeologica* 24, 1992, 177–86.

Jaʿfar b. Ḥarb: see Ps.-Nāshi'.

al-Jāḥiẓ (d. 255/869), *al-Bayān wa'l-tabyīn*, ed. ʿA.-S. M. Hārūn, 2nd printing, Cairo 1960–61.

al-Bukhalā', ed. Ṭ. al-Ḥājarī, Cairo 1958.

Kitāb al-Ḥayawān, ed. ʿA.-S. M. Hārūn, 7 vols., Cairo 1938–58.

'Kitāb al-qiyān', in ʿA.-S. M. Hārūn, *Rasā'il al-Jāḥiẓ*, II, Cairo 1385/1965, 139–82; tr. A. F. L. Beeston, *The Epistle on Singing Girls by Jāḥiẓ*, Warminster 1980.

al-Jahshiyārī (d. 331/942), *Kitāb al-wuzarā' wa'l-kuttāb*, ed. M. al-Saqqā *et al.*, Cairo 1938.

Jones, F. Stanley, 'The *Book of Elchasai* in its Relevance for Manichaean Institutions, with a Supplement: The *Book of Elchasai* Reconstructed and Translated', *Aram* 16, 2004, 179–215.
Review of Luttikhuizen, *Revelation of Elchasai*, in *Jahrburh für Antike und Christentum* 30, 1987, 200–209.
Jong, A. de, 'Animal Sacrifice in Ancient Zoroastrianism', in A. I. Baumgarten (ed.), *Sacrifice in Religious Experience*, Leiden 2002, 127–48.
'The First Sin: Zoroastrian Ideas about the Time before Zarathustra', in S. Shaked (ed.), *Genesis and Regeneration: Essays on Conceptions of Origins*, Jerusalem 2005, 192–209.
'One Nation under God', in G. Kratz and H. Spieckermann (eds.), *Götterbilder, Gottesbilder, Weltbilder: Polytheismus und Monotheismus in der Welt der Antike*, Tübingen 2006, I, 223–38.
'Shadow and Resurrection', *Bulletin of the Asia Institute* NS 9, 1995, 215–24.
'Sub Specie Maiestatis: Reflections on Sasanian Court Rituals', in M. Stausberg (ed.), *Zoroastrian Rituals in Context*, Leiden 2004, 345–65.
Traditions of the Magi: Zoroastrianism in Greek and Latin Literature, Leiden 1997.
Josephson, J., 'The "Sitz im Leben" of the Seventh Book of the *Dēnkart*', in C. G. Cereti, M. Maggi, and E. Provasi (eds.), *Religious Themes and Texts of Pre-Islamic Iran and Central Asia (Studies G. Gnoli)*, Wiesbaden 2003, 203–12.
Joyce, G. Hayward, *Christian Marriage: An Historical and Doctrinal Study*, London 1948.
Juergensmeyer, M., *Terror in the Mind of God: The Global Rise of Violence*, Berkeley, 2003.
Justi, F., *Iranisches Namenbuch*, Marburg 1895.
Juwaynī (d. 481/1283), *Tārīkh-i Jahāngushā*, ed. M. Qazvīnī, 3 vols., Leiden 1937 (repr. Tehran 1385) = *History of the World Conqueror*, tr. A. Boyle, 2 vols., Manchester 1958.
Kaabi, M., *Les Ṭāhirides*, 2 vols., Paris 1983.
Karamustafa, A., *God's Unruly Friends: Dervish Groups in the Islamic Later Middle Period, 1200–1500*, Salt Lake City 1994.
Sufism, the Formative Period, Edinburgh 2007.
Karev, Y., 'La politique d'Abū Muslim dans le Māwarā'annahr: nouvells données textuelles et archéologiques', *Der Islam* 79, 2002, 1–49.
Kāshānī (d. 736/1335f.), *Zubdat al-Tavārikh, bakhsh-i Fāṭimiyān va-Nizāriyān*, ed. M. T. Danishpazhuh, Tehran 1366 [1987].
al-Kashshī (fourth/tenth century), *al-Rijāl*, ed. A. al-Ḥusaynī, Karbalā' n.d.
Kasugai, S., 'Ancient Iranian Religion as it Appears in Buddhist Texts: Its Polyandry and Religious Practices', in *Proceedings of the IXth International Congress for the History of Religion*, Tokyo 1960, 112–15.
Kauṣītaki Upaniṣad: see *Upaniṣads*.
Kawasaki, S., 'A Reference to Maga in the Tibetan Translation of the *Tarkajvālā*', *Journal of Indian and Buddhist Studies* 23, 1975, 1097–1103.
Kay Kā'ūs (wr. 475/1082), *Qābūsnāma*, ed. S. Nafīsī, [Tehran] 1362 [1983]; tr. R. Levy, *A Mirror for Princes*, London 1951.

Kellens, J., 'L'eschatologie mazdénne ancienne', in S. Shaked and A. Netzer (eds.), *Irano-Judaica III*, Jerusalem 1994, 49–53.

Kennedy, H., *The Early Abbasid Caliphate*, London and Sydney 1981.

An Historical Atlas of Islam, Leiden 2002.

Kennedy, P. F., *Abu Nuwas*, Oxford 2005.

The Kephalaia of the Teacher, tr. I. Gardner, Leiden 1995. Cited by page and line number of the codex.

Khalʿatbarī, A., and ʿA. Z. Mihrwarz, *Junbish-i Bābak*, Tehran 1383/2004.

Khalīfa b. Khayyāṭ (d. 240/854), *Taʾrīkh*, ed. S. Zakkār, 2 vols. (continuous pagination), Damascus 1967–8.

Khan, G. (ed. and tr.), *Arabic Documents from Early Islamic Khurasan*, London 2007.

Khwāfī, Aḥmad b. Jalāl al-Dīn Faṣīh-i (b. 777/1375f.), *Mujmal-i Faṣīḥī*, ed. M. Farrūkh, 3 vols., Mashhad 1341 [1962f.].

Khwāfī, Majd al-Dīn (d. 834/1430f.), *Rawḍa-yi khuld*, ed. Ḥ. Khadīvjam, Tehran 1345 [1967].

al-Khwārizmī (wr. late fourth/tenth century), *Mafātīḥ al-ʿulūm*, ed. G. van Vloten, Leiden 1895 (repr. 1968).

al-Kindī (d. 350/961), *The Governors and Judges of Egypt*, ed. R. Guest, Leiden and London 1912.

King, K., *What is Gnosticism?*, Cambridge, Mass., and London 2003.

Kingsley, P., 'Meetings with Magi: Iranian Themes among the Greeks, from Xanthus of Lydia to Plato's Academy', *Journal of the Royal Asiatic Society*, third series, 5, 1995, 173–209.

Kister, M. J., 'Land, Property and *Jihād*', *Journal of the Economic and Social History of the Orient* 34, 1991, 270–311.

Kiyā, Ṣ, *Nuqṭaviyān yā Pasīkhāniyān*, Tehran [1320/1941].

Klijn, A. F. J. 'Alchasaios et *CMC*', in L. Cirillo and A. Roselli (eds.), *Codex Manichaicus Coloniensis*, Cosenza 1986, 140–52.

Jewish Christian Gospel Tradition, Leiden 1992.

Klijn, A. F. J. (tr.), *The Acts of Thomas*, 2nd edn., Leiden 2003.

Klijn, A. F. J. and G. J. Reinink, *Patristic Evidence for Jewish-Christian Sects*, Leiden 1973.

Klimkeit, H.-J., 'Buddhistische Übernahmen im iranischen und türkischen Manichäismus', in W. Heissig and H.-J. Klimkeit (eds.), *Synkretismus in den Religionen Zentralasiens*, Wiesbaden 1987, 58–75.

'Gestalt, Ungestalt, Gestaltwandel: Zum Gestaltprinzip im Manichäismus', in P. Bryder (ed.), *Manichaean Studies*, Lund 1988, 45–68.

Gnosis on the Silk Road: Gnostic Texts from Central Asia, San Francisco 1993.

Manichaean Art and Calligraphy, Leiden 1982.

'Manichäische und buddhistische Beichtformeln aus Turfan: Beobactungen zur Beziehung zwischen Gnosis und Mahāyana', *Zeitschrift für Religions- und Geistesgeschichte* 29, 1977, 193–228.

Kochnev, B., 'Les monnaies de Muqannaʿ', *Studia Iranica* 30, 2001, 143–50

Koenen, L., 'Augustine and Manichaeism in Light of the Cologne Mani Codex', *Illinois Classical Studies* 3, 1978, 154–95.

'How Dualistic is Mani's Dualism?', in L. Cirillo (ed.), *Codex Manichaicus Coloniensis*, Cosenza 1990, 1–34.
'From Baptism to the Gnosis of Manichaeism', in B. Layton (ed.), *The Rediscovery of Gnosticism*, ii (*Sethian Gnosticism*), Leiden 1981, 734–56.
'Manichaean Apocalypticism', in L. Cirillo and A. Roselli (eds.), *Codex Manichaicus Coloniensis*, Cosenza 1986, 285–332.
Kohlberg, E., 'Imam and Community in the pre-Ghayba Period', in S. A. Arjomand (ed.), *Authority and Political Culture in Shīʿism*, Albany 1988, 25–53 (repr. in his *Belief and Law in Imāmī Shīʿism*, Aldershot 1991, no. XIII).
'Rāwandiyya', in *EI*².
Review of Freitag, *Seelenwanderung*, in *Die Welt des Islams* 30, 1990, 237–9.
Koschaker, P., 'Adoptio in fratrem', in *Studi in onore di Salvatore Riccobono*, Palermo 1936, III, 359–76; repr. Aalen 1974.
Kotwal, F. M., and J. W. Boyd, *A Persian Offering. The Yasna: A Zoroastrian High Liturgy*, Paris 1991.
Kraft, H., 'Gab es einen Gnostiker Karpokrates?', *Theologische Zeitschrift* 8, 1952, 434–43.
Kraus, P. (ed. and tr.), 'Raziana I: La conduite du philosophe' (*al-sīra al-falsafiyya*), *Orientalia* 4, 1935, 300–34 (Arabic text reprinted, without preservation of the old pagination, in al-Rāzī, *al-Rasāʾil al-falsafiyya*, ed. P. Kraus, Cairo 1939, 97–111).
Kreyenbroek, P. G., 'Mithra and Ahreman in Iranian Cosmogonies', in J. R. Hinnels (ed.), *Studies in Mithraism*, Rome 1994, 173–82.
'Mithra and Ahreman, Binyamīn and Malak Ṭāwūs', in P. Gignoux (ed.), *Recurrent Patterns in Iranian Religions: From Mazdaism to Sufism*, Paris 1992, 57–79.
Yezidism: Its Background, Observances and Textual Tradition, London 1995.
Kruisheer, D., 'Theodore Bar Koni's *Keṯābā d-ʾeskolyon* as a Source for the Study of Early Mandaeism', *Jaarbericht ex Oriente Lux* 33, 1993–4, 151–69.
Kugel, J. L., *Traditions of the Bible: A Guide to the Bible as it was at the Start of the Common Era*, Cambridge, Mass., 1998.
al-Kulīnī (d. 329/941), *al-Kāfī*, ed. ʿA. A. al-Ghaffārī, 8 vols., Tehran 1362–3 [1983–4].
Landau-Tasseron, E., 'Alliances among the Arabs', *al-Qanṭara* 26, 2005, 141–73.
Landberg, le Comte de, *Etudes sur les dialectes de l'Arabie méridionale*, II (*Daṯîna*), Leiden 1905–9.
Landolt, H., "ʿAṭṭār, Sufism and Ismailism', in L. Lewisohn and C. Shackle (eds.), *ʿAṭṭār and the Persian Sufi Tradition*, London 2006, 3–26.
'Suhrawardī between Philosophy, Sufism and Ismailism: A Reappraisal', *Dāneshnāmeh* 1, Winter 2003, 13–29.
Langarūdī, R. R., *Junbishhā-yi ijtimāʿī va siyāsī dar Īrān pas az Islām*, Tehran 1385 [2006].
'Ustādhsīs', in *Dāʾirat al-Maʿārif-i Buzurg-i Islāmī*, ed. K. M. Bujnūrdī, Tehran 1367/1988–.
Langer, R., *Pīrān und Zeyāratgāh: Schreine und Wallfahrtstätten der Zarathustrier im neuzeitlischen Iran*, Leuven and Paris 2008.
Lanternari, V., *The Religions of the Oppressed: A Study of Modern Messianic Cults*, New York 1963.

Laurent, J., *L'Arménie entre Byzance et l'Islam depuis la conquête arabe jusque'en 886*, rev. M. Canard, Lisbon 1980.
Lazard, G., 'Pahlavi, Pârsi, Dari: les langues de l'Iran d'après Ibn al-Muqaffa'', in C. E. Bosworth (ed.), *Iran and Islam: A Volume in Memory of Vladimir Minorsky*, Edinburgh 1971, 361–91.
Lazarus-Yafeh, H., 'Some Neglected Aspects of Medieval Muslim Polemics against Christianity', *Harvard Theological Review* 89, 1996, 61–84.
Le Strange, G., *The Lands of the Eastern Caliphate*, London 1905.
Lee, A. D., 'Close-Kin Marriage in Late Antique Mesopotamia', *Greek, Roman, and Byzantine Studies* 29, 1988, 403–13.
Leriche, P., and S. Pidaev, 'Termez in Antiquity', in J. Cribb and G. Hermann (eds.), *After Alexander: Central Asia before Islam*, Oxford 2007, 177–211.
Lerner, J., 'Central Asians in Sixth-Century China: A Zoroastrian Funerary Rite', *Iranica Antiqua* 30, 1995, 179–89.
Leslie, D. D., 'Persian Temples in T'ang China', *Monumenta Serica* 35, 1981–3, 275–303.
Letsios, D., 'Theophilus and his "Khurramite" Policy: Some Considerations', in G. K. Livadas (ed.), *Graeco-Arabica: Festschrift in Honour of V. Christides*, Athens 2004, 249–72.
Levine, N. E., *The Dynamics of Polyandry: Kinship, Domesticity, and Population on the Tibetan Border*, Chicago and London 1988.
Lewis, B. (tr.), *Islam from the Prophet Muhammad to the Capture of Constantinople*, II (*Religion and Society*), New York and Oxford 1987.
Lidzbarski, M. (ed. and tr.), *Das Johannesbuch der Mandäer*, Giessen 1915.
Lieu, S. N. C., 'An Early Byzantine Formula for the Renunciation of Manichaeism', in his *Manichaeism*, 203–51; first publ. in *Jahrbuch für Antike und Christentum* 26, 1983, 152–218; updated and revised.
Manichaeism in Mesopotamia and the Roman East, Leiden 1994.
Lin Wushu, 'A Discussion about the Difference between the Heaven-God in the Qočo Kingdom and the High Deity of Zoroastrianism', *Zentralasiatische Studien* 23, 1992–3, 7–12.
Lindt, P. van, 'Remarks on the Use of *Skhēma* in the Coptic Manichaeica', in P. Bryder (ed.), *Manichaean Studies*, 1987, Lund 1988, 95–103.
Lindtner, C., 'Buddhist References to Old Iranian Religion', in *A Green Leaf: Papers in Honour of Professor Jes P. Asmussen* (Acta Iranica 28), Leiden 1988, 433–44.
Linton, R., 'Marquesan Culture', in A. Kardiner, with R. Linton, *The Individual and his Society: The Psychodynamics of Primitive Social Organization*, New York 1939, 137–96.
Loeffler, R., *Islam in Practice: Religious Beliefs in a Persian Village*, Albany 1988.
Lovejoy, A. O., and G. Boas, *Primitivism and Related Ideas in Antiquity*, Baltimore and London 1935.
Luneau, A., *L'histoire du salut chez les Pères de l'Église: la doctrine des ages du monde*, Paris 1964.
Luomanen, P., 'Nazarenes', in A. Marjanen and P. Luomanen (eds.), *A Companion to Second-Century Christian 'Heretics'*, Leiden 2008, 279–314.

Luttikhuizen, G. P., 'The Baptists of Mani's Youth and the Elchasaites', in his *Gnostic Revisions of Genesis Stories and Early Jesus Traditions*, Leiden 2006, 170–84.
'Elchasaites and their Book', in A. Marjanen and P. Luomanen (eds.), *A Companion to Second-Century Christian 'Heretics'*, Leiden 2008, 335–64.
The Revelation of Elchasai, Tübingen 1985.
Machinist, P., 'Kingship and Divinity in Imperial Assyria', in G. Beckman and T. J. Lewis (eds.), *Text, Artifact, and Image*, Providence 2006, 152–88.
MacKenzie, D. N., *A Concise Pahlavi Dictionary*, London 1986.
MacKenzie, D. N. (ed. and tr.), 'Kerdir's Inscription', in G. Herrmann (ed.), *The Sasanian Rock Reliefs at Naqsh-i Rustam* (Iranische Denkmäler, Iranische Felsreliefs, I), Berlin 1989, 35–72.
The 'Sūtra of the Causes and Effects of Actions' in Sogdian, Oxford 1970.
Sasanidische Rechtsbuch: see *MHD*.
Macuch, M., 'On the Treatment of Animals in Zoroastrian Law', in A. van Tongerloo (ed.), *Iranica Selecta: Studies in Honour of W. Skalmowski* (Silk Road Studies 8), Turnhout 2003, 167–90.
'The Use of Seals in Sasanian Jurisprudence', in R. Gyselen (ed.), *Sceaux d'Orient et leur emploi*, Bures-sur-Yvette 1997, 79–87.
'Zoroastrian Principles and the Structure of Kinship in Sasanian Iran', in C. G. Cereti, M. Maggi, and E. Provasi (eds.), *Religious Themes and Texts of Pre-Islamic Iran and Central Asia* (Studies G. Gnoli), Wiesbaden 2003, 231–45.
Madelung, W., 'Abū ʿĪsā al-Warrāq über die Bardesaniten, Marcioniten und Kantäer', in H. R. Roemer and A. Noth (eds.), *Studien zur Geschichte und Kultur des vorderen Orients: Festschrift für Berthold Spuler*, Leiden 1981, 210–24.
'Khurramiyya', in *EI*².
Religious Trends in Early Islamic Iran, Albany 1988.
'Was the Caliph al-Maʾmūn a Grandson of the Sectarian Leader Ustādhsīs?', in S. Leder *et al.* (eds.), *Studies in Arabic and Islam*, Leuven 2002, 485–90.
Madelung, W. and P. E. Walker (ed. and tr.), *An Ismaili Heresiography: The 'Bāb al-Shayṭān' from Abū Tammām's K. al-Shajara*, Leiden 1998.
MahFr = *Māh ī frawardīn rōz ī hordād*. See Grenet, 'Pahlavi Text'.
Mahler, J. G., *The Westerners among the Figurines of the T'ang Dynasty of China*, Rome 1959.
Majumdar, D. N., *Himalayan Polyandry*, Bombay 1962.
Malandra: see *Yašts*.
al-Malaṭī (d. 377/987), *Kitāb al-Tanbīh wa'l-radd ʿalā ahl al-ahwāʾ wa'l-bidaʿ*, ed. S. Dedering, Istanbul 1936.
Mansfeld, J., *Heresiography in Context: Hippolytus'* Elenchos *as a Source for Greek Philosophy*, Leiden 1992.
Maqātil, see Abū 'l-Faraj.
al-Maqdisī (wr. *c.* 355/966), *Kitāb al-badʾ wa'l-taʾrīkh*, ed. and tr. C. Huart, 6 vols., Paris 1899–1919; repr. without the translation n.p., n.d.
Marco Polo, *The Book of Ser Marco Polo*, tr. H. Yule, London 1875.
Marcus Aurelius (d. 180), *Meditations*, ed. and tr. A. S. L. Farquharson, Oxford 1944.

Markschies, C., *Gnosis: An Introduction*, tr. J. Bowden, London and New York 2003.
Marlow, L., *Hierarchy and Egalitarianism in Islamic Thought*, Cambridge 1997.
Marquart, J., and J. J. M. de Groot, 'Das Reich Zābul und der Gott Žun vom 6.–9. Jahrhundert', in G. Weil (ed.), *Festschrift Eduard Sachau*, Berlin 1915, 248–92.
Marshak, B. I., and V. I. Raspopova, 'Buddha Icon from Panjikent', *Silk Road Archaeology* 5, 1997–8, 297–305.
'Wall Paintings from a House with a Granary, Penjikent, 1st Quarter of the Eighth Century AD', *Silk Road Archaeology* 1, 1990, 123–76.
Martan Farrukh (fl. mid-third/ninth century), *Škand-Gūmānīk Vičār*, ed. and tr. P. J. de Ménasce, Fribourg-en-Suisse 1945.
Mashkūr, M. (ed.), *Haftād u sih millat*, Tehran 1962.
Mason, S., *Flavius Josephus on the Pharisees*, Leiden 1991.
al-Mas'ūdī (d. 345/956 or 346), *Kitāb al-tanbīh wa'l-ishrāf*, ed. M. J. de Goeje, Leiden 1894.
Murūj al-dhahab (abbreviated as MM), ed. and tr. C. Barbier de Meynard and A. J. B. Pavet de Courteille, 9 vols., Paris 1861–77 (cited in parenthesis, by volume and page); ed. C. Pellat, 7 vols., Beirut 1966–79 (cited first, by volume and paragraph).
Matthews, J., *The Roman Empire of Ammianus*, London 1989.
al-Māturīdī (d. *c.* 333/944), *Kitāb al-tawḥīd*, ed. F. Kholeif, Beirut 1970.
Ta'wīlāt al-Qur'ān, ed. H. İ. Kaçar and B. Topaloğlu, vol. X, Istanbul 2007.
McGuckin, J. A., 'The Changing Forms of Jesus', in L. Lies (ed.), *Origeniana Quarta*, Vienna 1987, 215–22.
McLeod, F. G., *The Image of God in the Antiochene Tradition*, Washington 1999.
Meeks, W. A., 'Moses as God and King', in J. Neusner (ed.), *Religions in Antiquity: Essays in Memory of Erwin Ramsdell Goodenough*, Leiden 1968, 354–71.
Mélikoff, I., *Abū Muslim, le 'Porte-Hache' du Khorassan*, Paris 1962.
Sur les traces su soufisme turc: recherches sur l'Islam populaire en Anatolie, Istanbul 1992.
Melville, C., 'Shah 'Abbas and the Pilgrimage to Mashhad', in C. Melville (ed.), *Safavid Persia*, London 1996, 191–229.
Ménasce, J. P. de, 'Autour d'un texte syriaque inédit', *Bulletin of the School of Oriental and African Studies* 9, 1937–9, 587–601.
'La conquête de l'Iranisme et la recuperation des mages héllénisés', *Annuaire de l'Ecole Pratique des Haute Etudes* 1956–7, 2–12.
'Early Evidence for the Symbolic Meaning of the Kustīk', in *Sir J. J. Zarthoshti Madressa Centenary Volume*, Bombay 1967, 17–18.
Une encyclopédie mazdéenne: le Dēnkart, Paris 1958.
'Kartak the Heretic and the Ordeal by Fire', *Studia Iranica* 15, 1986, 160–3.
Škand: see Martan Farrukh.
'Le témoignage de Jayhānī sur le mazdéisme', *Donum Natalium H. S. Nyberg Oblatum*, Uppsala 1954, 50–9.
Ménasce, J. P. de (tr.), *Le troisième livre du Dēnkart*, Paris 1973.
Mēnōg ī khrad, tr. E. W. West, *Pahlavi Books*, part iii (Sacred Books of the East, ed. F. M. Müller, vol. XXIV), Oxford 1885; repr. Delhi 1970.
Merkelbach, R., 'Die Täufer, bei denen Mani aufwuchs', in P. Bryder (ed.), *Manichaean Studies*, Lund 1988, 105–33.

MHD = *Mādagdān ī hazār dādastān*, ed. and tr. A. Perikhanian, *The Book of a Thousand Judgements (a Sasanian Law-Book)*, tr. from Russian by N. Garsoian, Costa Mesa, 1997. Part i refers to the first 55 folios of the manuscript, purchased by M. L. Hataria and published in facsimile by J. J. Modi; part ii refers to the 22 folios purchased by T. D. Anklesaria and published in facsimile by him. Perikhanian edits and translates both parts. The second part (marked A in Perikhanian) has also been edited with a German translation and extensive commentary by M. Macuch, *Das Sasanidische Rechtsbuch 'Mātakdān Ī Hazār Dātistān' (Teil II)*, Wiesbaden 1981.

Michael the Syrian (d. 1199), *Chronique*, ed. and tr. J. B. Chabot, 4 vols., Paris 1899–1910.

Miller, R. A. (tr.), *Accounts of Western Nations in the History of the Northern Chou Dynasty*, Berkeley and Los Angeles 1959.

Minorsky, V. (ed. and tr.), *Abū-Dulaf Misʿar ibn Muhalhil's Travels in Iran (c. AD 950)*, Cambridge 1955.

'Caucasica IV', *Bulletin of the School of Oriental and African Studies* 15, 1953, 504–29.

'Études sur les Ahl-i Haqq, I', *Revue de l'Histoire des Religions* 97, 1928, 90–105.

Notes sur la secte des Ahlé-Haqq, Paris [1922]; repr. from *Revue du Monde Musulman* 40, 1920, 20–97; and 44–5, 1921, 205–302. References are to the original pagination.

'The Older Preface to the *Shāh-nāma*', in *Studi Orientalistici in onore di Giorgio Levi della Vida*, Rome 1956, II, 159–79.

'Shaykh Bālī-Efendi on the Ṣafavids', *Bulletin of the School of Oriental and African Studies* 20, 1957, 437–50.

Mir-Hosseini, Z., 'Breaking the Seal: The New Face of the Ahl-e Haqq', in K. Kehl-Bodrogi, B. Kellner-Heinkele, and A. Otter-Beaujean (eds.), *Syncretistic Religious Communities in the Near East*, Leiden 1997, 175–94.

'Inner Truth and Outer History: The Two Worlds of the Ahl-i Ḥaqq of Kurdistan', *International Journal of Middle East Studies* 26, 1994, 267–85.

Mir-Kasimov, O., 'Notes sur deux textes ḥurûfi: le Jâvdân-nâma de Faḍlallâh Astarâbâdî et l'un de ses commentaries, le Maḥram-nâma de Sayyid Isḥâq,' *Studia Iranica* 35/2, 2006, 203–35.

Mīrkhwānd (d. 903/1498), *Tārīkh-i rawḍat al-ṣafā*, ed. J. Kiyānfar, 10 vols., Tehran 1380 [2001f.].

Miskawayh (d. 421/1030), *Tajārib al-umam*, in H. F. Amedroz and D. S. Margoliouth (eds. and trs.), *The Eclipse of the ʿAbbāsid Caliphate*, vols. I–II, IV–V, Oxford 1920–1.

Mitchell, S., 'An Apostle to Ankara from the New Jerusalem: Montanists and Jews in Late Roman Asia Minor', *Scripta Classica Israelica* 24, 2005, 207–23.

MM: see al-Masʿūdī.

Moerenhout, J. A., *Voyage aux îles du Grand Océan*, 2 vols., Paris 1837.

Mokri, M., 'Étude d'un titre de propriété du début du XVIe siècle provenant du Kurdistan', in his *Recherches de Kurdologie: Contribution scientifique aux études iraniennes*, Paris 1970, 301–30.

'L'idée de l'incarnation chez les Ahl-i Ḥaqq', in H. Franke (ed.), *Akten des vierundzwanzigsten internationalen Orientalisten-Kongresses München* (24 August–3 September 1957), Wiesbaden 1959, 496–8.
'Le Kalām gourani sur le pacte des Compagnons Fidèles de Verité au sein de la Perle Prémondiale', *Journal Asiatique* 265, 1977, 237–71.
Molé, M., 'Un ascétisme moral dans les livres pehlevis?', *Revue de l'Histoire des Religions* 155, 1959, 145–90.
Culte, Mythe et Cosmologie dans l'Iran ancien, Paris 1963.
'Deux aspects de la formation de l'orthodoxie zoroastrienne', *Annuaire de l'Institut de Philologie et d'Histoire Orientales et Slaves* 12, 1952, 289–324.
'Une histoire du mazdéisme est-elle possible?', *Revue de l'Histoire des Religions* 162, 1962, 45–67, 161–218.
'Le problème des sectes zoroastriennes dans les livres pehlevis', *Oriens* 13–14, 1961, 1–28.
(ed. and tr.), *La légende de Zoroastre selon les texts pehlevis*, Paris 1967.
Monnot, G., *Penseurs musulmans et religions iraniens*: see ʿAbd al-Jabbār, *Mughni*.
Morris, I., and W. Scheidel, *The Dynamics of Ancient Empires: State Power from Assyria to Byzantium*, Oxford 2009.
Morton, A. H., 'The *Chūb-i ṭarīq* and *Qizilbāsh* Ritual in Safavid Persia', in J. Calmard (ed.), *Etudes Safavides*, Paris and Tehran 1993, 225–45.
Mote, F. W., 'The Rise of the Ming Dynasty', in *Cambridge History of China*, VII, ed. F. W. Mote and D. Twitchett, Cambridge 1998, 11–57.
Mujmal al-tawārikh wa'l-qiṣaṣ (comp. 520/1126f.), ed. Malik al-Shuʿarāʾ Bahār, Tehran 1318 [1939].
Müller, K. E., *Kulturhistorische Studien zur Genese pseudo-islamischer Sektengebilde in Vorderasien*, Wiesbaden 1967.
al-Muqaddasī (wr. *c.* 375/985), *Aḥsan al-taqāsīm fī maʿrifat al-aqālīm*, ed. M. J. de Goeje, Leiden 1906; tr. B. A. Collins, Reading 1994 (not used). The correct form of the name is Maqdisī, but since there are so many authors of that name the old habit of calling him Muqaddasī is quite useful.
Mustawfī, Ḥamd Allāh (d. after 740/1339f.), *Tārīkh-i Guzīda*, ed. ʿA.-Ḥ. Navāʾī, Tehran 1362 [1983].
Muyldermans, J. (ed. and tr.), *La domination arabe en Arménie*, Louvain and Paris 1927.
al-Nābigha al-Jaʿdī (d. *c.* 63/683), *Dīwān*, ed. and tr. M. Nallino, Rome 1953.
Nafīsī, S., *Bābak-i Khurramdīn*, Tehran 1384 [first publ. 1342/1963].
Nallino, C. A., 'Intorno al divieto romano imperiale dell'affratellamento e ad alcuni paralleli arabi', in *Studi in onore di Salvatore Riccobono*, Palermo 1936, III, 319–57; repr. Aalen 1974.
Naquin, S., *Shantung Rebellion: The Wang Lun Uprising of 1774*, New Haven 1981.
Narsai (d. 502), *Homélies sur la création*, ed. and tr. P. Gignoux in F. Graffin (ed.), *Patrologia Orientalis*, Paris 1968.
Narshakhī: see *Tārīkh-i Bukhārā*.
al-Nasafī, Abū Ḥafṣ ʿUmar b. Muḥammad (d. 537/1142), *al-Qand fī dhikr ʿulamāʾ Samarqand*, ed. Y. al-Hādī, Tehran 1999.

al-Nāshiʾ al-Akbar (d. 293/905f.), *al-Kitāb al-awsaṭ*, in J. van Ess (ed.), *Frühe Muʿtazilitische Häresiographie*, Beirut 1971.
al-Nāshiʾ al-Akbar (attrib.), *Uṣūl*: see Pseudo-Nāshiʾ.
Nashwān al-Ḥimyarī (d. 573/1178), *al-Ḥūr al-ʿīn*, ed. K. Muṣṭafā, Baghdad 1948.
Naṣr b. Muzāḥim (d. 212/827), *Waqʿat Ṣiffīn*, ed. ʿA.-S. M. Hārūn, 2nd edn, Cairo 1382/1962.
al-Nawbakhtī (d. *c.* 300/912), *Firaq al-shīʿa*, ed. H. Ritter, Istanbul 1931.
Nawwābī, M. (ed. and tr. [Persian]), *Yādgār-i Buzurgmihr*, Tabriz n.d. (offprint from the Publications of the Faculty of Letters, Tabrīz, autumn, year 11 [1960]).
Naymark, A., 'Returning to Varakhsha', http://www.silk-road.com/newsletter/december/varakhsha.htm.
Naymark, A., and Treadwell, L., 'An Arab-Sogdian Coin of AH 160: an Ikhshid in Ishtihan?', *Numismatic Chronicle* 171, 2011.
Nestorius (d. *c.* 451), *Sermons*, tr. F. L. Battles and D. Sahas, Pittsburgh 1973.
Nicholson, R. A., *The Mystics of Islam*, London 1914.
Studies in Islamic Mysticism, Cambridge 1921.
Nihāyat al-irab fī taʾrīkh al-furs wa'l-ʿarab, ed. M. T. Dānishpazhūh, Tehran 1374 [1995].
Niẓām al-Mulk (d. 485/1092), *Siyāsatnāme*, ed. H. Darke, *Siyar al-mulūk*, 2nd edn, Tehran 1985 (abbreviated as *SN*); tr. H. Darke, *The Book of Government or Rules for Kings*, London 1960. Cited by chapter and paragraph division, usually followed by the page numbers in parenthesis because the absence of running heads makes it difficult to locate the chapters.
Nöldeke, T. (tr.), 'Burzōes Einleitung zu dem Buche Kalīla waDimna', *Schriften der Wissenschaftlichen Gesellschaft in Strassburg* 12, 1912, 1–27.
Nuʿaym b. Ḥammād (d. 228/843), *al-Fitan*, ed. S. Zakkār, Mecca 1991; ed. M. al-Shūrī, Beirut 1997. Cited in that order, divided by a slash.
O'Connell, J., K. Hawkes, and N. Blurton Jones, 'Hadza Scavenging: Implications for Plio/Pleistocene Hominid Subsistence', *Current Anthropology* 29, 1988, 356–63.
Oort, J. van, 'The Paraclete Mani as the Apostle of Jesus Christ and the Origins of a New Church', in A. Hilhorst (ed.), *The Apostolic Age in Patristic Thought*, Leiden 2004, 139–57.
Oppenheim, A. L., 'Akkadian *pul(u)ḫ(t)u* and *melammu*', *Journal of the American Oriental Society* 63, 1943, 31–4.
Origen (d. 254), *Contra Celsum*, tr. H. Chadwick, Cambridge 1953.
On First Principles, tr. G. W. Butterworth, New York 1936 (repr. 1966).
Otterbein, K. F., 'Marquesan Polyandry', *Marriage and Family Living* 25, 1963, 155–9.
Outmazian, H. M., 'Bābek et les princes de Siwnie', *Revue des Études Arménienne* 3, 1966, 205–24.
Özbayri, K., and J.-P. Roux, 'Quelques notes sur la religion des Tahtaci nomades bucherons de la Turquie méridionale', *Revue des Etudes Islamiques* 32, 1965, 49–86.
The Pahlavi Rivāyat accompanying the Dādestān ī Dēnīg, ed. and tr. A. V. Williams, 2 vols., Copenhagen 1990. Abbreviated as *PRDd*.

Panaino, A., 'The *Bayān* of the Frataraka: Gods or "Divine Kings"?', in C. G. Cereti, M. Maggi, and E. Provasi (eds.), *Religious Themes and Texts of Pre-Islamic Iran and Central Asia*, Wiesbaden 2003, 265–88.

'Manichaean Concepts in the Pahlavi Commentary of Māh Niyāyišn, par. 4?', in R. E. Emmerick, W. Sundermann, and P. Zieme (eds.), *Studia Manichaica*, Berlin 2000, 464–80.

Tištrya: see *Yašts*.

'Uranographia Iranica I: The Three Heavens in the Zoroastrian Tradition and the Mesopotamian Background', in R. Gyselen (ed.), *Au Carrefour des Religions: Mélanges offers à Philipper Gignoux*, Bures-sur-Yvette 1995, 205–25.

'The Zoroastrian Incestuous Unions', in C. Jullien (ed.), *Controverses des Chrétiens dans l'Iran sassanide*, Paris 2008, 69–87.

Paraphrase of Shem (CG VII, *l*), tr. M. Roberge and F. Wisse, in Robinson, *Nag Hammadi Library*, 339–61; ed. and tr. Roberge, *La paraphrase de Sem*, Québec and Paris 2000.

Parmar, Y. S., *Polyandry in the Himalayas*, Delhi 1975.

Payne, R., 'Christianity and Iranian Society in Late Antiquity, ca. 500–700', Ph.D. dissertation, Princeton 2009.

Pearson, B. A., 'The Figure of Seth in Gnostic Literature', in B. Layton (ed.), *The Rediscovery of Gnosticism*, II (*Sethian Gnosticism*), Leiden 1981, 472–504.

Gnosticism and Christianity in Roman and Coptic Egypt, New York and London 2004.

Pedersen, N. A., 'Early Manichaean Christology', in P. Bryder (ed.), *Manichaean Studies*, Lund 1988, 157–190.

Pellat, C., 'Le culte de Muʿāwiya au IIIe siècle de l'hégire', *Studia Islamica* 6, 1956, 53–66.

Pelliot, P., *Notes on Marco Polo*, I, Paris 1959.

Pembroke, S., 'Women in Charge: The Function of Alternatives in Early Greek Tradition and the Ancient Idea of Matriarchy', *Journal of the Warburg and Courtauld Institutes* 30, 1967, 1–35.

Perikhanian, A., 'Iranian Society and Law', in *Cambridge History of Iran* III/2, ed. E. Yarshater, Cambridge 1983, 627–80.

Perry, K., 'Vegetarianism in Late Antiquity and Byzantium: The Transmission of a Regimen', in W. Mayer and S. Trzcionka (eds.), *Feast, Fast or Famine: Food and Drink in Byzantium*, Brisbane 2005, 171–87.

Peter, Prince of Greece and Denmark, *A Study of Polyandry*, The Hague 1963.

Photius (d. c. 893), *Bibliothèque*, ed. and tr. R. Henry, VII, Paris 1974.

Pietro della Valle (d. 1652), *Viaggi*, ed. G. Gancia, Brighton 1843 [first publ. 1658].

Pines, S., 'Eschatology and the Concept of Time in the Slavonic Book of Enoch', in R. J. Zwi Werblowsky and C. J. Bleeker (eds.), *Types of Redemption*, Leiden 1970, 72–87.

Piras, P. (ed. and tr.), *Hādōxt Nask 2: il racconto zoroastriano della sorte dell'anima*, Rome 2000.

Plotinus (d. 270), *Enneads*, ed. and tr. A. H. Armstrong, 5 vols., Cambridge, Mass., and London 1966–89.

Plutarch (d. 120), *Cato the Younger, Lycurgus, Pompey*, in his *Lives*, ed. and tr. B. Perrin, 11 vols., Cambridge. Mass., and London 1914–26.

Polgreen, L., 'One Bride for Multiple Brothers: A Himalayan Custom Fades', *New York Times*, 17 July 2010, section A4.
Polybius (d. *c.* 120 BC), *The Histories*, ed. and tr. W. R. Paton, 6 vols. London and New York 1922–7.
Pomeroy, S. B., *Spartan Women*, Oxford and New York 2002.
Porphyry (d. *c.* 305), *On Abstinence from Killing Animals*, tr. G. Clark, Ithaca, NY, 2000.
The Cave of the Nymphs in the Odysee, ed. and tr. Seminar Classics 609, Arethusa Monographs, Dept of Classics, State University of New York at Buffalo 1969.
Pourshariati, P., *Decline and Fall of the Sasanian Empire*, London 2008.
PRDd: see *Pahlavi Rivāyat.*
Procopius (d. 565), *The Anecdota or Secret History*, ed. and tr. H. B. Dewing, London and Cambridge, Mass., 1969.
Pseudo-Clementines: see Clement (attrib.).
Pseudo-Dionysius (aka *Zuqnin Chronicle*), *Chronicon Pseudo-Dionysianum vulgo dicto*, II, tr. R. Hespel, Louvain 1989.
Ps(eudo)-Nāshi' (probably Ja'far b. Ḥarb, d. 236/850), *Kitāb uṣūl al-niḥal*, in J. van Ess (ed.), *Frühe Mu'tazilitische Häresiographie*, Beirut 1971. For the authorship, see W. Madelung, 'Frühe mu'tazilitische Häresiographie: das *Kitāb al-Uṣūl* des Ǧa'far b. Ḥarb?', *Der Islam* 57, 1980, 220–36.
Puech, H.-C., 'Fragments retrouvés de "l'Apocalypse d'Allogène"', *Annuaire de l'Institut de Philologie et d'Historie Orientales et Slaves (Bruxelles)* 4, 1936, 935–62.
Pulleyblank, E. G., *The Background of the Rebellion of An Lu-Shan*, London 1955.
Quispel, G., 'Gnosticism and the New Testament', *Vigiliae Christianae* 19, 1965, 65–85.
al-Qummī, Abū 'l-Ḥasan 'Alī b. Ibrāhīm (early fourth/tenth century), *Tafsīr*, 2 vols., Beirut 1991.
al-Qummī, Sa'd b. 'Abdallāh (d. *c.* 300/912), *Kitāb al-maqālāt wa'l-firaq*, ed. J. Mashkūr, Tehran 1963.
Radtke, B., 'How can Man Reach the Mystical Union? Ibn Ṭufayl and the Divine Spark', in L. I. Conrad (ed.), *The World of Ibn Ṭufayl*, Leiden 1996, 165–94.
Ragir, S., M. Rosenberg, and P. Tierno, 'Gut Morphology and the Avoidance of Carrion among Chimpanzees, Baboons, and Early Hominids', *Journal of Anthropological Research* 56, 2000, 477–512.
Raha, M. Kumar, and P. C. Coomar (eds.), *Polyandry in India*, Delhi 1987.
Ramelli, I. L. E., *Bardaisan of Edessa: A Reassessment of the Evidence and a New Interpretation*, Piscataway, N.J., 2009.
Rapp, C., *Holy Bishops in Late Antiquity*, Berkeley 2005.
Raschke, M. G., 'New Studies in Roman Commerce with the East', in H. Temporini and W. Haase (eds.), *Aufstieg und Niedergang der römischen Welt*, Berlin and New York 1975–91, II (*Principat*), ix/2, 604–1361.
Rashīd al-Dīn (d. *c.* 718/1318), *Javāmi' al-tavārīkh, qismat-i Ismā'īliyān u Faṭimiyān u Nizāriyān*, ed. M.T. Danishpazhuh and M. Modarressi Zanjānī, Tehran 1338 [1977].
al-Rāzī, Abū Bakr (d. 313/925), *Rasā'il falsafiyya*, Cairo 1939.

'Raziana I: La Conduite du Philosophe (*Sīra falsafiyya*)', *Orientalia* 4, 1935, 300–34; also tr. C. E. Butterworth, 'The Book of the Philosophic Life', *Interpretation* 20, 1993, 227–36.

al-Ṭibb al-rūḥānī, ed. 'A.-L. al-'Īd, Cairo 1978; tr. A. J. Arberry, *The Spiritual Physick of Rhazes*, London 1950.

al-Rāzī, Fakhr al-Dīn: see Fakhr al-Dīn.

Reck, C., 'Snatches of the Middle Iranian 'Tale of the Five Brothers'', in J. D. BeDuhn (ed.), *New Light on Manichaeism*, Leiden 2009, 241–57.

Recognitions: see Clement (attrib.).

Reed, A., '"Jewish Christianity" after the "Parting of the Ways"', in A. H. Becker and A. Y. Reed (eds.), *The Ways that Never Parted*, 2003, 189–231.

Reeves, J. C., 'Exploring the Afterlife of the Jewish Pseudepigrapha in Medieval Near Eastern Tradition: Some Initial Soundings', *Journal for the Study of Judaism* 30, 1999, 148–77.

Heralds of that Good Realm: Syro-Mesopotamian Gnosis and Jewish Traditions, Leiden 1996.

'Jewish Pseudepigrapha in Manichaean Literature: The Influence of the Enochic Library', in J. C. Reeves (ed.), *Tracing the Threads: Studies in the Vitality of Jewish Pseudepigrapha*, Atlanta 1994, 173–203.

'Reconsidering the "Prophecy of Zardūšt"', in B. G. Wright (ed.), *A Multiform Heritage: Studies in Early Judaism and Christianity in Honor of Robert A. Kraft*, Atlanta 1999, 167–182.

Rekaya, M., 'Le *Ḫurram-Dīn* et les mouvements *Ḫurramites* sous les 'Abbāsides', *Studia Islamica* 60, 1984, 5–57.

'Ḳārinids', in *EI*².

Māzyār: Résistance ou intégration d'une province iranienne au monde musulman au milieu du IXᵉ siècle ap. J.C.', *Studia Iranica* 2, 1973, 143–92.

'Mise au point sur Théphobe et l'alliance de Bâbek avec Théophile', *Byzantion* 44, 1974, 43–67.

'La place des provinces sud-caspiennes dans l'histoire de l'Iran de la conquête arabe à l'avènement des Zaydites (16–250 H/637–864 J.C.): particularisme régional ou rôle "national"?', *Rivista degli Studi Orientali* 48, 1974, 117–52.

Ritter, H., 'Die Anfänge der Ḥurūfīsekte (Studien zur Geschichte der islamischen Frömmigkeit, II)', *Oriens* 7, 1954, 1–54.

The Ocean of the Soul: Man, the World, and God in the Stories of Farīd al-Dīn 'Aṭṭār, Leiden and Boston 2003.

Robertson Smith, W., *Kinship and Marriage in Early Arabia*, 2nd edn., London 1907.

Robinson, C., *Empire and Elites after the Muslim Conquest*, Cambridge 2000.

Robinson, J. M. (ed.), *The Nag Hammadi Library in English*, 3rd edition, Leiden 1988.

Rossi, A. V., 'Perception et symbologie des couleurs dans le monde iranien et d'Asie Centrale', in *La Persia e l'Asia Centrale da Alessandro al X secolo* (Accademia Nazionale dei Lincei, Atti dei convegni lincei 127), Rome 1996, 87–97.

Rubin, U., 'Pre-existence and Light', *Israel Oriental Studies* 5, 1975, 62–119.

Rudolph, K., *Gnosis: The Nature and History of Gnosticism*, Edinburgh 1983.

Russell, J. R., *Zoroastrianism in Armenia*, Cambridge, Mass. 1987.

Sachau, E. (ed. and tr.), *Syrische Rechtsbücher*, 3 vols., Berlin 1907–14.
Sad dar, tr. E. W. West, *Pahlavi Books*, part iii (Sacred Books of the East, ed. F. M. Müller, vol. XXIV), Oxford 1885; repr. Delhi 1970.
Sadighi, G. H., *Les mouvements religieux iraniens au IIe et au IIIe siècle de l'hégire*, Paris 1938; Persian tr. G. Ṣadīghī, *Junbishhā-yi dīnī-yi īrānī dar qarnhā-yi duvvum va sivvum-i hijrī*, Tehran 1375 [1996]. References are given to both editions, separated by a slash, with the French original first.
Šahrestānīhā ī Ērānšahr, ed. and tr. J. J. Markwart, Rome 1931; ed. and tr. T. Daryaee, Costa Mesa 2002. Cited by paragraph number; all references are to Daryaee's edition unless otherwise indicated.
al-Samʿānī (d. 562/1166), *al-Ansāb*, 13 vols., Hyderabad 1962–82.
Sāmarāʾī, *al-Ghuluww wa'l-firaq al-ghāliya fi'l-ḥaḍāra al-islāmiyya*, Baghdad 1972.
Sanderson, A., 'Śaivism and Tantric Tradition', in S. Sutherland *et al.* (eds.), *The World's Religions*, London 1988, 660–704.
Savory, R., *Iran under the Safavids*, Cambridge 1980.
Šāyest nē šāyest, tr. E. W. West, *Pahlavi Books*, part i (Sacred Books of the East, ed. F. M. Müller, vol. V), Oxford 1880; repr. Delhi 1970.
Sayf b. ʿUmar (d. before 193/809), *Kitāb al-ridda wa'l-futūḥ wa-kitāb al-jamal wa maṣīr ʿAʾisha wa-ʿAlī*, ed. Q. al-Samarrai, Leiden 1995.
Schafer, E. H., 'Iranian Merchants in T'ang Dynasty Tales', in W. J. Fischel (ed.), *Semitic and Oriental Studies: A Volume Presented to William Popper*, Berkeley and Los Angeles 1951, 403–22.
Schenke, H.-M., 'The Phenomenon and Significance of Gnostic Sethianism', in B. Layton (ed.), *The Rediscovery of Gnosticism*, II (*Sethian Gnosticism*), Leiden 1981, 588–616.
Scher, A. (ed. and tr.), 'Histoire Nestorienne', part ii/1, in *Patrologia Orientalis* VII, Paris 1911, 97–201.
Schmidt, H.-P., 'The Non-Existence of Ahreman and the Mixture (*Gumēzišn*) of Good and Evil', in *K. R. Cama Oriental Institute: Second International Conference Proceedings*, Bombay 1996, 79–95.
Schneemelcher, W. (ed.), *New Testament Apocrypha*, rev. edn., 2 vols., Cambridge 1991–3.
Scholem, G., 'Redemption through Sin' in his *The Messianic Idea in Judaism and other Essays in Jewish Spirituality*, New York 1971.
The SCM Press A–Z of Origen, ed. J. A. McGuckin, Louisville, K.Y., 2004.
Scott, D. A., 'The Iranian Face of Buddhism', *East and West* 40, 1990, 43–77.
Sebeos (attrib.) (wr. *c.* 660?), *Histoire d'Héraclius*, tr. F. Macler, Paris 1904; tr. R. W. Thomson with historical commentary by J. H. Howard-Johnston and assistance from T. Greenwood, *The Armenian History Attributed to Sebeos*, Liverpool 1999, vol. I, translation; vol. II, commentary, continuous pagination.
Seiwert, H., and Ma Xisha, *Popular Religious Movements and Heterodox Sects in Chinese History*, Leiden 2003.
Selb and Kaufhold: see Syro-Roman Lawbook.
Serjeant, R. B., 'Zinā, some Forms of Marriage and Allied Topics in Western Arabia', in J. Heiss *et al.* (eds.), *Studies in Oriental Culture and History: Festschrift for Walter Dostal*, Frankfurt am Main 1993, 145–59.

Severus b. al-Muqaffaʿ (d. 987), *History of the Patriarchs of the Coptic Church of Alexandria*, ed. and tr. B. Evetts in *Patrologia Orientalis* I, V, X, Paris 1904–14.
Shaban, M. A., *The ʿAbbāsid Revolution*, Cambridge 1970.
al-Shābushtī (d. 388/988), *al-Diyārāt*, ed. G. ʿAwwād, Baghdad 1966.
Shafīʿī Kadkanī, M. R., *Guzīda-yi ghazaliyyāt-i Shams*, Tehran 1352 [1974].
Qalandariyya dar tārīkh, Tehran 1386 [2007].
Shahbazi, A. S., 'An Achaemenid Symbol. I: A Farewell to "Fravahr" and "Ahura Mazda"', *Archaeologische Mitteilungen aus Iran* 7, 1974, 135–44; 'II: Farnah "(God-given) Fortune" Symbolised', ibid., 13, 1980, 119–47.
'On Vārəγna the Royal Falcon', *Zeitschrift der Deutschen Morgenländischen Gesellschaft* 134, 1984, 314–17.
al-Shahrastānī (d. 548/1153), *Kitāb al-milal wa'l-niḥal*, ed. W. Cureton, 2 vols., London 1842–6; tr. D. Gimaret and G. Monnot, *Livres des religions et des sectes*, 2 vols., UNESCO 1986 (which preserves the paginations of both Badrān's and Cureton's editions).
Shaked, S., *Dualism in Transformation: Varieties of Religion in Sasanian Iran*, London 1994.
'Eschatology and the Goal of the Religious Life', in R. J. Z. Werblowsky and C. J. Bleeker (eds.), *Types of Redemption*, Leiden 1970, 223–30.
'Esoteric Trends in Zoroastrianism', *Proceedings of the Israel Academy of Sciences and Humanities* 3, 1969, 175–221.
'First Man, First King: Notes on Semitic-Iranian Syncretism and Iranian Mythological Transformations', in S. Shaked, D. Shulman, and G. G. Strousma (eds.), *Gigul: Essays on the Transformation, Revolution and Permanence in the History of Religion dedicated to J. Zwi Werblowsky*, Leiden 1987, 238–56.
'Mihr the Judge', *Jerusalem Studies in Arabic and Islam* 2, 1980, 1–31.
'The Moral Responsibility of Animals: Some Zoroastrian and Jewish Views on the Relation of Humans and Animals', in M. Stausberg (ed.), *Kontinuitäten und Brüche in der Religionsgeschichte (Festschrift für Anders Hultgård)*, Berlin and New York 2001, 578–95.
'The Myth of Zurvan: Cosmogony and Eschatology', in I. Gruenwald, S. Shaked, and G. G. Stroumsa (eds.), *Messiah and Christos: Studies in the Jewish Origins of Christianity presented to David Flusser*, Tübingen 1992, 219–37.
'The Notions of *Mēnōg* and *Gētīg* in the Pahlavi Texts and their Relation to Eschatology', *Acta Orientalia* 33, 1971, 59–107.
'Quests and Visionary Journeys in Sasanian Iran', in J. Assmann and G. G. Stroumsa (eds.), *Transformations of the Inner Self in Ancient Religions*, Leiden 1999, 65–87.
'Religion in the Late Sasanian Period: Eran, Aneran, and other Religious Designations', in V. S. Curtis and S. Stewart (eds.), *The Sasanian Era*, London 2008, 103–17.
'Some Notes on Ahreman, the Evil Spirit, and his Creation', in E. E. Urbach, R. J. Zwi Werblowsky, and C. Wirszubski: (eds.), *Studies in Mysticism and Religion presented to Gershom G. Scholem*, Jerusalem 1967, 227–34.

'The Yasna Ritual in Pahlavi Literature', in M. Stausberg (ed.), *Zoroastrian Rituals in Context*, Leiden 2004, 333–44.
Shaked, S. (tr.), *The Wisdom of the Sasanian Sages (Dēnkart VI)*, Boulder, Colo. 1979.
Shaki, M., 'On the Concept of Obligated Successorship in the Mādiyān ī Hazār Dādistān', in *Monumentum H. S. Nyberg*, II (Acta Iranica 5), Leiden 1975, 227–42.
'The Cosmogonical and Cosmological Teachings of Mazdak', in *Papers in Honour of Professor Mary Boyce*, II (Acta Iranica 25), Leiden 1985, 527–43.
'A Few Philosophical and Cosmogonical Chapters of the Dēnkart', *Archiv Orientální* 41, 1973, 133–64.
'The Sassanian Matrimonial Relations', *Archiv Orientální* 39, 1971, 322–45.
'The Social Doctrine of Mazdak in the Light of Middle Persian Evidence', *Archiv Orientální* 46, 1978, 289–306.
'Some Basic Tenets of the Eclectic Metaphysics of the *Dēnkart*', *Archiv Orientální* 38, 1970, 277–312.
Sharon, M., *Black Banners from the East: The Establishment of the 'Abbāsid State*, Jerusalem and Leiden 1983.
'Khidāsh', in *EI*[2].
Revolt: The Social and Military Aspects of the 'Abbāsid Revolution, Jerusalem 1990.
Shaw, B. D., 'Out on a Limb' (review of Bynum, *Resurrection of the Body*), *The New Republic*, 17 April 1995, 43–7.
'Ritual Brotherhood in Roman and Post-Roman Societies', *Traditio* 52, 1997, 327–55.
Shchuryk, O., '*L*ᵉ*bēš pagrā*' as the Language of "Incarnation" in the *Demonstrations* of Aphrahat the Persian Sage', *Ephemerides Theologicae Lovanienses* 83, 2007, 419–44.
Sheffield, D. J., 'The *Wizīgerd ī Dēnīg* and the Evil Spirit: Questions of Authenticity in Post-Classical Zoroastrianism', *Bulletin of the Asia Institute* 19, 2009, 181–9.
Shellrude, G. M., 'The Apocalypse of Adam: Evidence for a Christian Gnostic Provenance', in M. Krause (ed.), *Gnosis and Gnosticism*, Leiden 1981, 82–91.
Shepherd of Hermas (before 175), in M. W. Holmes (ed. and tr.), *The Apostolic Fathers*, Grand Rapids, Mich., 1992.
Shinji, M., 'The Zoroastrian Kingdoms in Māzandarān and the T'ang Empire', *Acta Asiatica* (Tokyo) 41, 1981, 29–46.
Sidner, S., 'Brothers Share Wife to Secure Family Property', at http://www.cnn.com/2008/WORLD/asiapcf/10/24/polygamy.investigation/index.html.
Silvanus = 'The Teachings of Silvanus (VII, 4)', tr. M. L. Peel and J. Zandee, in Robinson, *Nag Hammadi Library*, 379–95.
Silverstein, A. J., *Postal Systems in the Pre-Modern Islamic World*, Cambridge 2007.
Sims-Williams, N., 'From Babylon to China: Astrological and Epistolary Formulae across Two Millenia', in *La Persia e l'Asia Centrale da Alessandro al X secolo (Atti dei Convegni Lincei* 127), Rome 1996, 77–84.
'Christian Sogdian Texts from the Nachlass of Olaf Hansen, II: Fragments of Polemic and Prognostics', *Bulletin of the School of Oriental and African Studies* 58, 1995, 288–302.

'The Sogdian Fragments of the British Library', *Indo-Iranian Journal* 18, 1976, 43–82.
'The Sogdian Fragments of Leningrad', *Bulletin of the School of Oriental and African Studies* 44, 1981, 231–40.
'Some Reflections on Zoroastrianism in Sogdiana and Bactria', in D. Christian and C. Benjamin (eds.), *Realms of the Silk Roads: Ancient and Modern* (Silk Road Studies 4), Turnhout 2000, 1–12.
Sims-Williams, N. (ed. and tr.), *Bactrian Documents from Northern Afghanistan*, I (*Legal and Economic Documents*), Oxford 2000; II (*Letters and Buddhist Texts*), Oxford 2007.
Skjaervø, P. O., 'Iranian Elements in Manicheism: A Comparative Approach. Indo-Iranica I', in *Au Carrefour des religions: Mélanges offèrt à Philippe Gignoux*, Bures-sur-Yvette 1995, 263–84.
'Manichaean Polemical Hymns', *Bulletin of the Asia Institute* NS 9, 1995, 239–55.
'Venus and the Buddha, or How Many Steps to *Nirvana*? Some Buddhist Elements in Manichaean Literature', in P. Vavroušek (ed.), *Iranian and Indo-European Studies: Memorial Volume of Otokar Klíma*, Prague 1994, 239–54.
'Zoroastrian Dualism', in A. Lange, *et al.* (eds.), *Light Against Darkness: Dualism in Ancient Mediterranean Religion and the Contemporary World*, Göttingen 2011, 55–91.
Skjaervø, P. O. (tr.), '"Kirdir's Vision": Translation and Analysis', *Archaeologische Mitteilungen aus Iran* 16, 1983, 269–306.
Škand: see Martan Farrukh.
Škoda, V., 'Le culte du feu dans les sanctuaries de Pendžikent', in F. Grenet (ed.), *Cultes et momuments religieux dans l'Asie centrale préislamique*, Paris 1987, 63–72.
'Ein Śiva-Heiligtum in Pendžikent', *Archaeologische Mitteilungen aus Iran* 25, 1992, 319–27.
Skrbina, D., *Panpsychism in the West*, London 2005.
Smith, M., *Jesus the Magician*, New York 1978.
Smith, P., *The Babi and Baha'i Religions*, Cambridge 1987.
SN: see Niẓām al-Mulk.
Stahl, C., 'Derdekeas in the *Paraphrase of Shem*, NCH VII, 1, and the Manichaean Figure of Jesus, Two Interesting Parallels', in R. E. Emmerick, W. Sundermann, and P. Zieme (eds.), *Studia Manichaica: IV. Internationaler Kongress zum Manichaïsmus, Berlin, 14.–18. Juli 1997*, Berlin 2000, 572–81.
Stausberg, M., *Die Religion Zarathustras*, Stuttgart 2002–.
Zarathustra and Zoroastrianism, London 2008.
Staviskij, B. J., *La Bactriane sous le Kushans*, Paris 1986.
'Le problème des liens entre le bouddhisme bactrien, le zoroastrianisme et les cultres mazdéens locaux à la lumière des fouilles de Kara-tepe', in F. Grenet (ed.), *Cultes et monuments religieux dans l'Asie Centrale préislamique*, Paris 1987, 47–51.
Stead, F. M., 'The Ali Ilahi Sect in Persia', *The Moslem World* 22, 1932, 184–9.
Steinberg, S., 'Reform Judaism: The Origin and Evolution of a "Church Movement"', *Journal for the Scientific Study of Religion* 5, 1965, 117–29.

Stephens, M. E., 'Half a Wife is Better than None: A Practical Approach to Nonadelphic Polyandry', *Current Anthropology* **29**, 1988, 354–56.

Stern, S. M., 'Abū Ḥātim al-Rāzī on Persian religion', in his *Studies*, 30–46.

'Abū 'l-Qāsim al-Bustī and his refutation of Ismāʿīlism', in his *Studies*, 299–320 (first publ. in *Journal of the Royal Asiatic Society* 1961, 14–35).

'The Early Ismāʿīlī Missionaries in North-West Persia and in Khurāsān and Transoxania', in his *Studies*, 189–233 (repr. from *Bulletin of the School of Oriental and African Studies* 23, 1960, 56–90).

Studies in Early Ismāʿīlism, Jerusalem and Leiden 1983.

'Yaʿqūb the Coppersmith and Persian National Sentiment', in C. E. Bosworth (ed.), *Iran and Islam: A Volume in Memory of Vladimir Minorsky*, Edinburgh 1971, 535–64.

Strabo (d. *c.* 24), *Geography*, ed. and tr. H. L. Jones, 8 vols., Cambridge, Mass., and London 1960–70.

Stroumsa, S., 'From the Earliest Known Judaeo-Arabic Commentary on Genesis', *Jerusalem Studies on Arabic and Islam* **27**, 2002, 375–95.

Suhrawardī (d. 587/1191), *Ḥikmat al-ishrāq*, ed. and tr. J. Walbridge and H. Ziai, *The Philosophy of Illumination*, Provo, UT, 1999.

al-Sulamī (d. 412/1021), *Ḥaqā'iq al-tafsīr*, ed. S. ʿImrān, 2 vols., Beirut 2001.

al-Ṣūlī (d. 335/947), *Kitāb al-awrāq*, ed. V. Beliaev and A. Khalidov, St Petersburg 1998.

Sundermann, W., 'Die Bedeutung des Parthischen für die Verbreitung buddhistischer Wörter indischer Herkunft', *Altorientalische Forschungen* **9**, 1982, 99–113.

'Cosmogony and Cosmology, iii–iv'; 'Eschatology. II. Manichaean', in *EIr*.

'How Zoroastrian Is Mani's Dualism?', in L. Cirillo and A. van Tongerloo (eds.), *Atti del terzo Congresso Internazionale di Studi 'Manicheismo e Oriente Christiano Antico'*, Louvain 1997, 343–60.

'Iranische Lebensbeschreibungen Manis', *Acta Orientalia* **36**, 1974, 125–49.

'Mani', in *EIr*.

'Mani, India and the Manichaean Religion', *South Asian Studies* **2**, 1986, 11–19.

'Mani's Revelations in the Cologne Mani Codex and in Other Sources', in L. Cirillo and A. Roselli (eds.), *Codex Manichaicus Coloniensis*, Cosenza 1986, 205–14.

'Namen von Göttern, Dämonen und Menschen in iranischen Versionen des manichäischen Mythos', *Altorientalische Forschungen* **6**, 1979, 95–133.

'Der Paraklet in der ostmanichäischen Überlieferung', in P. Bryder (ed.), *Manichaean Studies*, Lund 1988, 201–12.

'Some More Remarks on Mithra in the Manichaean Pantheon', in *Études Mithraiques: Actes du 2e Congrès International, Téhéran 1–9 septembre 1975* (Acta Iranica 17), Leiden 1978, 485–99.

'Studien zur kirchengeschichtlichen Literatur der iranischen Manichäer II', *Altorientalische Forschungen* **18**, 1986, 239–317.

Sundkler, B., *Bantu Prophets in South Africa*, London 1948.

al-Suyūṭī (d. 911/1505), *al-Durr al-manthūr fī tafsīr al-ma'thūr*, 8 vols., Beirut 1983.

Ta'rīkh al-khulafā', ed. R. K. al-ʿAkkāwī, Beirut 1992.

Synodicon Orientale ou recueil de synods nestoriens, ed. and tr. J. B. Chabot, Paris 1902.

Syro-Roman Lawbook, ed. and tr. K. G. Bruns and E. Sachau, *Syrisch-römisches Rechtsbuch aus dem fuñften Jahrhundert*, Leipzig 1888 (repr. Aalan 1961); ed. and tr. W. Selb and H. Kaufhold, *Syrisch-römische Rechtsbuch*, 3 vols., Vienna 2002; ed. and tr. A. Vööbus, *The Syro-Roman Lawbook*, 2 vols., Stockholm 1982–3.

Tab. = al-Ṭabarī (d. 310/923), *Taʾrīkh al-rusul waʾl-mulūk*, ed. M. J. de Goeje and others, 3 series in 15 vols., Leiden 1879–1901; ed. M. A.-F. Ibrāhīm, 10 vols., Cairo 1960–[77]; preserves the Leiden pagination in the margin.

Tābān, T., 'Qiyām-i Muqannaʿ: junbish-i rustāʾī-yi sapīd jāmagān', *Iranshenasi* 1, 1989, 532–65.

Tabbernee, W., *Montanist Inscriptions and Testimonia: Epigraphic Sources Illustrating the History of Montanism*, Mercer, Ga., 1997.

Tabṣirat al-ʿawāmm, ed. ʿA. Iqbāl, Tehran 1313.

Tafazzoli, A., 'Observations sur le soi-disant Mazdak-Nāmag', *Acta Iranica* 23, 1984, 507–10.

Tambiah, S. J., 'Polyandry in Ceylon', in C. von Führer-Haimendorf (ed.), *Caste and Kin in Nepal, India and Ceylon*, New York 1966, 264–358.

Tansar's Epistle, ed. M. Minovi, Tehran 1932; tr. M. Boyce, Rome 1968.

al-Tanūkhī (384/994), *Nishwār al-muḥāḍara*, ed. ʿA. al-Shāljī, Beirut 1971–2; partial tr. by D. S. Margoliouth, *The Table-Talk of a Mesopotamian Judge* (part i), London 1922; parts ii and vii (repr. from *Islamic Culture* 3–6, 1929–32, Hyderabad n.d.).

Tarapore, J. C. (ed. and tr.), *Pahlavi Andarz-Nāmak*, Bombay 1933.

Tardieu, M., 'La diffusion du bouddhisme dans l'empire kouchan, l'Iran et la Chine, d'après un kephalaion manichéen inédit', *Studia Iranica* 17, 1988, 153–82.

Tārīkh-i Bukhārā (lost Arabic original by Narshakhī completed in 331/943f.; Persian tr. with additions by Qubāvī (522/1128f.)), ed. C. Schefer, Paris 1892; ed. M. Riḍawī, Tehran 1351; tr. R. N. Frye, *The History of Bukhara*, Cambridge, Mass., 1954. Cited in that order in the form *TB* 64/90 = 65.

Tārīkh-i Harāt, bih iḥtimāl az Shaykh ʿAbd al-Raḥmān Fāmī Hiravi (presumed author d. 546/1161), facsimile edn with an introduction by M. Mirhosseini and M. R. Abouyi Mehrizi, Tehran 1387 [2008].

Tārīkh-i Qumm (lost Arabic original by Hasan b. Muḥammad al-Qummī later fourth/tenth century; abridged Persian tr. 806/1403f.), ed. M. R. Anṣārī Qummī, Qumm 2006.

Tārīkh-i Sīstān (440s/1050s), ed. M. T. Bahār, Tehran 1314 [1935] (the edn of 1381, repr. 1387 [2008], is of limited scholarly use because it does not preserve the old pagination in the margin); tr. M. Gold, Rome 1976.

Tārīkhnāma-yi Ṭabarī gardānida-yi mansūb bih Balʿamī (text formed by accretion to Balʿamī's free translation, commissioned 352/963, of the early parts of Ṭabarī), ed. M. Rawshan, 5 vols., Tehran 1366/1987, repr. 1374 (abbreviated as *TN*). The repr. numbers the volumes differently from the first printing, but the pagination is unchanged. French tr. on the basis of a different edn, H. Zotenberg, Paris 1867–74; reissue of the chapters relating to the

ʿAbbāsids under the title *L'âge d'or des Abbasides: Extrait de la Chronique de Tabari traduite par Hermann Zotenberg*, Paris 1983. References in the form IV, 1258 = 181 are to the 1374 reprint of the text and the *L'âge d'or* translation.
Tautain, Le Dr [no initial given], 'Étude sur le mariage chez les polynésiens (Mao'i) des îles marquises', *L'Anthropologie* 6, 1895, 640–51.
TB: see *Tārīkh-i Bukhārā.*
Tendler Krieger, B., 'Marriage, Birth, and *Bāṭinī Ta'wīl*: A Study of Nuṣayrī Initiation Based on the *Kitāb al-Ḥāwī fī ʿIlm al-Fatāwī* of Abū Saʿīd Maymūn al-Ṭabarānī', *Arabica* 58, 2011, 53–75.
TG: see Ess, van.
al-Thaʿālibī (d. 429/1038), *Ādāb al-mulūk*, ed. J. al-ʿAṭiyya, Beirut 1990.
Ghurar akhbār mulūk al-furs wa-siyarihim, ed. and tr. H. Zotenberg, *Histoire des rois des perses*, Paris 1900; repr. Tehran 1963.
Thimār al-qulūb, ed. M. A.-F. Ibrāhīm, Cairo 1965.
Thekeparampil, J., 'Malkizedeq according to Jacob of Sarug', in R. Lavenant (ed.), *VI Symposium Syriacum 1992*, Rome 1994, 121–33.
Theodore Bar Koni (third/ninth century), *Livre des scolies (recension de Séert)*, ed. A. Scher, *Liber Scholiorum* (CSCO 55, 69/Syr. 19, 26), Paris 1910, 1912; tr. R. Hespel and R. Draguet (CSCO 431–2/Syr. 187–8), Louvain 1981–2.
Theodoret of Cyrus (d. *c.* 460), *On Providence*, tr. T. Halton, New York 1988.
Theophanes (d. 818), *The Chronicle of Theophanes the Confessor*, tr. C. Mango and R. Scott, with the assistance of G. Greatrex, Oxford 1997.
Theophilus of Antioch (d. *c.* 185), *Ad Autolycum*, tr. M. Dods (Ante-Nicene Father 2), New York 2007 [first publ. 1885]. Cited by book and chapter.
Thomassen, E., 'The Derivation of Matter in Monistic Gnosticism', in J. D. Turner and R. Majercik (eds.), *Gnosticism and Later Platonism*, Atlanta 2000, 1–17.
Tištar Yašt: see *Yašts*.
TN: see *Tārīkhnāma*.
Tor, D. G., *Violent Order: Religious Warfare, Chivalry, and the ʿAyyār Phenomenon in the Medieval Islamic World*, Würzburg 2007.
Treadgold, W., *The Byzantine Revival 780–842*, Stanford 1988.
Tremblay, X., 'Ostiran *vs* Westiran: Ein oder zwei Iran vor der islamischen Eroberung', in H. Eichner, B. G. Fragner, V. Sadovsky, and R. Schmitt (eds.), *Iranistik in Europa: gestern, heute, morgen*, Vienna 2006, 217–39.
TS: see *Tārīkh-i Sīstān*.
Tucci, G., 'Oriental Notes III: A Peculiar Image from Gandhāra', *East and West* 18, 1968, 289–92.
Tucker, W. F., *Mahdis and Millenarians: Shīʿite Extremists in Early Muslim Iraq*, Cambridge 2008.
Turcan, R., *Mithras Platonicus*, Leiden 1975.
Upaniṣads, tr. F. Max Müller, 2 vols., Oxford 1879–1884, repr. New York 1962.
ʿUyūn = *Kitab al-ʿUyūn wa'l-ḥadā'iq fī akhbār al-ḥaqā'iq*, part iii, ed. M. J. de Goeje, Leiden 1871.
Vaissière, É. de la, *Histoire des marchands sogdiens*, 2nd edn, Paris 2004.
Vaissière, É. de la, and P. Riboud, 'Les livres des Sogdiens', *Studia Iranica* 32, 2003, 127–36.

Vaissière, É. de la, and É. Trombert, 'Des Chinois et des Hu: migrations et intégration des Iraniens orientaux en milieu choinois durant le haut Moyen Âge', *Annales HSS* 59, 2004, 931–69.
Vajda, G., 'Le témoignage d'al-Māturīdī sur la doctrine des Manichéens, des Dayṣānites et des Marcionites', *Arabica* 3, 1966, 1–38.
Vd: see *Vendīdād*.
Vendīdād (Vīdēvdād), tr. J. Damesteter, *The Zend-Avesta*, part 1 (Sacred Books of the East, vol. IV), Oxford 1880 (repr. 2008). Abbreviated as *Vd*.
Vevaina, Y. Sohrab-Dinshaw, 'Resurrecting the Resurrection: Eschatology and Exegesis in Late Antique Zoroastrianism', *Bulletin of the Asia Institute* 19, 2005 (*Iranian and Zoroastrian Studies in Honor of Prods Oktor Skjærvø*), 215–23.
Vīdēvdād: see *Vendīdād*.
Wagner, E., *Abū Nuwās*, Wiesbaden 1965.
Waley, A., 'Some References to Iranian Temples in the Tun-Huang Region', *Bulletin of the Institute of the History of Philosophy*, Academia Sinica, 28, 1956, 123–28.
Walker, J. T., *The Legend of Mar Qardagh*, Berkeley 2006.
Wallace, A. F. C., 'Revitalization Movements', *American Anthropologist* 58, 1956, 264–81.
Walter, M. N., 'Sogdians and Buddhism', *Sino-Platonic Papers* 174, November 2006.
al-Wāsiṭī, Aslam b. Sahl (d. 292/905), *Ta'rīkh Wāsiṭ*, ed. G. ʿAwwād, Baghdad 1967.
Wasserstrom, S. M., 'The ʿĪsāwiyya Revisited', *Studia Islamica* 75, 1992, 57–80.
'The Moving Finger Writes: Mughīra b. Saʿīd's Islamic Gnosis and the Myth of its Rejection', *History of Religions* 25, 1985, 1–29.
Wellhausen, J., *The Arab Kingdom and its Fall*, London 1973 [German original Berlin 1902].
'Die Ehe bei den Arabern', *Nachrichten von der Königlichen Gesellschaft der Wissenschaften und der Georg-August-Universität zu Göttingen*, 11, 1893, 431–81.
'Die Religiös-politischen Oppositionsparteien im alten Islam', *Abhandlungen der Königlichen Gesellschaft der Wissenschaften zu Göttingen*, NF 5, no. 2, Berlin 1901, 1–99.
Wells, P. S., *The Battle that Stopped Rome: Emperor Augustus, Arminius, and the Slaughter of the Legions in Teutoburg Forest*, New York 2004.
West, M., 'Darius' Ascent to Paradise', *Indo-Iranian Journal* 45, 2002, 51–7.
Whitby, M. and M. (trs.), *The History of Theophylact Simocatta*, Oxford 1986.
White, D. G., *Kiss of the Yoginī*, Chicago and London 2003.
Widengren, G., 'Bābakīyah and the Mithraic Mysteries', in U. Bianchi (ed.), *Mysteria Mithrae*, Leiden 1979, 675–96.
'The Sacral Kingship of Iran', in *La Regalità sacra (Contributi al tema dell' VII Congresso Internazionale di Storia delle Religione), Roma, Aprile 1955)*, Rome 1959, 242–57.
''Synkretismus' in der syrischen Christenheit', in A. Dietrich (ed.), *Synkretismus im syrisch–persischen Kulturgebiet*, Göttingen 1975, 38–64.

Wiesehöfer, J., *Ancient Persia*, London 1996.
Wiessner, G., 'Zur Offenbarung im Manichäismus', in G. Wiessner and H.-J. Klimkeit (eds.), *Studia Manichaica: II. Internationaler Kongress zum Manichaïsmus, 6.–10. August 1989, St Augustin/Bonn*, Wiesbaden 1992, 151–58.
Williams, M. A., *Rethinking 'Gnosticism': An Argument for Dismantling a Dubious Category*, Princeton 1996.
Williams, P., and A. Tribe, *Buddhist Thought: A Complete Introduction to the Indian Tradition*, London and New York 2000.
Wilson, R. M., 'The Early History of the Exegesis of Gen. 1.26', in K. Aland and F. L. Cross (eds.), *Papers presented to the Second International Conference on Patristic Studies held at Christ Church*, Oxford, 1955 (Studia Patristica 1), Berlin 1957, 420–37.
Winter, I. J., '"Idols of the King": Royal Images as Recipients of Ritual Action in Ancient Mesopotamia', *Journal of Ritual Studies* 6, 1992, 13–42.
Witakowski, W., 'The Idea of *Septimana Mundi* and the Millenarian Typology of the Creation Week in Syriac Tradition', in R. Lavenant (ed.), *V Symposium Syriacum 1988* (Orientalia Christiana Analecta 236), Rome 1990, 93–109.
'The Magi in Syriac Tradition', in G. Kiraz (ed.), *Malphono w-Rabo d-Malphone: Studies in Honor of Sebastian P. Brock*, Piscataway, NJ, 2008, 809–43.
Worsley, P., *The Trumpet Shall Sound*, 2nd edn., New York 1968.
Yamamoto, Y., 'The Zoroastrian Temple Cult of Fire in Archaeology and Literature (II)', *Orient* (Tokyo) 17, 1981, 67–105.
Yamauchi, E. M., 'Cultic Prostitution', in H. A. Hoffner (ed.), *Orient and Occident: Essays Presented to Cyrus H. Gordon*, Neukirchen-Vluyn 1973, 213–22; Cambridge 1983, 991–1024.
Yang, H.-S., Y.-H. Jan, S. Iida, and L. W. Preston (eds. and trs.), *The Hye-Ch'o Diary: Memoir of the Pilgrimage to the Five Regions of India*, Seoul and Berkeley [c. 1984].
al-Yaʿqūbī (d. after 292/905), *Kitāb al-buldān*, ed. A. W. T. Juynboll and M. J. de Goeje (*BGA* VII), Leiden 1892; tr. G. Wiet, Cairo 1937. Abbreviated as YB.
Taʾrīkh, ed. M. T. Houtsma, 2 vols., Leiden 1883. Abbreviated as YT.
Yāqūt (d. 626/1229) *Muʿjam al-buldān*, ed. F. Wüstenfeld, 6 vols., Leipzig 1866–73.
Yarshater, E., 'Iranian National History', in *Cambridge History of Iran*, III (1), ed. E. Yarshater, Cambridge 1983, 359–477.
'Mazdakism', in *Cambridge History of Iran*, III (2), ed. E. Yarshater, Cambridge 1983, 991–1024.
Yašts, tr. J. Darmesteter, *The Zend Avesta*, part 2 (Sacred Books of the East, vol. XXIII), Oxford 1882; *Yašt* 8 (*Tištar Yašt*), ed. and tr. A. Panaino, *Tištrya*, i, *The Avestan Hymn to Sirius*, Rome, 1990; *Yašt* 13, ed. and tr. W. W. Malandra, 'The *Fravaši Yašt*', PhD dissertation, University of Pennsylvania 1971; *Yašt* 19, ed. and tr. (German) A. Hintze, *Zamyād Yašt*, Wiesbaden 1994 (an English translation without the edition and scholarly apparatus was also published): tr. (English) H. Humbach and P. R. Ichaporia, Wiesbaden 1998.

YB: see al-Yaʿqūbī, *Buldān*.
YT: see al-Yaʿqūbī, *Taʾrīkh*.
Yt: see *Yašts*.
Yūsofī, G.-Ḥ., 'Bābak Khorramī', in *EIr*.
Zādspram (alive 881), *Anthologie*, ed. and tr. P. Gignoux and A. Tafazzoli, Paris 1993.
Zaehner, R. C., *The Dawn and Twilight of Zoroastrianism*, London 1961.
'A Zervanite Apocalypse', parts I and II, *Bulletin of the School of Oriental and African Studies* 10, 1940–2, 377–98, 606–31.
Zurvan: A Zoroastrian Dilemma, Oxford 1955; repr. New York 1972.
'Zurvanica I', *Bulletin of the School of Oriental and African Studies* 9, 1937–9, 303–20.
Zakeri, M., *Sāsānid Soldiers in Early Muslim Society*, Wiesbaden 1995.
Zamyād Yašt: see *Yašts*.
Zand ī Wahman Yasn (aka *Bahman Yašt*), ed. and tr. C. G. Cereti, Rome 1995.
Zandee, J., '"The Teachings of Silvanus" (NHC VII,4) and Jewish Christianity', in R. van den Broek and M. J. Vermaseren (eds.), *Studies in Gnosticism and Hellenistic Religions presented to Gilles Quispel*, Leiden 1981, 498–585.
Zarrīnkūb, ʿA.-Ḥ., 'The Arab Conquest of Iran and its Aftermath', in *Cambridge History of Iran*, IV, ed. R. N. Frye, Cambridge 1975, 1–56.
Zaryāb Khūʾī, ʿA., 'Nukātī dar bāra-yi Muqannaʿ', in Y. Mahdavī and I. Afshār (eds.), *Haftād Maqāla: armaghān-i farhangi bah duktur Ghulāmḥusayn Ṣadīqī*, Tehran 1369, I, 81–92.

Index

The index is also a glossary. Bracketed numbers indictate pages where the subject is mentioned without being named.

CPSIA information can be obtained at www.ICGtesting.com
Printed in the USA
LVOW072117140413

329005LV00003B/3/P

9 781107 018792